PENGUIN

THE MODERN BRITISH NOVEL

Malcolm Bradbury was a novelist, critic, television dramatist and Emeritus Professor of American Studies at the University of East Anglia. He was the author of seven novels, including *The History Man* (1975), winner of the Royal Society of Literature Heinemann Prize, and *Rates of Exchange* (1983), which was short-listed for the Booker Prize. His other novels include *Doctor Criminale* (1992) and *To the Hermitage* (2000). He wrote short-fiction, satires and parodies. Among his many critical works are *The Modern British Novel* (Penguin, 1994; revised edition, 2001) and *Dangerous Pilgrimages: Trans-Atlantic Mythologies and the Novel* (Penguin, 1996). He also edited *The Penguin Book of Modern Short Stories* (Penguin, 1988), *Modernism* (with Professor James McFarlane; Penguin, 1991) and *The Atlas of Literature* (1997). For television he wrote two television novels about the European Community, *The Gravy Train* and *The Gravy Train Goes East*, and many episodes of *A Touch of Frost, Dalziel and Pasoce, Kavanagh Q.C.* and *Inspector Morse*. He also wrote the screenplays of Tom Sharpe's *Porterhouse Blue*, Kingsley Amis's *The Green Man* and Stella Gibbons's *Cold Comfort Farm*, now a feature film. In 1991 he was awarded the CBE and was knighted for services to literature in 2000.

Malcolm Bradbury died on 27 November 2000. Among the many tributes paid to him, the *Guardian* described him as 'one of the most prolific and influential novelists, critics and academics of his generation ... His death marks the close of half a century of academic and literary history, of which he was par excellence the chronicler.' David Lodge said of him in *The Times*: 'He was remarkable for the breadth of his writing. He was not only an important novelist, but a man of letters of a kind that is now rare. He covered the whole range of literary endeavour.'

In memory of
Angus Wilson, Angela Carter, William Golding and Iris Murdoch

Contents

Preface

This new edition of *The Modern British Novel* is about fiction in Britain from the end of the Victorian Age to the dawn of the twenty-first century and the birth of the third millennium: in other words, from one great age of the new to yet another. They called their time the Modern Age; we call ours the Postmodern Age. The two terms indicate there is an intricate connection. The book covers the novel in Britain over a century of radical innovation and novelty, political terror and shameless barbarism, rising human expectations and a serious loss of faith, deeply and rapidly changing images of selfhood, progress, psychology, science, the gene pool, the nature and future of our planet and the cosmos, enormous cultural change and a vast remixing of the national community. A century is a long time in the history of any literary or artistic genre; and this was a century of quite unprecedented change. It saw a sequence of major and deeply disastrous historical crises, when the existence of the planet itself was at risk, when the future could have gone in one of many different ways, toward freedom or servitude. The events and ideas of the century fractured an older sense of real, valuable, human and familiar. It upset the liberal belief in history, the human value of the person. It changed the logical evolution of British society – which as the twentieth century dawned was one of the most powerful societies in the world, empire spread wide, wealth vast, its innovations many, its place on the globe certain, its confidence despite rising tides of new politics of many kinds apparently secure.

Such were the changes that came in the next hundred years that not one of the terms in this book's title (with the possible exception of the definite article) can be considered safe. Today the word 'modern' has several meanings, both weak and strong. Often used to refer to the twentieth century – widely touted as 'the modern century', and its culture of unprecedented innovation – it is also used to refer to part of it, the first half, the age of the 'Modern movement', experimental, radical, avant-garde. If that is the Modern era, it follows that what comes next is the 'Postmodern' era – a convoluted but now common-place term used to denote both the more experimental arts of the second half of the century, and the natureless nature of its late capitalist, hi-tech, pluri-cultural culture. If the second half of the century is the Postmodern era, we might ask what comes next – Postpostmodernism? Or does a quite new epochal term for doings of the third millennium come into play? Certainly 'modern' has a weak (modern times) and a strong (Modernist avant-garde) meaning. One of the things that will interest us in this book is the complicated interplay that exists between the two.

'British' is far less safe a term. Used with splendid confidence as the century dawned and the map glowed pink, the Union Jack waved in many parts of the globe, the Union (mostly) flourished and most of the world's shipping sailed by need into London docks, it is a term of multiplying ambiguities in an age when the United Kingdom itself devolves and dissolves, the idea of Europe has acquired a quite different meaning and when the classic nineteenth-century nation state yields to new forms of political pluri-culturalism. Writing has always been cosmopolitan, and in literature the term was always open to considerable argument – not least because many of the writers sailing under this flag of convenience (British fiction, English litera-ture) were never British at all. Henry James was American, Conrad was Polish, George Moore, Sheridan Le Fanu, Oscar Wilde, James Joyce and Samuel Beckett were Irish, Robert Louis Stevenson and Arthur Conan Doyle were Scottish, Wyndham Lewis was simply born on a ship at sea. Now many of the writers we claim today under the rubric have names like Rushdie, de Bernières, Mo, Ishiguro, Okri, Kureishi and Zameenzad. Meanwhile many of the writers born in Britain chose – like D. H. Lawrence, Lawrence Durrell, Malcolm Lowry, Graham Greene, Anthony Burgess, Muriel Spark – to live, think and write elsewhere, and have often seen their land of origin and its literary tradition entirely from the outside. Parts of the British Isles that were in the Union have ceased, over the course of the century, to be so, leaving us with a complex and confusing paradox in the matter of Irish writing. In any case, however far back we care to go, the 'English' or to use the presently preferred (for how long?) term 'British', tradition has always been in some basic way international; Chaucer, Spenser, Shakespeare, Milton, Byron and Shelley are international, their writings having always been linked with travel, pilgrimage, exile, emigration, cultural pluralism, placelessness. In our own interfused and global village age, the idea of interpreting any literature, even as eclectic as that in Britain, in terms of a single national canon or sequence has obvious difficulties. And yet it does remain sensible to assume there are certain shaping aspects to a culture, definite characteristics and emphases, a national tradition, a variety of probable and recurrent subject-matters, however much it all fragments and diverges. In terms of inclusion or absence of writers, I have been pragmatic, including writers when they seem essential to the idea of a development or a tradition (James, Conrad, Joyce, Beckett) but not doing so when they seem better seen in the light of another lineage, like Flann O'Brien, Chinua Achebe, Patrick White, Michael Ondaatje, Nadine Gordimer or Thomas Keneally.

Next the tricky word 'novel'. As the term says, it exists to describe an original thing – a loose baggy monster, a form of fictional prose narrative of a certain length that contains infinite variety, assimilates many different sub-genres, draws on many origins, quite often to subvert them. Multiple-storied, containing many characters and discourses, it reaches across from reportage, social history, memoir and documentary to fantasy and romance, from the serious exploration of its own characteristics as a species of art to the most popular levels of commercial indulgence and generic repetition. It is truthful, it is false; it is high, it is low. The modern novel as we understand it is generally reckoned to date from Cervantes's *Don Quixote* (1605), that sceptical or deconstructive form of the old romance; though prose narrative had existed before, it here seems to encounter all the splendid scepticism of the modern world and modern prose. The novel became a popular form across Europe; in eighteenth-century Britain it became a key public expression of culture. In the age of Balzac, Hugo, Dickens, Thackeray, Tolstoy, Dostoevsky and Melville, it turned into the great social archive and moral record of the nineteenth century. In the work of the Brontës, Trollope, George Eliot and Mrs Gaskell, British fiction became a rolling opera, a rich source of social knowledge and entertainment, book of etiquette, moral tract, work of political criticism, voice of romantic sentiment, agent of reform. Then came the 'modern novel', which was in many respects an attempt to upturn the Victorian novel, challenging everything from its patriarchal morality, its high-minded principles and its sexual reticence to its representation of human nature and its claim to depict 'the real'. In the twentieth century the novel acquired a new experimentalism, a new psychological complexity and a new raunchiness. Today, as popular commercial product and a form of inquiring art, it is everywhere.

Yet throughout the course of the last century the borders and frontiers of fiction have been endlessly teased over and disputed. One very important part of the argument here is the entire question of what it is the novel is and does, how it survives and continues, and where it stands in times not just of cultural but technological change, when the book itself may be yielding to something else. The novel over the twentieth century served many functions, at many levels; it attracted to itself many great writers, and many kinds of writing. It would keep D. H. Lawrence endlessly poor and Jilly Cooper, Jeffrey Archer and Helen Fielding shamelessly rich. Its greatest books would generally sell in small quantities, or at least until they became classics; its smallest books would have the most massive sales. Novelists have constantly quarrelled over the very idea of the novel, and no form has been more analyzed and questioned. 'I have an idea that I will invent a new name for my books to supplant "novel",' wrote Virginia Woolf in her diary as she struggled with the great question. 'A new – by Virginia Woolf. But what? Elegy?' As usual, the new term is hard to come by; after all, what could be newer than 'novel' itself? Yet the frontier here can open out in so many ways: to lyricism, poetry, fantasy, to reportage, memoir, autobiography, to parody, elegy, dirge or faction. And, as we can challenge the idea of the novel as genre, so we can challenge the idea of the author, the voice of omniscience, the notion of the stable text, the confident faith in representation, the idea of fixed print on a continuous page, the idea of a publisher, the notion of the reader, the requirement that the story appear as a book. Again, the only way forward is to take to pragmatism; works of a good long length that develop fictional powers are what I shall take the novel to be.

One reason why the idea of the novel was so disputed is because it has been crucial to modern culture, especially modern British culture – and over a time when that culture has been changing radically, as has the wider world. So, briefly, what this book will be is a general survey of the development of the novel in Britain over a sequence of literary generations, from the dawn of the 'modern novel' to the plural, 'postmodern' scene of the recent present. To me it is one of the great and flourishing periods of writing, a time when the novel changed wonderfully in spirit and purpose, challenged poetry and drama for the high places of literary dominance, and then was itself challenged and transformed by new technological media – film, television, Internet – with which it has found the need to interact. Over this period it threw off a good deal of its historical framework and its Victorian constraints, formal and moral. It became an exploratory and discovering genre, and one of the fields of its exploration was the question of what the novel itself was and could do. The radical difficulty this presented for many readers – as they encountered major and baffling 'modern' works like James Joyce's *Ulysses*, Virginia Woolf's *Mrs Dalloway*, Malcolm Lowry's *Under the Volcano* or Beckett's *The Unnamable* – is a very important part of the story. Yet, as Stephen Spender argued in his book *The Struggle of the Modern* (1963), there are really two 'modern' traditions that need attention. One is the 'Modern', experimental and avant-garde; the other is the 'Contemporary', which is fiction and literary art at its familiar work of exploring the world as in general we see it, and the way we live now. Like many writers, I am fascinated by both traditions, and their constant interaction, for the popular is never far from the high, and the realistic and documentary from the grotesque or fantastic.

Until quite recently, this division was important in criticism. Once it became accepted that the 'Modern' was the radical art of the new century, the art of the great era of 'Make It New', it became a chief object of critical study. Since the most revolutionary period of experimentalism fell in the first half, or quarter, of the century, on each side of the Great War, that was the period of most critical attention. The Modern masters (James, Conrad, Joyce, Woolf, Lawrence, Forster) were key figures, along with their international contemporaries (Proust, Gide, Mann, Svevo, Hemingway, Faulkner), and became the taste which had to be understood. Far less attention was paid to other strands of fiction, and the 'Modern' dominated the more or less nameless era and cultural developments that have followed since. That division has implied a fundamental distinction over quality: the second generation was not like the first. That seems to me seriously misleading. It is true that many of the great writers of the century wrote in the first half of the century; but a major literature did develop in the second half, from writers who are still our contemporaries. The desire to do justice to that fact, and to give a portrait of the century as a whole, was one of the prime reasons for the writing of this book.

The relative neglect, until recently, of what we used to call the post-war period, and can perhaps now even call the postmodern period, has several sensible reasons. It is notoriously hard to judge our own contemporaries, as anyone who reads reviews can see; not least because they still have the means to judge us. Yet other countries and cultures are more confident about doing so; the contemporary in literature at least has never had that much of a name in Britain. Of course it takes time to see who the important contemporaries are, what are the most important directions. This is particularly true of the period after 1945, when there had been a major collapse of European culture, a slow uneasy process of cultural renewal, the international rise of a new politics of mass culture displacing the now traditional avant-garde. By comparison with the revolution of 1912, with its confident pronouncements of radical modernity, the post-war affair was muted and anxious. There was no aesthetic debate comparable to that of the early part of the century; critics paradoxically wrote of the arts of absurdity, the literature of silence. The roles of writer and critic divided; novelists went off to the marketplace, critics into the university (although it finally turned out to be in the market-place too). There were fewer campaigns, debates, clear tendencies or firmly defined milestones. That happened not least because the cultural origins and sources of writing were growing more diverse, harder to connect and trace. If the term 'postmodernism' has value it surely refers to the emergence of interfused styles, mixed cultural levels and layers, oddly intertwined traditions, multi-cultural pluralisms.

And if Modernism had challenged the tradition and attempted (as T. S. Eliot said) to reconstruct it out of the new contributions of the individual talent, the postmodern era, often taking its cue from narcissistic ignorance, seemed more inclined to dispense with traditions, canons and heritages entirely, unless for purposes of advertising or quotation. It wanted the immediate, the happening, the new (which never was); it dispensed – as Modernism never quite did – with judgement and the monumental. In my own view the post-war period in the British fictional line has been a striking, remarkable one; the very fact that we have turned the millennium and modern literature has moved from present to past, contemporary to classic, has made that fact even more visible. In recent years we have lost many of the leading contemporaries (some, being friends, mentioned in this preface). A simple inspection of the writers and titles listed at the end of this book might suggest the variety, the plurality and the overall significance of recent fiction, and also the way it has changed in the fifty post-war years: grown ever less parochial, ever more eclectic in its view of the world, ever more open to social, political, sexual, ethnic and cosmic change.

Perhaps there is another reason for the relative neglect of British fiction since the Fifties; it goes with the whole anxious notion of Britain's declining place in the world. When the era began, American literature was still perceived as a branch of British literature, and not until the post-war period did it come to be seen as equivalent or dominant. The idea that the novel – and above all the English novel – is dead has had a great deal of recent currency. Hence it is just worth remembering that this trope is not new; the novel has in fact been dead for every single decade of the century. The English novel was dead in the Edwardian 1900s: 'All modern books are bad,' E. M. Forster has his dry Cecil Vyse observe in *A Room With a View* (1907), '. . . Everyone writes for money these days.' Certainly, with a booming book trade, they could, and some like H. G. Wells, Arthur Conan Doyle and Elinor Glyn did; meanwhile the works of the late Henry James and Conrad, and the early James Joyce and D. H. Lawrence, were appearing. It was dead in the next decade: the banning and burning of Lawrence's *The Rainbow* in 1915 seemed, and not just to Lawrence himself, to mark the end of fictional experiment and the triumph of critical repression, though new works by James Joyce, Wyndham Lewis and Ford Madox Ford were transforming fiction. It was dead again in the Twenties, when T. S. Eliot now explained that Joyce's *Ulysses* had shown that 'the novel ended with Flaubert and with James', leaving the writer traditionless; and when Virginia Woolf, having in 1924 completed *Mrs Dalloway*, so much influenced by Joyce's novel, declared 'I'm glad to be quit this time of writing a "novel"; and hope never to be accused of it again.' We now, of course, acknowledge the Twenties as the major period of Modern fiction, largely on the strength of these novels that were not novels.

The novel was dead again in the Thirties, when the Marxist critics and writers saw the novel as a Victorian bourgeois prison, the burgher epic, to be dismissed on behalf of history and the modern reality; meanwhile they went on writing novels, and a new generation that included Evelyn Waugh, Graham Greene, Henry Green, George Orwell, Elizabeth Bowen and Rose Macaulay emerged. The novel was definitely dead by the coming of the Second World War, when Virginia Woolf declared its end in an essay called 'The Leaning Tower', and George Orwell announced, in another essay of 1940, 'Inside the Whale', that the writer had been left sitting on top of a melting iceberg: 'he is merely an anachronism, a hangover from the bourgeois age, as surely doomed as the hippopotamus.' As it so happened, the hippopotamus has survived, and so has the writer and the novelist. After 1945, the novel was even deader. Cyril Connolly, the editor of the magazine *Horizon*, announced 'closing time in the gardens of the West'. 'It is disheartening to think that twenty years ago saw the first novels of Hemingway, Faulkner, Elizabeth Bowen,

Rosamund Lehmann, Evelyn Waugh, Henry Green, Graham Greene,'
he commented in his usual twilight mood in a *Horizon* editorial of
1947, '. . . but no new crop of novelists has risen commensurate with
them.' This view persisted throughout the Fifties. In 1954 the *Observer*
newspaper ran an influential series, 'Is the Novel Dead?' It generated,
from a variety of critics and novelists, the same discouraging pronouncements: 'I do not see, therefore, that the conditions which render
fiction a relevant form of expression exist in the current generation,'
concluded, decisively, the voice of Bloomsbury, Harold Nicolson.
Meanwhile the careers of Angus Wilson, Doris Lessing, Anthony
Burgess, Muriel Spark, Iris Murdoch, William Golding, Kingsley
Amis, Brian Moore and Paul Scott began. And 1954, the year of these
conclusions, is now generally thought of as the key year for the
emergence of post-war British fiction, producing three major first
novels, one by an author, William Golding, who would win the Nobel
Prize for Literature.

What was wrong now? 'If the novel is truly no longer novel, then
many of our critical procedures for discussing it will need revision;
perhaps, even, we shall do well to think of another name for it,' wrote
the critic Bernard Bergonzi in 1970 in a fine though funereal study,
The Situation of the Novel, expressing a now familiar embarrassment.
It so happened as he wrote that another new generation of novelists,
including Angela Carter and John Fowles, was becoming established.
It was in the Seventies that the excellent lost literary magazine *The
New Review* ran a symposium in which it took nearly sixty British
novelists to get together and agree there was nothing at all going on
in the British novel. At just this time the careers of Martin Amis,
Julian Barnes, Peter Ackroyd, Pat Barker, Ian McEwan and many
other new writers who would dominate the Eighties started. When
that new decade dawned, another new literary magazine, *Granta*,
devoted its third issue (1980) to mourning 'The End of the English
Novel'. The same magazine went on to publish Amis, McEwan,
Barnes, Angela Carter, Bruce Chatwin, Jeannette Winterson, Colin
Thubron and John Berger. In 1983 it devoted an entire issue to 'The
Best of the Young British Novelists', listing more authors like Rose
Tremain and Kazuo Ishiguro. In 1993 it repeated the same exercise

again; and today Bill Buford, *Granta*'s then editor, prints the work of numerous British writers in *The New Yorker*. In 1993, the *Guardian* newspaper was convinced, as so often, that British fiction was dead and American literature better. 'British fiction, as everyone knows . . . is in a sad state,' wrote the literary editor, James Wood, in a sustained campaign against the new list that led him inevitably to the greater happiness of America. And now, plainly, things are about as bad, or good, as they ever were. The certainty of crisis has survived the millennium, a time of lists, for noting the ends of things and the beginnings of things. True, novels sell better than ever, but for how much longer, and of what quality, and won't the Internet change everything, and isn't the novel dead yet? Mourning is an old British disease. Meanwhile large numbers of new writers are published each year. London remains the world's prime publishing centre. Fiction flourishes, and even plays a primary role in modern British cultural life.

This new edition of *The Modern British Novel* has been very substantially revised in the light of what, in the longer view, we can now see and say about twentieth-century British fiction. All the material on the period from 1945 onward has been rewritten and greatly extended, and several new chapters added, with the aim of bringing the story to the turn of a second century and the dawn of a new millennium. The truth is that a century of wakes, dirges, odes, panegyrics and other funereal activities has no doubt changed but has certainly not yet buried the modern novel. We may still take it for granted that the novel (which was never one single thing, but an endlessly varied range of fictional explorations and fantastical inquiries) has survived, outliving so far the theoretical, political or other reasons for its 'inevitable' demise. It may be living on unusual drugs, but it has entered into the age of the Internet, the worldwide web, the digital revolution and the modem with some fair degree of splendour. It helps, perhaps, that it requires no complicated technology, is not subject to electronic breakdown and does not affect the technology on the flight deck. Like everything else in the shopping mall world, the cosmos of late universal capitalism, it has been refined as high-street, online or dot.com commodity. Yet, to a degree, it also remains as what we once thought it was: a major expression of moral, metaphysical, social, historical, political, sexual and aesthetic curiosity. It has explored – continues to explore – the nature, the stuff, the prospects, the mysteries of contemporary narrative. If there are no grand narratives any more, it still creates small ones, some of them opening the widest windows on present life and some on the meaning of stories. It constantly pushes at the margins and limits of the real, into the realm of fictions.

And, for the moment at least, and despite all the rapid change through which British society has passed, especially in the destabilizing years after 1945, when its world role changed, its values altered, its cultural funds grew ever more plural, we may still assume that there are significant lines and traditions which make sense of the idea of a British fiction, and give it a serious and important history in any modern account of writing. When I began writing the first version of this book in the early Nineties it reflected my double interests: as literary critic and teacher of literature and creative writing on the one side; as engaged writer of stories and screenplays but above all novels (the great form) on the other. Writers arise from writing, they depend on predecessors, role-models, peers, friends, contemporaries, successors, just as they depend on publishers, critics, reviewers, readers, and re-readers. For most of my life, in one way or another, I have been exploring and wandering this most inquiring of all the literary forms: its great storehouse of narratives, its enormous network of origins, its amazing celebrations both of the representational and the gloriously fictive. On the principle that a good writer should first be a good reader, I have tried to explore the novel as widely as possible, because we do indeed need both ancestors and traditions, rebellions and deconstructions to make up the vital history of the form.

Hence this book is eclectic. Once criticism liked to explore the narrow line of some great tradition (which by the time of F. R. Leavis had somehow closed down to five writers). Here there is no one great tradition, rather a wide range of options, possibilities, sub-genres, that cross over, intersect, interfuse. Still, in the end judgement is inevitable, preference inescapable and ignorance probable; which is why the book closes with a wider list of writers and works than is discussed within it. This is also part of a broader concern with the novel as international form, the nature of modern fiction, the general issues of Modernism and Postmodernism. Hence it relates to other books I have written: *The Social Context of Modern English Literature* (1971), *Modernism 1890–1930* (edited with Professor James McFarlane, rev. ed., 1990), *No, Not Bloomsbury* (1987), *The Modern World: Ten Great Writers* (1988), *The Modern American Novel* (rev. ed., 1990) and *From Puritanism to Postmodernism: A History of American Literature* (with Richard Ruland, 1991). In some places I have drawn on material from these, or from essays and reviews published elsewhere. I am greatly indebted to publishing and newspaper editors, as well as colleagues and friends, who have created conferences and congresses, asked for lectures, commissioned articles or reviews, or engaged in the great debate. They include Rudiger Ahrens, Guido Almansi, Bernard Bergonzi, Chris Bigsby, John Blackwell, Robert Boyars, Christopher Butler, Catherine Carver, Marc Chenetier, Jon Cook, Maurice Couturier, Jason Cowley, C. B. Cox, Haideh Daragahi, Diane DeBell, A. E. Dyson, Jay Halio, Ihab Hassan, Gerhard Hoffmann, Frank Kermode, Derwent May, Blake Morrison, Andrew Motion, Penny Perrick, Tom Rosenthal, Lorna Sage, Vic Sage, Mike Shaw, Anthony Thwaite, Richard Todd, Kristiaan Versluys, Erica Wagner, John Walsh, W. L. Webb, Harriet Harvey Wood and Heidi Ziegler, as well as many students and coming writers at the University of East Anglia. Then I thank the many writers I have talked to over the years, and who have discussed fiction or their own work with me: Walter Abish, Kingsley Amis, Martin Amis, Beryl Bainbridge, John Barth, Melvyn Bragg, Anthony Burgess, A. S. Byatt, Angela Carter, William Cooper, Jim Crace, E. L. Doctorow, Margaret Drabble, Ann Enright, Sebastian Faulks, Raymond Federman, John Fowles, William Gaddis, William Gass, William Golding, Wilson Harris, Joseph Heller, George V. Higgins, Kazuo Ishiguro, P. D. James, B. S. Johnson, Russell Celyn Jones, Doris Lessing, Toby Litt, David Lodge, Ian McEwan, Paul Micou, Arthur Miller, Timothy Mo, Iris Murdoch, Salman Rushdie, C. P. Snow, Muriel Spark, Graham Swift, Adam Thorpe, Rose Tremain, John Updike, John Wain,

Angus Wilson. I have been enormously indebted to my son, Dominic Bradbury, who has worked extensively on this revision of the text, and to my editor, Karen Whitlock. My agent, Mike Shaw, has been a major resource; so have many colleagues at the British Council, including Harriet Harvey Wood. The dedication names four writers who were especially important to me, and who have died recently. But the book is really dedicated to all who continue to believe in the art of fiction, the value of narrative, the future of the novel.

Malcolm Bradbury
Norwich, England, 2000

Part One: 1878–1945

1

The Turn of the Novel: 1878–1900

It has arrived, in truth, the novel, late at self-consciousness: but it has done its utmost ever since to make up for lost opportunities.   Henry James,
'The Future of the Novel' (1899)

The shift to which I refer was gradual, but it took place . . . with the greatest velocity at about the turn of this century . . . It was not merely plot, or characterization, or technique, or point of view, or thought, or symbolic organization that changed; it was not a matter of irreconcilable meanings, conflicting themes, or difficult problems. The change in the novel took place at a more fundamental level than these . . . The process which underlay the novel was itself disrupted and reorganized. The new flux of experience insisted on a new vision of existence; it stressed an ethical vision of continual expansion and virtually unrelieved openness in the experience of life.   Alan Friedman,
The Turn of the Novel (1966)

1

Just about every historian of British fiction would agree that, somewhere around the end of the nineteenth century or the start of the twentieth, there occurred a great 'turn of the novel'. The powerful tradition of Victorian fiction – moral, realistic, popular – began to die, and something different and more complex came to emerge: the tradition of what we now name the 'modern' novel. The change did not happen only in Britain; it was part of an international transforma- tion of the arts. Across Europe, more slowly in the United States, the form of the novel – which had emerged as a major genre of literature only in the seventeenth and eighteenth centuries, then become a crucial companion to the social and emotional expansion of the nineteenth – was moving through a great transition, as was all of Western humanist thought and culture itself. The change was in far more than fiction's subject-matter; deeper structures were reshaping too. The novel was aspiring to become a far more complex, various, open and self-conscious form, one which, in a new way, sought to be taken seriously as 'art'. The Spanish philosopher Ortega y Gasset, observing this in his 'Notes on the Novel' (1949), said fiction had shifted from being an Art of Adventures to an Art of Figures, from an art that told stories and reported life to a form that *created* form.[1] When Virginia Woolf wrote her important, audacious essay 'Modern Fiction' in 1919, she considered the modern novel was ready to claim a freedom from old convention that was just like a political revolution. 'If a writer were a free man and not a slave, if he could write what he chose and not what he must, if he could base his work upon his own feeling and not upon convention,' she argued, in her writers' version of the *Communist Manifesto*, 'there would be no plot, no comedy, no tragedy, no love interest or catastrophe in the accepted sense, and perhaps not a single button sewn on as the Bond Street tailors would have it.' Life was quite unlike the reality literature encoded; it was, she said, 'a luminous halo, a semi-transparent envelope surrounding us from the beginning of consciousness to the end' – and it was the task of the modern novelist to convey this fresh sense of life, with 'as little mixture of the alien and external as possible'. The modern novel, modern consciousness, would cast off its ancient chains and become free to deal with the strange plotless insubstantiality that was, in Woolf's vision, life or reality itself.

The modern change that came to fiction was not always so revolu-

1 José Ortega y Gasset, *The Dehumanization of Art, and Other Writings on Art and Culture* (Garden City, NY, 1956).

tionary, and was very much more complicated. For its coming we can find a great many reasons, and the critics have.[2] There were key social reasons: the growth of urban populations, the acceleration of technological change, the coming of improved education and literacy, the shifting relation of the classes, the expansion of leisure, the gradual increase in personal wealth. There were crucial intellectual reasons: the decline of a religious teleology and of the confident, theocentric, progressive Victorian world view, the rise of science and secular philosophies like sociology and psychology, the coming of a more material vision of life. There were important psychological reasons, as changing notions of the nature of the individual, social life, sex and gender relations, and rising awareness of the distinctive, increasingly mobile and fast-changing nature of experience in a modernizing age gave a new, more fluid view of consciousness and identity. There were important changes in the role of literature itself: the dying of the Victorian 'three-decker' novel, designed for libraries and associated with moral uplift, the rise of the literary marketplace and the development of the book as an item of purchase, the restratification of the cultural hierarchies in an age of increasing democracy, otherwise called the 'coming of the masses'. The explanations are many; all played their part in the changing character of the novel. But however we explain the change, the effects are apparent. The established form of the novel – fictional prose narrative – was acquiring a different kind of writer, a different kind of subject, a different kind of writing process, a different kind of reader, a different social and economic foundation. It was altering in length, appearance, price, and in social, moral and commercial purpose. It was multiplying, dividing its audience, reaching into new kinds of expression, undertaking daring new kinds of exploration, demanding new kinds of attention, claiming new freedoms of method and subject: new rights to social and sexual frankness, new complexities of discourse and form. Over the course

2 See, for example, Alan Friedman, *The Turn of the Novel: The Transition to Modern Fiction* (New York and London, 1966); Raymond Williams, *The English Novel from Dickens to Lawrence* (London, 1970); and Peter Keating's excellent *The Haunted Study: A Social History of the English Novel, 1875–1914* (London, 1989).

of the twentieth century – also called the 'modern' century – this transformation would continue. Changing, sub-dividing, springing from different cultural regions, reaching to very different audiences and new expressive functions, the novel would assume many roles. It would become a relaxing toy of leisure and fantasy, *and* a complex mechanism for imaginative and artistic discovery. It would serve as naive popular entertainment, and would transmit radical, often outrageous or surprising, visions and opinions. Above all it would become a central literary prototype, taking an importance it had never had as *the* literary medium of the age, dislodging poetry, to some degree even sidelining drama – until, later in the century, its dominance was in turn challenged by new technological media that promised or threatened to replace book-based culture with something more immediate, visual and serial. But even that great change in cultural technology the novel in general seems – so far – to have survived.

In consequence, the 'modern novel', an idea constantly discussed as the century closed, became a reality. A distinctive modern tradition developed, marked not just by modern themes, new techniques, wider availability, but by a firm break with past 'Victorian' conventions of narrative and literary morality, authorship and readership. But that break was never really to become complete. Many of the Victorian conventions and myths continued to haunt the radical surprise of the modern novel, and Victorian fiction – with its omniscient and godlike voice, its weighty realism, its chronological plotting, its presiding moral confidence, its role as the bourgeois epic – leaves its lasting imprint on British fiction to this moment. In the contemporary novels of Angus Wilson and Margaret Drabble, Marina Warner and David Lodge, Graham Swift and Peter Ackroyd its trace is clear, as the source of a modern social realism or as a traditional text the post-modern writer must unpick. In very self-conscious books like John Fowles's *The French Lieutenant's Woman* (1969) and A. S. Byatt's *Possession* (1990), we observe deliberate acts of homage to its presence, as from their different late twentieth-century perspectives these authors look back across the bridge between the Victorian and late-modern worlds, the Victorian and the late-modern novel. All these writers, all these books, acknowledge that some epochal change has occurred, in the representation of life, the angle of vision, the notion of Britain and culture. All of them see some continued if perhaps tricky connection between the age of Dickensian fogs and Darwinian crises and the nuclear age, the age of postmodern absurdity and the *nouveau roman.* 'The novelist is still a god, since he creates (and not even the most aleatory avant-garde modern novel has managed to extirpate its author completely),' writes Fowles in his meta-Victorian novel, which is both loving pastiche and critical parody, 'what has changed is that we are no longer the gods of the Victorian image, omniscient and decreeing; but in the new theological image, with freedom our first principle, not authority.' Byatt's book shows a greater nostalgia for a denser, richer time, and attempts a fuller possession. But it too deconstructs as well as reconstructs the sentimentalities and gender uncertainties that lay within Victorian solidity. 'The [Victorian] writers of the industrial novels were never able to resolve in fictional terms the ideological contradictions inherent in their own situation in society,' pronounces the critic Robyn Penrose in Lodge's *Nice Work* (1988), but she soon finds herself in a latter-day version of the same problem, as yet another contemporary fiction explores both the continuing affinity and the literary distance fiction and the world have travelled since the troubled closing of the Victorian age. The modern novel came, but the Victorian novel did not entirely go away; and that is one of the essential secrets of the modern novel.

2

That some epochal change occurred – in the role of the author, the spirit of the text, the shape of a story, the nature of a fiction – as the Victorian age ended can be more or less agreed. *How* it happened, *why* it happened, what it meant for the future of the novel, remain endlessly disputable. As for just *when* it happened, a variety of audacious dates has been put on offer. In 1899, as the new century turned, Henry James proudly announced the coming of a new 'self-consciousness' to the art of fiction: 'It can do simply everything, and that is its strength and its life.' 'On or about December 1910 human nature changed . . .,' Virginia Woolf said even more daringly in her essay 'Mr Bennett and Mrs Brown' (1924). '. . . All human relations shifted – those between masters and servants, husbands and wives, parents and children. And when human relations change there is at the same time a change in religion, conduct, politics, and literature.' Woolf's apocalyptic date is oddly precise, but there is a reason. She pinpoints her great shift in social relations and literary forms, her time of 'breaking and falling, crashing and destruction', to the end of the Edwardian period, the beginning of 'Georgianism' (as one critic had noticed, the British seemed to have long believed that kings and queens shape writing) – to the month of London's first exhibition of French Post-Impressionist and Cubist paintings, organized by her friend Roger Fry, when Britain saw Modernism's visual face, and 'Bloomsbury' went into the ascendant. 'It was in 1915 that the old world ended,' countered D. H. Lawrence in *Kangaroo* (1923), selecting for his transforming moment the second year of the Great War. He too had good reason: this was the year when apocalyptic signs showed in the sky (Zeppelins) and when his own work was suppressed by the British courts. Writing functions around epochal ideas, and all these key dates make sense. The millennial turn into the new and modern century, when science would reign; the ferment of avant-garde activity and new aesthetics that passed right through Europe in the immediately pre-war years; the crisis of war, that fundamental and revolutionary transformation that shattered the *belle époque*, broke down and transformed the European world map, and brought at least one revolutionary new ideology, Bolshevism, to political birth – all are among the important markers of modern European and world history, and of the modern novel.

In literature as in history, what looks sudden is usually born out of a long process. One reason we call the novel by that name is that it is a changing and discovering form, which alters with the new, and the news, and constantly struggles to express our shifting and developing inner and outer life. No one date will ever tell us when the 'modern novel', or the 'Modern movement', started, any more than we can know for sure when it ended, even though by calling ourselves 'post-modern' we clearly assume it has, more or less. What we can do is note the social, historical and artistic changes that made people think in a fresh way about society, culture, art and language, and make them view these things as uniquely 'modern' – a condition that has always existed, but that our own age of change and speed-up has highlighted, so that, as Karl Mannheim once said, what makes us modern is that we are always trying 'to tell by the cosmic clock of history what the time is'. Still, if we start looking for the time of greatest change, we are likely to go hunting a good deal earlier than any of the writers I have quoted. Something was reshaping the world, and the novel, long before 1900, 1910 or 1915. It was in the late Victorian years that what historians have called the 'Victorian synthesis' began to dissolve, and the cultural climate began to fragment. The progressive, optimistic view that had marked the earlier Victorian period was coming to an end, and it seemed the age had been not an institution but a revolution, a passage between a seemingly stable rural past and an infinite acceleration. Religious certainty declined under the pressure of the evolutionary theories of Charles Darwin, T. H. Huxley and Herbert Spencer. The fading of the old rural order and the rise of new urban masses, the march of 'progress' and 'reform', the surge of new technologies and communications, were altering, shrinking and cosmopolitanizing the world. The map of Europe was reshaping (the first German Reich was founded in 1871), and various European empires reaching a point of crisis or internal disintegration. New and revolutionary political movements – socialism, and the Communist philosophies of Marx and Engels – disturbed the comfortable surface of a bourgeois age. Materialism prospered, but in a climate of great historical uncertainty; it was hard to read where the world was going next. New technologies – the incandescent lamp, the electric street car, the internal combustion engine, the 'dynamo revolution' – offered amazing promises of change and prospects for the future; at the same time they indicated that the world was now governed by massive processes that increasingly dwarfed individual lives. Well before the end of the century, there was intense awareness of deep-seated and eternal change, and the idea of a 'coming of the modern' became a Europe-wide phenomenon. 'Only the day after tomorrow belongs to me,' announced Friedrich Nietzsche, the philosopher of the modern. 'Some men are born posthumously.'

The remaking of human ideas and expectations round the turn of modern centuries is not new. The last decades of the previous century had seen a sequence of revolutions: the American and the French, the Industrial and the Romantic. Now, as the nineteenth century came toward its close, and industrial, technological and economic development accelerated, a similar restless transformation was in the air. Advance in science, the speeding up of invention and futuristic discovery, the boom in world trade, the rise in European and American imperial and economic power, created a time of innovation. New forms and styles were shaping everywhere. European cities spent imperial wealth on a vast grandiosity; their streets filled with new technologies and architectures, with tramways and electric streetlights, *art nouveau* and *Jugendstil*. The idea of the Modern took on more and more meaning: there was talk of the modern city, modern architecture, modern science, modern man, the modern woman, modern consciousness, the modern soul. Writers and thinkers weighed the 'modern' question. 'Late-Victorian' sages like Flaubert, John Stuart Mill, Zola, Ibsen, Tolstoy, Kierkegaard and Nietzsche – the world-historical figures the Danish critic Georg Brandes called the 'men of the Modern Breakthrough' – aimed to express and explore the distinctive character of the new: its break with past ties, customs, faiths and traditions, its will to bring new consciousness to birth. The belief that a new age was emerging spread across Europe and America; as H. Stuart Hughes says in *Consciousness and Society* (1958), 'Nearly all students of the last years of the nineteenth century have sensed in some form or other a profound psychological change.'[3] Sociological thinkers like Weber, Durkheim and Pareto explored the underlying systems of the social world. Thinkers in the different realm of consciousness and psychology – William James, Henri Bergson, Sigmund Freud – began reconceiving the structures of the inner life. The Modern could be progressive and 'advanced'; it could also be introverted and decadent. But whatever it was, few doubted it was on its

3 H. Stuart Hughes, *Consciousness and Society: The Reorientation of European Social Thought, 1890–1930* (New York, 1958; London, 1959).

way, bringing a decisive break with the past, and new consciousness, new expression, new forms of art.

By the later years of the nineteenth century, especially in Britain, the novel had become a central means of exploration of the state of the nation, the feel of the culture, the relationship between personal and historical life. From mid-century on, as the age of Romanticism began to fade, it had increasingly moved toward realism – a democratizing, empirical way of writing that opened fiction out to social discovery, a wide reportage, a sympathetic responsiveness to the daily feel of ordinary lives. After the liberal revolutions that ran through Europe in 1848, the year of the *Communist Manifesto*, and the powerful impact of Darwin's *Origin of Species* in 1859, Realism became the great movement in art and fiction. Its report grew ever more socially exploratory, analytic, scientific, attentive to new laws of social evolution, the coming of new classes and masses; this was the tendency Zola called 'Naturalism'. As the century came toward its close, Naturalism too was challenged, by rising aesthetic preoccupations and deepened concern with human consciousness, distrust of the certainties of progress and the laws of social determinism. Thus it began to conflict or cross over with the movements we call Symbolism, Aestheticism and Decadence. The Modern movement really came in as a wave of movements, which oscillated between sociology and psychology, the progressive and the decadent, the objective and the subjective, the deterministic and the indeterminate. Its changes paralleled deep changes in other spheres where uncertainty was emerging: religion and morality, science and medicine, philosophy and physics. This general transition of literary consciousness was so great and so various that no single date can ever capture it. But dates can be useful, can sharpen the meaning of things. That is why, in the hunt for the modern in the novel, there is much to be said for considering what happened – or rather did not happen – on 1 November 1878, and, to be quite precise, at tea-time.

3

Just two years earlier, an ambitious young American novelist, Henry James – a child of New York, Albany, Boston, Harvard, and the cosmopolitan James family – decided to settle in Europe: indeed in London, the place where, for the novelist who took social manners and human behaviour as his subject, there was, he said, the most in the world to observe. Born in New York in 1843, James had been brought to Europe as a child for his 'sensuous education', returned to see his nation divided by a terrible Civil War, begun to write in an unhappy America where the pre-Civil War era of 'the American Renaissance' – the age of Emerson, Thoreau, Hawthorne and Melville – was over. While his American contemporaries of the Reconstruction era, like William Dean Howells, Mark Twain and Walt Whitman, chose to stay in their plain new nation to write of its past and future, James, a natural cosmopolitan, began travelling widely to look for an ideal city of art. He tried Rome, where earlier American writers and artists had sought escape from American provincialism and puritanism, and explored his aesthetic quest in his novel *Roderick Hudson* (USA, 1875), mostly written in Europe. Rome was somehow *too* aesthetic: he returned home to 'try New York', but by 1875 he was back trying Paris – where, through his Russian friend and fellow exile Ivan Turgenev, he met many of the important authors, including Flaubert, Maupassant, the Goncourt brothers, Zola, representatives of the new realist movement of the day. James held himself a realist, but one large theme of his realism was in fact the American romance, above all focused on Europe itself. This is the romance that draws not only Roderick Hudson, but the various characters of his stories in *A Passionate Pilgrim and Other Tales* (1875), and Christopher Newman, the American businessman 'stepping forth in his innocence and his might, gazing a while at this poor corrupt old world and then sweeping down on it', who also tries Paris in his first major novel *The American* in 1877.

Late in 1876 James found his European base, decided to make London his home, and settled in Bolton Street off Piccadilly. He was to remain in Britain for most of the rest of his life, and the major phase of his writing. 'My choice is the Old World – my choice, my need, my life,' he wrote in a letter home, adding:

For one who takes it as I take it, London is on the whole the most possible form of life. I take it as an artist and a bachelor; as one who has the passion of observation and whose business is the study of human life. It is the biggest aggregation of human life – the most complete compendium of the world.

James had based his 'choice' on sound realist reasons. In a claim that upset Howells and Twain, he described American society as 'thin', and argued that 'the flower of art only blooms where the soil is deep, that it takes a great deal of history to produce a little literature, that it needs a complex social machinery to set the novelist into motion.' London offered what the realist needed: a textured society, a world of manners, a 'great numerosity' of lives. So James became a British writer: or almost – for, as he rightly explained, 'I find myself more of a cosmopolitan (thanks to that combination of the continent and the USA that has formed my lot) than the average Briton of culture.' That meant he saw Britain as part of Europe: and Europe as a world of deepened experience which began, he said, as an 'enlarged and uplifted gape', and became 'a banquet of initiation which was in the event to prolong itself through years and years'. The theme of emotional and cultural initiation, entry through art and social complication into the deeper realms of experience, became the key to his fiction. In *Roderick Hudson*, the sculptor Roderick creates a statue of a boy drinking deep from the cup of experience. In *The American*, the symbolically named Christopher Newman, the 'great Western barbarian', risks his innocent values to encounter the mannered, deceptive, experienced world of French society. In *Daisy Miller* (1878), the book that made his reputation, the central figure transforms into the young, free, formless American girl, the heiress to all the ages, encountering the miasmic corruptions of Rome. James had found his 'international theme', and by *The Europeans* (also 1878) he was confident enough to reverse it, taking a group of sophisticated European travellers on a reverse journey across the Atlantic to plain, puritan New England – as if to show the transaction worked two ways: European experience could learn from American innocence, an American writer could perform equally in the realm of the American and the European novel.

But if London and English life seemed solid and deep, the society in which James settled with such pleasure was hardly settled itself. Nor was the state of the literary form in which he sought to express himself. Certainly, as the 1870s started, the lineage of the Victorian novel – the expansive social form that had developed to explore and challenge the confident urbanizing age of industrial, imperial, world-powerful Britain – seemed secure enough. With the achievement of Dickens and Thackeray, Trollope and Bulwer-Lytton, Disraeli and Mrs Gaskell, it had become the expression of a sturdy, self-critical bourgeois culture in an age of growth, widening commerce, shifting class relations. It dealt, often realistically, sometimes romantically, generally rather sentimentally, with the changing relations of past and present, town and country, class and class, wealth and poverty. It explored religious duties, moral anxieties and social issues, told entertaining and moving stories. At times it attacked the social problems and divisions of the age, and in the 1860s what came to be called 'the Condition of England' novel challenged harsh industrialism and moral indifference, social suffering and ideological contradiction. Victorian novels came in prolix variety, but they were generally capacious, multi-narratived and episodic, and made no great claim as works of art. Then, in 1870, the leading figure of Victorian fiction, Charles Dickens, died suddenly at his home at Gad's Hill; the age of Thackeray and Trollope, the Brontës and Bulwer-Lytton, Mrs Gaskell and Wilkie Collins drew to a close. Collins wrote on to attain his greatest fame, though not for his best novels. Trollope kept writing to the decade's end, and in 1875 produced one of his finest and bitterest works, tellingly called *The Way We Live Now*, about an age that was losing all community and values, all but an economic purpose. In 1871 Charles Darwin published *The Descent of Man*, his second challenging account of human evolution, in 1873 Herbert Spencer his *Study of Sociology*; the age was beginning to revolt against itself. And the newer voices exploring the way we lived now saw a world shaped by Darwin and Spencer, Marx and John Stuart Mill – a world of fading religious certainties, evolutionary theories, political transformation, rising scientific discovery, quickening technological growth. In 1872, Samuel Butler published his dystopian fantasy *Erewhon* (it – almost – spells 'nowhere' backwards), a deeply ironic vision of an age devoted to money and machines which mocked many of the values of high Victorianism. He went further in his next novel, *The Way of All Flesh*, an attack on Victorian patriarchy, parenthood, hypocrisy and religious complacency so iconoclastic it could not be published until after Butler's death in 1903 – making it, in effect, the first Edwardian novel. According to George Meredith, it was time to expose the moral tone of the times to the searchlight of what he called 'the comic spirit'; he did just that in his novel of Victorian moral hypocrisy *The Egoist* (1879). Many new and different voices sounded in the 1870s, and none more striking than Thomas Hardy, who came to notice with his third novel *Far From the Madding Crowd* in 1874, and whose underlying note was modern tragedy, the tragedy of passage from a religious to a materialist age.

Still, it was plain to see who, after the death of Dickens, was *the* great novelist of the changing late Victorian world. 'George Eliot' – Marian Evans – was the moral conscience and artistic arbiter of British fiction. A woman writer working under a man's name, she reinforced the splendid androgyny of the novel, reconciling domestic and public, the sentimental and intellectual, the realist and romantic in one voice. She considered the novel a serious form and claimed it for moral reflection and human sympathy. She was a regional writer with a cosmopolitan mind, a historical novelist with a clear vision of the secular, humanistic process of the present, a writer who understood the great historical transformation of the age. In 1859, the year of *Origin of Species*, she published *Adam Bede*, a work that did much to give British fiction the same spirit of realism that was sweeping through the European fiction of Flaubert and Turgenev and Tolstoy. She explained her kind of art by comparing herself with the Dutch genre painters, realists of the commonplace. 'All honour and reverence to the divine beauty of form!' she wrote in *Adam Bede*:

Let us cultivate it to the utmost in men, women, and children – in our gardens and our houses. But let us love the other beauty too, which lies in no secret of proportion, but in the secret of deep human sympathy. Paint us an angel, if you can, with a floating violet robe, and a face paled with celestial light; paint us yet oftener a Madonna, turning her mild face upward and opening her arms to welcome the divine glory; but do not impose on us any aesthetic rules which shall banish from the region of Art those old women scraping carrots with their workworn hands, those heavy clowns taking holiday in a dingy pothouse, those rounded backs and stupid weather-beaten faces that have bent over the spade and done the rough work of the world . . .

Eliot's was a realism of the middle ground, less a theory than a progressive social attitude. She explored the common, the customary, the provincial, finding 'a course of delicious sympathy' in 'faithful pictures of a monotonous homely existence, which has been the fate of so many more among my fellow-mortals than a life of pomp or absolute indigence, of tragic suffering or world-shaking actions'. She wrote less of fashionable people or city life than the regions, usually the Midlands, setting many of her stories in the past, though they often showed her characters, especially her strong heroines, aspiring to the freedoms of the present and the future. If she could write felt provincial tragedy in *The Mill on the Floss* (1860), she could deal knowingly and directly with social problems and political reform in *Felix Holt, The Radical* (1866), a 'Condition of England' novel that put her with Dickens and Disraeli. In 1872, when she published *Middlemarch*, subtitled 'Scenes from Provincial Life', it was acknowledged her powers had reached their peak. The book looked vastly across the Victorian era, surveying the age of the first Reform Bill from the age of the second, capturing the time when liberalism, suffrage, the coming of the railways, the remaking of community, were issues, when the age she wrote in was beginning to take on its powerful shape. In 1876, the year James arrived in Britain, she published what proved her final novel, *Daniel Deronda*, a modern story set in the 1860s. It was her first treatment of the international social scene and political life, and James admired it. It was, he said, 'full of the world'.

James met Eliot on his previous visit to Britain in 1869, and was smitten. She was the 'one marvel' of his visit, and he declared himself 'literally in love with this great horse-faced blue-stocking', with 'a larger circumference than any woman I have ever seen'. He wrote warmly of her work, which he saw as the British equivalent to Flaubert, Turgenev and Tolstoy. She might lack the aesthetic exactness of a Flaubert, the scientific note of a Zola, the vast sweep of a Tolstoy; at times her plots could be mechanical, her devices clumsy. But she was an intellectual writer, who gave fiction emotional seriousness and profound moral reflection, whose concern was with the 'rare, precious quality of truthfulness'. Where the Victorian novel had often been ill-structured, episodic, a bundle of fragments, she saw the novel as an organic form (even though, he admitted, *Middlemarch* made 'an indifferent whole'). Qualities like this would later lead Lord David Cecil, in his *Early Victorian Novelists* (1934), to call Eliot 'the first modern novelist' – the writer who in the interests of truth to life and character, broke free of the schematic plots, sentimental moral convention, religious sentiments and melodramatic devices so characteristic of Victorian fiction, her plots finding their own course through the exacting development of a character or a moral idea. James would have nodded. In the line of British fiction, to which he meant to contribute, she was the great example, the creator of the organic novel, made of truth to life and experience. Not surprisingly he set out to renew acquaintance, and on 1 November 1878 he called on her with a companion at her house in Witley, where she kept a famously unconventional ménage with her literary adviser and sexual partner George Henry Lewes. From James's account in his memoir *The Middle Years* (1917), he clearly had high hopes of the encounter. He knew Eliot, admired her, celebrated her in print. He plainly hoped that some acknowledgement of descent, some apostolic laying on of hands, would occur – that she would recognize, as he put it, that he was doing 'her sort of work'.[4]

---

4 Henry James, *Autobiography*, ed. F. W. Dupee (New York, 1956), contains *A Small Boy and Others* (1913), *Notes of a Son and Brother* (1914), *The Middle Years* (1917). The story is also told in Gordon S. Haight, *George Eliot: A Biography* (Oxford, 1968).

The occasion, alas, did not go as planned. Tea was, James noted, 'a conceivable feature of the hour'; it was not served. The visit was brief, then, as James and his companion were going, Lewes told them to wait a moment, left, and returned with two books, saying, 'Ah, those books – take them away, please, away, away!' The books, when inspected outside, proved to be the two volumes of *The Europeans*, James's new novel, which his companion had thoughtfully sent in advance. The episode upset James, though when he recorded it many years later it was to reach a finely Jamesian explanation: 'there was positively a fine thrill in thinking of persons – or at least of a person, for any fact about Lewes was but derivative – engaged in my own pursuit and yet detached, by what I conceived, detached by a pitch of intellectual life, from all that had made it actual to myself.' So he read what happened as proof of Eliot's purity and high intellectual detachment, an abstraction from the mundane so complete that the custom of writer calling on writer scarcely interested her. Indeed the event confirmed his belief, he said, that she was the one English novelist who possessed 'a constant sense of the universal', the secret of her power. She was the novelist as moral perceiver, analytic observer, judge of values, the writer who always responded to the immense variety of life while always knowing the difficulties 'with which on every side the treatment of reality bristles'. Her characters had minds, their minds had feelings; she put 'stirred intelligence' and 'moral consciousness' at the centre of literature's actions. What did it matter about tea?

The afternoon probably had a sadder explanation. Lewes was seriously ill, and died later that month. Eliot's last novel was already written; she died in 1880, the last great Victorian novelist. Many of the great Victorian sages – Robert Browning, Herbert Spencer, T. H. Huxley – attended her notable funeral, and an age was done. But the tea-less tea-time had lasting effect on James. The next spring he sat down to write what would prove his best early novel, *The Portrait of a Lady*. It is his first real treatment of Britain, and it is probably no accident that it opens with a famous reference to the British tea-time: 'Under certain circumstances, there are few hours in life more agreeable than the hour dedicated to the ceremony known as afternoon tea. There are circumstances in which, whether you partake of the tea or not – some people of course never do, – the situation is in itself delightful.' The trace of Eliot shows strongly on the novel, and when James wrote its preface – one of the remarkable series of self-conscious prefaces he sketched for the New York Edition of 1907–17 – he made the debt clear. The book's theme – 'a certain young woman affronting her destiny' – comes, he said, from the freedom of action Eliot grants characters like Dorothea Brooke and Gwendolen Harleth, and the way she uses female consciousness as a discovering means for exploring moral and social experience. Just as important is the idea of the novel as an open form rather than a work of plotted convention, its self-discovering design coming from a character set 'free' by the author – so in James's story Ralph Touchett sets Isabel Archer financially free to 'affront' her destiny, though with ironic results. And when James famously speaks of 'the perfect dependence of the "moral" sense of a work of art on the amount of felt life concerned in producing it', he is plainly thinking of Eliot's dense realism, and claiming his own place in the same tradition. James's homage to Eliot was seriously meant, part of his ambition to be seen as a European realist, not an American romancer. Yet, like the tea-time episode itself, it reveals the considerable gap between them. The fact was that Eliot was a British Victorian writer at the close of her career, James an exiled modern novelist at the start of his.

Over the next four decades – James wrote on till his death in 1916 – his work would change fundamentally, and when he was done the British novel would be a very different creature, not least because of the way he had transformed it. For all her cosmopolitanism, George Eliot wrote from deep inside British culture. James possessed his different cosmopolitanism – what he called the American 'joke', which knows that however real and dense European society is, it is not everything, in life or fiction. He knew 'reality' in fiction was a created semblance of the real, not a direct representation of it, that the novel did not have to be a 'loose, baggy monster', but could also be a fine formal thing, an art of selection, composition, refined aesthetic intelligence. The gap was even apparent in the painterly comparisons each writer employed. Eliot's *Scenes from Provincial Life* followed the manner of past figurative Dutch genre painters: James's *Portrait of a Lady* was done in the fashion of a Whistler or a Sargent, followers of 'Impressionism', announced in Paris in the 1870s (his preface explains the book is not intended as 'an impersonal account of the affair in hand', but is 'an account of somebody's impression of it'). In fact this whole later preface is no statement from a writer of Victorian moral seriousness, but from a self-conscious modern artist first aware of his own creative method. It celebrates Eliot, but deploys an aesthetic language we at once identify as modern: 'The spreading field, the human scene, is the "choice of subject", the pierced aperture, either broad or balconied or slit-like and low-browed, is the "literary form"; but they are, singly or together, as nothing without the posted presence of the watcher – without, in other words, the consciousness of the artist,' James announces: 'Tell me what the artist is, and I will tell you of what he has *been* conscious. Thereby I shall express to you at once his boundless freedom and his "moral" reference.' For James, the morality of fiction is itself an artistic construct, realism an aesthetic project that steeps 'the whole matter in the element of reality'. Above all the posted presence of the watcher, the artist ever-present in the text, is the guarantee of value. George Eliot's tea-less tea-party may have been an afternoon of Victorian social confusions. It is also as good a place as any for observing the great turn of the novel – the continuity and discontinuity, the bridge and the chasm, that moved fiction out of Victorianism and into the spirit of the modern.

4

A jaundiced critic once divided Henry James's five decades of work into three phases: James the First, James the Second and James the Old Pretender. We don't have to agree with the complaint to accept the notion – that James's work was a development through distinct and remarkable stages into an art of high complexity and modern difficulties. The first phase, largely devoted to James's exploration of the 'international theme', takes us from the early slight *Watch and Ward* (1871), through the sharp irony of James's very New York novel *Washington Square* (1880), to *The Portrait of a Lady* (1881) – his first great book, recognizably a fiction in transition. *Washington Square* is an ironic tale of female imprisonment, about the romantic dreams of Catherine Sloper, who ends the book trapped and doing 'basket-work for life'. *The Portrait of a Lady*, though, has Isabel Archer as the young, strong-willed American girl set free, in motion through three different European societies – aristocratic Britain, socialite France, aesthetic Italy. Her search for experience is darkened, her freedom finally trapped, by the aesthetic sterility of Gilbert Osmond and the corrupt cunning of Madame Merle. The method is contemporary realism, what James called 'solidity of specification', using exterior representation, authorial omniscience, an objectively 'rounded' view of character. But the book is already 'modern' in ways Eliot's are not – filled with displaced aristocrats, wealthy American tourists, businessmen and journalists, train timetables and the tele-graph. Isabel is a 'New Woman', and when she challenges Madame Merle's insistence that we are merely what society says we are, we see James's very American presumption that consciousness precedes social actuality. And in James concern with consciousness – the felt life and experiential consciousness of the characters, and the self-consciousness of the artist, the 'posted watcher' in the text – is everywhere an issue. 'The centre of interest throughout *Roderick [Hudson]* is Rowland Mallett's consciousness, and the drama is the very drama of that consciousness,' James's preface notes of this early novel. The drama of consciousness in its struggle with the weight of society, fed by James's American awareness of the ambiguity of social codes and institutions, would lead his work through the phases that followed, out of his early realism toward the 'modern' itself.

George Eliot's death in 1880 effectively marked the end of the Victorian novel. The 1870s had been a time of transition; the 1880s were a time of literary transformation, and writer after writer asserted the need to break free of Victorian conventions. Social theories were changing, rising expectations coupled with economic downturn fuelled political unrest, the logic of positivism and social determinism was increasingly accepted. New writers found the Victorian tradition both aesthetically and morally constraining, and they looked else-where, above all to Paris – where, in 1880, two writers well known to James published highly influential works. Guy de Maupassant brought out his frank tale of a fat working-class girl, *Boule de Suif*, and Emile Zola his sexually scandalous *Nana*, as well as the essay *Le Roman expérimental* (*The Experimental Novel*), a literary manifesto for the rising trend of Naturalism. Zola used the term 'experimental novel' in a different, more scientific, sense than we would now expect. His experiment was sociological and deterministic; he urged that, using laboratory-style methods and documentary and journalistic techniques, novelists should explore systems and processes, the laws of economics, heredity, environment and social evolution, to deter-mine the fate of typical, representative characters. 'A symmetry is established,' he claimed, 'the story composes itself out of all the collected observations, all the notes, one leading to another by the very enchainment of the characters, and the conclusion is nothing more than a natural and inevitable consequence.' This was realism schematized; individuals were subject to universal systems, typified general laws; as Zola noted, 'A like determinism will govern the stones of the roadway and the brain of man.' Naturalism moved away from the liberal and the moral novel, the novel of independent conscious-ness; it acknowledged genetic drives, the power of heredity, economic determinism, the force of sexual instinct, the *bête humaine*, the animal in man. It perceived the age of the mass, the machine, the crowded and inhuman city; it looked at the ghettos, the age of commodities, rising department stores, the industrial conditions of workers, the visible aspects and processes of the modern itself. It claimed scientific rationality rather than religious or moral wisdom; it was the art of the direct, the frank, the free, the contemporary – the modern tone itself.

For new British writers of the 1880s, Naturalism offered an explor-ing frankness and set a new mood. George Moore, from Ireland, was a painter as well as a novelist; he studied in Paris, and picked up Naturalism at first hand. 'The idea of a new art based on science . . . an art that should explain all things and embrace modern life in its entirety . . . filled me with wonder,' he said. He called his clever, erotic novel of bohemian life *A Modern Lover* (1883), presenting the Naturalist spirit as the spirit of the modern itself. *A Mummer's Wife* (1885) mixed determinist assumptions, aesthetic themes and sexual frankness, and was fiercely attacked. In a notorious response, *Literature at Nurse* (1885), Moore assaulted the moralistic and repressive views held by British critics of fiction. For the rest of the decade the 'novel' became a field of controversy, not least because sexual representation was central to the issue. Part of the question was frankness in representing sexual activities; this became known as 'Zolaism'. But, as greater social, emotional and sexual opportunities for women grew, 'New Woman' novels by writers like 'John Law' (Margaret Harkness), feminist socialist author of *A City Girl: A Realistic Story* (1887), 'George Egerton' (Mary Chavelita Bright), 'Sarah Grand' (Francis Clark), 'Iota' (Kathleen Caffyn), Charlotte Mew and Ada Leverson challenged George Eliot's portrait of passive female suffering with radical different images of women's needs and experience. What Thomas Hardy called 'the immortal puzzle – given the man and woman, how to find a basis for their sexual relation', in other words the question of 'modern marriage', became a central theme, creating a new explicitness that offended church, press, the lending libraries. The novel again became a place for treating dark social problems or engaging controversial issues, and, following the Naturalist code, it adventured freely into the world of the unexplored, the unexpressed, the unwritten, the unclassed. For George Gissing, the Yorkshire radical whose life was always to be marked by poverty and a sense of exclusion, Naturalism was less a form of art than a bitter social cry, the voice of the unrecorded, the 'nether world'. 'We must dig deeper, get into untouched social strata,' he said, and in books like *Workers in the Dawn* (1880), *The Unclassed* (1884), *Demos* (1886), and *The Nether World* (1889) – the very titles reveal their social themes – he did, exploring the facts of 'grinding poverty', the pressures of the 'competitive system', the bleak trapped lives and the grim struggle of the new urban melting-pot, creating 'the working-class novel'. For such writers and those who came after, like Arnold Bennett, Somerset Maugham and Robert Tressell, author of *The Ragged-Trousered Philanthropists* (1914), Naturalism marked the opening of the novel into an exploration of the social pains and contradictions of the bourgeois age.

James was no Naturalist. Impressed as he was by what he called its 'magnificent treadmill of the pigeon-holed and the documented', he argued that the real adventures of the artistic spirit were precisely what was not reducible to 'notes', that the novel's 'air of reality' did not come from transcribed facts, that Naturalism was a realism wanting in reality, a simplification of fiction: 'The individual life is, if not wholly absent, reflected in coarse and common, in generalized terms.' Still, as over the Eighties controversy about the novel grew, he sided with the new trends, arguing that Naturalism had made the novel into a form at last open to artistic argument. As he put it in his key essay 'The Art of Fiction' (1884): 'Only a short while ago it might have been supposed that the English novel was not what the French call *discutable*. It had no air of having a theory, a conviction, a consciousness of itself behind it – of being the expression of an artistic faith, the result of choice and comparison . . . Art lives upon discussion, upon experiment, upon curiosity, upon variety of attempt . . .' On his own fiction the effect was plain. In 1884 he was indeed himself out on the magnificent treadmill, researching a novel about the political confusion, the social immensity, and the hard detail of contemporary London: 'I have been all morning at Millbank prison (horrible place) collecting notes for a fictional scene,' he wrote in a letter. 'You see I am quite the Naturalist.' That novel, *The Princess Casamassima*, and a second, *The Bostonians*, both came out in 1886; they mark a fundamental change in his work, and are the two chief novels of his middle period, James the Second. Both are novels of contemporary society, with strongly political themes. *The Bostonians*, set entirely in contemporary America, deals with the conflicting forces of American culture: art and commerce, North and South, men and women. 'I wished to write a very American tale . . . and I asked myself what was the most salient and peculiar point in our social life,' he noted. 'The answer was: the situation of women, the decline of the sentiment of sex, the agitation on their behalf.' The story is an ironically told tale of the battle for Verena Tarrant's soul between a radical New England feminist and a Southern gentleman, a tale of gender war. But it is also a novel about the modern city, about a Boston leaving the age of the old New England social and cultural ascendancy and becoming something new: a Boston divided between 'chimneys and steeples, straight, sordid tubes of factories and engine-shops, or the spare, heaven-ward finger of the New England meeting house'.

In the same way James's London novel *The Princess Casamassima* – probably his most under-estimated work – is a very political novel about the modern city in the age of 'horrible numerosities'. It portrays an age when the spectre of international terrorism was rising across Europe, as anarchist and Fenian outrages increased, a climate Joseph Conrad returned to in *The Secret Agent* twenty years later. A poor young man, Hyacinth Robinson, is caught up in an international revolutionary conspiracy; as his name suggests, he finds himself split, between culture and anarchy, wealth and poverty, 'Society' and those (some of them from 'Society') who want to destroy society. It is a story of London as 'the greatest aggregation in the world', a 'great grey Babylon', divided between wealth and poverty, those who possess culture and those kept alien from it and who represent 'the sick, eternal misery crying out of the darkness in vain'. These are Naturalist themes, but in fact James's is less a Naturalist's city than an Impressionist's: 'London damp: the way the winter fog blurred and suffused the whole place, made it seem bigger and more crowded, produced halos and dim radiations, trickles and evaporations, on the panes of glass.' The impressions – 'the assault directly made by the great city on an imagination quick to react' – are, James explains in his preface, primarily those of Hyacinth Robinson, an 'obscure intelligent creature whose education should be almost wholly derived from them, capable of profiting by all the civilization, all the accumulation to which they testify, yet condemned to see these things only from outside'. James rejects the great Naturalist sweep, and prefers 'intensity' ('Without intensity where is vividness, and without vividness where is presentability?' he asks us). He moves close in, using what he called 'concentrated individual notation', the world seen through the minds that live in it, so 'placing in the middle of the light, the most polished of possible mirrors of the subject'. *The Princess Casamassima* is a complex political novel, about strong social ideas and the unfolding of revolutionary events. But it is also about the paradox of culture, which is art and humanity, but also accumulation, wealth and style as power, enfolded in the fog of resentful poverty and exclusion. In fact James creates a modernist city novel, which takes its place with other works – Conrad's *The Secret Agent*, Biely's *Saint Petersburg*, Joyce's *Ulysses*, John Dos Passos's *Manhattan Transfer* – about the vast, fragmentary, many-cultured, many-voiced, Babylonian modern metropolis, which can only be seen as fleeting, synchronic, beyond wholeness or unity.

His novels of the Eighties began to lose James his public. The darkening of his social vision, the fragmentation of his once more solid world, the growing technical complexity and verbal density, the fact that his characters now seemed ambiguous rather than sympathetic, all made him seem difficult, and the reviewers attacked: 'I have entered upon evil days,' he noted. With his next book *The Tragic Muse* (1890) he returned to a more familiar subject, a portrait of upper middle-class society, only to reveal how much his view of society had changed – it was no longer a place of experience and moral opportunity, but of concealments, deceptions, hypocrisies and shadows. The book depends on what the social psychologist Erving Goffman – in his *The Presentation of Self in Everyday Life* (1959) – names 'the dramaturgical analogy'. In this view of the world the self is an actor and society a theatre, a stage where we present, through changing performances and false masks, the fiction that passes for our so-called substantial self. In the book Miriam Rooth is 'a series of masks' – 'her character was simply to hold you by the particular spell; any other – the good-nature of home, the relation to her mother, her friends, her lovers, her debts – was not worth speaking of . . . These things were the fiction and shadows; the representation was the deep substance.' His fine short stories of this time show how preoccupied James had become with the question of 'the real thing' – whether there was a solid observable reality, or whether all is art, artifice, illusion. The qualities James once called the stuff of fiction – 'solidity of specification', 'accumulated characters', 'thickness of motive' – now took on a new ambiguity. Characters grow more self-conscious, less solid; art spreads from the artist to take in his subjects. It was this increasing sense of life's theatricality, as well as the relative failure of his recent novels, that took James off into the unfortunate adventures of writing for the stage. For several years in the early Nineties, thinking his kind of novel was dead, he did his main work for the theatre, an unhappy diversion of his talents which culminated in the failure of his play *Guy Domville* in 1895.

In retrospect this choice seems tragic. For the novel was now moving James's way, departing the Naturalism and political urgencies of the Eighties for the Aesthetic renewal of the Nineties. In 1891 the Zola disciple Paul Alexis availed himself of an important new technology and sent a famous literary telegram to an inquiring Parisian journalist (inquiring journalists were another phenomenon of the age). 'Naturalism not dead,' he wired. 'Letter follows.' In the letter that followed, Alexis claimed the scientific, reforming vision marked by Naturalism would come to mark twentieth-century literature. And Naturalism was not dead; Ibsen represented it in theatre (though his later works were already moving toward Symbolism), and young writers in Britain, America and Russia advanced its message. From Gissing and Arthur Morrison (*A Child of the Jago*, 1896) to Arnold Bennett and H. G. Wells, it would be a way of detailing the world of slum and provincial life, the experience of the rising lower middle class and the changes in sexual *mores*, the social problems and aspirations of the age. Even so, the magnificent treadmill was beginning to turn more slowly. Writers were wearying of prolix documentary, and life was proving a commodity in endless supply. Max Beerbohm smartly summed up the fact-sodden Eighties – 'To give an accurate and exhaustive account of that period would require a far less brilliant pen than mine,' he wrote – and Oscar Wilde in 1889 produced his anti-realist manifesto 'The Decay of Lying', complaining about novels 'so lifelike that no one can possibly believe in their probability'. In the *fin-de-siècle* shadows, Aestheticism, Art for Art's Sake, Decadence gathered. France again showed the way. In 1884 J-K. Huysmans brought out his mannered portrait of aristocratic decadence *A rebours* (*Against the Grain*), which influenced Wilde; in 1890 P. A. Villiers de l'Isle-Adam produced his visionary prose-drama *Axel* ('Live? our servants will do that for us . . . Oh, the external world! Let us not be made dupes by the old slave'). New writers of 'consciousness' like Paul Bourget and Edouard Dujardin – deviser of the 'interior monologue' developed by James Joyce – came to attention; the philosopher Henri Bergson was elaborating his philosophy of 'interior time', interposing between individual and interior world a concept of consciousness and inner memory that would strongly influence fiction (including that of his cousin by marriage, Marcel Proust). In 1890 Henry's brother William published his *Principles of Psychology*, not only an exploration of the new science revolutionizing modern thought – Sigmund Freud in Vienna was already exploring the notion of a secret and recessive unconscious forging human behaviour – but also the source of a famous literary phrase. Arguing that the mind is not the mirror of matter, but has its own motions and structures apprehending experience, James proposed: 'In talking of it hereafter, let us call it the stream of thought, of consciousness, or of the subjective life.' Interior monologue, stream of consciousness, aesthetic subjectivity, creative intuition, the labyrinthine indirection of meaning, the shifting and impressionistic nature of registered reality – all became key preoccupations of the 1890s. If, as James said in 'The Art of Fiction', the only thing we can demand of the novel in advance is that it be interesting, if novels 'are as various as the temperament of man, and . . . successful in proportion as they reveal a particular mind, different from others', if the novel, in its broadest sense 'a personal, a direct impression of life', was now coming to 'self-consciousness', then the brew from which this 'modern novel' would come was already forming in the aesthetic climate of the early Nineties.

Other deep changes were transforming fiction too. The lending libraries were losing their moral control, printing and publishing technologies were changing, the commercial marketplace was growing fast. 'Cheap fiction' meant a new stratification of the audience (when George Gissing published his *New Grub Street* in 1891, the 'nether world' he explored was not the urban poor but the new proletariat of writing itself), and 'difficult fiction' grew harder to sell, though it was also increasingly acknowledged as 'conscious art'. All this increased James's dismay. But in 1897 he returned triumphantly to the novel, with two short, remarkable works, *The Spoils of Poynton* and *What Maisie Knew*. And now, in the changing climate, the point began to be seen, certainly by two of the most promising writers of the next generation, Joseph Conrad and Ford Madox Ford, who recognized *The Spoils* . . . as 'the technical high-water mark of all James's work', and developed his methods. Even reviewers, notorious for being late, began to get it; one hailed *What Maisie Knew* as adding 'a whole new conception of reality to the art of fiction'. Not everyone welcomed late James, James the Old Pretender; even his friends admitted his gift for difficulty. Conrad agreed the man in the street would never read him; his good friend Edith Wharton, who generously diverted some of her own royalties to subsidize the badly selling New York Edition, said even she couldn't read the final works, even though some people thought she had written them. Thomas Hardy felt he had 'a ponderously warm manner of saying nothing in infinite sentences'; his once good friend H. G. Wells later attacked him viciously. The sense of difficulty was understandable. Some – not all – of the late books that followed are labyrinthine and indirect; his method of dictating them did not always help. But the important thing was that James's 'painting' was losing its direct mimesis, becoming ever more an 'impression', stressing, like contemporary painters, the dominance of the medium over the content, the way of seeing over the subject. The novel, James now emphasized, was not a reported 'adventure'. It was a composition, an 'affair', a 'doing' that composed its own vision, its illusion of reality. Realism had not left his work entirely, but the observed reality was no longer that of a moral community, an agreed common culture. It was a refracted thing, seen through angles of vision, through the evolving consciousness of its perceivers. And it was not so much a 'dense society' that set a novelist in motion, but the 'Things, always the splendid Things', that in *The Spoils of Poynton* make up 'the sum of the world'. Culture dissolves into possessions, commodities, *objets d'art*, generally with a price-tag attached. Similarly, sexual relations are not a sphere of romantic discovery but are complex transactions about things, rights, possession.

James's new, fragmentary, darkened world of experience comes out clearly in *What Maisie Knew*, the most cunning of his new novels. The title tells all; the key to the tale, the preface explains, is the young girl Maisie, the 'central vessel of consciousness', through whose eyes the story is seen. What she knows or in childish 'innocence' does not know – all she sees, feels, senses, registers or avoids – is what we get by way of story. The adult reader can intuit those things, above all sexual things, that Maisie does not know, though by the end we are not clear how much knowledge she possesses. For knowing is itself ambiguous, and the book itself refuses to provide its reader with a complete 'knowledge'. This is a tale of innocence not learning from but corrupted or blocked by experience; by limiting his tale to one 'knowing' consciousness James has upturned the social spread and moral breadth of his earlier fiction. Innocence is a toy – Maisie is used as a token, a plaything, a message, by her adulterous and corrupt parents – and experience is not wisdom, which means innocence is itself an ambiguity. That theme passed on to the great ghost story James would tell as the century ended, *The Turn of the Screw* (1898). James was now fascinated with what one critic calls 'the haunted house of Victorian culture', the shadow world behind the social façade that other writers like Stevenson (*Dr Jekyll and Mr Hyde*) and Wilde (*The Picture of Dorian Gray*) were exploring, and Gothic and the ghost story were becoming ever more popular as the age examined its own hidden spaces. James accepts many of the Gothic conventions: the strange country house, the governess, ambiguously placed between the master, her charges and the other servants, her responsibility for protecting 'innocence' while harbouring romantic dreams, her acceptance of mysterious duties. The great change he makes is to make this a 'psychological' ghost story, based on odd angles of perception and ambiguous states of mind and emotion, as well as on the dangerous border between childish 'innocence' and adult sexuality. The tale is deceptive; as the second narrator Douglas says, 'The story *won't* tell . . . not in any literal vulgar way.' The governess narrator may be repressed or deluded, and the story is filled with blanks and indirections, and finally refuses the conventional finality of fiction (it creates an 'incomplete signification', as the modern critics say). In fact it leaves us, as James would say, within 'the beautiful difficulties of art'. Its ambiguities point to the problems of many later modern fictions and modern creativity – how 'whole' is a story? how much of it should be told? where and why does closure come? is completeness desirable, since life and consciousness do not have concluded shapes? how do we make stories appear 'true'? As James wrote his essay 'The Future of the Novel' in 1899, looking round him as the century turned, he had good reason to say that the novel was at last coming to self-consciousness, and becoming a complex, speculative and modern art.

And if so he was becoming the modern master, the writer who had gone through the passage from realism and Naturalism, and come to aestheticism and now, increasingly, to Modernism. Living now at Rye in Sussex, he produced, over the turning of the century, and in a great creative burst, some of his most remarkable works. By now he had accepted he would never be a popular novelist, but he would be a discovering one. He produced the wry mannered social comedy of *The Awkward Age* (1899), the baffling ambiguity of *The Sacred Fount* (1901) – a work of incomplete investigation about the problem of reading and decoding human relations that has rightly been compared with the French *nouveau roman*. There was the symbolist *The Wings of the Dove* (1902), with its famous techniques of grammatical indirection ('She waited, Kate Croy, for her father to come in . . .'), with its implication for the indirectness of all human subjectivities and all human relations, but also the far more accessible *The Ambassadors* (1903), the tale of Lambert Strether, the man who comes to Europe in quest of a young artist and learns at last to see, to discover the nature of the impression, and so to live, learning the book's lesson: 'Live all you can; it's a mistake not to.' He returned to and rewrote the international novel in *The Golden Bowl* (1904), with its central image of the cracked bowl of loving human relations, which is related to similar cracks in all objects of desire. Here the social depth of Europe, the discovering innocence of America, turn back on themselves: the European aristocrat has the name of Prince Amerigo, while wealthy Americans collect and commodify the arts of Europe. In their different ways these books express the indirection of James's late discourse, 'those sentences which delay exact significance to the end and even leave it problematic then, casting the reader on his impressions like a boat surrendered to a stream' – the discourse that is not just a way of telling the story, but *is* the story.[5] In all of them, as he said in his preface to *The Ambassadors*, there are hence two fundamental stories: 'There is the story of one's hero and then, thanks to the intimate connection of things, the story of one's story itself.'

'I sat for a long while with the closed volume in my hand going over the preface in my mind and thinking – that is how it began, that's how it was done,' Conrad wrote on receiving the first volumes of the New York Edition, which came out alongside the final novels. James was now unmistakably the Master. What he sought to do was apparent not just in the fiction he wrote, but in what he wrote about fiction – in the key essays 'The Art of Fiction' (1884), 'The Future of the Novel' (1899) and 'The New Novel' (1914); in these prefaces to the twenty-four-volume New York Edition (1907–17); in the extraordinary records he kept in his notebooks of his 'germs' and '*données*', now available to us.[6] His late novels, as some contemporaries saw, are modern because they present a late nineteenth- and early twentieth-century world adrift from the old anchors and certainties, filled with anxieties of consciousness and unexpected structures of discovery. It is a world of impressionism, but also hard materialism, *belle-époque* lives and sudden wealth, businessmen and tycoons and poor European princes, rising cultural anxieties about the blankness of experience and the cultureless void on which culture or meaning is overlaid. In all this James had come a long way from George Eliot's tea-less tea-time of 1878, his later books amending, subverting or creatively misreading his earlier vision of realism. He had found, as he said, that the house of fiction had many windows, and reality was to be seen from many standpoints. The novel was no plain report on life, and its rules were born from within, from the potential of creative making. Novelists do not report but create, discover and compose and dramatize, and it is art that makes life and creates importance. Stories are

5 Millicent Bell, *Meaning in Henry James* (Cambridge, Mass., and London, 1991).
6 F. O. Matthiessen and Kenneth B. Murdock (eds.), *The Notebooks of Henry James* (New York, 1947).

purpose, greedily rewrites and reinterprets another. Hardy thus became one of the great antecedents of modern British fiction, as indeed he did of modern poetry, and for Lawrence he marked the passage out of Victorian fiction to his kind of novel, just as James did for Conrad and Ford. James and Hardy belonged to the same literary generation, started their major work in the 1870s, and shared a mutual influence in George Eliot. Beyond that, they seemingly had little in common, and the paths away from them also seem to divide. Neither admired the work of the other. James spoke of 'good little Thomas Hardy', but found his novels technically naive; Hardy said 'James's subjects are those one could be interested in when there is nothing larger to think of.' This was not surprising, for if they shared some common influence in George Eliot they drew on quite different sides of her work. James was the cosmopolitan who chose his own relation to the British tradition; Hardy was the provincial writer who by art and instinct extended what he saw as an already founded heritage of themes, concerns, communities, communal language. The son of an American Swedenborgian whose 'native land' was the wandering James family, and the builder's son from Dorset who lived and largely wrote from within the confines of the West Country, came to writing from different places, and developed different destinies for themselves, finally becoming probably the two great opposites of the late nineteenth-century novel in Britain. James had his 'international theme' and Hardy had his indurant Wessex. James was the formalist, the writer of what Mark Schorer calls 'technique as discovery', while Hardy wrote grainily about an ordinary world people recognized and hardships and sufferings they daily faced. James challenged and tested the role of the storyteller; Hardy accepted it, writing in an omniscient, choric, sometimes God-like way in what he considered a Godless world. James saw fiction as a discovery of knowledge, a careful apprehension of experience, and hungered for the sensations of 'felt life', reached through art. Hardy felt experience as the ominous weight of life itself, and brooded tragically or stoically before it, making his characters not so much discover experience as suffer it. James let his plots discover themselves from their infant germs; Hardy subjected his characters to his inexorable plots, those plots to cosmic ironies.

James's novels claim the freedom of form; Hardy's are schematically made, are written, as one admirer, Marcel Proust, observed, with the solid geometry of the master stonemason.

If Lawrence rightly considered Hardy to be a 'modern' writer, it was for reasons quite different from those we tie to James. It had to do with his vision of a modern fate, a vision Lawrence quarrelled with but entirely understood. As E. M. Forster once said, 'The fate above us, not the fate working through us – that is what is eminent and memorable in the Wessex novels'; Hardy had largely resolved the nature of the human condition, acknowledged the human irony, before he began his books. It was his aim of making fiction the field of a modern metaphysic, however arguable, that for Lawrence made him a writer to contend with. Hardy started off in a familiar world of culture, nature and British history, and turned it into drama, metaphor and crisis, making his Wessex not only a large regional landscape but a primal scene, a place of nature and of culture, of eternity and of social change. When, in late life, he produced his 'Wessex Edition', he too divided his novels into three groups – very different, though, from those applied to James. There were the novels of 'Character and Environment', the 'Romances and Fantasies', the 'Novels of Ingenuity', and Wessex was stage to all. He might write of it joyously, as in *Under the Greenwood Tree* (1872), his story of the Mellstock choir, a pleasant rural comedy with a sub-title that shadows George Eliot, 'A Rural Painting of the Dutch School'. But it could equally be the field for a very modern tragedy, as in *Jude the Obscure* (1895). With his third novel *Far From the Madding Crowd* (1874) he laid full claim to his region, making it what William Faulkner, constructing his own distinctive region of Mississippi in the next century, called his own 'postage stamp of soil', on which all kinds of story could unfold. The writer – Hardy explained, when he tried to draw his novels together for the Wessex Edition – needs a 'territorial definition of some sort to lend unity', a place part real and part dream, which would permit 'a deeper, more essential, more transcendent handling'. For 'that which is apparently local should be really universal', he said, expressing the faith of the local-colour movement that played so large a part in late nineteenth-century fiction right across Europe. But Wessex was not just an indurant land of nature; as Raymond Williams has said, it was a 'border country . . . between custom and education, between work and ideas, between love of place and experience of change'.[8]

Lawrence was surely right. From *Far From the Madding Crowd* onward, Hardy was a 'modern' novelist, even if the mostly tragic fortunes of modernity were to be played out on a pastoral Wessex stage. That book's title, from Gray's 'Elegy in a Country Churchyard', makes Hardy's claim to pastoral clear at once. This is a tale set in a space apart, and the name of the central character, Gabriel Oak, the long-enduring sheep farmer, tells us that some at least of the characters are imbued with nature's spirit. But it is plain that Wessex is a wide stage, onto which come figures and influences from the world elsewhere; it is also plain that the nature Hardy is reflecting on is not the illuminating guide and wise friend of the British Romantic poets. It is prehistoric, born of a druidic, pagan past. It is subject to the cosmic workings of an indifferent and irrational universe, a place of vast transitions and modernizing change, suffering the shifts of consciousness that move us painfully from one historical age to another. Hardy may not have been a highly educated writer; that shows in the heavy hand of some of his prose. But he was widely read, above all in the writers of nineteenth-century pessimism: Darwin, Spencer, Mill, Schopenhauer, von Hartmann, the philosophers of the age of blind evolution, random process, the Unconscious Will. With the publication of Darwin's *Origin of Species* (1859) and *The Descent of Man* (1871), conceptions of progress had turned to theories of chance, humanist hopes into cosmic anxieties, eternal purpose into random selection. In an age caught between God and science, continuity and unbidden change, new troubled speculations about individuality and process began to arise. As William James would observe in 1895: 'the visible surfaces of heaven and earth refuse to be brought by us into any intelligible unity at all. Every phenomenon that we could praise there exists cheek by jowl with some contrary phenomenon that cancels all its religious effect on the mind. Deity . . . rolls all things together to a common doom.' Hardy could have written this; it may

8 Raymond Williams, *The English Novel from Dickens to Lawrence* (London, 1970).

well have been guided by his pervasive, gloomy vision; but, for many more than Hardy, this was the age of 'pessimism'.

Over three decades and fourteen extremely various novels – comedies, tragedies, romances, tales of ingenuity – Hardy went on to explore the British world under the gaze of that dark vision. *The Return of the Native* (1878), the first of the great novels, is set back in the 1840s; like many Victorians Hardy constantly returned to the historical novel. The book is dominated by the primal scene of Egdon Heath, with 'its lonely face, suggesting tragic possibilities', which will emerge. On the heath, individuals are 'solitary atoms of life', and live in a dangerous natural and cosmic space: 'Above the plain rose the hill, above the hill rose the barrow, and above the barrow rose the figure. Above the figure was nothing that could be mapped elsewhere than on a celestial globe.' Individuals like the 'figure', Eustacia Vye, either struggle aspiringly up from nature into that larger space, or, like the cosmopolitan traveller Clym Yeobright ('Mentally he was in a provincial future, that is, he was in many points abreast with the central town thinkers of his date'), are blindly returned to nature, with their burden of 'modern nerves'. They live in a universe neither moral nor immoral, but unmoral ('there may be consciousness, infinitely far off, at the other end of the chain of phenomena, always striving to express itself, and always baffled and blundering, just as the spirits seem to be,' Hardy once wrote). They perform some evolutionary task, Darwinian or Lamarckian, but it is not clear by what need or to what end; meanwhile the mind is 'adrift on change, and harassed by the irrepressible new', for the eternal space is also a changing history, a passage, Hardy says here, 'from the bucolic to the intellectual life'. His pessimism was not entire, nor was it universal. When readers disliked the grimness of *The Return of the Native*, he gave them one of his light romantic works, *The Trumpet Major* (1880), set back in the Napoleonic Wars. Still, it was that pessimism, that sense of the futile evolution of history, that awareness of life's struggle and humanity's ironic fate, that made him one of the deepest as well as most dissenting voices of late-Victorian fiction.

Like James's, Hardy's work was plainly changed by the changed fictional climate of the 1880s. No more than James could he be a conventional Naturalist; his view of irony, fate and chance was distinctive, and nothing like Zola's environmental or genetic determinism. It came from a kind of cosmic brooding, an innate pessimism, which Lawrence correctly saw as a tragic metaphor of the human condition. He certainly did not write a fictional documentary, and observed that ' "realism" is not art.' His fiction was architectural, poetic, symbolistic, and at times surreal, and utterly distinguished from most Naturalism by the cosmic vastness of the stage on which it is set. Naturalism, too, was generally an affair of cities, crowds and masses; it could be said that Hardy returned it to the world of nature it had, after all, come from. But even while he espoused its sexual frankness, Hardy was not concerned, as such, with the *bête humaine*; indeed it was precisely the struggle of consciousness away from the animal about which he wrote best.[9] For all their tales of sexuality, erroneous desire, misplaced passion and modern marriage leading to modern divorce, for all that the aspirations of his characters are repeatedly held in check by the failure of the evolutionary struggle for growth and survival, that struggle is always felt within, by the living and self-conscious mind, as it develops its own desires and dreams, its hungers of consciousness, its distinctive individualisms. Admittedly, while humankind has consciousness, the forces that control it have not, or at least they reject human intention. In *Two on a Tower* (1882), he attempted to treat this lyrically, aiming to set 'the emotional history of two infinitesimal lives against the stupendous background of the stellar universe'. But with the final group of late novels – *The Mayor of Casterbridge* (1886), *The Woodlanders* (1887), *Tess of the D'Urbervilles* (1891), *Jude the Obscure* (1895) – which form the major era of his work, he acknowledged that for his central theme the real mode was tragedy.

In these books themes that plainly belong to the age of Naturalism

9 What was the *bête humaine*? Zola gave one important explanation in the preface he wrote for *Thérèse Raquin* (1867): 'I had only one desire: given a highly sexed man and an unsatisfied woman, to uncover the animal side of them and that alone, then throw them together and note down with scrupulous care the sensations and actions of these creatures. I simply applied to two living bodies the analytical method that surgeons apply to corpses . . .'

emerge as something larger. Here Wessex, as a choric stage, dissolves into a general modernizing process. And these are stories of isolated individuals, struggling for consciousness against the changing world: modern tragedies, works of ironic fatality, temperamental passion. The drunkenness, intemperate anger and stubbornness that eventually destroy the aspiring Michael Henchard in *The Mayor of Casterbridge* can be seen as Naturalist forces as much as tragic inner flaws, and chance and circumstance conspire in his downfall; but so does the historical cycle and the rise of the new order represented by Farfrae. *The Woodlanders* is an oddly sunny book for late Hardy, and his own favourite, but it too is about a world blighted by destiny, blind chance, corrupted growth, failed sexual relations. Above all there is the 'Unfulfilled Intention': 'Here as everywhere, the Unfulfilled Intention, which makes life what it is, was as obvious as it could be among the depraved crowds of a city slum. The leaf was deformed, the curve was crippled, the taper was interrupted; the lichen ate the vigour of the stalk, and the ivy slowly strangled to death the promising sapling.' Tess of the D'Urbervilles is, as the subtitle defiantly says, 'a pure woman,' a victimized social heroine of nineteenth-century fiction, trapped between nature and public morality – a familiar Naturalist theme – but equally the victim of 'the Unfulfilled Intention'. As both Durbeyfield and D'Urberville, she is divided both in her social and her genetic inheritance, and she equally suffers from 'the mutually destructive interdependence of flesh and spirit'. Seduced and betrayed, she finally hangs for murder, in what Hardy sees as a tragic cycle: 'The President of the Immortals (in the Aeschylean phrase) had ended his sport with Tess.' *Jude the Obscure* is also about the 'deadly war waged between flesh and spirit', and is 'a tragedy of unfulfilled aims'. Jude Fawley is again seeking to evolve from a primitive to a civilized existence, only to be defeated by what seem eternal forces. Some are social, born of the pressures of class and the limits of education, 'the artificial system of things'; others are larger powers – crossed destinies, the competing energies of survival and destruction, nature as rank abundance and nature as rank deceit, 'man and senseless circumstance', which has its way in the end.

But, as Lawrence, reading Hardy for his own purposes, noticed, these 'modern tragedies' are important and modern not simply for their sense of social victimization, nor their vision of cosmic gloom and life's little ironies. Their strength lay in the instinct of the modern itself – Hardy's sensuous understanding of the living struggle of human consciousness, the battle of the human flesh and spirit, and the metaphysical force with which he saw the relation between the world of social experience and individual felt experience of being, both in society and in nature. Hardy's work was praised, or blamed, for its Olympian detachment, its highly plotted narrative, its familiar philosophizing: 'What,' asked Edmund Gosse in his review of *Jude*, 'has Providence done to Mr Hardy that he should rise up in the arable land of Wessex and shake his fist at his Creator?' But Lawrence noticed something different, an intense intimacy between the author and the inner life of his created characters. Tess herself acknowledges the world to be 'a psychological phenomenon'; meanwhile Hardy intimately follows her as she intensifies 'the natural processes around her until they seemed part of her own story'. Similarly Jude Fawley's fate may be plainly plotted from without, but it is also deeply felt from within, as a state of consciousness. As a child growing up toward adult awareness, Jude looks out from under his straw hat and feels life as 'a sort of shuddering': 'All around you there seemed to be something glaring, garish, rattling, and the noises and glares hit upon the little cell called your life, and shook it, and warped it.' Hardy's novels, especially the late ones, were, as Lawrence saw, about the struggling aspiration of human consciousness and its vital energy to grow away from nature or Wessex and become more than it is. In the event that aspiration is stifled, by social convention or moral conditioning, by blind chance and universal fatality, or else by what in *Tess* is called 'the chronic melancholy which is taking hold of the civilized races with the decline of belief in a beneficent Power'. By Lawrence's more modern, more vitalist, more Nietzschean view of things, this means that what holds his characters, and the world of nature and society, back from emergence and realization is on the one hand their own 'weak life-flow', and on the other Hardy's flawed metaphysic, his post-Darwinian pessimism. At the same time they contain the essential struggle, the energy and desire of human consciousness and human evolution to pass from the pre-modern to the modern age. Lawrence's own books could therefore take up the story, and they do, only to develop, in a process of evolutionary return, toward tragedy, the tragedy of consciousness that invests his own late books forty years on.

This is Lawrence's Hardy, but it points us to what was so modern in his work. For modernity is indeed one of Hardy's most essential themes, especially in the late fiction. *Jude the Obscure*, his last and most powerful novel, is the story of the endeavour to reach a new awareness, through social advancement, through education, through new emotion. Jude, with his orphaned, suffering, struggling consciousness, is an uprooted modern self, seeking a new culture that will lift him out of primal nature into spirituality and civilization, from Arabella to Christminster. Sue calls herself a 'modernist', and is Hardy's vision of the 'New Woman', educated, sexually tense, strangely fragile, potentially destructive, making her break with the past yet haunted by fatality. Both of them see themselves as 'pioneers', only to find the time is not yet ripe: 'Our ideas were fifty years too soon to be any good to us.' 'We are horribly sensitive, that's what's wrong with us,' explains Jude. It is a novel of lost roots and rapid motion, of parts of the culture in contrast and conflict, of quick passage, by train, from one world to another. Jude begins obscure, and ends obscured; his life and desires are not completed but curtailed, his significance is never fulfilled – or not in the novel that bears his half-cancelled name, though later fiction would be filled with Judes no longer obscure. Hardy sees him as a modern hero, Sue as a version of the modern heroine, but both live in a world that returns them to fatality and insignificance. In a parable of human wishes aborted, the story ends on the grim spectacle of child suicide, a sign of the 'coming universal wish not to live'. This is almost too apocalyptic, except that modern fiction since has again and again returned, like Hardy, to cosmic irony and darkness.

It is relevant that Hardy's own hopes for the novel as a form were aborted too. *Tess* was his endeavour to write of a publicly victimized woman, and not surprisingly it was attacked as such: 'if this sort of thing continues, no more novel-writing for me,' Hardy noted in his journal. Yet *Jude*, his novel not of the New Woman but of the New Man, struggling against 'men and senseless circumstance', was a yet greater challenge, with its ironic contrast 'between the ideal life a man wished to lead and the squalid real life he was fated to lead'. It was widely read, and widely attacked, in part for its sexual frankness – the famous hog's pizzle thrown at Jude by Arabella – and its decadent 'morbidity' – the killing of the young children by 'Father Time', who obviously embodies that spirit of *fin du globe* that Max Nordau attacked in his book *Degeneration*, published in the same year. Hardy's novel was assaulted as immoral by the critics ('Even Euripides, had he been given to the writing of novels, might well have faltered before such a tremendous undertaking,' said one), rejected by the lending libraries, condemned by the church, burned by an Anglican bishop; 'the experience completely curing me of further interest in novel-writing,' Hardy explained later in a bitter preface. There was in fact one more notable novel, *The Well-Beloved* (1897), which was admired by Proust, but it had mostly been written in 1892. Thus from 1895 to his death in January 1928, Hardy concentrated on poetry, the form in which he felt happiest, and here he did some of his finest work. His *Wessex Poems* came out in 1898; today he is acknowledged as among the most important of our early modern poets. It seems ironic, if not Hardyesque, that, just before the novel really began to lay full claim to its new freedoms, just before James's career opened out into its late phase, Hardy's collapsed – meaning that he will always be seen as essentially a late-Victorian novelist. As his career in fiction ended, H. G. Wells's began, and the story of those Judes who no longer felt so obscure began to be written. But the essential onward link was indeed with Lawrence, who was able to convert Hardy's vision of social, sexual and vitalist aspiration, of the new self struggling toward birth out of the historical culture, into a new modern myth. Hence 'where *Jude* ends *The Rainbow* begins', it has been said.[10] By the end of the century James had already begun one tradition of exploratory modernity in the novel, the novel as self-consciousness, the novel as 'affair'. Hardy had bequeathed

10 In Ian Gregor, *The Great Web: The Form of Hardy's Major Fiction* (London, 1974).

another, more communal and choric, its sense of crisis differently affirmed, and that went on too, through Lawrence and into contemporary fiction, including that of David Storey, John Berger and Raymond Williams, writers for whom the struggle of consciousness out of nature, into culture, has been essential to the modern British novel.

6

By the mid 1880s, the state and nature of the novel was a matter of public argument. James's essay 'The Art of Fiction' (1884) was a reply to a lecture by Walter Besant, and proposed a much wider and more open view of the genre: 'We must grant the novelist his subject, his idea, his *donnée*; our criticism is applied only to what it makes of it.' This essay in turn provoked a reply, or rather 'A Humble Remonstrance', from a young Scots novelist, Robert Louis Stevenson, who wanted to widen the definition further. The remonstrance was probably humble because James had gone out of his way to praise Stevenson's romance of the year before, *Treasure Island* (1883), as 'delightful, because it seems to me to have succeeded wonderfully in what it attempts', and the two writers in fact became close friends. But Stevenson was keen to establish that what he was attempting, the 'romance', was indeed as important and central to fiction as the 'solidity of specification' and 'the intense illusion of reality' commended by James. Romance, action and escape were also essential fictional materials: 'The novel which is a work of art exists, not by its resemblances to life, which are forced and material, as a shoe must still consist of leather, but by its immeasurable distance from life, which is designed and significant, and is both the method and the meaning of the work.' As a Scot, Stevenson was a follower of Scott and the romance tradition, and he was in reaction against the social and moral emphasis of what even the American James called 'the English novel'. He was also a Scot in revolt, against the Presbyterian realism of his Edinburgh childhood, and during the 1870s he had won a reputation with accounts of his adventurous European travels. He delighted in the world of daydream and fantasy as a means of escape into the life of the imagination: 'Fiction is to grown men what play is to a child,' he said. He made his love of the wonderworld of story plain in his early collection *The New Arabian Nights* (1882), while *Treasure Island* – a story of, as James nicely put it, 'murders, mysteries, islands of dreadful renown, hairbreadth escapes, miraculous coincidences and buried doubloons' – proved one of the most successful novels of its day, and made even the boys' book seem worthy of serious attention. When *Kidnapped* (1886), set in the Jacobite Rebellion, appeared, James was again warm in his praise, saying the book showed a high 'imagination of physical states'. *Kidnapped* merged the boys' book with the Scots historical romance; seeing the story from the standpoint of the boy David Balfour, Stevenson was able to give the book a dream-like motion and a sense of adventurous action that still renders it legendary.

Though he admitted that his novels, which were enormously popular, had a considerable element of 'Tushery', Stevenson was determined to establish that he was no naive storyteller but a self-conscious artist. In fact, so prolix and various were the subjects of his writing that, right up to his death at the age of forty-four, he still seemed to be in search of his essential style and theme. Nonetheless he was enormously productive, the exemplary popular novelist, a writer who created or reconstructed a wide variety of different fictional genres. There was the genre of the regional romance, developed in *The Master of Ballantrae* (1889), *Catriona*, sequel to *Kidnapped* (1893), and the unfinished *Weir of Hermiston* (1896), which conferred on Scots historical writing a whole new identity. There were works of fantasy, children's tales, stories of travel and high adventure, like *The Black Arrow* (1888). Indeed there were many Stevensons, from the author of the thrilling boys' book to the artist of complex literary sophistication. His claims for 'romance', as a primal space for imaginative discovery, and indeed as a region where action and intellect, technique and flamboyant fantasy, highly literary and highly popular forms could happily lie down together, did a great deal to reverse the drive toward realism and Naturalism that had shaped most serious fiction ever since the 1850s; the cause of 'romance' influenced not simply the popular novelists – the Hentys and the Haggards – but James and Conrad. Throughout the twentieth century Stevenson has continued to win important admirers, not the least of them that master of postmodern fantasy and early magic realism, Jorge Luis Borges. Meanwhile his own life became an adventurous travelling romance, a search – like his fictions – for worlds elsewhere, which led him finally to Samoa, as distant as possible from the Scots origins he both honoured and revolted against; here he died suddenly of a brain haemorrhage in 1894.

But no book was more important to modern fiction, nor more revealing of the divided nature of its author's imagination, than the book that became one of the most successful, expressive works of the 1880s, *The Strange Case of Doctor Jekyll and Mr Hyde* (1886). In it Stevenson went back into the tradition of Gothic romance, with its awareness of mirrored lives, threatening doubles, strange powers released by the abuse of science, which lead the mind out of the world of reality and reason and into darkness, duplicity, otherness, metamorphosis. But, just as James was, Stevenson was looking inside 'the haunted house of Victorian culture', and this tale of the *homo duplex* – the man split between a respectable public self and a hidden, violent and animal double – was a fable that touched some of the deeper moral anxieties of the age. The book's essential message is 'Man is not truly one, but truly two', and it touched many chords. It acknowledges the Naturalist concern with the animal in man, the *bête humaine*, but it equally shares the decadent fascination with narcissism so strong in Aestheticism. Jekyll himself expounds on 'the profound duplicity of life', and the book engaged with increasing scientific curiosity about the unconscious self, the hidden *id*, unspoken in an age of repression and strict morality, that Freud would soon explore. If the theme is sensational, the subject is psychological, the technique complex. This is, like many Gothic novels, the story of an investigation, and prefigures the rising popularity of the detective story; in fact Arthur Conan Doyle would introduce the public to his 'unofficial detective' Sherlock Holmes, man of medicine, science, and deduction, chasing strange crimes in the London fog, in *A Study in Scarlet* the next year. So the plot involves yet more doubling: the lawyer Utterson, who investigates the mystery, explains 'If he be Mr Hyde . . . I shall be Mr Seek.' There is yet another doubling: beneath the social surface of bourgeois London life lies a darker world, and the city of civilization hides in its heart dark secrets and criminal selves. Creating his doubled world, Stevenson was introducing late-Victorian culture to one of its strongest themes, one which would obsess the dying of the century and the entire spirit of Decadence itself, and compound its sense of unease. The theme of the doubled self in the doubled city would appear in its Decadent form in Oscar Wilde's *The Picture of Dorian Gray* (1891), where the ambiguity is brought into the centre of art itself. In Wilde's version, Dorian becomes ever more corrupt in life, but holds on to his golden youth. Meanwhile his portrait in the attic ages and decays, art expressing the reality as the reality turns into art. The portrait becomes the double; when it must be destroyed ('It had been like a conscience to him . . . He would destroy it'), Dorian himself ages and dies.

Stevenson's importance lay in his challenge to realism, his clear proof that the age of documentary Naturalism was also open to myth and exotic fantasy. His defence of the 'romance' and his re-exploration of Gothic were important campaigns of the 1880s, and encouraged the proliferation of forms that followed as the popular market for fiction expanded. It was because of the enormous success of *Treasure Island* that H. Rider Haggard embarked on *King Solomon's Mines* (1885), a boys' tale of male quest through the adventurous landscape of Africa. Haggard's book – there would be many more of the kind, from the adventures of G. A. Henty to the novels of Kipling – depended on the fact that the late-Victorian age was one of expanding imperial horizons, as an ever greater part of the world map came under Western political, economic or imaginative domination. As a result what Martin Green calls 'dreams of adventure, deeds of empire' became key fables of the age.[11] Both in Britain and the no less imperialistic USA, tales of manly or boyish adventuring into the unknown and the

---

11 Martin Green, *Dreams of Adventure, Deeds of Empire* (London, 1980): 'My argument will be that the adventure tales that formed the light reading of Englishmen for two hundred years and more after *Robinson Crusoe* were, in fact, the energizing myth of English imperialism.' See also Alan Sandison, *The Wheel of Empire: A Study of the Imperial Idea in Some Late Nineteenth Century and Early Twentieth Century Fiction* (London and New York, 1967).

dangerous – into distant landscapes, new frontiers, far-off wars and tribal conflicts – became a highly popular form, and the lost city, the missing treasure, the hidden tomb, the undiscovered tribe, the law of the jungle and the call of the wild, recaptured their place in fiction. What Stevenson called 'romance' need no longer be set in history; it could follow the reaches of Empire, the tracks of exploration, the battlegrounds of imperial wars. 'Romance' was no story of love, but of adventure and travel, an exploration, a voyage into mythic space, a tale of discovery or heroism. The new boys' papers promoted it, in part as an antithesis to the 'morbid realism' and the *fin-de-siècle* sensibilities that seemed to be infecting life, and fiction, at home. When Nordau's *Degeneration* appeared in 1895, many read it as a warning against the kind of novels Hardy and Wilde wrote, to which works of spirited adventure, like Rider Haggard's, offered a very welcome contrast.

'Ah! this civilization, what does it all come to?' asks Allan 'Hunter' Quatermain, the African explorer and Haggard's narrator in *King Solomon's Mines*, putting the big question of the day. His answer – escape into nature in the form of the African wild – proved so popular Quatermain came back in fourteen more tales, a frontiersman almost as popular as Fenimore Cooper's 'Leatherstocking', that free spirit who had wandered the American frontier a hundred years before. In the second story, *Allan Quatermain* (1887), Haggard spelled out his message of nature against modern civilization even more clearly. 'Nineteen parts of our nature are savage, the twentieth civilized, but the last is spread out over the rest like the blacking on a boot, or the veneer over a table; it is on the savage that we fall back in emergencies.' Haggard, like his fellow writers of the modern adventure, Henty and Kipling, was maybe not so far from Naturalism after all. And as for the 'emergencies' in question, Elaine Showalter is no doubt right to suggest that one of them is indicated by the very title of *She* (1887); they were women.[12] This was Haggard's most successful novel, and the story of a quest for the eternal woman, Ayesha, the white queen of the mysterious African land of Kor, 'she who must be obeyed'. With

12 See Elaine Showalter, *Sexual Anarchy: Gender and Culture at the Fin de Siècle* (London, 1991).

her secret of eternal life, she constructs an everlasting matriarchy, an ageless female principle. But though she must be worshipped, she can be challenged and defeated when things go too far. Like Dorian Gray, she finally perishes from her own eternal beauty, burned up in her own flame. However, the rules of romance are generally permissive. When her story proved enormously successful, she managed to reappear for the sequel, *Ayesha*, in 1905.

7

The fictional arguments that raged through the 1880s – about Realism and Naturalism, Aestheticism and Romance – were really part of a larger issue of the time: the very nature and spirit of the 'modern' or the 'new' itself. When Walter Pater in his study *The Renaissance* (1873) talked of 'modern sensations', or George Moore called his novel of 1883 *A Modern Lover*, or that same year Georg Brandes celebrated the 'men of the modern breakthrough', people knew more or less what was meant: an alertness to the fragile moods of a time of change, a sense of transition and transience, a new manner of behaviour, a fresh reaching out to the forces that would shape the future. By the end of the decade, as a new century loomed closer, the issue intensified. 'New' was the new word of 1889. Right across Europe belief grew that thinkers like Ibsen, Zola, Nietzsche, Weber and Durkheim were opening wide the doors to a time of transformation, a 'new age'. That was the year Europe saw *Ghosts*, Ibsen's powerful play about the way the past can taint the sunlit hopes of the present. It was the year Nietzsche went mad, still publishing his apocalyptic works: 'Only the day after tomorrow belongs to me.' In that year the French celebrated the Centennial of the French Revolution by erecting the Eiffel Tower, which the historian Roger Shattuck has described as 'in its truculent stance . . . the first monument of Modernism'.[13] It was a work of mechanical abstraction, later much

13 See Roger Shattuck, *The Banquet Years: The Origins of the Avant Garde in France, 1885 to World War I* (New York, rev.ed., 1968).

celebrated by those who called themselves 'Futurists', built to dominate a great Exposition of a kind with which the century had grown
familiar, designed to display the emerging technologies that marked
the new stage the industrial revolution had reached, and were bringing
fresh inventions and systems into every city, street and home. Indeed
the hero of the Exposition was not a Frenchman at all, but an
American, Thomas Alva Edison, 'the Wizard of Menlo Park', the
'Magician of the Century', inventor of the telegraph, the phonograph
and the electric tramway. Edison's incandescent bulbs lit up the fair,
as they would light the streets of most of the European cities before
long; meanwhile that year Edison was developing the Kinetoscope,
the source of modern film. Evidently the modern meant not just new
sensibilities but new technologies. Hence 'future fiction' – in the wake
of Jules Verne – was becoming the rage, and Edison appeared in that
too. In 1886 Villiers de l'Isle Adam, aesthete and influence on Oscar
Wilde, in his novel *L'Eve future* (*The Future Eve*), has Edison inventing
a female android to give the hero, a British nobleman, the sexual
solace he cannot find in human form. As the American historian
Henry Adams, a tireless visitor to the great exhibitions of the end of
the century, observed, the human race was moving from the age of
the Virgin to the age of the Dynamo, and from the universe to the
multiverse.

The 'new' came even to Britain. Admittedly the British book of
1889 was Jerome K. Jerome's *Three Men in a Boat*, a suburban clerkly
comedy that would lead on to George and Weedon Grossmith's *The
Diary of a Nobody* (1892), the very ordinary and politely bourgeois
story of Mr Pooter, of The Laurels, Brickfield Terrace, Holloway.
British suburbanism flourished, but 'The Red Flag' was written, after
a dock strike. Ernest Vizetelly, publisher of Zola and Maupassant,
was sent to prison for foulness; but George Gissing published his
Naturalist classic *The Nether World* and G. B. Shaw his *Fabian
Essays*. Aestheticism declared itself with Wilde's *The Decay of Lying*,
which asserted that 'Art is our spirited protest, our attempt to teach
Nature her proper place.' 'The Nineties began in 1889 and ended in
1895,' Richard Ellmann has noted, writing of the space between
Wilde's triumph and his trial. 'At least the Wildean Nineties did so,

and without Wilde the decade would never have found its character.'[14] In 1889 a writer James dubbed 'the infant monster' came from nowhere (in fact from the imperial outpost of Lahore, India) with several already published books hot and ready for British reissue; so Rudyard Kipling won sudden fame with *Plain Tales from the Hills* and *Soldiers Three*. That year a Polish sea captain calling himself 'Joseph Conrad' resigned command of the *Otago* and, awaiting a vessel to take him up the Congo, rented a villa in Pimlico and began work on an imperial romance about the Malay archipelago, *Almayer's Folly*. The 'new' in fact was everywhere: 'The range of the adjective gradually spread until it embraced the ideas of the whole period, and we find innumerable references to the "New Spirit", the "New Humour", the "New Realism", the "New Hedonism", the "New Unionism", the "New Party", and the "New Woman",' reports Holbrook Jackson in his brilliant book *The Eighteen Nineties* (1913).[15] It meant many things, from the Victorian and Celtic Twilight to the New Jingoism, from Decadence to 'future fiction'. The 'new arts' were forever in the news: there were many more newspapers, and the 'New Journalism' flourished in a decade that saw the yellow press as well as the *Yellow Book*. This was a time of dawns and twilights, aubades and nocturnes. Naturalism continued, reinforced by the new socialism and the new sociology, dealing with all that went unexplored and unacknowledged: poverty, prostitution, the provinces. But it intersected with the arts of a time intensely self-conscious about style, mannerism, fragile sensation, veiled symbols, sexual ambiguities. This was, said Jackson, a 'decade of a thousand movements', of Naturalism and Impressionism, Aestheticism and Symbolism, the 'novel' and the 'romance', which generally meant a division not just in form but in the literary marketplace, for the 'novel', like 'aestheticism', stood for high art and 'romance' for popular literature.

14 Richard Ellmann, *Oscar Wilde* (London, 1987). Also see John Stokes, *In the Nineties* (New York and London, 1989), and Malcolm Bradbury, David Palmer and Ian Fletcher (eds.), *Decadence and the 1890s* (London, 1979).
15 Holbrook Jackson, *The Eighteen Nineties: A Review of Art and Ideas at the Close of the Nineteenth Century* (London, 1913; reissued 1988, with an introduction by the present author).

For other things were new. The entire marketplace of the novel was shifting, as the lending libraries declined in influence and the cheap book increasingly appeared on the new bookstalls meaning that novels could now be slim and elegant productions from opulent publishers or cheap volumes sold from the news agencies. The number of new novels doubled over a decade that saw the rise of the literary agent and the growth of literary commerce, at which some writers were good and others were not. So there was what George Gissing announced as 'New Grub Street' in his novel of that title in 1891. Now the poverty Gissing naturalistically examined was literary poverty, as various kinds of writers in different ways confronted the facts of literary commerce (the hero Edward Reardon refuses to supply 'good, coarse, marketable stuff for the world's vulgar', while his wife protests that 'Art must be practised as a trade, at all events in our time. This is the age of trade'). Meanwhile in the wake of new theories of consciousness, like those of William James in 1890, Naturalism was losing a good deal of its faith in the purely scientific or analytical vision. In 1894 George Moore produced his best book yet, *Esther Waters*, the moving story of a London servant girl with an illegitimate child, which immediately provoked comparisons with Hardy's Tess. It has Naturalist impulses, but Moore had now really broken with Naturalism. He complained that Zola was too concerned 'with the externalities of life', that Naturalism was a 'handful of dry facts instead of a passionate impression of life in the envelope of mystery and suggestion', that art's aim was 'not truth but beauty'. Other writers explored Naturalism less as a deterministic method or a social protest than an aesthetic in itself. In 1898 Arnold Bennett came to literary notice with his *A Man from the North*, the story of a provincial young man like himself who comes from the Potteries to an indifferent London to write and seek his sexual freedom. Bennett's method is self-consciously flat and banal, but then he was, he explained, 'the latest disciple of the Goncourts', in other words a Naturalist. He also insisted on his strong aesthetic standpoint, and collectively rejected his Victorian antecedents for lack of artistry in almost Jamesian language: 'As regards fiction, it seems to me that only within the last few years have we absorbed from France that passion for artistic shapely presentation of truth, and that feeling for words as words, which animated Flaubert, the Goncourts, and Maupassant . . . An artist must be interested in presentment, not in the thing presented. He must have a passion for technique, a great love for form . . .' – in other words those qualities that Virginia Woolf accused Bennett of not having when she joined battle with him twenty years later.

The fact was that during the 1890s, a time of aesthetic reconsideration, many things – Naturalism and Symbolism, Socialism and Decadence, the 'thing in front of us' and 'presentment . . . not the thing presented' – were shading into each other, as the novel took on a fresh genetic variety and a widening variety of tones, themes, audiences. The whole map of literature widened, just like the Empire itself. This was very visible in the treatment of London, James's 'biggest aggregation'. In 1890 the explorer and journalist H. M. Stanley wrote about the Belgian Congo in his powerful report *In Darkest Africa*. That year General William Booth, founder of the Salvation Army, also new, countered with *In Darkest England and the Way Out*, showing London's East End as another dark continent awaiting the ministrations of the explorer and the missionary ('As in Africa it is all trees, trees, trees with no other world conceivable, so it is here – it is all vice and poverty and crime'). 'Darkest London', already there in James and Stevenson and Gissing's 'nether world', became a motif of fiction. It was the world of slum life Arthur Morrison naturalistically explored in *Tales of Mean Streets* (1892) and *A Child of the Jago* (1896), and W. Somerset Maugham in *Liza of Lambeth* (1897); Jack London, the American Naturalist, would stalk through it again in his *People of the Abyss* (1903) to show life as endless Darwinian struggle. But in the age of the 'impression' London also offered many other shades: the foggy urban world of the crime and detective fiction into which Sherlock Holmes adventured as he penetrated 'the lowest portions of the city', but also the crepuscular mists of the urban nocturne, painting in prose – Wilde, Herbert Crackenthorpe, Aubrey Beardsley – what Whistler painted in pastel. Then there was the green London that William Morris prospects in *News from Nowhere* (1890), a reformist Utopian work in which, in the arcadian twentieth century, the fogs, poverty and industrial problems of his own London have somehow gone: 'The soap-works with their smoke-vomiting chimneys were gone; the engineers' works were gone; the lead works were gone . . .'. Writers now 'reasserted the romance of London in their new-found love of the artificial', Jackson notes; and the London they explored could equally be a world of grim poverty and Darwinian struggle or a flickering city of strange impressions, glimpses, contrasts, a rich urban artifice. Like Dr Jekyll, the detective story and the ghost story drew together different worlds, wealth and poverty, surface and underside, opening out windows from one to the other. London, like so much else in the decade, was mirrored, doubled: the great world capital of empire and trade was also the heartland of poverty, crime and anarchy, representing at once civilization, art and artifice, and its secret sharer, darkness and disorder.

This was the image brought together at the decade's end by Joseph Conrad in *Heart of Darkness* (1899), which draws on most of these motifs. Conrad, the Polish sea captain whose spoken English stayed so poor he would be briefly picked up as a German spy in the Great War, began as a novelist of Empire when he published *Almayer's Folly* (1895) and *An Outcast of the Islands* (1896), two stories of the distant Malayan archipelago where nature met culture. *Heart of Darkness*, his symbolist novella about the ambiguity secreted in the imperial mission, brings all this much closer to home. The story starts on the Thames in the port of London; this is 'the biggest, and greatest, town on earth' and also 'this monstrous town', which, says the narrator, Marlow, suddenly, 'has been one of the dark places of the earth'. The story then moves through a circuitous, labyrinthine descent from this river to another, the Congo, in 'darkest Africa', and through the layers of indifference, futility, corruption, barbarism and inhuman cruelty to empty evil, the world of 'exterminate the brutes', and 'the horror, the horror'. From here on, Conrad's fiction would construct a universe in which everything is mirrored and doubled, as London mirrors and refracts the Congo: courage and cowardice, faith and betrayal, culture and nature, individualism and tribalism, light and darkness. In each mirror is a glimpse of the abyss and a need to preserve the fidelity of the surface. This moral and metaphysical ambiguity is one mark of the writing of the 1890s, one of its chief gifts to the Modernist vision. 'Man is not truly one, but truly two,' Jekyll had said in Stevenson's Gothic fable of his *homo duplex*. Wilde's *Dorian Gray*, a work both of the New Aestheticism and the New Hedonism, converts these Gothic materials into a fable about art and reality. Such Gothic deceptions became an essential part of the popular writing of the 1890s, which produced two of the great fables of modern Gothic sensationalism from the haunted house of late-Victorian culture. George du Maurier's *Trilby* (1894) is set in bohemia, the world of Parisian artists, where the threat comes with Svengali, who uses a popular science, Mesmerism, as his instrument of control over others. But it is when the conventional young solicitor Jonathan Harker unwisely chooses to do some conveyancing work in darkest somewhere, and travels to Transylvania, land of Vlad the Impaler ('It seems to me that the further East you go the more unpunctual are the trains,' he is soon complaining), that the dark shadows just beyond the edge of culture find their strongest popular treatment. Transylvania, in Bram Stoker's *Dracula* (1897), is another land at the heart of darkness, where the writ of modern reason does not run: 'the old centuries had, and have, powers of their own that mere "modernity" cannot kill', Harker learns. The vampire, culled from old fictions, strikes back; it takes a mirror, a Christian cross, decapitation and a stake through the heart to lay the fear of the undead, which still satisfies the living today. Or the ghost may be just across another border: 'No one would have believed in the last year of the nineteenth century that human affairs were being watched keenly and closely by intelligences greater than man's and yet as mortal as their own,' began H. G. Wells's *The War of the Worlds* (1898), a 'scientific romance' about an invasion from Mars. The age of scientific reason and social analysis was also the age of the sensational romance, the mythology of a time filled with a sense of contradiction, uncertainty and transition, and perturbed by what lay at its borders, or in the future. So it provided the 'new' popular culture which would pass on, a mythology endlessly to be rewritten, into our modern mass media – born out of Edison's Kinetoscope of 1889.

8

It has often been pointed out that, if the writing of the early 1890s was given to arts of mannered style, evanescent impression and veiled meaning, and opened into labyrinthine uncertainties about civilization and darkness, the self and the other, then this had – as in the contemporary work of Freud and Breuer themselves – a great deal to do with a growing sense of sexual ambiguity. As Elaine Showalter has put it, 'when sexual certainties broke down, fictional certainties changed as well'.[16] For now both feminism and a half-veiled gay writing flourished, and a good deal of high-minded eroticism entered literature, as in Wilde's *Dorian Gray*, where the innocent face conceals not just corruption but sexual ambiguity, in Aubrey Beardsley's work, not least his pornographic *Under the Hill*, or in *My Secret Life*, which was simply written by Anonymous. Beyond this was a fundamental change in the refracted image of the sexes themselves. Naturalism had frankly explored the power of the sexual instinct ('I simply applied to two living bodies the analytical method that surgeons apply to corpses,' in Zola's version), and faced, as in Hardy's *Jude*, the 'marriage question'. Strong feminist works, most importantly Olive Schreiner's *The Story of an African Farm* (1883), had been part of the Naturalist campaign of the 1880s. Now 'New Woman' fiction – that term was invented by the popular novelist 'Ouida' in the 1890s – looked at the way women, offered greater independence by improving educational and work opportunities, changing *mores* and better birth control, began, in life and fiction too, to claim more control of their lives and aspirations. This then was another essential 'modern' theme, explored in works like Sarah Grand's *The Heavenly Twins* (1893) and 'George Egerton's' stories *Keynotes* (also 1893). Egerton, having lived in Scandinavia and imbibed the influence of Ibsen and Hamsun, wrote about women's lives in a newly passionate prose: Mona Caird, in *The Daughters of Danaus* (1894), explored the struggles of women

[16] Elaine Showalter, *Sexual Anarchy: Gender and Culture at the Fin de Siècle* (London, 1991).

who attempted to produce serious art; Ellen Hepworth Dixon produced her feminist *The Story of a Modern Woman* (1894). And 'New Woman' fiction also included works like Hardy's *Tess*, Moore's *Esther Waters* and Gissing's *The Odd Women* (1893). Writers male and female were arguing, if in different voices, much the same issues: modern marriage, free love, the nature and balance of the sexual instincts, the imprisonment of moral codes, eroticism and 'New Hedonism'. When Grant Allan, who proselytized for the latter, published his *The Woman Who Did* (1895), a fiction of free love, it was quickly countered by 'Victoria Cross' (Vivian Cory) in *The Woman Who Didn't* (also 1895), which put the case for female purity; book talked back to book. These were fundamental themes of the late-Victorian dissolution, and they duly passed their concerns onward to more powerful writers from H. G. Wells and D. H. Lawrence to Virginia Woolf, May Sinclair, Dorothy Richardson and Rebecca West.

But often the choice was simpler, and the readers of the time were offered a choice of male or female worlds: worlds of empire and adventure, or worlds of social and domestic pressure at home. For once, this was an age when it was women writers who wrote bitter realism and men who wrote romance. Above all there was Rudyard Kipling, the 'Imperial Laureate', the first British writer to be awarded the Nobel Prize. In our own plain and post-imperial times, it is sometimes hard to see why he was regarded by so many as the most important and representative British writer of the age, but no writer was more closely in touch with the energies that were making the age what it was. On the one hand there was the vast commercial and governmental task of empire, on the other there were the oily jobs of the machine age; Kipling wrote about both, celebrating daily things and routine work. Born in Bombay in 1865, he was schooled in Britain, then returned to India as a journalist. He knew the Empire not as a traveller, but as one who lived its workaday life and lived its daily pan-racial relations. It was in India that he laid the solid grounding for the career that followed; when he moved back to Britain in 1889 to earn his living as a writer, he had seven books, mostly of short stories, already finished. They include some of his finest work;

James was right to call him the 'infant monster'. These include complex stories of sexuality like 'Without Benefit of Clergy', and 'The Man Born to be King' (1888), about two rogue adventurers who try to set up a version of the Empire in 'Kaffiristan', finally with grim and ironic results. The two voice imperial high dreams, but expressed in the vernacular; Kipling's vernacular language often has a power like Mark Twain's of expressing a vision of the world comically undermining the one that has been politely written down. Like Twain, it offers us the sense of a well observed, honest and half-comic vision; from this comes the jangling, popular voice of his fiction and poetry, which would sound out over the following decades. The novel he wrote on return to England, *The Light That Failed* (1890), is really a fable about his literary choice. It is set in the Sudan and in London: the world of war and action, and the world of art and bohemia. The central character, a painter and an adventurer, loses his sight, and this dangerously returns him to the world of action; the fable seems to represent Kipling's own choice, of public forms over private ones, the world of doing over domestic and aesthetic life. From then on his tales of adventure, action and work began to dominate the decade. Stronger in the short story than the novel, he could write modernist fiction, as his story 'Mrs Bathurst' proves. But his two great treasures lay in childhood life – he had the statutory unhappy childhood of so many writers – and India (to which, in fact, he did not return, living in Britain and the United States). So he could create the unhappy, wonderful, above all tribal world of school and childhood in *Stalky & Co.* (1899), of India in what is probably his best book, *Kim* (1901). He wrote many excellent stories, like 'Wireless' and 'Mary Postgate'; his Indian stories for children – *The Jungle Books* (1894, 1895) and *The Just So Stories* (1902) – won him youthful audiences that never left him after. Altogether, his sense of the struggle of life, the battle for experience, the ways of tribes and races, the dangerous adventure of the age of the Gatling gun and the Imperial mission, made him central to his unsettled, expanding age.

At the same time his artistic grasp began to diminish. James had the highest hopes of this 'infant monster'; his mind changed later. 'I thought he perhaps contained the seeds of an English Balzac, but I have given that up in proportion as he has come down steadily from the simple in subject to the more simple – from the Anglo-Saxons to the natives, from the natives to the Tommies, from the Tommies to the quadrupeds, from the quadrupeds to the fish, and from the fish to the engines and screws.' What's more, he complained, his work had 'almost nothing of the complicated soul or of the female form or of any question of *shades*'. Kipling did write simply, but he wasn't simple; his best work possesses a clear aesthetic subtlety. But he lacked Conrad's moral subtlety, and firmly belonged to the imperial age, the age of the race and the tribe, of the savage and the white man's burden, the age of the machine. Still, he wrote with a sense of social and psychological complexity, an awareness of the power of the natural and the savage, and a view of life through the eyes of the underdog, seen against the importance of a great empire and the worth of the rule of law. When he wrote across the races, it was sometimes with condescension, but at others with real sympathy and understanding. His fiction is born in romance, but filled with a distinctive Naturalism; he possessed the pessimism of the age, its abiding anxiety about the future, and he understood the burden of ordinary daily life and work, the subjection of the footsoldier to the regiment or the machine, the life of 'engines and screws'. More than most, he understood the power of the machine, and wrote finely about the craftsmen and engineers of the time of technical change, when machines made machines. As Holbrook Jackson also observes, he also gained his power from a deep shift in the spirit of the 1890s. For around 1895, the era that had begun with Wilde, aestheticism and decadence shifted toward something else. Wilde's trial and imprisonment in 1895 – which coincided with the publication of Nordau's *Degeneration*, and the silencing of Thomas Hardy in fiction – was a crucial moment: 'The aesthetic cult, in his nasty form, is over,' announced the *News of the World*, though perhaps so too was the Victorian age. According to Jackson, the decade fell into two clear halves, the first 'remarkable for a literary and artistic renaissance, degenerating into decadence; the second for a new sense of patriotism degenerating into jingoism', and ending in 'that indulgence of blatant aspirations', Mafeking Night in 1900.[17] Yet, he adds, the impulse of the decade had always been double. If there was *fin de siècle*, there was also *aube de siècle*; if there was 'degeneration', there was also 'regeneration'. Many writers were themselves versions of *homo duplex*. In the same year as *Dorian Gray*, Wilde could write *The Soul of Man Under Socialism*. Writers who understood the 'beautiful difficulties of art' also produced commercial successes, like Stevenson or Du Maurier. Kipling himself was aesthete as well as imperial laureate, experimental prose writer as well as conservative jingoist: another complicated voice of the Modern.

And so was another new author who, in 1895, seemed to come from nowhere and became not just one of the most popular writers of the day, but the voice of things to come. H. G. Wells, born in 1866, the son of a cricketer-shopkeeper and a lady's maid, was a Jude who had no intention of being obscure. He got his technocratic education at the Royal College of Science, coming under the influence of T. H. Huxley, and a political education from Socialism. Then in the year of *Jude* he published his *The Time Machine*, a work of what was then called 'scientific romance' or perhaps 'future fiction', and we know simply as 'SF'. What Wells showed was that there were directions the mind – and the romance – could travel in other than spatially, through the Empire, down the Congo, backward into the historical past. Utopian and dystopian predictions existed in plenty, most recently in Edward Bellamy's *Looking Backward* (1888) and William Morris's *News from Nowhere*, but they were mostly versions of pastoral, and lacked scientific insight or a real gift for historical anticipation. Prophecies of future war had also been increasing in number (there was, for instance, the famous *The Battle of Dorking*, 1871, by Sir George Tomkyns Chesney), and works about the cities of the future.[18] But Wells's was a work of the age of Edison and Eiffel, which perhaps owed most to Jules Verne; above all he brought to the form

17 Holbrook Jackson, *The Eighteen Nineties: A Review of Art and Ideas at the Close of the Nineteenth Century* (London, 1913; reissued 1988 with an introduction by the present author).
18 See I. F. Clarke, *The Pattern of Expectation, 1644–2001* (London, 1979), for details.

a distinctive scientific clarity. He could foresee the heat-death of the solar system, and propose 'a fourth dimension' in which his 'Time Traveller' could bicycle forward to the year 802,701, to find a world divided between an aesthetic class and an eternal underclass, the Eloi and the Morlocks. This was Wells's political theme, already important, and to develop through the novels, social fantasies and anticipatory works of the next decade. As G. K. Chesterton, who also tried the form in his *The Napoleon of Notting Hill* (1904), would say, Wells's 'first importance was that he wrote adventure stories in the new world the men of science had discovered', and he had the capacity to excite his readers about the hopes and dangers of the future. Indeed he virtually invented science fiction in its modern form, and in its modern variety – as futuristic exploration, as satirical fable, as scientific prophecy, as grim warning.

Wells was a serious novelist, who set off on his work with high artistic ambitions. During the 1890s he became a close friend of Henry James, Joseph Conrad, Stephen Crane – writers we would plainly acknowledge as 'moderns'. Wells saw himself as a modernist too, but in a very different way. He wrote in popular forms for a popular audience, often inventing extravagant action and excitement. For the genre he opened with his early work was popular scientific romance, a fiction not of modern techniques but of the modernizing process itself. If he was a Socialist, it was not of an arcadian, William Morris kind; what he believed in was reform through science and politics, through free thought, free love, evolutionary biology, political foresight, space travel, the coming world state. He envisioned a world where technology was changing everything, from the relation of the sexes and the races to the accessibility of the solar system to space travel, and dispensing with Old England and the Victorian age. The books he wrote up to the turn of the century – *The Island of Doctor Moreau* (1896), *The Invisible Man* (1897), the disturbing invasion prophecy *The War of the Worlds* (1898), which depicted not only Martian invasion but technological warfare, *The First Men in the Moon* (1901) and more – were filled with amazing inventions, extraordinary machines, scientific discoveries, future wars. But though their content was frequently highly fantastic, they drew, excitingly, on real scientific and military possibilities: spaceships, killer rays, collisions of competing world powers. They foresaw remarkable prospects – there was a strong note of social optimism – but also new terrors – world war, social collapse, racial conflict. Henry James admired Wells, and even offered to join in 'doing Mars' with him; it remains one of literary history's most unlikely collaborations. As the century turned, his attention moved closer in, to contemporary English life and the potential of personal and social change, though his themes were never less than world-historical. As he would write in *A Modern Utopia* (1905): 'The almost cataclysmic development of new machinery, the discovery of new materials, and the appearance of new social possibilities through the pursuit of material science, have given enormous and unprecedented facilities to the spirit of innovation.' The story of the new sorts of lives evolving in the age of change and innovation – the lives of the ordinary 'new' young men and women, the Mr Kippses and Mr Pollys and Ann Veronicas, typical figures seizing modern opportunities – became an exemplary form of Edwardian fiction. If, as James said, the novel as the century turned was coming to a new self-consciousness, it was clear there would be many shapes to the shape of fictional things to come.

9

By 1900 many elements of the modern novel in Britain were already in place. It was becoming a voice of modernity, and had shaken loose from many of the elements that had seemed to confine it: the lending libraries, dutiful and religious morality, even the confident notion of grand authorial omniscience. It had claimed the right to freedom and frankness of expression, an issue that would ensure many conflicts and censorings over the years; it had also begun to claim another freedom, the aesthetic right to complexity and obscurity we associate with Modernism. It was developing an avant-garde independence from the popular audience, but also using popular techniques to reach deeper into that audience. It was reaching outward, into documentary and social and journalistic concerns, and it was reaching inward, into the recesses of consciousness and psychology that would give it a whole new language of awareness. It was spreading in subject-matter, into the realms of boyish and imperial adventure. It frequently looked backward, in a decadent world-weariness, to the wonderlands of the past, but it also looked forward, into the techno-wonderland of the age of things to come. It was beginning to leave behind those crises of religious and moral conscience, those dramas of damnation or redemption, that filled the pages of much Victorian fiction; its new dramas were dramas of social and sexual relations, modern marriage, generational struggle, represented less in the discourse of religion or morality than that of sociology or aestheticism. It had begun to break, in several different ways, with the conventions of realism and familiarity, of subjectivity and objectivity, of time and space, that governed most previous fiction. In an age when the old gods were indeed dying, and new powers and convictions were to be summoned, it came to seem, at best, to be itself a form of human discovery, creative evolution, a quest for knowledge in an age when what was knowable was itself becoming indeterminate. By the turn of the century, writers had increasingly come to see that, as Frank Kermode has put it, 'a text might have to stand in a new relation to reality to be truthful'.[19]

The novel was becoming a radical art, but also an important new commodity, an adventure in the marketplace. Books got cheaper, literacy grew, adventurous themes raised the interest of the reading public and the number of new novels published jumped, from 381 in 1870 to 1,825 in 1899. As authors like Haggard and Henty, Wells and Bennett, Chesterton and John Buchan demonstrated, writing novels became a fine way to earn a crust, a grand and profitable adventure: 'The last decade of the nineteenth century was an extraordinarily favourable time for new writers . . .' Wells was to say; 'Below and above alike there was opportunity. More public, more publicity, more publishers and more patronage.' This began to drive a wedge, all too familiar now, between the novelists who saw fiction as an art, an affair of high impressions and fine technique, like painting, and those who saw it as a profitable and influential commodity, like soap. By

19 See Frank Kermode, *Essays on Fiction: 1971–82* (London, 1983).

the 1900s, said Ford Madox Ford (Hueffer), fiction in Britain was counterpoised between the artistic and the blatantly commercial. Henry James watched his reputation soar and his royalties diminish; Arnold Bennett, who made a fortune from writing, could declare, 'I am a writer, just as I might be a hotel-keeper, a solicitor, a doctor, a grocer, or an earthenware manufacturer' (no doubt making the kind of commodity the characters in James could not bear to mention). But even popular writers do not usually like to admit they are writing down to the market; what they are doing, of course, is elevating the market up to them by going down to it. Bennett freely wrote 'art', and rubbish; and he, and Wells, and many more, thought that just as much as James they were undertaking a 'modern experiment'. This matter famously came to a head in 1915 (Lawrence's 'year the old world ended') in a quarrel between James and Wells, those former friends who had once thought of 'doing Mars' together. James's late essay 'The New Fiction' – originally titled 'The Younger Generation' in the *TLS* in 1914 – had taken a sweep of his literary contemporaries, and he complained the novel was dissolving into artless art, an art of 'saturation' by life. Wells, like Bennett, was one of the saturators mentioned in the piece, and took his revenge in his novel *Boon* (1915), a work totally unremarkable for anything but this, by satirizing James's late fiction: 'It is like a church lit but without a congregation to distract you, with every light and line focused on the high altar. And on the altar, very reverently placed, intensely there, is a dead kitten, an eggshell, a bit of string.' James defended his view of fiction, replying, 'It is art that *makes* life, makes importance, for our consideration and application of these things, and I know of no substitute whatever for the force and beauty of its process.' Wells retorted he preferred to be seen as a journalist, not an artist: 'To you, literature, like painting, is an end, to me literature like architecture is a means, it has a use.'[20]

To this episode, many ironies attach. Wells had already in effect

---

20 This splendid quarrel is recorded in Leon Edel and Gordon N. Ray (eds.), *Henry James and H. G. Wells: A Record of Their Friendship, Their Debate on the Art of Fiction, and Their Quarrel* (London, 1958). Stephen Spender's comments are in his *The Struggle of the Modern* (London, 1963).

left the novel behind, and was into the future of science and the world state; he lived on till 1946, to see Hiroshima and the Mind at the End of Its Tether. James was also leaving the novel behind; he died the next year. The Great War had begun, and after it novels would be written in new ways, neither with Wellsian optimism nor the Jamesian sense of the labyrinthine complexity of society. The work of D. H. Lawrence, named in the controversy, would be censored, and many of the most important novels to follow would come out of avant-garde exile. Generally the future of fiction would confirm the viewpoint of James; the highest value of modern fiction is as a form of challenging discovery, not as an instrument of saturation or report – the newer media can give us that in plenty. There is generally no shortage of records of life, people with a pen and a story; there is a general dearth of real artistic explorers, makers of radical form and imagination. But the argument opened up then was destined to be repeated over and over, in other similar quarrels – Virginia Woolf *v.* Arnold Bennett, D. H. Lawrence *v.* John Galsworthy – and to become, as Stephen Spender put it, an ongoing conflict between 'moderns' – the aesthetic explorers – and 'contemporaries' – the recorders, explorers and critics of contemporary life. The issue has lasted beyond the wars of Modernism, and remains, a powerful oscillation in the history of the novel, to this day. Iris Murdoch distinguishes between 'crystalline' (neo-symbolist) and 'journalistic' novels; David Lodge sees the late modern novelist eternally returned to the crossroads, ever choosing between the paths of realism and experiment.[21] If as the new century came there was indeed a new age for the novel coming in Britain, it did not point a single direction, did not declare a single aesthetic, did not claim a single audience, or emerge from a single tradition. What had been willed to the modern novel was not a tradition but a mixture of traditions, not a clear fictional culture but a multi-layered variety of them, not a clarified view of life but a confusion of visions, impressions, social apprehensions, future feelings. The twentieth century

---

21 Iris Murdoch, 'Against Dryness' (1961), and David Lodge, 'The Novelist at the Crossroads' (1969), both reprinted in Malcolm Bradbury (ed.), *The Novel Today: Contemporary Writers on Modern Fiction* (London, new edition, 1990).

would not have a style; it would be an age in ceaseless quest for a style, an aesthetic battlefield. As the inheritors of James's 'self-consciousness' found and showed over the years ahead, what they had been bequeathed was a confusing, various, rich bundle of prospects that would lead to the multi-faceted, multi-layered, multi-cultural fictional phenomenon we call the novel today.

2

The Opening World:
1900–1915

Millennium! Millennium!
The wondrous world that is to come.
    William Ford Stanley, 'Millennium! Millennium!' (1903)

It was – truly – like an opening world ... For, if you have
worried your poor dear brain for at least a quarter of a century
over the hopelessness of finding, in Anglo-Saxondom, any
traces of the operations of conscious art – it was amazing to
find these young creatures not only evolving theories of writing
and the plastic arts, but receiving in addition an immense
amount of what is called 'public support'.
    Ford Madox Ford (Hueffer), *Thus to Revisit* (1921)

1

The 'opening world' Ford Madox Ford, formerly Ford Madox
Hueffer, is here recalling – as he gazes backward across the deep
murderous trench of the Great War, across a time when everything,
even his own name, has changed – is the patch of London years
between 1908 and 1914, a major era of the experimental arts in Britain.
It was, everyone agreed, a Modernist wonderland – a time when
British philistinism and provincialism wonderfully dissolved, and for a
brief few years new arts, new ideas, new movements were everywhere.
'Europe was full of titanic stirrings and snortings – a new art coming
into flower to celebrate or announce a "new age",' recalled another
famous survivor of the era of experiment and wartime, Wyndham

Lewis, the writer, painter, and founder of Vorticism, in his bitter memoir *Blasting and Bombardiering* (1937). What had happened, he claimed, was that between 1908 and 1914 an entire new school was in formation, right across Europe. It was more significant than the Romantic Revolution, not just recreating the arts but transforming all the philosophical rudiments of life, and heralding great social and political changes. And then, he reports, 'down came the lid – the day was lost, for art, at Sarajevo'. His was one of many reports. 'It was an age of noise, and every new effort had to be announced with a blare of trumpets,' recalled another writer, R. A. Scott-James, who was also looking back from the Depression disappointments of the 1930s, when all this was a distant past: 'It was a sort of *micarême* festival of big drums and little tin whistles and fancy dress. A new show of Post-Impressionist pictures had much the same character and purposes as the marches of flustered suffragettes on Whitehall.' 'If we had no Offenbach to set everyone whirling frantically to tunes in which mad gaiety blended with the tom-toms of death,' declared, even more extravagantly, another participant, Douglas Goldring, 'there was nonetheless a close resemblance between the last days of the Third Empire and the London which woke with a hangover to face the deluge of blood in 1914.' This, said Virginia Woolf, was the time when everyone behaved differently, thought differently, voted differently, felt differently and – very importantly – loved differently. In fact human character changed. 'The first signs of it are recorded in the books of Samuel Butler, in *The Way of All Flesh* in particular; the plays of Bernard Shaw continue to record it.' But it all came to a peak, she famously said, in December, 1910.[1]

If almost every survivor seems to have a story to tell about the pre-war Modernist wonderland, when so many careers, ideas and -isms, so much artistic activity in so many spheres, came to the boil, that partly has to do with the extraordinary stir of excitement the

[1] Ford Madox Ford, *Thus To Revisit* (London, 1921); Wyndham Lewis, *Blasting and Bombardiering* (London, 1937); R. A. Scott-James, 'Modern Accents in English Literature', *The Bookman* (NY), Sept. 1931; Douglas Goldring, *South Lodge* (London, 1943); and Virginia Woolf, 'Modern Fiction' (1919), in Leonard Woolf (ed.), *Collected Essays of Virginia Woolf* (4 vols., London, 1966–7).

British version of the Modern revolution generated, the extraordinary new personalities it threw up, the fact that the whole idea of an era of New Arts in philistine Britain – all artists knew as an act of ultimate faith that Britain was philistine – came as a shock of surprise. Ever since 1895, the year of Wilde's trial, of Hardy's withdrawal from fiction, of Wells's emergence, the tide of experiment that had been seen at the opening of the decade, with Aestheticism and Decadence, had appeared to be ebbing fast. 'The decade of [the Nineties] began with a dash for life and ended with a retreat,' Holbrook Jackson said in *The Eighteen Nineties*, which appropriately appeared in 1913, reminding the new generation of experimentalists that others now forgotten had been most of this way before. The avant-garde and decadent arguments, the mannerist forms and elegant styles, the sexual frankness and ambiguity, the surging sense of modern transition, that had quickened the early Nineties all seemed well past, leaving the mauve decade marooned as a time of lost possibilities, evanescent moments, eternal transition. The careers, and in quite a number of cases the lives, of the main participants had faded fast too. In 1900 Nietzsche, who had called on the 1890s to 'transvalue their values', died mad in Jena, and never saw the age of the Superman he had tried to summon; that same year Oscar Wilde died in lonely disgrace in Paris; Emile Zola, having fought the battle of the Dreyfus case, died there two years later, suffocated by the fumes of a charcoal stove. The new century that everyone called 'modern' came, but, as W. B. Yeats explained in a famous comment, 'everybody got down off his stilts; henceforth nobody drank absinthe with his black coffee; nobody went mad; nobody committed suicide; nobody joined the Catholic Church; or if they did I have forgotten.'[2] The *fin de siècle* was over, like the *siècle* itself, and a plainer, less decorated, more confidently, perhaps smugly modern twentieth-century age dawned. Then, in 1901, the Victorian Era, which had been closing for such a long time, did truly close. Queen Victoria, the very image of Britain, died, after over sixty years on her imperial throne. Edward VII succeeded her; the 'Edwardian Era', Britain's brief *belle époque*, began.

2 W. B. Yeats, 'Introduction' to *The Oxford Book of Modern Verse* (Oxford, 1936).

Except in the diary of country ladies, Edwardianism would never really have a good literary press. As Richard Ellmann rightly said, 'the phrase Edwardian literature is not often heard,' and when it is, it is generally in a note of Bloomsbury disparagement.[3] It has never been a period held notable for its writing, though this considerably mistaken impression is largely due to the excitement the age that followed next – Hueffer/Ford's 'opening world' – has had for literary historians, who rightly see in it the roots of Anglo-American modernism, fanning out into William Carlos Williams and the future of the American arts. But the fact is that much that was important for the modern movement in fiction and poetry – James's late phase, Conrad's finest fiction, the founding work of James Joyce, Virginia Woolf, D. H. Lawrence, the growth of poetic Imagism – was initiated in the Edwardian age, even though some of the most significant was not actually published then. It has simply not been considered to typify it, because in so many cases the publications or the recognitions did get delayed, as is common with those arts that call themselves avant-garde. What instead has been thought to typify it were just those things many of the new writers were in revolt against – the last gasps of Victorian moralism, the formal social conventions and hypocrisies, the bourgeois-philistine mood, the culture of commercialism and the literature of profit. Certainly these were commercial, material, imperial times, when Kipling sounded and British power and trade still ruled the world. They were also reforming times, an era of political upheaval, welfare attitudes, income tax and state intervention. Quite a lot of the fiction seemed formed out of a happy mixture of the two, a radical adventure in commercialism, as the boom-careers of writers like H. G. Wells and Arnold Bennett, G. K. Chesterton and Rudyard Kipling, showed. Typical books seemed to be brooding works of distant travel – W. H. Hudson, R. B. Cunningham-Grahame – or boyish or manly adventure by Henty and Deeping and Merriman and Le Queux. Women writers produced pieces of well-done tosh – there was Elinor Glyn's *Three Weeks*, sex

3 Richard Ellmann, 'Two Faces of Edward', in R. Ellmann (ed.), *Edwardians and Late Victorians* (New York, 1960).

on a tigerskin in the age of imperialism, Florence Barclay's *The Rosary*, a sentimental tract, Marie Corelli's *The Treasure of Heaven*. But far more biting women writers were emerging: Ada Leverson produced the sharp social satire *The Twelfth Hour* (1907), May Sinclair a grim glance at marriage in *The Helpmate* (also 1907) and Virginia Woolf, around this same time, began her first novel. It was an age of the bluff bookman, and bookish people found writers like G. K. Chesterton, who linked his Catholicism to the detective story in the 'Father Brown' tales, and parodied *fin-de-siècle* pessimism in *The Man Who Was Thursday* (1908), W. H. Hudson, author of the lush, and pleasing, Venezuelan romance *Green Mansions* (1904), Walter de la Mare, John Masefield, Hugh Walpole, John Galsworthy or Hilaire Belloc among the great glories of English literature. They were not, though often they were good. Meanwhile James and Conrad struggled for an audience, while James Joyce, who had more or less completed *Dubliners* in 1904–5, was decisively silenced by the caution of British and Irish publishers. When the liberal politician C. F. Masterman, in his influential *The Condition of England* (1909), suggested that the Condition of England and the Condition of the English Novel were related, both seemed to give cause for concern.

That the Condition of England and the Condition of the English Novel were indeed related – and in more complicated ways than is sometimes supposed – was shown in a brilliant essay by Frank Kermode, 'The English Novel, *Circa* 1907'.[4] In Edwardian times, he notes, there was much popular commercial writing, but also much talk about matters of technique and purpose in the novel, and broad consideration of how much further the novel could go in the direction of art, innovation, and sexual frankness. The social, sexual, generational and class issues that stirred the late Victorian era still remained at the forefront of fiction. Samuel Butler's *The Way of All Flesh* (posthumously published in 1903) and then Edmund Gosse's *Father and Son* (1907), both clear, critical farewells to the pre-Darwinian age and the rule of the Victorian paterfamilias, made it plain that the

---

4 Collected in Frank Kermode, *Essays on Fiction, 1971–82* (London, 1983).

theocentric age was over, a secular one in progress, and what came next was an age of machines, materialism and money. These books were seized on by many younger writers, who agreed that sons, and daughters too, were in revolt against the Victorian fathers, and that the time had come for an end to reticence, a return to the heart, a new equation of feeling. In intellectual circles religion had mostly given way (apart from Chesterton and Belloc) to science and socialism, as H. G. Wells made plain in his novels, and Bernard Shaw in his plays. New writers like E. M. Forster, whose first book *Where Angels Fear to Tread* appeared in 1905, might acknowledge that they belonged to 'the fag-end of Victorian liberalism' but they looked for a new view of life and culture, based on personal relations, the reform of the heart, on passion and paganism. The 'Condition of England' concerned many writers. H. G. Wells explored it, with brilliant satire, in his *Tono-Bungay* of 1909; Forster confronted it in his balanced, liberal moral comedy *Howards End* of 1910. Liberalism, as a Whig programme of progress and reform, was dissolving, as the nation split between commercial and imperial Toryism and a spirit of scientific socialism; and this was the time of what historians call 'the strange death of Liberal England'. But as it declined as a public politics, liberalism was emerging as something more, or else, as the 'liberal imagination', a critical, reforming desire to examine and reconceive the nature of public and private life, confront what Forster called the 'inner darkness that comes with a commercial age', and challenge the cultureless, philistine Condition of England itself.

In Edwardian times there was no shortage of writers called 'modern'. The difference between the 'Edwardian' writers and those, many of the same generation, who achieved influence after was a disagreement about where the heart of the modern lay. Thus Joseph Conrad, writing his strange version of imperial romance, did not at the time seem notably modern, while, to the critics confronting what Henry James in his preface to *The Golden Bowl* (1904) nicely described as the 'marked inveteracy of a certain indirect and oblique view of my presented action', the late great novels that were now appearing seemed works of contorted and willed obscurity. On the other hand H. G. Wells – now directly portraying Edwardian life with its commercial enterprise, its new social types and possibilities, and speaking up for the new classes, the new men and women, and the new spirit of sex, all of this seen in the light of a great world-historical vision – seemed a prototype of the modern. So did Arnold Bennett and John Galsworthy, exploring the social texture of a changing age that had now left Victorianism well behind. James and Conrad wrote aesthetically, indirectly, from within; Wells and Bennett and Galsworthy wrote from without, as vivid, objective, 'realist' observers of a time in rapid change. They were materialist writers for materialist times, recorders of its new opportunities and dulling limitations, its sexual and emotional aspirations and its moral and class hypocrisies. Commerce and free love, business and socialism, were all modern. This was a time of department stores and aeroplanes and new opportunities, calling for adventurous writers. In *Tono-Bungay*, Wells celebrated 'the romantic element in modern commerce': 'We became part of what is now quite an important element in the confusion of our world, that multitude of economically ascendent people who are learning how to spend money,' his narrator explains: 'With enormous astonished zest they begin *shopping* . . .' New technologies were modern. The car and its goggled driver ('a short figure, compactly immense, hugely goggled, wearing a sort of brown rubber proboscis, and surrounded by a tableland of motoring cap'), the aeroplane and the destroyer are there in *Tono-Bungay*; cars moving at 60 m.p.h. allow the Wilcox family to hurtle across the old pastoral England without noticing it in *Howards End*; trains of virgin newness which move as smoothly 'as British gilt-edged securities' symbolize the age for Ford Madox Ford in his retrospective war novel *Some Do Not . . .* (1924). This was an age of statism and social planning, and the businessmen, bureaucrats, mandarins and scientific social thinkers, the people who 'administered the world', appear again and again in the fiction of Wells, Galsworthy, Forster and Hueffer/ Ford. And so do new young men from the lower classes seeking their rightful place in culture, from Wells's Mr Polly to Forster's Leonard Bast, along with the new young women demanding will and independence, like Wells's Ann Veronica. Masterman defined the 'Condition of England' as a set of contradictions, where it seemed impossible to reconcile old interests and new politics, past institutions and new vitality, the instincts of individualism and the demands of welfare, the desires of culture and the needs of the nation-state in a time of fast change, political uncertainty and rising international competition. He called on writers for a new, overarching cultural vision – something that a good many writers, from the socialist Wells to the liberal Forster to the Nietzschean D. H. Lawrence, did not fail to provide.

A great deal was stirring, then, in the brief Edwardian period, between 1901 and 1910. But what the Edwardians had really not decided, as many of their successors more confidently did, was the meaning of the word 'modern', the kind of artistic claim and commitment it seemed to require. In 1904 James Joyce (that Irish Edwardian, who set his most famous novel on a June day in this same Edwardian year) began *Stephen Hero* – a *Kunstlerroman*, or fictional 'portrait of the artist', a type of novel that had flourished greatly in the Decadence – as in Huysmans's *A rebours*, Wilde's *Picture of Dorian Gray*, Thomas Mann's *Buddenbrooks*. The story of the artist emerging from the material world of bourgeois reality has many dimensions, but one of them, said Joyce, was to enter the unknown arts, and be 'modern', or 'vivisective'. 'The ancient method investigated law with the lantern of justice, morality with the lantern of revelation, art with the lantern of tradition,' Joyce's young artist Stephen Dedalus explains. 'But all these lanterns have magical properties; they transform and disfigure. The modern method examines its territory by the light of day.' Examining 'by the light of day' meant both a voyage into the 'unknown arts' and a changed and radical conception of the artist: 'I will tell you what I will do and what I will not do,' Joyce has Stephen say in a later, aesthetically more refined version of the book, *A Portrait of the Artist as a Young Man* (1916): 'I will not serve that in which I no longer believe, whether it call itself my home, my fatherland, or my church: and I will try to express myself in some mode of life or art as freely as I can and as wholly as I can, using for my defence the only arms I allow myself to use, silence, exile and cunning.' The price of Joyce's artistic revolt was soon clear – silence and exile. The stories of *Dubliners*, offered to publishers in 1905, were rejected for indelicacy and possible libel. Set in galley in 1912, they were again suppressed, and did not appear until 1914, when modernist small press culture began to emerge, and the artist could declare his claim to an experimental modern vision.

What was missing in British culture, according to Hueffer/Ford, was the 'critical attitude', and so in 1908 he founded his excellent *English Review*, devoted to 'the arts, to letters, and to ideas', a sequence, he acknowledged, of almost hopeless causes, to promote just that. It seems odd now, when there is too much of it, that everyone then was asking for criticism. It was 'criticism, on other than infantile lines', that James cried for, and this was one reason he wrote the prefaces to the New York Edition, which appeared alongside his late great novels. Conrad requested something similar, growing ever more irritable with the 'inconceivable stupidity' of a childish reading public that could only tolerate clear plots and simple endings. D. H. Lawrence and Virginia Woolf had both begun writing fiction by now, he in 1906, she in 1908; both were experimenting with forms of fiction where consciousness and psychology created not clear plots and simple endings, but a structure and texture distinct and belonging only to itself. Around this same time, a new, 'harder' poetry was beginning to emerge, as the romantic shell and the divine afflatus were cast off, and the poem became a node, an event in language. And, just as the 'inner' poem was beginning to throw off the case of the 'outer' one, so an 'inner novel' was beginning to be disclosed. 'Story', 'plot' and 'description' were the stuff of the outer novel; but 'Yes, yes – but is this *all*?' Henry James was begging the reader to ask. 'These are the circumstances of the interest – we see, we see; but where is the interest itself, where and what is its centre, and how are we to measure it in relation to *that*?' Most Edwardian readers did not yet know the answer, but in fact it lay in some variant of the word 'form'. You could also try 'design', 'pattern', 'technique', 'revelation', 'epiphany' or 'consciousness'. It may not quite have been what Arnold Bennett was after when he told his tales of Bursley (though he was interested in the question), or H. G. Wells when he explored that great new romp called modern life. But it was at the centre of what was increasingly being named 'the art of fiction', which assumed, along with

James, that part of the essential subject of the novel was the story of its own making or becoming. And the age of 'the art of fiction' was clearly in the air when, in May 1910, King Edward VII died, King George V ascended to the throne, and the Georgian age began.

2

It was no doubt of all this Virginia Woolf was thinking when she pronounced, in her essay 'Mr Bennett and Mrs Brown' (1923), that 'in or about December 1910 human character changed', and along with it everything else, including religion, politics, conduct, values and literature. Up to 1910, she explained, there was no British novelist from whom a new writer could learn his or her serious business. James was an American, Conrad was a Pole, Dostoevsky was a Russian and Joyce simply remained invisible above his unpublished handiwork, paring his fingernails. The leading British novelists were Arnold Bennett, H. G. Wells and John Galsworthy, and they had educated the public into understanding what the novel was – a material thing, made of flat realities, exteriorly seen characters, broad social history, plainly charted plots. Going to them to learn how to write modern fiction, she said, was 'like going to a bootmaker and asking him to teach you how to make a watch'. Their books had nothing to do with the way in which life was really known and felt, certainly not as she herself knew and felt it. 'Is life like this? Must novels be like this?' she demanded. By 1910 it seemed clear, if the lessons of Cubist painting, of Einstein's relativity or of Dostoevsky's novels were any guide, that life was not really like this at all; it was filled with angles, recesses, indeterminacies, fragments. After attending the exhibition of French Post-Impressionist paintings ('Manet and the Post-Impressionists') organized by Woolf's friend Roger Fry at the Grafton Galleries, in December 1910, which included works by Van Gogh, Cézanne, Picasso and Matisse, even Arnold Bennett seemed inclined to agree: 'Noting in myself that a regular contemplation of these pictures inspires a weariness of all other pictures that are not absolutely first-rate . . . I have permitted myself to suspect that, supposing some writer were to come along and do in words what these men have done in paint, I might conceivably be disgusted with the whole of modern fiction, and I might have to begin again.'[5] Novels, then, did not necessarily have to be like 'this'. In that year, 1910, Bennett's own *Clayhanger* and Wells's *The History of Mr Polly* had appeared, and they were two of the stronger works of Edwardian realism. But so had E. M. Forster's most important pre-war novel *Howards End*, where realism is shot through with symbolism, and Hueffer's *A Call*, a novel of the telephone. Then in 1911 came D. H. Lawrence's sensuous first novel *The White Peacock*, Katherine Mansfield's volume of subtle and highly Chekhovian stories *In a German Pension* and a first novel, *Dolores*, later to be disowned, by another new writer, I. Compton-Burnett, who would duly turn the old Victorian world into an eternal stage set for her biting modern art. Hueffer now published his volume of essays, *The Critical Attitude*, and Virginia Woolf was herself becoming widely influential as a very critical literary critic, the modern equivalent of her father Leslie Stephen (in its way Bloomsbury too belonged to the fag-end of Victorian liberalism). A new generation of 'Georgians' was already emerging, leaving the Edwardian novel behind in its 'unreality', and, said Woolf, with 'a sound of breaking and falling, crashing and destruction', starting to break free.

So 1910 became a folkloric Bloomsbury date, and it was certainly the year when Bloomsbury itself, famous for its intellectual and aesthetic novelty and high sensitivity, started to acquire both its name and its artistic identity. But Fry's exhibition was essentially a reminder to the largely uncomprehending British ('The mild tragedy of the thing is that London is infinitely too self-complacent even to suspect that it is London and not the exhibition which is making itself ridiculous,' wrote Bennett) that the avant-garde tendencies and aesthetic inquiries that had been growing from the later nineteenth century had really not expired. The first decade of the century had been a flourishing, discovering period for the international Modern

---

5 'Jacob Tonson' (Arnold Bennett), 'Neo-Impressionism and Literature', *The New Age*, 8 December 1910; reprinted in Arnold Bennett, *Books and Persons* (London, 1917).

movement, which grew more international by the day. It was born in an appetite for transformation, the need to transcend and triumph over the past, following the Nietzschean imperative to create the world anew, in an endless sequence of creative discovery. By 1908 a modern avant-garde had plainly emerged, covering a new bohemian map that spanned from Moscow to Chicago, Rome to Oslo, Trieste to Dublin. It had resolved itself into a complex web of tendencies and causes, some of them closely inter-related, others deeply hostile to each other. In Paris by 1908 Pablo Picasso had painted *Les Demoiselles d'Avignon*, Cubism had been declared, Gertrude Stein had begun the uncertain adventure of writing Cubist prose and Proust had started *A la recherche du temps perdu*. In Germany, the art critic Wilhelm Worringer had defined 'abstraction' rather than 'empathy' as the key of modern art, and Expressionism had begun. In Vienna Musil, Schnitzler and Hoffmannsthal were writing, and Freud had published *The Psychopathology of Everyday Life*. In Italy Marinetti had started announcing Futurism; in February 1909 the *Futurist Manifesto* appeared, calling for the destruction of the cities and the art of the past ('Flood the museums!'), and celebrating new forms based on the automobile, the aeroplane and war. In pre-Revolutionary Russia, where Chekhov was writing his late plays, it found its parallel in Constructivism. All these movements were claiming history for themselves: announcing new psychologies of creation, new principles of form, new modes of perception, new attitudes to the future in the age of brute modernity, and declaring that artistic styles were not derived from accepted practices and conventions, but had to be newly sought and freshly made. The Modern movement was in essence an international affair, founded on exile, the movement of the arts, ideas and forms from one bohemia to another. And even in 'philistine' but imperial and hospitable pre-war Britain it now was starting to find a homeless home. Marinetti toured the country, declaiming his outrageous manifestos, and many artistic expatriates and exiles from elsewhere, drawn by its imperial vitality, were starting to flood in. In 1908 Ezra Pound arrived from the United States, determined to start a 'mouvemong' on the French model, and he found a group of poets, now well remembered as 'the Forgotten School of 1909', to support

Les Jeunes, as they chronologically presented themselves to us, were Mr Pound, Mr D. H. Lawrence, Mr Norman Douglas, Mr [F. S.] Flint, 'H. D.', Mr Richard Aldington, Mr T. S. Eliot . . . in our Editorial Salons they found chaises-longues and sofas on which to stretch themselves while they discussed the fate of already fermenting Europe. So, for three or four years, culminating in the London season of 1914, they made a great deal of noise in a city that was preparing to reverberate with the echoes of blasts still greater. They stood for the Non-Representational in the Arts; for *Vers Libre*; for symbols in Prose, *tapage* in Life, and death to Impressionism.

Over the two years of his editorship the paper comfortably printed, side by side with the Edwardians, nearly all the above, and the magazine marks a moment of strong literary transition. The movement came, the critical attitude flourished. Hueffer's instincts were right, and he had chosen his moment well. In the sphere of the literary arts, there was – truly – an 'opening world'.

3

Virginia Woolf's sound of 'breaking and falling, crashing and destruction', was therefore real enough. In the four years between the beginning of Georgianism and the outbreak of the Great War, the 'modern spirit', the sense of avant-garde adventure, of new forms opening new windows on a changed world, had once again begun to take hold. New and powerful influences, Dostoevsky and Chekhov, Ibsen and Nietzsche, Bergson and Sorel and Freud, began affecting British writing. For the moment London was recognizably a major centre of artistic cosmopolitanism, and writers and forms flooded in, in what is now remembered as a period of high cultural hospitality and internationalism rare in the modern British arts. Everyone slipped off to Paris. Hueffer came to see himself as German, or French, indeed anything but English. Then there were the expatriates and exiles: Conrad and Gaudier-Brzeska from Poland, S. S. Koteliansky from Russia, Yeats, Shaw and George Moore from Ireland (Joyce took his exile further afield, to the old Habsburg port of Trieste); James,

Pound, 'H. D.', and later the quiet T. S. Eliot from the USA; Katherine Mansfield from New Zealand and Wyndham Lewis from God alone knew where (he was appropriately born on a ship at sea). Lawrence made Nottinghamshire sound like a place of exile, followed German literature with passion, and began, like Joyce, on the path of wandering. Now more and more little magazines, generally with strange typographies and abstract covers, began their insecure publication; more and more movements and manifestos appeared (Imagism, Vorticism), calling in their different ways for energy, explosion, destruction and recommencement, aiming to blast down the past in the hope of blessing the future. The arts were in a mood of rebellious warfare, and their flamboyant putsches, campaigns and counter-putsches won public attention.[8]

Woolf's term for this, 'Georgian', was perhaps less than satisfactory. She was speaking of a double revolt, against 'Victorianism' and 'Edwardianism', but in fact the new movements and tendencies split in many directions, in which Georgianism – everything now was an 'ism' – was just one voice. In 1912 came Edward Marsh's *Georgian Poetry*, printing a variety of poets and generations, and claiming that the Georgian period might 'take rank in due time with the several great poetic ages of the past'. To D. H. Lawrence, who was both in it and reviewed it, the new 'Georgian' spirit was one of Nietzschean hope: 'The nihilists, the intellectual, hopeless people – Ibsen, Flaubert, Thomas Hardy – represent the dream we are waking from. It was a dream of demolition . . . But we are awake again, our lungs are full of new air, our eyes of morning.' Others were less sure. Georgianism in verse was soon challenged by Imagism, which was then challenged by Vorticism, each of them with a different view of the distilling form – 'image', 'vortex' or whatever – of the new. Dreams of the great demolition, the crashing and falling, continued. When Wyndham Lewis started a Vorticist manifesto-magazine in 1914 he called it *Blast*: and in a volley of brief, violent curses and benedictions he blasted the

---

8 A good recent record of this era is Julian Symons, *Makers of the New: the Revolution of Literature, 1912–1939* (London, 1987). Also see Frank Swinnerton's bluff but interesting *The Georgian Literary Scene* (London, 1938).

Victorians, rejected Romanticism for Classicism, Georgianism for something harder, tougher, more to do with machines than nature, and blessed the age of the abstract vortex and the cleansing modern explosion. The new excitements intensified year by year, and some of those who had called themselves simply moderns now knew they were Modernists, claiming that a most momentous transformation was fully under way. Small groups gathered, experimental enclaves flourished, hard experimental art-works multiplied, and new small presses and little magazines appeared to exhibit the avant-garde, printing works by writers whose work seemed to have been shamefully denied, from the new feminists to the exiled James Joyce. Hueffer, who once called himself an 'Impressionist', in the manner of Conrad, now called himself a 'Vorticist', and used Vorticist methods for his novel *The Good Soldier*, a section of which in turn appeared in *Blast*. *The Egoist*, once a feminist magazine, now had acquired Pound as literary editor; it promoted the movement of 'Imagism', and then in 1914, over twenty-four episodes, ran Joyce's *A Portrait of the Artist as a Young Man*. It was a rare and remarkable period in British writing, in prose and poetry, and in painting and sculpture and dance, all of which linked together in common cause. A pre-war Modernist wonderland did exist, and it was indeed like an opening world.

Even so, it is quite possible that all this could have been a brief and seasonal adventure, were it not for one terrible fact. The pre-war writers did not know they *were* pre-war writers, though sometimes it seems they half-intuited what was to come. The avant-garde, for all its modern prophecies, was not aware of what it was really *avant*. 1914, the year of Joyce's *Dubliners* and the serialization of *A Portrait* . . ., saw the excitement reach its peak. Then in August, between the first and second issues of *Blast*, the real blasts sounded. The collapse of imperial Europe, following the assassination of the Habsburg Archduke in Sarajevo, started; the Great War began. Soon the vortex of new energy ran free, and the young were all transforming themselves into Good Soldiers. Many, including T. E. Hulme, voice of the hard new classicism, and Gaudier-Brzeska, who had declared in *Blast* 'The War is a great remedy', died at the front. The abstract metallic explosions, the bursting mechanical violence, the new kinetic energy, became realities; the bombing of the old art cities, the flooding of the museums, that the Futurists had called for turned into fact. Over several literary generations writers had been prophesying the coming of the New Age, the violent end of an epoch, the rule of the destructive element, a war of the worlds. Now an era that thought it was beginning also found that it was ending, that even the spring-time new hopes were dashed. An era in culture, the arts and civilization was now in crisis, as Henry James, now at the close of his life, saw. He wrote his story 'A Dream of Armageddon', and reflected in a letter of August 1914 to his friend Howard Sturgis 'the plunge of civilization into this abyss of blood and darkness . . . is a thing that so gives away the whole long age in which we have supposed the world to be, with whatever abatement, gradually bettering, that to have to take it all now for what the treacherous years were all the while really making for and *meaning* is too tragic for any words.' Indeed, he noted, 'the war has used up words'. It was a notion that would resurface grimly after the Holocaust of the Second World War. The words, of course, would come in time. But the realization that they would have to be new words, that the war had drained most of the old ones of signification, that a different language, pared of most of the old romantic and cultural associations, would have to be found, grew as the terrible Great War went on. So it was that the war itself completed what pre-war Modernists had begun to imagine: the sweeping away of Victorianism and Edwardianism. Georgianism, its eyes full of morning, went too. The war smashed romanticism and sentimentalism, naive notions of patriotism and imperial adventure; they did not outlast the conflict. But, paradoxically, some of the complex aesthetic ideas that had stirred in the years between 1910 and 1914 – 'hardness', 'abstraction', 'collage', 'fragmentation', 'dehumanization' – and the key themes of chaotic history, Dionysian energy, the 'destructive element', did help to provide the discourse and forms of the world to come.

1915 – the year the war settled into the futility of trench warfare, and Zeppelin airships arrived to bomb London – was the culminating year, both in the war and in the transition of the arts. Some of the key books of the years of experiment appeared, marking a deep change in fictional climate. Conrad's emphatically titled *Victory* came out; so did John Buchan's classic spy story, *The 39 Steps*. Hueffer's farewell to the *belle époque*, the book that he had intended to call *The Saddest Story* (in accordance with its famous opening line, 'This is the saddest story I have ever heard'), appeared under the new wartime title of *The Good Soldier*. Virginia Woolf's long-delayed first novel appeared at last as *The Voyage Out*, and Dorothy Richardson opened her long experimental sequence 'Pilgrimage' with the volume *Pointed Roofs*. D. H. Lawrence, who had proved himself a writer always interested in apocalyptic moments and signs, the leap from the ruins, the personal resurrection, found the growing darkness of his vision confirmed. Before the war, he had started his most ambitious project so far, *The Sisters*, aided by his reading of Thomas Hardy. Now he divided it into two, to take account of what was happening. 'I knew I was writing a destructive work . . .,' he explained later, 'And I knew, as I revised the book, that it was a kind of working up to the dark sensual or Dionysic or Aphrodisic ecstasy, which actually does burst the world, burst the world-consciousness in every individual. What I did through individuals, the world has done through the war. But alas, in the world of Europe I see no Rainbow.' In 1915 the first segment of the book, which was called *The Rainbow*, the rainbow being an apocalyptic sign, appeared. It was a work both of crisis and Dionysic sensual ecstasy, developing both in optimism and pessimism on from Hardy. The critics were shocked, perhaps in part by its apparent indifference to the war itself. One thousand and eleven copies were seized and destroyed by the police, and it was banned under the Obscene Publications Act. 'The world is gone, extinguished,' Lawrence bitterly noted, already planning the path of post-war exile; 'It was in 1915 that the old world ended.' Many of the fruits of the pre-war experiment had come to birth. So had a new world, bitter and empty, made out of cultural disorder and European ruins. It might be a modern, but it was no longer an opening, world.

4

It is hardly surprising that the immediately pre-war years became folkloric, for the participants and then for the later critics; so much that is important to the idea of modern literature stirred into existence then. In retrospect, said Wyndham Lewis, looking back from 1937, when he had himself become the 'Enemy', at odds with most of what happened thereafter to the Modern movement, it would all appear 'an island of incomparable bliss, dwelt by strange shapes labelled "Pound", "Joyce", "Weaver", "Hulme" . . . As people look back at them, out of a very humdrum, cautious, disillusioned society . . . the critics of the future will rub their eyes. They will look, to them, so hopelessly avant garde!, so almost madly up and coming! What energy! – what impossibly spartan standards, men will exclaim! . . . *We are the first men of a future that has not materialized!*' Whether this is self-serving or not, it is certainly true that we cannot write the history of modern fiction without looking with some care at many of his strange shapes. And there is no doubt that one of the strangest, and most representative, was the one then labelled 'Hueffer', though later known as 'Ford'. Hueffer/Ford always had a gift for metamorphosis, and this brought him into close contact with nearly everything that was interesting and significant about the Modern movement. Lewis, whom he discovered, called him 'a flabby lemon and pink giant, who hung his mouth open as though he were an animal at the Zoo inviting buns – especially when ladies were present' (they often were); H. G. Wells, first his friend, then his enemy, described him as 'a great system of assumed persona and dramatized selves'. Indeed it was true his manner often appeared a disguise, and there somehow seemed to be two or more of him. He was the British writer incarnate, but he was also German, or French. Sometimes he was the foreign bohemian adrift among British philistines; sometimes he was the last British Tory, condemned to travel the great wilderness known as 'abroad'. At various times he was the Last Pre-Raphaelite, the first Impressionist, a Post-Impressionist, a Vorticist and a soldier of the Parisian 'Revolution of the Word'. He wrote extensively about the 'critical attitude', but was not a theorist (his companion of the Twenties, Stella Bowen, described him as 'a writer – a complete writer – and nothing but a writer'). He collaborated with Conrad, wrote well on James and had literary friendships (though they often turned, as such things do, into enmities) with most of the major figures of the era – Conrad, James, Hardy, Wells, Pound, Lawrence, Violet Hunt, Rebecca West, May Sinclair, Joyce, Stein, Jean Rhys and Robert Lowell, helping many of them to publication. He was close to every major movement, from Pre-Raphaelitism to Dada, over the fifty years of his writing life. He wrote over eighty books in innumerable genres, children's stories to advanced poetry, from the early 1890s to 1939, the year of his death; thus his writing life more or less matched the main span of Modernism.

He both enacted Modernism's story, and told it – not always accurately, but he was an 'Impressionist' – in many books of criticism and reminiscence. He was born in 1873, in a Pre-Raphaelite bohemian household; his father was a German music critic just arrived in Britain, his mother was daughter to the painter Ford Madox Brown. At eighteen, as the Nineties started, he published his first book *The Brown Owl*, a fairy story that owed something to Stevenson, and by 1898, after several more books, met the still little-known Conrad. They collaborated on three commercial novels, *The Inheritors* (1901), *Romance* (1903) and *The Nature of a Crime* (1924), and Hueffer also had a hand in *Heart of Darkness* and *Nostromo*, two of Conrad's finest works. Drawing on the theories of Flaubert, Maupassant and James, they agreed together on the method of 'Impressionism': 'We accepted the name of impressionists because we saw that life did not narrate but made Impressions on our brains,' he later explained. 'We in turn, if we wished to produce an effect of life, must not narrate but render impressions.'[9] He was also writing novels of his own, and making important literary friendships, with Henry James, H. G. Wells, John Galsworthy and Stephen Crane, the American author of *The Red Badge of Courage*, now living in Britain. Most of these were gathered together, as if for experimental literary security, in the same general area of Kent and Sussex; they visited each other frequently –

9 Ford Madox Ford, *Joseph Conrad: A Personal Reminiscence* (London, 1924).

James on his bicycle, Crane with his six-gun – and formed an important seedbed for the cultivation of the modern, a meeting-place for many of its main ideas and, indeed, its future quarrels.

Between the century's turn and the coming of war, Hueffer – a writer's writer who wrote every day – produced almost forty books, from memoirs and children's books to historical and social novels. Several were in the typical Edwardian form of the 'Condition of Engand' novel, explorations of the contemporary social order and its conflicts. But he explored them with 'impressionist' techniques, as he did, more surprisingly, the historical romance – above all his fine *Fifth Queen* trilogy, about Catherine Howard, which he completed in 1908, just as he was founding *The English Review*. That magazine brought him into close contact with an entire new generation of writers, including Pound, Lewis and D. H. Lawrence, all of whom he 'discovered': 'Ford Madox Hueffer discovered I was a genius,' Lawrence wrote, ' – don't be alarmed, Hueffer would discover *anything* if he wanted to.' He championed the new because it *was* new, original, innovative; the process helped make his own work new. He began to see that an experimental bridge could be built between the older writers of the 1890s and the younger innovators, even those at odds with his own literary philosophy. A declared Impressionist, he gladly published those like Pound who cried 'Death to Impressionism'. Though he had total contempt for the Novel With a Purpose ('A novel should render, not draw morals'), he published Wells, who after 1900 wrote little else – and before he was done Hueffer wrote Novels With a Purpose too (his post-war 'Parade's End' sequence had, he said, for its purpose 'the obviating of all future wars'). He believed in Flaubertian French perfection, but he advanced expressionistic neo-Nietzscheans like D. H. Lawrence. He saw and wrote of an age of looming sexual chaos, but assisted New Feminist writers like Violet Hunt (translator of Casanova, and author of the interesting novel of the life of working women, *The Workaday Woman*, 1906), Rebecca West, Stella Bowen and later Jean Rhys. Sometimes his assistance went a very long way, and led to various unconventional ménages; generally he received either too little or too much in the way of gratitude. It didn't matter; what counted was 'perfection', the 'critical attitude', the 'serious artist', the 'spirit of modern life'. In 1912, he finally and grandly announced his farewell to literature, to leave the field to newer writers 'whose claim or whose need for recognition and what recognitions bring was greater than my own'.

Fortunately, and typically, he soon changed his mind, and so in 1913, on his fortieth birthday, he resolved to give himself one last chance. 'I had always been mad about writing – about the way writing should be done and partly alone, partly with the companionship of Conrad, I had even at that date made exhaustive studies into how words should be handled and books constructed,' he explained, but 'I had never really put into any novel of mine *all* that I knew about writing.' That aim went into his new book, which proved his finest, his great contribution to the New Novel. He followed the method of Conrad and later James by dictating some of his story, which doubtless added to its hesitancies and indirections, its air of fracture and tension. Excited by Vorticism, he borrowed its 'hard' technique, and made the book polished, 'like a steel helmet'. Responding to the mood of the time, he made his theme the dying of the European *belle-époque* world, which he presented with bitter irony. He gave the book an ambiguous, American narrator, Dowell, a deceived husband, who declares 'Six months ago I had never been to England, and, certainly, I had never sounded the depths of an English heart.' The novel's theme is sounding the false beat of the pre-war English heart, and the book contains its own ominous warning. Hueffer ensured that the chief events occur on 4 August of various years – the date of the outbreak of the Great War, which came as he worked on the novel.

The book, *The Good Soldier*, therefore appeared in 1915, along with other key books of the pre-war modern movement. The peak of his experiment, it was also the end of an era. Despite its title, it is a novel not of war but pre-war. Set mostly in the German spa town of Nauheim (in enemy territory by the time the book appeared), the story is about a man of honour corrupted by sexuality and the social deceits and hypocrisies which surround and disguise it. Two central couples, the British Ashburnhams, the American Dowells, have *mariages blancs*, unconsummated marriages; for different reasons the wives want to protect their sexual sanctity. They pretend to 'heart disease' so that, at the spa, various polygamous arrangements can be made. Ashburnham, who seems especially honourable, is the British 'good soldier'. But married love is conducted through surrogates and intricate systems of deception. Only Dowell, the cuck-old narrator, seems unaware of them; the story he tells as it were deceives him. His method of indirect narration also deceives us ('I have, I am aware, told this story in a very rambling way so that it may be difficult for anyone to find their path through what may be a sort of maze. I cannot help it . . . when one discusses an affair – a long, sad affair – one goes back, one goes forward . . .'). If, as he says, the book's social world is 'secret', 'subtle', 'subterranean', the workings of the sexual world are more obscure still; one critic of the book has remarked that its sexual activity seems always the echo of an echo – now you see it, now you don't. The innocent Dowell is left to unravel the impressions and deceits confronting him. The word 'impression' is crucial to the story – there are 'all-round impressions', 'first impressions', 'false impressions'. The baffled decoding of impres-sions – learnt from James and Conrad – gives the difficult fragmented technique. *The Good Soldier* has been called the best French novel in the English language; it is easy to see why. It is what the French critic Roland Barthes calls *scriptible*; we are always aware of the self-conscious method of the writing, the writerly nature of the text. In Jamesian terms (which Hueffer adopted), the story is an 'affair', the telling is a 'treatment', the method displays James's 'baffled relationship between the subject-matter and its emergence'. James here was referring to Conrad, but Hueffer takes matters one step further, making his narrator the victim of the story he tells. But in a world of false social surfaces, where everything is deliberately unspoken, it takes an art of great indirection to get to, well, the heart of the matter.

The Good Soldier, one of the culminating books of the pre-war modern movement, was Hueffer's last novel as Hueffer. When he came back from the front he changed his name to Ford; domestic troubles were part of the reason, but, as he rightly said, all identities had changed in the war. He still had twenty more years of writing life, some thirty more books to bring to print, including the excellent

'Parade's End' sequence (1924–8), of which more later on. But part of its importance is that it explores the difficult passage, through the battlefields of the Somme, from pre-war to post-war Britain, and suggests why the Condition of England was no longer an easily available subject, why modern forms continued to fragment. By now he was an exile in France; for the 'opening world' had plainly closed by now, the London experiment had virtually died, and Britain had banned, silenced or alienated many of its finest and most demanding writers. He would never live permanently in Britain again, and his main work hereafter was done in France, amid the experimental excitements of the Twenties. And by now the modern novel had ceased to be an 'affair'; it had become the expression of a historical crisis. The future had indeed materialized, but not in the way its prophets had expected. Hueffer/Ford died in France in 1939, when the Modern experiment was as good as over. Hueffer had seen one half of it; Ford had seen the other. Each had written a major modern work: Hueffer the pre-war *The Good Soldier*, and Ford the post-war 'Parade's End'. His own reputation had declined by now, but he had done what he meant to do – bring a French perfection to the English novel and support the changing experiment of British writing. He had crossed with nearly everything that was significant, and midwived many of the main achievements, from start to finish, from Conrad's *Nostromo* and Lawrence's *The White Peacock* to Stein's *The Making of Americans* and Joyce's *Finnegans Wake*. He had written good books and bad ones, and, as he confessed, not done all he intended. But in Modernism's discontinuous continuity he still remains a central figure.

5

If the young Ford Madox Hueffer who met and collaborated with Joseph Conrad in 1898 was not always to remain Hueffer, the forty-year-old Polish émigré his path had crossed with had certainly not always been Joseph Conrad. The disorders of imperial middle Europe had brought about his change of name and cultural identity, and they left their mark on all his work. He was born Josef Teodor Konrad Nalecz Korzeniowski, the child of Polish gentry in 1857 in the Russian-occupied Polish Ukraine, a 'country that was not a country'. His father Apollo was a romantic nationalist who fought against the Tsarist domination, and when he was sent into Russian penal exile he took the young child with him. From this time onward 'Conrad' would always remain to some degree exiled and stateless; so would the fiction he came to write. As he grew up he wandered in Europe – he moved to France, went to sea, fought a duel, engaged in gun-running, spent a fortune, attempted suicide. To avoid conscription in the Russian army, he joined the British merchant navy, and sailed the seaways of the imperial and mercantile world, from the Pacific to South America, the British coastal ports to the Congo. That gave him British citizenship, but never quite perfect English; the fiction he started now would always have, in language as well as vision, a touch of the foreign and the exiled about it. Nonetheless, in a time that was turning to the imperial romance, he evidently possessed perfect exotic material, and a chance meeting with John Galsworthy on an Eastern voyage led him to think of writing a novel. He began a tale about outcast Europeans in the Malayan archipelago, based on personal experience, which he carried about the world; it appeared in 1895 as *Almayer's Folly*. In 1896 he followed it with another similar story of the Pacific, also about Europeans split between two worlds, *An Outcast of the Islands*. Both were romances, but both have a haunting sense of life on its frontier, of existence as isolation and extremity. And a distinctive Conradian note is already struck in a passage in the second novel where he speaks of 'the tremendous fact of our isolation, of the loneliness impenetrable and transparent, elusive and everlasting; of the indestructible loneliness that surrounds, envelops, clothes every soul from the cradle to the grave, and perhaps, beyond.'

Then in 1898, just round the time Hueffer met him, he produced a quite different kind of book. Today it is uncomfortably dated by its title, *The Nigger of the 'Narcissus'*, but it remains a work of unmistakable modernity, the beginning of his major fiction. The story of a homeward voyage from Bombay to London, it tells of nihilistic forces set loose on the ship during the passage, and of the final, necessary restoration of order. Like many of Conrad's later books, it is also a myth – possibly influenced by Herman Melville's remarkable sea-fable 'Benito Cereno' (1856) – about an unreliable and doubled world. It was the first of many tales he would set on merchant vessels, seen as microcosms of the social, moral, indeed metaphysical world, where the need for order and discipline conflict with wilderness and threat, not only from the 'terrible sea' and the anarchy of life, but from the inner ambiguity of human nature itself. Shipboard society becomes a space where the 'essential' values – honour, duty, courage, fidelity ('Those who read me know my conviction that the world, the temporal world, rests on a few simple ideas; so simple they must be as old as the hills,' Conrad observed: 'It rests notably, among others, on the idea of Fidelity') – are tested to extremity. Pervading the stories is a fearful scepticism, the awareness that civilization soon finds its limits, light turns into darkness, virtue and courage are always at risk, behind every face there is a secret sharer, behind every man there is a darker double. When David Daiches hailed Conrad as 'the first important modern novelist in English', it was because of the distinctive timbre of his metaphysical vision, which means that 'the world of significance he creates is at the furthest remove from the world of public significance created by the great Victorian and eighteenth-century novelists.' Like the Russian fiction of Dostoevsky, whose work Conrad claimed to detest ('I don't know what Dostoevsky stands for or reveals, but I do know he is too Russian for me,' he said, in a remark that peculiarly resembled the complaints of some critics about his own novels), his novels implanted into social or romantic themes an existential crisis. And with that modern spirit went a modern method, part-born from this alien, metaphysical tone of his writing – a method always indirect, deferring, bred of his dark conviction that he wrote of a gloomy unstable universe in which, as he said, 'no explanation is final'.

So quite as famous as *The Nigger of the 'Narcissus'* is its preface, now taken as one of the most important manifestos of the modern way in fiction. Perhaps stung by H. G. Wells's charge of 'obscurity', probably influenced by Stevenson's defence of the 'web . . . or the pattern' at the heart of fiction ('a web at once sensuous and logical, an elegant and pregnant texture: that is style, that is the foundation of the art of literature'), Conrad made the case for a novel that unified form and content by searching inwardly, self-consciously for its own logic and coherence. A famous phrase declares the symbolist credo: 'A work that aspires, however humbly, to the condition of art should carry its justification in every line.' A novel should have the magical suggestiveness of music and the plastic arts, should be 'an impression conveyed through the senses'. And the task of the novelist was to 'render'. 'My task which I am trying to achieve is, by the power of the written word to make you feel – it is, before all, to make you *see*. That – and no more, and it is everything. If I succeed, you shall find there according to your deserts: encouragement, consolation, fear, charm – all you demand – and, perhaps, also that glimpse of truth for which you have forgotten to ask.' The aim of art, just like that of life, 'is inspiring, difficult – obscured by mists. It is not in the clear logic of a triumphant conclusion; it is not in the unveiling of one of those heartless secrets which are called the Laws of Nature.' Art grew not from statement or narrative completeness; it grew from rendering, figuration, 'impressions', the pursuit of the symbol. If some unhappy readers thought this simply produced novels that were themselves obscured by mists, others felt this was indeed what James called the new self-consciousness of fiction.

What Conrad had in mind perhaps grew a little clearer when he set off directly for the heart of his darkness. *Heart of Darkness*, the powerful long novella of imperialism he published in magazine form in 1899, and collected in the volume *Youth* in 1902, starts in the gloomy light of London, the imperial city; it returns safely back at last to the drawing-rooms of social fiction. Between comes a cunning allegory of light falling into darkness, a descent through the heart of Africa into human horror and the black places of the soul. In 1890 Conrad had taken part in the new scramble for Africa, sailing to the imperial Belgian outpost in the Congo; he returned ill, shaken, morally outraged by the cruelties and corruption he had seen. 'Before the Congo I was only a simple animal,' he said. The story follows his experience almost exactly, taking its narrator, Marlow, on a 'night journey' from London, via a sinister Brussels, to the grim Congo and the 'Inner Station' – a journey that moves from civilization through futility and carelessness to evil, darkness, exploitation and 'the earliest beginnings of the world'. In the Congo Marlow finds his tragic double, Mr Kurtz, an idealist who had dreamt of bringing civilization to Africa, been drawn into its savagery – 'The wilderness had patted him on the head' – and comes to the ultimate abyss, declared in his dying cry of 'The horror! The horror!' Kurtz bequeaths Marlow a moral dilemma; when he returns to London he has to report his death to Kurtz's fiancée, 'the Intended', who asks what his last words were. Marlow chooses a saving lie over a revelation of the moral anarchy he has seen: 'The last word he spoke was – your name,' he says. But the story contains a second story, of its own telling. Marlow recounts it all, on a ship in a London port, to a chosen audience, an Imperial trio: a Lawyer, an Accountant and a Director of Companies, to whom he reveals that London too has been, is, one of the earth's dark places. Marlow – the angled, ironic narrator who first appeared in the earlier story 'Youth' – is the key to the tale. He is, Conrad explained, a man 'with whom my relations have grown very intimate in the course of years . . . He haunts my hours of solitude when, in silence, we lay our heads together in great comfort and harmony; but as we part at the end of a tale I am never sure that it may not be for the last time.' He is, effectively, the storyteller as method, not just the experiencer of the tale, but its constructor, interpreter, investigator, decoder, an intruded presence between tale and reader. He has his own view of story: 'The meaning of an episode is not inside like a kernel but outside, enveloping the tale which brought it out only as a glow brings out a haze, in the likeness of one of those misty halos that sometimes are made visible by the spectral illumination of moonshine.' This may sound like a defence of Romanticism, but the point, of course, is that 'episodes' do not have one simple meaning, but are refracted. This was what readers otherwise admiring of Conrad often challenged. 'Is there not also a central obscurity, something noble, heroic, beautiful, inspiring half-a-dozen great books, but obscure, obscure?' asked E. M. Forster. To others this became the essence of modern fiction itself, what James, also writing of Conrad, called the baffled relation between the story and its emergence, which made the novel not an action but an 'affair'.

A novel should be not a 'superficial how' but a 'fundamental why', suggests Marlow, when he returns, one of several narrators, to tell the story of *Lord Jim* (1900). Jim, the hero who fails to be a hero, abandons his vessel, the *Patna*, loaded with pilgrims en route for Mecca, when he thinks it is sinking, and so violates a fundamental law of duty and responsibility. The ship is rescued, and his cowardice and shame exposed, at an official enquiry. But this fails to satisfy Marlow, who sees Jim as 'one of us' and looks for what this tells us about human nature: 'Why I longed to go grubbing after the deplorable details of an occurrence which, after all, concerned me no more than as a member of an obscure body of men [sailors] held together by a community of inglorious toil and by fidelity to a certain standard of conduct, I can't explain,' he tells us: '. . . Perhaps, unconsciously, I hoped I would find that something, some profound and redeeming cause, some merciful explanation, some convincing shadow of an excuse.' The book changes from seafaring adventure into a psychological and metaphysical investigation, and develops not to a final resolution but to a deep uncertainty about human complexity. Marlow teases the story backward and forward, seeking the essence among the multiplied meanings of Jim – coward and hero, outcast and *tuan*, the man who tries to redeem his moral crime by confronting the 'destructive element', and finally meets the positive and negative faces of his own self in an apparently senseless act of sacrifice. The book's time-scale, and its viewpoint, move back and forth, through indirections and curious retellings. These indirect methods are of the essence, functioning in the story just as Marlow does: to fill out an expanding world of values and ambiguities against which Jim is tested, and has tested himself, and which leaves him and the story 'inscrutable at heart', real and yet disembodied.

Later in life Conrad would describe his art as lying 'almost wholly in my unconventional grouping and perspective', explain that he was concerned for 'effects' rather than 'mere directness of narrative'. Complexity was becoming the essence of his novels; like his own Captain Giles in *The Shadow Line* (1917), Conrad had chosen to be an expert in 'intricate navigation'. If readers found them difficult, as they did, this was not only because of oblique tactics – his breaking of conventional time-codes, his refusal of safe endings, his multiplication of viewpoints – nor because of his sense that life and human action were enigmatic, 'inscrutable at heart'. There was also something that could aptly be called 'foreign' about his writing, a double vision, displayed in the spirit of irony – a spirit seemingly at odds with the best hopes and public themes of the Edwardian age, when in fact he produced his finest work. *Nostromo* (1904) is often thought his best novel, an ultimate fable of New World imperialism. It is set in the imaginary South American republic of Costaguana – otherwise 'the dung coast', dominated by its silver mine, the ever-ambiguous symbol of New World adventuring – and written in the mode of what we now call 'magical realism'. Conrad gives his imaginary land a complex Borgesian history, drawn, he says, from Don José Avellanos's *History of Fifty Years of Misrule*, a lost work whose pages float away across the harbour in the course of the novel. 'I am in fact the only person in the world possessed of its contents,' Conrad says in the preface, '. . . I hope my accuracy can be trusted.' It has to be, since, as he also says, 'There was not a single brick, stone, or grain of sand in its soil I had not placed into position with my own hands.' Like the New World itself, Costaguana is an invented space of history and myth: it is pastoral, virgin land, the placid gulf, an American dream, a half-blank page on which history is still to be written, 'a twilight country . . . with its high shadowy Sierra and its misty campo for mute witness of events flowing from the passions of men short-sighted in good and evil.'

It also has a very modern politics, and if its history is still being written, many try to write it: the old colonists and the new European adventurers, who bring the usual mixtures of idealism and materialism, buccaneering exploitation and liberal dreams, social reform and violent revolution, hope and depravity, 'violent efforts for an idea and sullen acquiescence in every form of corruption'. 'Liberals! The words one knows so well have a nightmarish meaning in this country,' we learn; all the causes prove to have 'a flavour of folly and murder', and no one survives very long. Western civilization intrudes with its apparent principles of order and reason, bringing the steamship company, the railroad, the exploitation of the San Tomé silver mine, otherwise known as 'material interests'. 'Silver' is the novel's key word, intricately coded into the book. It is a moral ideal, and a source of European and North American wealth; a dream of redemption and the corrupting instrument of an age of capitalism and individualism. The source of identity, it destroys everyone – Charles Gould, Decoud, above all Nostromo, 'our man', the Man of the People, the figure of 'unbroken fidelity, rectitude and courage' whose fidelity and bravery are corrupted and rendered an artifice: 'Nostromo had lost his peace; the genuineness of all his qualities was destroyed.' Nature and civilization becalm each other, producing a collapse of ideals and dreams, love and will, creating indifference and nihilism. *Nostromo* is a dark book – in its vision of human nature and desire, its view of modern history, its doubt of all political systems. At the end the United States still waits in the wings ('We shall run the world's business whether the world likes it or not'), and the name of the corrupted Nostromo still rings ambiguously over the dark gulf. This is the work of a man who sees that history does not work by progressive liberal evolution nor by revolution, that idealistic virtues and political dreams rarely survive pure but betray or are betrayed from within or without: an ironist indeed.

His next book, *The Secret Agent* (1907), brought that irony far closer to home. He turned to a British subject, given him by Hueffer, with a Russian flavour, explaining his conception like this: 'The vision of an enormous town presented itself, of a monstrous town more populous than some continents and in its man-made might as if indifferent to heaven's frowns and smiles: a cruel devourer of the world's light. There was room enough here to place any story, depth enough for any passion, variety enough there for any setting, darkness enough to bury five millions of lives.' The 'monstrous town' is London, the darkness holds grim political secrets as well as obscure and furtive lives. The theme is anarchism, the central situation based on a bizarre and futile attempt made in 1894 on Greenwich Observatory – the sailor's sanctuary, the place where the temporal mean is set – when the terrorist had been blown up by his own bomb. This was the stuff of the sensational novel and the detective story; Conrad described his task as one of 'applying an ironic method to a subject of this kind'. The irony he applied is universal: there is irony of character (all the figures in the book are somehow examples of paradox, contradiction and futility), irony of plot (nothing ever works out as intended), irony of narrative perspective (the outcome of the story is an emotional nihilism), irony of existence (life, as Mrs Verloc discovers, is not worth looking into). Anarchism unwraps into the empty void of its own nihilism and is in any case the product of safe bourgeois values; the book distances all the human agents, even the gentle simpleton Stevie, and spares neither civilization nor the revolutionary aspirations that threaten it. Frank Kermode describes the book as 'a story with an enormous hole in the plot'; other critics have seen it as a novel without a hero, and a work without a perspective. But as Thomas Mann saw, when he wrote the preface for the German translation, the perspective is that of irony itself. It was a work neither of political liberalism nor revolutionary utopianism, both tempting attitudes of the day; it uses what Mann calls the method of 'the tragic grotesque', the viewpoint of dismayed distance, the modern tone. There was one further irony; Conrad had subtitled the book 'a simple tale', and hoped his melodrama would lift his disappointing sales; it did not. Chesterton was affronted enough to counter the book with his *The Man Who Was Thursday*; it may well have stimulated Wells, to whom it is dedicated, to write his more buoyant version of the monstrous town in *Tono-Bungay*. Conrad explained the book to Galsworthy as 'an honourable failure . . . I suppose there is something in me that is unsympathetic to the general public . . . Foreignness, I suppose.'

And 'foreignness', the fact that not all the world is to be seen under Western eyes, was the theme of his next novel, *Under Western Eyes* (1911). This surely is Conrad's real masterpiece, even though it has its obvious imperfections, enough to drive its author to a nervous breakdown after writing it. It is an exile's book, in which he returns to the source of his own exile, Russia, that land of heroic romance and empty futility, tyranny and anarchy, 'spectral dreams and disembodied aspirations', a work that links his fiction back to

Dostoevsky and forward to Nabokov. Conrad added a preface to the book after the Bolshevik Revolution of 1917, explaining its underlying prophecy: an autocratic state founded on total moral anarchism had now been upturned by its 'imbecile opposite', a proletarian and utopian revolution that went for destruction as the first means to hand. The book unlocks the hidden implication behind many of his other novels – that, if you happen to see the world with not quite Western eyes, not with the conventional assumptions of British liberalism or good-hearted reform, political order is generally a thin film on the top of chaos, and political sentiment quickly leads to a world of guilt and treachery. For all that he dismissed the works of Dostoevsky (just being translated in Britain as his book appeared), his fiction, and the tradition of the Russian novel, is imprinted on this novel: in the divided ideology, split between conservatism and revolution, in the romantic turmoil of soul and the search for a metaphysic between contradictory, violent extremes. Razumov, the book's central character, directly recalls the Raskolnikov of *Crime and Punishment*, with his introspective and tormented consciousness, and his need to confess and purge the crime he has committed; both writers deal with the theme of the psychological purging of the self in a world that itself lacks all moral substance – a modern existential theme that has been central to the modern novel.

But there is one essential and fundamental difference, which makes the book into a dual text (as Nabokov's *Ada*, imprinting the landscape of Russia on America, the Russian novel on the American novel, is a dual text). The vivid tale of Razumov's student life, his encounter with revolution and his betrayal in Saint Petersburg, and then his confession and expiation among the revolutionary exiles of the city of exiles, Geneva, is a Russian story. But the story is told to be interpreted and read under Western eyes. The book's narrator, a British teacher of languages in Geneva, is a latter-day Marlow, trying to tell and read the tale that has come his way. 'To the teacher of languages there comes a time when the world is but a place of many words and man appears to be a mere talking animal not much more wonderful than a parrot,' he tells us at the start; words are, he confesses, 'the great foes of reality'. It is his distance from the inner secrets of so many words that make him a less than reliable narrator, for though he is a student of many grammars there is much he cannot see with his 'Western eyes'. Thus the book layers two stories, from two narrative traditions, two different political and moral cultures. There is the language teacher's story, and that of Razumov, which he draws from his written confessions or his partial witnessing of events. The story is filled with hidden secrets, which he doubly attempts to decode: making what sense he can of Razumov's tale, and making the experience understandable to readers who have only Western eyes. He uses Razumov's diary to extend his eye-witness material, but also develops and comments on it. The difficulty, not always narratively successful, becomes part of the virtuosity of the telling. It was not entirely surprising that British readers had some trouble with Conrad's 'obscurity'. When his own narrator has such problems in reading and interpreting a tale so dense with confusions and secrets, when that story concerns a different and alien world with a different sense of history, then it takes care and time to read with Western eyes a story that questions the gaze of Western eyes.

Conrad's obscurity, in short, was more than a technical obscurity; it had also to do with a challenge to Western culture his readers took some time to accept. Nonetheless they did accept it; with his next novel, *Chance* (1913), Conrad had at last his first popular success. Thereafter his audience magically widened. His last group of books – *Victory* (1915), *The Shadow Line* (1917), *The Arrow of Gold* (1919), *The Rescue* (1920), *The Rover* (1920) – satisfied the audience at last; where earlier books had runs of less than 3,500 copies, *The Rescue* had a first run of 25,000. By now he had returned, largely, to sea stories, and his famous obscurity seemed to have turned into a dense and satisfying Romantic haze. His technique had muted, turning into what one great admirer, Virginia Woolf, called 'old nobilities and sonorities . . . a little wearily reiterated, as if times had changed'. In his final years he became one of Britain's most famous writers, revered abroad, offered a knighthood (mysteriously refused) in 1924; he died later that year. His greatest importance as a writer had lain in two things. One was the vision of a world of disorder, which challenged our sense of humanity and politics, and demanded an obscure new

similar themes, all about the excitement of life in a time of change and promise. Wells was above all readable; he was the novelist of ordinariness and familiarity, which he made excitingly unordinary and unfamiliar. His stories were mostly based on autobiographical materials, born out of the lower-middle-class London suburban world from which he came, tales of aspiring, opportunity-seeking young men and women who were taking on the adventure of social, educational, commercial and sexual self-transformation. The basic plot is plain: a young person from modest beginnings is helped by political awareness, scientific knowledge and sexual openness to face the widening prospects of life, challenging convention and the stuffy inheritance of the British past in the process. There is usually a Big Idea on hand – Science, Evolution, Socialism, Feminism, Free Love, Modernity or just a great new commercial invention. Some of the stories, like *Kipps* (1905) or *The History of Mr Polly* (1910), are larky and Dickensian, and Wells brought a welcome note of comic relief to the general solemnity of fiction. Others, like *Ann Veronica* (1909), a portrait of a free new woman who takes what she wants, or *Tono-Bungay* (also 1909), a remarkable analysis of contemporary British culture, are more deeply serious. The Wellsian message is also unmistakable. If we are timid or unlucky, we return to the prison of convention or dull domesticity, but the real promise is the rule of positive evolution, stated in *The History of Mr Polly*: '. . . when a man has once broken through the paper walls of everyday circumstance, those unsubstantial walls that hold so many of us securely prisoned from the cradle to the grave, he has made a discovery,' Wells tells us: 'If the world does not please you, *you can change it.*'

Wells, we know, along with Arnold Bennett, John Galsworthy and some others, wrote the Edwardian novel. But what then was the Edwardian novel? Plainly it was not the new self-conscious fiction James, Conrad and Hueffer were commonly expounding. But this did not mean its authors were ignorant of the claim that the novel was, as James said, an 'affair'. Wells had kept good company with 'the immense artistic preoccupations' of these writers, and had given some considerable support to them; for example, he hailed Stephen Crane's highly Impressionist *The Red Badge of Courage* (1895) as a new kind of writing, 'the expression in art of certain enormous repudiations'. He sustained his friendship with Conrad, who dedicated *The Secret Agent* to Wells as 'the historian of ages to come' (he likewise dedicated *Nostromo* to John Galsworthy, who had indeed encouraged him to begin writing). Wells believed he was constructing a radical experiment in fiction, as did Galsworthy and above all Bennett, who had signalled himself as 'the latest disciple of the Goncourts', had devoted himself during the 1890s to what he called 'conscious pleasure in technique' and always asserted there was no conflict between experimental artist and commercial literary adventurer. The experiment was above all a revolt against Victorianism, the nineteenth-century notion of the novelist. The question was the direction in which that revolt led the new writer. While the authors of 'immense artistic preoccupations' followed the course of Impressionism, the Edwardians felt they had inherited the sweeping, reforming spirit of Naturalism. For a period in the 1890s the two seemed to be reconciled. By the early twentieth century the choice seemed to be between the one or the other: on the one hand 'the beautiful difficulties of art', which dissolved materiality in fiction, and on the other the reforming passion born of Nietzscheanism, which moved on beyond Darwinian pessimism to a new evolutionary optimism. If the Symbolists claimed 'art', the Edwardians claimed life: as Wells put it, imperially, 'Before we have done, we will have all life within the scope of the novel.'

'Life', from the Naturalists on, obviously meant more than just life, ongoing existence. It meant evolutionary energies, people seen in their environment and history, as representatives of the workings of the world; it was love and death and sex and marriage, plainly and frankly, objectively and critically seen. It was material mass, houses and goods and class relations, detail on detail amassed and considered and ordered. It was material in another sense, the telling facts of social activity and human behaviour the writer had noted, by being there and finding out. It was the world with all its facts challenged and its statements investigated, everything checked and taken down in evidence. It was literature supported by the investigative skills of journalism, the scepticism of science; it was not sentimental, or if it was sentimental it was in the interest of radical expectations. Readers then and since agreed that life was, indeed, just like this.[11] One thing was clear; it was not seeking a Flaubertian perfection of art. 'Literature is not jewelry, it has quite other aims than perfection, and the more one thinks of "how it is done" the less one gets it done,' said Wells: 'These critical indulgences lie along a fatal path . . .' 'What I'm trying to render is nothing more or less than Life,' explains George Ponderevo, the very self-conscious narrator of *Tono-Bungay*. Arnold Bennett entitled an entire section of *The Old Wives' Tale* (1908) 'What Life Is' – the answer was in fact a long, slow, melancholy decline into age and death – and insisted his first concern was with life's feel and texture, 'the interestingness of existence'. Amongst other things it was clear that what life required of the writer was not aesthetic wholeness or even Conradian incompleteness but a plain openness. 'I fail to see how I can be other than a lax, undisciplined storyteller,' asserts George Ponderevo. 'I must sprawl and flounder, comment and theorize, if I am to get the thing out I have in mind.' Where James said that art made life, these writers purposefully insisted that life, observed, made art. And when Virginia Woolf said that the novel is not like that because life is not like that, she was arguing against writers who had already made their own confident declaration of what life actually is.

But equally this was not a return to the middle ground of Victorian realism, even though these novels do often inspire reference back to Dickens or Hardy. For Wells, the open 'sprawling' method was a way of dealing with the shapelessness and lack of social coherence that was Edwardian England, when 'all that is modern and different has come in as a thing intruded or as a gloss upon [the] predominant formula.' As he put it himself, the traditional English novel has been formed within a fixed social frame; now, with 'the new instability', that frame had splintered and itself become part of the picture. As Raymond Williams explains it, the Victorian novel was created out

---

11 'I can feel with this [Wells's creative energy] strongly, as I felt strongly with Lewisham many years ago making schedules for exams: the first character in fiction I ever fully identified with.' Raymond Williams, *The English Novel from Dickens to Lawrence* (London, 1970).

of community, a social and moral compact that linked individual and social life; in the Edwardian period the communicable society had dissolved, and individual and society lived in a fluid and atomized world. If the Edwardian novel carried realism forward, it carried it into new social conditions. God the benevolently omniscient narrator was still there, but now He was God the Scientist, God the Sociologist, God the Journalist. He was interested in progress, evolution and social change, and was always a meticulous external observer of the world as it worked. In Edwardian fiction – and it goes on being written still – the observer is everywhere, a presence between writer and reader. 'The opening chapter does not concern itself with Love – indeed that antagonist does not appear until the third – and Mr Lewisham is seen at his studies,' begins *Love and Mr Lewisham*, telling us about Mr Lewisham at his studies. 'Those privileged to be present at a family festival of the Forsytes have seen that charming and instructive sight – an upper middle class family in full plumage,' announces Galsworthy the novelist at the start of *The Man of Property* (1906), going on to tell us that these observers would see a spectacle 'not only delightful in itself, but illustrative of an obscure human problem'; in fact they would have 'a vision of the dim road of social progress'. 'On an autumn afternoon of 1919 a hatless man with a slight limp might have been observed ascending the gentle, broad declivity of Riceyman Steps,' commences Arnold Bennett's *Riceyman Steps* (1923), and this positioned observer is kept busily moving and, of course, observing, for the rest of this objectified novel.

In Edwardian fiction, chapters concern themselves with topics, obscure human problems are illustrated, visions of the dim road of social progress are regularly offered. Characters are seen from the exterior, their dominant characteristics signalled ('a hatless man with a slight limp'), as if they exist more for their social representativeness than any felt life within. They live unconsciously as symptoms of a larger case, become what D. H. Lawrence, writing on Galsworthy, called 'a subjective-objective reality, a divided being hinged together, but not strictly individual'. 'A character has to be conventionalized,' Bennett explained: 'You can't put the whole of a character in a book, unless the book were of inordinate length and the reader of infinite patience. You must select traits . . .' 'I have come to see myself from outside, my country from outside – without illusions,' says Ponderevo. The result of this is a distinctive way of writing fiction, no less fictional, of course, than any other. It is, as Virginia Woolf fairly says, material realism – dense with social life, rich in illustrative detail, filled with exteriorized observations which are also generalizations, dealing with social types in a transforming political order. It also mirrors a sense of change as an involuntary and formless growth. In many of the novels of the Nineties, and in the fiction of James and Conrad, individuals, living in a world of 'things' or 'material interests', are often drawn back into an existential subjectivity. In Edwardian fiction, the individual, though often solitary and exposed, is generally caught up completely in the padded mahogany furniture, the busy streets and commerce, of an age of materiality. It could be said that 'Edwardian fiction' not only revived realism, but ensured its survival as a means of twentieth-century writing. Like the work of Dreiser in the United States, it created a dialectic with a more abstract modernity that has remained powerful in the evolution of modern fiction.

That said, it becomes apparent when we look more closely at the best Edwardian fiction – and it seems fair to take Galsworthy's *The Man of Property* (1906), Bennett's *The Old Wives' Tale* (1908) and Wells's *Tono-Bungay* (1909) as eminent examples – that 'Edwardian fiction' was never a single thing, as those who challenged it later sometimes suggested. John Galsworthy's *The Man of Property* – which by a very appropriate process of dynastic evolution turned first into the three and then the nine volumes of 'The Forsyte Saga' (1906–34) – is a still readable family saga that details the disintegration of the property-owning middle classes from the mid 1880s to the 1930s, and it chronicles a significant social change. '*The Forsyte Saga* has great importance as the mirror of the British high bourgeoisie,' observes Herr Birenbaum, a character in Angus Wilson's novel *No Laughing Matter* (1967), which both pastiches and parodies the form. If, as has so often been said, the English novel is first and foremost the burgher epic, then this is that form in a kind of self-conscious disintegration. The Forsytes start as the representatives of the rising class of their age: 'the middlemen, the commercials, the pillars of society, the corner-stones of convention', the people whose wealth and security makes everything possible, 'makes your art possible, makes literature, science, even religion, possible. Without the Forsytes, who believe in none of these things, where should we be?' Galsworthy catches them at the peak of their power, which is corrupted from within by the possessive code of property, and threatened from outside by what usually threatens such things – adulterous love and divorce. Like Thomas Mann in his remarkable *Buddenbrooks* (1900), Galsworthy at first seemed to write the story of the collapse of the bourgeois age, as historical forces undermine it, and his observation is initially detached and highly ironic. And perhaps, if there had been a major social revolution in Britain, Galsworthy would have been its great chronicler. But Britain remained and remains a bourgeois society, and as the sequence evolved the tone grew less critical, as the characters became more attractive to the readers and clearly to their author. The critique of a class turns into a family saga, following the family over three generations, through peace to war and uncomfortable peace again. Because the fundamental world remains whole, there is no crisis of form (as there is in Mann's fiction), and Galsworthy stayed an Edwardian novelist into post-Edwardian times. He became the great chronicler of middle Britain, and as such won the Nobel Prize for literature in 1932.

Bennett's social history has quite different cultural roots. He was above all the self-made author, the solicitor's son from the Five Towns who watched the dissolution of the weighty, moral, confining Victorian age through the eyes of someone who has been carried upward by social change and his own effective career. The story of an age in motion from limited provincial lower-middle-class life to the promises and disappointments of the 'newfangled days' is the heart of his theme as a serious writer, the most memorable part of his large human comedy. He belonged to the age of regional realism, that opening out of the wider world to honest literary treatment that was one urgent justification for Naturalism; he brought the spirit of the Goncourt brothers to the British literary provinces, and British provincial fiction has depended on this ever since. But he divested the task of much of its theory, in accordance, no doubt, with his own claim that 'The novelist should cherish and burnish this faculty of seeing crudely, simply, artlessly, ignorantly.' At best this made him a novelist of deep social honesty, at worst an aspiring vulgarian. In 1902 he produced two utterly contrasting works. One was *Anna of the Five Towns*, the story of a miser's daughter in the Potteries of his childhood, intimately charting a process of social change from the 1880s to the present; the other was *The Grand Babylon Hotel*, a high-life fantasy obviously written to display sophistication and frankly written for money. His work went up and down in quality, but onward and upward in commercial success; he admitted he had set out to become 'an engine for the production of literature', and he made his literary fortune. In that same year he moved to Paris, which provided him with the essential contrast of one of his finest books, *The Old Wives' Tale*. It began, his preface tells us, in Paris in 1903, in the Naturalist way; observing a ridiculous old woman in a Paris restaurant, he realized she had once been slim and beautiful. To explore her story, he gave her a sister, also fat; one of the sisters would live 'ordinarily', fulfilling a life of provincial virtue, the other would become a Parisian and a whore. 'Neither has any imagination,' he noted. 'The two lives would intertwine.' Constance and Sophia Baines, daughters of a Bursley draper, with their two very different, ageing lives, were born from these thoughts. The story of dutiful Constance, who stays at home, and rebellious Sophia, lured by a travelling salesman to Paris, becomes a long, loving chronicle over the forty years from the 1860s to the 1900s; at first a shared heredity and environment appear to produce two quite different destinies, but they unwind, over the slow and erosive passage of time, and through the later stages of the industrial revolution and through the French empire, to one common human fate. The novel skilfully bridges not just British provincial and French experience, but French techniques and a British subject-matter, the commonplace Staffordshire world becoming ever more brightly lit in the gaze from Paris. As Henry James admiringly said, this was all done clearly and effortlessly and became the method of 'saturation', achieved with a power of demonstration 'so familiar and quiet that truth and poetry . . . melt utterly together'. It also showed the limitations of the method of 'hugging the shores of the real'. But it is not when he hugs the shores of the real – as he so successfully did here, and again in *Clayhanger* (1910) and *Riceyman Steps* (1923) – but when he sets sail on the sea of the fanciful that Bennett is disappointing; and 'hugging the shores of the real', disclosing the novel as a felt moral and social history, is, as John Updike has said, one of the essences of fiction.

Bennett, of course, did not see his art as artless; and no more did Wells when he wrote *Tono-Bungay*, the book in which he put the largest part of his vision, and which lies at the heart of his claim on fiction. It owed, he said, something to Balzac, certainly a good deal to Dickens, and, in its comedy of impertinence, something also to Mark Twain, who also wrote of the age of the entrepreneur and advertising – above all in the mocking comedy of *A Connecticut Yankee in King Arthur's Court* (1889), where the era of the machine and the bomb violently intrudes into the timeless chivalric wonderland of Camelot, so reassuring to Victorian imaginations. In Wells the land of timeless Englishness is the 'Bladesover System' – 'great house, the church, the village, and the labourers and the servants in their stations and degrees . . .' – in which nonetheless change moves unseen, even though 'all that is modern and different has come in as a thing intruded or as a gloss on this predominant formula, either impertinently or apologetically.' This is really the principle of the novel, which takes the 'predominant formula', equally found in fiction, and subjects it to impertinence and rewriting. For, as the narrator George Ponderevo tells us, this is a story of 'this immense process of social disintegration in which we live'; the 'ordered scheme' is going. Bladesover has been 'outgrown and overgrown', and a 'modern mercantile investing civilization' has rapidly taken its place. The book that Ponderevo now writes is thus 'something in the nature of a novel', its apparent formlessness resembling the condition of England itself. Formlessness is in fact not just the method of the book, but its central metaphor. 'I suppose what I'm really trying to render is nothing more or less than Life – as one man has found it,' George tells us in the now familiar way, adding, 'I want to tell – *myself*, and my impressions of the thing as a whole, to say things I have come to feel intensely of the laws, traditions, usages, and ideas we call society, and how we poor individuals get driven and lured among these windy, perplexing shoals and channels.' So his book is 'just an agglomeration', 'not a constructed tale'. It is the lively, funny story of George's Uncle Edward Ponderevo, a Mr Toad-like entrepreneur and adventurer, 'the Napoleon of domestic conveniences', who pursues wealth, fame, power and social position by peddling a worthless, maybe even harmful, patent medicine that offers to cure the new ailments of the changing age. As Uncle Teddy deceives a society that has already begun to deceive itself, George himself turns into a scientific inventor, a figure out of Wells's earlier 'future fiction' who is involved in the invention of a flying machine, a radioactive compound called 'quap' and at last a 'destroyer' on which everyone can sail away after the collapse of the artificial Tono-Bungay empire. Like the earlier scientific romances, the book contains an important social allegory about the splits, divisions and conflicting, potentially destructive forces of an age dissolving into the future.

Tono-Bungay is, of course, a 'Condition of England' novel, and one of the finest, a panoramic satire of its age. Its random energy is displayed best in its portrait of London itself, in a version that contrasts interestingly with Conrad's in *The Secret Agent*. Here is 'the richest town in the world, the biggest port, the greatest manufacturing town, the Imperial city – the centre of civilization, the heart of the world!' The 'whole illimitable place' teems with 'suggestions of indefinite and sometimes outrageous possibility, of hidden but magnificent meanings', but it is also a tentacular chaos, spreading, teeming, 'unstructured' and 'cancerous'. 'Factory chimneys smoke right against Westminster with an air of carelessly not having permission, and the whole effect of industrial London and of all London east of Temple Bar and of the huge dingy immensity of London port, is to me of something disproportionately large, something morbidly expanded, without plan or intention,' George reports, creating an analogy between the city and the activities of the two Ponderevos themselves. 'All these aspects have suggested to my mind ... the unorganized, abundant substance of some tumourous growth-process ... To this day I ask myself will those masses ever become structural, will they indeed shape into anything new whatever ...' London too is formless, but filled with chaotic energies, which Wells presents with a delighted wonder, opening the story up to include science and shopping, the building of fortunes and the building of houses, loveless marriages and so 'freer' sexual relations, social contrast and the implicit danger of war. But, for all that it needs reform, modern life remains a great and 'impertinent' adventure. And it is on further formlessness that the book ends: 'I fell into a thought that was nearly formless,' George declares, as he departs the shores of Britain on his 'destroyer', looking for something else new. The solution, of course, lies where Wells himself would put it, in science, machinery and invention. 'I decided that in power and knowledge lay the salvation of my life; the secret that would fill my need; that to these things I would give myself,' he concludes.

This could, in its way, be taken as Wells's own farewell to the real experiment of the novel, even though he wrote a good many more. *Ann Veronica*, also published in 1909, created a public scandal with its story of a free woman seeking free love; he retrieved his comic reputation with *The History of Mr Polly* in 1910, another story about the little man breaking loose. However Wells was increasingly giving himself elsewhere, to science, political prophecy, world visions, and the bounds of the novel were proving too small. *The New Machiavelli* in 1911 is an endeavour to write a political novel about the making of the state: 'The state-making dream is a very old dream indeed in the world's history,' says its narrator: 'It plays too small a part in novels.' The book deals with the struggle between a Great Idea and a Great Love, with feminism and the transformation of the modern family, with military policy and apocalyptic warnings – all to come true – about war with Germany and the break-up of Empire; it has a chaotic force, but none of the aesthetic care that was shaping other novels of the modern. That year Wells declared his position in a lecture on 'The Contemporary Novel', in which he attacked the cult of 'artistic perfection', separated himself from the self-conscious artists, and urged that the task of fiction was to deal with 'political questions and religious questions and social questions'. Here was the basis for the famous quarrel of 1915 with Henry James; for Wells was, in effect, now taking on the whole idea of the 'literary imagination' itself, and the way in which it stood apart from 'the world'. The 'world', as Wells saw it, meant science and technology, politics and history, the formation of new societies and the shaping of the new world order. The novels he wrote, and continued to write, if with diminishing force, toward the year of his death in 1946, were, as he said, frankly instrumental, means in a larger argument. It became an argument between literature and science ('the two cultures'), between pessimism and optimism, between the moral crisis of progress and progress itself. It was part of a split in the fortunes of the modern novel which was also a split in British culture itself, one to which writers would continually return. To understand the novels of Wells, and Bennett and Galsworthy, you had merely to read them and perceive their view of life, society and politics. But to understand the work of James, Conrad, Woolf and Joyce, you needed to grasp an entire conception of art itself, and its distinctive modern task.

7

If the British novel and the British culture of 1910 seemed split and in need of reconciliation, then it was offered one kind of answer in the work of E. M. Forster, whose *Howards End* – with its epigraph of 'Only connect . . .' ('Only connect the prose and the passion') – appeared that year. Forster, who said he belonged to 'the fag-end of Victorian liberalism', the late-Victorian dissenting intelligentsia whose members included 'philanthropists, bishops, clergy, members of parliament, Miss Hannah Moore', possessed an Arnoldian desire to see life steadily and see it whole. He had been (like many of the Bloomsbury Group, with whom he was half-associated) at Cambridge, and come under the influence of the philosopher G. E. Moore, who emphasized 'aesthetic states' and 'personal relations' as the standards of life; he had read and been shaped by the works of Samuel Butler, with his 'undogmatic outlook', and George Meredith, who urged that 'the cause of comedy and the cause of truth are the same'. By 1910 he had already published three social comedies – *Where Angels Fear to Tread* (1905), *The Longest Journey* (1907) and *A Room With a View* (1908) – which challenged social dullness and philistinism, sexual convention and the undeveloped English heart, and emerged as an important comic voice of a new humanism. His moral comedy was illuminated by a sharp liberal intelligence and a symbolist inclination, and these three were novels of new feeling. But it was plain that with *Howards End* a new ambitiousness had entered his fiction, and that here was a work that confronted Masterman's 'Condition of England', and not with the larky splendour of Wells's *Tono-Bungay* but with an urgent desire to relate and unify a formless culture split in many directions: between class and class, culture and commerce, materialism and idealism, head and heart, muddle and mystery, society and consciousness, or culture seen as cancerous and formless and culture as meaning and wholeness.

The question at the heart of *Howards End* was 'Who shall inherit England?' – a question to which it gave complex answers. 'Does she belong to those who have moulded her and made her feared by other lands, or to those who have added nothing to her power, but have somehow seen her, seen the whole island at once, lying as a jewel in a silver sea, sailing as a ship of souls, with all the brave world's fleet accompanying her towards eternity?' the book asks. Like Wells, it acknowledges that something new is happening to England: in the 'Age of Property', a new 'civilization of luggage' is advancing, and modern discontinuity is accelerating, driven by commercial enterprise, new industrialism and technology, and the potential clash of world imperialism. Here too there is a tentacular growth, as the 'red rust' of London's suburbia spreads over the land and sprawls toward Howards End, the ancient farmhouse that is the central symbol of the novel. Forster embodies this split world in a story of two families. There are the Wilcoxes, energetic people, male-dominated, rushing by car round the nation to do the work of Empire; and there are the Schlegels, represented by two sisters – the intelligent Margaret, the impulsive Helen – who are emancipated, humane, of foreign stock and devoted to ideas. They take from their German father a sense of idealism and a faith that materialism can be dissolved by 'the mild intellectual light', and 'In their own fashion they cared deeply about politics, but not as the politicians would have us think; they desired that public life should mirror whatever is good in the life within.' The book's theme is the relation of these two, and of both to a third. For at Howards End lives Mrs Wilcox, different from them all. She has faint mystical properties, is linked not with the busy present but with the yeoman past, and attached to some of the book's main 'symbols' – the house Howards End, with its Druidic spirit, the wych-elm tree, and the hay in the meadow – though these symbols are carefully contained within the human: 'House and tree ... kept within the limits of the human. Their message was not of eternity, but of hope on this side of the grave.'

The novel is the story of these two families, who are drawn toward each other through various personal relationships, but become divided. When Mrs Wilcox dies she wills Howards End to Margaret, hoping for a reconciliation. Margaret eventually marries the widower Mr Wilcox, and an ambiguous unity is achieved. Meanwhile her sister Helen has had an affair with a lowly Wellsian clerk, Leonard Bast, and had an illegitimate child. At first Mr Wilcox refuses to give any help. But the story ends with Mr Wilcox ill, Margaret triumphant and Helen's child likely to inherit Howards End. Barely told, the story sounds schematic, but the book is a complex and ironic comedy, and in Forster's world nothing is simple. For this is a world split in many ways, between the whole and the part, the eternal and the 'flux', 'infinity' and 'panic and emptiness', the note of spiritual anarchy that sounds out of Beethoven's Fifth Symphony. And Forster gives the novel a large panoramic sweep. It is deeply set in the Edwardian period (it *is* an Edwardian novel) and amid the forces active in it: the economic race with Germany, the process of imperial expansion and commercial growth, the technological destructions of the motor car, the intellectual pressures shifting people from liberalism to socialism. In the three main settings of the book – the metropolitan intellectual world of the Schlegels, the commuter world of the Wilcoxes, the clerkly suburbia of Leonard Bast – change is moving fast. A key theme of the novel is moving house and rebuilding; Wickham Place, where the Schlegels live, is to be pulled down for flats ('Can what we call civilization be right if people mayn't die where they were born?' asks Mrs Wilcox), and 'the civilization of luggage' is nearing Howards End, as the nearby railway station shows ('The station ... struck an indeterminate note. Into which country will it lead, England or Suburbia? It was new, it had island platforms and a subway, and the superficial comfort exacted by business men . . .'). Margaret looks for 'infinity' in King's Cross station, and hopes to 'live in fragments no longer'; but she too lives the life of 'gibbering monkeys', and zig-zags 'with her friends over Thought and Art'. Motion and muddle threaten any idea of culture or the infinite, and Margaret sees that the places of solid life are 'survivals, and the melting-pot was being prepared for them. Logically, they had no right to be alive. One's hope was in the weakness of logic.' Forster's endeavour is to reconcile two worlds not naturally akin, the worlds of 'life by time' and 'life by value', and recognizes – it is an essential part of his comic vision – that they rarely converge.

As the American critic Lionel Trilling was later to see, Forster is one of the great novelists of modern liberalism, a writer of checks and balances, who extends his liberal scepticism even to the most cherished of liberal principles, like the Wellsian faith in progress or science. In *Howards End* nothing is eternally reconciled; history upsets eternity, muddle upsets mystery, and panic and emptiness question the symbols of wholeness that float through the book. The will to vision, the liberal wish for right reason, the claim of the holiness of the heart's affections – all are consistently confronted with ambiguity. The same scepticism applies to his style, which is always dialectical. Forster had not dispensed with realism and familiarity, but opened it out to wider things. So poetry resides with comedy, symbolism with realism, and, says Trilling, where 'the plot speaks of clear certainties, the manner resolutely insists that nothing can be so simple'.[12] *Howards End* lies, 'liberally', midway between Wells's assertively progressive novel, the carrier of history, and the symbolist novel of late James or Woolf, the carrier of form, between social and moral comedy and something more symbolist or metaphysical. The book works in a double form – an attempt to connect not only the prose to the passion of life, but

---

12 See Lionel Trilling, *E. M. Forster* (Norfolk, Conn., 1943; London, 1944). And also see the essays of his collection *The Liberal Imagination: Essays on Literature and Society* (New York, 1950).

realism to the 'musicalization' of fiction. And so one way the book can be read is as Forster's attempt to reconcile, through his distinctive comic humanism, the two directions in which the novel was now pulling: toward social and political realism, and pure wholeness of form. 'Yes – oh dear, yes – the novel tells a story,' Forster was to say in his admirable study *Aspects of the Novel* (1927), and that means it must satisfy realism, familiar recognition and story's narrative 'and then . . . and then . . .' But the novel can also be a form of 'pattern' and 'rhythm', and reach for 'expansion': 'That is the idea the novelist must cling to. Not completion. Not rounding off but opening out.' By the time Forster returned to the public with his novel of Empire *A Passage to India* in 1924, the world of his Edwardian novel had already dissolved. British empiricism and German idealism had not met, or not in the way he imagined; the civilization of luggage, and 'panic and emptiness', were here to stay. Symbolism has become more ambiguous, confronting a greater nullity; the machine of civilization persistently breaks down and turns into stone, and not just the political world but the earth itself resists wholeness. Keeping his saving comic irony, his belief in the moral world of personal relations, Forster had passed from being a liberal novelist to a Modernist. Thereafter, from 1924 till his death in 1970, he wrote no more novels, saying that the world his fiction comprehended had gone. But he also had a striking influence on his successors; writer after writer, from Christopher Isherwood to Angus Wilson and Doris Lessing, has since returned to the mode of the liberal novel. And this still left *Howards End* a classic of pre-war liberal fiction, *A Passage to India* a classic of Modernist fiction: two of the more important British novels of the century.

8

'How do you know I'm not dead?' Forster asked D. H. Lawrence in 1922, when Lawrence was saying that all the English were dead. 'Well, you can't be dead, since here's your script,' Lawrence replied: 'But I think you *did* make a nearly deadly mistake glorifying those *business* people in *Howards End*. Business is no good.' Forster's sceptical

humanism was in the opposite spirit to Lawrence's passionate apoca-
lypticism, and yet these were two writers who shared a great deal in
common. Both were novelists who were seeking to unite the spectrum
of the English soul, Forster under the roof of Howards End, Lawrence
under the apocalyptic sign of his rainbow. The 'red rust' of suburbia
spreading toward Howards End resembles the 'hard cutting edges of
the new houses' that sprawl in 'a dry, brittle, terrible corruption'
across the countryside at the end of *The Rainbow*, and both books
seek a great new social and emotional union. The pagan Italians who
redeem the undeveloped English heart in *A Room With a View* in
turn resemble the various figures, Italians, Indians, gypsies, who
attempt to rescue the dead soul in so many of Lawrence's novels.
And, from start to finish of his writing life, Lawrence too wrote the
'Condition of England' novel. But it was an England in a different
condition, seen from a different social standpoint, needing a different
redemption. Hence it called for a different, a new kind of novel: a
sensuously radical document, a 'bright book of life', a work that could
'get the whole hog'. 'I am man alive, and as long as I can I intend to
go on being man alive,' Lawrence declared. 'For this reason I am a
novelist. And being a novelist, I consider myself superior to the saint,
the scientist, the philosopher and the poet, who are all masters of
different bits of man alive, but never get the whole hog.' That meant
the novelist was a prophet: not Wells's scientific and political prophet,
not Forster's tolerant humanist, but an emotional, visionary Nietzschean prophet, a prophet of the new imagination. Hence, he said,
'Each work of art has its own form, which has no relation to any
other form.' Forster understood this, and acknowledged Lawrence as
'the greatest imaginative novelist of his generation'. He was not alone:
among many writers and thinkers of the day, if not with the general
public or the censor, it was widely agreed that in Lawrence England
had found its difficult modern genius.

   Once again it was Hueffer at *The English Review* who found him.
According to his version, he one day received from an unknown
Nottinghamshire author and provincial schoolteacher a short story,
'Odour of Chrysanthemums', about the death of a miner in an acci-
dent. This is not quite accurate; in fact Lawrence's friend Jessie

Chambers had sent Hueffer some poems, which got him into print. But Hueffer had seen in his new author, the son of an Eastwood collier and an educated mother, that precious thing a 'working-class writer', a writer equivalent to Arnold Bennett in his power to capture the ordinary working life of his origins, and the story duly appeared in the review. Hueffer and his then companion Violet Hunt introduced Lawrence to London literary life, and he also read the manuscript of the novel Lawrence had been working on since 1906, saying that although it 'sins against any canon of art as I conceive it', it presaged a great future. He directed the book toward Heinemann, from whom it appeared in 1911 as *The White Peacock*. It was hardly the working-class romance Hueffer thought it was; but then it took editors, publishers and critics a long time to come to grips with the difficult, poetical, deeply individualized spirit of Lawrence's writing. The book is set on home ground, the Nottinghamshire–Derbyshire border, but the miners' lives, the bleak pitheads, the grim red houses that would sprawl in later fiction are not here. It is a story of provincial intellectual life, set close to the fecund world of the Moorgreen reservoir, where an ancient fertility is under threat. The sensual writing of the opening lines, written in an inward, vividly felt prose, displayed its freshness: 'I stood watching the shadowy fish slide through the gloom of the mill-pond. They were grey, descendants of the silvery things that had darted away from the monks, in the young days when the valley was lusty. The whole place was gathered in the musing of old age. The thick-piled trees on the far shore were too dark and sober to dally with the sun, the weeds stood crowded and motionless.' The code of words is already Lawrentian: the grey dying of a lusty age, the crowding of the weeds and the failure of the trees to dally with the sun. There is a stirring sense of revolt, emotional 'jerking awake', in what follows. The characters are ordinary, but radical, self-educated and bookish, like the people of the world from which Lawrence came. Other seeds of dissolution are here too. For another code of the book is the voice of prophecy, as Lawrence draws in the figure of Annable, the educated gamekeeper, a 'man of one idea: – that all civilization was the painted fungus of rottenness.' If Annable seems something of an intrusion into the book, and dies before the tale is done, he is already a sign of the urgent passion that would make Lawrence into the bitter prophet of his age. He is also the antecedent of Lawrence's later gamekeeper hero, the Mellors of *Lady Chatterley's Lover* (1928), his last real novel and the book where, in his exile, he would return once again to the Nottinghamshire landscape to make his historical reckoning.

The Trespasser (1912), Lawrence's second novel, was part-written with Helen Corke, and remains something of a botched conception. It is based on her story of an affair with a music teacher on the Isle of Wight (Corke published her version as *Neutral Ground* in 1934), but its interest now lies less in the affair and its erotics, or the sexual radicalism of the New Woman. The key figure is Siegmund, the music teacher, a Wagnerian hero who is suicidally trapped between erotics and death, and hungering for 'a breaking of the bonds, a severing of blood-ties, a sort of new birth'. As his name and nationality suggest, the book is full of Germanic echoes. Lawrence had a powerful self-education, like many of his heroes, and had been reading avidly in continental ideas. But where most of his contemporaries were looking to the French, where Bennett was seeking his 'Naturalism', or Hueffer his Flaubertian notions of 'rendering' and 'impersonality', Lawrence was exploring elsewhere. He concerned himself with Nietzschean ideas of will, dissolution and renewal, with German Expressionist notions of inward and self-revealing form ('He doesn't see, he envisions,' explains one critic about the Expressionist artist: 'He doesn't decipher, he experiences'). There was the basis for a literary argument here, since most of his literary friends were Francophile and Russophile – his editor Edward Garnett, for instance – and looked in his novels for an objectivity and formalism he had already begun to distrust. (Hueffer did find *The Trespasser* 'execrably bad art', though Garnett was more encouraging.) Something else developed from his German interests; he thought of becoming a lektor in Germany, and began visiting Ernest Weekley, the Professor of Modern Languages at Nottingham University, and so met his wife, Frieda von Richthofen Weekley. In 1912, close to the time *The Trespasser* appeared, the two eloped together to Germany.

Frieda, Germany and the state of independent artistic exile Lawrence now found himself in had everything to do with the making of
Sons and Lovers, the highly autobiographical novel he now finished
with her assistance. It would prove his first mature book, and many
critics still regard it as his best. It promises in its first half to be a
powerful, realistic and socially evocative story of British provincial
life in the mining village of 'Bestwood'. It starts off in grainy realism
('The Bottoms succeeded to Hell Row') though without the familiar
Naturalistic distance, but it soon turns into a war of archetypal
emotions, as the educated miner's wife Mrs Morel transfers to her
sons her sense of aspiration for both higher and deeper things. Frieda,
and the artistic exile that Lawrence now found himself in, undoubtedly
had a great deal to do with *Sons and Lovers*. The struggles of parents
and children, flesh and spirit, are presented in an immediate, felt
language and with a kind of sensuous physical apprehension not seen
before in British fiction: '. . . the dusky, golden softness of this man's
sensuous flame of life, that flowed off his flesh like the flame from a
candle, not baffled and gripped into incandescence by thought and
spirit as her life was, seemed to her something wonderful, beyond
her.' Written out of the senses, the book has all the intensity of
an autobiographical charge: indeed it is, in Expressionist terms, an
'I-drama', a tale of coming to being. And the work is also vividly
sexual. 'I never did read Freud, but I have heard about him since I
was in Germany,' Lawrence observed. He had indeed; Frieda had
been through psychoanalysis, and she was guiding the struggles of the
rewriting, and giving new meaning to the psycho-sexual struggles of
the book and the portraiture of, especially, the women characters.
The book's essential theme became something much more than autobiographical realism, even if that was how many of its readers read
it. It was the story of the attempted escape of Paul Morel, through
the struggles of his own individuation, from the binding relationship
with his mother to sexual self-discovery, from the deathly psychic
web where a divided consciousness and culture had trapped him into
a different realm. The discovery is essentially pursued through the
process of writing or rather rewriting the book; and a myth that lay
well beyond familiar realism thus took on Oedipal force, as the

struggles of mothers who are lovers of their sons, sons who are lovers of their mothers, push onward toward the making of a whole identity. Whether new consciousness is truly achieved is not completely clear. Lawrence called the book a tragedy – 'the tragedy of thousands of young men in England . . . The name of the old son-lover was Oedipus. The name of the new one is legion' – and seemed to suppose he had left the ending still pointing toward death and extinction: 'He is left in the end naked of everything, with the drift towards death. It is a great tragedy.' By the end of the book Lawrence feels the need to place Paul behind him. But the text on the page surely points toward rebirth, self-discovery, coming through. In front of Paul the city of Nottingham shimmers: 'But no, he would not give in. Turning sharply, he walked towards the city's golden phosphorescence. His fists were shut, his mouth set fast. He would not take that direction, to the darkness, to follow her. He walked towards the faintly humming, glowing town, quickly.'[13]

This, perhaps, is because *Sons and Lovers* has another key theme – the casting off of the past, of mother, class and home, to forge the birth of the artist. Like Joyce's *A Portrait of the Artist as a Young Man* – written around the same time, though not published till 1916 – it is about the artist who through an Oedipal break is self-exiled from his own past and his maternal birth, and re-born in separation and apprehensive openness into a dubious freedom, facing new books, new worlds, new forms and new emotions to come. And the form of the novel had itself been born through such a struggle: 'I tell you it has got form – *form*; haven't I made it patiently, out of sweat as well as blood,' he wrote urgently to his editor Garnett, who in fact saved the book, when Heinemann turned it down, by taking it to another publisher, Duckworth: 'If *you* can't see the development – which is slow, like growth – I can.' It was this search for new and inwardly energized form that became the preoccupation driving his work in a

---

13 The story has been excellently told in John Worthen's *D. H. Lawrence: The Early Years 1885–1912* (Cambridge, 1991), which in turn has been able to benefit from the autobiographical materials of Lawrence's posthumously published novel *Mr Noon* (Cambridge, 1984), and from the uncensored texts of the novels in their new 'definitive' Cambridge editions.

different direction from Joyce – not toward the self-consciousness of experimental modernist epic, but into the deep envelope of feeling, the great felt psycho-myth of cultural and sexual relations, and a distinctive mythology of creation through disintegration, which became both the source and the inner myth of the novels themselves. In Italy with Frieda, and feeling free of the limitations of his origins, he began a remarkable new burst of production, starting on many things – *The Lost Girl* (1920), much important poetry, but above all a large new project he called *The Sisters*, which went through four hard-worked drafts over 1913–14. 'It is very different from *Sons and Lovers*; written in another language almost,' he wrote to Garnett. 'I shan't write in the same manner as *Sons and Lovers* again, I think – in that hard violent style full of sensation and presentation.' In another letter he declared the theme of the project; it was to be 'the relationship between men and women. After all, it is *the* problem of today, the establishment of a new relation, or the readjustment of the old one, between man and woman.' Through version after version, the book struggled into existence. Lawrence was discarding nearly all his mentors, including Garnett. He began the idiosyncratic study of Hardy, following out the struggle of consciousness in his characters, even as he rejected the controlling plots. He read and dismissed Bennett: 'Tragedy ought to be a great kick at misery. But *Anna of the Five Towns* seems like an acceptance – so does all the modern stuff since Flaubert. I hate it.' 'Tell Arnold Bennett that all rules of construction hold good only for novels which are copies of other novels,' he wrote to his agent. 'A book which is not a copy of other books has its own construction, and what he calls faults, he being an old imitator, I call characteristics.' What he was doing lay beyond explanation, and he told Garnett that the book was 'like a novel in a foreign language I don't know very well – I can only just make out what it is about'.

By mid 1914 the book was called *The Wedding Ring*, and he was comparing the spirit of it with Marinetti's Futurism, which he had been following with excitement. He wrote to Garnett, who disliked the draft, explaining that what should be understood was that he had dispensed with previous forms, above all with the old, conventional idea of character, 'the old-fashioned human element', in favour of a

Futurist 'inhuman will', or 'physiology of matter'. 'I don't so much care about what the woman *is* – what she IS – inhumanly, physiologically, materially – according to the use of the word: but for me, what she *is* as a phenomenon (or as representing some greater inhuman will), instead of what she feels according to the human conception . . . You mustn't look in my novel for the old stable *ego* – of the character. There is another *ego*, according to whose action the individual is unrecognizable, and passes through, as it were, allotropic states which it needs a deeper sense than any we've been used to exercise, to discover are states of the same single radically unchanged element.' But where Marinetti and the Futurists were seeking vitality within mechanism, Lawrence was looking toward something almost the opposite: he was a prophet of the redeeming flesh, seeking an 'inhuman' vitalistic energy born out of blood rhythms, states of consciousness, the solar plexus – in other words, something nearer the eternal human unconscious. But what, he said, was important about his new novel was that it no longer followed the rule of development through individual characters, but through the relation between individuation and the collective motions of consciousness: 'the characters all fall into the form of some other rhythmic form, as when one draws a fiddle-bow across a fine tray delicately sanded, the sand takes lines unknown.' If *The Wedding Ring* was a move toward a greater self-expression, it was also a move toward a greater abstraction, indeed a post-humanist form of writing.

At last the book split into two parts, one becoming *The Rainbow* (1915), the other *Women in Love* (1920) – an Old Testament and a New. Lawrence had written his study of Hardy, and also read Thomas Mann's dynastic *Buddenbrooks*; both may have encouraged his late decision to drive his new story backward over several generations. So *The Rainbow* became a historical novel, the story of three generations of the Brangwen family, from the pastoral, creational age of the 1840s and through into the deathly, decultured modern world. The book opens at Marsh Farm to traditional, indeed Biblical rhythms, filled with fertility and sensuousness: 'They felt the rush of the sap in spring, they knew the wave that cannot halt, but every year throws forward the seed to begetting, and, falling back, leaves the young-born on the earth. They knew the intercourse between heaven and earth, sunshine drawn into the breast and bowels, the rain sucked up in the daytime, nakedness that comes under the wind in autumn.' But the powers of historical change are there, as canals, railways, collieries come, planting dead mechanism into the land. And the powers of change are also there in the eternal division of consciousness between the men, rooted in their soil, and the women, who 'looked out from the heated, blind intercourse of farm-life, to the spoken world beyond . . . They strained to listen,' reaching toward 'the magic land . . . where secrets were made known and desires fulfilled.' Possibly with hints from *Howards End*, *The Rainbow* merges two kinds of novel, the historical novel and the novel of consciousness, and works in two different languages. One retains many of the solid elements of realism, and deals with the familiar workings of the world; the other is concerned with sexual dialectics and the flow of human consciousness, and requires a sensualized, symbolist mode of expression.

Many readers have sensed a crossover point in the novel, where one language yields dominance to the other, realism to psycho-symbolism. Frank Kermode calls the method 'palimpsest', meaning that the writing is less chronological and developmental than 'layered' – 'historical chapters' interweave with 'symbolic' chapters, time and timelessness merge into each other, especially in moments of erotic stasis or emotional arrest, and each new generation revisits the experience of the past in the form of a revised commentary. What unites the language of realism and the language of sensuality and symbolism is a third voice, the language of prophecy. For, as Kermode also points out, the book is held together by another scriptural code founded on the Apocalyptic types: the myth of crisis and rebirth, of last things and first, Genesis turning to Revelation. Lawrence's largest theme is the modern dying of the world, and the birthing of the new individual and a new sensual creation out of the crisis of the age. This is symbolized by the book's overarching image, the rainbow itself, which takes on a sequence of meanings, as salvation, religious architecture, cultural union, sexual congress, finally the architecture of consciousness itself. At the end, which was to be the beginning of the second book, Ursula Brangwen – the modern woman who inherits the story, as well as the sensual rebellion and the chaotic sterility of modern times – has passed 'outside the pale of the old world', and is looking for 'a new germination'. The key image takes its last form: 'She saw in the rainbow the earth's new architecture, the old, brittle corruption of houses and factories swept away, the world built up in a living fabric of Truth, fitting to the overarching heavens.'[14]

The book about crisis – a crisis of history, consciousness, sexuality, gender and literary form – appeared in 1915, a time of crisis. Lawrence claimed the book was 'written and named in Italy . . . before there was any thought of war'. This was not quite so; he revised the book further in wartime, darkening some passages to suit, but it still ends on a note of promise. The crisis became personal; soon after publication (by Methuen), the book was seized for obscenity, and banned with the publishers' consent. In wartime conditions, when literary experiment no longer seemed urgent, Lawrence found few defenders. Meanwhile, as a tubercular non-combatant with a German wife, he was harried and persecuted by the authorities, and refused a passport for the United States. All this and the deathliness he saw everywhere convinced him that the apocalyptic signs were real, that the book was an accurate prophecy. 'It was in 1915 the old world ended,' he said, and 'What I did through individuals, the world has done through war.' His sense of crisis, his bitterness, his dismay with history, his sense of universal death-flow, a 'process of active corruption', his weariness with humanity, his belief in the dominance of the mechanical – all this went into the rewriting of *Women in Love* he undertook in 1916, recasting most of the material (the book was re-issued, expurgated, by Martin Secker in 1921). His wartime experiences entered the story, the hard futurist dimension of the book intensified, and, though it remains set in the immediately pre-war world of Britain and Europe, it moves inexorably toward the age's dance of death, its chosen oblivion in the snow. Lawrence was always to insist that the two works were one, and made an organic whole, and there is great unity of theme: the apocalyptic dissolution of an

---

14 See Frank Kermode, *Lawrence* (London, rev. ed., 1985), and his essay 'Lawrence and the Apocalyptic Types', in *Continuities* (London, 1968).

older order, the struggle of consciousness through sexual and gender relations, the summoning of a new age and its destructive and bitter birth. But *The Rainbow* retains a deep texture of realism, while *Women in Love* – he thought of calling it *Dies Irae*, or *The Last Days* – is a vastly more radical work, a full-blown experiment in uniting experience with doctrinal passions, a post-humanist novel of the unstable ego, of disintegrative form and emotion, a tale of the tragic present. He himself called it 'purely destructive, not like *The Rainbow*, destructive-consummating'. For all the connections, *The Rainbow* remains a pre-war novel, and *Women in Love* – written, like so many of the key works of Modernism, across the war – is a post-war novel, filled with the wound of war and the renewed encounter with disintegration; it is discussed again later. Lawrence, unable 'to write of England any more', despairing of the white soul, sought his dark gods, his apocalypse, his sexual and sensual salvation, the phoenix of rebirth elsewhere, leaving behind the coffin of England. He became an exile, to Italy, Sardinia, Australia, New Mexico, Mexico and France, where he died in 1930. He did return to Britain and his Nottinghamshire countryside for a final summation in his 'Condition of England' novel, *Lady Chatterley's Lover*, a last cry of disaster and sensual rebirth. Published in Italy, the book too was exiled, and stayed banned in Britain until the Sixties – when it returned to British culture, along with its author's reputation as, at last, a major revolutionary maker of modern British fiction.

9

Perhaps what was most remarkable about the fiction of the immediately pre-war years was not simply the individual achievements (many of which had been separately born a good deal earlier) but the sudden convergence – in a single time, and in so many fields of activity, from poetry and painting to philosophy and music – of so many radical ideas of art and the artist. With them, too, went another notion, that of the artist as the self-exile. No writer was to display all this more plainly, deeply or mythically than James Joyce. If the artist could now be his or her own hero, indeed Stephen Hero, then 'silence, exile, and cunning' – the means and methods Stephen Dedalus prescribes for himself when he makes his famous *non serviam* in *A Portrait of the Artist as a Young Man* – increasingly came to seem the foundations of the necessary rebellion: the means of experiment, the source of the long critical distance and the great struggle with culture, form and language the modern writer, unaccepted by his own society, needed to undertake in order to break open the meaning of his history, his origins and his world. It was in the year of his exile, 1904, that almost everything in Joyce started, and to which almost everything came back. Even his greatest work, *Ulysses* (1922) – which T. S. Eliot said explored the panorama of futility and anarchy which was post-war history – is set on a single day, now called Bloomsday, 16 June, in that same year of 1904, when Joyce was still only twenty-two. It was the year of choice, of sudden creativity; the year of his meeting with Nora Barnacle ('she'll stick to him,' they said), the year of his artistic vocation, the year he finally left Ireland 'to forge the uncreated conscience of my race'. In that year, writing quickly, he sketched out many of the short stories of *Dubliners*, the poems of *Chamber Music*, and began *Stephen Hero* (written in 1904–6, posthumously published in 1944), the artist's autobiography that eventually turned into *A Portrait of the Artist as a Young Man*. But between these beginnings, when the largest part of Joyce's projects for a lifetime were to take shape, and the ultimate moment of publication fell a very large gap. A version of *Dubliners* was ready for publication in 1905, but twice rejected, in London and then Dublin, because of anxieties over obscenity and libel; the book did not come out until 1914. *Stephen Hero* went through various drafts, emerged in new form from the revision of 1911 as *A Portrait of the Artist . . .*, and was serialized in *The Egoist* in 1914–15. But Lawrence's problems with *The Rainbow* made publishers anxious; it appeared in an American edition only in 1916, then an English edition in 1917. Also around 1904, Joyce sketched a tale about a Wandering Jew in Dublin, which he returned to in 1914. So began the great project of *Ulysses*, a book written and published in exile. Serialization began in 1918, but not until 1922 did it finally come out in a limited edition from a Paris bookshop, banned for some long time in Britain, the USA, above all in the Ireland it was about. It could be said that the Dublin of 1904 spawned almost all of Joyce. It could also be said that if, after 1904, he made a stateless exile of himself – in Pola, in Trieste, in Rome, Zürich, Paris – the Irish-English culture he grew up in also made an exile of him.

Hence, of all the English-language writers, Joyce seems most to exemplify the myth of the modern, rebellious, fractured journey into the 'unknown arts', the orphan birthing of the new. But that journey had started even earlier, in the late nineteenth-century climate of Naturalism and Impressionism, Decadence and the Celtic Twilight. From the symbolist aesthetic debates of that time (and the influence of W. B. Yeats) came many of the arguments of *Stephen Hero*, which shows his interest in the spirit of a Paterian aestheticism. But he was also drawn toward Naturalism, and it was his admiration for the 'modern' and 'vivisective' spirit of Ibsen (he learned Danish to read him) that began his quarrels with the authorities and his break with the Catholic Church. Explaining his intentions for *Dubliners*, he phrased them in highly Naturalist terms: 'My intention was to write a chapter in the moral history of my country and I chose Dublin for the scene because the city seemed to me to be the centre of paralysis,' he explained: 'I have written it for the most part in a style of scrupulous meanness and with the conviction that he is a bold man who dares to alter the presentment, still more to deform, whatever he has seen and heard.' In fact the style is frequently poetic, the intention symbolist, the spirit not one of 'scrupulous meanness' – though realism remains the essential code. The fifteen stories are linked in a cycle where the connections come not from the separate reported lives but from an overall view of Dublin's stasis and paralysis. Hence all these lives are in some way trapped – by limitation, circumstance, inarticulacy, historical inertia, a failure to act on dreams and possibilities. Paralysis occurs 'literally' in the first story, 'The Sisters', about a dying priest, and carries through to the last image of the last story, 'The Dead', of the snow that is 'general all over Ireland' and hems in all lives. In 'The Dead', Gabriel Conroy has a glimpse of something larger, as he observes his wife on the stairs, listening to music, 'with grace and mystery in her attitude as if she were a symbol of something'. But the image is one of love lost in death, of living and dead becoming one; meanwhile the solid world itself fades to nothingness and nullity, 'dissolving and dwindling'. But if the characters cannot reach freedom or a full revelation, that task passes elsewhere, to the visionary revelation of the story itself, which radiates naturalist events with symbolist implications.

In fact the unspoken figure of the stories is already the artist, the priest of sensation, revelation, ecstatic discovery, who sees such ordinary things of life in sacramental, symbolist or transcendental terms, and this story too had to be told. Joyce began it in *Stephen Hero*, about the artist-hero Stephen Daedalus as, he stressed, a young man. Stephen shares Joyce's history: born in the 1880s in shabby-genteel late-Victorian Dublin, the first city of Ireland, second city of the British Empire, seventh city of Christendom, and in a state of 'paraplegia' after the fall of Parnell. Born of a spendthrift father and a religious mother, he goes to Clongowes seminary, following his mother's desire to see him become a priest, but resentment of discipline, dissent and even his bad sight change him. At sixteen, he commits a 'cardinal sin' of the senses, has an emotional and sensory rebellion, and seeks to create 'life out of light'. So he rebels against the maternal religion by becoming a priest of art, both intensely engaged in and apart from what he sees. 'The spectacle of the world in thrall filled him with the fire of courage. He at last, though living at the farthest remove from the centre of European culture, marooned on an island in the ocean, though inheriting a will broken by doubt and a soul the steadfastness of whose hate became as weak as water in siren arms, would lead his own life according to what he recognized as the voice of a new humanity, active, unafraid, and unashamed.' He also realizes that 'though he was nominally in amity with the order of society into which he had been born, he would not be able to continue so'. Joyce gives him the name of Daedalus (later Dedalus) after the 'fabulous artificer' who built the Minoan labyrinth and escaped on wings he had himself constructed, and is hence 'a symbol of the artist forging anew in his workshop out of the sluggish matter of the earth a new strong imperishable impalpable being'. This is the basis for his new vocation, his secular, symbolist priesthood. The key word that links the two vocations is 'epiphany': 'By an epiphany he meant a sudden spiritual manifestation, whether in the vulgarity of speech or gesture or a memorable phrase of the mind itself. He believed it was for the man of letters to record these epiphanies with extreme care, seeing that they themselves are the most delicate and evanescent of moments.'

The two basic versions of this tale are two variant autobiographies of the young artist in pursuit of the modern. Both are *Kunstlerroman*, stories about artistic emergence or aesthetic discovery, much practised at the time in works like Huysmans's *A rebours*, Mann's *Buddenbrooks*, Lawrence's *Sons and Lovers* and Proust's *A la recherche du temps perdu*, a good deal of which was written contemporaneously with *A Portrait of the Artist* ... But the difference between the versions itself displays the subtly shifting nature of these developments in Joyce himself. Each is a search for the supreme artist: 'the artist who could disentangle the subtle soul of the image from its mesh of defining circumstances most exactly and re-embody it in artistic circumstances chosen as the most exact for its new office, he was the supreme artist.' Both question existing concepts of fictional creation: 'When we come to the phenomena of artistic conception, artistic gestation and artistic reproduction I require a new terminology and a new personal experience,' says Stephen in *A Portrait* ... But that meant that the work itself had to be commensurate with just this ideal. The first version was an uncomfortable mixture of Naturalism and Impressionism, autobiography and exposition – a third-person omniscient picaresque tale based on the ballad 'Turpin Hero', external and social rather than inward and psychological. But Joyce was now beginning to acknowledge that art stands beyond the autobiography and personality of the artist, and should grow from its own psychology of creation. Stephen himself is seen acknowledging this, accepting that while art may begin as artistic cry it must turn into epic and dramatic narrative – so that the artist starts to refine himself out of existence, producing pure form, and 'The mystery of aesthetic like that of material creation is accomplished. The artist, like the God of creation, remains within or behind or beyond or above his handiwork, invisible, refined out of existence, indifferent, paring his fingernails.'

By now Joyce is already beginning to see the book that followed, and Stephen is cast in his role as the eternal aesthete. So, in the revision that becomes *A Portrait* . . . the method becomes psychological, fluid and self-conscious. It begins in a world of childish consciousness which is also a Modernist synaesthesia: 'Once upon a time and a very good time it was there was a moocow coming down along the road and this moocow that was down along the road met a nicens little boy named boy tuckoo . . . His father told him that story . . .' The technique follows the various human stages of internal awareness by which life is not so much recorded as apprehended. The human senses and the various discourses of awareness begin to interseam with one another, giving a coherence to the developing language itself, which generates a complex web of motifs, images, symbols. The result of this aesthetic growth is acceptance ('Welcome, O life!') but also exile, as Stephen, doing what Joyce had done in 1902, finally sets off to his artistic exile in Paris, in order 'to forge in the smithy of my soul the uncreated conscience of my race'.

There were, in fact, two exiles. Joyce himself would return to Dublin, witness the death of his mother and then depart again, on the second, permanent, exile of 1904. This return is what we learn of in *Ulysses*, in which the next aesthetic step on the journey is taken. For that novel is not a work of symbolist naturalism, like *Dubliners*, nor even a psychological lyric, like *A Portrait* . . . It is, as Joyce explained, a work written 'from eighteen different points of view and in as many styles, all apparently unknown or undiscovered by my fellow tradesmen'. Though Stephen the artist is still present, reading the signatures of unknown things, he is a character among characters, a consciousness among consciousnesses. Other principles of creation and generation – Leopold Bloom's, and his wife Molly's – take a central place. Everything that happens – and everything happens, birth and death, defecation and menstruation, masturbation and lovemaking, past and present, history and historylessness – occurs on a single day. Myth has come in, through the story of Homer's *Odyssey*, both the material for parody and the source of new and deeper mythmaking. The methods of the modern interiorization of story – 'interior monologue', 'free association', 'stream of consciousness' –

consort with the linguistic devices that make a text self-consciously a text. Above all *Ulysses*, like *Finnegans Wake* to follow, was a fable of creation in process, a text seamlessly at work reading the signs of the world. 'If it is not a novel, that is simply because the novel is a form which will no longer serve,' wrote T. S. Eliot; 'it is because the novel, instead of being a form, was simply the expression of an age which had not sufficiently lost all form to feel the need of something stricter.' It was another stage of aesthetic self-discovery and self-begetting creation, expressionistically born, like the novels Lawrence was writing at around the same date. *Ulysses* – which is discussed more fully later – was to become not just Dublin's book but everybody's, in fact the Novel of the Century in the age of the Death of the Novel. The phrase that Samuel Beckett, who carried on Joyce's lineage, used to explain it is famous and central: 'His writing is not *about* something; *it is that something itself*.' It applies to what Lawrence was trying to do, and others in the period around 1914, when it seemed the novel had indeed 'lost all form' and had to win, out of creation itself, a new one. And, for the moment at least, this was the 'modern novel'.

3

The Exciting Age: 1915–1930

'I don't see that it would be possible to live in a more exciting age,' said Calamy. 'The sense that everything's perfectly provisional and temporary – everything, from social institutions to what we've hitherto regarded as the most sacred scientific truths – the feeling that nothing from the Treaty of Versailles to the rationally explicable universe, is really safe, the intimate conviction that anything may happen, anything may be discovered – another war, the artificial creation of life, the proof of continued existence after death – why it is all infinitely exhilarating.'

'And the possibility that everything may be destroyed?' questioned Mr Cardan.

'That's exhilarating too,' Calamy answered, smiling.

Aldous Huxley, *Those Barren Leaves* (1925)

Ours is essentially a tragic age, so we refuse to take it tragically. The cataclysm has happened, we are among the ruins, we start to build up new little habits, to have new little hopes. It is rather hard work: there is now no smooth road into the future; but we go round, or scramble over the obstacles. We've got to live, no matter how many skies have fallen.

D. H. Lawrence, *Lady Chatterley's Lover* (1928)

1

So large was the change in fiction's tone and temper after the Great War ended that it is best to start off with a roll-call. In the middle of the war, in 1915, the year he said the old world ended, D. H. Lawrence published *The Rainbow*, and Ford Madox Hueffer brought out *The Good Soldier*, just before leaving for the Front himself. Virginia Woolf signalled her forthcoming career as a novelist of the Twenties with her first novel *The Voyage Out* (Lytton Strachey praised it as 'very un-Victorian') and Dorothy Richardson began her long thirteen-book experimental sequence 'Pilgrimage' (collected together in four volumes in 1967) by publishing its first volume or 'chapter', *Pointed Roofs*. This was a work which Woolf described as inventing 'a sentence which we might call the sentence of the feminine gender', and May Sinclair called 'stream of consciousness going on and on' (as, to be frank, it rather did); between them these two books marked the beginnings of a distinctive feminist modernism. Then in 1916, the year when Henry James died, James Joyce's aesthetic and psychological novel of voyage into the unknown arts, *A Portrait of the Artist as a Young Man*, came out in book form in New York, and was reprinted in Britain the next year by the small Egoist Press. In that year, 1917, Conrad published *The Shadow Line* and Norman Douglas *South Wind*. It was a year of experiment in poetry – T. S. Eliot printed his first volume *Prufrock and Other Observations* and W. B. Yeats *Wild Swans at Coole* – and in publishing. Small avant-garde magazines and presses were multiplying, and Leonard and Virginia Woolf began the Hogarth Press, which would sponsor many important and experimental works over the next decade, from Eliot, Rilke, Freud, Rebecca West, Gertrude Stein, Italo Svevo and more. In 1918, the year the war ended, Wyndham Lewis published his hard Vorticist novel *Tarr*, and 'Rebecca West' (Cecily Fairfield), best known as a polemicist, turned to fiction with a topical novel about shellshock, *The Return of the Soldier*. 'Bloomsbury' declared itself a major power with what has been called 'the first book of the Twenties', Lytton Strachey's *Eminent Victorians*: a mocking demolition of four Victorian sages (Cardinal

Manning, Thomas Arnold, Florence Nightingale and General Gordon), a celebration of the witty deconstructive present, a firm repudiation of the past.

1919, a year when writers were already starting to look round in disillusion at the post-war age, saw Virginia Woolf's second novel *Night and Day*, and, possibly even more importantly, her influential essay 'Modern Fiction', where she demanded a new realism based on consciousness: 'Life is not a series of gig-lamps symmetrically arranged; but a luminous halo, a semi-transparent envelope surrounding us from the beginning of consciousness to the end,' she wrote; 'Is it not the task of the novelist to convey this varying, this unknown and uncircumscribed spirit, whatever aberration or complexity it may display, with as little mixture of the alien and external as possible?' Ronald Firbank published his ornately decadent *Valmouth: A Romantic Novel* and May Sinclair her experimental, autobiographical *Mary Olivier*. In 1920 Conrad brought out *The Rescue*, Katherine Mansfield produced her first collection of very Chekhovian short stories, *Bliss*, and from a New York private press came Lawrence's *Women in Love* – which, he explained, 'does contain the results in one's soul of the war'. In 1921 Lawrence's book appeared in Britain, and Aldous Huxley, who was satirized in it, published his clever first novel, *Crome Yellow*, about the psychoses of the post-war intelligentsia. Galsworthy completed the first trilogy of 'The Forsyte Saga' with *To Let*, set in the post-war world and acknowledging that 'The waters of change were foaming in, carrying the promise of new forms only when their destructive flood should have passed its full.' But Galsworthy now stood for an older spirit in a fiction that, like post-war poetry, was prepared to be rebellious, experimental, 'new'. That grew plain in 1922, Modernism's year – the *annus mirabilis* of the modern movement, Harry Levin has called it. In Paris Proust died that year; however on 2 February, his fortieth birthday, James Joyce brought out, in a half-hidden limited edition of a thousand signed copies from a small English-language bookshop, his vast novel *Ulysses*. For all it was banned in Britain and the USA, the book dominated experimental fiction for the rest of the Twenties. T. S. Eliot, whose crisis-laden modernist poem *The Waste Land* appeared the same year, spelt out the work's meaning in an essay, 'Ulysses, Order and Myth' (1923), saying Joyce had finally broken the mould of the old novel: 'The novel ended with Flaubert and with James.' Referring to his use of the framework myth of *The Odyssey*, he said: 'No one else has ever built a novel on such a foundation before . . . In using the myth, in manipulating a continuous parallel between contemporaneity and antiquity, Mr Joyce is pursuing a method which others must pursue after him.' Joyce, he claimed, had found 'a way of controlling, of ordering, of giving a shape and a significance to the immense panorama of futility and anarchy which is contemporary history . . . Instead of the narrative method, we may now use the mythic method. It is, I seriously believe, a step toward making the modern world possible for art . . .'

Virginia Woolf, whose own *Jacob's Room* appeared that year, considered the book 'underbred', but she did recognize Joyce's importance in the making of 'modern fiction'. That year, too, Lawrence published *Aaron's Rod* and Katherine Mansfield the fine-tuned stories of *The Garden Party*. Two notable novels about the war experience, a key theme of the Twenties, William Gerhardie's *Futility* (set in Russia around the time of the Revolution) and C. E. Montague's *Disenchantment*, also came out, and their titles said it all. Of course the 'old' novel had not ended with Flaubert and James; it has not ended still. Wells, Galsworthy and Bennett still remained the leading literary novelists, and in 1923 Bennett published his excellent and highly realist *Riceyman Steps*. But the campaign for 'modern fiction' now intensified, and Woolf fiercely attacked him and his fellow materialists in her essay 'Mr Bennett and Mrs Brown', where she suggested he saw everything and understood nothing, and announced the great change of 1910. By now it was growing much easier to see what she meant. In 1924 – the year of Thomas Mann's *Buddenbrooks* and Ernest Hemingway's *In Our Time* – E. M. Forster published his finest, most innovative and final novel, *A Passage to India*, Ford Madox Ford opened his remarkable four-volume experimental sequence about wartime, 'Parade's End', with *Some Do Not . . .*, Michael Arlen won fame with his smartly modern *The Green Hat* and Firbank published the very camp *Prancing Nigger*. All were modern in their different ways: modern in form, modern in subject and smartness, modern in their awareness of psychoanalysis, decadent cynicism or Spenglerian despair. In 1925 Virginia Woolf published her finest novel to date, *Mrs Dalloway*, showing she had made good use of the Joycean lesson, Lawrence his novella *St Mawr*, Aldous Huxley *Those Barren Leaves* and I. – Ivy, it turned out – Compton-Burnett her *Pastors and Masters*, which converted the patriarchal Victorian family into a timeless *mise-en-scène* for the eternal tragi-comedy of domestic life.

New American fiction, especially from expatriate Paris, was increasingly influencing European writing. Three important experimental works, Gertrude Stein's word-novel *The Making of Americans*, John Dos Passos's expressionist city novel *Manhattan Transfer* and F. Scott Fitzgerald's *The Great Gatsby* all came out that year, and over the next two or three years Hemingway and Faulkner made their mark. And in Britain too, by the second half of the Twenties, a fresh, distinctively post-war generation, mostly born in the twentieth century, was changing the tone and spirit of the novel. Modern conventions were now becoming commonplace. When, in 1927, E. M. Forster published his study *Aspects of the Novel* and said 'Yes – oh dear, yes – the novel tells a story,' as if this were just the smallest part of its work, modern writers and readers now knew just what he meant. In 1926 a young Oxford undergraduate Henry Green (Henry Yorke) published his experimental, 'sightless' novel *Blindness*, and Rose Macaulay a witty tale of a 'modern' independent woman, *Crewe Train*. In 1927 Virginia Woolf published *To the Lighthouse*, the storyless story of a trip untaken to a Hebridean lighthouse, Rosamund Lehmann her psychological story of a girl's growing up, *Dusty Answer*, and Elizabeth Bowen *The Hotel*. All these were novels where sensibility ('pattern', 'rhythm', 'poetry') rather than story were in charge, part of what Woolf saw as a 'feminization' of the novel that was to flourish in the following years. The avant-garde prospered, as writers fled Victorianism, puritanism and their parents for the independent country of art, and bohemian communities themselves became common subjects in fiction. There was Hemingway's story of lost-generation Montparnasse *The Sun Also Rises* in 1926, and

Lawrence showed the wandering bohemia of Twenties artists in many of his fictions. 1927 saw Wyndham Lewis's vast artistic satire *The Childermass*, and Jean Rhys's story of drifting and writing on the Left Bank, *Postures* (later called *Quartet*). Bohemia led to sexual scandal; in 1928 Lawrence brought out *Lady Chatterley's Lover* – a tale of shattered bohemian lives in the modern 'tragic age', a book so sexually frank it had to be published privately in Italy, and 'Radclyffe Hall' her novel of lesbianism *The Well of Loneliness*, which was banned and not reissued until 1949. Popular fiction flourished now, above all the thriller and the cerebral detective story. In 1928 the Dantean scholar Dorothy Sayers set Purgatory aside to unravel a number of mysterious deaths at which *Lord Peter Views the Body*, and Agatha Christie ingeniously solved *The Mystery of the Blue Train*.

As the decade began to close, a large group of brilliant new writers appeared, very much the products of the post-war climate. In 1928 Evelyn Waugh emerged with his black-comic novel of the age's 'bright young things', *Decline and Fall: An Illustrated Novelette*; Christopher Isherwood published *All the Conspirators*, about, he said, the Second 'Great War', by which he meant the war of the old and the young, which led the way on to the work of the 'Auden Generation'. In 1929 Graham Greene appeared as a novelist with his historical novel *The Man Within*, starting a fictional career that would last eight decades. The decade closed with a sudden burst of disillusioned war fiction, Richard Aldington's *The Death of a Hero*, Robert Graves's *Goodbye to All That*, and many more; the futility of the Great War now seemed ever more apparent, and the post-war generation felt somehow betrayed. Henry Green published his 'industrial novel' *Living*, a mixture of experimentalism and social conscience, and John Cowper Powys *Wolf Solent*. Then in October 1929 the American stock market crashed, the Depression which had already begun was confirmed, and the entire mood changed. 'The modern decade' became the dislocated, lost decade; George Orwell condemned it from the Thirties as 'a period of irresponsibility such as the world has never before seen' – though he would also condemn his own decade in much the same way. The excitement of Modernism, the aesthetic excitement that had peaked between 1922 and 1929, began to fade, grim fears for the future grew, Europe entered an era of new and terrible disorder, and writers looked to society, reality and political commitment. It grew harder now to acknowledge the achievement of the immediately post-war decade, even though so much new writing had begun in it. Yet it was another period of the 'New Arts', and quite as important as any. It was also the time when the 'modern novel' ceased to be a shock of surprise, and became an artistic convention.

2

I have given this roll-call to show how deeply the flavour of literary culture changed over the Twenties, the decade of the general triumph of the 'modern'. Many of the epic books at the heart of the Modern movement – *Women in Love* and *Ulysses, A Passage to India* and 'Parade's End', *Mrs Dalloway* and *The Childermass* – came out at this time, and were paralleled with similar work in French, German and American fiction. The concept of the novel, the very language of fiction, changed, and it seemed that the experimental spirit that had been developing from the 1880s on was now fully confirmed. In fact the tone of modern experiment had altered greatly in the wake of the war; the mood was no longer that exhilarated excitement in new forms and avant-garde possibilities that Hueffer could celebrate as 'the opening world'. 'Modern' became a widespread term, though it now seemed less to suggest an exciting adventure, more a dark historical necessity. The 'modern' experiment took on a bleaker, more decadent, more fragile, even more terminal mood. If it stood for a breaking of reticences, a freeing of forms, a poetic opening out of the inwardness of narrative, a new voyage into consciousness (as it was to Virginia Woolf), it was also a dismayed reaction to the fragmentation of culture, to a catastrophic history, to the pervasive sense of psychic crisis, to modern violence and dislocation. The difference between the experimental expansiveness of Woolf's first novel *The Voyage Out* and the psychic fragility of *Mrs Dalloway*, where Clarissa's crisis is intimately linked with the shellshocked mind of Septimus Smith, is telling. The 'post-war novel' had arrived, and lives as well as novels, history as well as literary form, had been modernized during the war. If the new modern epics were often works of deep inner fragmentation (fragments shored against the ruins, as Eliot said in 'The Waste Land'), of broken myths and history aestheticized into form, that was because the very nature of culture and its myths had deeply changed over wartime, and had to be rewritten, pared down, recovered, reconstructed.

So, as a post-war generation used the arts to survey and catch at a different and shattered world, Twenties experiment took on a character all its own. Today we see the Twenties as the first truly modern decade we have behind us – modern not just in its art-forms, but because in life and fiction alike we see modern lives lived in modern ways. It was, as Strachey's *Eminent Victorians* showed, an age of the 'younger generation', who saw Victorianism far behind in the past, and thought they had passed through a great and terrible historical initiation. The moral certainty, the monumental attitude, the progressive view of history, the sense of cultural stability, that still remained in the experimental works of the Edwardian and early Georgian era had now largely gone. War, battlefield slaughter, the loss of a whole part of a generation, political uncertainty, historical doubt, sexual freedom, psychic tension, the sense reported in Aldous Huxley's *Those Barren Leaves* that 'everything's perfectly provisional and temporary', the belief in what Lawrence's *Lady Chatterley* named a 'tragic age', gave a feeling of passage through a momentous change. The war *was* modernity, and modernity meant not just free verse, stream-of-consciousness prose, fragments shored against the ruins, the revolution of the word, abstraction, surrealism or Dada, but also life speeded up, flattened out, stripped of something. It meant radio and cinema and the telephone, the new popular technologies, the accelerated pace of daily life, the culture of a generation that was already rejecting its parents. As Isherwood said of his *All the Conspirators*, the motto of the day was 'My Generation – right or wrong.' But the age declared itself less through politics or passion for reform than through avant-garde rebellion, self-conscious independence of style and *mores*, revolution of the sensibility. Style meant form, meant fashion, meant self-conscious initiation, a new manner of being, and the new tastes, the new amusements, the new public roles and identities all became part of the changing style of the arts themselves. Sexual *mores* had changed greatly; there was new independence for women, as the trimmed figures and capped hairdos showed. There was a search for vitalism, primitivism, passion, a faith in the unconscious and the libido, a rejection of 'puritan' codes.

To be 'modern' meant many different things. It indicated the abstract difficulty, the fragmentation and syncopation of free verse or the stream-of-consciousness novel, but also the generational revolution in morals and values, the mood of decadent disenchantment, that came so often from the young. As Hemingway in *The Sun Also Rises* had his 'lost generation', Evelyn Waugh had the 'bright young things' of *Decline and Fall* and *Vile Bodies*, while among their elders the topic of the Younger Generation 'spread like a yawn'. For to be modern also meant disenchantment with history, living for the instant, life seen as just like the Big Wheel at Luna Park in Waugh's *Decline and Fall*: 'They're all trying to sit on the wheel, and they keep getting flung off, and that makes them laugh, and you laugh too.' Or it was the headlong rush toward disaster, the 'faster, faster' of the parties, instant love affairs and motor races of his *Vile Bodies* (1930), which ends, like several Twenties novels, and many in the early Thirties, with an apocalyptic premonition of future war. A cynical rejection of all that was romantic, traditional or 'Victorian' linked with harder styles, hero-less stories and pacey, flickering narrative to change and speed up the narrative voice of Twenties fiction. This owed not a little to the coming of the most modern, and popular, type of narrative of all: first silent cinema, with its narrative method of montage and rapid cutting, and then in 1927, in a sudden technological acceleration, the sound movie, with its dialogue as well as visual action. All of these things entered the spirit of modern style in writing, became steps in making the modern world possible for art.

It is useful to distinguish two 'modern' generations in Twenties fiction, each with a different impact on the lineage of the modern British novel. One is the Modernist generation, who really represent a radical development of the experimental writing that had begun before the turn of the century and seemed to peak as war began;

the second was the younger generation of writers who established themselves during the Twenties, for whom modern experiment was already a birthright. By around 1915 there was already a growing consent in intellectual, artistic and literary circles that a modern revolution, of form and sensibility, was transforming the arts. The fiction of James and Conrad, Ford, Lawrence, Joyce and, soon, Woolf was seen to come from an era that had come to acknowledge the power of the evolutionary modernizing processes foreseen by Marx and Darwin, the new imperative of Nietzsche, the impassioned modern consciousness of Dostoevsky ('Confound all these young fellows,' Galsworthy wrote, 'how they have gloated over Dostoevsky'), the sexual unconscious of Freud. A variety of movement names were found for what was happening – Post-Impressionism, Expressionism, Imagism, Vorticism, or, said the philosopher T. E. Hulme, 'let us agree to call it classicism' – and ideas like Worringer's 'abstraction', Fry's 'significant form', Joyce's 'epiphany', Eliot's 'impersonality', Woolf's 'luminous halo', were increasingly accepted. Writers increasingly saw the artist's own vision and consciousness, rather than some exterior reported reality, or some eternal law of story, as art's prime source, regarded narrative not as reporting or telling but 'presenting' or 'rendering', considered that art followed the self-made laws of its own aesthetic goals. If this *was* the Modern revolution, it could indeed be argued that in Britain it was largely done by 1915. A good many artists saw it like this, going off to Paris in the Twenties to find the stateless capital of Bohemia, where experiment ran freer, sexual *mores* were franker, censorship less, the parties and the drinks better, and the avant-garde had its own best home. But the social changes of the Twenties transformed the literary environment, the mood of post-war crisis induced its own new decadence, and, without necessarily being avant-garde, writers back at home were also developing their own new arts. In this, they had, at least for a time, the leadership of experiment's British outpost, 'Bloomsbury', and a general culture that self-consciously accepted that the world, and modern society, had been transformed and modernized by the war.

For, whether you wrote in avant-garde Paris or at home, it was clear enough that the war did represent, or serve as the great metaphor of, an epochal transition. Pre-war fiction – for all its interest in the 'new', the 'abstract', the 'inhuman' – generally had the spirit of liberal humanism as its companion. It accepted progress in history, human development, the advance of the spirit as the motors of culture, and sought to see it 'whole'. Even if the human self was proving to have deep recesses of unconscious behaviour, or was submitted to the blind powers of heredity, environment or libido, or the dehumanizing forces of modern mechanization, there was a faith in the rounded character and the general density of personal life. But war seemed to abstract and empty life itself, creating a landscape of violence and uncertainty in which the human figure was no longer a constant, the individual self no longer connected naturally with the universe, the word no longer attached to the thing. Culture now seemed a bundle of fragments, history no longer moved progressively, but cyclically, toward a Viconian eternal return – or more likely toward Spenglerian decline; no wonder history was, as Stephen Dedalus says in *Ulysses*, a 'nightmare from which I am trying to awake', or Eliot's 'immense panorama of futility and anarchy'. Life came randomly to consciousness, so that, said Virginia Woolf in 'How It Strikes a Contemporary' (1923), the modern writer 'cannot make a world, cannot generalize'. The ancient echo that Mrs Moore hears in the caves of *A Passage to India*, which says 'Everything exists, nothing has value', sounded for many writers of the Twenties, helping to create that 'twilight of the gods' feeling, that 'destructive element', that George Orwell and Stephen Spender read in post-war literature. If abstraction, collage and fragmentation provided the mode of many works in the Twenties, if many of them were parodic versions of previous forms, this surely had something to do with crisis and cataclysm. As a result Modernism now began to look, especially in European writing, less like joyous experiment than grim prophecy, and pre-war discovery turned into post-war disillusion.

From the 1890s onward, it is true, fiction had been filling with prophecies of future wars, often linked with belief in (or fear of) the limitless powers of science and speculation about the social or racial future of the planet. There were Wellsian Wars of the Worlds, imaginary battles of or invasions by European powers, wars between machines and men.[1] Similarly fiction had expressed rising suspicions of a universal anarchy underlying culture, that 'destructive element' that Conrad speaks of in *Lord Jim*. The metaphor of life as warfare underlay a good deal of Naturalism; even literature was often seen as a kind of modern warfare. The term avant-garde is after all a military analogy, and it was scarcely an accident that Wyndham Lewis should title his pre-war Vorticist magazine *Blast*, and declare that 'Dehumanization is the chief diagnostic of the modern world.' But the uneasy sense of prophecy that preceded the Great War bore only small relation to the reality. When it came, it proved more terrible, more dehumanizing, than any prophecy, more violently destructive than any dystopian fantasy, more damaging to the European political and social order than any prediction. The writers who were there to record it, at or away from the front, found they had to forgo all lyricism, sentimentality or romanticism, that the language of impression, macabre irony, abstraction, fragmentation and dehumanization frequently served them best to express their own sense of powerlessness.[2] The war was a crisis not simply for the subject-matter of fiction – heroism and bravery, the value of individual life and social history – but for its very power of representation. It is understandable that many critics have found this the epochal moment when literature took on modern sensibility, as social representation was fragmented, language decentred, reality de-realized. So John McCormick, in his *American Literature: 1919–1932* (1971), argues that the war 'smashed

1 A brilliant study of all this is I. F. Clarke's *Voices Prophesying War: Future Wars 1763–3749* (Oxford and New York, rev. ed., 1992). Clarke's bibliography lists an enormous number of titles, some by 'serious writers', others popular fantasies, others by military men, accelerating in quantity as 1914 approaches. Since 1914, of course, the genre has multiplied and become part of the convention of science fiction.
2 'The passage of these literary characters [the soldiers who wrote about the war] from pre-war freedom to wartime bondage, frustration and absurdity signals just as surely as does the experience of Joyce's Bloom, Hemingway's Frederic Henry, or Kafka's Joseph K. the passage of modern writing from one mode to another, from the low mimetic of the plausible and the social to the ironic of the outrageous, the ridiculous, and the murderous,' writes Paul Fussell in *The Great War and Modern Memory* (London and New York, 1975), p. 312. And he quotes H. M. Tomlinson's comment that 'the parapet, the wire, and the mud' are now 'permanent features of human existence'.

all the Stendhalian mirrors', forcing literature to shift away from representation of society toward a shattered representation of the self; Frederick J. Hoffman says in *The Mortal No: Death and the Modern Imagination* (1964) that – though all war depersonalizes – the Great War, with its mass slaughter without victory, challenged every traditional idea of warfare, and overthrew the decorums within which all writing of war and death had previously been contained. But the most vivid comment is by the German critic Walter Benjamin: 'men returned from the battlefield grown silent – not richer but poorer in communicable experience,' he notes. 'A generation that had gone to school on a horse-drawn streetcar now stood under the open sky in a countryside in which nothing remained unchanged but the clouds, and beneath those clouds, in a field of force of destructive torrents and explosions, was the tiny, fragile human body.'[3]

The deep change plain in the temper of post-war fiction deserves such an explanation, even though some, at least, of the shifts of style and vision often commented on were clearly present in the novel well before the war. But the war and its historical and psychological impact was one of the chief stories the post-war writer was forced to tell. For one reason or another, most of the leading modernists – Joyce, Woolf and Lawrence, Pound, Eliot and Yeats – did not take up arms or go to the front. Even so the fiction of the Twenties was indeed dominated by the war novel; by 1930, it's estimated, some seven hundred books had been written on the war. Even in the works of writers who had not directly seen the battlefront horrors the war is omnipresent, appearing as wound, cultural fracture, violence and intrusion, modern revolution (Gerhardie's *Futility* is about waiting for the one in Russia), the moment of severance, the confirmation of the modern as a state of cultural crisis. In Woolf's *Mrs Dalloway*, war has destroyed the mind and peace of Septimus Smith, who is a surrogate of Clarissa Dalloway herself; in *To the Lighthouse* it is the great destructive

3 John McCormick, *American Literature, 1919–1932: A Comparative History* (London, 1971); Frederick J. Hoffman, *The Mortal No: Death and the Modern Imagination* (Princeton, 1964); and Walter Benjamin, 'The Storyteller', in *Illuminations* (London, 1973). Also see Holger Klein (ed.), *The First World War in Fiction: A Collection of Critical Essays* (London, 1976).

vacancy at the book's centre, blankly removing many of the characters. It is there in the home-based fiction of Rebecca West and Elizabeth Bowen. War and its wound destroys the past and the identity of Christopher Tietjens in Ford Madox Ford's 'Parade's End', which takes the story to the battlefront. It brings the castrating wound that, literally and symbolically, sterilizes Sir Clifford Chatterley in *Lady Chatterley's Lover* – a book that is, Lawrence tells us, dominated by 'the false inhuman bruise of war', and already senses the next one. Sir Clifford writes stories too, 'clever, rather spiteful, and yet in some mysterious way, meaningless', but 'curiously true to modern life, to modern psychology, that is'. Lawrence acknowledges this new style even as he tries to subvert it with a language of vernacular sexual 'tenderness'; that is the reason for his famous 'frankness'. But clever, spiteful stories, curiously true to modern psychology, certainly did dominate the Twenties. Impersonal dehumanized techniques – Wyndham Lewis celebrated them as the method of 'the Great Without' – went along with the sense of the human creature as an absurd machine of being, irrationally split between thought and passion. Harder, sharper, more detached methods matched the sense of transitoriness, accelerating pace, the 'faster, faster', the collapse into danger or death. Directly or indirectly, the wound of war was everywhere in the post-war novel, explaining the note of sharp generational change, historical weariness, waste-land vision and rootless psychological tension so plain in much of the best fiction.

Some of the finest of these books were by writers who, having already established pre-war literary reputations, produced their classic works, works of most extreme disturbance, across the bridge of the war: Joyce's *Ulysses*, Forster's *A Passage to India*, Proust's *A la recherche du temps perdu* (*Remembrance of Things Past*), Gertrude Stein's *The Making of Americans*, Thomas Mann's *Buddenbrooks*, Franz Kafka's *The Trial*, in fact some of the key texts of early Twenties Modernism. These works, begun in one historical climate, finished in another, offered their monumental lessons (if not their actual monumentalism) to younger writers. And by the mid Twenties Modernism had become, in effect, an institution. Stein, Pound and Ford gave their masterclasses in Paris; in Britain 'Bloomsbury' was now less an outrage than an influential cultural elite; the Modernist T. S. Eliot edited the leading respectable literary magazine, *The Criterion*. Works like Percy Lubbock's *The Craft of Fiction* (1921) and Forster's *Aspects of the Novel* (1927) treated Jamesian notions of 'point of view', 'pattern', 'rhythm' as agreed literary convention. Hence for newer writers like Aldous Huxley, Evelyn Waugh, Ronald Firbank and Michael Arlen, most too young for the war, the modern was no obscure artistic 'affair', but a condition of life to be reported. The age of great Modernist epics or anti-epics – *Women in Love, Ulysses*, 'Parade's End', *A la recherche du temps perdu, Buddenbrooks* – was thus also an age when life became fragile, love became brittle, art became amusing, style became manner, when everything was an 'experiment'. Being 'modern' meant being close to the sharpest tastes of the age – the flappers and car rides, the nightclubs and parties, the yawning boredoms and weary affairs, the orgies and cynicisms, the despair and the *nada*, for immersion in the present, giving oneself to the intensifying if senseless pace of history, was one way of dealing with post-war things, of telling by the clock of history what the time was. This helped create the smart exoticism of Arlen, the febrility of Firbank, the mixture of involvement and satirical detachment in Huxley or Waugh, where the very senselessness and loss of meaning becomes a sad comedy. And then, around 1930, when new terrors showed on the horizon, history became not a post-war amusement but a pre-war horror, and exile and violence came to seem the universals of contemporary life, the 'Modern' grew boring. Or rather, in fiction, it began to turn into something else, the contemporary realist novel of the surreal dark twentieth century.

3

Twenties poetry had the shock of Eliot's 'The Waste Land'; Twenties fiction had the shock of Joyce's *Ulysses*. Despite, maybe because of, its Parisian publication, and its famed difficulty and obscurity, it became the book serious modern writers (and readers) had to take in, learning its lesson and imbibing its influence. It was a compendium of the modern genres, a stylebook for the age; banned from Britain and the United States, it was smuggled into both disguised as *The Complete Works of William Shakespeare*, which it was as big as. And, coming from an Irish exile, printed by a Dijon printer, and published by a small Paris bookstore, it helped establish 'modern English literature' as something quite independent of a single nation, as Hugh Kenner has observed. If it was not an English novel, nor an American novel, it was not quite an Irish novel either. The famous last words of the book, Molly Bloom's great erotic cry of sexual and human acquiescence 'yes and I drew him down to me so he could feel my breasts all perfume yes and his heart was going like mad and yes I said yes I will Yes,' are not quite the last words. They are followed by a byline, 'Trieste-Zürich-Paris 1914–1921', the byline of a modern literary exile. *Ulysses* is the great novel of Dublin, but it is about a Wandering Jew, based on another famous wanderer, Ulysses, and written by another wanderer, who having finally chosen Paris as his home died in Zürich. This was certainly a novel written across the war. Our first glimpse of it goes back to a postcard of 1906 ('I have a new story for *Dubliners* in my head. It deals with Mr Hunter') sent by Joyce from Rome to his brother Stanislaus. But this germ for a short story about a Jewish cuckold in Dublin, to which he later adds the title 'Ulysses', was not to find its way into *Dubliners*. In early 1914 Joyce was encouraged by the successful London serialization of *A Portrait* . . . to think of extending the story of Stephen Daedalus, and setting his Stephen Hero in a larger myth. By now Joyce was in Trieste, the Adriatic outlet of the dying Austro-Hungarian empire, teaching languages and learning them. He had made many cosmopolitan literary friendships with, for instance, Italo Svevo, the sardonic Triestian modernist who wrote *The Confessions of Zeno*, had become in effect a middle-European writer who wrote in the press on the affairs of the region, and was writing a play aptly called *Exiles*. When war broke out from events very close to hand (Trieste is not so far from Sarajevo), he was immersed in the difficult working out of his book, and professed indifference. By 1915 Stanislaus was interned in Austria, and he himself, paroled by the Austrians, moved to new exile in neutral Zürich, haven, as Tom Stoppard readers will know, to revolutionary exiles of many dispositions, including Lenin, Tristan Tzara, founder of the movement of Dada, and Joyce himself, brooding a revolution of his own.

In Zürich a good deal of the novel *Ulysses*, that great paperchase, was written, and Joyce expressed many of his underlying ideas to Frank Budgen, a friend he made there. He recorded them in *James Joyce and the Making of 'Ulysses'* (1934), a study that makes it clear how the work changed enormously in the writing, taking in new narrative, new schemata, becoming an ever more ambitious and elaborately coded text. By now it was no longer another tale for *Dubliners*, or even a supplement for *A Portrait* . . .; it had become a major new project, the book of books. When early chapters were serialized, in Britain and the USA, in 1918, Virginia Woolf read them and acknowledged that, in an age of materialist fiction, 'Mr Joyce is spiritual; he is concerned at all costs to reveal the flickerings of that innermost flame which flashes its messages through the brain . . .' The book was, she said, 'important', 'difficult' and 'unpleasant'. The 'unpleasantness', the concern with bodily functions, with defecation and urination and menstruation, led to its banning; the serial instalments were never completed. When the war ended, Joyce briefly returned to Trieste.

Then in 1920 he met Ezra Pound, who had helped get the work published and arranged financial support for him. He suggested Joyce move to Paris, explaining that it was 'the cheapest place last year', and he already had a large avant-garde reputation there. It was the best of advice; later that year Joyce came to Paris, then alive with post-war experimental tendencies, Dada and Surrealism, and, with its cheap franc and its available wine, attracting young writers from Britain and the United States, tired of Victorianism, Anglo-Saxonism, Puritanism and, in America, Prohibition. It was the ideal place both to finish *Ulysses* and publish it in an environment that could accept it. Moving from apartment to apartment, Joyce completed the book, now acknowledged as the greatest Modernist novel of the century, at 5 Boulevard Raspail in October 1921. He had met the American bookseller Sylvia Beach, who thought him a genius, and the book that could no longer be published in Britain or the USA appeared from her small bookstore Shakespeare and Company in the Rue de l'Odéon. The death of Proust that year had left an experimental vacancy. Joyce filled it, and *Ulysses* was hailed both as a great work of experimental Paris and a major emblem of the Modern movement.

It is still worth asking how its vast reputation arose. At first glance *Ulysses* is not a contemporary novel. It is set back on one long June day and night in the distant Dublin of twenty years before, just at the point when its author departed the city, more or less for good. It was already a historical novel, about a Dublin that no longer existed, except in Joyce's own vivid memory and through his own meticulous research. Friend after friend had checked every detail, answering the questions that the writing had thrown up. The Imperial Dublin in which the book was set was over and done with; in the year of publication the Irish Free State was declared. History, in the book, is omnipresent, yet history is the nightmare from which Stephen Dedalus (the spelling of his name had changed) is desperately trying to awake, into another realm entirely, the transubstantiated realm of art. This, perhaps, is why the story is held tight to one single day in Dublin, the city of paralysed stasis, and why the narrative code is not sequential, as in most novels, but synchronic. But history, under another rule, is there nonetheless: as immediate sense-data, as newspaper report ('Sufficient unto the day is the newspaper thereof'), contemporary popular song, endless Nationalist demands for republican political engagement, which Stephen Dedalus and Leopold Bloom (as Hunter had become) hear but are not engaged by, having their own other interests. History lives over again in the meticulous detailing of the city's advertising signs, its tramway routes, its water and sewer system ('through a subterranean aqueduct of filter mains of single and double pipeage constructed at an initial plant cost of £5 per linear yard'). For the immediacy of life and the transformations of art are the contradictory, countervailing powers in this story. As Anthony Burgess says, *Ulysses* is a great comic novel which achieves 'the solemnization of drab days and the sanctification of the ordinary'.[4] Joyce had

4 Anthony Burgess, *Here Comes Everybody: An Introduction to Joyce for the Ordinary Reader* (London and New York, 1965).

so carefully prized his accuracy, stored his memories, checked his facts that, he claimed, if the Dublin of 1904 were destroyed, it would be possible to recreate it from the book. But this Dublin is more than Dublin, as Eliot's London in 'The Waste Land' is more than London. Joyce remarked that 'if he could get to the heart of Dublin he could get to the heart of all the cities of the world'; and *Ulysses* is an exemplary modern city novel, one of those works of experiment where the city, any city, becomes an open space for the flickering collage that is modern experience. But above all it is a modern city where, as Eliot said, history is amended by myth: a classic myth of home and homelessness, of sons lost and fathers found, of faithful/faithless wives and cuckold/loving husbands, of departure and return. The myth teases the commonplace city; the commonplace city challenges but gives human substance to the modern myth.

Back in Zürich, Joyce had wisely told Budgen his elaborate mythic intentions. In selecting Ulysses as his heroic prototype (rather than Jesus, or Hamlet, or Faust), he had picked a complete man with a complete and rounded life, a man who was son and father, husband and lover, soldier and family man, hero and victim, someone who would transfer into the very contemporary figure of Leopold Bloom, the ordinary yet also marvellously rich Jewish advertisement canvasser whose local wanderings are set in counterpoint to those of Stephen Dedalus, the modern artist-aesthete. But Joyce was not aiming to retell the story of the wily Ulysses in modern-day terms; his aim was to create a complex system of correspondences. Each separate chapter of the book had, he explained, an exact Homeric parallel, and was written in its own distinctive language. Each episode had a linguistic and stylistic character appropriate to its subject; the book was also an epic of the parts of the human body, and structured with musical and colour codes. It was thanks, then, to Budgen, and later to Stuart Gilbert, another respectful and loyal interpreter, that modern readers/interpreters (one did not just read *Ulysses*) were made to understand that the dense social, domestic and sexual detail of this encyclopedic book was deep-coded with complex systems of parallelism and correspondence: that the novel was both a reasonably open, though difficult, story of Dublin life and a very hermetic text, awaiting

its professorial exegetes.[5] Joyce laid down other guides to an interpretation, as Eliot did with 'The Waste Land', a poem with footnotes.
Thus he wrote in a letter: 'It is an epic of two races (Israelite–Irish)
and at the same time the cycle of the human body as well as a little
story of a day . . . It is also a sort of encyclopaedia. My intention is to
transpose the myth *sub specie temporis nostri*. Each adventure (that
is, every hour, every organ, every art being interconnected and inter-
related in the structural scheme of the whole) should not only condition but even create its own technique . . .' Of the many things
that seemed new about *Ulysses*, one was its power to construct and
interweave an entire universe inside itself. Joyce told Budgen that the
English language was wonderfully rich in words, but they were not
all the right ones; hence the book is filled with linguistic invention.
He also said that the problem was not so much finding the right
words, but putting them in the right order; so it is also filled with
multiple types of discourse, distinctive and self-created grammars. The
resulting constructions – the unusual verbal amalgams, the literary
echoes, parodies and pastiches, the allusions and the lists, the quotations, interlocutions and interrogations – made *Ulysses* the great
word-book of Modern literature. Unlike, say, Gertrude Stein's *The
Making of Americans* (1925), another 'text' (the term became inevitable) of 'the Revolution of the Word', Joyce's novel is unrandom,
God-like, self-consciously made throughout. It is one reason why part
of the Modernist tradition is made of hermeneutic texts: texts as
interpretation, that continue to require interpretation. Joyce was not
only constructing a modern book; he was constructing, with it, the
modern deconstructive reader.

But this is not the only way we can read *Ulysses*: it is made in many
layers, constructed in many registers. There is no shortage of ordinary
Naturalism ('Mr Leopold Bloom ate with relish the inner organs of
beasts and fowls. He liked thick giblet soup, nutty gizzards, a stuffed

5 See Frank Budgen, *James Joyce and the Making of 'Ulysses' and Other Writings*
(London, rev. ed., 1972 [originally published 1934]), and Stuart Gilbert, *James Joyce's
'Ulysses'* (New York, rev. ed., 1952 [originally published 1930]). Harry Blamires, *The
Bloomsday Book: A Guide Through Joyce's 'Ulysses'* (London and New York, 1966),
is also recommended.

roast heart, liverslices fried with breadcrumbs, fried hencods' roes. Most of all he liked grilled mutton kidneys which gave to his palate a fine tang of faintly scented urine'), even though it is so mannered and careful in its making that it does not read like innocent Naturalism. There is, thanks to the vividly given consciousness of Stephen Dedalus, a portrait of the artist as a slightly older man, a great deal of Aestheticism, and the lore of Aestheticism ('Ineluctable modality of the visible: at least that if no more, thought through my eyes. Signatures of all things I am here to read, seaspawn and seawrack, the nearing tide, that rusty boot. Snotgreen, blue-silver, rust: coloured signs. Limits of the diaphane'), but it is not quite the Aestheticism a late nineteenth-century reader would recognize. Modern readers read popular romances (and so does Molly Bloom), so the intonations of Ouida and Paul de Kock ('nice name he has') are there ('The hero folded her willowy form in a loving embrace murmuring fondly *Sheila, my own*. Encouraged by this use of her christian name she kissed passionately all the various suitable areas of his person which the decencies of prison garb permitted her ardour to reach'), though this is not the level of writing we are asked to believe in. Innumerable popular languages – the languages of newspaper reporting, political speechmaking, advertising, commercial jingle ('What is home without/Plumtree's Potted Meat?/Incomplete./With it an abode of bliss') – are incorporated into the collage, as is the endless chatter of Dublin, that city of gabbers. The different registers, brought together, all function just off register, making a text that shifts freely between representation and pastiche or parody. Language opens out into gaps and fractures, allusion and borrowing, so that we must read this writing as writing, not, as with so many novels, simply looking through the word to the world it seems to stand for. The world itself becomes a book, and a book to be read. Yet the work never ceases to be other than vividly real, because it never loses touch with character or the density and physicality of the human self. The great and mythic triad of characters – Stephen, now mourning the accusing death of his mother; Bloom, formerly Virag, alias Henry Flower, Wandering Jew, cuckold husband, good Samaritan; Molly, the unmothering mother, the unfaithful wife, weaver of the web of myth, sometimes claimed as the most deeply felt female character in fiction – are themselves both psychologically deep and multi-layered, fragmentary, floating on sensation and consciousness, fed by their random thoughts and their half-conscious dream worlds. Collectively, they form a psychic unity, of father, mother, and surrogate son, of husband, wife, and eternal desire.[6]

The dominant role taken by *Ulysses* in the making of modern fiction (and for that matter modern criticism) is testament to a deeply changing conception of literature, and it had many implications, forward and back. The idea of the novel as a self-creating artefact was vindicated, giving a new sense of tradition to the line of literary self-consciousness that had developed from James. Most serious modern novelists, faced with the task of creating a twentieth-century fiction, feel the need to confront *Ulysses* – not just as the day-book of Dublin perpetuated, but the book of the modern genres in their relation and juxtaposition. As Eliot suggested, it seemed to mark the end of the Old Novel, to propose that the modern century summoned a different fictional discourse. Whether true or not (and many writers have found it possible to reconstruct some effective linkage with the novel of nineteenth-century realism), the book proposed a challenge to literary practice that has never gone away. Joyce remained resident in Paris for twenty years, and became there the exemplary author of an age of expatriate writing, when novelists and poets from Britain and Ireland, the United States and Russia, and many more countries sought less to write a literature of nationality than of a new avant-garde internationalism. With *Ulysses* written and published, he went on in 1923 to start the open-ended project he called simply 'Work in Progress', publishing influential segments in various magazines over the Twenties; only late in the day was the text finally given the title *Finnegans Wake*. When he was asked how long *Ulysses* took to write, he said five years, and a lifetime. 'Work in Progress', *Finnegans Wake*, took sixteen years to produce, the second half of a lifetime, and Joyce was to suggest that if it took that long to write it should also take that long to read. But *Finnegans Wake* challenges interpretation at a level

6 I have discussed *Ulysses* in more detail in Chapter 7 of *The Modern World: Ten Great Writers* (London, 1988).

beyond *Ulysses*, as it was meant to; one critic has aptly described the book, and the reading of the book, as a 'life sentence'. It was, exactly, a work in progress, a dream-like adventure in writing itself that, being cyclical, has no clear principle of closure. If *Ulysses* can be reasonably described as a 'stream of consciousness' (the stream, of course, is carefully managed and metered), then *Finnegans Wake* is the great flowing river itself, moving onward yet eternally renewing itself from the source. If *Ulysses* grew out of wandering exile, *Finnegans Wake* grew out of the concentration and distillation of the avant-garde in its own chosen capital city, and flourished on its controversies; when many critics attacked the project for its obscurity, Eugene Jolas rallied the troops of his 'Revolution of the Word' to produce *Our Exagmination Round his Factification for Incamination of 'Work in Progress'*, which Shakespeare and Company published in 1929, offering, long before the work was complete, one of the now many guidebooks to the riddling novel that was not to appear until seventeen years to the day after publication of *Ulysses*; it came out in New York on 1 February 1939.

From its opening pages, *Finnegans Wake* promises an endless cycle of return: 'riverrun, past Eve and Adam's, from swerve of shore to bend of bay, brings us by a commodius vicus of recirculation back to Howth Castle and Environs,' it begins. The river is the Liffey, Dublin's river, but is also Life, and it starts in Genesis, or Paradise, on its journey of Viconian renewal. Down it everything flows, or everything that, using the multi-referential resources of human language, Joyce could manage to incorporate or coalesce into its cycle of motion and stillness, birth and death, beginning and ending and beginning again. The flow is a flow of language, but it is a new and self-composing language, a connective tissue of semiotic relations and punning release. Every word in the book is a word in the making, and alludes or refers in multiple directions. Each letter is a sign and a promise: thus HCE = Howth Castle and Environs = H. C. Earwicker = Here Comes Everybody. The letters throw up a cast of characters: Earwicker the Father, Anna Livia Plurabelle (ALP) the Mother, and the sons Shem ('the penman') and Shaun, all of whom have multiple and often contradictory stories and functions, spinning off in many directions.

Language exists in the condition of Babel; this is a polyglot text in which all languages known to the author merge into one. In one sense the work seems to reject the role of author, replacing him with the book. In another sense this book can belong to one author only, and be his own private mode of speech. *Finnegans Wake* is the hermetic text of the Modern movement, at once the most complete and incomplete of the modern novels, the book of books, the book beyond books, which we do not so much read as decode.

Where *Ulysses* disseminated its radical methods here and there through modern writing – variously affecting the fiction of Virginia Woolf, John Dos Passos, William Faulkner, André Gide and so many more – *Finnegans Wake* functioned differently. It has been suggested that where *Ulysses* is a key text of Modernism, the later novel is the key early text of Postmodernism, the era of multi-culturalism, depthless juxtaposition, parodic quotation, collage. In more than one sense, the work really was a Wake, a party for the end of something. Significantly it appeared in the year Europe collapsed again, and in that collapse the Modern movement itself began to die – its writers thrown into yet newer exiles, its avant-garde dissipated, its cultural vision thrown under new political questioning, its key figures reaching the end of their writing lives. But more than Modernism was dying in 1939; so was the Europe of the first half of the century, whose radical art this had been, whose crisis it had come to express. Later that year, the Second World War began, and avant-garde Paris was vacated. Joyce's most obvious successor and fellow Irish exile, Samuel Beckett, who helped him transcribe *Finnegans Wake*, joined the French Resistance; the novels he in turn wrote during and after the war are works of radical silence, of language frequently attenuating to nothing, of lost names and voiceless voices, of an eternal waiting for the messages that do not arrive. The world after the Wake was a darkly different world, and Joyce too found himself once again in flight. In 1940, with the German occupation of Paris, he returned again to neutral Zürich, where *Ulysses* had once taken shape. Here, on 13 January 1941, he died of a perforated ulcer, leaving many serious writers to think they would always be writing in the wake of his Wake.

4

For part of modern British literature at least, Paris in the Twenties was to become the centre of continuing avant-garde development. As Ezra Pound, who moved there from London ('an old bitch gone in the teeth') in 1920, put it, it became the post-war 'laboratory of experiment in the arts'. Where London seemed to shrink back toward provinciality, Paris, where living was cheap and the excitements of post-war culture flourished, attracted innumerable English-language writers to the avant-garde ferments of Montparnasse. Many came from the United States, finding the Left Bank an invaluable extension of Greenwich Village, and with them they brought their own bookshops, magazines, small presses and social community, which proved one of the essential supports for Joyce. The post-war movements, Tristan Tzara's Dadaism and André Breton's Surrealism, extensions of Modernism into post-war chaos and the age of psychoanalysis, flourished – along with strident manifestations, dramatic manifestos and parades that stopped the traffic asking 'Do you want to slap a corpse?' Young American writers like Ernest Hemingway, William Carlos Williams and Robert McAlmon arrived from 1920 on to learn the Modernist lesson from Stein, Pound and Joyce, and British writers from 'Bryher' to Jean Rhys came there too. Marcel Proust, writing in his cork-lined room on the Boulevard Haussmann, extended right through the war the multi-volumed novel of time and subjective memory that he had begun in 1909 and called *A la recherche du temps perdu*; he was still writing it to the day of his death in 1922. The arrival of James Joyce in 1920 made these two into contrasting monuments of the modern spirit in the novel, though they affected not to know of each other: 'I regret I do not know M. Joyce's work,' said Proust; 'I have never read M. Proust,' remarked Joyce. When Proust was buried, in the French way, with full military honours, Joyce was present at the great funeral; thereafter he largely inherited Proust's mantle as the *doyen* of fictional experiment.

Also among the mourners that day was Ford Madox Ford. He had finally dropped the Germanic name of Hueffer, not though in wartime but in 1919, after his demobilization from the British army, when, he claimed, writers were let go last, along with window-cleaners. He had returned in dismay to what he claimed was an increasingly philistine Britain that was pulling down Regent Street, and losing sight of the great experiment of the pre-war years. There was also the embarrassing fact that he was being pursued by not one but two Mrs Hueffers, and he wished to restart his life with a new companion, the writer and painter Stella Bowen. So he too moved to France, and came to Paris in 1922, too late to meet Proust in the flesh, but just in time to attend his funeral, and consider the momentous question of the Proustian succession. In Ford's eyes, Proust had been the true fictional historian of his age, the creator of what he called, approvingly, 'the ponderous novel', and Proust's death, he asserted grandly in his memoir *It Was the Nightingale* (1934), was what 'made it certain I should again take up a serious pen'. The future of the ponderous novel needed to be ensured, and he declared there was now work to be done. That work included creating and editing the excellent magazine *The Transatlantic Review*, which would print some of Gertrude Stein's *The Making of Americans*, some of Joyce's *Work in Progress* and early pieces by Hemingway. But the chief project that came from Proust's funeral was his own four-volume *roman-fleuve*, 'Parade's End', started in 1922, and completed in New York in 1927. Initially it was to consist of three novels, *Some Do Not . . .* (1924), *No More Parades* (1925) and *A Man Could Stand Up –* (1926), but, pressed by a friend to reveal 'what became of Tietjens', the hero, he added a fourth, *The Last Post* (1928). He explained the project thus: 'The work that at that time – and now – I wanted to see done was something on an immense scale, a little cloudy in immediate attack, but with the salient points and the final impression extraordinarily clear. I wanted the Novelist in fact to appear in his really proud position as historian of his own time . . . The "subject" was the world as it culminated in the war.' He meant it as a work of Impressionist 'rendering', a book written 'without passion', but also as something he had long despised, the Novel With a Purpose: 'I sinned against my gods to the extent of saying that I was going . . . to write a book that would have for its purpose the obviating of all future wars.'

'Parade's End' did not, we know, obviate all future wars, but it did fulfil the aim, which he called 'Proustian', of writing an epic novel about 'the public events of a decade'. His first thought was to use the method by which 'all the characters should be great masses of people – or interests', in which case we might well have had an expressionist sequence like John Dos Passos's *USA* (1934). But he then changed his mind, deciding to focus the story round a single central character who suffers the tribulations of war and peacetime. Experience of the Front had produced what he called the 'singular conclusion' that what preyed most on non-professional soldiers at the front was not the horrors ('you either endure them or you do not') but 'what was happening at home'. What Ford saw happening at home between 1912 and 1918 was a vast change in the social and moral order, in public values, gender relations, class attitudes. So he created his suffering hero Christopher Tietjens, the 'mealsack elephant', the 'last Tory', a Christian gentleman with an English estate and an oddly Germanic name, someone who had a place in peace and war: a '*homo duplex*', he explained, a 'poor fellow whose body is tied in one place, but whose mind and personality brood eternally over another distant locality'. Officer and gentleman, country squire and Whitehall mandarin, Tietjens indeed could intersect with most realms of British life in peace and wartime: 'I seemed to see him stand in some high places in France during the period of hostilities taking in not only what was visible but all the causes and all the motive powers of infinitely distant places.' The representative of a feudal and social inheritance, a man of 'clear Eighteenth Century mind', living out the contradictions of that code to their ultimate conclusion, he carries history, and suffers for it. Whether the novel really owes much to Proust, as its author claimed, is doubtful – though it is a Modernist work, concerned with inner psychology, time-shift and the involuntary operations of the memory. It is certainly a 'Condition of England' novel, at a time when that form seems at the end of its tether, and what the Hungarian Marxist critic Georgy Lukacs would call a 'historical novel': a novel, that is, which carries the contradictory processes of an age and the struggles of class in an evolving culture. The result is that 'Parade's End' is a panoramic epic, or anti-epic, engaged with history in a way that, say, Virginia Woolf's novels, even her panoramic *The Years*, could never be. Ford uses modern methods, but he sustains many of the nineteenth-century interests of fiction: in public life, the social web, the state of the nation. The techniques then are techniques for presenting large-scale dispositions of experience and historical time, of bringing the large and the small into relation. 'Parade's End' is a historical allegory with a psychological centre, a 'Condition of England' work about an individual whose psychic and social collapse and fragile renewal *enacts* history.

Despite impressive competition – C. E. Montague's *Disenchantment* (1922), R. H. Mottram's 'Spanish Farm' trilogy (1924–6), Richard Aldington's *Death of a Hero* (1929) and more – 'Parade's End' is as a result surely the finest English novel we have to deal, both directly and indirectly, with the Great War and its effects. Indirect, angled, fractured in technique, it tells of the collapsing of a culture and the closing of an epoch, of a society that is pushed into fragmentation and passes through fundamental revolution as the guns boom on the front. If this is an Impressionist novel, it is not Impressionism as either Proust or Woolf would define it: not Proust's 'inner book of unknown symbols', Woolf's 'the atoms as they fall'. The aim is not to bring the story under the control of some metaphor, or produce a sense of aesthetic luminosity, but to tell a social allegory about the fate of an age, and draw the elements of history together before a total disunity sets in. So the book tells two stories, set side by side. One is the social story, the story of 'the public wants of a decade', which involves the replacement of the old ruling class by the new mandarins, the careerists and climbers, and of a felt, historic national identity with the cult of National Efficiency, all of this encouraged by the war. The other is the psychological story, the story of the collapse of a representative individual, the British gentleman as sacrificial victim, who goes to battle, passes through the purgatory of the front, and progresses, through madness and memory loss, into the new post-war world, where he has to learn to live again. Ford is able to manage this because he takes as the centre of his 'affair' a character who wants to hold these two worlds in relation, though the result is an unbearable strain; indeed he suggests that he is the last man who would try to do so. Tietjens is the good gentleman who bears the burden of his class – 'Our station in society naturally forms a rather close ring,' he observes – but, as an old feudalist, is also separated from its values. He is the last of his line, a figure of romance caught at the point of extinction, and after him there will be no more men 'who do not'. To some extent he is an absurd and comic figure, with a perverted creed, masochistically sustaining his own identity while questioning the society he lives in.

In Ford's allegory of change, his agony precedes the war; indeed the strains already there in the bodies politic and sexual make the war a necessary purgatory. The crisis is there from the novel's beginning, in 1912, and comes from the false, unhappy marriage Tietjens has made with his unfaithful wife Sylvia, pregnant by another man. That 'chivalric' act not only throws his heritage into doubt, but provokes Sylvia, one of fiction's more frightening and vengeful immoralists, into challenging his chivalry in every way possible, as she tries to bring him down to human scale. This same assault on the chivalric disposition (caught symbolically when the car driven by General Campion hits the horse Tietjens is riding) intensifies when the story moves, by sudden time-shift, from the relatively secure world of 1912 to the world at war – a war of mismanagement, bureaucracy, corrupt politics and red tape, where the enemy is less the opposing Germans than the 'swine in the corridors of Whitehall', his own government, the High Command and Sylvia, now entrenched with the General's party in France. Three wars – world war, social war, sex war – are intimately related; 'War is inevitable as divorce,' Tietjens says prophetically at the start, and the two are aspects of each other. But the war turns the cycle, and bleakly begins to open a new life for Tietjens. He collapses toward madness and amnesia, but at last is able to make the break with his own past, and find a life beyond chivalry, glory and parades. In the historical allegory, the aristocrat gives way to the bureaucrat, the chivalric to the mechanical, the age of values and convictions to the age of individual survival. Finally, like Guy Crouchback in Evelyn Waugh's 'Sword of Honour', the equivalent trilogy for the Second World War, Tietjens halts his epic pilgrimage and makes ironic peace with what is.

It is matched in the ironic tone of the text itself. Ford's technique of 'aloofness', the concern with registration he drew from Flaubert, sets the story at a distance. It begins on a note of objective social realism, capturing the Georgian social scene of 1912. 'The two young men – they were of the English public official class – sat in the perfectly appointed railway carriage,' runs the famous opening: 'The leather straps to the windows were of virgin newness; the mirrors beneath the new luggage racks immaculate as if they had reflected very little; the bulging upholstery in its luxuriant, regulated curves was scarlet and yellow in an intricate, minute dragon design, the design of a geometrician in Cologne. The compartment smelt faintly, hygienically of admirable varnish; the train ran as smoothly – Tietjens remembered thinking – as British gilt-edged securities . . .' These two young men are administrators of a well-managed, very British world ('If they saw a policeman misbehave, railway porters lack civility, an insufficiency of street lamps, defects in public services or in foreign countries, they saw to it either with nonchalant Balliol voices or with letters to *The Times*, asking with regretful indignation, "Has the British This or That come to *this*?"'), but the imagery tells us it is already dissolving. The train has a brittle newness; there is a hard foreign abstraction to the decor. This is a world of surfaces without depths, of hypocrisies laid over sexual corruptions, the England of National Efficiency and Imperial statistics. Soon the knackers' cart comes round the corner, and, by the Modernist device of time-shift, the action dissolves to the battlefront of 1917, with a war-wounded Tietjens lost amongst the chaos he had once thought to control. From social realism the method moves toward greater Impressionism, representing the fragmentation of war, society, consciousness itself. In *It Was the Nightingale*, Ford tells us that it is the nature of war to take away all confidence in social substance: 'A social system had crumbled . . . Nay, it was revealed to you that beneath Ordered Life itself was stretched, the merest film with, beneath it, the Abysses of Chaos. One had come from the frail shelters of the Line to a world that was more frail than a canvas hut.' This dissolving world justifies the fragmentary method: time-breaks, flashbacks and flashforwards, rapid cuts from scene to scene to generate a cumulative impression, or relate the world of the front to the world of 'money, women, testamentary bothers' back home. In *No More Parades*, Tietjens is buried, gassed, wounded, and his own inner realities begin to dissolve. *A Man Could Stand Up* – cuts between battlefield and the Armistice, between amnesia-stricken Tietjens and the life of his new female friend, who is also a 'New Woman', Valentine Wannop. Tietjens has lost his old values, his old heaven, his world of parades. 'Feudalism was finished; its last vestiges were gone. It held no place for him,' he reflects. In the final volume, *The Last Post*, which Ford was never sure whether to keep in the main sequence, Tietjens is only partly glimpsed as a character, and the end of the feudal world is shown; an entire social heritage gives way to an age of individualized values in which there are no more chivalries, no more parades, though perhaps a vague agrarian hope.

'Parade's End' is, no doubt, a very British version of Modernism, indirect yet social, complex yet accessible, a large cultural history as well as a work of consciousness (but then so are the novels of William Faulkner). And it shows Ford, like his hero, making a transition from one age to another: from the age of the modern novel as an 'affair' to one of a fiction made fragmentary by the very history of cultural collapse it concerns itself with. As in Ezra Pound's poem 'Hugh Selwyn Mauberley', the methods of collage, juxtaposition and fragmentation are now techniques for creating the distance, hard irony, disorder and historical dismay suited to a darkened age, and led on to the note of 'fictional indifference' that marked much Twenties and then Thirties writing. Ford played a serious part in British Modernism, significantly influencing other writers from Jean Rhys to Graham Greene and Evelyn Waugh. In Paris in the Twenties, in American universities during the Thirties, he advanced the cause of experiment, still writing prolifically, but never again with the force that produced *The Good Soldier* just before the war, 'Parade's End' just after it. He died, after a lifetime of involvement in the Modern movement, in June 1939, in Deauville in France, just a few weeks before the beginning of the Second World War his novels did not obviate. So much, he would doubtless have said, for Novels with a Purpose; always a true Modernist, he never really believed in them anyway.

5

Meanwhile, if Paris in the Twenties had Montparnasse, London had Bloomsbury. It was no area of boulevard cafés and zinc-topped bars where writers stopped to write a little and discuss the Revolution of the Word, no centre of salons and small presses and dramatic moments and manifestations. It was a postal district, around the British Museum, mostly noted for bookshops and Georgian terraces. Bloomsbury did not interrupt the opera with noise and protests, or invite you to slap a corpse; it generally lived behind closed Georgian doors, and disappeared to cottages in Sussex in the summer. The intellectuals and writers who increasingly chose to live in this part of London were largely an established network of friends, an already known elite who now commanded many of the magazines and the presses and set the critical tone. Bloomsbury, in fact, was a distinctive caste, though also a state of mind. It stood for what was avant-garde and experimental, not just in writing and publishing, but in sexual relations, economics, painting, politics, philosophy, biography and interior design. But it was unquestionably a social as well as an artistic phenomenon, an educated social caste that could read its genealogies back to the heart of the Victorian intelligentsia, to Thackeray and the Clapham Sect, to the Pre-Raphaelites and Pater. If Lytton Strachey's *Eminent Victorians* typified the great quarrel it conducted with the Victorian past, this frequently resembled a family quarrel, of sons and daughters against fathers and mothers, conducted in public. Bloomsbury was amongst other things a shared social and family background, a web of family relations, friendships, a network of complex sexual liaisons, an elite with a body of agreed social and cultural assumptions and standards. Essential to this was an 'aesthetic' attitude to the world itself, which involved a celebration of the 'modern'. Bloomsbury had its own tribal assumptions about creative personal relations and emotional states, and about the aesthetic deliverances art afforded. It helped to have read Walter Pater, who emphasized the power of impressions and of 'quickened, multiplied consciousness'. It was wise to have gone to Cambridge, perhaps been an 'Apostle' there, and certainly to have studied with or read the philosopher G. E. Moore – whose *Principia Ethica* (1903) reminded a whole generation that 'By far the most valuable things we know or can imagine are certain states of consciousness, which may roughly be described as the pleasures of human intercourse and the enjoyment of beautiful objects.'

Bloomsbury was unmistakably descended from the liberal, critical Victorian intelligentsia, and knew its own cultural authority. With its 'taste for truth and beauty', its freedom and frankness of personal and sexual relations, its powerful intellectualism, it was a revolt against the Establishment that soon became a new, formidable Establishment itself. It had taken shape before the war, when Roger Fry supported the new Cubist painters and developed his philosophy of 'significant form', and Virginia Woolf, daughter of Sir Leslie Stephen, took over his role as a major literary critic. It had Fry and Clive Bell as its Post-Impressionist aestheticians, Lytton Strachey as its biographer-historian, Maynard Keynes as its economic thinker, Bertrand Russell as its philosopher, Duncan Grant, Vanessa Bell, 'Carrington' and Mark Gertler as its painters, Lady Ottoline Morrell as one of its chief social patrons, E. M. Forster, to begin with, as its novelist, Virginia Woolf as its literary, critical and social conscience. Being a daughter, Virginia had not gone to Cambridge, which outraged her; but she wrote and thought much as if she had. When she, her sister Vanessa and her brothers Thoby and Adrian, settled in 1904 at 46 Gordon Square, north of the British Museum, 'Bloomsbury' began to acquire a local habitation and a name. Virginia called it 'the most beautiful, the most exciting, the most romantic place in the world', where 'Everything was going to be new; everything was going to be different.' In literary terms, what was to be 'new' and 'different' she explored in her criticism, much of it for *The Times Literary Supplement*, where she took particular interest in the past and future of the novel, looking back at the British fictional tradition, but equally at the cosmopolitan heritage of Dostoevsky, Chekhov, James and Conrad. Her brilliant, if at times mannered, critical essays, written over the following years, were key works of modern interpretation, and, collected under the title of *The Common Reader* (1925), they much affected the Twenties. But Woolf was no common reader; this was a subtle and specialized journey in quest of her own new and rigorous notion of 'contemporary fiction' and 'the modern novel'. Many of her ideas of a new 'poetic' modern fiction were thus largely formed before she completed her own first novel *The Voyage Out*, begun in 1908, accepted for publication in 1913, not published till 1915. As she explained: 'It is not that life is more complex or difficult now than at any other period, but that for each generation the point of interest shifts, the old forms put the interest in the wrong places, and in searching out the severed and submerged part of what to us constitutes form we seem to be throwing fragments together at random and disdaining the very thing we are trying our best to rescue from the chaos.' The search for a new form elicited from fragments, the opening of a new expressive awareness, the creation of a transformed and poeticized contemporary sensibility, was also a struggle of consciousness. It was also, importantly, a sexual battle, part of the 'fight between the fathers and the daughters'.

Bloomsbury – which has been sentimentalized and exoticized in recent literary commentary, to the point of excess[7] – both expanded and constrained British literary culture, and some of the literary exile and political and artistic anger that shaped the British writings of the Twenties and the Thirties was plainly an attempt to get away from it. D. H. Lawrence came close to, then vehemently rejected, Bloomsbury in his troubled wartime years. That goes into *Women in Love* (1920), his exploration of 'the results in one's soul of the war'. This is, like all Lawrence's books from here on, a modernist work – a radical work born out of artistic turmoil, written not so much to narrate its story as to distil, in moments of neo-symbolist concentration, the merging moments of sexuality and radical purging – but

7 As Noel Annan put it nicely in *The New York Review of Books* in 1978: 'It seems that almost everyone who ever spoke to the denizens of Gordon Square has found an amanuensis. As the critical studies and reminiscences mount, you are seized with panic and exhaustion and go down on your knees begging to be spared yet another account of the Pattle sisters, of Sir Leslie [Stephen] groaning, of the Midnight Society and the Apostles in 1900, and of the familiar anecdotes repeated in every account. Yet what we are witnessing is the documentation in detail of a kind never before seen in English letters: so that by the time it is completed we shall know more about the members of the Bloomsbury Group than of any other set of people in literary history . . .'

also a darkly prophetic one, well summarized (it is difficult if not impossible to summarize) by John Middleton Murry.[8] It is the novel where Lawrence breaks loose from ideas about the novel as anything other than 'the bright book of life', where fiction is made to invigorate and enflesh essential ideas, instinctualism becomes an incantatory prophecy about life in a sterilized and tragic age, as Birkin struggles through 'decay and decomposition' and 'dark, potent secrets' to a new subconscious unity of the sensual and spiritual, and the role of the writer is 'leadership'. But though it is essentially a major modern text of social and sexual dissolution, *Women in Love* is also a savage satire on British literary and artistic culture, following a theme that would recur through many of his impassioned works of the Twenties, from *Saint Mawr* to *Lady Chatterley's Lover*, as Lawrence seeks to explore what has poisoned the springs of creation and consciousness. Old personal scores are settled; a number of the characters are identifiable, including Bertrand Russell, Murry and Lady Ottoline Morrell; and Bloomsbury, in both its social tone and its aesthetic idealism, is 'a menagerie of apeish degraded souls', who display the enervation both of British social *mores* and artistic values, failing to respond to the tragic implication of the tragic age. 'Comes over one an absolute necessity to move,' Lawrence announced now, and spent most of the Twenties in a wandering exile, through Italy, New Mexico and Mexico, looking for the presence in the world of a new primitive soul, natural and animal. His bitter charges about the decay of the English soul and spirit, alike in its intellectuals and its working class, would resound through his fiction of the decade through to his death in Vence in 1930. If *The Lost Girl* (1920), which Virginia Woolf reviewed, suggesting that Lawrence was reverting to the spirit of Arnold Bennett,

---

8 'It is easy enough to understand Lawrence's intention in *Women in Love*: to present first the contrast between a man who immolates himself to the mechanism of modern civilization and one who is in dynamic revolt against it; and also to present the fatal influence on the man–woman relation of the inward sterility of Gerald [Crich], and the gleam of hope in the "love" that is based on Ursula's response to the vitality with which Birkin conquers his own despair. The theme is profound and prophetic. But much of its working out is mysterious . . .' John Middleton Murry, review of F. R. Leavis, *D. H. Lawrence: Novelist, TLS,* 1955; reprinted in John Gross (ed.), *The Modern Movement* (London, 1992).

and new-found works like *Mr Noon* show him capable of continuing to write a distinctive social history of Britain, other novels insistently direct their observation at the British aesthetic intelligentsia as symbol of the decline of the Western mind and spirit: the stories of *England, My England* (1922), the political prophecies of *Kangaroo* (1923), the historical despair of *Lady Chatterley's Lover* (1928) and the sexual resurrection of *The Virgin and the Gypsy* (1930) all pursue the theme. No doubt there was an element of class hostility in this (to return among the writers of the Fifties), but above all it was an argument about culture; the Bloomsbury compound – aestheticism, sensitivity, self-awareness, liberal social reformism – summoned Lawrence's resentment and despair.

Not surprisingly, Bloomsbury hardly took to Lawrence, though Woolf would admit his powerful originality and contribution to the new psychology of the novel. There were different reservations about Joyce. In 1918 he offered *Ulysses* to the Hogarth Press, but it was hard to find a printer who would risk it. In any case, Virginia Woolf, who had praised *A Portrait* . . ., did not like it, finding it naturalistic and sensual, filled with too much of 'the alien and external': 'the scratching of the pimples on the body of the bootboy at Claridge's', in fact. Later she acknowledged its 'greatness' – though greatness 'of the inferior water' – and drew on it for *Mrs Dalloway*, perhaps even hoping to suggest what its true experiment should have been. But Bloomsbury did like Proust: not Ford's creator of 'the ponderous novel', but the Proust who had rescued form and consciousness from the dross of materialism, pursued the modern quest for 'significant form'. It was Roger Fry – who disliked novels that were choked with 'criticisms of life, of manners or of morals', which most novels are – who introduced Proust in Britain before the war, as he introduced the Post-Impressionist painters. He drew him to Woolf's attention: 'Oh, if only I could write like that!' she wrote back enthusiastically. 'I try. And at the moment such is the astonishing vibration and the saturation and intensification that he procures – there's something sexual in it – that I feel I *can* write like that, and seize my pen and then I *can't* write like that. Scarcely anyone so stimulates the nerves of language in me; it becomes an obsession.' At work on *Mrs Dalloway*, she notes in her journal: 'I wonder if this next lap will be influenced by Proust? I think his French language, tradition, &c., prevents that: yet his command of every resource is so extravagant that one can hardly fail to profit, & must not flinch, through cowardice.'

Likewise E. M. Forster celebrated Proust in a key section of *Aspects of the Novel* (1927), observing the importance for the low, recalcitrant form of the novel of his use of 'rhythm' and 'pattern', those neo-musical elements that, stitching a work together from within, gave it aesthetic harmony. Forster was not quite Bloomsbury, but very close to it: he shared similar social and intellectual origins in 'the fag-end of Victorian liberalism', a Cambridge education, a belief in the primacy of personal relations, and a neo-symbolist view of art – 'the one orderly product our muddling race has produced', 'the only material object in the universe which may possess internal harmony'. But he also, believed that, oh dear yes, the novel tells a story, that, unlike poetry, it must respond to the laws of narrative, acknowledge the interest of society and history, incorporate 'the immense richness of material which life provides'. Here he fell out with Virginia Woolf, who reviewed *Aspects of the Novel* and made her difference plain. He had written 'The novelist who betrays too much interest in his own method can never be more than interesting; he has given up the creation of character and summoned us to help analyse his own mind . . .'; she disagreed, rejecting the 'assumption that fiction is more intimately and humbly associated to the service of human beings than the other arts . . . though it is impossible to imagine a book on painting in which not a word should be said about the medium in which a painter works, a wise and brilliant book about fiction, like Mr Forster's, can be written without saying more than a sentence or two about the medium in which the novelist works. Almost nothing is said about words . . . In England at any rate the novel is not a work of art.' That was the true Bloomsbury argument: what Woolf meant to do, in her long critical campaign, was exactly to make the novel in England a work of art, a work of self-conscious method.

The difference between them was not great; background, close friendship and generation linked them. But, though only three years separated their ages, Forster would remain an exemplary figure from the early part of the century, an Edwardian and Georgian writer who wrote nearly all his fiction before the First World War and then became a Modernist, a liberal humanist novelist for whom the essence of fiction lay in its concern with manners, morals and humane values, though he also knew it must aspire to wholeness of form. And he did achieve one magnificent Modernist work. After completing *Howards End* in 1910, he had difficulty in developing the next stage of his fiction. He tentatively started the novel *Arctic Summer*, but never completed it; he wrote *Maurice*, which he did complete but, since it was a frank story of a homosexual revolt against family, friends and culture, it could only come out posthumously in 1971. Then in 1912–13 he visited India, which had a profound effect on him, and began a novel about it, which he also set aside, finding the subject too vast for the governing imagination (when the book came at last, this would be its theme). The war, which he spent largely doing Red Cross work in Alexandria, also blocked it, but widened his experience of the non-British world. In 1921 he returned to India and took up the novel again, now conscious of new influences, Proust above all. 'I learned ways of looking at character from him. The modern subconscious way. He gave me as much of the modern way as I could take,' he later told an interviewer; the 'modern way' was undoubtedly the use of rhythmic composition and symbolist structure for the linear and social plot. Walt Whitman's all-embracing poem 'A Passage to India', about the great westering dream of American democratic imperialism ('The earth to be spann'd, connected by network/ The races, neighbours, to marry and be given in marriage/ The oceans to be cross'd, the distant brought near/ The lands to be welded together'), gave him his title. *A Passage to India*, the book he had struggled with right across the war, appeared at last in 1924.

A Passage to India is his most ambitious work, and surely one of the classic modern English novels, a work both of modern chaos and modern aesthetic order. The echo in the Marabar Caves ('ou-boum') levels all meanings to one, declares 'Everything exists; nothing has value', enforces that 'twilight of the double vision' in which the Janus-face of the universe is visible, where its horror and smallness are simultaneously known, where we can 'neither ignore nor respect

Infinity'. At the same time Forster's aspiration for rhythmic wholeness draws together the book and makes it a symbolist unity. This is the work that most embodies the neo-symbolist aspirations of *Aspects of the Novel*, giving it an imaginative texture different from the pre-war novels. Yet many of the same liberal themes continue: here once more are those powers in social life and nature – the claims of public and private, seen and unseen, social conventions and personal desires and relations which divide the universe and produce the need for reconciliation. Forster's basic moral sympathies are here too: the book is based in the testing-ground of human relationships, in the need of the liberal mind, of 'good will plus culture and intelligence', to overcome the grids of interest, ignorance and custom that divide individual from individual and race from race. So are his basic literary methods, the moving between poetic evocation of mystery and the comic world of human muddle, maintaining both a symbolist and a social mode of fiction. But the balance has changed. For some critics, *A Passage to India* is Forster's most affirmative book, his declaration that 'unity and harmony are the ultimate promises of life', according to Wilfred Stone. Others have seen the opposite: a novel about the final gap between chaotic human life and the intractable infinite.⁹ What is clear is that Forster's social observation is fuller and finer than before, his sense of human mystery is deeper, his theme of far greater vastness. This is surely the best novel by an Englishman to deal with the weight of the Imperial experience, and the confusing, spiritually demanding nature of the world its imperial net is laid over.

So on one level – yes, oh dear yes – the novel tells us a story, a social and political story told in a spirit of comedy and human muddle, about the life of the British Raj, the strict, bloodless conventions of British behaviour, the rituals of class, the rules of behaviour and racial duty. The British mean well, and do their task – 'to do justice and keep the peace' – effectively. They hold 'bridge parties' with the Indians, but they dissolve into misunderstanding; even those who try

9 See, for example, Wilfred Stone, *The Cave and the Mountain: A Study of E. M. Forster* (Stanford and London, 1966), and James McConkey, *The Novels of E. M. Forster* (Ithaca, NY, 1957).

harder, like the mystical Mrs Moore or the liberal schoolteacher Fielding, fail to encompass the sum that India represents. 'Nothing embraces the whole of India, nothing, nothing,' says the young Hindu doctor, Aziz. Sects and races are divided among themselves; so is the earth itself: 'The fissures in the Indian soil are infinite: Hinduism, so solid from a distance, is riven into sects and clan, which radiate and join, and change their names according to the aspect from which they are approached.' The 'extraordinary' awaits, and India invites cosmic meanings. But Beauty is absent, Nature rejects Romantic engagement: 'not the unattainable friend, either of men or birds or other suns . . . not the eternal promise, the never-withdrawn suggestion that haunts our consciousness; . . . merely a creature, like the rest, and so debarred from glory.' The human never quite touches the infinite: 'Trees of poor quality bordered the road, indeed the whole scene was inferior and suggested that the countryside was too vast to admit of excellence. In vain did each item in it call, "Come, come." There was not enough god to go round.' Mrs Moore and Fielding try hard; Forster as novelist tries harder, seeking to incorporate everything, not with a Whitmanesque barbaric yawp, but with a wry sense of human comedy, which sees how we generally fail when we seek to grasp diversity.

The human plot – set largely round the city of Chandrapore, evidently in the Twenties – hinges on Adela Quested, who comes to India to marry, has doubts when she sees what Indian service has made of her fiancé, and tries to see more. She goes on an expedition with her fiancé's mother Mrs Moore to the Marabar Caves, arranged by the friendly Indian doctor Aziz. In one cave she thinks she is sexually attacked by him (in an early draft she is); meanwhile Mrs Moore hears her echo, and suffers her 'twilight of the double vision'. Adela accuses Aziz of attempted rape, and though she retracts this at the trial the incident sows discord and exposes the political stresses and the racial crisis in the country. While Fielding seeks for personal and political reconciliation, Mrs Moore, haunted by her glimpse of the eternal abyss, dies on the way home, and Adela returns to Britain unwed. Both stories seem to fail, but, as Lionel Trilling once wisely remarked about the book, 'The characters are of sufficient size for the plot; they are not large enough for the story – and indeed that is the point of the story.'[10] Progressing through three large blocks of experience – Mosque, Caves and Temple – and through circle after circle of the Indian infinity, the story, following various heavenly invitations, moves away from its human plot toward the goal of 'completeness not reconstruction', 'expansion, not completion'. It opens – through the figure of the Hindu mystic Professor Godbole, the Hindu ceremony and the strange return of the spirit of Mrs Moore among the Indian crowds – on a hint of wholeness. What it does not offer is the certainty of it. At the close of the book, the earth still says 'No, not yet,' and the sky says, 'No, not there.' The echo at the edge of Fielding's consciousness persists: 'Everything echoes now; there's no stopping the echo. The original sound may be harmless, but the echo is always evil.' The two aspects of the novel – the social realism, the comedy of the human plot, and the patterned, symbolist hunger for the 'one orderly product' – remain in suspension, and that too is the point of the story. Forster avoids the closure of the realist plot, but he equally avoids the closure of the symbolist plot; both material realism and symbolism ask, in their different ways, for everything to be included, and Forster did neither. *A Passage to India* – Forster's last brilliant work of fiction, for though he lived until 1970 he produced no more novels – remains a humanist novel, accepting its own contradiction and its own dualism, as the novel so often has: the world is both a mystery and a muddle. This did not quite suit Virginia Woolf, even though she admired the book for its modernity, and acknowledged it was going in the right direction: 'though it is true there are ambiguities in important places, moments of imperfect symbolism, a greater accumulation of facts than the imagination is able to deal with, it seems as if the double vision which troubles us in the earlier books is in process of becoming single,' she wrote. But Forster, she had to confess, was a materialist novelist, 'too susceptible to the influence of time': in other words he felt the need to admit social life, history and contradiction into his universe. Forster was good, but he was still not quite Bloomsbury.

10 Lionel Trilling, *E. M. Forster* (Norfolk, Conn., 1943; London, 1944).

6

If Virginia Woolf had problems with Forster's view of the novel ('too susceptible to the influence of time'), it was not surprising he had a reverse problem with hers. 'You're in a very special position, I feel; you seem to be experimenting in the direction of poetry, and might carry fiction into a region where it will glow and contract,' he wrote. Forster's critical judgement on her books was one she highly valued; he in turn had to confess, as others of her friends, like Lytton Strachey, also did, that they missed from them many of the thicker densities of life. 'Elegant arabesques,' said Strachey, while Forster observed, 'she is always stretching out from her enchanted tree and snatching bits of the flux of daily life as it floats past, and out of these bits she builds novels.' He, it seemed, still respected the old novel; she wrote the 'new' one, the insubstantized novel. He was an Edwardian, she a 'modern', who came later to fiction, in a different spirit, beginning her work at a time when the day of the material novel was over, or at least incapable of conveying any meaningful sense of life as it had become. As for Woolf's own sense of life, it was clear, vivid, subjective; it sparkled in moments, shifted between mind and mind. 'Examine for a moment an ordinary mind on an ordinary day,' she said in 'Modern Fiction' in 1919. 'The mind receives a myriad impressions – trivial, fantastic, evanescent, or engraved with the sharpness of steel. From all sides they come, an incessant shower of innumerable atoms; and, as they fall, as they shape themselves into life of Monday or Tuesday, the accent falls differently from of old . . .' Not all of us would say that this is the life of the ordinary mind on an ordinary day; it is more like the life of an aesthete's mind on a symbolist day. For Woolf's atoms are more than random or contingent; they form into glimpses, sudden revelations, which become the essences of fiction, the basis for a quite different sort of story, about an utterly different 'that'. 'For the moderns "that", the point of interest, lies very likely in the dark places of psychology,' she explained: 'At once then, the accent falls a little differently, the emphasis is on something hitherto ignored; at once a different outline of form becomes

necessary, difficult for us to grasp, incomprehensible to our predecessors.' Thus the novelist's task was to dematerialize what was
material, de-create form as it had been, make the novel a self-creating
species, writing a decomposition as well as a composition. Maybe
what she was seeking was not even a novel at all. 'I have an idea that
I will invent a new name for my books to supplant "novel"', she put
in her diary in July 1925, as she planned *To the Lighthouse*. 'A new –
by Virginia Woolf. But what? Elegy?'

In fact Woolf's kind of 'insubstantized' novel can be traced back,
maybe to Walter Pater, certainly to William James's insistence in
Principles of Psychology (1890) that reality was not an objective given,
but was subjectively perceived through consciousness. From then on,
in experimental poetic fiction, we find 'consciousness' constantly
interposed between the world and the individual 'subject', creating a
new kind of gaze. Sometimes this produces psychological realism,
sometimes a highly aesthetic or poetic self-consciousness; mostly it
produces a merger between the two. As Dostoevsky became better
known in Europe, as James exerted his influence, as Freud and Bergson
came to be generally read, the claims of the psycho-aesthetic vision
intensified. The claims of aesthetics to provide an overview of human,
especially modern, experience were put forward with missionary
energy, and Bloomsbury founded its distinctive secular religion on
aligning sensitivities of art and form with intensity in personal
relationships. The idea of a 'new' composition spun from a sensitive
authorial consciousness whose own psychology was so finely attuned
as to produce a symbolist metamorphosis, an aesthetic epiphany,
underlies many of the novels of sensibility, psychology and poetry
that began appearing in the second decade of the century – when there
was a growing revolt against the scientific positivism of Wells and
Shaw, and many fresh notions of the need to evaluate experience
through consciousness. In 1913 the first two volumes of Proust's
eight-volume *A la recherche* . . . came out, to Bloomsbury interest. In
1914–15, twenty-four instalments of Joyce's *A Portrait of the Artist*
. . . appeared in serial form in the British magazine *The Egoist*, and
won Woolf's admiration. In 1915, the year of Woolf's own first novel
A Voyage Out, Dorothy Richardson's *Pointed Roofs* appeared, the

first 'chapter' of her *roman fleuve* 'Pilgrimage', quickly followed by several more (*Backwater*, 1916; *Honeycomb*, 1917; etc.), which Woolf found exciting, though egotistical and hence formless. What links all these together is that they are simultaneously psychological and experimental novels, their structure won from orders drawn from interior rather than historical time. As Richardson justly pointed out, not all these books could have influenced each other: 'An interesting point for the critic who finds common qualities in the work of Proust, James Joyce, Virginia Woolf and D. R. is the fact that they were all using the "new method" though differently, simultaneously.'[11] Something else must have linked them together, a new attitude to art and literature itself.

There was also something else – feminism, or at least a concern with the development of a distinctive feminine, or differently engendered, vision. *The Egoist*, the magazine where much experimental new work, including Joyce, Eliot and Pound, appeared, where the poetic movement of Imagism was announced, was a feminist paper, first called *The New Freewoman*. Richardson herself was a 'New Woman' who had broken with her once wealthy family, taught in Germany, been a suffragette, worked in London as a typist, had the almost statutory affair with H. G. Wells. *Pilgrimage*, the slowly, seamlessly unfolding tale of Miriam Henderson, is virtually autobiographical, following out an independent, struggling life like the author's over the course of the years through thirteen deeply felt 'chapters'. Richardson defined her aim as 'to produce a feminine equivalent of the current masculine realism', but rejected the narrative methods of established novelists, who 'left out certain essentials and dramatized life misleadingly. Horizontally. Assembling their characters, the novelists developed situations, devised events, climax and conclusion. I could not accept these finalities.' It was another important feminist novelist and critic, May Sinclair, who, in *The Egoist* in 1918, took a key phrase from William James to describe what she was doing. This was, she

---

11 All this is usefully recorded in Leon Edel, *The Psychological Novel: 1900–1950* (New York and London, 1955), and Morris Beja, *Epiphany in the Novel: Revelation as Art* (Seattle and London, 1971).

said, the method of 'stream-of-consciousness', depending on 'moments tense with vibration, moments drawn out fine, almost to snapping point'. Woolf, who thought her methods less egotistical and far more refined, did not relish the comparisons made between her work and Richardson's, but she increasingly acknowledged the centrality of the feminine vision. In *To the Lighthouse* she would look beyond the men who 'negotiated treaties, ruled India, controlled finance', to sensibilities, female sensibilities, distinctively attuned to 'little daily miracles, illuminations . . .' And female radiating characters like Clarissa Dalloway and Mrs Ramsay helped point the way to the 'new' novel – the novel of flowing consciousness, 'moments tense with vibration', life's shimmer, psychological intensity, released from the rule of time and identity. Perhaps, she suggested in her *A Room of One's Own* (1929), and yet more forcefully in *Three Guineas* (1932), it was because women were not supposed to write novels that they could break free of convention, beyond social constraint into what she elsewhere called 'queer individuality'. In any case, she promised in her essay 'Women in Fiction' (1929), women writers could be less absorbed than men in facts, and no doubt in the future they 'will look beyond the personal and political relationships to the wider questions which the poet tries to solve – of our destiny and the meaning of life'.

In Woolf's vision, the modern novelist was free: but free to do what? In her two key essays 'Modern Fiction' and 'Mr Bennett and Mrs Brown' she spoke for the writer released from traditional views of time, identity and reality, and stressed three elements of new fiction: the novel, through the withering away of old conventions, becomes more 'itself'; it manifests a new mode of perception; it reveals the real spirit of 'life' once dross and materiality have been discarded. Life is, she says, 'a luminous halo, surrounding us from the beginning of consciousness to the end', and this the novelist should convey, with 'as little mixture of the alien and external as possible'. But if the novelist was concerned with 'consciousness', what Woolf meant by that term was not quite what other novelists made of it. For some, from James to Joyce and Faulkner, the method of consciousness served to reveal the contingency, the chaos, the underlying stress, of a life from which all wholeness and coherence had gone, and displayed the problem of finding order in a disordered age. In James it is the ordeal of fine minds in a specific social environment, and a partial instrument of understanding; in Lawrence it is the means to break up the 'old stable ego' and explore the energies, vitalistic or deathly, that pass among individuals in an apocalyptic time. In Joyce stream-of-consciousness is both aesthetic (Stephen's reflections) and subterranean (Molly's soliloquy), and by *Finnegans Wake* it has become a dream-like substratum of myths, images and linguistic associations. In Woolf, consciousness is flowing, poetic, feminine, above all painterlike and aesthetic – the means by which art can enter the realm of intuition, imaginative pattern, heightened responsiveness, a reverie of the *ego* rather than an emanation of the *id*. In her novels consciousness flows, not only backward and forward in time, and spatially, from this place to that, but among and above the characters, who often share a strange intuitive relation to some common symbol: the lighthouse, the waves. And consciousness does more than apprehend the 'shower of innumerable atoms', or 'the luminous halo'; it reaches to the edge of eternal revelation, to moments of vision, 'little daily miracles, illuminations, matches struck unexpectedly in the dark'. Woolf can create flux in its terrifying enormity, as with Septimus Smith in *Mrs Dalloway*, who, shellshocked in war, accepts that 'it might be possible that the world itself is without meaning', or Eleanor in *The Waves* who acknowledges that atoms that 'danced apart and massed themselves' might hardly construct 'what people called a life'. From the start her novels never lack pain or melancholy, her note of 'elegy'. But the quest does point to some symbolist wholeness; consciousness can ultimately reveal form, penetrate the curtain. Thus the reflection of Mrs Ramsay in *To the Lighthouse*:

there is a coherence in things; a stability; something, she meant, is immune from change, and shines out (she glanced at the window with its ripple of reflected lights) in the face of the flowing, the fleeting, the spectral, like a ruby; so that again tonight she had the feeling she had once today, of peace, of rest. Of such moments, she thought, the thing is made that endures.

It is the vision remembered in turn by Lily Briscoe, ten years on: 'In the midst of chaos there was shape; this eternal passing and flowing (she looked at the clouds going and the leaves shaking) was struck into stability. Life stand still here, Mrs Ramsay said.'

Woolf pursued this quest for the revealed shape in the midst of chaos through eight novels, written over five decades. Her first book, *The Voyage Out*, began as *Melymbrosia* as early as 1908; her last, the mature *Between the Acts*, appeared just after her death by suicide in 1941. From 1915 on she kept a detailed, vivid diary recording – along with much else of her daily life and thought – the progress of this endeavour toward 'some queer individuality'. One of the great compositional records, it does much to illuminate not just her own, but the modern, creative instinct in an age of critical self-consciousness. With her third novel, *Jacob's Room* (1922), a meditation on the life and the room of a dead soldier ('Let us suppose that the Room will hold it together,' say her notes), comes the breakthrough; she remarks 'I have found out how to begin (at 40) to say something in my own voice.' Critics agree in seeing the group of books that followed – *Mrs Dalloway* (1924), *To the Lighthouse* (1927) and *The Waves* (1931) – as the centre of her work, the heart of her contribution to Modernism. *Mrs Dalloway* – originally called *The Hours*, and set over seventeen chimed hours of one day in London in 1923 – is a portrait of a fifty-two-year-old society hostess preparing a party. Her gift is to 'kindle and illuminate', despite illness, sexual loneliness ('Narrower and narrower would her bed be'), intimations of death. Juxtaposed with her story is that of Septimus Smith, a spirit from a different London, racked and broken by the war. His death by suicide coincides with Clarissa's party, and resonates through the final scenes. Otherwise the two do not come directly together, other than by the flowing motions of the prose, the rhythms of consciousness that move through the city, pick up the crowds, the walkers in the street, the nursemaids in the park, the moments from various individual pasts that distil in the present. As she wrote it, from 1922 to 1924, Woolf recorded its joys and depressions in her diary. She shows the need for a planned design, then the need to upturn it; she records the discovery of 'my tunnelling process, by which I tell the past in instalments, as I have need of it'; she declares her final conviction that the book has passed beyond mere accomplishment: 'it seemed to leave me plunged deep in the richest strata of my mind. I can write and write and write now: the happiest feeling in the world.' All this is matched in the rhythm of the book, which plainly progresses through a series of inner aesthetic gratifications, concluding with the obvious sense of artistic fulfilment in the famous final sentence: 'For there she was.'[12]

One critic has nicely called Clarissa a 'metaphysical hostess', a figure who distils the experience of others and is an equivalent to form and life itself. So is Mrs Ramsay (based on Woolf's own mother) in her next book, *To the Lighthouse*. She is a pulsing, radiating centre of life, a 'lighthouse' herself, a unified sensibility, living 'in beauty':

Mrs Ramsay, who had been sitting loosely, folding her son in her arm, braced herself, and, half turning, seemed to raise herself with an effort, and at once to pour into the air a rain of energy, a column of spray, looking at the same time animated and alive as if all her energies were being fused into force, burning and illuminating (quietly though she sat taking up the stocking again), and into this delicious fecundity, this fountain and spray of life, the fatal sterility of the male plunged itself, like a beak of brass, barren and bare.

The book's two episodes, an evening and a morning ten years apart, split by an interlude which sets those ten years of history into a parenthesis, describe a world with Mrs Ramsay and a world without her. Like *A Passage to India* the book is structured as a triptych: the first part, 'The Window', is gently celebrative; the second part, 'Time Passes', evokes the decay of the house over the period of the Great War, during which two of the Ramsay children die, and Mrs Ramsay; the third, 'The Lighthouse', treats a world of absence, redeemed by art. A lighthouse trip is achieved, Lily Briscoe finishes her painting: '. . . she drew a line there, in the centre. It was done; it was finished. Yes, she thought, laying her brush down in extreme fatigue, I have had my vision.' The human has passed into the aesthetic; out of

---

12 I have discussed *Mrs Dalloway* more thoroughly in Chapter 10 of *The Modern World: Ten Great Writers* (London, 1988).

blobby experience a harmony has been captured, some answer to Lily's large question 'What is the meaning of life?' The aesthetic is also an intuitive metaphysic, culminating in a unity called form. What Lily may be presumed to do is draw together the multiple moments of vision that make the novel. Woolf is never a narrative novelist, and this is a book of constant stases, moments of visionary gazing, contemplation, rapture: Charles Tansley seeing Mrs Ramsay's beauty plain; Lily perceiving human thought as a scrubbed kitchen table in a tree; Mrs Ramsay going on a spit of land 'which the sea is slowly eating away, and there to stand, like a desolate sea-bird, alone'. In different ways the task of 'merging and flowing and creating' is assigned to all parties; as the characters halt for moments of reflection and veneration, the narration enriches this with an elaborate iconography, in which, however, 'nothing was simply one thing'. The novel ends on Lily's brushstroke, which finally becomes a composition; so, while the flux may be the flux of human consciousness, it reaches a coherence not of life or thought but of aesthetic completion. Pattern emerges, the pattern of art, the Cézanne-like shape in the midst of chaos, giving form to the absences, vacancies and obscurities of the human world.

Woolf followed the book with a squib, *Orlando* (1928), a playful exercise in androgyny. She herself called it an 'escapade', though it proved curiously successful commercially. But 'as usual I am bored by narrative', she wrote in her diary in 1929. So started the next major project, an emerging new book that was first called *The Moths* and finally appeared as *The Waves* (1931). She noted: 'I am not trying to tell a story ... A mind thinking. They might be islands of light – islands in the stream that I am trying to convey: life itself going on.' Life going on, as it moves against narrative, against the steady dead beat of the clock, against history's familiar line of progress, against all that was dead and material, against conventional notions of human identity and personality: this was what her new work was trying to convey. *The Moths*, or *The Waves*, would be a prose poem, a flow, a novel beyond the novel, a work where every atom is saturated, a 'combination of thought; sensation; the voice of the sea', a book written to a rhythm, not a plot. Six identities merge into a common lyrical and elegiac rhythm of experience, and the book is the culmin-

contribution was not only to Modernism's experimental adventure, which began to expire in the Thirties as political issues rose (she resisted, saying that art was in jeopardy when 'rage and personal grievances' came into it, while accepting that the idea that the artist was 'absolved from political duties' in order to have 'freedom of mind, security of person, immunity from practical affairs', was now fundamentally challenged). It was also to the making of a new feminine novel, the writing of 'Shakespeare's sister'. Indeed she was a leading figure in a new tendency that developed powerfully during the Twenties in the work of May Sinclair, Dorothy Richardson, Katherine Mansfield, Rebecca West, Jean Rhys, Rosamund Lehmann, Elizabeth Bowen and more. For the 'new methods' had released into fiction a deepened psychology, a more profound female portraiture, a richer discourse of inner life, a vital sense of aspiration – and a conviction that there is no presiding rule, no 'proper stuff of fiction', that 'the story might wobble, the plot might crumble, ruin might seize upon the characters. The novel, in short, might become a work of art.'

During the Thirties, when personal stories increasingly yielded to public and political ones, Woolf produced two more novels, *The Years* (1937) and *Between the Acts* (1941), works of panoramic historical intention, but less fundamental originality. The waning of art was in fact a theme of the age, and the air of crisis that had touched her work became more intense. In January 1941, with a new war going on round her, she noted in her diary James Joyce's death – 'Joyce about a fortnight younger than I am.' She recalled reading *Ulysses*, in its blue and white cover, with 'spasms of wonder, of discovery, and then again the long lapses of intense boredom . . . And now all the gents are furbishing up their opinions, and the books, I suppose, take their place in the long procession.' She wrote her essay 'The Leaning Tower', a reflection of the decline of art in an age of politics, and a challenge to the younger generation who had found important historical issues, but had not written great books. Her own tragic death followed just after, in March, when, shattered again by the new war, she drowned herself in the river at Rodmell. Her own books, with their aesthetic intensity, high poetry, felt femininity, their struggle to complete identity both in art and life, were indeed, as she put it herself in *To the Lighthouse*, forms beyond experience, 'one of those globed compacted things over which thought lingers, and love plays'. And they too now took their own much argued, though increasingly respected, place in 'the long procession', where history and criticism would go on doing their complicated work.

7

The fiction of high aesthetic intensity, of inwardly felt 'globed compact things' that offer through art a wholeness not there in life, was never the only aim of the contentious Modern movement. According to Ortega y Gasset's famous essay, a prime feature of Modern fiction was its move toward dehumanization – its departure from romanticism, realism and humanism toward perspective, abstraction, ironic observation, defamiliarization, away from the centrality of the human figure. Lawrence saw his novels firmly moving away from human representation in the direction of the greater inhuman will. In Woolf's *To the Lighthouse*, Mrs Ramsay's presence is replaced by her absence, and in *The Waves* individual identities give ground to the endless rhythm of life and death itself, a world beyond the self: 'The difference we make so much of, this identity we so feverishly cherish, was overcome,' Woolf wrote at the end of that book. In Joyce's *Ulysses*, human figures yield ground to the verbal life of the busy text they inhabit; even in Forster's humanistic *A Passage to India*, individuals are like 'dwarfs shaking hands' in the obscure mystery of the landscape, and the human plot gives way to the symbolic one. As in painting, the represented human figure was losing its place at the centre of the world, the romantic self yielding to modern collectivity and impersonality.[14] 'The primal artistic impulse has nothing to do

14 Wyllie Sypher offers a brilliant study of this in his *Loss of the Self in Modern Literature and Art* (New York, 1962), which draws the lesson that in the age of collectivity, science and the vanishing individual any new humanism 'must come to terms with our sense of the anonymity of the self, must therefore get beyond any romantic notions of selfhood. The importance of recent painting and literature is here, for both suggest that we must no longer confuse humanism with romantic individuality

with the rendering of nature,' the German art critic Wilhelm Worringer wrote in *Abstraction and Empathy* in 1908; 'It seeks after pure abstraction as the only possibility of repose within the confusions and obscurity of the world-picture . . .' All this, as critics have often noted, increasingly led at least one part of modern fiction in the direction of a pervasive irony, reflecting the sense of fading identity in a nihilistic, destructive and depersonalizing age. It was not surprising that this spirit of irony intensified in the post-war years, responding to the incongruity and horror of life with a vision of the modern as the age of meaninglessness and absurdity. Detachment, abstraction, impersonality, not realism or romantic subjectivity – surely these were the essentials of the modern method in the age of the machine and mechanical war?

That was certainly the view of 'the Enemy', Wyndham Lewis, proponent of the Vorticist method of 'the Great Without'. Born in 1882, educated at the Slade School of Art, then in Munich and Paris, Lewis was both painter and writer, and an active power in the early international Modern movement. Back in London in 1909, he was taken up by Hueffer/Ford for the *English Review*, and after that played a key part in the pre-war British avant-garde. A central moment was his split with Roger Fry and his Post-Impressionist Omega Workshop; Lewis was attracted by the violent energy of Marinetti and the Futurists, and set up his own Rebel Arts Centre – from which, with the support of Pound, came Vorticism, celebrating the radical mechanical vortex of energy at the centre of art, and its magazine *Blast*. By 1911 he had started a Vorticist novel, *Tarr*, set in Paris's artistic bohemia, about the war between the artist and the rational philosopher, displaying many of his essential ideas about art in the age of the modern machine. Like other important works of the time, it was completed in wartime, when Lewis served on the front as a gunner, serialized in *The Egoist* in 1916–17, published in 1918. *Tarr*

---

or with an anthropomorphic view that put the self at the centre of things. I take the phrase from Jean Grenier's essay on the disappearance of man from art: 'We now walk in a universe where there is no echo of "I".' The image of the self held in past eras has been effaced from the universe in which even nature seems an abstraction.'

is an art of 'polished and resistant surfaces', a comedy of machines, in which the characters are automata, human mechanisms seen in absurd performance. They acknowledge this themselves: 'Deadness is the first condition of art,' announces Tarr. 'The second is the absence of soul, in the human and sentimental sense ... good art must have no inside.' The hard external manner is stark, what many would call 'modern':

Tarr possessed no deft hand or economy of force: his muscles rose unnecessarily on his arm to lift a wine-glass to his lips: he had no social machinery at all at his disposal and was compelled to get along as well as he could with the cumbrous one of the intellect. With this he danced about it is true: but it was full of sinister piston-rods, organ-like shapes, heavy drills ...

From the start Lewis rejected 'fiction from the inside', the interiorized novel of psychology that romanticized consciousness, as did Virginia Woolf's. 'The *external* approach to things (relying on the evidence of the *eye* rather than on the more emotional organs of sense) can make "the grotesque" a healthy and attractive companion,' he explained; 'Dogmatically, then, I am for the Great Without, the method of external approach.'

As the dismaying Twenties developed, and the Modernist excitement turned to something else, Lewis's hard aesthetic detachment shifted to a plainer satirical disgust. He claimed that the pre-war rebellion had lost its direction, and Bloomsbury's ascent in the Twenties increased his disputatious rage. He became 'the Enemy', the adversary of false experimental traditions, scoffing at the clownish age. Like Lawrence, he saw the Twenties as a time in crisis, unable to reconcile mechanical and human, reason and passion. Unlike Lawrence, he rejected the Romantic solution, the retreat into primitivism, intuitionalism, vitalism and 'the wild body'. He condemned the novels of Joyce, Lawrence, Stein and Woolf alike for what he saw as their sentimentalization of experience and consciousness. And his answer was comedy; modern literature should be satirical or comic, meeting dehumanization with dehumanization. 'The root of the comic,' he says in *The Wild Body* (1927), following Bergson, 'is to be sought in the sensations of a thing behaving like a person. But from that point of view all men are necessarily comic; for they are all things, or physical bodies, behaving like persons.' Two remarkable works – *The Childermass* (1928), an abstract comedy of ideas set on the arid steppe at the threshold of heaven, and *The Apes of God* (1930), a bitter satire directed at a Britain 'dead as mutton', above all at the contemporary artistic scene and especially the Bloomsbury intelligentsia, that 'general rabble that collects under the equivocal banner of ART' – put the method into practice. These are works of vivid prose, powerful social observation, hard satirical rage. This is satire that enjoys all the Swiftian mechanics of disgust. Thus, from *The Apes of God*, this passage about the aged Lady Fredigonde Follett, symbol for the whole culture, rising from her chair:

The unsteady solid rose a few inches, like the levitation of a narwhal. Seconded by alpenstock and body-servant (holding her humble breath), the escaping half began to move out from the deep vent. It abstracted itself slowly. Something imperfectly animate had cast off from a portion of itself. It was departing, with a grim paralytical toddle, elsewhere. The socket of the enormous chair yawned just short of her hindparts . . .

Lewis – who remains an under-estimated writer, in part because his political ironies at the expense of the fashionable Left led him too close to Fascism for a time, and who kept on writing through the Fifties – is a novelist of extraordinary force, at his best capable of the rage of a Lawrence at the progressive enfeeblement of the culture, at his worst a writer who is chaotically prejudiced, painfully personal and shrill. But he also stays important for what he exemplifies: the rise of detached, objectively satirical methods and forms as a way of representing the grim modern experience in art. For the method of 'the Great Without' was what many modern writers saw the point of. Robert Musil's 'man without qualities', Italo Svevo's weatherless heroes, Kafka's self-victimizing victims, belong to a new age of ironic texts and characterless characters, writers of a world where the human was emptying out as the subject of art.

Sean O'Faolain, in *The Vanishing Hero* (1956), his interesting study of some of the best writers of the Twenties and Thirties (Joyce, Woolf, Hemingway, Faulkner, Aldous Huxley, Evelyn Waugh, Graham Greene, Elizabeth Bowen), explains that 'The one constant in them all is the virtual disappearance of that focal character of the classical novel, the Conceptual Hero.'[15] In his view, the novel of the Twenties sees the end of earlier fictional humanism and of the socially approved hero, who becomes instead the anti-hero, the self-creator, the nonentity, the rebel, the misfit or the 'galvanized puppets of their authors' transcendental ideas'. And the humanist framework of the novel was indeed weakening, not only because of the movement toward symbolism and poetic fiction, or toward Lawrence's 'inhuman self', but for more directly historical reasons: the war itself had eroded heroism in the scale of its mass slaughter, and the post-war weakening of public values, and social and psychological stability, accelerated the process. Heroes were falling off their monuments in the Twenties, and public values decaying; Wyndham Lewis was doubtless right to see that one of the mechanisms for dealing with this was a new comedy of manners and of ideas, which in fact the novelists of the Twenties give us in considerable profusion. There were the bright social comedies of Michael Arlen, the camp comedies of Ronald Firbank, above all the fiction of Aldous Huxley, the most underlyingly serious of them. Huxley, born in 1894, grandson of the Darwinian T. H. Huxley, wrote four fine novels over the Twenties – *Crome Yellow* (1921), a brilliant debut, mocking Lady Ottoline Morrell's Garsington and filled with invention and wit; *Antic Hay* (1923), a highly satirical portrait of London's cynical bohemia; *Those Barren Leaves* (1925), which was set among expatriates in Italy; and *Point Counterpoint* (1928), a novel of ideas about writing a novel of ideas. A presiding theme is the very nature of the modern itself. 'Living modernly's living quickly,' explains Lucy Tantamount in *Point Counterpoint*: 'You can't cart a wagonload of ideals and romanticisms around with you these days. When you travel by airplane, you must leave your heavy baggage behind. The good old-fashioned soul was

---

15 See Sean O'Faolain, *The Vanishing Hero: Studies in Novelists of the Twenties* (London, 1956).

all right when people lived slowly. But it's too ponderous nowadays. There's no room for it in the airplane.' The good old-fashioned soul disappears from Huxley's novels; these are characters who are quite used to crisis. 'I don't see that it would be possible to live in a more exciting age,' says Calamy in Aldous Huxley's *Those Barren Leaves* (1925): 'The sense that everything's perfectly provisional and temporary . . . the feeling that nothing . . . is really safe, the intimate conviction that anything may happen, anything may be discovered – another war, the artificial creation of life, the proof of continued existence after death – why it is all infinitely exhilarating.'

It was little wonder that Huxley's novels came to be seen as works of modern cynicism. His characters appeared powerless to act, their relationships incapable of taking shape, their ideas circular and pointing to eventual futility. These are novels of ideas that set no store by the salvation of ideas. When, in *Point Counterpoint*, Philip Quarles sets out to write a book for the times, it is indeed a novel of ideas. 'Novel of ideas . . .,' he notes. 'The chief defect about the novel of ideas is that you must write about people who have ideas to express,' in other words intellectuals, who are disappointing and futile in their own ways. Quarles also thinks it a good idea to put a novelist in the novel ('He also justifies experiment. Specimens of his work may illustrate other possible or impossible ways of telling a story'), which of course is just what Huxley himself had done; these books are nothing if not self-conscious. As for the ideas themselves, they generally turn on notions of crisis and desires for primitivism, the products of an age of lost ideals and universal boredom in which barbarism and Freudian libido become solutions to an intellectual sterility (which is why, of course, the ideas turn into comedy). Huxley knew well he was one of the people he was himself satirizing, living in a 'pointless landscape' (or what D. H. Lawrence, himself satirized in *Point Counterpoint* as Rampion, called the 'slow suicide of inertia'), in a world where things are either exciting or boring, when humanity is a wearisome condition. Behind them is a sense of the failure of history and the collapse of secular progress, so that only irrational solutions are possible. Perhaps it was inevitable that Huxley's next and most famous book would be *Brave New World* (1932), written when the processes Huxley was writing about had gone yet further. A dystopian, anti-Wellsian novel about the future, set in the seventh century AF (After Ford), a Butler-like satire on a world where science, mechanism and reason have triumphed over human nature, it makes clear that, though Huxley's novels were regarded as indifferent and cynical, the underlying pain, anxiety and humanism were real enough. And Huxley spent his later years in the USA, as a modern thinker rather than a novelist, watching, as his eyesight failed, a good many of his bleaker predictions and prophecies come true in the age of science and mechanization.

Still, there was no doubt who the writer was who distilled modern comedy, and best caught the mood of the later Twenties. Evelyn Waugh, born in 1903, the son of Arthur Waugh, the literary journalist and publisher's editor, was a schoolboy at Lancing during the Great War, and so belonged to the distinctively post-war generation. He went up to Oxford in 1922, the year of *Ulysses* and *The Waste Land*, the peak year of the Modern movement, and in it he took a great interest; indeed the influence of Eliot is plain on his work, and he later took the title of *A Handful of Dust* (1934) from his famous poem. Toward the end of the decade he began writing fiction which reflected this interest. He had also been reading Hemingway, a younger American writer then working experimentally in Paris, whose very post-war story of futility, modern pain and 'the lost generation', *The Sun Also Rises*, with its tight, understated and economical prose, appeared in 1926, around the time Waugh began writing. His interests were eclectic. He admired Max Beerbohm, whose witty if highly romantic comedy of Oxford life, *Zuleika Dobson*, appeared in 1911; the novels of P. G. Wodehouse, with their utterly distinctive, timeless, comfortingly British comic world, supported by the excellent Jeeves; the novels of Ronald Firbank, whose *Valmouth* appeared in 1919 and his *Prancing Nigger* in 1924 (he died in 1926). Waugh was a writer in search of a distinctive modern style, and he found one. Writing on Firbank just after he had published his first novel *Decline and Fall* (1928), in an essay in 1929, he explored the modern technique of Firbank's fiction. Effect, he noted, was presented without cause; his art balanced 'the wildest extravagances and the most austere economy'; presentation was done through dialogue rather than characterization, extravagant action and the pace and cross-cutting of film. And, like Lewis, Waugh had evidently read his Nietzsche and Bergson, whose ideas are expressed by Professor Silenus in *Decline and Fall*, where he speaks of a world of the purely mechanical, uninvaded by the mischief that is called man. Waugh is a writer who has been consistently under-estimated because his work seems to offer no intellectual analysis of the modern condition, but simply represents it as an absurd situation. But that was the point: he had found his modern style, entirely distinctive and original. It was an absurdist humour; indeed he can be taken as the chief creator of the spirit of black humour in modern British fiction. His early novels (written, as Edmund Wilson once remarked, in the spirit of Jowett's advice to the British gentleman: 'Never apologize, never explain') are remarkable for the completeness of their comic vision, the pure anarchy of their world, the concentration of their modern comic form.

Decline and Fall: An Illustrated Novelette is a brightly modern picaresque comedy about the adventures of an innocent young man, a twentieth-century Candide, from the time he is unjustly sent down from his Oxford college to the time just over a year later when he returns to it, having been witness to a modern world fantastic in its nature and challenging to all his liberal assumptions. Meantime everything has happened to him, and also nothing. He has taught at a rogue school, met a great variety of confusingly anarchic characters, spent a 'very modern night of love' with Margot Beste-Chetwynde, a society lady who doubles as a brothel-keeper, gone to prison, and been mysteriously released. He finally discovers the 'still small voice' of conscience, which means that he doesn't really belong in the anarchic modern world at all, and ends back exactly as he began. But he too is not a hero, as Waugh carefully explains in the text: 'the whole of this book is really an account of the mysterious disappearance of Paul Pennyfeather, so that readers must not complain if the shadow which took his name does not amply fill out the important part of hero for which he was originally cast.' He is not a hero because this is not a world for heroes, and also because the disappearance of the human element is part of the story of the modern world – as Professor

Silenus, the voice of modernity, explains: 'What an immature, self-destructive, antiquated mischief is man! ... on the one side the harmonious instincts and balanced responses of the animal, on the other the inflexible purpose of the machine, and between them man, equally alien from the *being* of Nature and the *doing* of the machine, this vile *becoming*!' Silenus sees the problem of art as 'the elimination of the human element from the consideration of form'.

And so in his way does Waugh. His achievement was indeed the creation of a complete style, an impassive, ethically neutral, modern comic form. The writer stands at the centre of his comedy, omniscient but evasive, surrounded by his own distinct universe of outrage and absurdity. His world passes by as an impression, a mad collage without psychological depth, flickering, quickly rendered, made with short scenes, rapid pace, comically vivid and yet characterless characters whose lives and reality do not detain us. His characters deliberately lack deep psychology, and live in a world that operates according to whim, chance or fortune, an anarchic 'modern' universe beyond moral law. Waugh's later work gives a history to this state of modern alienation and human meaninglessness. His early work simply represents it, as a plain state of affairs. And while in *Decline and Fall* Paul can simply leave the anarchic world, in the next novels there is no escape. In *Vile Bodies* (1930) the worlds of black comedy and contemporary history exactly overlap. Despite his name, Adam, the central character, is no innocent, and has to manage his survival within the world of vile bodies, 'faster, faster', mad motor races, flimsy affairs, brief marriages, economic chaos, dead religion, a 'radical instability of the world order'. The vision is of the last days, the impulse is toward herd-suicide; the novel closes on a war between unspecified parties on 'the biggest battlefield in the history of the world'. And so it was onward into Waugh's remarkable fiction of the Thirties, which is discussed in the next chapter.

The fiction of the Twenties can be seen in two ways: as a consolidation of the Modern movement, the realization of a series of artistic developments that had been taking place over twenty-five years; or as its opposite, the product of an apocalyptic moment that had fractured all traditions, even the Modern one, leaving the writer with a new kind of task, as Lawrence claimed in his wartime and post-war comments. 'Ours is essentially a tragic age, so we refuse to take it tragically,' begins his *Lady Chatterley's Lover* (1928), the book in which he attempted to take the age both tragically and comically (it is filled with satirical social observation), and his largest culture-reading of the post-war age. 'The cataclysm has happened, we are among the ruins, we start to build up new little habits, to have new little hopes . . . This was more or less Constance Chatterley's position. The war had brought the roof down over her head. And she had realized one must live and learn.' This had been the theme of his writing since *Women in Love*. In *Aaron's Rod* (1922), which starts with the end of the war, in *Kangaroo* (1923), a political novel set in Australia, and *The Plumed Serpent* (1926), a mythic romance set in Mexico, he had sought new transformations, looked for new social orders, new forms of leadership, new depths of primitivism, to salvage the age or the individual. These are novels of a long search through darkness and the irrational that has been bred, as much as anything, by the war itself. *Lady Chatterley* . . . was his last major work of fiction, written and published in Italy, and in its full form it was kept from British and American audiences until the 1950s. In it he returned home again, to the English Midlands and its natural and social landscape, to the 'Condition of England' novel, and to much of the spirit of his earlier writing, except that his world is now entirely dominated by the 'bruise of the false inhuman war'. This has cancelled 'all the great words', love, joy, happiness, even sex: 'the last of the great words, it was just a cocktail term for an excitement that bucked you up for a while, then left you more raggy than ever.'

Lady Chatterley . . . is a dark fable of social and sexual sterility, a story of the 'gap in the continuity of consciousness' that makes the modern person a creature of mechanism rather than feeling, producing the thin post-cataclysmic sensibility that forms the flavour of the novel, and against which Mellors, the good soldier-survivor, revolts. The book went through three distinct drafts, playing the story in different ways, and offering, in the earlier versions, some promise of a political solution to the crisis afflicting an England divided between the classes, between the industrial and pastoral, the mechanical and passional, and flowing toward death. In the decisive final version this is withdrawn, and the bad time is coming still; it is only the language of intimate personal tenderness, and the vernacular sexual language of that tenderness, that offers an answer, though one that itself does not satisfy; the end is still nigh. The apocalyptic message is strong, here as in much else that came from the later Twenties. It can be long argued whether the darkened apocalyptic mood of Twenties Modernism represented an essential spirit or, as some American writers like William Carlos Williams argued, a gloomy European diversion away from its artistic promises. Later critics, notably George Orwell, came to question this Twilight of the Gods feeling in a different way, as an aesthete's attempt to reject history by substituting art for real politics, though in the end history was to prove no better muse. What is true is that during the Twenties the direction of fiction sharply changed, and the Modernist adventure that had been growing from the later nineteenth century generally took on a new apocalyptic note. The fact remains that some of the greatest, and also the most various, works of modern British fiction came from the moment, and they have retained their power over the fate and fortune of the novel ever since.

4

Closing Time in the Gardens: 1930–1945

Nina looked down and saw inclined at an odd angle a horizon of straggling red suburb; arterial roads dotted with little cars; factories, some of them working, others empty and decaying; a disused canal; some distant hills sown with bungalows; wireless masts and overhead power cables; men and women were indiscernible except as tiny spots; they were marrying and shopping and making money and having children. The scene lurched and tilted again as the aeroplane struck a current of air.

'I think I'm going to be sick,' said Nina.

'Poor little girl,' said Ginger. 'That's what the paper bags are for.'
Evelyn Waugh,
Vile Bodies (1930)

'Nothing dreadful is ever done with, no bad thing gets any better; you can't be too serious.' This is the message of the Forties from which, alas, there seems no escape, for it is closing time in the gardens of the West and from now on an artist will be judged only by the resonance of his solitude or the quality of his despair.
Cyril Connolly, 'Editorial',
Horizon (Dec. 1949/Jan. 1950)

1

It was one of the implications of the post-war Modern movement that the Crisis of the Word and the Crisis of the World were intimately linked. This is why, when we revisit many of the great works of the early Twenties, we can scarcely miss the way they seem shaken into being by crisis and change, the disaster of war and the feelings of historical chaos and futility that followed it, which gave them both their mood of despair, loss and exile, and their artistic tactics of fracture, fragmentation, and linguistic crisis. Yet, in the early Twenties, the consequence of this visible 'crisis' is frequently a new adventure into form, an excited rediscovery of art, a rejection of the decadence of history for the lasting value of aesthetic space. During the rest of the decade, this aesthetic but despairing view of 'modern' writing, the famous 'Waste Land' sensibility, penetrated a good part of the serious literature of Europe – though in the United States a more optimistic view of the alliance between futuristic progress and modern form was often felt. By the decade's end, when it became even clearer how little the war had achieved in creating European stability or worthwhile social change, the climate of historical dismay, impotent outrage and anxious pessimism greatly increased. It was made plain in a whole sequence of war, or rather anti-war, books – Edmund Blunden's *Undertones of War*, Siegfried Sassoon's *Memoirs of a Fox-Hunting Man* and R. C. Sherriff's *Journey's End* in 1928, Richard Aldington's *Death of a Hero*, Robert Graves's *Goodbye to All That*, Henry Williamson's *The Wet Flanders Plain*, Erich Maria Remarque's *All Quiet on the Western Front* and Hemingway's *A Farewell to Arms* in 1929, Frederic Manning's *Her Privates We*, H. M. Tomlinson's *All Our Yesterdays* and Hašek's *The Good Soldier Schweik* in 1930, and so on – which indicated all the war had done was to leave its survivors and successors in a shattered, unmanageable, directionless world. Novels like Waugh's *Decline and Fall*, Lawrence's *Lady Chatterley's Lover*, both published in 1928, were already exploring the still more terrible thought that the age lay *entre deux guerres*, between two world wars; and in 1929 a friend of W. H. Auden was 'talking excitedly of a final war'. Younger novelists, like Waugh, Christopher Isherwood (*All the Conspirators*, 1928) and Graham Greene (*The Man Within*, 1929), and the poets who would soon be known as 'the Auden generation', writers who had been born in the first years of the century and inherited the Twenties from the deeds of their elders, were already writing of and in a shattered, historically hopeless, morally damaged world. And, much as those same elders had felt themselves in revolt against the Victorians, so they felt their own revolt was one against the Edwardian and early Georgian age. They consciously belonged to a new generation, with a new and damaged history. And, claimed Isherwood in his fictionalized autobiography *Lions and Shadows: An Education in the Twenties* (1938), 'we young writers of the middle 'twenties were all suffering, more or less subconsciously, from a feeling of shame that we had not been old enough to take part in the European war.'

The mood of generational change was plain well before the Twenties were over. 'Only from about the year 1926 did the features of the post-war world begin to emerge – and not only in the sphere of politics,' wrote T. S. Eliot in January 1939, in a sad final editorial for his review *The Criterion*, when the war these new writers had imaginatively prospected was about to begin: 'From about that date one began slowly to realize that the intellectual and artistic output of the previous seven years [the peak years of Modernism] had been rather the last efforts of an old world, than the struggles of the new.' By the mid Twenties, the great 'Shock of the New' had already passed: 'modern' experience and material was now familiar matter in art, fashionable as bobbed hair, and the opening of a Museum of Modern Art in New York in 1929 marked a clear acceptance of what was once thought avant-garde and totally outrageous. The avant-garde was already set to become a modern institution, and a number of the writers whose work began from small presses in Paris were turning into popular authors. A writing of civilized misery, historical sterility and class uncertainty became common; as Erich Auerbach said in *Mimesis* (1953), one increasingly found in writing 'a hatred of culture and civilization, brought about by the subtlest artistic devices culture and civilization have developed, and often a radical and fanatical urge to destroy'.

But, as the Thirties dawned, the note of ominous disorder and historical nervousness grew ever stronger. This is what W. H. Auden, the poet whose tight economy and wit of image did so much to give a language to the Thirties, indicates in his famous 'diagnostic' poem '1929': 'It is time for the destruction of error. / The chairs are being brought in from the garden, / The summer talk stopped on that savage coast . . . / In the sanatoriums they laugh less and less, / Less certain of cure; and the loud madman / Sinks now into a terrible calm.' 1929 was a key date for obvious reasons – the year in which a condition of political modernity perhaps seventy years in the making suddenly jolted forward toward totalitarianism, dictatorship, rearmament, disaster. Politics were back: in a climate of deep social and economic unease, a General Strike and a growth of poverty, Labour's second Government came to office in Britain that year. Then a decade that had opened with one historical crisis, the uneasy armistice at the end of a Great War, ended on yet another, the coming of the Great Crash; in November that year the American stock market failed. By the end of the year, and on more than the calendar, the Twenties were over, their moral, stylistic and psychological credit exhausted, their tinsel settling to earth – as one of their best interpreters, F. Scott Fitzgerald, observed. Capitalism seemed to be entering a terminal decline; economic realities – if anything to do with economics can ever be called a reality – took over. And so did totalistic political solutions: Stalin's Bolshevik Russia radiated its powerful ideological and modernizing influence, a Germany enfeebled by punitive war reparations, inflation and class disintegration bred a new era of national socialism, Nazism, and in Mussolini's Italy the highly Futuristic movement of Fascism rose. All modern histories were now globally interconnected, and the European crisis was reflected and repeated in Britain itself. In 1931 the nation came off the Gold Standard; in 1932 unemployment peaked at 2.8 million, Oswald Mosley founded the British Union of Fascists and Communist Party membership multiplied. In 1933 Hitler became German Chancellor, and the Communist International prophesied 'a new round of revolutions and wars'. In 1934 Fascists took over in Austria; in 1936 came the Spanish Civil War – the war which, thanks to outside intervention, became the battlefield of the 'modern' ideologies, the harbinger of the greater European war that emerged fully-fledged in 1939.

By 1930 the Twenties was already a distinct decade, slipping away into history. But it quickly seemed the Thirties was shaping up to be another equally distinctive decade, a trough between Great Crash and future crisis. In the event, its cycle would last almost exactly ten years too, from the Slump of autumn 1929 to the outbreak of World War in autumn 1939. This time there was no doubt at all that the war had been imaginatively prefigured; matters of peace and war, violence and disorder, politics and ideology, dominated most of the writing of the decade. The writers of the Twenties had thought of themselves as a generation, probably a 'lost' generation. The writers of the Thirties soon saw themselves as one too: the 'Thirties Generation', or, eventually, taking the name of the most influential of the 'diagnostic' poets (poetry played a big part in the writing of the decade), the 'Auden Generation'. For, just like the decade itself, notable for its terrifying massing of groups, armies, crowds, parades, causes and ideologies, it was their instinct to be collective – one reason why so many modern studies of this time treat them collectively.[1] For the novel at least, the term 'Auden generation' is plainly too narrow; but it does help remind us that the generational, collective climate in writing was not simply a matter of the grouping tendencies of the decade. It also came from the intimate networking of writers, who so often shared backgrounds – schools, famous universities (Oxford and Cambridge, or Oxbridge), friendships, partners, homosexual brotherhoods – in common, and frequently commented on, or collaborated in, each other's work. We think of the Thirties as an age of 'proletarian' writing, and important figures like Lewis Grassic Gibbon, Walter Greenwood, James Hanley, Walter Brierley, Sid Chaplin and others wrote fine working-class fiction during the decade. It seemed the social origins of literary writing were changing, and there were other writers, above all C. P. Snow and William Cooper (Harry Hoff) who were exploring society from the near-Wellsian standpoint of the provincial, grammar-school, scientifically trained meritocracy, while regional fiction grew in importance. The fact

1 See, for instance, Samuel Hynes's *The Auden Generation: Literature and Politics in England in the 1930s* (Princeton, 1976), and Valentine Cunningham's wonderfully capacious *British Writers of the Thirties* (Oxford and New York, 1989), as well as the many memoirs by Christopher Isherwood, Stephen Spender, John Lehmann, Louis MacNeice, Cyril Connolly, George Orwell, Graham Greene, Evelyn Waugh, Henry Green and others.

remains that never before in British writing had a particular cadre, the socially connected, well-educated, public-school and university intelligentsia, been so obviously influential. A large proportion of the dominant authors were sons or daughters of doctors, army officers, literary journalists, academics, Anglican ministers or earlier writers. The world of their social and educational background – Waugh's Oxford, Isherwood's Cambridge, Greene's Berkhamsted school, Orwell's St Cyprian's – became part of the literary landscape, one reason, no doubt, why narratives set in lesser-known schools and redbrick or new universities provided some of the key contradictory myths of the fiction of the Fifties.[2] If anything, in these left-wing and political times, British fiction narrowed rather than widened in social source, though it broadened widely in other ways – through travel, through increased consciousness of European and world politics, through extensive social observation, through large-scale historical 'diagnosis'. But the shared social culture and background does so much to explain the private cadences and allusions of quite a lot of writing, to the point where Cyril Connolly once suggested that the writers of the period were held in a state of permanent adolescence, still eternally at their prep and public schools. One result of this was a pervasive note of class guilt, as social and economic change, a conviction of long-term historical crisis, and generational anger was applied to that most elegant and intricate of human artifices, the British class system, which has given so much to the nature of the novel. An air of social anxiety, political instability, liberal dismay, crypto-exile, runs through the writing of an era, as an old

---

2 In his *Children of the Sun: A Narrative of 'Decadence' in England After 1918* (London, 1977), Martin Green offers an interesting list, noting that of the writers, artists and political figures he deals with, many went to similar prep schools, and similar or the same public schools: 'Waugh and [Tom] Driberg went to Lancing: [John] Betjeman, [Louis] MacNeice, [T. C.] Worsley, and [Anthony] Blunt went to Marlborough. And to Eton went . . . [George] Orwell, [Harold] Acton, [Brian] Howard, [Robert] Byron, [Cyril] Connolly, [Henry] Green, [Anthony] Powell, [Oliver] Messel, [Alan] Pryce-Jones, [John] Lehmann, [Ian] Fleming, [Randolph] Churchill and [Guy] Burgess. From there most went on either to Oxford or Cambridge.' Humphrey Carpenter also follows the Oxford story in *The Brideshead Generation*. Also see my *The Social Context of Modern English Literature* (Oxford and New York, 1971).

establishment sought to disestablish itself, and find a different place in, a fresh angle on, history.

2

No wonder that this was the age of the 'writer's dilemma', and that, whatever the writer's origins, the belief that a new literary accounting was necessary grew widespread. It was a time when, as Jean-Paul Sartre proposed in *What Is Literature?* (1947), writers hesitated between proclaiming the new world and being the gravediggers of the old, when 'Historicity flowed in upon us'. The Thirties was a nightmare decade, and produced a nightmare literature, a daydreaming on the edge of the real world, where even the fabric of daily commonplace experience – schooldays, family life, suburban domesticity – generally acquired a surreal aspect of estrangement and horror. In Graham Greene's distinctive and intensely autobiographical universe, as in Isherwood's, there are always corruptions in the dorm, deceits in the passageways, strange creatures beneath the garden, a gun in the bathroom cupboard. Writing filled with sinister, Gothic images ('the hooded women, the hump-backed surgeons,/ And the Scissor Man' of Auden's 'The Witnesses'). Writers assumed poses of disguise and self-concealment, found themselves ever crossing both sides of the social, moral and sexual borders, thought of themselves as exiles or spies in their own countries ('Our hopes were set still on the spies' career,' wrote Auden, ever good with a line; one result of all this was the spy scandals and Moscow flights of the Fifties and the Sixties). They hid names and backgrounds behind pseudonyms; the Etonian Eric Blair who turned into the proletarian George Orwell, and was scarred by the birthmark of his origins, was by no means the only dramatic self-transformer. They surveyed their landscape with an aerial detachment (Auden saw himself as 'the helmeted airman'), and travelled to live their lives in secret abroad. These detached aerial views oscillated with painful psychological frankness; Auden revealed his 'neural itch', Stephen Spender was suitably described as 'redeeming the world by introspection'.

Meanwhile History itself had taken over from the artist as the great experimentalist, and writers felt passive before it. If the serious writers of the Twenties had generally seen themselves as a vanguard, advancing, individualistically, aesthetically, apolitically, under the banner of the experimental arts, those of the Thirties often saw themselves as inert agents driven by 'inevitable', 'necessary' forces beyond their own individuality, requiring collective homage (what, asked Louis MacNeice, 'would we have history say/ Of us who walked in our sleep and died on our Quest?'). In the Twenties History was a fool that knew nothing, a nightmare from which the artist was trying to awake. In the Thirties the writer was, it seemed, inescapably inside the nightmare, so that novelty in literature increasingly came from a 'diagnostic' or 'psychological' response to the strangenesses, terrors and irrationality of the historical world. From this chaos, politics seemed, for a time, to offer an escape. In a recurrent Thirties enterprise writers 'took sides', fighting each other, and the bourgeois class from which they generally came. The aesthetic revolts of the Twenties turned into the class wars and ideological confrontations of a new decade when (as the new critical magazine *Scrutiny* ironically observed) the question 'Under Which King, Bezonian?' was endlessly asked. 'As an Englishman I am not in the predicament of choosing between two evils,' Evelyn Waugh answered when the *Left Review* polled writers' allegiances during the Spanish Civil War. 'I am not a Fascist nor shall I become one unless it were the only alternative to Marxism. It is mischievous to suggest such a choice is imminent.' But this was bold and unusual; for most writers the choice *was* imminent, already made for them by History, in advance. Most looked Left, going 'forward from Liberalism' via anti-Fascism to Communism and the Party, or somewhere 'committed' close by. Especially later in the decade, some (Julian Bell, John Cornford, Christopher Caudwell) forgot preliminaries and were militant Marxists from the start. Others looked Right, like T. S. Eliot, with his Anglo-Catholic/Classicist/ Royalist sympathies, or Wyndham Lewis. Others (like Waugh and Greene) looked up, to God, especially when Catholic, searching beyond left and right or right and wrong to good and evil.

According to Stephen Spender, in his very typical, and very liberal, polemical work *Forward from Liberalism* (1937), the death of liberalism and hence the forthcoming alliance between the writer and Marxism was the crucial issue. 'The Individual has died before . . .' resignedly announced MacNeice in his 'Epitaph for Liberal Poets'. If this was true (there were many writers who never did feel it was), then it is also notable how variously un-Marxist much of the best writing of the decade finally is. For one thing, many of these writers had actually started their careers in the Twenties, and done their literary apprenticeship with *Ulysses* and 'The Waste Land', the poem disturbingly read out at Oxford in Waugh's powerful retrospect of the doubled Twenties-and-Thirties era, *Brideshead Revisited* (1945). The fiction of the Thirties echoes with Joycean sounds – in early Isherwood and Henry Green, in Samuel Beckett and Malcolm Lowry, who freely confessed he was 'Joyced with his own petard' – just as the poetry is filled with Eliotic remnants. Modernism and Thirties writing existed in uneasy coalition right through the decade, and Bloomsbury remained a power in the land well into the Fifties. T. S. Eliot's *Criterion* published, in January 1930, Auden's charade 'Paid on Both Sides', generally seen as the first testimonial statement of Thirties writing, and, for all its 'classicist' line, went on supporting the new writers (even printing Hugh McDiarmid's 'Hymn to Lenin'). Leonard and Virginia Woolf's Hogarth Press published the Michael Roberts anthologies *New Signatures* (1932) and *New Country* (1933) which set out the younger writers collectively; and it also brought out many of their books (Isherwood's, Henry Green's), thanks largely to John Lehmann, the supporter of 'new writing' who worked for the press. Quarrels came: Eliot challenged the Marxists and ideologists; Virginia Woolf expressed her criticism of the new Leftists looking out from their leaning tower, built on parental gold, in a forceful last essay of 1940 'The Leaning Tower'.

Similarly, the new writers found Modernism a 'distortion' or an 'irrelevance', Eliot a 'reactionary' and Woolf's fiction of the Thirties over-aesthetic, precious and 'unsocial' ('elegant arabesques', as even Lytton Strachey put it). But certain links were plain; in a way it was the darkness in Modernism that excused the 'dream of violence' of the 'new' Thirties writing. So when Spender wrote his study of modern writing *The Destructive Element* (1935), he took his title from a potent phrase of Conrad's, and, in a convenient rewriting, acknowledged a basic continuity between the Modern movement, with its Twenties note of Waste Land sensibility and Spenglerian decline, and his own contemporaries. However, where the Moderns wrote 'subjectively', in an age without belief or clear values, the new generation, he claimed, had produced a writing that was 'objective and social'. Later, after the Marxist God had failed, he observed in his autobiography *World Within World* (1951): 'perhaps, after all, the qualities that distinguished us from the writers of the previous decade lay not in ourselves, but in the events to which we reacted.' Perhaps so: the pervasive note of a good deal of Thirties writing is not, finally, its political engagement but the spectacle of its liberal experimentalists trying and failing to be engaged. 'Writers were scared now, and very rightly too,' Pamela Hansford Johnson once brusquely commented. 'For the first time since 1918 they had to face the fact that *they personally* might be starved, degraded, tortured, murdered. They had to write for their lives: and in the face of that necessity, "art for art's sake" became to them temporarily without meaning.' This may be too hard, but much Thirties writing is a battlefield of liberal anxiety, where crisis in history and politics is also a crisis of self and identity. This then led on to that distinguishing air of secrecy, self-concealment, wanderlust, exile, infidelity, existential crisis, seediness, inauthenticity and betrayal, all perhaps to be solved by 'commitment', political, religious, psychoanalytic, existential, that runs through so much of the writing of the whole decade. In fact we can already find in Thirties writing much of that dark existential disquiet, about the lost soul caught in the sink of history, that would return in much writing after the new, 'absurdist' crisis of the Second World War.

One useful marker of the transition from Twenties to Thirties is the passage from the very Twenties word 'modern' to the very Thirties word 'new'. During the Twenties all that was experimental was also 'modern'; in the Thirties nearly all the various magazines and anthologies that attempted to capture the changing climate sported the word 'new' somewhere in the title. In 1932 Michael Roberts's famous anthology *New Signatures*, printing poetry by Auden,

Spender, Cecil Day Lewis, William Empson and others, proclaimed editorially that this was not just work of a 'new' generation, but a fresh unesoteric poetry where 'imagery taken from contemporary life consistently appeared as the natural and spontaneous expression of the poet's thought and feeling'. That year F. R. Leavis published *New Bearings in English Poetry*, emphasizing a different but no less radical lineage, focused on Eliot; his wife Q. D. Leavis published her *Fiction and the Reading Public*, looking at the impact of the new mass culture on the novel; and they both started the Cambridge critical magazine *Scrutiny*, which became a central voice of what would be called 'New Criticism'. Oxford, better known for writers than critics, came out with the left-wing *New Oxford Outlook*. In 1933 Roberts produced his second anthology *New Country*, adding 'new' prose by Isherwood and Edward Upward, and a marked steer to the Left; the editorial announced that as the writer sees 'his interests are bound up with those of the working-class, so will his writing clear itself from the complexity and introspection, the doubt and cynicism, of recent years'. (It never did.) That year Geoffrey Grigson started *New Verse*; in 1934 H. E. Bates and others began *New Stories*. In 1936, as the Spanish Civil War began, the 'new' endeavour was pulled together in John Lehmann's elegantly produced *New Writing*, later extended into *Folios of New Writing* and *New Writing and Daylight*. Publishing poetry, fiction, criticism and reportage, displaying a strong leftward emphasis as well as a strong European dimension, it printed much that was remarkable: Isherwood's *The Nowaks*, Edward Upward's *The Border Line*, Rex Warner's *The Wild Goose Chase*, George Orwell's *Shooting an Elephant*, notable working-class writing by James Hanley, George Garrett, Sid Chaplin and B. L. Coombes, important European work by Boris Pasternak, Bertolt Brecht, Ignazio Silone and Jean-Paul Sartre. These would provide valuable funds when, in 1940, with war begun, the venture developed into *Penguin New Writing*, a cheap paperback magazine with many of the same writers, and large wartime sales, which kept the creative and reportorial record of the dark years and the period of Cold War, rationing and austerity that followed. It closed in 1950.

3

What, then, was 'new'? Plainly quite a lot of the best writing of the Thirties was not, if only because it was 'modern'. It was a writing that came directly from change, responding to the rising political disorder, ideological confrontation and crowd frenzy of what had become an age not of the avant-garde but of the cumulative modern masses. It aspired in its own way to be a 'mass', or at least a 'public', writing, as Lehmann explained in his Penguin volume *New Writing in Europe*, published in 1940, where he sought to place it in what was now a historical perspective. He recorded the growth, in the early Thirties, of 'a group of poets and prose-writers who were conscious of the great social, political and moral changes going on around them, and who became increasingly convinced that it was their business to communicate their vision of this process, not merely to the so-called highbrow intellectual public to which their predecessors had addressed themselves, but to the widest possible circles of ordinary people engaged in the daily struggle for existence'. 'New writing', he said, marked an extension of the Modernist rebellion past the crisis of 1929–31. This 'cracked the world of the twenties beyond repair', demanding a fresh awareness of historical realities and progressive aims, a move beyond aesthetic humanism to social realism and report-age, a need to search for a 'proletarian' writing (and *New Writing* encouraged a good many working-class writers, though never to the point where they dominated). The result was often a strange, uneasy marriage between 'Bloomsbury' and 'public writing', aestheticism and social realism. The chief 'new writers' frequently emerged both as bour-geois and anti-bourgeois, scientists and subjects of their own experi-ment, diagnosticians and their own patients, in what Auden called 'this country of ours where no one is well'. Reportage, sociology, 'mass observation' provided one important discourse; so did the new gurus of psychoanalysis, above all Georg Groddeck and Homer Lane, special-ists in various forms of the 'neural itch'. 'New writing' was the product of a decade essentially, 'inevitably', preoccupied with itself, and in that very fact it proved to be what it intended to be, 'symptomatic'.

'New writing' was not alone in its distinctive characterization of the nightmare decade, in which history became a machine, society a battlefield and neurosis the typical inner condition. Writers left and right explored chaos, the 'destructive element', and the systems, rational and irrational, that might control it. They travelled, everywhere, until they generally became foreign travellers at home, or proto-Europeans in their own land. Isherwood, the passive camera, went to homosexual – which also, as the wheel of history turned, proved Fascist – Berlin; others, from Greene to Waugh to Malcolm Lowry, went to Abyssinia, Mexico or wherever the age's borderlands – frontiers of right and left, God and dialectical materialism, civilization and barbarism – lay. The dangerous border, the risky frontier, the barbed-wire fence, the local revolution, indeed became the grand metaphors for the age, and the view from the air, or some other angle of detachment, became ever more important. Meanwhile Lawrence's 'bad time coming' and Waugh's 'biggest battlefield in the history of the world' ran like a lode-bearing seam through the literature of the era, moving from surreal fantasy toward historical actuality. '*It's going to happen*,' George Orwell wrote in *Coming Up for Air* in gloomy 1939. 'All the things you've got at the back of your mind, the things you're terrified of, the things you tell yourself are just a nightmare or only happen in foreign countries.' In the time of nightmare, writers, and writing itself, increasingly aspired to action: travelling, flying, hiking, climbing, bicycling, and going – as by 1936 many were ready to do – to war. With the Spanish Civil War, Thirties writing, and especially 'new writing', found both its moment and its crisis. Many went to report or participate, a significant number died, and others, like George Orwell, returned disillusioned, the agreed ideological certainties already half-dissolved.

'I proceed like a somnambulist,' Adolf Hitler, who dominated the decade, once declared. So, in its later half, did most of the writers of the Thirties. Lehmann meant his *New Writing in Europe* to show, he said, how 'the seed which lay at the heart of the whole movement, – to put it shortly, the idea of a *public* writing, of speaking to the people and with the people in their struggle for a better world, – reached its full flowering during the early part of the Spanish [Civil] War.' But he also says that it was now the programme began to collapse – 'the real disintegration started before the War was over' – and the spirit of the Thirties changed into something else. History did this too. In March 1938 Hitler assumed the powers of War Minister, and marched into Austria; Mussolini won international support for his annexation of Abyssinia; Franco was beginning to triumph in Spain; in the Soviet Union that spring, Stalin's show trials revealed him as yet another totalitarian dictator. The troubled fantasies and prophecies that already filled poetry and fiction became actuality; dictators and gener-alissimos were taking charge; jackboots and strutting armies, street parades and saluting masses, rolling tanks and overflying bombers dominated not just imaginative fiction, as they already had, but European reality. In the autumn of 1938 Chamberlain went to Munich and won his famous piece of paper; German troops entered the Sudetenland. Right across Europe, air-raid shelters were dug, gas-masks issued, doors broken down; midnight arrests took place, books were burned – those of the German Nobel prizewinner Thomas Mann in his own country, as he joined the flight of displaced persons, persecuted races and literary exiles for the United States. 'If I were asked,' Lehmann writes, 'I would say the first date in the disintegration [of the Thirties consensus] was the Munich agreement of September 1938, the second the final overthrow of the Spanish Republic in the following spring, and the third the outbreak of international war in September 1939, – or the Russo-German pact which preceded it.' As he said later in his memoir *The Whispering Gallery* (1955), a hangover had set in, and now the best books were those that illuminated 'not the cruelties of fascism and the perversions of fascist thinking, but the equally menacing ideals that fanatical left-wing idealism could lead to'. The coming of war and new militarization completed the process. By the time Lehmann summed up the 'new', it had already transmuted into something else: a reportage of battle, the struggle of shaving through the Blitz, the fear of universal totalitarianism. Lehmann turned his eyes from Russia to America, as did a good number of Thirties writers. By early 1939 Auden and Isherwood had already joined the rising tide of European exiles departing Europe for the States, and their later work largely became a revisionist version, a fundamental rewriting, of their writing of the Thirties. It was not very long before the Thirties turned from an age of political progress to the 'low dishonest decade'.

This changing viewpoint can be read in the very form of the fiction of the period. The Thirties had begun with a hunger for historical realism. But, as J. A. Morris convincingly argues, the political and military developments of the later decade, and the gradual collapse of the Marxist argument for 'proletarian realism', released many of the under-movements that were always apparent in the writing of the decade: satire, allegory, parable, fable and fantasy.[3] Modern history now seemed less a conflict of clearly defined ideological forces than a mass psychosis. The novels of Kafka were translated into English, by Edwin and Willa Muir, across the decade: *The Castle* in 1930, *The Trial* in 1937, *America* in 1938. In a world itself grown – the term found extensive employment – 'Kafkaesque', Kafka seemed, of all the moderns, the most relevant, his strangely gothicized and psychological forms the most useful, his extreme inner exile the most telling of prophecies. 'Balzac carried a cane on which was written the legend: I smash all obstacles,' he had written in his diary: 'my legend runs: every obstacle smashes me.' He had expressed, ambiguously, a wish to suppress his books at his death in 1924. Now the suppression his executor Max Brod had refused was happening; his books were banned in Germany, then in his own Czechoslovakia, occupied in 1939, and he was one of the age's many silenced writers. By the decade's end his metaphysical fantasy of modern exposure and absurdity entered much new writing. 1938 saw the publication in Paris of Jean-Paul Sartre's novel *La Nausée* (*Nausea*), perhaps the first true work of modern existentialism ('The word remains on my lips; it refuses to go and rest upon the thing'), Samuel Beckett's work of philosophical absurdism *Murphy* and Lawrence Durrell's surrealist

---

3 J. A. Morris, *Writers and Politics in Modern Britain, 1880–1950* (London, 1977), which argues: 'Indicative of the shift from commitment to an inward-looking, self-questioning debate on where man stood in society, in the world or even in the universe, is the variety of literary styles to appear in the late thirties . . . By the late 1930s and early 1940s generic terms such as allegory, satire, parody, fable, pastiche had become increasingly applicable.'

The Black Book. Graham Greene published his most existential novel *Brighton Rock*, Rex Warner his surreal fantasy of persecution *The Professor*, Edward Upward his no less surreal fable of the bourgeois spirit *Journey to the Border*, Eric Ambler his thriller *Epitaph for a Spy*; and the year also saw Auden and Isherwood's play *On the Frontier* and Spender's *The Trial of a Judge*. 1939 brought not only war and the summative masterwork of the Modern movement, Joyce's *Finnegans Wake*, but Orwell's grim war prophecy *Coming Up for Air*, Isherwood's *Goodbye to Berlin* and Henry Green's ironic fantasy *Party-Going* ('what targets – what targets for a bomb'). And in 1940, Arthur Koestler published his truly Kafkaesque novel of the modern Marxist state *Darkness at Noon*, intimately linking the world of inner and outer crisis ('when the two officials of the People's Commissariat of the Interior were hammering on Rubashov's door, in order to arrest him, Rubashov was just dreaming that he was being arrested').

When an earlier generation of writers confronted the coming of the Great War, some at least saw it as heroic on the one hand, or cleansing and futuristic on the other. The mood across Europe as the Second World War approached was quite different. In his autobiography *World Within World* (1951) Stephen Spender emphasizes the mood of emotional and aesthetic passivity, taking a telling note from his diary: 'Peter Watson travelled from Paris to Calais a few days ago in a troop train. The compartment was crowded with soldiers. They sat all the way in absolute silence, no one saying a word.' The passivity resembled the sense of an art swamped by events that had grown through the decade – in, for instance, the deliberately enfeebled, flatly observing, camera-eye of Isherwood's Berlin stories. For the age of historical enormity, journalism, reportage, the diary and the memoir seemed the only proper instruments; in fact they would occupy many of *Penguin New Writing*'s pages in the wartime years. The First World War provoked new vortices of artistic energy; the Second did not – perhaps because, as the poet Keith Douglas said, the same horrors cannot be written twice. A fiction long haunted by images of the barbed-wire frontier, the marauding raid, the aerial bombardment, the shattered factory, plastic false teeth, ersatz sausages, the food queue, the ration book, the gas-mask and fumbling Waste Land lusts

– 'the slogans, the enormous faces, the machine-guns spurting out of bedroom windows' that Orwell had foreseen in *Coming Up for Air* – turned into reported actuality, as the sirens sounded over London, the air-raids began and soldiers went to war. All this was background to Orwell's essay 'Inside the Whale' (1940), written as war began, where he claimed that an age of totalitarianism had silenced writing, and shown 'the impossibility of any major literature until the world has shaken itself into a new shape'. Looking back across writing since the Great War, he observed three possible postures for the writer. One was Modernism, with its Twilight of the Gods feeling, which he found 'reactionary'; another was the 'committed' writing of the Thirties, which he challenged for its 'orthodoxy-sniffing'; the third was quietism, the response of the writer who, imprisoned in the womb of history, trapped inside the whale, makes a passive, obscene, impotent protest, as the American writer Henry Miller, much admired by Orwell (who borrowed his jacket to go to Spain), had done. The age of liberalism was over, in the time of totalitarian dictatorships and the militarized state: 'The literature of liberalism is coming to an end and the literature of totalitarianism has not yet appeared and is barely imaginable,' he wrote: 'As for the writer, he is sitting on a melting iceberg: he is merely an anachronism, a hangover from the bourgeois age, as surely doomed as the hippopotamus.'

By one of the better fortunes of modern history, this was to prove excessive. Universal totalitarianism did not prevail, however much the grim modern century pointed toward it; and one of the first works of the post-war era was Orwell's own *Animal Farm* (1945), a satire on totalitarianism addressed to liberal readers. But the gloom he expressed was widespread. It had been encouraged by the murder of writers in Russia and Germany, the exiling of many more, the sudden deaths of yet others – including Yeats, Freud, Joyce and Virginia Woolf, now seen as some of the key figures of the Modern movement. 'Periods end when we are not looking,' wrote Cyril Connolly (who actually aimed to rescue the situation by bringing over a hundred writers and intellectuals from the USA) in his magazine *Horizon* in August 1941; 'The last two years have been a turning point; an epidemic of dying has ended many movements.' But it was not only

Modernism that was reaching its dying fall. So was the political writing of the Thirties. Orwell was only early in renouncing Communism for patriotism. Committed writers were now exiling themselves from history, uncommitting their commitments; six of them famously announced their ideological withdrawal from the church of Marx in *The God That Failed* in 1949. Others fell silent, or audibly theorized about silence. Evelyn Waugh best caught the mood in *Work Suspended* (1941), a novel under way as war began which he symbolically left unfinished – 'all our lives, as we have constructed them, quietly came to an end,' says the narrator; 'Our story, like my novel, remained unfinished – a heap of neglected foolscap at the back of a drawer.' But not all novels remained unfinished: a number of writers, including Graham Greene and Henry Green, Elizabeth Bowen and V. S. Pritchett, and indeed Orwell and Waugh, produced some of their best work in or around the war. The war and the Blitz made Greene's seedy Greeneland seem entirely natural, and it reinforced the shattered fragility of Bowen's writing. New writers of war appeared, mostly in short fiction – Alun Lewis, Denton Welch, J. Maclaren-Ross. Nonetheless something seeped from writing as the war began, and in quite different ways from in 1914; the Forties is for good reason the least remembered literary decade. Like the historical Thirties themselves, the fictional Thirties ended in dismay, disorder, lost causes and weary apostasies. They soon became Auden's 'low dishonest decade', Orwell's 'scenic railway ending in a torture chamber', Leavis's 'Marxizing decade', a decade effectively defeated by the history it had hoped to seize. And so strong was the general air of collapse that, when the task of the novel resumed in post-war conditions, it resembled the task of beginning all over again.

4

The great break between Thirties fiction and post-war writing seems in retrospect a pity, for a good deal of important fiction, a good many important writers, emerged from the surprising variety of the anxious decade. It was no doubt the concern with history, society and the public self that made the age one that appeared drably committed to reportorial realism; ironically enough, much of its best work is a deviation from that form. The realism that the Thirties writers and critics so often argued for was not, in fact, the middle-ground social and moral realism of George Eliot, nor even the sociological documentary of Zola and Gissing, or the progressive materialism of Bennett and Wells. It was shaped by a changed and more ideological brand of argument: the Marxist case for 'proletarian writing' or 'Proletcult', the sociological argument for 'mass observation', or the journalistic argument for 'reportage'. The growth of a mass audience, the impact on the arts of the age of mechanical reproduction, the pressure of film, the weight of history and travel into history, all played their part. So, particularly, did the Marxist argument about the need for the bourgeois writer to accommodate to progress and the people after the false aesthetic adventure of Modernism. This was a fashionable opinion, to be found even among some former Modernists in the United States and elsewhere, and it was strongly put in several works of polemical criticism in Britain. So the Marxist critic Ralph Fox, himself a novelist, argued in his *The Novel and the People* (1937) that lack of dialectical philosophy had led fiction off on a false trail; he advised writers to follow the practice of ancient tyrants who 'mingled at night-time with their subjects, carefully disguised as common men', if they were to return to the 'active life' of the age, and called for a new epic of the age of history. The no less Marxist Edward Upward argued in *The Mind in Chains* (1937) that the writer could no longer share the life of a bourgeois class that could not solve the problems confronting it, and only if he moved to the progressive side of the conflict 'will it be possible for his writing to give a true picture of the world'.[4] The 'true picture' frequently meant a populist picture, or a proletarian picture; in fact it more or less came to mean what the Hungarian Marxist critic György Lukács would call 'contemporary realism', or 'the realism of the future', deriving from the alliance between the writer, the working class and the revolutionary objectivity

---

4 Ralph Fox, *The Novel and the People* (London 1937; reissued 1979); C. Day Lewis (ed.), *The Mind in Chains: Socialism and the Cultural Revolution* (London, 1937).

of History, the great progressive machine that knew exactly what it was doing.[5]

And a significant body of 'proletarian writing' – by no means all of it by proletarian writers – did appear, much of it in the earlier Thirties, when unemployment peaked and national and regional social problems predominated; one result of this was not just a new and bitter social and political documentary but a powerful strengthening of regional and industrial fiction. The vivid Scots novels of Lewis Grassic Gibbon (*A Scots Quair*, 1932–34) with their powerful vernacular voice, the Salford fiction of Walter Greenwood (*Love on the Dole*, 1933), the sea stories of James Hanley (*Boy*, 1931), the Durham mining stories of Sid Chaplin, the Derbyshire miner Walter Brierley's *Means Test Man* (1935) or the Welsh miner Lewis Jones's *Cymardy* (1937), are works that come closest to a serious working-class fiction, extending the tradition of *The Ragged-Trousered Philanthropists*. But a good deal else under the 'proletarian' banner followed the propagandistic and melodramatic formulae – hard facts, gross and evil bosses, heroic workers – of what Arthur Koestler called 'the pink novel', the work of 'a period in which novels read like dispatches by war-correspondents from the fronts of the class struggle. The characters seemed to be flat, two-dimensional beings, fighting their shadow battles against a lurid background. People in the pink novel had a class-dimension (length), plus, say, a sex-dimension (width); the third, irrational dimension (depth) was missing or atrophied.'[6] Another significant part of 'working-class fiction' was the writing of bourgeois writers who, following Lawrence, frequently looked to working-class, or rural, men and women as the embodiment of vigour, libido or cultural alternative, as did writers as various as Malcolm

---

5 György Lukács, *The Meaning of Contemporary Realism* (1957; London, 1963). 'A correct aesthetic understanding of social and historical reality is the precondition of realism . . .,' he says: '. . . it may appear that critical and socialist realism are virtually indistinguishable. But in spite of the similarities, there are important qualitative differences. These derive from that hard-and-fast perspective of the future, that "true consciousness", which socialist realism by definition possesses . . . In no other aesthetic does truthful depiction of reality have so central a place as in Marxism.'
6 Arthur Koestler, 'The Novelist's Temptations', in *The Yogi and the Commissar and Other Essays* (London, 1945).

Lowry and Christopher Isherwood, J. B. Priestley and H. E. Bates, Sylvia Townsend Warner and Mary Webb. (The great parody of the overlush darling buds of May-ness this sometimes produced was Stella Gibbons's *Cold Comfort Farm*, 1932, an ironic juxtaposition of smart metropolitan Lambeth and the world of phallic shoots and something nasty in the woodshed.) Undoubtedly the writer who gave most sense and strength to the idea of honest social realism was George Orwell (one reason why his work had such an impact on the younger writers of the Fifties). He merged many of the fundamental period elements: the Naturalistic reportage of the working-class novel and a high awareness of that complex structural ladder in British society that is called 'class'; experience of travel and that of hard descent into 'ordinary' working life; the historical urgency and socialist polemic and the aesthetic concern of one fearful for the misuse of language; radical sympathies and a blunt John Bullish Englishness – all of this dramatized in the complex character of his invented self, 'George Orwell'. Good prose might be a window pane, as Orwell claimed, but he also knew that realism is never simply life observed, but something constructed, structured, argued, placed, to create its consensus about, to assemble its agreed working model of, 'the real'. His persuasive, elaborate, plain-speaking codes of resemblance were managed objects, but they constructed an effective renewal of the realist and descriptive tradition itself.

Generally, though, the realism the Thirties talked much of was not a realism of social report but a realism of history; and since history itself was surreal, absurd, nightmarish and threatening, so too was much of the fiction. Hence what most good fiction of the time betrays is an anxiously unstable relationship with realism, and it often turns into a formal or an emotional revolt against it. The pervasive unreality of the modern historical realities concerned most of the writers of the day. 'As imagined thrillers, even as authentic revelation of the Chicago underworld or the international drug traffic serialized in the Sunday newspapers, the Moscow Trials might pass; but as part of the everyday lives of ordinary people, they were disconcerting,' Malcolm Muggeridge observed in his impressionistic study *The Thirties* (1940). 'The policeman on his beat, scrutinizing doorways, bundling along a drunk and incapable; the horseguards, spendid and immobile in Whitehall; Cabinet Ministers assembling in Downing Street . . . Was it possible that they too might become terrible and strange? In their ways, secret and bloodthirsty?' In the imagination of Thirties fiction, a great deal grew terrible and strange, became a kind of collective landscape – a 'menacing dream-experience', Rosamund Lehmann called it – shared by writers left and right, materialist and religious. *It's a Battlefield*, Graham Greene titled one of his novels of seedy desolate London in 1934. The panorama of suburbia and decay Nina sees from the plane in Waugh's *Vile Bodies* (1930) – which closely resembles Auden's panorama of 'Smokeless chimneys, damaged bridges, rotting wharves and choked canals' of 'Get There If You Can', published in the same turn-of-decade year – was to turn into the typical Thirties fictional landscape. In Orwell's work, suburbia, spreading over England, becomes intricately linked with the disorders of elsewhere, 'the things you tell yourself are just a nightmare or only happen in foreign countries'. Engagement and disdain, commitment and detachment, become common codes: the daily world grew nearer, but also further away, a world of ersatz sausages, Bakelite ashtrays, cheap music, arterial roads, abandoned pitstocks, rusting machinery and decaying vicarages. In an age of the mass, crowds and mob motion fill many novels: gathering for strikes or protests, aimlessly watching a film or a parade. Human figures grew cheaper, bodies more vile: little Lord Tangent had already been disposed of, at a tangent, in two or three brief sentences of Waugh's *Decline and Fall*, but now sudden death and random violence became commonplace material, popular Gothic. So did ominous travels, journeys to world frontiers, dangerous quests, soldiers at checkpoints, threatening military machines, walls of barbed wire, the strange landscapes of Rex Warner's novels. Aeroplanes flew over with lethal or absurd cargoes, like the dog dropped from the air to explode on the rooftop terrace in Aldous Huxley's *Eyeless in Gaza* (1936). The world was littered with violence and casualties, from the wounded of the Great War or the clubbed strikers of Grassic Gibbon's *A Scots Quair* to the many psychological victims of the age. For a sense not just of social crisis but psychic danger filled the novel. Most writers shared, it seemed, a guilty self-suppression, a sense of betraying or having betrayed. Psychology offered a solution, or if not a solution then an explanation, or a mythological accountancy, for the errant desires, the vulnerable passivities, the lack of moral focus, the unheroic selves of the day, and in some writers like Graham Greene seediness, lovelessness and betrayal became a metaphysical modern condition. Indeed one result of all this was a heightening of the metaphysics of fiction in the face of absurdity, Pascal's 'endless territory of death'. So realism merged with surrealism, objective reportage with subjective confession, to construct the style of the 'new' fiction in what was inescapably a nightmare age, and it left the modern novel with an enduring legacy.

5

If there really was a distinct Thirties fictional climate, which significantly shifted the direction of the new or modern novel, then one of the writers who most evidently embodied it was Christopher Isherwood, who, while still a student at Cambridge in the mid Twenties, was – according to Spender – already presciently being considered 'the Novelist' of his generation, just as his friend Auden at Oxford was being considered 'the Poet'. At Cambridge Isherwood was to produce the most famous piece of unpublished fiction to come out of the period, the sequence of stories he wrote in collaboration with another friend, Edward Upward, called 'Mortmere' (the matricidal implication is deliberate). Collaboration was another common concern of the Thirties, when individual voices wondered if they were enough; Isherwood would produce some of his most interesting work with Auden, using the common ground of Expressionist poetic drama. As Isherwood tells it in *Lions and Shadows*, the Mortmere tales were 'a dream, a nightmare, about the English', set in an 'anarchist paradise' which was 'a private place of retreat from the rules and conventions of university life'. The chief surviving fragment is Upward's 'The Railway Accident' (finally published, after much private circulation, in his *The Railway Accident and Other Stories*, 1969), and it shows the intended spirit of surreal fantasy very clearly. This is fiction that reaches out of a failing bourgeois world to the gap in the pavement, the door in the wall, that would lead into an 'other world' of fiction that could be superimposed on the real one. 'Mortmere' already displays that distorted, half-psychological, half-political texture of prose that would become so familiar in the Thirties, when distinctive moral and existential domains (Greene's Greeneland) were so often laid over the almost familiar 'real' world. It is also appropriate that 'Mortmere' is an aborted, uncompleted work. So, in fact, were all Isherwood's early fictions, which, according to his own account, always came from something much larger – a massive unfinished project that history, or personal weakness, never allowed him to complete.

When he left Cambridge, Isherwood planned another large-scale project, an 'immense novel' that would be called *The North-West Passage*. All that survives is the intention: it would be a large portrait of the post-war generation, seen from the standpoint of the 'Truly Weak Man', the anti-hero making his indirect and deviant journey toward the America of life. If it remained unwritten, that was part of the point; the modern writer was indeed the Truly Weak Man, no longer in control of life. Nonetheless it was undoubtedly this that spawned his first two published novels, *All the Conspirators* (1928) and *The Memorial: A Portrait of a Family* (1932). Both return to many of the 'Mortmere' themes, above all the struggle with the repressive mother and domestic and bourgeois life. In *All the Conspirators* the young would-be artist Philip Lindsay struggles against the conspiracy of the old with his new, distinctly neurotic, conspiracy of the new. The method now is not surreal but naturalistic, but various Modernist devices are also used; as Isherwood commented, 'there were several "thought-stream" passages in the fashionable neo-Joyce manner which yielded nothing, in obscurity, to the work of the master himself.' Thirty-five years later, Isherwood, now in Hollywood, returned to this phase of his life and writing in the retrospective novel *Down There On a Visit* (1962), and targeted the key theme and flavour of both of these novels in defining his own character: 'Perhaps his strongest negative emotion is ancestor hatred. He had vowed to disappoint, disgrace and disown his ancestors.' The second, better, novel *The Memorial* treats the same demonumentalizing theme with somewhat more sympathy. Isherwood confessed a debt to E. M. Forster, who dealt with large themes in terms of personal relations, and called this a 'potted epic . . . disguised as a drawing room comedy'. This is another novel of attempted escape from the monumentality of the past, an anti-war book in which all those left behind by the war become the modern wounded, 'living on in a new world, unwanted, among enemies'. The novel ends by following out Isherwood's own course, as its anti-hero escapes to the Berlin of the Weimar period. During the writing of the book Isherwood, on Auden's enthusiastic recommendation, made the same journey, which in the event was to prove a voyage toward his most fundamental material. For the land of homosexual freedom, sun worship, oiled male bodies and Weimar decadence, his natural destination, was also the place where contemporary history was unfolding. Isherwood remained in Berlin from 1929 to 1933; over that period Nazism rose, and Hitler became Germany's Chancellor. A relationship could be forged between the figure through which he perceived himself, that of the weak and enfeebled modern writer, and the rising crisis of the age.

Another large project was planned, a novel called *The Lost*, which would deal with life in Weimar Berlin over the five years up to Hitler's coming to power. This too was never finished, but the shattered fragments from the larger idea would produce Isherwood's major work. Over the course of several years there emerged a network of novels and stories – *Mr Norris Changes Trains* (1935), *The Nowaks* (in *New Writing*, 1936), *Sally Bowles* (1937), *Goodbye to Berlin* (1939) – which were at last collectively presented as *The Berlin Stories* in 1946. They formed an essential narrative of the Thirties, though the main material belongs to the dying of the Weimar age, the Modernist decadence. Lehmann (who plainly thought the work brilliant, but felt it could do with ideological improvement) accounts for it in *New Writing in Europe* as a work whose 'implication' is revolutionary, even though Isherwood disappointingly avoids dealing with 'revolutionaries' and 'almost invariably prefers, on the contrary, to take eccentric and fantastic characters as his central pivots, the extreme products of the anarchy and pathological condition of modern society'. Yes, indeed. Lehmann also uncomfortably admits that 'one

is forced to read the last few pages [of *Mr Norris* . . .] shaking with
laughter. While this is a source of disappointment to one part of Mr
Isherwood's public, I cannot help suspecting it is the secret of his
popularity with the other.' It is also, of course, the secret of success,
but in the Thirties History was not to be laughed at, and historical
satire not always an easily understood form. The point about all these
stories is that they are rendered on a note of almost neurotic passivity,
with a first-person, plainly autobiographical narrator variously
rendered as 'William Bradshaw' and 'Herr Issyvoo', who describes
himself as 'a half-hearted renegade from my own class, my feeling
muddled by anarchism talked at Cambridge, by slogans from the
confirmation service, by the tunes the band played when father's
regiment marched to the railway station, seventeen years ago'. He is
ostensibly the reporter, or, more passively still, 'a camera'. 'I am a
camera with its shutter open, quite passive, recording, not thinking,'
he notes in *Goodbye to Berlin*. 'Recording the man shaving at the
window opposite and the woman with the kimono washing her hair.
Some day all this will have to be developed, carefully printed, fixed.'
Meanwhile, though, it stays, as intended, provisional, immediate,
almost improvised. As the German critic Walter Benjamin wrote in
his *Small History of Photography* in 1931: ' "In our age there is no
work of art that is looked at so closely as a photograph of oneself,
one's closest relatives and friends, one's sweetheart," wrote Lichtwark
back in 1907, thereby moving the inquiry out of the realm of aesthetic
distinctions and into social functions. Only now this vantage point
can be carried further.' Isherwood, we can say, does.[7] The camera, of

---

[7] It was as if Isherwood was deliberately reflecting the condition examined by Walter
Benjamin in his famous essay 'The Work of Art in the Age of Mechanical Reproduction'
(1936; reprinted in *Illuminations* [London, 1970]): '. . . that which withers in the age of
mechanical reproduction is the aura of the work of art. This is a symptomatic process
whose significance points beyond the realm of art . . . Unmistakably, reproduction as
offered by picture magazines or newsreels differs from the image seen by the unarmed
eye. Uniqueness and permanence are as closely linked in the latter as are transitoriness
and reproducibility in the former.' He later adds that mankind's self-alienation 'has
reached such a degree that it can experience its own destruction as an aesthetic pleasure
of the first order. This is the situation of politics which Fascism is rendering aesthetic.
Communism responds by politicizing art.'

course, does not simply record; it is an object from the age of mechanical reproduction, challenging the authority of art by its instantaneous collusion with its subject. It has lenses, angles, shutter speeds; it quotes from reality, renders life as instant; it snaps, magnifies, distorts, frames and excludes, creating, here, a variety of mixed and almost random images from an age of surreal absurdity, when life is already reportage and will soon be history. So beyond the woman in the kimono and the man shaving, or the English nightclub whore Sally Bowles, the fastidious British adventurer Mr Norris, with his wigs and whips, the wandering expatriates seeking decadence, the gay young men seeking the sun, the Nowaks and the Lindauers, are the racial tensions, the rising hatreds, the glimpse of the baton and the concentration camp; a nightmare evolution from reality to decadence to violence is unfolding.

'Youth always demands its nightmares,' Isherwood noted in 1939, '. . . Germany supplied them.' Without any artistic formality history suddenly enters the passively visual narrative. 'Berlin was in a state of civil war,' we suddenly learn in *Mr Norris* . . . 'Hate exploded suddenly, without warning, out of nowhere; at street corners, in restaurants, cinemas, dance-halls, swimming-baths; at midnight, after breakfast, in the middle of the afternoon. Knives were whipped out, blows were dealt with spiked rings, beer-mugs, chair-legs or leaded clubs; bullets slashed the advertisements on the poster-columns . . . Frl. Schroeder's astrologer foretold the end of the world.' By the end Hitler is in power, Mr Norris has become that primal figure of the age, the double agent, daily life goes on in its usual daily snapshots in the cafés – and Herr Issyvoo, 'smiling', is ready to leave, his last photographs taken and ready to be developed. What makes these Berlin tales remarkable is not only the radical historical moment they capture through fragments, a moment which entered the English imagination as the sign of the way the world was moving, and provided the landscape of nightmares to come. It is also their frank aesthetic passivity, which emerges as an apparently flat reportage rendered to us by a narrator whose very passivity is a product of the way history is affecting artistic consciousness. They mark Isherwood's move out of an interest in Modernist mannerism to an endeavour in what came to be 'reportage', but was also an experiment in self-cancelling autobiography set in history, the writing of a time when, Isherwood said, 'everyone must be his own guinea-pig'. They also made him a writer peculiarly dependent on the history to which he might bear witness, and when he moved to peculiarly historyless California in 1939, his subject largely died. Walter Allen once called Isherwood the great disappointment of the modern novel. But this is not because of the half-aborted tales he produced in the Twenties and Thirties; it was because his later life never allowed him the same peculiar intimacy between historical crisis and the neurotically conceived artistic self. Isherwood remained a camera: his next book, *Prater Violet* (1945), deals with an *émigré* European film-maker, and the making of a film, a story of the moving picture; he himself became an important Hollywood screenwriter. But the later fiction is work essentially of personal narrative rather than historical diagnosis. *The World in the Evening* (1954) deals with what is really sexual boredom in the Cold-War, comfortably alienating USA. *Down There on a Visit* (1962) returns him to his old life in the Twenties and Thirties, but acknowledges his role as essentially that of the tourist in history. *A Single Man* (1964), a work of vivid present-tense neurosis, is a tale of a historyless America and the portrait of a single man who cannot build a full identity and has chosen not to mature. Isherwood, as he knew himself, stayed eternally a novelist of the Thirties, a novelist whose work was focused and historicized by a decade.

The same is true of Edward Upward, the 'Chalmers' of *Lions and Shadows* and the collaborator on 'Mortmere'. The first of the Auden group to join the Communist Party, he published various important short stories and worked slowly on his novel *Journey to the Border*, which appeared in 1938. This is another work from the nightmare world, showing the influence of 'Mortmere', the story of a neurotic young tutor, working for a rich British family, who finds the familiar social world distorted to the point of surreal extremity. But, though Upward feels obliged finally to justify his point in *The Mind in Chains* that neurosis might disappear if one took the standpoint of the workers, the book's essential theme is not political but psychoanalytical, indeed neurotic. The 'border' was the final place of Thirties fiction (and Auden and Isherwood published their related play *On the*

Frontier in the same year), the bridge not simply between self and history but between identity and neurosis, reality and unreality; it is the margin of consciousness itself. The force of the book lies in the (Kafkaesque) way the worlds within and without erode each other, and the border tested is that of fictional realism itself. Upward, still Marxist, returned to fiction in the Sixties, with the novels about the historically struggling poet Alan Sebrill that form the trilogy 'The Spiral Ascent' (*In the Thirties*, 1962; *The Rotten Elements*, 1969; *No Home But the Struggle*, 1977). It is a serious yet finally laboured work of modern realism, recording Sebrill's sequence of battles to balance art and Party membership through the political and emotional vagaries of the Thirties, wartime and the Cold War years. But this time the subject failed to yield a strong imaginative form of expression, unlike Doris Lessing's *The Golden Notebook*, one of the most notable of post-war novels, and a work in which the struggles of art, Marxist politics, sexuality and consciousness generate a radical literary form – which happened to appear in the same year as Upward's first volume, and showed the stylistic transition from age to age.

6

Journey to the Border, though, remains one of the key works of the psycho-political allegory that fascinated the later Thirties, when, in fact, the novel was moving away from and not toward what Upward called 'the true picture'. For, as Irving Howe has said, from the Russian Revolution to the end of the Thirties, the political novel had passed from being a work of revolutionary excitement, Utopian possibility and proletarian promise to a work of psychosis, terror and victimization, following a dark descent, 'an increasingly precipitous fall into despair'.[8] An important indication of this is the fiction of Rex Warner, the poet and classicist who, as the decade closed, wrote three powerful allegorical novels, *The Wild Goose Chase* (1937), *The*

8 Irving Howe, *Politics and the Novel* (New York, 1957; London, 1961), a work that follows the course of the political novel on a European scale.

Professor (1938) and *The Aerodrome* (1941), which expressionistically explored the rising power of the masses and the machine, of modern totalitarianism and tyranny. These are political novels in more than a proletarian, and certainly more than a British, sense, dealing with the ideas, the powers and the political structures of an age of European tragedy; 'I do not aim at realism,' Warner observed. *The Wild Goose Chase* is a 'fable' of ethical and existential quest, filled with strong scenes, flavoured with the spirit of Marx and Freud, influenced by Kafka. *The Professor*, the most notable of these works, is set in an imaginary Eastern European country threatened by its neighbours and Fascist forces within (the situation closely resembles that in the Czechoslovakia of the day), and which is another borderland, a dream world of terrible actuality, where moral and political drama is set against inexorable and hideous fact. The central character, Professor A., is a world-famous scholar who believes in the Greek *polis*, the liberal democratic state which can summon the high values of civilization to resist the barbarian at the gates. But it, and he, are about to be overthrown, as he is summoned to take leading political office. It is a fable of his defeat as 'metal was to be proved harder than his flesh, stupidity and fanaticism more influential than his gentlest syllogisms'; the age of force beyond civilization prevails. *The Aerodrome* was written in wartime, and allegorically shows the corruption of war. Militaristic Fascism from the nearby aerodrome overlays the seemingly familiar world of the British village; images of nature yield to those of the machine, man yields to metal, honour yields to power, love to cold political reason. At the same time this is a story of domestic crimes and tragedies, drawing on the structures of Greek tragedy as well as those of the Expressionist drama of the day. But these novels are also contemporary political fables, in that they are about the modern *polis*, the state that threatens human reason and life's complexity with violence, terror and power.

Of similar power and importance are Arthur Koestler's *The Gladiators* (1939), *Darkness at Noon* (1940) and *Arrival and Departure* (1943), three political novels by a Hungarian-born journalist and former member of the German Communist Party who had been imprisoned in both Spain and France before he escaped to Britain in

1941. Koestler described his fiction as being about whether a noble End justifies the use of ignoble Means, and about the relentless logic in both Marxism and Fascism which ensures that its own intellectual leaders are sacrificed 'in the death camps of Utopia'. *Darkness at Noon*, the most notable of them, written first in German, tells the story of the Bolshevik Rubashov, who confesses to crimes he has not committed in Stalin's totalitarian state. In a world where victims collude with executors in the belief that 'Everyone with a goal in front is forced to its baleful track', Rubashov no longer knows whether he is in an actual history or an eternal nightmare, and he is finally brought to the point, under questioning, where nightmare and reality actually merge and he becomes capable of Doublethink. This is a psychological as well as an ideological tale, but also a vividly precise, historically exact political story about the lies, slogans, betrayals, imprisonments, interrogations, tortures, psychological deceptions, false confessions and executions that had become the standard weapons of the totalitarian state, as well as about the 'grammatical fiction' of modern ideology, which destroys the I in the We. Here we see the modern political novel acquiring a terrible new meaning, as the intellectual life corrupts itself, and revolutionary politics become not a matter of hope but of moral despair. George Orwell, in a notable essay on Koestler, indicated his importance: 'One development of the last ten years has been the appearance of the "political book", a sort of enlarged pamphlet combining history with political criticism, as an important literary form,' he said, adding that its most remarkable writers had been European 'renegades from one or another extremist party, who have seen totalitarianism at close quarters and known the meaning of exile and persecution'. And he noted the difference between Koestler and other left-wing writers, who 'have always wanted to be anti-Fascist without being anti-totalitarian'.

There is no doubt that Koestler's work in turn influenced Orwell's late fiction, the two anti-Utopian political satires *Animal Farm* (1945) and *Nineteen Eighty-Four* (1949), which are likewise stories of the harsh, recognizable realities of totalitarian states, and their horrifying promise of a post-humanist future in which the jackboot comes down on the human face forever. The link between the two writers was, personally and artistically, close, though Orwell was as patriotic as he was socialist, as deeply English as Koestler was European. But Orwell's writing and ideas were interwoven by a European and internationalist view of history and politics, to a degree surely unusual in British fiction. 'What I have most wanted to do throughout the past ten years is to make political writing into an art,' he explained in 1946. 'My starting point is always a feeling of partisanship, a sense of injustice.' He wrote, he said, 'because there are some lies I want to expose, some fact to which I want to draw attention' – though he did add that the work must be 'also an aesthetic experience'. 'So long as I remain alive and well I shall continue to feel strongly about prose style, to love the surface of the earth, and to take pleasure in solid objects and scraps of useful information,' he also observed: 'The job is to reconcile my ingrained likes and dislikes with the essential public, non-individual activities that this age forces on all of us.' The result of all this is a complicated balancing of a fictional tradition bred from the 'Condition of England' novel and the work of the Naturalists – he admired Gissing and Kipling, Wells, Bennett and Galsworthy – with a fiction of political experience and intellect: a kind of novel which is often highly traditional, but which could, and would, leave realism behind and move toward moral and anti-Utopian satire. Orwell saw himself not as primarily a novelist but a political writer, a writer of engrained Englishness who has rebelled against Britain as 'a family with the wrong members in control', and a social history he felt the moral need to change. Born Eric Blair in British India in 1903, the son of a colonial official, and so belonging, as he explained it with his familiar precision, to the 'lower upper middle class', he was returned to England for his schooling. At prep school, then as a scholarship boy at Eton, he acquired, he said, much of the snobbery of his class, but also a sense of social displacement and loneliness that marked him later, politically, emotionally, stylistically. In 1921 he went to Burma as a colonial policeman, and was divided again, 'stuck between my hatred of the Empire I served and my rage against the evil-spirited little bastards who tried to make my job impossible'. He came back in 1927 to a Britain in the aftermath of the general strike, and determined to fulfil his ambition to be a writer. A period of economic deprivation and vagrancy followed in which he worked in Paris hotels and tried to survive in the London of the Depression, all this recorded in the neo-documentary *Down and Out in Paris and London* (1933). With this he became no longer Eric Blair but 'George Orwell', a name he took partly to spare his family, but also as a badge of escape and rebellion ('the only thing to do in the world of twentieth-century barbarism was to rebel').

His first novel *Burmese Days* (1934) returned to his experience in Burma, and his anti-hero Flory is significantly scarred with an ugly birthmark, signifying his own anxious curse of birth and class and his 'outcast' state. He published three more novels over the decade, *A Clergyman's Daughter* (1935), *Keep the Aspidistra Flying* (1936) and *Coming up for Air* (1939) – novels of considerable but not the highest quality, in part because their purpose is sometimes too plainly instrumental. But with them are interwoven two crucial non-fiction books: *The Road to Wigan Pier* (1937), a journey into the working-class Condition of England which is also a work of intense self-analysis, and *Homage to Catalonia* (1938), his remarkable account of his experiences in Spain with the POUM forces during the Civil War (in which he was almost fatally wounded) and from which he returned in disillusion both with Communist tactics and the attitude of the British left-wing intellectuals – the 'orthodoxy-sniffers' – who had supported them. It was as much from such works, and his critical and political essays, as from fiction that there came the rigorous, spiky, critical, collective identity that was Orwell. He had been down and out in Paris and London, followed the road to Wigan Pier, fought in Spain, made his political homage to Catalonia. He had modulated the old Etonian Eric Blair into the plainer George Orwell, and made himself a central and deeply immersed recorder of the economic, social, political and historical problems of the age. Half in resistance to aestheticized writing, he had perfected his famous plain style, the no-nonsense manner that united the British common sense and decency with the revolutionary propagandist so easily that his voice sounded as if it were the truth frankly declaring itself. He had known poverty and pain, challenged imperialism and capitalism, tried several forms of social identification, and come to speak not only for the unemployed and deprived of Depression Britain but for the new half-life of Thirties British suburbia, with all its respectable constraints and limitations. He had come to a radical, vivid, often deeply idiosyncratic yet loving reading of his culture in its contradiction and variety, while seeing that culture in a world-historical frame as part of an ongoing and universal crisis. Out of this he had come to devise both a form of writing and a form of politics, a sometimes strange, frequently volatile mixture of radical socialism and intimate identification with lasting British decencies, a liking and loathing. His realistic writing is experienced and plain ('good prose is like a window pane') and he believed in the task of telling the historical truth against the orthodoxy-makers. His pursuit of a critical social representation – he saw a 'death of society', a Britain ruined by class, poverty, sterility and unemployment, where what had collapsed was not just an economic but a cultural structure – never lost sight of the dense experience of British life, of which he was a compelling reporter. Glimpses of that life at its best are to be seen: in rural life, in the traditional working-class home, in comic seaside postcards, in the 'Great Peace' of Edwardian society, all now subject to inexorable erosion and decay. Present realities are judged from a double perspective: one that of the historical past, which sees current reality in the light of historical continuity or discontinuity, the other that of the political future, which turns the real into instant history, a quickly passing and apocalyptic world.

Orwell's Thirties novels are works of rebellion, against class limitation, money-centred capitalism and the sterile erosion of British culture itself, portraits of a dying society, a failing nation, in which social detail and milieu, rather than the fortunes of the protagonist, finally dominate. *Keep the Aspidistra Flying* is a story of a would-be rebel, Gordon Comstock, a character who prefigures some of the angry rebels of fiction twenty years later. He has ambitions to be a poet, but above all is in revolt against society, advertising, and that flag of British lower-class respectability, the aspidistra in the window, as well as against 'the futility, the bloodiness, the deathliness of modern life'. He takes a downward path ('He wanted to go down, deep down, into some world where decency no longer mattered; to cut the strings of his self-respect; to submerge himself, to sink') which is also a willing self-degradation. 'The sense of disintegration, of decay, that is endemic in our time, was strong on him,' and he reads in his fellow human beings 'The great death-wish of the modern world. Suicide pacts. Heads stuck in gas-ovens in lonely maisonettes. French letters and Amen Pills. And the reverberations of future wars.' The rebellion is incomplete, and like many of his successors in fiction he becomes a creator of the advertising slogans he has despised ('It was what, in his secret heart, he had desired'). In *Coming Up for Air* (1939), told in the first person in a grainy and even comic vernacular, the horrors underlying the social surface have come even closer, the angry disgust and violence are yet plainer: 'Everything's streamlined these days, even the bullet Hitler's keeping for you.' Orwell warningly wrote it when he knew war was coming, and the book mingles this apocalyptic knowledge with images from an idyllic Edwardian Thames Valley childhood which cannot be recreated, and a few glimpses of hope in the common decencies of ordinary people. It was written close to the essay 'Inside the Whale', where he was already developing his 'totalitarian hypothesis' that the two oligarchies of Communism and Fascism would come together, and that the writer was being returned to a grim passivity, trying to write amid the ruins. Nonetheless just after war started he began to incubate a large English family saga, to be called either *The Lion and the Unicorn* or *The Quick and the Dead* – which, like so many books of the time, was never written.

What was written instead during wartime was *Animal Farm: A Fairy Story*, though it did not appear until 1945. He had conceived the original idea in 1937 in Spain, and he wrote it over a period of three months in late 1943 and early 1944, at a time when the Russians were beginning to throw off the German advance, when Churchill, Roosevelt and Stalin met in Teheran to plan the Nazi overthrow, and Stalin stood high in British popular esteem. The book is a plain allegory of the betrayal of the Russian Revolution by Stalin and his cohorts, of the treacherous treatment of Trotsky, the purges and Show Trials, and the exploitation of the populace for party survival and advantage. Publishers whether left or right were unwilling to publish; T. S. Eliot at Faber acknowledged the book's Swiftian power, but said that the house did not believe that 'this is the right point of view from which to criticize the political situation at the present time'. These infuriating delays and obstructions in fact favoured the book, which appeared as the war closed, so that instead of dramatizing the recriminations of the Thirties it captured the atmosphere of liberal crisis and the new fear of continued totalitarianism that outlasted the conflict. '*Animal Farm* is the first book in which I tried, with full consciousness of what I was doing, to fuse political purpose and artistic purpose into one whole,' Orwell said; and now a work that in wartime might have been read solely as political polemic could be seen as something more. It carried forward, as few political works from the Thirties did, the moral as well as political energy that could be salvaged from the Thirties; it also attacked some of its darker illusions. It united satirical and political rage with the vivid near-timelessness of mythic writing, helped in this by the old satiric form of the animal fable. It expressed itself less as political venom than moral vitality. It took the official versions and authorized texts of modern ideology and subjected them to ultimate scepticism; oppressive fictions become the fictions they are, set against 'human' (here animal) decency. Orwell held on to his socialist hope in a revolution that could truly transform society; but the book was essentially a liberal text, about the need to raise people over systems, ordinariness against power, decency against historical inevitability, scepticism against authority, prose against propaganda. And the publication of *Nineteen Eighty-Four* (1949) reinforced the point that Orwell's later fiction was not simply a warning against Stalin, but about the corruptions of power, the weaponry of propaganda, the structure of terror, the nature of authoritarianism, the use of scapegoats and victims, and the defeat of language itself. These books may have been the last novels of the Thirties; but they also became in effect the first British post-war novels, a fundamental line of continuity between the fiction of the Thirties and the writing of a post-Holocaust future.

7

Even so, it was as well for the fortunes of modern British fiction that not every writer set out to accept bourgeois guilt, see history through the eyes of the workers, or provide Upward's 'true picture of the world'. One of the most notable writers of the age was Evelyn Waugh, a writer never considered distinguished for his political virtue, finally a lasting goad to the Left. Waugh, to my view, was a major modern writer, though in a quite different way from Joyce, with his intricate new discourse, or Woolf, with her complex vision of consciousness. His power lay in a pure vision of comedy so complete that it became a compelling modern style, a style that seemed to spring fully-grown from the early fiction and served him well until the 1960s. Comedy is more than a mode of amusement; it is a vision of life in both its romantic possibility and its darkness and grim absurdity. It is a high self-consciousness of style, of the play of form and language, and Waugh constructed it in its mode of modern satire, through which the compulsive claim of history itself can be challenged through a mixture of anarchistic delight in ephemeral follies and sheer indifference to externally imposed fictional and ideological orders. In later life he chose to dramatize this by inhabiting the mask of testy colonel which he analyses (and mocks) so well in *The Ordeal of Gilbert Pinfold* (1957). Pinfold is the man who presents himself to others as infuriated by all that has happened in his own lifetime ('His strongest tastes were negative. He abhorred plastics, Picasso, sunbathing and jazz – everything that had happened in his own lifetime . . . There was a phrase in the 30s: "It is later than you think," which was designed to cause uneasiness. It was never later than Mr Pinfold thought'). Yet to begin with Waugh was a modernist stylist, who at Oxford in 1922 had been greatly taken by the vogue for literary experiment, was concerned with the transition out of Victorian form, and wrote an admirable book on Dante Gabriel Rossetti on that theme. There is a clear influence of Hemingway on his early work, while his essay on Firbank is an analysis of the modern method of narrative, noting how his books are 'almost wholly devoid of any attributions of cause to effect; there is the barest minimum of direct description; his compositions are built up, intricately and with a balanced alternation of the wildest extravagance and the most austere economy.' Both writers taught Waugh the modern value of stylized dialogue, descriptive economy, and cinematic pace. Waugh's novels are, needless to say, a radical critique of the age about which he wrote; they also contain a dense social history of the period from the early Twenties to the age of the post-war Welfare State. Indeed they embody the climate and discomfort of the times as deeply as do Isherwood's or Orwell's. But in them what is plainly a dark moral vision converts into a delighted comic anarchy; if the age has condemned itself to barbarism, the barbaric age deserves a vision of itself in which comic outrage is a norm.

Reviewing *Vile Bodies* (1930), Waugh's first novel of the Thirties, Rebecca West identified its highly radical technique. It was, she said, 'a further stage in the contemporary literature of disillusionment'; its narrative method, conducted largely through tight, monosyllabic dialogue, did 'something as technically astonishing as the dialogues in Mr Ernest Hemingway's *A Farewell to Arms*, so cunningly does he persuade the barest formula to carry a weight of intense emotion'. The debt to Hemingway's *In Our Time* and *The Sun Also Rises* is clear, not only because of the hard new dialogue but for the lost-generation subject-matter, though here the situation is played less as modern tragedy than absurdist comedy. The Bright Young Things are (as usual) in rebellion against their elders, convention, and the older world of 'Anchorage House', a revolt of the 'amusing' against the 'bogus' which is, as one critic puts it, 'not experimental, but fashionable', part of 'a revolution of manners, stabilized, popularized, flattened out'. There is also, as the slightly sinister Jesuit priest Father Rothschild explains, 'a radical instability in our whole world order', though also 'a fatal hunger for permanence'. The novel begins on a cross-channel ferry with all the main characters suffering, 'unhappy about the weather' ('to avert the terrors of seasickness they indulged in every kind of civilized witchcraft, but they were lacking in faith'), and ends with a fantastic World War between unnamed powers, 'the biggest battlefield in the history of the world'. Salvation of various kinds is on offer: there is Father Rothschild's Catholicism; the evangelism of Mrs Melrose Ape (based on Aimée Semple Macpherson) and her tattered choir of angels; Shepheard's Hotel in Dover Street where, 'parched with modernity', the Bright Young Things can go and 'draw up, cool and uncontaminated, great healing draughts from the well of Edwardian certainty'. Meanwhile they seek satisfaction in action and fun, the endless round of parties (Agatha Runcible 'heard someone say something about an Independent Labour Party and was furious that she had not been asked'), travel, speed ('faster, faster'), sexual carelessness and 'vile bodies' ('Masked parties, Savage parties, Victorian parties . . . dull dances in London and comic dances in Scotland and disgusting dances in Paris – all that succession and repetition of massed humanity . . . Those vile bodies . . .'). Civilization is running rapidly off the rails; politics are surrealistically in chaos (they were), Prime Ministers keep changing (they did), and, as the hero Adam Fenwyck-Symes murmurs, 'things can't go on much longer' (they didn't). Waugh implies, but does not state, his deep disenchantment with the smart, metropolitan, cynical world where 'certainty', 'permanence', 'faith' and 'honourable people' are all set in the past. But he identifies with the comic follies of the present, and the comic spirit of the book is, it has been said, a 'joyfully insolent defiance of reason and right'.

Waugh's novels always give us a detailed social history of their period of writing, and in the next book, *Black Mischief* (1932), the Bright Young Things are already changing ('Everyone's getting poorer and it's making them duller'), the barbarism of the world increasing. The novel is chiefly set in 'Azania' (based on Abyssinia, which Waugh had recently visited, writing a travel book), one of the modern borderlands that fascinated the Thirties imagination. Here Basil Seal, the book's insolent and amoral hero, a natural survivor, meets the Emperor Seth – Chief of Chiefs of the Sakuyu, Lord of Wanda and Tyrant of the Seas, Bachelor of the Arts of Oxford University – who, trying to shake off the jungle that surrounds him, believes in Western Progress: 'I have been to Europe . . . I have read modern books – Shaw, Arlen, Priestley . . . at my stirrups run woman's suffrage, vaccination, and vivisection. I am the New Age. I am the Future.' It need hardly be said that progress brings nothing but trouble. 'I think I've had enough of barbarism for a bit,' Basil admits at the end, after he has inadvertently eaten his fiancée at a cannibal feast ('I'd like to eat you,' he has unwisely said to the ill-named Prudence), and seen the death of Seth; but progress offers no better. 'The story deals with the conflict of civilization, with all its attendant and deplorable ills, and barbarism,' Waugh wrote in a letter of explanation to the Catholic Church he had now joined; 'the plan of my book throughout was to keep the darker aspects of barbarism continually and unobtrusively present, a black and mischievous background against which the civilized and semi-civilized characters performed their parts; I wished it to be like the continuous, remote throbbing of hand drums, constantly audible, never visible . . .' At the end Sonia Trumpington complains 'I've got a tiny fear that Basil is going to turn serious on us too'; and this now increasingly applied to Waugh himself. And, though he explained in his next travel book *Ninety-Two Days* (1934) that he had become interested in 'distant and barbarous places, and particularly in the borderlands of conflicting cultures and states of development, where ideas, uprooted from their traditions, become oddly changed in transplantation', it is clear that the border was closer to home.

That is apparent in his next novel, *A Handful of Dust* (1934), which Waugh thought his best; it is. It takes its title from 'The Waste Land' ('I have seen fear in a handful of dust') and is a modern Gothic comi-tragedy. The shape of the fable is clear. The aptly named hero Tony Last is in every way the last of his line. He loses his son and heir in a hunting accident, his wife by divorce, his loved ancestral home by deception, and ends his search for the ideal city in the South American jungle endlessly reading Dickens to the mad, and ominously named, Mr Todd. The agents of destruction, mother and son, are called the Beavers, who administer the new world, taking a commission on everything, preying on the misfortunes and boredoms of Society. Society itself has new fads; osteopathy, reducing diets, fortune-telling and maisonette flats are the vogue. Hetton, the house Tony loves, is itself no ancestral mansion, but a Victorian pile rebuilt in 1864 ('I'd blow it sky-high,' says one observer), and he is no aristocrat, though his wife Brenda is. But she is seen by her London friends as 'the imprisoned princess in a fairy story', and takes John Beaver as her lover. Hetton and everything Tony associates with it – Victorian architecture, Victorian marriage, the Victorian nursery – have no value in the age of chrome plating and easy adultery, and are fated to be lost: 'hard cheese for Tony', but 'nobody's fault'. Barbarism, indifference and the rule of the jungle prevail, and Tony is subjected to an ever-accelerating cycle of horrors: 'for a month now he had lived in a world suddenly bereft of order; it was as though the whole reasonable and decent constitution of things, the sum of all he had experienced or learned to expect, were an inconspicuous, inconsiderable object mislaid somewhere on a dressing table; no outrageous circumstance in which he found himself, no new, mad thing brought to his notice, could add a jot to the all-encompassing chaos that shrieked about his ears.' The book, for all its grim and Gothic material, remains wonderfully funny, but it establishes a new sympathy for its protagonist and indeed for Brenda; suffering is now implicated in absurdity. Its fable is condemnation of the moral chaos of the world; the book, Waugh said, dealt 'entirely with behaviour. It was humanist and contained all I had to say about humanism' – presumably that human nature is beyond the explanation of the humanist, that it led to egotism and the endless vanity of human wishes, the deception of secular dreams. But what was tragic to the moralist was still rewarding to the comic writer; the mixture of these two things makes it Waugh's most subtle book.

With his next work of fiction, *Scoop: A Novel About Journalists* (1938), Waugh left behind this intricate structure and returned to high farce. A satire on the modern press and exotic press travel to foreign wars, it remains one of the best novels on the modern media ever written. The book's action takes place in a world of dangerous international politics, finance and intrigue, all seen through the eyes of one of his most innocent and Candide-like heroes, William Boot, a writer of small newspaper pieces about nature ('Feather-footed through the plashy fen passes the questing vole . . .') who lives in a world of 'change and decay'. Boot is sent by error to cover the war in Ishmaelia (Abyssinia again, but now changed in meaning by the Italian occupation), and, like his precursor Paul Pennyfeather, he undergoes a fantastic series of adventures, visits 'lush places', falls in love, meets pure evil, and finally gladly returns to the place of change and decay where it all began. But Waugh was no longer satisfied by satire; no longer a bright young thing attracted to modernity, he craved to write a more intimately serious book. He intended the book that was eventually published as *Work Suspended* (1941) to mark the end of his youth, and of an era; it did, far more dramatically than he suspected. The story is set in what proved to be the last days of peace, in a London of vanishing houses, rising flats, crude commercial travellers and communist fellow-travellers. The story, very close to autobiography, is told by Waugh's first first-person narrator, John Plant, a writer of detective stories, and deals with intimate things: the death of a father, falling in love, the birth of a child ('To write of someone loved, of oneself loving, above all of oneself being loved – how can these things be done with propriety? How can they be done at all?') It is about altering social and artistic conditions, about a man who is robbed of an ordered life because he is deprived of the things that make it possible; it expresses a direct dismay with the world. In the event war prevented the completion of the book, and this is another of the aborted works of the age. Plant adds his postcript, explaining that the new life he had sought was given him 'not by my contrivance . . . all our lives, as we had constructed them, quietly came to an end. Our story, like my novel, remained unfinished – a heap of neglected manuscript at the back of a drawer.'

In fact it took two more books to complete this phase of Waugh's work. He dealt with the Phoney War period in *Put Out More Flags* (1942), a satire where the Bright Young Things, now ageing and growing responsible, make their peace with war. Then he grasped at the entire period of the *entre deux guerres* in *Brideshead Revisited: The Sacred and Profane Memoirs of Captain Charles Ryder* (1945). The book, which is hardly comic, was partly written on war service in Yugoslavia, and shows a gluttonous appetite for the past ('I piled it on rather,' he admitted) and for the glories of Oxford and British country-house life. It is also his first explicitly Catholic novel. But it is also something else: a complex social and moral history of an entire period which runs from youthful hope and artistic promise through decline to death, from Arcadia to that of which Arcadia reminds us, the memento mori. The social history covers the General Strike, the disorders of the Thirties, the rise of the press barons making politics and war, the ascent of the common man. It is a story of people falling apart 'into separate worlds, little spinning planets of personal relationships', of an era when 'man had deserted his post and the jungle was creeping back into its old strongholds', of the nomadic, aesthetic, decadent and dandified life of art and the yearning for social and religious security. Charles Ryder, who tells the story, and who Waugh stressed was not himself ('I am not I'), is ultimately used by a higher plotter for higher ends. The central image is of the great baroque house Brideshead, with its small chapel. Waugh by now plainly thought that what was already there in England was better than anything that reform or revolution could bring to it, and the book is suffused with historical nostalgia. But Brideshead is an image not solely of English aristocratic life but Arcadia itself, the paradisal, innocent world of beatific vision, which does not however yield grace. The house and its meanings end up, as most meanings in Waugh do, in another, chaotic, wartime world, as an army camp with a lunatic asylum at its gates, 'quite remote from anything the builders had intended', but still an indirect, ambiguous symbol of an essence. If *A Handful of Dust* is Waugh's finest, most completed novel of the period, *Brideshead Revisited* is the great social recapitulation, clearing the ground for Waugh's embittered encounter with the post-war world to follow.

8

If Waugh seemed to spring fully-fledged as a writer with a style, Graham Greene seemed to spring fully-fledged as a writer with a subject, a vision, a world of his own so distinctive that it came to be called Greeneland ('that last-chance waterfront where the vultures clatter down like thunder from heaven on the tin roof beneath which a drunken doctor and corrupt police chief exchange brown concubines and confidences about losing their faith at preparatory school', one critic calls it). Greene, who was born in 1904, the son of the headmaster of Berkhamsted School, always believed that writerly imagination, like misery and faithlessness, started in childhood; and his own certainly did. The imprint of young unhappiness and a youthful attempt at suicide laid a version of life over his fiction – the fiction of an ever distinctive world of 'misery's graduates', spies and adulterers, betrayers and sinners, where temporal disorder is universal, civilization never on offer, redemption ambiguous and death certain, which, shifting from one form to another, he would always write. One striking thing about Greene in retrospect (he died in 1991) is the sheer scale of his production: over twenty-five novels, over fifty books, several plays and important film scripts, like *The Third Man* (1950), with its famous chase through the sewers of life, which would change directions in modern cinema. Greene was influenced by several strands of Modernism, and possessed particular admiration for Conrad and Ford, though also for much more popular writers like John Buchan, Marjorie Bowen and Eric Ambler, who opened up many of the landscapes of his work. But he was essentially a writer formed in the Thirties, and his writing gradually rejects Modernist mannerism for a vividly metaphoric realism, drawing on journalism, travel writing and popular forms. His work, with its spyings and treacheries, seedy landscapes and dangerous frontiers, its wastes of moral and political confusion and its high metaphysical anxieties, its European and internationalist texture, always remained born out of that decade, even though more than any other novelist he would carry forward the vision through the era of the Cold War and the superpower age and right into the New World Order. Some of his best books belong there, though also some of his worst. His first novel *The Man Within* (1929), written when he was a recent Catholic convert, is a historical novel which opens out some of his essential themes – betrayal, pursuit, the manhunt, the inner burden of guilt and anxiety – but remains slight; his next two novels were failures and were later withheld from the Collected Edition. But over the Thirties his fiction realized the forms it needed for itself, and the sequence of novels he produced just before, around and immediately after the war – *Brighton Rock* (1938), *The Confidential Agent* (1939), *The Power and the Glory* (1940), *The*

Ministry of Fear (1943), *The Heart of the Matter* (1948) and *The End of the Affair* (1951) – surely form the recognizable centre of his fiction.

Greene's first successful novels – artistically as well as commercially – were in fact his 'entertainments', borrowings from the popular and sensational forms from the crime novel to the psychological thriller which, in the Thirties, suddenly acquired a moral, political and metaphysical relevance. He called his first really successful novel *Stamboul Train* (1932) an entertainment (it was written for money); the book borrowed from Agatha Christie's *The Mystery of the Blue Train* (1928) and elsewhere those ever more familiar themes of crossing risky frontiers and the borders of civilization, of espionage and sudden arrests, seduction and meetings with strange emissaries of foreign powers, all born from a Europe in terrible unrest, which flavoured so much of the fiction of the Thirties, from Isherwood to Elizabeth Bowen (*The House in Paris*, 1935). *A Gun for Sale* (1936) – another 'entertainment', though now meant more seriously – is the story, set in a world fearful of war, of a harelipped political assassin, Raven, who says 'There has always been a war for me,' and whose complex amoral mixture of loyalty and treachery gives the novel not only its dark flavour but a metaphysical theme. David Lodge has noted how in Greene's work 'the properties of realism – the sharp visual images presented through cinematic devices of montage and close-up, the catalogues of significant particulars, the keen rendering of sensation, the touches of local colour laid on with so skilled a hand – seem to cluster around the nucleus of some ambiguous moral concept which is "the heart of the matter" and which is represented by some word or words recurring as insistently as a drumbeat.' In *A Gun for Sale* the word is 'betrayal', in his next novel *It's a Battlefield* (1934) it is 'justice', in *The Confidential Agent* (1939), Greene's third entertainment, it is 'trust', in *The Heart of the Matter* (1948) it is 'pity', in *The Human Factor* (1978) it is 'gratitude'. They indicate the deepening moral and metaphysical thrust of his writing, indeed its emerging religiosity. They remind us too of Conrad, by whom he was technically and morally influenced, and *It's a Battlefield* – set around the police investigation of a political crime, in a vividly rendered, grimly desolate contemporary London which is indeed a social, political and moral battlefield, and concerned, Greene said, with the inadequacy of human justice – is Greene's most direct homage to him.

For, like Conrad, Greene was becoming a novelist of the gloomier moral flavours, of fidelity and infidelity, trust and betrayal; after all the writer was at heart, he said, 'a man given over to an obsession'. Also like Conrad, he was a writer who never seemed quite at home with the familiar, and who sought out the dark places of the earth. Even when he wrote of English life – the desolate London of the political rally in *It's a Battlefield* or in parts of *England Made Me*, seedy bedsitter Nottingham in *A Gun for Sale*, the Brighton of the pre-war razor gangs in *Brighton Rock* (1938) – it appeared a foreign and distanced place, part of a larger European map, increasingly a world map, of pain and compassion, guilt and sin, betrayal and obscure redemption. It feels, increasingly, an abandoned world, a ruined place where life is damned or fallen, though there is always 'someone who has betrayed one's natural distrust of human nature, someone one has loved'. Bridging the gap between popular and serious writer, storyteller and experimentalist, he was progressively coming to see the novel as a narrative for telling stories of heroes or, more often, anti-heroes who, in the dark and confusing passages of modern history, faced some difficult yet eternal trial, succeeded or, more probably, failed in some existential and metaphysical quest. It was a journey without maps in a landscape where the secret agent and the private detective, the spy and the traitor, stalked through the mean streets of an ill-lit world, where kindness and compassion frequently led to self-betrayal and despair, where, it has been said, characters have discovered a sense of sin but not set their feet on the way of salvation, and where life is a gamble with a death that has its own obscure yet strangely radical theology of hell and redemption. With this comes a Conradian understanding, even a sympathy or moral identification, with those who have not managed to keep faith, or have committed treachery.

Brighton Rock is the novel where the theme of faith emerges clearly in Greene's fiction, as it does in Waugh's with *Brideshead Revisited*. It started as yet another entertainment, with the seventeen-year-old racecourse hoodlum Pinkie a villain from the same world as Raven;

but by setting the book in a world in which good and evil become a common country, apart from conventional right and wrong, the themes of salvation and damnation are significantly released ('She was good, he'd discovered that, and he was damned; they were made for each other'). This is played against structures taken from the crime novel and the thriller movie, with an element of chase and detection; it shares with *noir* fiction like Patrick Hamilton's the notion that life is throughout a dingy world ('Why, this is Hell, nor are we out of it,' says Mr Drewitt in the book). Ida, who thinks otherwise and believes in 'human nature' ('Bite all the way down, you'll still read Brighton,' she says, comparing life to Brighton rock, 'that's human nature'), is thus not the novel's heroine, but a blowsily good-hearted figure of farce; Rose, who supports Pinkie throughout, despite his cold evil ('no more human contacts', he dreams), much as Pinkie accepts his own damnation, is the moral focus. The novel surprises, even shocks, because of the moral frame in which its action is interpreted; at times, indeed, it becomes difficult to grant the author his Greenean God on which so much depends. These are lawless roads, where the hunter is a narrower human being than the hunted, the rule of law is less than the rule of salvation and damnation, and the marked man can become the alien or demonic hero, dependent at the last on the 'strangeness of the mercy of God'. If, as Greene said, he had learned from Marjorie Bowen to write of 'perfect evil walking the world where perfect good could never walk again', here was the book to prove it. With his next, *The Confidential Agent* (1939), Greene offered another, and far less weighty, entertainment that really goes back to Conrad and *The Secret Agent*, though it draws on the Spanish Civil War for its political atmosphere and its angle of foreignness. But with *The Power and the Glory* (1940), 'the only book I have ever written to a thesis', Greene's religious theme returned in all its force.

Basing the novel on his travels in revolutionary Mexico over two months in 1938, Greene here extraordinarily creates the physical, moral and religious landscape of central America in a period of cruel anti-clericalism. It is a fitting Greenean setting to the drama of his nameless whisky priest, the seedy lover and alcoholic who fails as a man but succeeds in his office, so that at once he descends into darkness and ascends into martyrdom. He is one of the central characters of Greene's fiction, one, he said, that 'had emerged from some part of me, from the depths'. His failings are many, but they teach him human love; he can still fulfil his function, and in Greene's interpretation become that much more the saintly man. For increasingly Greene was turning to the paradoxes of his Catholic religion, the metaphysical ironies and enigmas of faith, the portrait of a Pascalian, absurd world from which God seemed absconded, but in which obscure acts of faith constitute something midway between a humanist and a religious – in other words an existential – salvation. There was another entertainment, *The Ministry of Fear* (1943), now most notable for its evocation of London in the Blitz; but the larger theme returned again in *The Heart of the Matter* (1948), a novel set in expatriate Africa in wartime, in which the colonial policeman Scobie attempts to take on the world's evil and suffering, and finally dies by suicide. Set in a West Africa where 'Heaven remained rigidly on the other side of death, and on this side flourished the injustices, the cruelties, the meanness that elsewhere people so cleverly hushed up,' where love is a response to human unattractiveness, where what Scobie offers up to God is his own damnation, this is one of the most complete of the 'Greeneland' social, moral and metaphysical landscapes, a central work that, lacking the sensationalized crime aspects of *Brighton Rock*, or the political persecution of *The Power and the Glory*, becomes the interpretation of a psychology. With these three novels Greene had laid out his central themes, established his distinctive flavour, and turned what had begun as sensational popular fiction (his work was never entirely to lose that flavour) into the novel of existential crisis. And what had begun as a fiction written, as he said, against 'the economic background of the thirties and that sense of capitalism staggering from crisis to crisis', a fiction in which the social order has been destabilized and existence is lived according to hellish rules, had become a universal theme, a bleak overall accountancy of the twentieth-century condition, a metaphysical setting. The fictional world has become a universe, with Greene its neo-divine creator – the maker of its plots, the deviser of its obscure governing moral and metaphysical rules, the dispenser of its strange spiritual destinies, working in collusion with a yet higher plotter still. This created some of the fictionalist ambiguities of his next novel *The End of the Affair*, a book strangely split between the human and divine author, so that the first is able to assign a miracle to the second. Greene's highly ordained, metaphysically terrible, historically seedy universe was in place, all ready to sustain him over more than thirty more years of influential and central writing.

9

'What a decade!' wrote George Orwell in 1940, in what looked like a relieved farewell to the entire Thirties: 'A riot of appalling folly that suddenly becomes a nightmare, a scenic railway ending in a torture chamber.' The obituaries on the 'low, dishonest decade' started almost at once. If the times had a dominant form, it was elegy; and the striking poetic elegies Auden wrote for the deaths of two of the great 'Moderns', Sigmund Freud ('To us he is no more a person/ But a whole climate of opinion') and W. B. Yeats ('In the nightmare of the dark,/ All the dogs of Europe bark,/ And the living nations wait,/ Each sequestered in its hate'), just as he left for the United States appeared to sum up the prevailing mood. Dismay and the funereal note were now clearly dominant in the arts. In the pages of *Horizon*, Cyril Connolly announced that it was 'closing time in the gardens of the West', and mourned the dying not just of one but of two eras of writing: the Modernist era, and the 'new writing of the Thirties'. There was, he noted, an intimate link between 'the Twilight of the Arts and the twilight of a civilization', and, though this artistic as well as historical gloom might have seemed the personal pessimism of a legendary decadent, it was widely shared by others. In *Penguin New Writing* in 1942, John Lehmann complained that 'this war has found no writer in prose and verse to interpret it with anything like ... depth and power,' and saw writing in general decline, virtually mute; so did most commentators. War and a new patriotic feeling had not made writing flourish. The Forties started out with *Finnegans Wake* and *No Orchids for Miss Blandish*, the terminal experiment and the seedy grim thriller. Where fiction was written, its map of contemporary life was almost universally one of frustration, bewilderment, maladjustment, disintegration, anxiety. Kafka and his heirs cast their influence wide, from the political novels of Koestler, Warner and Alex Comfort (*The Powerhouse*, 1944) to the entertainments of Graham Greene, which became now a report from the unfamiliar on the entirely familiar, and so on into the popular thriller – now a widely read form of escape from yet grimmer actuality. Meanwhile the terminal mood of the commentators reinforced the belief that all the darker aspects of Thirties fiction – the death of the hero, the self-cancelling of the author, the growing conviction of the irrelevance of art in the age of great History, vast masses, and the age of mechanical reproduction – had all the time been signalling the end of literature, the death of the novel itself, just as Orwell's 'Inside the Whale' prophesied. The decade of the Thirties may have started in realism, but it ended in surrealism; no wonder it handed on to the writing that did actually follow an intense awareness of a grotesque and absurd world which has never since disappeared from the climate of fiction.

This apocalyptic reading of the end of the arts was, of course, understandable, even though in time it proved too grim. Modernism had faded, and the movement had been robbed of some of its dominant figures; the later sadness in Woolf's work, the terminal mood of *Finnegans Wake*, reflected not just personal dismays but experiment's fading fortunes. Even so, the spirit of experiment had by no means departed entirely from fiction. One of the more striking novelists of the Thirties was Henry Green (Henry Yorke), whose insistently fictionalist, very textual works have lately attracted the attention of deconstructionist critics because of their playful linguistic texture, their verbal idiosyncrasy and enigmatic spaces. But his early *Living* (1929) was, for all its textural complexity, an important industrial novel set around a Birmingham foundry-works, part of the reincorporation of the industrial world into literature that went on developing during the Thirties. Then came *Party-Going* (1939), a remarkable work about a party of rich young people befogged, in society, stasis and the arbitrariness of words themselves, as well as bad weather, in a very Saussurian railway station. *Party-Going* was plainly a Thirties political novel, a work of social criticism by a writer on the Left; but it was also a mannerist work about a crisis of expression and moral obscurity. Like many books of this date it prefigured the war, and some of Green's best work came with wartime, in which he served as a London fireman. *Caught* (1943), about London in the air-raids, is one of the most vivid and effective of British wartime novels; *Loving* (1945), by contrast, is a dense and complex fable set in a castle in neutral Ireland, while *Back* (1946) is about a soldier back from the wars. The Forties were Green's most productive decade, and seven novels appeared between 1939 and 1952. His fiction hovers between realism and pure text, a writing of dense texture and narrative incompleteness; it has remained important to writers and lovers of self-conscious fiction ever since, as an important expansion of the Modern experiment.

'Experiment', then, certainly did outlast the Thirties. There was, for example, Malcolm Lowry, author of *Ultramarine* (1933; revised ed., 1962), a youthful novel about a bourgeois young man who ships as a deckhand on voyage to the Far East, and who is looking both for human solidarity and for his own artistic solitude and identity. It is filled with Expressionist scenes and strong literary echoes; typically the manuscript was stolen and had to be rewritten, for Lowry was the unluckiest of writers. Even after publication Lowry wrote it again, trying to incorporate it into the larger adventure of his fiction, his 'voyage that never ends'. Lowry actually drafted a good deal of his fiction over the Thirties, though most of it was not published until much later, quite a lot of it after his death in 1957. So there was the much more Expressionist *Lunar Caustic* (1962), a wild, jazz-like evocation of the modernist city, based on his experience of being hospitalized for drunkenness in New York's Bellevue Hospital, and there was *In Ballast to the White Sea*, unpublished and destroyed in a fire in 1944. Then there was the book Lowry started in Mexico in 1936 as a political parable, and which turned through many rewritings into one of the great mythic novels of the age, *Under the Volcano*; published at last in 1947, it was to become one of the most important of post-war novels. Samuel Beckett – who had worked as amanuensis to Joyce, and translated part of *Finnegans Wake* into French – was born as a writer into the climate of Modernism. He published the clever playful stories of *More Pricks Than Kicks* in 1934, and then in 1938 a major absurdist novel *Murphy* – in which Murphy enters the Magdalen Mental Mercyseat, a mental hospital roughly equivalent to the solipsistic space of his own mind ('life in his mind gave him pleasure, such pleasure that pleasure was not the word'). In 1942–4, while working with the Resistance in France, he produced his next novel *Watt*, which opened the way toward a new and productive phase of his writing, and the central part he played in the post-war literature of 'absurdity'. Also in 1938, Lawrence Durrell, likewise working in Modernist Paris, published *The Black Book*, a surrealist work that was banned in Britain, a rhetorical flux of images of death and rebirth, obsessed with the evolution of consciousness from its regressive state in a world of nightmare realities. Durrell too was to become one of the most important post-war writers, and, like Lowry and Beckett, he continued the experimental tradition into his novels of the Fifties and Sixties.

And there were other ways of writing history, and other ways of reading the history of the novel. Anthony Powell was a notable writer of the Thirties: his *Afternoon Men* (1931) is a splendid novel about the Bright Young Things entirely comparable with the fiction of his friend Evelyn Waugh, while *Venusberg* (1932), a cinematic and surreal comedy about the affairs of a Baltic country (Finland), remains one of the overlooked classics of the period; Powell, later, would become one of the great recorders of the social, moral and artistic history of the century. C. P. Snow produced in *The Search* (1934) a fine novel, about the provincial life of a lower-middle-class young man who has chosen science as his vocation, that developed the tradition of Wells and Bennett, and would form the basis of his later social fiction; his friend H. S. Hoff produced three novels under his own name before turning into the post-war writer 'William Cooper'. Joyce Cary wrote four excellent novels based on his African colonial experience over the Thirties, the finest of which are *Aissa Saved* (1932), *The African Witch* (1936) and *Mister Johnson* (1939). Henry Williamson wrote several notable nature novels (*Tarka the Otter*, 1927; *Salar the Salmon*, 1935), and a key war novel (*A Patriot's Progress*, 1930); he also got unpleasantly close to Nazism.

Around or soon after the end of the Thirties, all these writers started work on major *romans-fleuves*, long-flowing sequences that suggested that some significant line of connection and development linked the inter-war, the wartime and the post-war world. So there now began to appear Snow's eleven-volume 'Strangers and Brothers' sequence (1940–70), which would duly track the coming of the post-war welfare state and the atomic age. Cary's 'Gully Jimpson' trilogy (*Herself Surprised*, 1941; *To Be a Pilgrim*, 1942; *The Horse's Mouth*, 1944) would follow the fate of British artistic bohemia in its story of a wild and inventive artist, and it was succeeded by a second important trilogy in the Fifties (*Prisoner of Grace*, 1952; *Except the Lord*, 1953; *Not Honour More*, 1955), the story of a religious upbringing and its consequences. William Cooper traced the development of an autobiographical hero who moves from provincial life to the world of metropolitan power in his four-volume 'Scenes from Life' sequence (*Scenes from Provincial Life*, 1950; *Scenes from Married Life*, 1961; *Scenes from Metropolitan Life*, 1982; *Scenes from Later Life*, 1983). Anthony Powell would produce one of the key narrative records of the century in his splendidly funny and wonderfully well-observed twelve-volume 'Dance to the Music of Time' sequence (1951–75), and Henry Williamson would go on to write the even vaster fifteen-volume 'A Chronicle of Ancient Sunlight' (1951–69), a record of an autobiographical hero, a 'passionate pilgrim of our age', that epically covers the period from the close of the Victorian age to the Sixties. These *romans-fleuves* are more than retrospects, though most of them are about the remembrance of things past (most of these writers, even the more realistic, acknowledged the importance of Proust); they were to represent a continuity of style that would help define the social material and the public scope of subsequent fiction.

Meanwhile another essentially continuous body of human experience, the world of love, sexuality and loneliness, was explored in the fiction of several very notable women writers. Most of them began work during the Twenties, developed during the Thirties, and had considerable influence on writing after the war. Rose Macaulay, a writer of great wit and observation, producer of thirty-six books, some of them satires on the literary world, did some of her finest work in the Thirties – for instance her Spanish Civil War novel *And No Man's Wit* (1940) – and continued to write fiction into the Fifties. The Anglo-Irish novelist Elizabeth Bowen established herself with her first novel *The Hotel* in 1927, and with *The Last September* (1929), a felt, poetic novel about the Irish Troubles in the early Twenties. She wrote several powerful novels over the Thirties, above all *The House in Paris* (1935) and *The Death of the Heart* (1939), about the impact of public on private worlds, centred on individual female sensibilities in a socially shattered world, and concerned, as she said, with poetic truths caught in non-poetic statements. Bowen's manner was self-consciously feminine, fragmented, concentrated in sharp moments, good on loneliness ('I have isolated, I have made for the particular, spot-lighting faces or cutting out gestures that are not even the faces or gestures of great sufferers'). It particularly suited the experience of wartime; her Forties short stories like 'Mysterious Kor', and her war novel *The Heat of the Day* (1949), set in a time of bombings, conspiracies and double agents, when the disorder always implicit in her best novels is a clear reality, are among her finest work. Rosamund Lehmann first established herself with *Dusty Answer* (1927), a bold story of schooldays lesbianism; then, during the Thirties, she was active with her brother John Lehmann in the 'new writing' movement, and continued to publish a significant, strongly realistic fiction of the crises of sexuality and solitude. Her fiction, too, powerfully extended across and beyond the war, and her two late books, *The Ballad and the Source* (1944), a child's perspective on adult sexuality, and *The Echoing Grove* (1953), a subtle treatment of adultery, remain among her best.

And then, above all, there was Jean Rhys, born in the West Indies, and a friend in Paris of Ford Madox Ford. He wrote the preface to her first story collection, *The Left Bank* (1927), noting her knowledge of 'many of the Left Banks of the world', and became one of the subjects of her *Postures* (1928). Rhys moved to London in 1927, and produced her novel *After Leaving Mr Mackenzie* (1930), a vivid portrait of sexual drifting and half-survival in Paris and London. The theme of the woman identityless and adrift, floating like flotsam in a random social world, became the chief subject of her Thirties fiction.

Then, after *Good Morning, Midnight* (1939), about another woman drifting in Paris, Rhys was silent, 'disappeared', for twenty-seven years till the Sixties – when she produced the remarkable *Wide Sargasso Sea* (1966), her complex rewriting and recoding of *Jane Eyre*, exploring its 'hidden' story, the life of the crazed Creole wife locked away in the attic of Thornfield Hall, providing her with a past, a history of dislocation and loneliness, an aberrant identity, missing from the original novel. Her work, like that of the Australian Christina Stead and the Canadian Elizabeth Smart, came from the sense of endless displacement, as a colonial and as a woman, and offered a bohemian answer to it; it greatly influenced the women writers of the Sixties, providing them with a missing culture of creativity. Like certain elements of the Modernist tradition, the tradition of feminine experimentalism also outlasted the war.

There was an even more glorious way to deal with the ominous idea of History that sounded through the Thirties. And that was flamboyantly to set it aside, substituting a quite different era and idea of history for it. This is what Ivy Compton-Burnett does in her remarkable novels, which are among the finest of the period. Compton-Burnett had published her first novel *Dolores* in 1911, but she later disowned it; her last novel was published after her death in 1969. This made a career of twenty remarkably similar novels, her mature work starting with her second book *Pastors and Masters*, which came out in 1925, one of the peak years of Modernism. Modernism was what, on the face of it, Compton-Burnett seemed to have little to do with; her work over forty years scarcely changed in subject or background, and each of her books is set in a fixed historical time and a ritualized fictional space. The time is less that of late-Victorian life than the late-Victorian novel, which Compton-Burnett does not reject but subvert, preserving it in an eternal stasis, for repeated decoding. This is the eternal world of Samuel Butler's *The Way of All Flesh* and Edmund Gosse's *Father and Son*, and Butler's deep irony and Gosse's sense of patriarchal crisis are both essential elements of her method. The titles of some of her novels suggest both their world and their highly dramatic material of conflict: *Brothers and Sisters* (1929), *Men and Wives* (1931), *A House and Its Head* (1935),

A Family and a Fortune (1939), *Manservant and Maidservant* (1947), *A Father and His Fate* (1957), *A Heritage and Its History* (1959), *The Mighty and Their Fall* (1961), and so on. This is a completely patriarchal, hierarchical world, where the landed gentry rule forever, though they generally hold their ancestral estates in reduced and difficult circumstances. The social rules and customs are precise; these patriarchs and masters have butlers and governesses, menservants and maidservants, imperious wives (often several), unreliable children and normally rebellious dependents. Society is totally important, though never in the Thirties sense of that word. So is history, though here it means the weight of the past and the power of custom, not Marx's revolutionary process. In this world religion is observed, and other classes do not normally impinge; indeed almost everything outside the designated family space – the classic space of Greek tragedy – is excluded, and the main powers of change are social, sexual and generational. Struggles for love, power and influence, and for fortune, precedence and inheritance dominate; the crimes and sins are the classic ones, of pride and hatred, of bigamy, incest, murder, child abuse and fraud. The dissecting, deconstructive irony that Compton-Burnett brings to this realm of domestic comedy and tragedy is generally shared by the very self-aware participants themselves ('What a day it has been! . . . There is material for an epic. The fall of Lavinia; the return of Ransom; the uplift of Ninian,' says Hugh in *The Mighty and Their Fall*). And material for an epic, moral and ironic, comic and tragic, there is indeed.

Suppose, Compton-Burnett's novels suggest to us, that on or about December 1910 human nature did *not* change, and all human relations, 'those between masters and servants, husbands and wives, parents and children', did *not* shift, as Virginia Woolf had claimed in her famous essay of 1924 – one year before the special world of Compton-Burnett emerged. That world is a stylized version of the eternal drama of human experience, which has been carefully placed in one selected phase of historical evolution. Compton-Burnett had, we know, read Engels's *The History of the Family*, and she seems to have turned it into a universal landscape. And if history has been stylized, so has her literary method. Almost everything is represented in the form of abbreviated, self-knowing dialogue, a dramatic ritual that is shared by all of the characters, whose lives are consciously presented as purified forms of social art. It is the distance that makes all the difference; this is family life rendered totally unfamiliar, made universalized and emblematic, a consensual fiction. Compton-Burnett's books are neither realistic nor social, and they are not historical either. They treat the 'past' as if it were the 'present', 'history' as if it were 'modernity', one fiction laid over another. But they are intensely modern in form, and seamed with contemporary experience, even as they insist on remaining fictions and refuse competition with reality. As Angus Wilson once put it, 'In the age of the concentration camp, when from 1935 to 1947 or so, she wrote her very best novels, no writer did more to illumine the springs of human cruelty, suffering and bravery.' And as another critic (Wolfgang Iser) has observed, 'the more artificial her technique of presentation, the more possibilities she unfolds'. Compton-Burnett is a wonderful reminder of the fact that fiction is a power on its own account, and that, even amid the omnipresent historical realities and social arguments of the Thirties, the Victorian novel, if sufficiently decoded, was by no means dead. It was a heritage and a history, a father and a fate, a family and a fortune, there to be struggled with, so that a very modern writer, if sufficiently cunning, could question it and then re-create it as a form of contemporary moral and human truth. Like many of the novelists who succeeded in outlasting the oppressive historical pressure of the Thirties, Compton-Burnett challenged simple and doctrinal history; instead she rendered history as radical style. It was a style that went on to serve her, with little change, right through into the Sixties, by which time she had become a leading novelist of a totally different age.

Part Two: 1945–2001

than the disaster of 1914–18, of which it was an extension. It can be claimed as the most horrific war in modern history. It started in the troubles of Europe, the results of the Armistice of 1918, the German determination to avenge humiliation, the deep-seated economic problems that swept across Europe and the world in the Great Depression. But it acquired its own distinctive horror, and came to enfold nearly every portion of the globe. It emerged from the age of dictatorships and harsh modern ideologies that developed through the Twenties and into the Thirties. In times of economic disorder, the Thirties became an age of dictators, extreme solutions, political terrors and purges; yet these were to prove a small foretaste of the terrors released by war itself. The Second World War saw unprecedented barbarism. Dreaming of a slave-holding Third Reich that reached as far as the Pacific, the Nazis enslaved huge populations, set up extermination camps for mass genocide. The Soviets purged their own generals and officials, shot their own soldiers; Stalin killed as many Russians as the Germans did. The Japanese starved and beheaded their prisoners. Great cities from Dresden to Hiroshima were firebombed, their civilian populations incinerated or subjected to nuclear radiation. The war produced more dead than any in recorded history: 46 million people died, mostly civilian. Methods of war included blitzkrieg, or violent and merciless rapid attack; saturation bombing; the sinking of civilian ships; scorched earth tactics; horrific reprisals against innocent civilians; vast deportations; death marches; slave labour; mass atrocities; public hangings and executions; the killing of unarmed prisoners; kamikaze suicide attacks; the genocidal elimination of whole races and categories; the forced sterilization of the unfit; the release of atomic energy with agonizing consequences. Refugees and displaced persons remained a problem for decades. Entire communities that had experienced genocidal suffering came to regard themselves simply as 'survivors'.

Hitler's intentions were plain enough ever since he published his Aryan bible, *Mein Kampf*, in 1925. 'The boundaries of the year 1914 mean nothing for the German future,' he declared. His new Reich demanded occupation of much of Europe and Russia as land for Germans to live in, *Lebensraum*; he sought the elimination of non-

Aryan races. 'Now I dream of the Great German Reich of which great poets have dreamed,' he declared. As, after the Russian revolution, ideologies hardened and a modern model of the totalitarian state developed, Hitler, who rose to power as Chancellor in 1933, used its methods, equally well developed by Stalin, to ensure his position. A bloody purge of his Nazi party in 1933 left him in secure control, allowing him to undertake the 'Nazification' of German life, and start a massive rearmament. Despite his blustering threats ('I am one of the hardest men Germany has had for decades, perhaps for centuries, equipped with the greatest authority of any German leader') and his territorial pushes into Austria and Czechoslovakia, other powers still felt they could do business with him. The great conflict flared on 3 September 1939, after Hitler invaded Poland, and Britain and France declared war. Hitler's response was swift and formidable; much of Western Europe was quickly occupied. The retreat of May 1940 from Dunkirk left Britain, under Churchill, standing alone under threat of invasion, the economy drained, the nation facing likely defeat. When Japan, expanding its empire in the Pacific, attacked the American fleet at Pearl Harbor, Hawaii, in December 1941, the USA was drawn into the war. By the time the conflict was over, it had engulfed many of the nations and powers of the globe. It was fought everywhere: across Europe, in Russia, North Africa, the Balkans, Greece and Arab lands, Burma, Malaya, right across the Pacific. Its impact on the history of the century was vast, far greater in its way than the crisis of European history and culture left by the conflict of just twenty-five years earlier.

After the war's outbreak, nightmarish fantasies worse than any Thirties writers imagined soon began to unfold. On the biggest battle-field in the history of the world, tanks rolled, jackboots marched, death squads prowled, prison camps filled and bombers flew between searchlight and flak to smash great cities to rubble. Vast regions of Europe and Russia saw occupation by foreign troops, with attendant cruelties, including public hangings and executions. The rifle, flame-thrower, knout and lash took over; the intentions of the totalitarian regimes proved more terrible than most Western imaginations could have envisaged. When the Allies won victory in Europe in May 1945

(VE Day) most European capitals were gutted, vast areas of the continent lay in ruins, industrial activity ceased, harvests lay unreaped. Every border was unsettled, millions were displaced and many more millions starving. War crimes continued to the moment of surrender and beyond. Emaciated and shattered survivors wandered the ruins from place to place: former slave labourers, displaced persons, prisoners of war, fleeing troops. As Donald Watt said of the Allied victory: 'Rejoicing was doled out in small bundles which were instantly engulfed in horror about the past and the present and usually in grim foreboding about the future too ... realism, if not actual disillusionment, was the order of the day.' More was to come. The European death toll had been vast: 15 million killed in action, another 4 million dead as prisoners of war, 5 million killed in air raids, 10 million murdered in massacres. Unbelievable facts about the deportations, massacres and acts of genocide that occurred in labour and death camps like Buchenwald and Auschwitz began to emerge. The Nuremberg Trials of Nazi war crimes in 1946 revealed the apocalyptic scale of the 'final solution' planned by the Reich. Six million Jews perished in this 'Holocaust'; millions of others, Jewish and non-Jewish, had been deported to slave labour and death. Many never returned, and new killings began as more hatreds and political conflicts were settled. Repatriated prisoners were slaughtered; so were Russians and Poles sent back under Stalin's rule. Western consciences were hardly clear. In the Pacific intense fighting island by island continued until August, when two atomic bombs were dropped on the mainland Japanese cities of Hiroshima and Nagasaki, so ending the war but initiating the nuclear age. The Second World War was over; its legacy of terror, dictatorship, totalitarianism and atrocity was not. The end of the Hot War was the beginning of the Cold War; the sense of historical disaster was deepened by a widespread sense of horror. The Allied victory was also the dawn of the Atomic Age, the age of Mutually Assured Destruction and the possibility of universal self-annihilation.

In 1947 W. H. Auden, now an exile in New York, wrote a 'diagnostic' long poem, *The Age of Anxiety*, into which he poured many of the deeper anxieties of the time. His earlier poem 'September 1, 1939' set the scene and the mood: 'Faces along the bar/ Cling to their average day:/ The lights must never go out/ The music must always play . . . / Lest we should see where we are, / Lost in a haunted wood, / Children afraid of the night, / Who have never been happy or good.' Auden's verse diagnostics summed up the post-war atmosphere on both sides of the Atlantic. Peace of sorts had arrived, and in America a new plenty, since war production had driven away the Depression. So had a new atmosphere of disturbance and demoralization. A sense of the 'absurdity' of modern existence was growing. As the French novelist-philosopher Albert Camus put it in *The Myth of Sisyphus*, published in German-occupied Paris in 1942, 'In a universe suddenly deprived of illusions and of light, man now feels a stranger . . . The divorce between man and his life, the actor and his setting, truly constitutes the feeling of Absurdity.' The Holocaust imprinted its lesson everywhere. Forty years on Martin Amis still proclaimed he wrote in a time of 'Einstein's Monsters', his work shaped by the Holocaust and the nuclear age: 'It is the highest subject and it is the lowest subject. It is disgraceful, and exalted. Everywhere you look there is a great irony: tragic irony, pathetic irony, even the irony of black comedy or farce; and there is the irony that is simply violent, unprecedentedly violent. The mushroom cloud over Hiroshima was a beautiful spectacle, even though it owed its colour to a kiloton of human blood.' Holocaust and nuclear cloud dominated the entire sensibility of the post-war period. And, as political tensions sharpened and multiplied, communism and capitalism moved into stand-off, turning post-war into non-peace, the mood of anxiety, absurdity, political horror, historical uncertainty increased.

In 1947, too, a cold bitter winter brought home to Britons the severity of their economic and political plight. The war had massively curtailed Britain's role as the great imperial power, and as part of the wartime Anglo-American alliance Churchill had had to accept the prospect of retreat from empire. In 1947 the Raj ended, as Britain handed over India at one minute past midnight on 15 August, after two hundred years of engagement in the subcontinent. Truman declared the 'Truman doctrine'; the Marshall Plan, for massive American economic aid to Europe, was approved. Robert Hathaway in his book on post-war Anglo-American relations, *Ambiguous Partnership*, sums up the atmosphere of the year:

Shortly after the turn of the year an unusually severe blizzard, the worst in memory, buffeted Britain. Coupled with an acute shortage of coal, it brought the economic life of the country to a virtual standstill and emphasized how vulnerable the once proud island had become. Prime Minister Attlee's announcement in the House of Commons during the height of the storm of plans for the final British withdrawal from India only reiterated that slide from the pinnacle of power. In February the British government turned the bewildering puzzle of Palestine over to the United Nations, at once admitting it could no longer handle a problem squarely in the middle of an area traditionally considered a British preserve ... These months also saw the merging of the British and American zones of occupation in Germany, and finally, the formulation and enunciation of what was to become known as the Truman Doctrine, with all its implications of an American assumption of British responsibilities. Many Englishmen, stunned at the momentous import of these events, believed they were witnessing the end of an era.[1]

The Cold War had begun; the term was first used that year. In the ruins of defeated Berlin there was already talk of an 'iron curtain' falling across Europe as a result of Russian post-war intentions; in 1946 Winston Churchill used the phrase in a famous speech at Fulton, Missouri, saying that an Iron Curtain had descended across Europe 'from Stettin in the Baltic to Trieste in the Adriatic'. Behind its totalitarian line of control lay, he observed, the great capitals of the ancient states of Central Europe: Warsaw, Berlin, Prague, Vienna, Budapest, Belgrade, Sofia, now lost to the Western world. The post-war world had arrived, and would last a very long time – certainly until the collapse of the Iron Curtain and of the Communist threat in

---

1 Robert M. Hathaway, *Ambiguous Partnership: Britain and America, 1944-1947* (New York, 1981). Though Hathaway's book is primarily about political relations between Britain and America in the post-war climate, and the emergence of American dominance, it indicates the climate in which contemporary American writing – the work of writers like Saul Bellow, Norman Mailer, J. D. Salinger and Mary MacCarthy – became of new interest to British readers (and writers).

Eastern Europe in 1989. If there had truly been, as writers of the inter-war years used to claim, a 'mind of Europe', it was now irrevocably divided. So was the ideological map of the world. Europe was not just split geographically, with wire fences, armed guards and concrete walls, but between two systems which Stalin proclaimed incompatible: communism and capitalism. Soon, in an era of suspicion and espionage, both would become atomically equipped superpowers, world influence divided between them. Each represented a fundamental modern ideology, born from the intellectual arguments of modernity itself: one from the tradition of progressive democratic liberalism, the other of revolutionary proletarian totalitarianism. In a web of confusions, conspiracies and mutual suspicions, the post-war world started, in a stasis that would end (if it did end) only forty-five years later, when the Berlin Wall raised in 1961 came down at last.

2

The period from September 1939, the outbreak of war, to November 1989, when the Cold War ended, is half a century long: as long as the period from the dawn of the 1890s to 1939, roughly the lifespan of the Modern movement. But the second half of the century was already proving in all respects quite unlike the first. Deep decisive events interrupted the age of Modernism, which began amid the liberal expectations and the artistic excitements of the *belle époque*, but dissolved into the world of Fascism, the age of dictators, an era of revolutionary totalitarianism. A fresh and terrible age of politics had taken over, and the historical optimism that was once part of the dream of modernity had long since failed. As the second half of the century turned to grim and menacing stand-off, the progressive hopes and ideological Utopias that had attracted many in the Thirties seemed at best naive illusions, at worst forms of treachery and betrayal, corrupting allegiances. If in Europe's capitals, entire political systems, industrial foundations and economic structures lay in ruins, so did European intellectual and religious values, ideological and metaphysical beliefs, ideas of selfhood and community, individual and state, history, culture, art, good and evil. The theologian Reinhold Niebuhr expressed the metaphysical shock when he warned that progressive liberal morality could no longer cope 'with the ultimately religious problem of the evil in man'. Others warned that the Enlightenment idea of the open society was in peril, the age of totalitarianism, as Orwell foresaw, here to stay.

In countries that had been defeated or occupied (that included most of Europe) and were still in crisis, or in some cases ceased to exist, the intellectual, cultural and moral tradition of literature and the arts had to be constructed afresh. Accusations of treachery, betrayal, collaboration, *trahison des clercs*, were widespread; the figure of the tainted intellectual would stay a potent symbol for the rest of the century. Ezra Pound, the prophet of 'Make It New', one of the great organizers of Modernism, was in a Washington mental hospital, unfit to plead on a treason charge, having broadcast from Italy for Mussolini during the conflict. In Germany great figures like Martin Heidegger were discredited by association with Nazism. In France leading writers like Céline were judged collaborators. In Eastern Europe developing events made the question of freedom and ideology ever more urgent. Stalin's armies had, in the emollient phrase, 'liberated' many countries, installing puppet regimes beholden to Moscow that suppressed intellectual argument and silenced, imprisoned and murdered political leaders and writers, all in the interests of history's proletarian revolution. A new form of *kulturkampf* emerged, provoking complex questions of intellectual and ideological allegiance. Many who had been on the progressive or revolutionary Left during the Thirties, up to and including the Spanish Civil War, rescinded their allegiance. A notable sign was the publication in 1949 of *The God that Failed*; six key writers, including Stephen Spender, Arthur Koestler, André Gide and Ignazio Silone, explored their rejection of Marxism and totalitarianism, as Orwell had in the years just before the War.[2]

2 Richard H. Crossman (ed.), *The God that Failed* (London, 1949): 'In this book, six intellectuals describe the journey into Communism, and the return,' comments Crossman in his introduction, noting that their conversion to Communism was 'rooted in despair – a despair of Western values', and their return was largely shaped by the refusal of Soviet Communism to respond to Western humanistic values. This was one of a

Yet Marxist sympathies, overt or covert, had not ceased entirely. Influential figures, dismayed by America's sole possession of atomic power, became spies for Russia, creating a complex web of dual allegiance, betrayal, intrigue. The CIA, founded out of wartime security and intelligence services in 1947, became embroiled in intellectual as well as international politics. The American anti-communist witchhunts of the Fifties, and the rise of the 'military-industrial complex', complicated allegiances and suggested to many on the Left a fundamental corruption of liberal democracy. Yet if Western Europe was to be preserved from communism it could only be through support from the United States. So complete was this second collapse of the European order that the post-war world essentially belonged to the two superpowers.

The post-war world that came into being after 1945 and lasted through decades of long anxious stalemate knew it was many things. It was post-Holocaust and post-atomic, post-ideological and post-political, post-humanist and, declared many, post-modern. The age of Modernism was surely over; the term 'postmodernism' begins to acquire currency round this date.[3] It was not just over; it was tainted. 'We come *after*, and that is the nerve of our condition,' wrote George

---

number of books that had a powerful impact on the post-war intellectual climate, others being Friedrich Hayek's *The Road to Serfdom* (1944), Arthur Koestler's *The Yogi and the Commissar* (1945), Arthur Schlesinger's *The Vital Center* (1949), Lionel Trilling's *The Liberal Imagination* (1950) and Hannah Arendt's *The Origins of Totalitarianism* (1951). *The God that Failed* received much American governmental support and circulation, since it desirably showed the new emergence of a 'non-Communist left' in Western Europe and the USA. For the general background of Cold War political conspiracy and *kulturkampf*, see Frances Stonor Saunders's fascinating (if sometimes exaggerated) *Who Paid the Piper?: The CIA and the Cultural Cold War* (London, 1999).

3 As Margaret A. Rose usefully shows in *The Post-Modern and the Post-Industrial* (Cambridge, 1991), the term 'post-modern' has been used by Arnold Toynbee in his *Study of History* (1939) to define the historical period inaugurated by the Great War (1914–18). It was used after 1945 by various commentators, including Irving Howe and C. Wright Mills, to describe the post-war politico-cultural climate and the revolt against Modernism. Like many such terms, it quickly transformed in meaning. Today, associated with 'the cultural logic of late capitalism', it suggests the pluralism, multiculturalism, relativism, self-ironizing discourse and cultural crossover of contemporary art and the knowing pluralism of contemporary society.

Steiner in *Language and Silence* (1967); 'After the unprecedented ruin of humane values and hopes by the political bestiality of our age.' The deaths of many great figures – Yeats, Freud, Joyce, Benjamin, Woolf – reinforced the feeling that a cultural era had ended. In critical circles it was already being historicized and monumentalized, made part of the history of the past. Experiment continued, in the work of writers like Samuel Beckett or Malcolm Lowry, but the day of the European avant-garde had died. The dominant tones in Western culture became those of existential anxiety and chastened liberalism, a guilty, vigilant 'new liberalism' sometimes not clearly distinguishable from conservatism or religiosity. As the American critic Lionel Trilling put it in his influential book *The Liberal Imagination* (1950), the times called for 'moral realism': a recovered awareness of the dangers of history, ideology, extreme allegiance; a deepened sense of the complexity and unreliability of human nature, and a return to the 'tragic sense of life'. As some looked to religion, Trilling looked to literature, above all to the novel, D. H. Lawrence's 'bright book of life'. What was needed was no longer politics and ideology: a Thirties inheritance now discredited. It was the novel, with its sense of difficulty, complexity, ambiguity, and its dialogic spirit, that, for Trilling, spoke to the difficult age.

Yet many writers felt nearer to muteness. If the coming of war had forced many into silence, its end seemed to prolong silence into perpetuity. Literature in much of Europe and Russia had been suppressed already, by dictatorship, oppression and control. Collaboration and new political instability further corrupted the climate. So did the difficulty of the truths that now had to be told. 'No poetry after Auschwitz,' said Theodor Adorno, the German philosopher who escaped to the USA during the war, warning that it was dangerous to aestheticize an evil history. In Germany itself literature had died under Nazism – until, after 1947, a changing intellectual and political order allowed a new writing to take shape. In Italy post-war writing came largely from those who had been communists or partisans during the war, or had survived the death camps: Ignazio Silone, Alberto Moravia, Cesare Pavese, Primo Levi and Italo Calvino became the key figures of a new literature. In France, where issues of wartime collaboration dominated, the movement of Existentialism raised fundamental questions of commitment and allegiance. When across Europe a post-war literature did begin to emerge, its writers often found their task difficult and paradoxical, their traditional humanism put to trial, their language and forms inadequate to deal with the horrors that had been witnessed and the sense of nihilism and absurdity they felt. 'There is nothing to paint and nothing to paint with,' one key figure of the post-war scene in Paris, Samuel Beckett, told Georges Duthuit in the late Forties, prefiguring the minimalism, simplicity and namelessness of his writing in fiction and theatre in the Fifties. It was not surprising that the writings of the time were deeply touched with history, marked by a spirit of absurdity and extremity, an air of nihilism and an instinct toward the minimal: as if human nature had betrayed itself, human character had collapsed, the human scene had gone. If, after 1945, there was already a 'postmodern condition', then at that time these were the things that notion then implied.

3

Little wonder that the most influential expression of Western thought and sensibility in the early post-war years was Existentialism: the thought of Kierkegaard, Heidegger, Jaspers, Husserl, above all Jean-Paul Sartre – the Parisian philosopher who had resisted the Germans, measured from the heart of war and occupation the key questions of moral responsibility, whose vision of anguish, forlornness and despair in L'Être et le néant (Being and Nothingness, 1943) expressed a philosophical spirit based as much on the contemporary historical situation as on the collapse of the Enlightenment traditions of humanism and reason. Similarly, in his wartime study The Myth of Sisyphus (1942), Albert Camus explored the sense of absurdity that overwhelmed the person in an age of inhumanity and futility. Both were novelists and playwrights as well as philosophers, and their fiction sounded the depths of the philosophies they explored. In Sartre's famous novel of alienation and contingency, La Nausée (Nausea, also

The Diary of Antoine Roquentin), begun as early as 1931, though not published till 1938, Antoine Roquentin lives in a world divided between swooning abundance and non-existence, unable to realize himself as essence; he seeks a philosophical discovery. As Iris Murdoch – writing brilliantly about the book as she started her own first novel *Under the Net* – observes, it is an intensely philosophical novel of bad faith, about a man with no proper human attachments.[4] It opens the way to Sartre's crucial occupation trilogy *Les Chemins de la liberté* (1945–9), translated as *The Roads to Freedom* (1947–50), which takes its hero from a condition of 'nothingness' (*le néant*) to the moment when, gun in his hand, ideas become actions, existence essence, and he can assert 'Freedom is exile, and I am condemned to be free.' Camus too published a wartime novel *L'Etranger* (1942, translated both as *The Outsider* and *The Stranger*), set in Oran, Algeria, about an aimless *acte gratuit*: the anti-hero Meursault commits a pointless murder to test the limits of his being and his capacity for sensation. *La Peste* (1947, *The Plague*) is again set in Oran, at a time when it is invaded by a bubonic plague; it is plainly an allegory about the German occupation. Here the weary hero Dr Rieux acknowledges that he too suffers from the 'present sickness', is 'sick and tired of the world he lives in'; put to the test, he tries to find enough humanism to counter the world of disease, bureaucracy and meaninglessness. The theme is echoed in Camus's philosophical study *The Rebel* (1951), which tries to answer Fascism's 'nihilist revolution' with a spirit of humanist rebellion. It passes on into the fiction of Samuel Beckett, with its sense of contingency and the absurd.

For the post-war years Existentialism was the crucial philosophy, and Sartre, Camus and Beckett profound influences on new writing, in Britain and the United States as well as Europe. Their impact had everything to do with the fact that they came from a land that experienced a German occupation which had produced both a brave resistance and a clear *trahison des clercs* among notable writers. Existentialism was a philosophy and a literature (many of the most

4 Iris Murdoch, *Sartre: Romantic Rationalist* (London, 1953). This was Iris Murdoch's first published book.

powerful novels, poems and plays bore its influence, not least the 'Theatre of the Absurd'); it was also an ideology, a climate, and a lifestyle. Its writings bore a sombre, absurdist message, about the loss of essence, the fragmentation of self, the hell of others, the blank vacancy of existence. Yet it also seemed to affirm the possibility of a humanist recovery, and explicitly put the writer to the test. Hence for writers Sartre's most influential book was probably *Qu'est-ce que la littérature?* (1947; *What is Literature?*, 1950), which affirms the aim of art as 'to recover this world by giving it to be seen as it is, but as if it had its source in human freedom'. In an argument resembling that of Orwell's in 'Inside the Whale', Sartre is concerned to define the responsibility of a writer of his own generation, the 'third generation' of modern literature, who has inherited a task from two generations who have failed: the bourgeois modernists of pre-1914, who aestheticized modern art, and the writers of the Surrealist revolution of the inter-war years, who failed to determine whether they were the voice of a new world or the gravediggers of the old. All were writers from the bourgeois age of 'the fat cows'; 'in the time of the lean cows they have nothing more to say'. Now the writer should act as if he were a free man, addressing free men, and could have 'only one subject – freedom'. The task was nothing less than the recovery of the word itself: a restoration of meaning. 'The war of 1914 precipitated a crisis of language,' Sartre says. 'I would say the war of 1940 has revalorized it.' He hence calls for a 'renewal of the sign', in effect a revival of political realism, and he counts above all on the novel: 'The empire of signs is prose.' (In a wonderfully odd passage he exempts British writers from his comments, since, living in a land which has never considered its writers as intellectuals, they can 'make a virtue of necessity and by aggrandizing the oddness of their ways attempt to claim as a free choice the isolation that has always been imposed on them by the structure of their society').

Like many empires after 1947, Sartre's 'empire of signs' was far from secure. His 'existential realism', like his later Marxism, was based on an act of faith. Reality could be determined through sign and discourse; the meaning of literature lay in its instrument, language; all it took was an act of 'engagement', re-authentification, to replenish sign with meaning. When the subsequent arguments of Structuralism, Post-Structuralism and Deconstruction had finished with all this, Sartre's 'revalorization' was left seriously challenged. But for the moment Existentialism was the intellectual necessity of a whole generation. After oppression and totalitarianism, it affirmed a new humanism; and it was not hard to see why, after wartime horrors, it was felt the age called for an authentic naming, a truer history. If it depended on an obscure act of 'good faith', it also encountered the darkness, the struggle of being and nothingness, the sense that the alien or the outsider had the power to struggle to new meaning. In France the work of Sartre, Camus, Malraux and others marked a way back to moral and political action. In post-war Western Germany a group of writers, *Gruppe 47*, including Günther Grass and Heinrich Böll, took up the task of replacing propaganda with fictional truth, falsehood with reality. (Grass tells the story of the writers' duty allegorically in *The Meeting at Telgte*, 1979, a novel about writers gathering after the Thirty Years' War to 'bring back the long war as word-butchery'). In Italy writers like Silone and the young Italo Calvino looked to 'neo-realism' to tell the story of wartime, then of Italy's post-war poverty and political chaos. Existential realism also flourished in American writing: in the fiction of black writers like Richard Wright (*The Outsider*, 1940), above all in the Jewish-American fiction of such authors as Saul Bellow, Bernard Malamud and Norman Mailer, who felt compelled to confront in fiction the moral meaning of the Holocaust. And, in a Britain deeply concerned with its own problems, aware that it was passing through a significant social revolution, writers followed George Orwell in the pursuit of social reportage and plain language, a return to the honest word. When over a decade later critics like Bernard Bergonzi (*The Situation of the Novel*, 1970) complained that the novel in Britain was 'no longer novel', this recovery of realism was generally what they meant.

Today, the history of twentieth-century literature is quite often written in two broad strokes: there was Modernism, then Postmodernism, and these represent the two key periods in the twentieth-century experiment. Yet as an account of the history of modern literature this seriously misleads. Right through the century there has run a major line of realistic, historical and political fiction-writing, against which Modernists and Postmodernists both reacted (every avant-garde needs a convention or tradition to overthrow). Often the result was merger: realism and surrealism formed an effective compound for many writers in the Thirties. Many of them who, following James, rejected the fiction that was too devotedly 'hugging the shores of the real', also professed it. James argued for 'solidity of specification'; Woolf, prophet of the insubstantial, also required us to 'examine life on an ordinary day'. Modern writing has consistently challenged realism's borders, examined its sense of fact or claim to veracity, doubted its phenomenology, rejected its materialism. But it has also affirmed its pursuit of a new or changed reality, and in Twenties Modernism there lies a fundamental search for the *mot juste*, a pared-down precise language, a Revolution of the Word to match the Revolution of the World. One result of the war was that in some ways the situation seemed reversed. Language had been a weapon of war, and had been corrupted; recovery of the sign was an urgent need. The hard and true facts of history, terrible beyond belief, needed revealing; a moral assessment had to be made. Against the case for silence there was the case for plain honest truth. In *Nineteen Eighty-Four* (1949), George Orwell closed his dystopian tale of the modern state with an appendix on the fate of words under totalitarianism. In the 'Ingsoc' of the future, life would be controlled by 'Newspeak', using the spin-doctoring techniques of Doublespeak, Newthink and Crimestop ('The purpose of Newspeak was not only to provide a medium of expression for the world-view and mental habits proper to the devotees of Ingsoc, but to make all other modes of thought impossible').

The 'return to realism' that formed a powerful trend in post-war fiction came in part from the desire to return damaged words to useful meanings, to make new modes of thought possible. Seeking to name reality when it was no longer the familiar friend but the threatening enemy, it represented less a rejection of Modernist experiment than a need to reactivate Nietzsche's 'sixth sense' – awareness of the commanding power of history – in the fiction of the post-war, post-nuclear age. It duly provoked its own reaction in the Sixties, as philosophers returned to the language issues posed earlier in

4

For all Sartre's wry words about the odd nature of British society and writing, the Second World War was as great a watershed for Britain as for any other European country. Though the British mainland remained uninvaded throughout, the threat came close; American entry into the war in December 1941 relieved a disastrous situation ('I went to bed and slept the sleep of the saved and the thankful,' wrote Winston Churchill of the night of the attack on Pearl Harbor). Britain emerged from the conflict a victor, but a much depleted one. War had not divided the nation but united it, and the accusations and guilts afflicting other European countries did not apply. But the long destructive air-raids had left major cities severely damaged, infra-structure and housing stock depleted, reserves and resources heavily spent; war had destroyed a quarter of the national wealth. Edmund Wilson, the American critic, visiting the ruins of Europe just after the war, concluded that Britain, with its bomb-damage, rationing, austerity and wartime military organization, felt like a defeated country, though one struggling to hold on to its historic and imperial pride. This was not the same nation as the Britain of the Thirties. War brought fundamental social change. While Churchill advanced the war, Labour and Liberal politicians had been planning the domestic peace: a post-war 'New Jerusalem'. As he tried to influence the post-war settlement at the Potsdam Conference, the general election of July 1945 swept Labour under Clement Attlee, his coalition deputy, to a landslide victory ('I won the race – and now they have warned me off the turf,' Churchill said). The common endeavours of wartime brought unstoppable demands for change, and in the aftermath of war Britain went through a deep and fundamental revolution, a shift of social power. New legislation planned during wartime, with greater equality, wider educational and economic opportunities, was advanced; but rationing and austerity became if anything more severe. The Labour government was committed to the 'Welfare State', and to 'nationalization' (state control) of many sectors of the economy. The Beveridge Plan of 1942 was now administered as a programme of 'cradle to grave' social welfare and benefit support; the Butler Education Act of 1944 had already opened new doors of educational and social opportunity. Heavy taxation flattened incomes and was used as a class equalizer; 'We are the masters now,' proclaimed Hartley Shawcross. The power of trade unions grew massively; wartime controls and bureaucracies remained in place.

New Jerusalem was not easily built. Whilst the new legislation widened opportunities for all, the high taxes were a heavy burden. In the Attlee period austerity ruled: coal shortages, food shortages, steel shortages, housing shortages, travel shortages. Britain sat in victorious poverty, in a time of slender means: 'Long ago in 1945 all the nice people in England were poor, allowing for exceptions,' wrote Muriel Spark, one of the great fictional recorders of this era, in *Girls of Slender Means* (1963). With foreign travel restricted, even the great travel writers of the Thirties found themselves stuck at home. Horizons narrowed: a Britain that had ranged the world imperially in the first part of the century and had then been engaged on front after front now shrank within tighter borders, as it lost its economic power as well as its imperial role. Yet what it lost in hard power it sought to hold through moral influence. As the symbolically austere Sir Stafford Cripps, Labour Chancellor of the Exchequer, put it: 'The world crisis is . . . in my view basically a moral rather than a political or economic crisis.' Unfortunately the British moral empire hardly compensated for loss of world role and economic strength. The future of the nation was uncertain. Europe as the scene of recent terrors hardly beckoned, though there were already plans for the 'United States of Europe' which eventually became the European Community. Yet, following on the wartime 'Special Relationship', Britain looked above all to the USA. And it was post-war American support through Marshall Aid that played a fundamental role in reviving Britain's, and Europe's, fortunes, in due time creating among Western allies the post-war version of the consumerist liberal capitalist economy which began to evolve during the Fifties, when Conservative governments returned and, according to Prime Minister Harold Macmillan toward the end of the decade, Britons had 'never had it so good'.

Not surprisingly, in many quarters, not least literary ones, pessimism was widespread. 'England as a great power is done for . . .,' Evelyn Waugh wrote in his diary in 1946, 'the loss of possessions, the claim of the English proletariat to be a privileged race, sloth and envy, must produce an increasing poverty . . . until only a proletariat and a bureaucracy survive.' Those of more liberal viewpoint looked with hope to the world of Beveridge, Butler, Bevan and the Welfare State. Yet the political mood of populism, bureaucracy and austerity encouraged cultural grimness and a drab general anti-intellectualism. Except in forms of official celebration (the most famous being the 1951 Festival of Britain), the arts seemed out of place. By 1950 magazines like John Lehmann's *Penguin New Writing* and Cyril Connolly's *Horizon* had folded in dismay. It was soon noted that, whereas the Great War had been followed quickly by the Modernist explosion, nothing similar was emerging from Britain post-1945. Cyril Connolly, that elegant pessimist, refined his pessimism further in his book *The Unquiet Grave* in 1944: 'Flaubert, Henry James, Proust, Joyce and Virginia Woolf have finished off the novel. Now all will have to be re-invented from the beginning.' In 1946 in *Horizon* he saw no sign of any such re-invention in Britain, 'not because of a decline in talent, but on account of the gradual dissolution of the environment in which it ripens'. In 1947 he added: 'It is disheartening to think that twenty years ago saw the first novels of Hemingway, Faulkner, Elizabeth Bowen, Rosamund Lehmann, Evelyn Waugh, Henry Green, Graham Greene . . . but no new crop of novelists has risen commensurate with them.' The arts were not supported, the literate bourgeoisie disappearing or in reduced circumstances and 'such a thing asavant-garde has ceased to exist'. He warned: 'There is an intimate connection between the Twilight of the Arts and the twilight of a civilization.' The sense that the post-war era represented 'the Twilight of the Arts' went on well into the Fifties. And it was certainly true that the pre-war avant-garde spirit that had nurtured Bloomsbury and Fitzrovia for the past three decades showed small sign of returning.

It should be said that similar views – that the era of the avant-garde was over, the cultural climate had diminished, the age grown drab, oppressive, bureaucratic and critical – were expressed elsewhere, not least in the USA where, in fact, a significant new generation of writers that included Saul Bellow, Norman Mailer, John Updike, Gore Vidal and Mary MacCarthy was emerging into national and then into international notice. In Britain, critics grown used to the writings of the Bloomsbury and Auden generations were quick to deplore the absence of talent and the lack of a new *Ulysses*. Yet many of the writers of the previous generation were now central figures of post-war literature: every one of the authors Connolly listed as the creative inventors of twenty years earlier was still writing. So were George Orwell, Christopher Isherwood, Aldous Huxley, I. Compton-Burnett, Anthony Powell, Joyce Cary (*The Horse's Mouth*, 1944), William Sansom (*Something Terrible, Something Lovely*, 1948), Elizabeth Bowen (*The Heat of the Day*, 1949), L. P. Hartley (*The Go-Between*, 1953), C. P. Snow, the brilliant story writer V. S. Pritchett, Vita Sackville-West and many more. What was missing was the 'new crop', the fresh generation. Those who did begin to emerge, Evelyn Waugh suggested sourly, were mostly state-aided, production-line specimens in National Health Service spectacles, as austere and grim as Stafford Cripps himself. And it was to prove true that the new generation often did have a grammar school and red-brick university scholarship boy look to it, and was a good deal more inclined to a Leavisite moral seriousness than to bohemianism, dandyism, alcoholism or camp. And a certain tone of moral rigour was encouraged by the powerful educational and critical influence of magazines like Leavis's austere and demanding *Scrutiny*, or Raymond William's socialist *Politics and Letters*, which had much of the puritan severity of contemporary socialism, and which seemed far more important than the half-faded literary journals. Most were devoted to encouraging the new genera-tion to cast away childish things – not least Bloomsbury, and some would say literature itself.[6]

6 An interesting personal account of this by a former pupil of Leavis at Cambridge is Martin Green's *A Mirror for Anglo-Saxons* (London, 1960), a serious attempt to analyze the intellectual, cultural and political mood of the times – and, not least, the appeal of the USA, to which Green moved as a teacher and writer.

The literary pessimism that developed in Britain over the Forties long outlasted its season; there are many signs of it to this day.[7] Thus in *After the War* (1993), D. J. Taylor, an interesting novelist as well as an active newspaper critic, argues that British fiction after 1945 has been dominantly preoccupied with notions of national decline and the issues and problematics of Englishness, creating a current of dissatisfaction that underlies most post-war British fiction to the present. As he also notes, in a wide-ranging survey of contemporary novelists, the war itself, and its inordinate power of social and historical disruption, was to remain a persistent reference point for British fiction.[8] And certainly, fed by strong feelings of literary transition and cultural insecurity, a distinctive image of British fiction began to grow widely familiar, undoubtedly fed by images of post-war Britain itself. Thus, as England sank giggling into the sea, its power fading, its economy in decline, it was inclined to look back, exploiting what it had most of: the past. It could still produce fiction of the traditional kind, the novel's equivalent to the Burberry raincoat or the Harris Tweed sports jacket. It could still produce wild invention and radical style, fiction's equivalent of Swinging London or the Beatles; but as fiction elsewhere grew more experimental and postmodern, it 'hung on' to the traditional virtues, sidetracking Modernism and maintaining a continuity with the realistic novel of the past. In truth, though Modernism had begun to disappear, not least because of many of its class and ideological associations, it had also never been more influential. Post-war 'New Criticism' began to monumentalize it, burnish its statues and icons, give it name, shape, order and significance, distil its overall importance. It became a heritage: in Leavis's criticism, the line of new

[7] Thus, in 2000, Ian McEwan on why Salman Rushdie wishes to move from London to New York City: 'It's the difference between being stuck in a remote foggy island off the northwest coast of Europe in AD 50 and being in Rome.'

[8] D. J. Taylor, *After the War: The Novel and England Since 1945* (London, 1993): 'The public debate about England's role in a post-war world which fizzes on through the post-war period, is consistently reflected in the fiction of the time, occasionally manifesting itself in unexpected ways but always providing a thin current of dissatisfaction flowing beneath the surface of individual lives.'

bearings in English poetry, the canonical order of the Great Tradition. And at the same time the modern novel acquired a new centrality, replacing poem or play as the exemplary literary object; it was now that writers like James, Conrad, Lawrence, Woolf and Joyce became objects of veneration.

Post-war fiction – not only in Britain – appeared regressive by comparison. Avant-garde urgencies had died; novels were marked by a return to realism, reportage, materialism, character, plot, setting and theme, linearity and narrative order – all the Modern movement had surely set in question. It likewise reverted to humanism; it rediscovered provinciality; rejecting the shock of the new, it hunted the shore of the real. The novel in Britain was no longer an enterprise in radical experiment; in fact it was 'no longer novel' – in technique or subject. For Evelyn Waugh this was a result of the drabness of the age: a golden age had now been followed by a silver one, which showed no radical innovation but could still be acknowledged 'for elegance and variety of contrivance'. To writers of more radical viewpoint, the problem lay in failure to change, in the conservative traditionalism of British life that, if in very paradoxical form, Waugh himself rather splendidly embodied. Meantime, this line of argument often went, real experiment was occurring in fiction elsewhere: the USA, Latin America, anywhere but Britain. This was the view that began to acquire long-term critical currency, leading to the over-emphasized notion that British fiction was realistic, provincial and anti-experimental: a view that has overlooked its interest and variety, as well as the rewriting of the tradition and the modern experiment that has actually taken place. It was true that the post-war atmosphere in Britain, well into the Sixties, was not encouraging to contemporary literature. University courses scarcely studied modern writing; academic critics, holding the same view of writers that the US cavalry had toward Indians – 'the only good one is a dead one' – devoted small attention to current fiction (though, strangely enough, many of those who wrote it were now in universities, which replaced bohemia as a literary setting). 'The most discouraging thing about writing novels ... for a young novelist in this country', complained the novelist and playwright David Storey, author of *This Sporting Life* (1960), 'is the fact that they have no importance, I mean they have no intellectual currency.'

In truth, a great many of the post-war novelists were in no way intrinsically anti-experimental or anti-Modernist; they were defined as that by the critics who read and interpreted them. The three best books on post-war British fiction were by American critics, who, however sympathetically, were inclined to perceive a Britain in thrall to history, tradition and anti-Modernism. In his pioneering *A Reader's Guide to the Contemporary English Novel* (1959), Frederick R. Karl noted that 'we have been reminded with alarming frequency that the English novel of the last thirty years [i.e. 1929–59] has diminished in scale', and that its novelists have implied that 'the experimental novel . . . is no longer viable and that retreat is perhaps expedient. The contemporary novel is clearly no longer "modern".' James Gindin's early survey *Postwar British Fiction: New Accents and Attitudes* (1962) saw the dominant subject-matter as class and social conduct, though he did emphasize the powerful influence of French Existentialism on British writers. And in *The Reaction Against Experiment in the English Novel, 1950–1960* (1967), Rubin Rabinowitz rightly drew attention to a general withdrawal from Modernism and the influence of the Bloomsbury Modernists in Fifties fiction, and an emphasis on the importance of the older, Victorian tradition of the English novel. This was a line of argument summed up later by the British critic Bernard Bergonzi in *The Situation of the Novel* (1970), where he held that British novelists had settled for 'the ideology of being English', accepted 'the nineteenth century as a going concern' as far as writing fiction was concerned, and hence were failing to write the 'fiction of the Human Condition' that had developed elsewhere, in France or the USA. From these accounts it could be judged that British fiction of at least the Forties and Fifties rejected all formal experiment, was predominantly national or provincial in its tone, had recuperated the tradition of Victorian fiction and was dedicated to social realism. Its technique was that of documentary social reportage; its characteristic tale was a story of a working-class or lower-middle-class young man wandering in a state of alienation along a canal bank in Wakefield or Nottingham.[9]

Happily more recent studies have noticed the incompleteness and narrowness of these accounts. Neil McEwan in *The Survival of the Novel* (London, 1981) remarks that the post-war relationship with Victorian fiction is a complex, critical and deconstructive one, and also that realism is far from being the dominant spirit of British fiction: 'Our fiction is strong in fantasy, in scandal and sexual humour, in eccentric forms of life, in philosophical and intellectual comedy, in its radical social irreverences; and in its attitude to genre, its parodies, and its attitude to the verbal nature of the novel.'[10] Other critics, like Robert Scholes in *The Fabulators* (1967), noted this plurality. The argument, clearly, had a truth to it; but it was always far too narrow, and soon exceeded its sell-by date. British fiction had hardly 'returned' to realism, since it had been a base-line for most fiction in the century.

---

9 Frederick R. Karl, *A Reader's Guide to the Contemporary English Novel* (New York, 1959; rev. ed., London, 1963); James Gindin, *Postwar British Fiction: New Accents and Attitudes* (London and Berkeley, Ca., 1962); Rubin Rabinowitz, *The Reaction Against Experiment in the English Novel* (New York, 1967); Bernard Bergonzi, *The Situation of the Novel* (London, 1970). Karl's useful study covers 1930–59 and considers writers including Graham Greene, Evelyn Waugh, Henry Green, Elizabeth Bowen and Joyce Cary, as well as the 'Angry' writers of the Fifties. It concludes that British fiction has chosen to be 'restrictive rather than extensive, to bring back character and plot rather than to seek the inexpressible; in brief, to return to a more self-contained matter while retaining, however, many of the technical developments of the major moderns.' Gindin's concern is largely with representation of class and conduct, and explores multiple perspectives on contemporary society. Rabinowitz is essentially concerned with the Fifties revolt against Bloomsbury. Bergonzi is interested in the late twentieth century crises of humanism and the nature of identity in modern fiction, and contrasts the way British writers have sustained a concern with humanist and liberal values while American 'comic-apocalyptic fiction' has taken a more extreme view of changing historical identity. All these books were of great importance in sustaining a debate about contemporary British fiction when it was largely neglected by British critics themselves.

10 Neil McEwan, *The Survival of the Novel: British Fiction in the Later Twentieth Century* (London, 1981). McEwan adds: 'The Victorian novel appeared, a generation after Joyce, as a vast and orderly genre reflecting a coherent society, which had since broken up, leaving its surviving relics in an uncertain world . . . Postmodernist disruptiveness is meaningless when it loses contact with literary convention. However conscious of their unviability, modern fiction has depended on Victorian rules for its own sense of freedom.'

If many post-war novels displayed strong social preoccupations, that was hardly surprising in a time of historical crisis and moral and ideological change. If the preoccupations were with class, region and identity, that too was unsurprising when new groups, classes and constituencies were finding their place in British life. But British fiction was not resigned to a new provinciality; nor was it immune to influences from elsewhere. As fiction revived, slowly during the Forties, with growing energy during the Fifties, the wish to record social changes and new attitudes did drive many young writers to the pen. The political anxieties and alienations of a time of moral and ideological confusion, and later themes of affluent nonconformity, clearly entered fiction. There was a search for popular vernacular, a vigorous renewal of language. Yet the view that British post-war fiction was, for several decades, primarily devoted to sociological realism is far too simple, and had the effect of narrowing the range of writers who became subjects of critical study, and the critical ideas by which they were judged.

In fact British fiction during the later Forties and the Fifties was enjoying a significant revival, and this period is when many of the most significant of post-war novelistic careers began. And far from moving in one single and backward direction, the novel was moving in many: toward realism, but also toward fresh experiment; toward provincialism or regionalism, but also toward cosmopolitanism; toward social documentation, but also into allegory, fantasy, Gothic and metafiction. In Britain, as elsewhere, this was a period when no one movement really prevailed, when no single style or aesthetic manner was dominant, when the range of heritages writers had access to multiplied, and the imaginary museum that feeds the modern arts expanded. Cultural layers and stratifications changed, as did audiences and methods of publishing. The emergence of the popular mass media, above all television, changed cultural values, and what A. Alvarez defined as an age of 'No Style' emerged. There were distinctive directions. By the Fifties British fiction increasingly reflected two things. One was a desire to reconstruct a form of humane liberalism, which led to connections with certain central novelists of the past, not least E. M. Forster, still alive and a significant influence.

Another was the need to confront the spectacle of the age of anxiety, the era of barbarism, which meant acknowledging some of the most fundamental insights of modern literature: the work of Dostoevsky, Mann, Kafka. Many of the most interesting works of the post-war years – they include Malcolm Lowry's *Under the Volcano* (1947), Orwell's *Nineteen Eighty-Four* (1949), Beckett's *Molloy* (1951), Angus Wilson's *Hemlock and After* (1951), William Golding's *Lord of the Flies* (1954) – deal, in a variety of forms from political or moral allegory to vivid social realism, with such problems of continuity and crisis. The 'return to realism' was just one element in the broader story of how, in a time of great social, cultural and artistic change, British post-war fiction took shape.

5

There can be little doubt which was Britain's first post-war novel. On 17 August 1945 – in the month atomic bombs annihilated Hiroshima and Nagasaki, followed by the Japanese surrender, which brought four years of ferocious fighting in the Pacific and the war itself to an end – George Orwell published a 'fairy story', *Animal Farm*. The book was completed in 1944, but publication had been delayed, since this tale that seemed a fable for children was in fact about Britain's wartime ally, Stalin, as his regime grew more brutal and his terror increased. This was no book written from 'inside the whale', in resigned passivity; Orwell had learned his disillusion with communism the hard way, through his experiences in the Spanish Civil War, and he now feared that though Nazism had been defeated, totalitarianism had not. *Animal Farm* seems the most English of novels, set in the decaying, traditional English countryside; but its real subject is Soviet Russia. It uses an old form, the animal fable, but for a completely contemporary purpose: the story of what happens when a popular modern revolution (here the revolt of the oppressed animals of Manor Farm, subsequently Animal Farm) goes wrong. A benign new order turns into a totalitarian system run by an apparatus of dictatorship, militarism, terror, betrayal, propaganda, the stuff of the new age.

Napoleon had commanded that once a week there should be held something called a Spontaneous Demonstration, the object of which was to celebrate the struggles and triumphs of Animal Farm. At the appointed time the animals would leave their work and march round the precincts of the farm in military formation, with the pigs leading . . . The sheep were the greatest devotees of the Spontaneous Demonstration, and if anyone complained . . . the sheep were sure to silence him with a tremendous bleating of 'Four legs good, two legs bad!'

Orwell explained he meant the book not as anti-revolutionary, but as a warning of how revolution can be corrupted – by modern illiberalism, the one-party state, unprincipled leaders, corrupt and servile apparatchiks, exploitation of the deluded masses, strict management of all thought. The book is most 'realistic' in the sense that it is written with Swiftian certainty: plainly and simply told, it depends on the value of the honest word.

So does Orwell's final book *Nineteen Eighty-Four* (1949). Shaped by the drab post-war Britain of shortage and austerity, its story is set forty years on (Orwell set it first in 1980, but as writing dragged on its title-date moved to 1982, then 1984), it comes from the time when Cold War had begun in earnest; it was published as China went Communist, and Russia exploded a nuclear bomb identical to the American one. It is a classic tale of dystopia, the dangers and disorders of the present fantastically projected onto the larger screen of the future. It is realism made displaced and extreme, as the shock of its famous first line shows: 'It was a bright, cold day in April, and the clocks were striking thirteen.' In 1984 Britain has become 'Airship One', part of the totalitarian state of Oceania, run by Big Brother. This is the world of Doublespeak, where reality is transformed to fiction, truth is falsehood, facts are lies. Appropriately the 'hero', Winston Smith, works in the Ministry of Truth, the source of its opposite. If realism has to do with the world of the familiar, Winston belongs in a world where the apparatus is directed at the destruction of all that is familiar – family, love, friendship, loyalty, brotherhood, even time itself. If at moments crudely extreme, the book acquires its greatness from Orwell's deep and modern understanding of the mechanisms of terror, brainwashing and psychological invasion: all the means by which the new 'reality' is imprinted on top of the old. The first weapon is language. The state depends on 'Newspeak', the abbreviated, corrupted, cryptographic language of so-called 'justice' and 'progress', which distorts everything and disguises the frightful reality. With it goes corruption of history and human memory. Big Brother, O'Brien, explains the totality of modern revolution: it cannot be overthrown. For this is 'oligarchical collectivism', where the first aim is not progress or revolution but power itself: 'We are not interested in the good of others; we are interested solely in power . . . We are different from all oligarchies of the past, in that we know what we are doing . . . We know that nobody ever seizes power with the intention of relinquishing it . . . One does not establish a dictatorship in order to safeguard a revolution; one makes the revolution in order to establish the dictatorship.' So had both Stalin and Hitler proceeded, offering a grim lesson to the totalitarian leader. O'Brien sums the future up finally, in a way quite understandable in the climate of 1949, and many times since: 'If you want a picture of the future, imagine a boot stamping on a human face – for ever.' In January 1950, seven months after the book appeared, Orwell died of tuberculosis in University College Hospital in London, another major writer lost to the post-war scene.

When the year 1984 arrived at last, it was generally said that Orwell's prophecies had been proven less than true. Yet the force of the book lies not in the definition of the future of Western Europe but in the marginal prophecies: the pervasive destruction of the familiar, the penetration and influencing of the human mind and conscience, the vast spin-doctoring of language and the loss of stable meanings, the manipulations of the historical record, the pollution or undermining of discourse, the nature of oligarchical collectivism. In this Orwell's novels, read right across the world, except in those countries where they were banned, were very British tales. They presume an empirical common sense, a sensible and democratic view of society and the rights of the individual, a conviction of access to a shared and honest language, even as they explore the conditions of an extreme, dehumanizing, totalitarian age and state. It is because Britain is hardly yet like Orwell's Ingsoc that the book is powerful: so powerful that it was possible to add the adjective 'Orwellian' to another literary adjective, 'Kafkaesque', to describe the direction in which certain societies, mostly those in the Communist orbit (where, as one Soviet historian put it, 'The presence of 6.5 million Soviet soldiers buttressed Soviet claims'), were developing. Orwell's two post-war novels were indeed very British tales, in their settings and liberal vision of human beings themselves, but they quickly became modern classics and international Cold War literature, *samizdat*, undercover writings from the age of the Show Trial and the Gulag. In Britain their meaning was a little different; they sustained a tradition of decent liberalism and common sense that came out of the progressive tradition, a work of complex political speculation as well as a warning for the future (another proposed title for *Nineteen Eighty-Four* had been *The Last Man in Europe*). Like Forster, Orwell had a large influence on the post-war mood: his books affected a generation, sustained the liberal political novel, encouraged moral realism and shaped many of the dystopian and large historical anxieties that ran through British fiction thereafter, from William Golding to J. G. Ballard.

6

'I should have loved to have seen them together,' wrote Malcolm Muggeridge of the very civil meetings that finally occurred between Evelyn Waugh and George Orwell, when Orwell was in a sanatorium and dying, 'his country gentleman's outfit and Orwell's proletarian one, straight out of back numbers of *Punch*.' And, if Orwell was a writer-survivor from the Thirties who handed on a significant tradition to his heirs and successors, so did Evelyn Waugh, though in a very different way. Waugh was no friend at all to the post-war world, which, in turn, was no friend to him. 'I have no message. I had a message . . . I do not believe in this brave new world,' Churchill had said sadly just before the election of 1945. Waugh had similar sentiments. He did not like the resigned atmosphere of decline, the drabness, the egalitarianism, the progressive pieties; like Churchill, he took up a comically pugnacious stand against it. Back in *Brideshead Revisited* (like *Animal Farm*, the book was written in wartime but published to massive success in 1945), he had made a lush farewell to the now distant inter-war years, displaced and destroyed in the tragi-comic chaos of wartime. The book, about the social and religious value of a symbolic house from the British and Catholic past as it was taken into the state-run world, was a splendid success, making Waugh potentially wealthy just at a time when such profits were being taken back by the state. Beyond the lost world of Brideshead lay the new world of 'modern Europe', and in *Scott-King's Modern Europe* (1947) he gave his views in yet another bitter satire of the world of dictators and revolutionary leaders. The book is the story of a British history teacher invited to the state of Neutralia (a cross between Yugoslavia and Franco's Spain) to attend a bogus national festival designed to win support and justification for the regime. He sees a revolution, has several sinister adventures and then returns to his English public school, to find it is now proposing to 'fit its boys for the modern world'. Scott-King objects, observing that *not* to fit a boy for the modern world is 'the most long-sighted view it is possible to take'. Waugh clearly concurred with his hero. The splendour of his best late fiction is that it simply accepts the absurdity of the new world order as a ridiculous comic spectacle, a universe from which all intelligent meaning has clearly leached. In response he offered a theatrically aristocratic stance, a splendid disdain, rejecting almost everything in sight, from modern marriage to modern plastic, from progressive notions to the spirit of Americanization, the culture of classless equality to the writers who succeeded him. This allowed him to witness everything with an enraged and testy comic delight. The post-war world obliged by giving him every possible opportunity; there was never any shortage of subjects.

The great opportunity came in the grim year of 1947, when Waugh was invited to sail across the Atlantic and visit Hollywood to consider a screen version of *Brideshead Revisited*; the book had been a massive success in the USA. 'I mean to do business with the Californian savages if it is possible,' Waugh announced. On shipboard he discovered the new social order: the British aristocracy now travelling steerage and

GI brides going first class. This baroque film project was aborted (the successful version was done on British television in the early Eighties), but Waugh, the only man in Los Angeles wearing a bowler hat, had meanwhile discovered what he called 'a deep mine of literary gold'. He was taken to see Forest Lawn, Los Angeles's fanciful theme-park cemetery, created by undertaker-salvationist Dr Eaton, and to this day a prime site of Postmodernism.[11] As Waugh delightedly observed, its founder was 'the first man to offer eternal salvation at an inclusive charge as part of his undertaking service': mortality as commerce. The result of his visit to the famous death-park, with its green swards, expensive graves, multi-cultural and pluri-historical chapels and enlarged version of Da Vinci's *Last Supper*, was *The Loved One: An Anglo-American Tragedy* (1948). The topic was a timely one in the age of the Marshall Plan; the spirit was that of post-war black comedy. In the new order, when American innocence meets European experience, innocence, not knowing itself, wins every time. The 'tragedy' is set round Hollywood's famed 'Whispering Glades' cemetery, with its depthless borrowings from the stuff of European culture ('The Wee Kirk o' the Heather', 'The Lake Isle of Innisfree'), and its presiding genius, the cosmetician Mr Joyboy. The place has its own parodic counterpart in the nearby pet cemetery, which provides similar services for our animal friends ('Dog that is born of bitch hath but a short time to live . . .'). Waugh's wonderfully Gothic text, and his delighted reaction to the bland, film-set, self-falsifying, narcissistic plasticization of California, the new Arcadia of eternal life and perfect death, where culture does not even go skin-deep, is more than condescending. Other later British writers were to find deeper treasures and

11 Thus see Umberto Eco, 'Travels in Hyperreality', in *Faith in Fakes: Essays* (London, 1986): 'But to understand the Last Beach theme we must go back to California and the Forest Lawn-Glendales cemetery. The founder's idea was that Forest Lawn, at its various sites, should be a place not of grief but serenity . . . To see the Last Supper, admitted at fixed times as if for a theatre performance, you have to take your seat, facing a curtain, with the Pieta on your left and the Medici Tombs sculptures on your right. Before the curtain rises, you have to hear a long speech that explains how in fact this crypt is the new Westminster Abbey and contains the graves of Gutzon Borglum, Jan Styke, Carrie Jacobs Bond, and Robert Andrews Millikan . . . In the construction of immortal fame you need first of all a cosmic shamelessness.'

more fundamental relationships in the Anglo-American connection, and other American writers would strike deeper into the empty alienations of the world of the Lonely Crowd. But to Waugh, the great modern black humorist, it was all an emblematic visit to the universe of modern unrealities, a world that had failed to confront all that mattered to Waugh himself: history, culture, rank, identity, faith, death and the true Last Things. In a sense it was perfect, as his writer hero Dennis sees, as he contemplates the death and cremation (at the Animal Cemetery) of his own loved one:

On his last evening in Los Angeles, Dennis knew he was a favourite of Fortune . . . He was adding his bit to the wreckage, his young heart, and was carrying back instead the artist's load, a great, shapeless chunk of experience; bearing it home to his ancient and comfortless shore; to work on it hard and long, for God knew how long. For that moment of vision a lifetime is often too short. He picked up the novel which Miss Poski had left on his desk and settled down to wait his loved one's final combustion.

By now not just Waugh's reaction to the madhouse of contemporary society but also his Catholic faith was becoming a key element in his fiction. *Helena* (1950) is a seriously pious work, 'done in anagrams and ciphers', the story of the British saint's discovery of the True Cross. But it is important mostly as a historical pre-treatment of his major post-war trilogy 'Sword of Honour' (*Men at Arms*, 1952, *Officers and Gentlemen*, 1955, *Unconditional Surrender*, 1961), surely the most important British fiction to come out of the Second World War. It is based on his own courageous if unconventional service (the Commandos, the Horse Guards, the Middle East, in then-Yugoslavia with the partisans), and has (deliberate) echoes of Ford Madox Ford's Great War sequence 'Parade's End'. Waugh's hero, Guy Crouchback, is created in his own image, but he, like Ford's Tietjens, is a chivalric gentleman, the last in his line, an old-fashioned and nostalgic (Catholic) Christian with an estate and the desire to serve in a just war on a true crusade. When he goes to war, what he finds are ignominious things, political treacheries, low values, corrupt alliances; this is no just war, simply a sequence of absurd and shameful mistakes, social and military disasters. The work is wonderfully rich in characters and episodes, filled with glorious comic set-pieces (Apthorpe's Thunder Box, etc.), and the book's quest for meaning, Guy's pilgrimage, is conducted amid a splendid chaos of wartime events. After all, war consists of strange alliances of interest, odd meetings of men. Meanwhile at home Guy's faithless and corrupt wife Virginia (she owes something to Tietjens's wife Sylvia) has an affair with the commonplace Trimmer; sex and class are corrupting, as in Waugh's earlier tragi-comic fiction. The true crusade proves false in nearly every respect. When the Ribbentrop–Molotov Pact is signed, the enemy is 'plain in view, all disguise cast off': it is Fascism and Communism, the 'Modern Age in Arms'. When British and Soviets become allies after Hitler invades Russia, the true cross is falsified and becomes the Sword of Stalingrad, while the war becomes 'the people's war'. Disasters in Crete and the Mediterranean lead Guy through a purgatorial underworld. The betrayals continue; in Yugoslavia the British give their support to Tito. Meanwhile a strange Providence plays a part, intervening sometimes on Guy's behalf, sometimes against him. The story is dominated by a myth of social decline and failed quest; in the end, like Tietjens, Guy stoically accepts his fate. Perhaps there are no just wars, just a common death-wish; and Providence may not be at all concerned with what happens to the British Catholic aristocracy. Guy makes a disappointed peace, takes up residence in the Lesser House on his estate, remarries Virginia (with her 'faint, indelible signature of failure, degradation and despair') and accepts her child by Trimmer. Unlike 'Parade's End', all ends as sombre comedy: 'Half an hour's scramble on the beach near Dakar; an ignominious rout in Crete. That had been his war.' Meanwhile 'monstrous constructions appeared on the South Bank', the Festival of Britain, celebrating the modern age.

By now Waugh was reaching the 'dangerous age' of fifty, falling out with his friends and many of his public, waiting, he said, for death. His bitter and jaundiced political opinions, his disdain for many of his successors (though he was generous in praise of Angus Wilson and Muriel Spark) and his frequent public rudenesses unsurprisingly made him unpopular with the ranks of the hypersensitive, the progressively enlightened, the politically correct. Yet one fundamental clue to the nature of his genius came in his last major book, *The Ordeal of Gilbert Pinfold*, published in 1957, midway through 'Sword of Honour', but reflecting an experience some years earlier. Though Gilbert Pinfold writes books 'quite external to himself', this novel is virtually an undisguised confession. Pinfold, the central character, is a middle-aged, dandyish, self-conscious writer tired of life and believing he lives in a declining age of letters. Like his creator, he has adopted the mask of testy don and eccentric colonel, and feels an aristocratic disdain for everything that has happened in his own lifetime. On a cruise to the Far East, he finds himself mysteriously persecuted by a great variety of strange, accusing voices, from the Right as well as the Left, who attack him for every kind of sin and deviance, threaten him with death and disaster. Finally he recovers from this ordeal, a paranoiac near-madness, brought on by the use of chloral. At last he recovers his reason and his 'modesty', his carapace of disguise, which has always protected him. Now, though, he realizes that 'a mocking slave always stood beside him in his chariot reminding him of his mortality'. Mortality was never something Waugh had neglected; the memento mori runs through all his work (and it is certainly to the point that Muriel Spark's book of that title, much influenced by Waugh, appeared in 1959). The 'Sword of Honour' trilogy would be his last major work. In April 1966, after he had attended church, the mocking slave he was long expecting called; Waugh died suddenly, in his own toilet, at the age of sixty-three.

Waugh is a major writer – still undervalued, in part because his politics, though far more complex than generally understood, were at odds with the run of the post-war world. In truth he was always a writer of the gloomy vision, the novelist of decline and fall. From *Decline and Fall* onward, his books share a similar vision, though in the early works the novelist is comically urbane and detached, and the crisis is seen pure. By *A Handful of Dust* the social comedy has become a personal tragedy, comically seen. In *Brideshead Revisited* the disaster has become complete and historical; by the late novels, the author himself is implicated – he either suffers like Guy Crouchback, turning to faith for endurance, or like Gilbert Pinfold, suffering paranoiacally. The story is imbued with despair, personal disappointment, hidden tragedy; perhaps it always was. It also becomes part of a Catholic recusant history, generating a sense that British history failed centuries back. In Waugh's world the barbarian is always at the gates, and in the light of eternity history is folly, the notion of progress ever absurd. This dark grim humour of absurdity is one of Waugh's greatest gifts to modern fiction. It revived an essential, neo-classical tradition of fictional satirical comedy that went back to Swift and Sterne. It was Waugh who gave it the appropriate place in the modern world, challenging many of modernity's expectations and illusions. In curious ways it became a central presence in modern British fiction, which has always sustained an essential and deep-rooted line of comedy. It passed to novelists of many persuasions. It is as present in the biting, liberal social satire of Angus Wilson as it is in the Catholic ironies of Muriel Spark, in the social observation of Simon Raven and Frederick Raphael, the prejudiced comedy of Kingsley Amis, whether early or late (Amis inherited the fundamental motto of the satirist: 'Never apologize, never explain'). It persists in the fiction of Martin Amis, William Boyd, Julian Barnes, Kazuo Ishiguro. It crossed the Atlantic into the American black humour of the Sixties: the work of Terry Southern, Kurt Vonnegut, Joseph Heller – writers who realized that in the late twentieth-century world black humour is never wasted, as Waugh so clearly saw.

As for his last major project, the 'Sword of Honour' trilogy, this became one of a whole sequence of post-war *romans-fleuves* that would deal with Britain, the war and the transition into the new order. In 1951 Waugh's friend Anthony Powell published the first volume of his sequence 'A Dance to the Music Of Time' (1951–75). At first meant to run to six volumes, it would eventually run, over the years, to twelve, and become one of the great comic social records of a large span of the century. Powell's is – like Waugh's – an insider's story, the world seen from the wide and high reaches of British society. The narrator, Nicholas Jenkins, has been everywhere, known all ranks, departments, corners of society, taken part in great decisions and small relationships, and watched the world change as it dances over long years to the fatal music of time. Like Waugh's trilogy, the sequence too offers a wonderful portrait of the wartime years, when lives disappear into the obscurities, betrayals and disasters of blitz and battle, and when the British social order changes. Here again a suspect hero-villain – the much-humiliated Widmerpool – ascends through the ranks to prominence, and is able to take his revenge for old humiliations, finally climbing to the highest office in the post-war world. Powell's open structure – the books, written over a twenty-five-year span, chronicle six decades of English life – allows for a fine rambling delight to be taken in recording changing attitudes, the ups and downs of social and sexual fortunes, the great comic gallery of British types. Life is a mordant comedy, where ambitions twist, promises fail, sexual desire corrupts and many fall by the wayside. Poverty links hands with industry, pleasure with poverty, the endless dance turning slowly to the music of time.[12] As in Waugh, wartime upsets the order, confusedly bringing together upstarts and decadents, aristocrats and artists, eccentrics, bureaucrats, soldiers, spies, spivs. In another major double sequence, 'The Balkan Trilogy' (1960–65) and 'The Levant Trilogy' (1977–80), Olivia Manning gave a powerful account (televised as *The Fortunes of War*) of a different warfront, the Balkans and Mediterranean, lands dear to the British imagination. Her story of the wartime experiences of a group of British teachers, first in Romania as it approaches war, then in Egypt, is another classic record of the world at war. Around the same time, C. P. Snow was extending his *roman-fleuve*, 'Strangers and Brothers', into the wartime years, when his Whitehall scientists were involved with the mysteries of the atom. Paul Scott would soon begin chronicling the Empire's end in the 'Raj Quartet', Doris Lessing the winds of change in colonial Africa in the five-volume 'Children of Violence'. In one fashion or

---

12 As the first novel, *A Question of Upbringing* (1951), already foresees it, in an observation both about the social whirl of the novels and the literary technique: 'The image of Time brought thoughts of mortality, of human beings, facing outward like the Seasons, moving hand in hand in intricate measure . . . breaking into mysterious gyrations, while partners disappear only to reappear again, once more giving pattern to the spectacle; unable to control the melody, unable, perhaps, to control the steps of the dance.'

another, these were extended tales of fundamental social change and many of them also stories of decline and fall.

7

Still, the writer from the Thirties who passed through the wartime years as if it were his territory-in-waiting, and then went on to capture the climate of the post-war years in their moral anxiety and sensibility of conspiracy and betrayal, was Graham Greene, Evelyn Waugh's strange co-religionist. Greene (who called Waugh 'the greatest writer of my generation'), was a writer of quite different slant. One of Sartre's 'second generation', a literary contemporary of Malraux, Bernados and Mauriac, his real impact belonged to the third. Indeed, the longest stretch of his writing life came in the years after the war, and though that, as he might have said himself, was basically a matter of longevity (he died in 1991 at the age of eighty-seven), it is also a testament to his imaginative vitality and his vigorous sense of history, for his writing never ceased to be topical or relevant. Not just the largest but the best part of it fell around or after the war; it was as if, for all its force, his fiction of the Thirties was a preparation. By 1960 he was widely acknowledged as the best novelist Britain had, unlucky not to be awarded the Nobel Prize. By the Seventies he had offended enough political figures across the post-war world to make himself a dangerous presence. On his death in Switzerland (he never ceased to be an exile), William Golding acknowledged him as 'the ultimate chronicler of twentieth-century man's consciousness and anxiety'. By this time he had worked in nearly all the available genres – spy novel and thriller, the tale *noir*, the religious romance, the political novel, the foreign mystery, the social comedy, as well as the screenplay and the stage play. If some of his works were entertainments, he made all the genres relevant, accessible to his complex religious and metaphysical vision and to an age perceived as one of spiritual chaos and historical dislocation. His free use of form and genre led some critics to suppose he had never quite found the right form for his fiction; in fact these were just those forms. In a notable novel from wartime, *The Ministry of Fear* (1943), set in the Blitz, Greene has a character reflect on this as bombs rain down: 'You used to laugh at the books Miss Savage read – about spies, and murders, and violence, and wild motor-car chases, but dear, that's real life . . . The world has been made by William Le Queux.' Greene was right: the world of immediate wartime realities (and, as it would turn out, his post-war and Cold War concerns) had already been formed in fiction by the spy novelists from William Le Queux to John Buchan, detective-story writers from Conan Doyle and E. L. Trent to Nicholas Blake and Margery Allingham, and the creators of the modern metaphysical thriller, from François Mauriac to Patrick Hamilton and Raymond Chandler.

Spy fiction in particular was becoming one of the great modern genres, not least because its development coincided with a rising atmosphere of international intrigue and conspiracy, and the growth of secret police systems and foreign intelligence-gathering enterprises, in which writers, intellectuals, academics and journalists played a significant part. Modern spy fiction, like most of the modern spy services, developed in the years just before the Great War, in the fiction of William Le Queux (1864–1927), who was probably (like Greene) a spy himself. Le Queux wrote *Guilty Bonds* (1890), *A Secret Service* (1896) and *Spies of the Kaiser* (1909), dramatic and patriotic stuff that provided warning of a likely German invasion, a theme taken up by Erskine Childers's famous *The Riddle of the Sands* in 1903. A more complex treatment of such materials, arising from times of political assassins, anarchist and Fenian conspiracies, was Conrad's *The Secret Agent* (1907), another book Greene admired. The Great War caused spy tales to prosper: John Buchan's *The 39 Steps* (1915) was hastily written, proposing a German plot to infiltrate the British establishment and presenting the patriotic British spycatcher Richard Hannay.[13] By the Thirties – as political order collapsed, internal secret

---

13 'An early hero of mine was John Buchan, but when I reopened his books I found I could no longer get the same pleasures from Richard Hannay,' Greene wrote in *Ways of Escape* (London, 1980). 'More than the dialogue and situation had dated; the moral climate was no longer that of my boyhood. Patriotism had lost its appeal, even for a schoolboy . . . The hunger marchers seemed more real than the politicians. It was no longer a Buchan world.'

police forces flourished, international espionage grew in scale, moral and ideological allegiance grew more ambiguous – the spy or the double agent was everywhere in fiction. Somerset Maugham, one of a number of writers who had actually worked in Intelligence during the Great War, introduced his own urbane spy hero in *Ashenden: Or the British Agent* in 1928. Christopher Isherwood showed the spy in different guise and in a much more corrupted world of fascism and bolshevism in the form of the clownish Arthur Norris in *Mr Norris Changes Trains* (1935). Eric Ambler wrote splendidly of espionage in *Epitaph for a Spy* (1938) and *The Mask of Dimitrios* (1939). And Greene himself, in his early books, which were by no means about the old Buchan world, caught the pervasive and duplicitous atmosphere of danger and conspiracy, loyalty and betrayal, alliance and misalliance, in *Stamboul Train* (1932) (" "'E's a spy," Mr Savory added, " 'E 'as to see everything and pass unnoticed'"), *England Made Me* (1935), *A Gun For Sale* (1936) and *The Confidential Agent* (1939). The spy, like the sinner or the failed priest, was a figure out of the contemporary morality play as the world darkened and cosmic intention grew peculiarly obscure.

Greene proved a natural novelist of wartime. He served in the conflict with characteristic obscurity, working for the Foreign Office and being sent on 'special duty' for MI6 to Freetown in Sierra Leone, where he wrote *The Ministry of Fear*, and which became the setting for *The Heart of the Matter* (1948). On his return he worked for the SIS under Kim Philby (who became a close friend), running agents and disinformation in Spain and Portugal. He grew fascinated by the mood of treachery, double-dealing and divided allegiances that led to some of the great spy scandals of the Cold War years; suspicions that he was involved with the intelligence services (but whose?) lasted right up to his death in 1991. Duplicity, divided loyalties, split allegiances and guilty betrayals were his theme and calling card, right from his schooldays on. As he said himself: 'The writer should be a somewhat mysterious figure; he owes it to his readers. It is what he writes that matters, not the personality of the writer.' Like Waugh, Greene saw the history of his times as debased, corrupt, senseless, human life at odds with the world, cut off from the obscurely divine, leaving despair and guilt everywhere. Innocents turn into murderers, loving husbands to spies, helpless men to hunted creatures. Unlike Waugh, he reacted to this not with aristocratic dismay but political knowingness, the eye of the world-weary initiate who always has access to the hidden door, always knows the intimate secret. His world of seedy landscapes, bombed cities, invaded lands, vulture-haunted tin shacks, failed loves, dishonoured marriages, political, sexual and religious faithlessness, moral and metaphysical guilt, was the product of a complex Catholic conscience, but over time it also strangely came to match the objective condition of the world, the crises of an age of existential anguish. And it also came to match almost exactly the distinctive landscape of confrontational ideology, treachery, mutual suspicion and intricate intimacy that became the international landscape of the Age of Cold War.

Thus Greene's stained, anxious, Gothic realism somehow moved ever closer to the centre of modern writing as the dark years rolled by, the Cold War got colder, the nuclear stand-off grew. As in the famous screenplay for *The Third Man* (1949) (later turned into a book), the story of Harry Lime, the smuggler of penicillin through the tunnels of Vienna in that four-power occupied and divided city (the character was probably based on Philby), his writing shifted to take full account of the new ideological divide, the shattered cities, the chaos of lives caught up in one way or another in the great undercover superpower game. A Catholic who could fully sympathize with Communism, to the point where he often seemed to presume a mutual identity between the two, a writer who saw sinners as capable of sainthood, traitors as capable of honour, innocents as capable of sin, patriotism as debased, disloyalty as part of a higher loyalty, he at last succeeded in transforming his own special landscape that started in his schooldays – we call it Greeneland – into a simulacrum of the Cold War world itself. In that world he then became an indefatigible traveller, appearing in its flashpoints and trouble spots (never a short-age of those), capturing its aromas and its local colours, creating them as real places that could still belong inside his distinctive moral and metaphysical world. Greene insisted that he was not a novelist of social realism, and only a small part of his work is about Britain. Nor, quite, are his novels religious novels; rather they were written in some aftermath, the shadowy moral and geographical wastelands that had been left behind after the death of order and reason and the departure of a just God. The significance of the religious novel, Greene explained, was that it sustained something central to fiction, the human factor: 'with the religious sense went the importance of the human act'. And it is the religious sense that dominates in the novels he wrote around wartime and the immediate aftermath – one of the strongest periods of his work, and the highest period of his fame.

The Heart of the Matter, set in the Sierra Leone Greene knew as an intelligence officer in the war, appeared in 1948, and seemed to complete the sequence of novels that had begun with *Brighton Rock*. Scobie, the colonial policeman, a weak man who sins out of human compassion, and is led along the path to adultery, blasphemy, then suicide, wants to reach 'the heart of the matter', confront the evil and suffering of the world. His 'presumption' brings his self-sacrifice, for himself or perhaps even for the world. Significantly the novel, though religious in subject, is also the portrait of a dying empire where all law is in decay: a typical landscape from the later fiction. *The End of the Affair* (1951), with an epigraph from Léon Bloy ('Man has places in his heart which do not yet exist, and into them enters suffering, that they may have existence'), has some claim to be Greene's best novel (Waugh thought so). Set in London during the Blitz, it is a story told by the writer Bendrix; a strange religious fable, it is also a self-conscious fiction about the nature of fiction. Bendrix is no religious man but a cynical humanist. He is having an affair with Sarah, a married woman, and becomes convinced she has another lover he must pursue. A theological detective fable begins; it turns out that the suspect lover is God, to whom Sarah has turned again in adulterous guilt. In a metaphysical wager, after seeing Bendrix's body lying in a bombed house, she has promised God to give him up for good if he can only live. God of course is a far higher plotter than Bendrix, and in his great game of sin and redemption, saints and sinners, Bendrix can only have the most minor of roles. The story turns into a battle of plotters, which Bendrix is bound to lose. 'We are inexorably bound to the plot,' he bitterly concludes, 'and wearily

God forces us, here and there, according to his intention, characters without poetry, without free will, whose only importance is that somewhere, at some time, we help furnish the scene in which a living character moves and speaks.' It is the book in which Greene comes closest to displaying his hand as a writer, and his fictional aesthetic: the novelist is God-like, perhaps acting with Him or against Him, but creating human lives, choices, dilemmas of love and compassion. Greene's fullest examination of love of God and desire for eternity, of the gambles we make with God, this is also his closest look at the paradoxes of narrative. 'If this book of mine fails to take a straight course, it is because I am lost in a strange region; I have no map,' Bendrix confesses. Greene's most blatantly Catholic novel is also his most metafictional.

For the moment this fine novel marked the end of that particular affair. By the early Fifties the Cold War had become highly confrontational. Key dates were the Truman Doctrine (1947), the Berlin Blockade (1948–9), the proclamation of East Germany (DDR) as a separate state in 1949, the year the USSR tested a nuclear bomb, the start of the Korean War in 1950, the Russian invasion of Hungary in 1956 and the beginning of US involvement in Vietnam in 1965. This darkening of world history was mirrored in Greene's fiction. In the early Fifties he several times visited French Indochina (Vietnam) as the French resisted insurgent nationalists led by Ho Chi Minh. This (and Greene's problems in getting an American visa because of youthful Communist Party membership) produced his novel *The Quiet American* in 1955. The quiet American is Alden Pyle, a young man who works for the American Embassy and is engaged in covert operations. He is satirically treated: sexually and politically naive, he has read too many books with long titles, believes neither in a colonial nor a communist Vietnam, wants all the world to be like America. The cynical British journalist Fowler, Pyle's rival for a Vietnamese girl, is at first taken by his simplicity but finally concludes 'Innocence is a kind of insanity.' He conspires in Pyle's death at the hands of the rebels, and ends the book in a state of mild Catholic guilt. The book reveals Greene's ambiguous allegiances. It also conceals the fact that he had undertaken various SIS engagements since his official departure from the organization in 1944, suggesting his own engagement in a nether-world of counter-intelligence – where, as in love and religion, duty is obscure, innocence has no value, loyalty becomes blurred. It opened out to a sequence of books, in various styles from comic to tragic, which took Greene to scenes of modern political turmoil – onto which he grafted his political observation, experienced cynicism, concern with guilt and innocence, radical hopes and religious doubts and beliefs. A visit to Batista's Cuba ('a comedy of errors') yielded material for *Our Man in Havana* (1958), a conspiratorial spoof about the absurdities of the British intelligence community, drawing on Greene's experience of running a double agent in Portugal whose cast of informants was entirely fictional. When 'Our Man in Havana', a vacuum cleaner salesman named Wormwold, wanting to buy a pony for his daughter, is recruited, he becomes first comically then dangerously involved in the hard trade of spycraft, which he sees is like 'the cruel and inexplicable world of childhood'.

The world of modern espionage, superpower politics and Third World revolutions would remain close to Greene's attention. And by the early Sixties the spy novel had become a genre deeply suited to the times. In 1953 the most famous spy of them all – 007, James Bond – appeared in *Casino Royale* and a sequence of Ian Fleming novels where he loved every woman, used every gadget, defeated every sinister foreign conspiracy, blocked every apocalyptic endeavour to blow up the world. Greater books appeared: John Le Carré introduced his quiet spymaster George Smiley in *Call for the Dead* (1961), and became a bestselling author in 1963 with *The Spy Who Came in from the Cold*, about a fake defector sent into East Germany. In such books and the work of Len Deighton (*The Ipcress File*, 1962, *Funeral in Berlin*, 1964) and Adam Hall (*The Quiller Memorandum*, 1965), the serious post-war spy novel, a labyrinthine fable of the Cold War age, was born. Greene's fiction undoubtedly helped create this world, though he had not fully dispensed with his religious concerns, as his next novel shows. *A Burnt-Out Case* (1961) is set well out of the world, in a leper colony in the Congo. For some reason Greene felt this would be his last novel, that he too was a burnt-out case. Hence the book was meant to be a final statement, 'an attempt to give dramatic expression to various types of belief, half-belief and non-belief'. The once famous architect Querry, builder of fine churches, now feels himself to be a burnt-out case, just like a leper who has passed through the disease. He goes to the colony to leave behind worldly success, only to win new fame as a humanitarian, and then die as a result of a false accusation of seduction.

In fact, it was the religious theme that burnt out in the novel; Greene had many more books to write. He returned to fiction in *The Comedians* (1966), set in 'Papa Doc' Duvalier's corrupt Haiti, with its seedy dictator and his force of Tontons Macoutes. Evil is rampant, terror universal, but the theme is comedy; when the world is so absurd, perhaps the individual can only be a comedian. As the character Brown puts it: 'We are the faithless; we admire the dedicated . . . for their integrity, their fidelity to a cause, but through timidity, or lack of sufficient zest, we find ourselves the only ones truly committed – committed to a whole world of good and evil, to the wise and the foolish, the indifferent and the mistaken.' Finally there is an absurd revolution on the part of the comedians; the book was a sufficient provocation to make 'Papa Doc' into a literary critic, condemning Greene's work and attitudes. But tactics of survival in the still dark world of modern politics were now a key Greene theme. *The Honorary Consul* (1973) more seriously explores the world of the South American dictatorships, following the kidnapping activities of guerillas in Argentina and Paraguay, and considers the morality of political terrorism. The victim of kidnapping is a British nonentity, Charlie Fortnum, the drunken British honorary consul, a Greene-ian version of Malcolm Lowry's Geoffrey Firmin. Spying forms the basis of *The Human Factor* (1978), which is partly based on the case of Greene's friend and former spy-boss Kim Philby, now fled to Moscow: a very British spy. The book is a compassionate account of that complex figure, the double agent. Castle, the central character, has a history not unlike Greene's own, and when he defects to Moscow the novel seeks to follow his quest onward past God and Marx, faith and disloyalty, to eventual peace of mind. Greene's sense of the post-war ideological paradox lasted to the end. In *Monsieur Quixote* (1982), his revisionist version of the great novel from which all novels spring,

Cervantes's *Don Quixote*, the scene is modern Spain and Quixote and Panza are a Catholic priest and a Communist mayor. The wind-mills and mirages they pursue are the modern ideologies, which turn them into adversaries. But as they enjoy their adventures and debate their metaphysical and social positions, they find they just might be going in the same direction after all. As Father Quixote reflects, 'sharing a sense of doubt can bring men together perhaps even more than having a faith'.

A decade later, after eight decades of writing, Greene died; he was still the contemporary British writer the critics and the British tradition found hardest to deal with. His work had never gelled into one single shape or form. It had never established a fixed level of seriousness. Yet it was all collectively Greene-ian, constructing in every case a pervasive atmosphere, social and moral, metaphysical and religious. No single book summed it up, though there were classics: *Brighton Rock*, *The Power and the Glory*, *The Heart of the Matter*, *The End of the Affair*. His writing was essentially filmic, and it was essentially international. Greene never seemed fully at home in his native land-scape, and reached into powerful images of entire continents just as he did into the darkest places of the human condition, leaving those who attempted to track him on a biographical quest ever floundering in his wake. It was a journey without maps, he said, but he mapped it with his own pen. Yet for all the travels and the eternal hints of disloyalty and faithlessness, there remained a kind of Conradian solidity, which was also a kind of Britishness. His writer's sense of exile was never total; and if, like Waugh, he disputed with progressive liberalism he plainly had a sense of the need for political change in the world. In all, his fiction – remarkably various, drifting freely among the genres – amounts to one of the most complete of modern writing lives. He had moved from the bitter political age of Depression crisis through wartime horrors to the no less dark and ugly world of Cold War and superpower rivalries, where the spy novel became a kind of cultural necessity. He moved from thrillers and entertainments to become an explorer of modern politics and a speculator of contem-porary dilemmas of faith and justice; when asked, he was content to be thought 'a good popular writer'.

The writer who said he would rather end his days in a Russian Gulag than California was not to every taste: he was not without humour, not without cynicism and certainly not without sin. He cultivated a grand air of deviousness, and some readers found his blend of faith and politics, idiosyncratic Catholicism and idiosyncratic Marxism dismaying. Some thought his vision of a world where compassion often led to self-destruction, goodness to evil, no maps are safe and the survival of the human factor seems an arbitrary matter, too contorted a mystery. In fact over his fifty books he left his trace everywhere on British fiction, and writers who have no other reference point in common seem to find one in him: Malcolm Lowry, John Le Carré, Muriel Spark, Anthony Burgess, P. D. James, Len Deighton, Brian Moore, David Lodge, Beryl Bainbridge, Ian McEwan and Martin Amis. Greene certainly shaped the future of the dark crime novel, the psycho-thriller which captured the seediness of the world at war or uneasy peace. He steered the spirit of post-war spy fiction, which did so much to capture the mood of duplicity and conspiracy, the whole looking-glass world, that marked the Cold War age. When Len Deighton published *The Ipcress File* in 1962, John Le Carré *The Spy Who Came in from the Cold* in 1963, both were in the shadow of Greene. He certainly shaped the future of the modern religious novel: the novels of Muriel Spark, another writer who shares the sense of God or Providence as a cunning plotter who is testing the world of author, novel and story, and the complex Catholic comedies of Anthony Burgess. At best his books assume that what he called 'popular' fiction (he was an unerring bestseller) can possess the same density, moral challenge and human depth as the works of Conrad or Mauriac, two of his heroes. He was a major and enduring writer: even if some of his books were slight or feeble, all were fed by a vision almost too large for his own interpretation of the difficult and seemingly meaningless age of secularity, religious disorder, metaphysical paradox, bleak history and the ever troubling 'human factor': the times through which he lived.

8

In Waugh and Greene, post-war Britain had two great popular writers. But was Modernism dead now, the age of the avant-garde over – as critics like Cyril Connolly argued? Few signs of experimentalist passion were, it was true, emerging from the young writers of Welfare State Britain. But could it be that Modernism was alive, well and living in exile, as it always mostly had – and possibly turning into something quite fresh, a new era of experiment? Paris was the classic location, and in Paris there was Samuel Beckett: a Protestant Irishman of Huguenot descent, who had now chosen to work in the French language. He was thus at several angles to the British tradition, working on what would prove to be some of the most important writing of the post-war era, though its importance would take some time to grow fully visible. Born near Dublin in 1906, he had a fine education in languages and a highly philosophical disposition; in 1928, having taught in Ireland, he went to Paris as a language tutor at the École Normale Supérieure. He found himself part of the Modernist expatriate community, and became a good friend of James Joyce, publishing an essay on his work-in-progress, *Finnegans Wake*. Joyce greatly influenced his decision to become a writer: 'I realized that I couldn't go down that same road,' he observed – though it took some time to break free of direct influence. He wrote experimental stories for the little English-language Paris magazines, a long poem *Whoroscope*, and in London published a short, quirky, interesting study of Proust. He wrote an early novel containing a good deal of autobiographical material, *Dream of Fair to Middling Women*, not to be published until 1992, well after his death. The book showed continued indebtedness to Joyce, as well as to Sterne, Diderot and Rabelais. A collection of bleakly comic short stories, *More Pricks Than Kicks*, appeared in 1934 in London. Beckett was now living in London, and undergoing psychotherapy for depression at the Tavistock Clinic. Out of this episode came his London novel *Murphy*, published in Britain in 1938, his first truly original as well as his funniest work of fiction. The novel, set around the streets of London and a mental hospital, is a work of elaborate playfulness and learned allusion that can fairly be compared with Flann O'Brien's *At Swim-Two-Birds*, another splendidly playful language-based novel that came out the next year. Seen against the span of Beckett's subsequent work, it appears as his densest and most social fiction. Murphy's split, imploding being – social body, hermetically sealed mind, the silence of one being needed for the life of the other – remains a Cartesian comic essence basic to all Beckett's work. *Murphy* was to acquire considerable cult reputation; it is surely one of the sources for Iris Murdoch's first novel *Under the Net*, which appeared in 1954.

Meanwhile Beckett's disturbed rootlessness increased. During 1936–7, still awaiting acceptance of *Murphy*, he wandered round the cities and art galleries of Nazi Germany. After an unhappy homecoming to Dublin, he moved back to Paris. He then chose to remain there during the war, returning there from a visit home to Ireland on the very day hostilities broke out. As an Irish neutral he was allowed residence in Paris, where he worked for the Resistance, risking arrest and execution by the Gestapo after the cell for which he worked was broken; he then took refuge in Roussillon. Through this dangerous time he continued writing; the result was *Watt*, published in Paris in 1953. Set in the Dublin of his own youth, the book is a parody of the methods of reason. With the war over, Beckett briefly returned to Dublin, but only before making his return to Paris with two fundamental decisions made. One was how to respond to the Modernist influences left him by Joyce: 'I realized Joyce had gone as far as one could in the direction of knowing more, in control of one's material . . . I realized that my own way was in impoverishment, in lack of knowledge and in taking away, in subtracting rather than in adding.' His world would be one of impoverishment, failure, loss, diminution; his aesthetic was declared. The other great decision was to write in French ('it was more exciting for me') and become, in effect, a French writer. A period of amazing productivity ('a frenzy of writing') followed, shaped, in effect, by the vision that it was now impossible to write. The central body of new work began in 1946, with *Mercier et Camier* (not published till 1970). There were four novellas, now collected as *First Love and Other Novellas*. Between May 1947 and January 1950 he produced the great fictional trilogy: *Molloy* (Paris, 1951; New York, 1955), *Malone Dies* (Paris, 1951; New York, 1956; London, 1958) and *The Unnamable* (Paris, 1953; New York, 1958; London, 1959). He also produced *Texts From Nothing* (Paris, 1955; New York, 1957), and the most powerful of all the post-war plays, *En Attendant Godot* (*Waiting for Godot*), the story of two tramps on a bare stage awaiting the arrival of a figure who never comes, first performed in 1953 when his fame soared and his primary work moved to the theatre.

This was the key body of his work: was it Modernism or something new? As the critic Christopher Butler puts it, these were works from 'after the wake' (*Finnegans Wake*), and they form a brilliant and purist progress (regress?) onward from Modernism. Coming from a bohemian expatriate background, they adapt to the post-war crisis, intensifying the irony, the intellectual comedy, the solipsism of experi-ence, the waste of reason, to the point of creating a quite new absurdist fictional world, which was also a fresh kind of fictional text. These were obviously works from Modernism's afterlife, and in time it became particularly appropriate to call them 'postmodern'.[14] His fiction had grown by a kind of fundamental process of reduction, reducing the novel's human and familiar content, meanwhile ques-tioning the nature of reason, the status of language, the lineage of writing, the meaning of the word, as well as the basis of the fictional act itself and the power of the imagination to imagine. *Murphy*, the

---

14 Christopher Butler, *After the Wake: An Essay on the Contemporary Avant Garde* (Oxford, 1980). The book is an interesting exploration of the post-war experiment across all the arts. Butler notes that it is Beckett's supreme achievement 'to take an experimental technique and use it, not to play a game which perpetually refers back to the author's own procedures or language, but to create an imaginary world and a structure for it whose halting suspension in time revives for us one of the most terrifying and yet traditional images of the human condition: that of hell on earth.' In *The Modes of Modern Writing* (London, 1977), David Lodge similarly identifies Beckett and others who broke away from Joyce and Proust as 'postmodernist', who were then followed by writers like John Barth, Thomas Pynchon, John Fowles and Muriel Spark, the 'new postmodernists'. Also see John Fletcher's *Claude Simon and Fiction Now* (London, 1945), which observes the links between experimental writing in France (Beckett, the *nouveau roman*) and British experimental writing.

first, pre-war novel, starts sombrely enough ('The sun shone, having no alternative, on the nothing new') and its 'hero', the seedy solipsist Murphy, spends much time in his rocking chair. But this is plainly a work of Irish black humour, in the tradition of Swift and Sterne, and for all its solipsism a work of play, parody and punning. It is set in a defined place, London, in the Magdalen Mental Mercyseat; it has a defined central character, the mental nurse Murphy, with his bohemian friends and odd sexual contacts; it even has something like a continuous plot, about Murphy's quest for success in life and his chess-like movement toward self-extinction. The novel ends with his death, or rather extends to deal with the fate of his remains, destined to be flushed down the toilet (the necessary house) of the Abbey Theatre in London, but finally scattered among the butts and vomit of a London pub floor. Murphy is a split being: this is a very funny tragi-comedy of Cartesian anxieties, and consciousness and intellect are absurd manifestations. If the body, like the poor, is always with us, it is the life of the mind that gives Murphy pleasure: such pleasure that pleasure is not the word. And it is this that gives author and reader pleasure too: in parody, misplaced logic, obscure metaphysics, the mockery of literary form.

The wartime book *Watt* – a question demanding an answer – takes matters further. Watt is blocked by a succession of quandaries (how do you name an object, feed a dog?) and ends within the caged confines of the house of his opposite, Mr Knott, surviving comically amid negatives. Thereafter the terms of minimal survival become a central theme of Beckett's work, as increasingly the sense of absurd, or late modern, tragedy arises. The vision grows ever more purgatorial, the characters turn into 'lost ones', caught in obscure, parodic, circular questions, struggling to maintain human motion in a world of travel without destination, otherwise the human condition. 'If it begins to mean something, I can't help it,' Beckett once wrote; but meaning is an obscurity. That grows clearer over the course of the trilogy itself as, following the course of his developing vision of absurdity, the terms of narrative slow, and we move from character toward the absence of character, from naming to unnaming. In *Molloy* the central character is poor, old, impotent, caught in a scarcely defined (though

Irish) landscape with a minimum of objects: a bicycle, a few stones in his pocket. He is hunting for his mother, while apparently a second character, Moran, a private detective, is hunting Molloy. Both of these quests are parodic and circular, progression not being possible. Even so things change. Molloy loses his bicycle and crutches, is left to crawl onward, remarking: 'But I am human, I fancy, and my progress suffered, from this state of affairs, and from the slow and painful progress it has always been, whatever may have been said to the contrary, was changed, saving your presence, to a veritable calvary, with no limit to its stations and no hope of crucifixion.' Words change a little too, toward gloom: Moran's narrative circles back to its own first sentence, but with new negatives added. In *Malone Dies*, the quandaries of narrative increase. Malone, dying, tries to fill his days with fictional time, which might dispose the facts differently. The act of writing serves a purpose rather like the stones Molloy had tried to structure and combine in the previous novel; it is a combinatorial game, a fictionalist attempt to construct a system.

With *The Unnamable*, language moves a good deal nearer to silence, losing many of its signifying powers. The hero virtually disappears; only words make him. The gradual taking away of whatever makes an identity reaches the point where a name is in question, and only the physical body is left. Characterless characters, they are minds that can just claim an independent activity, that of creating words. Meanwhile the landscape dissolves and the material world is reduced to a very small number of permutable objects. Character and author become an identityless agent producing text without certainties. Language grows closer to gabble, or babble; it takes on the character of an imperfect or obscured set of named memories that are incapable of being clearly invoked. The result is an agonized comedy about writing itself, one that asks many of the deeper questions that lie behind the inquiries of late modern fiction. Beckett's work now clearly belonged to the Age of the Absurd – *Waiting for Godot* became the founding play of the Theatre of the Absurd – and the era of Existentialism. Yet somehow the implication went further, into that fading of signification, the death of the self and the author, that is predicated in structuralist critics like Roland Barthes and Michel

Foucault. A key phrase from *Molloy* – 'There are no things but nameless things, no names but thingless names' – calls up an entire debate, matching Barthes's view that modern fiction was a text written against an 'essential enemy, the bourgeois norm', which meant that it was reduced to being a problematics of language. Likewise in Beckett the author grows authorless, the text grows both textually dense and highly unreliable, and writing is written by others than the writer himself. At the end of *Molloy* writing overturns itself, as Moran notes: 'Then I went back to the house and wrote, It is midnight. The rain is beating on the windows. It was not midnight. It was not raining.' Trying to write the story of his own death, Malone ends in the silence of writing itself. *The Unnamable* is written from the silence, and challenges the earlier writing of the trilogy: 'All these Murphys, Molloys and Malones do not fool me. They have made me waste my time, suffer for nothing, speak of them when, in order to stop speaking, I should have spoken of me and me alone.' The book ends: 'it will be the silence, where I am, I don't know, in the silence you don't know, you must go on, I can't go on, I'll go on.' Beckett, of course, did go on – into more fiction, major plays and stage monologues. But he was not done with fiction: in *How It Is* (Paris, 1961; London, 1964) he took a further step. At the centre of the narrative is a naked being crawling forward through mud, in a world now down to the most minimal names and objects (mud, sack, can-opener, cans). The book, like some of Beckett's later stories, depends on the permutation of a limited but still variable set of signs which can often turn to pure gabble ('quaqua'). The story itself is untrue; yet it is not irrelevant, for there is a kind of survivor's humanism, the minimum of signification: 'something happened yes'. Or, as a shorter prose work put it: 'imagination dead imagine'.

As *Godot* reshaped post-war world theatre, so Beckett's fiction, especially the trilogy, affected the novel, not least in Britain. Beckett should probably be called an Irish or a French writer (it's said that to understand him properly a green Irish passport is required). Yet, like Nabokov and Borges, experimental writers with whom he is best compared, his impact on post-war fiction was huge. All were internationalists; all were ex-Modernists who carried their work into post-war circumstances; all expressed many developments central to the idea of 'postmodernism'. By the mid Fifties many in Britain and the United States were reading Beckett; his silence had become an amazing noise. For British writers from Iris Murdoch to John Wain and Anthony Burgess, in whom his trace clearly adheres, it was probably his note of strained humanism that mattered most; for American writers his linguistic play was central. For all, he came to express the problematics and experiments of fiction in an age when the very stuff of human existence appeared challenged, the human subject cast into doubt, the signifying power of language brought into question. Beckett's work served as a central reminder that realism is no stable entity, a novel is a fiction made by an organizing imagination, from a language whose power to assert, investigate or denote recollection is itself in question. If narrative is a 'going on', then the idea of progression is itself in doubt, self-cancelling. Yet Beckett is also a brilliant comedian of modern ideas; it is his wonderful clowning that makes his plays alive. In many respects Beckett has always been a highly individualized writer, his despair and disgust at once classical and teasing, his vision of life's purgatorio idiosyncratically his own. Yet once *Waiting for Godot* had been staged in Britain in 1955, and the trilogy made available in English, Beckett became the best example of contemporary avant-garde writing there was. In the Sixties John Fletcher wrote: 'He is there, looming large and inescapable on the literary landscape; the games which he has been playing for over thirty years have become matters of immediate relevancy to us. His extraordinary hero roams about in our consciousness, a haunting and troublesome shadow.' In latter-day circumstances he had done what Joyce earlier did: found a form and discourse not now for the chaotic plenitude of modernity, but for its purgatorial and denuded futility, its dark humour. In 1969 Beckett, now seen as one of the greatest writers of the age, won the Nobel Prize for Literature – in, of course, his absence. He died, still in Paris, in December 1989.

9

Other writers carried the spirit of Modernism into the post-war world. One was Lawrence Durrell, another graduate of the experimental Paris of the Thirties. Here he had worked with the American writer Henry Miller, been a convert to Surrealism and produced a significant experimental novel, *The Black Book* (1938), described by Miller as 'a good little chronicle of the English death . . . a book Huxley could have written if he were a mixture of Lawrence and Shakespeare.' Miller approved the vision of decadence, the social surrealism and sexual realism; Durrell shared Miller's fascination with psycho-sexual occultism and the eternal regression to the womb. Unsurprisingly given its sexual content, the book had to be published in Paris. Born in India, Durrell remained a lifelong expatriate: in the Thirties living in Paris and Corfu, over the war years working as a government press officer in Egypt, then in Greece and Yugoslavia, before settling in Provence. This splendid cosmopolitanism lay behind the sequence of novels that secured his fame, 'The Alexandria Quartet', consisting of *Justine* (1957), *Balthazar* (1958), *Mountolive* (1958) and *Clea* (1960). They reflected his own experiences in Egypt during and after the war; they also returned to the surrealism, eroticism and psycho-sexual fantasy of previous fiction and poetry. A wonderful reminder of the erotic, exotic 'Arabian' sources of fiction and storytelling, the sequence makes a complex set of mirror-novels about a complex set of sexual relationships. It was based, Durrell liked to explain, on the Freudian rule that every sexual relationship involves four people. Hence it was 'a four-dimensional dance, a relativity poem', a 'four-card trick in the form of a novel' which 'might raise in human terms the problems of causality or indeterminacy'. The novels function against each other in space and time, one fictive narrative challenging or amending another. The sequence undoubtedly appealed to austere times less for its experimental methods than its Egyptian richness and its splendid exoticism. Yet Durrell's perspectivized method of narration, where different narrators tell different volumes, and many of them are writers, utterly self-conscious about the act of writing, makes this a fiction of mirrored narcissism. Later sequences – *Tunc* (1968) and *Nunquam* (1970), set in a Turkish harem, and 'The Avignon Quartet' (1974–85) – are less successful, but they do develop another essential note in Durrell's always poetic and part-mystical fiction: the notion that the novel is not just an erotic world of mirrors but a metaphysical site, open to forms of knowledge beyond Western protestant rationalism.

Another major writer carried an experimental and expatriate career from the Thirties over into the post-war world. This was Malcolm Lowry, born in the Wirral in 1909. He fell out with his stockbroker father, read English at Cambridge in the early Thirties in the heyday of I. A. Richards, William Empson and F. R. Leavis, and became, it has been said, Cambridge's greatest novelist since Forster. But the spirit of Cambridge was only partly on him; life, as he saw it, was a romantic adventure, a voyage that never ends – deep into the spirit, the world, the chaos. His favourite writers were themselves mostly writers of voyage: Melville, Conrad, Faulkner, Conrad Aitken, Nordahl Grieg. His early novel *Ultramarine* (1933; rev. ed., 1963) tells his own story, of a middle-class young man who signs on as a deckhand aboard a ship on an Eastern voyage. As in many a Thirties novel, he is taunted by the crew but finally accepted; more crucially the book lays down the notion that was to last Lowry a lifetime, of an endless mythic journey which is the journey of the romantic artist into art. Lowry took his own journey to Paris in the Thirties, like Beckett and Durrell, though with different consequences: he married an American, the left-wing actress and writer Jan Gabrial. Soon he was heading for the USA, following the track of two of his heroes, Herman Melville and Bix Biederbecke, chasing the general spirit of American literature, hunting, he said, his own white whale. This journey halted for a time in Bellevue Mental Hospital, where his chronic alcoholism required treatment; the surreal story is told in the short novel *Lunar Caustic*, set in New York, the 'last frontier', a 'city of dreadful night without splendour'. The story, his one American tale, was written in 1934, but went through several variants and was not published until 1968, after Lowry's death. The point was that Manhattan was one step in a larger literary journey, which now led to Mexico, where D. H.

Lawrence and Hart Crane had gone before. In September 1936 he and Jan set sail for Mexico, arriving – at least according to his own legend – on a crucial date, the Day of the Dead: the Mexican All Souls, a time of pagan-Christian carnival, a grotesque, violent, complex display of faith and mortality, involving magic and mystery, a day that ties the living to the dead.[15]

They rented a house in Cuernavaca, a historic town fifty miles south of Mexico City under the twin volcanoes of Popocatépetl and Ixtacihuatl. Here Jan left him, he went on a sequence of major drinking binges and was three times imprisoned for expressing pro-Communist opinions among Fascist sympathizers. Here he began a vast epic about the Faustian damnation of an alcoholic British hero, the consul Geoffrey Firmin, whose abuse of his 'magical powers' leads to his death in a barranca, a ravine, at the hands of a local Fascist gang. The story is set over twelve hours on the Day of the Dead in 1938, after the signing of the Munich Agreement; it is filled with the echoes and consequences of international politics, and was meant as a mid-century tragedy. The events are seen from the same day a year later, November 1939, when the world is now at war. The book struggled through draft after draft, from 1937 to 1944, by which time Lowry had married Margerie Bonner, moved to a squatters' shack in British Columbia and begun the vast, exiled writing enterprise that occupied the rest of his life. He completed a version in 1941; it was widely rejected. Much re-redrafted, *Under the Volcano* was finally accepted by Cape in London and appeared in 1947, surely the greatest novel to appear in Britain in the immediate post-war years. The story of Geoffrey Firmin, 'a Faustian gent', 'a poor sort of good man', the tragic hero who spirals down to death in an atmosphere of historical

---

15 In his excellent introduction to the Penguin Classics edition of *Under the Volcano* (2000), Michael Schmidt quotes from the chapter on the Day of the Dead in Octavio Paz, *The Labyrinth of Solitude* (1950): 'Our Fiestas, like our intimacies, our loves, and our attempts to reorder our society, are violent breaches with the old and the established. Each time we wish to express ourselves we must break with ourselves . . . The Mexican, gloomy being that he is, confined within himself, suddenly bursts, opens his bosom and reveals himself with a degree of complacency, lingering on the shameful or terrible crannies of intimacy . . . It releases us into the void, a self-immolating drunkenness, a shot into the air, an artificial fire.'

crisis, political corruption, betrayal and infidelity, sexual despair, romantic self-destructiveness and a haze of beer, tequila and mescal, clearly has a historical allegory behind it. Lowry wrote grandly to his publishers that the book was a parable about 'the universal drunkenness of mankind during the war, or during the years immediately preceding it, which is almost the same thing', but he offered many explanations of the complex mythic and structural underpinnings of the novel.

In this letter, 'the brilliant defence', he called the book a symphony, an opera, a horse-opera, a 'sort of machine' based on the number 12. It was a work of modern epic aspirations, a multivalent text like *Ulysses*, a Dante-an voyage to the heart of darkness, like Conrad's novella. It was extensively filled with 'borrowings, echoes, design-governing postures', or what we now call 'intertextuality', with codes and hidden readings the scholars are still decrypting. It was also an occult text, filled with references to the Kabbala and other hermetic texts, mathematics, astronomy, mysticism. It drew on Homer, the Inferno of Dante, the Faust legend of Marlowe and Goethe; it had the classic twelve-book epic structure. Melville, Kafka and the Modernists were there too; so were the modern writers of Mexico, above all D. H. Lawrence and B. Traven. The Joycean echoes are strong: Lowry said he was 'Joyced with his own petard.' There are many references to Lowry's own fiction, to *Ultramarine* and books not yet published. The story is set over a single day; he explained it was 'a wheel with twelve spokes, the motion of which was something like that . . . of time itself'. It depends on a complex use of consciousness, fragmentation, collage, strange signs, symbols, signals; the consul is a man following imperfectly understood runes as he wanders through Cuernavaca ('You like this garden? Why it yours? We evict those who destroy!' – or perhaps the sign doesn't mean quite that). As Lowry informed his probably only half-comprehending publishers, the book was 'so designed, counter-designed and interwelded that it could be read an indefinite number of times and still not have yielded all its meanings or its drama or its poetry' – perfectly true.

Altogether he had meant it, he explains, as 'a prophecy, a political warning, a cryptogram, a preposterous movie, and a writing on the wall'. All these things are there, and the book stays a cryptic Enigma machine. But it is also, and above all, intensely physical, bringing Mexico to life with a compelling immediacy of scene and atmosphere. Yet the Mexican infernal paradise is deeply linked to other worlds: the Civil War in Spain, which prefigures what is coming, Liverpool and the escorted convoys leaving, the Birkenhead Empire, the ships with their questing sailors sailing the world. In the story movies play a big part, and radio signals from Texas, all the signs of danger emerging as the world moves toward conflict between the liberal democracies and the huge powers of Fascism. Everything has its sinister parallels and echoes in Mexico, and the book can now be read as a very remarkable novel from the moment of mid-century crisis as well as a complex and experimental text. In Modernist fashion it is structured against rather than alongside historical time. History is fundamental to the story, but history is also recurrence. So the book opens out into myth and symbol, and its destructive cycle is part of an eternal Faustian damnation ('The stars move still; time runs; the clock will strike. / The Devil will come, and Faustus must be damned') as well as a contemporary crisis. Yet it is in the immediacies – the Mexican textures, the houses, the streets, the barrancas, the vultures, the random thoughts, the anxious connections, the haunting feeling of world crisis – that the book works. With publication obstructed by war, and with his old literary contacts broken by Canadian exile, Lowry allowed the book to spiral. The text grew ever more complex, but Lowry had no intention of letting the journey end there. Damnation implied redemption; inferno could be followed by purgatory and paradise. His writing was to be a lifelong ambitious scheme, called 'The Voyage That Never Ends'. This ever-varying project would grow to incorporate six or seven books, novels and stories, exploring versions of the artistic imagination struggling with the world, introducing the Modernist themes of the war between fiction and reality, and the need for a text to be 'open', or eternally unfinished and self-questioning.

Alas, the book won small recognition and few good reviews; there was the disturbing suspicion that another novel about a great alcoholic bender, Charles Jackson's *The Lost Weekend*, had scooped all popular attention. For ten years after the book came out, Lowry, living in impermanent conditions in British Columbia, worked on and on. Scarcely a day passed without writing; nothing he produced ever seemed to find a proper home. He had no clear place in English literature, none in American, and Canadian literature scarcely existed. In his last decade he became a vast creator of manuscript, one text leading on to another. *Under the Volcano* became part of the greater scheme. So did *Lunar Caustic*, written back on the New York drinking binge but now heavily revised. In 1945, with *Under the Volcano* finished, he returned to the scene of the crime, Mexico, for five months, ran into the usual difficulties that dogged him, and wrote a sequel, *Dark as the Grave Wherein My Friend is Laid*, posthumously published from drafts in 1968; unfinished and unshaped, it makes a disappointing variant on the earlier novel. Other books figured in the sequence, like *In Ballast to the White Sea*, a lost manuscript he sought to rewrite. *Under the Volcano*, which would stand in the middle, was now described as written not by Lowry but by one of the several alter egos he cooked up for himself, Sigborn Wilderness. Rather like Beckett, if for different reasons, Lowry wanted book to refract book, make the problems of art, the crisis of writing, the details of his own life, his failures and silences, part of the narrative. The last project, as the overall plan shifted yet again, was *October Ferry to Gabriola* (published posthumously, 1970). Set in Canada, where he was now living permanently, it deals again with expulsion from the paradisal garden and the corruption of the wilderness. Completed after his death by Margerie Bonner, it is, like a good deal of his late writing, an interesting book, with much in it that is important. But nothing of this late, contorted, generally uncompleted writing comes anywhere near the power of his masterpiece. *Under the Volcano* is a modern classic, still too little valued.

Three plots seemed to lead Lowry onward: the plot of his own life, a tale of a *poète maudit* whose drive for creation was also a talent for destruction; the plot of his art, which turned into a labyrinthine mystery; and the plot of his age, which had become ungovernable. In all the stories there is something infernal, born of the darkness of the Thirties and the wartime years. Yet perhaps in them there is a code,

in the official handbook as representing 'one united act of national reassessment, and one corporate re-affirmation of faith in the nation's future'. The aim was to unify the nation and bring a new hope after years of war and post-war crisis; the Labour government invited 'spontaneous expressions of citizenship' to celebrate the event. A tall aluminium Skylon, an emblem of modern style, a kind of lightweight and temporary Eiffel Tower, rose in the air without obvious moorings (as critics said, like Britain itself it had no visible means of support); a Dome of Discovery presented some of the current wonders of British invention, which included radar and the jet engine; there were signs of a whole new age of design. But the still fog-bound city of London round about remained heavily battered and bomb-damaged, though hastily designed prefabricated blocks of brick or concrete now began to rehouse some of the Londoners displaced by six years of bombing, or living in insanitary Victorian slums. Saint Paul's Cathedral, the great symbol of wartime survival, now began to disappear behind high-rises and office towers. The Festival itself was successful, but temporary, intended to initiate the cultural development of the bomb-flattened South Bank of the river. So a foundation stone for a National Theatre was laid, though it took many more years and generations of effort for the project to flower. For all the assertions of official hope, the England of post-war socialism still felt a drab, austere and defeated place, suffering constant shortages, plagued by strikes and the 'dollar gap' – one reason, perhaps, why the general election that November saw the Conservatives, still led by an ageing Winston Churchill, come to office. In 1953, following the death of King George VI, the coronation of a young Queen Elizabeth – seen by many of the people on their newly acquired television sets – offered a larger symbol of promise, for thus, the British were assured, was inaugurated a New Elizabethan Age. Promising as this was, the economy remained weak, rationing and military conscription continued, the international situation was frighteningly unstable, the nuclear threat grew as more and more weapons were tested, and the role of Britain as a world power seemed in serious doubt, above all with the Suez Crisis of 1956. The death of Stalin in 1953 and the appointment of Khrushchev as his successor did not reduce international tensions. The Cold War extended, there was conflict in Korea, Indo-China, Cyprus and Malaya. In 1956 Russian tanks stormed Budapest to suppress the Hungarian Revolution, producing a new wave of refugees to the West. Meanwhile the USA, which had promoted European decolonization as an enlightened new order for the post-war world, found itself inheriting the post-imperial mantle across much of the globe.

Still, the Fifties was the decade when the post-war generation began to feel itself as a generation, and this was reflected in the cultural mood. Some of the first signs of new energy appeared in theatre. Though this was the decade when the Theatre of the Absurd made its mark and established its influence in Britain, some of the most important drama was political. In London's East End, at the other Stratford, Joan Littlewood in 1953 founded her left-wing Theatre Workshop, which discovered new playwrights like Brendan Behan and Shelagh Delaney, and mounted the satirical anti-war musical *Oh What a Lovely War!* (satire became one of the motifs of the decade). And at the other end of London, in Sloane Square, the Royal Court Theatre mounted new radical drama from playwrights like Arnold Wesker and above all John Osborne, whose *Look Back in Anger* became – in the year after *Waiting for Godot* was seen in London – the theatrical sensation of 1956. 'By putting the sex war and the class war onto one stage, Mr Osborne gave the drama a tremendous nudge forward,' announced the critic Ken Tynan, the warmest supporter of the new theatre. But the play also captured the mood of a new generation, and a culture that became the culture of 'Anger', an Anglo-equivalent to the American Beat Generation. Anger spilled in 1956, the year of Suez and the Hungarian Revolution. In the same year the young Colin Wilson published a polemical book, *The Outsider*, a self-consciously youthful work about Nietzsche, Sartre, Van Gogh and Nijinsky, a celebration of the rebel, the bohemian, the outside view, that turned into a surprise bestseller, rather like Byron's early poetry. Tynan was one of many to see the signs of a new movement that linked these playwrights, some new novelists, including Kingsley Amis, Doris Lessing and John Wain, 'kitchen-sink painters' such as John Bratby and film-makers like Lindsay Anderson and John Schlesinger as a generation who 'came of age under a Socialist government and found the class system was still mysteriously intact'.

There were other important directions to the culture of Fifties Britain. In 1957, for instance, Harold Pinter produced his first play, *The Room*, quickly followed by *The Birthday Party*; but that major play ran for only a short London season, and it took time for his original drama, about 'the recognizable reality of absurdity', to win attention. Protest and class were the great Fifties themes. The voices of the new generation were drawn together – if not in opinion, at least under the same set of covers – in the volume *Declaration* (1957), edited by Tom Maschler, where voices from Osborne to Lessing and Wain to Tynan very variously expressed their rebellion and their anti-establishment sensibilities. 'They have little in common, except youth, and a shared striving to change many of the values which have held good in recent years,' reflected the review in *The Times*. 'They are vigorous, uninhibited, aggressive, and most of them have already tasted success.' Protest, declaration, commitment: these things were in season, and spilled far beyond theatre, fiction or polemic. The Campaign for Nuclear Disarmament flourished. The Suez Crisis of 1956, when Britain, France and Israel sent troops into Egypt to prevent Nasser's nationalization of the Suez Canal (the old lifeline of Empire, so carefully protected by Churchill during the war), brought a protesting younger generation onto the streets. For them the imperial age was already over. As Osborne's play challenged the older generation with the rage of disenchanted youth, so an older version of British society, as class, hierarchy and national confidence, was rejected in newer styles and fashions: Teddy Boys, the New Look, Rock and Roll; youth culture, jazz clubs, American chic. Yet in the end the essential revolution of the Fifties was economic. Though Britain was losing its position as a trading power, and productivity was declining fast, material prospects were improving as the Western European economy, reinvigorated by the Marshall Plan, began to boom. Rationing ended, travel opportunities grew and personal incomes generally began to rise. It became just possible to think of owning a telephone, a television set, a car, a refrigerator, and entering the age of egalitarian consumer affluence. Many things were changing in post-war Britain; and they too became part of the literature.

Class factors played a considerable part in British culture over the Fifties. In the pages of the American-financed intellectual magazine *Encounter*, the left-wing Thirties poet Stephen Spender noted the new mood, spotting 'a rebellion of the lower middlebrows', which had 'an aroma of inferiority about its protest'. Spender was right to suppose there was a clear rebellion taking place against the Bloomsbury culture of the Twenties and Thirties. Thus the social as well as the cultural foundations that had supported the Modern movement had weakened; as D. H. Lawrence had observed much earlier, the notes of Modernism were often sounded in British upper-class accents. So too had the Marxist politics of the Thirties, in which Spender himself had participated. Post-war writers were increasingly drawn from fresh social origins – lower-middle-class or working-class backgrounds; educations in grammar schools and red-brick universities – and modern literary culture seemed founded on the class relations of groups to which they did not belong. It bred a puritan or Leavisite suspicion about the dominant metropolitan literary scene, the Modern movement itself and the romantic experimental bohemia of the previous generation, exemplified by writers like the rebel poet Dylan Thomas (who died in New York in 1953) and Malcolm Lowry. The Modernist rebellion had led to an urbane cosmopolitanism which excluded much from fiction, including much of provincial and regional life. So the new writing spoke not for romantic experimentalism but for sense and realism. It moved toward a more popular and plainer tone, a more direct and classical view of art, a greater concern with social depiction, a politics of liberalism. For good or ill this was an important part of the atmosphere of the British Fifties, which had much influence on the future of the novel.[1]

1 Peter Lewis, in *The Fifties* (London, 1978), gives a vivid and detailed portrait of the culture and events of the era.

2

If the Fifties were the time of the appearance of a new post-war theatre, it was also the time of the emergence of the post-war novel. During the decade many of the major figures and chief directions of British fiction emerged, shaping and influencing the novel to this day. There was indeed a conscious new mood. Cyril Connolly had said that the Modernists – James, Joyce, Proust, Woolf – had 'finished off' the novel, and that 'all would have to be re-invented from the very beginning'. New writers attempted to oblige. The early signs came very shortly after the war, when two youthful novels appeared from a new writer who a decade on would become famous in another genre. In 1946 Philip Larkin published a fine first novel, *Jill*, set in an Oxford college distant from the Brideshead world of Evelyn Waugh, in drab times during the war. The central character was a clumsy working-class boy from Lancashire, whose educational aspirations and social dreams are contrasted with the plain facts of his northern background. The book is based on an unequivocal and stoical accept-ance of the routine and the ordinary; in Larkin's work dreams would rarely become realities. A year later Larkin (who became a librarian in red-brick universities) followed it with a second novel, *A Girl in Winter*, about a young girl from an unnamed foreign country who comes to Britain to work in the library of a provincial town. She has high, dream-like expectations of the place she comes to, the people she meets. Instead she finds herself coming to terms with something different, simple unromantic ordinariness and contingency, 'the flat landscape, wry and rather small' of British life. The book has a vivid truth; this is realism as ironic understatement, with an insistent refusal to inflate, romanticize, fantasize, to breed unreal hopes and expect-ations. The tone is without protest, simply the affirmation of a vision, like the paintings of L. S. Lowry, depicting the half-forlorn and yet valued texture of ordinary British life. During the Fifties Larkin departed the novel for poetry, and published in 1955 a verse-collection appropriately called *The Less Deceived*. The undeceived eye, the flat universe, the conventions of ordinary life, the provincial scene, the climate of unglamorous towns, the distinctive and half-visible English 'here', where 'only salesmen and relations come', would be his essential material: minor matter turned to a major theme. In poetry Larkin established himself as the most important, most direct and unexperimental, most sure-footed and most plainly English of the post-war poets. He rejected Modernism, the influence of *The Waste Land*, the voices of *vers libre* and high technical experiment, and looked instead to a usable tradition that reached back to Hardy and the Georgians. His influence on fiction was similar, and considerable: *Jill* is dedicated to Larkin's close college friend Kingsley Amis, at St John's College, Oxford, at the same time as John Wain; here were two of the important novelists of the Fifties.

It was in the Forties too that Angus Wilson emerged as the *enfant terrible* of post-war fiction. In fact when he started to write he was already in his mid thirties, and had taken up fiction after working during wartime in code-breaking and signals intelligence at the highly secret 'Station X' at Bletchley Park, where Alan Turing worked on the Enigma codes and began work on the modern computer. Wilson, a striking and camp figure with a great gift for mimicry, suffered a breakdown under the pressure; writing was recommended as therapy. In November 1946 he produced a highly satirical short story, 'Raspberry Jam', and a year later Cyril Connolly printed a further story in *Horizon*. Wilson had a natural subject-matter: born a late child to shabby-genteel parents with high pretensions (his father described himself as 'a gentleman of no occupation', his mother was daughter to a rich South African jeweller), he had grown up in faded hotels among 'darling dodos' (he described himself as 'a lonely and spoilt child, learning about the nature of the world from unhappy, pseudo-sophisticated, *déclassé* adults'). It was a world where childhood unhappiness and insecurity were compensated for by theatrical games; there was a similarity with the childhood of Charles Dickens, which Wilson was always to feel as he re-explored the situation. By the post-war years the darling dodos represented a dying class, left adrift on a sea of social change, rising egalitarianism, penal taxation, genteel poverty, *déclassé* anxieties and post-colonial dismays. In one form and another they appear again and again in Wilson's early stories, which are vivid, social and often wonderfully cruel. They have a Waugh-like edge, but also a reforming bite. Novels in miniature, they point in two directions: against the dodos themselves, a bitter elderly bourgeoisie trying to preserve old privileges in indigent and egalitarian circumstances; and against the new, rational, humourless bureaucrats who, with their *realpolitik*, administer the rites of the Welfare State ('We are the masters now'). By 1949 a collection of twelve of them, *The Wrong Set*, appeared; the next year eleven more made up the successor volume *Such Darling Dodos*. Unusually in Britain, Wilson established a major literary reputation on the strength of short stories, as the gadfly writer of the post-war world.

In 1950 another important book appeared. William Cooper, who under his real name of H. S. Hoff had published fiction in the Thirties, produced *Scenes from Provincial Life*, a splendid work of regional realism and wry comedy that influenced many younger writers. The story is set in a Midlands city based on Leicester at the close of the Thirties, around the time of the Munich agreement, as the world moved into war. Behind the story are strong political implications, about how close Britain and its way of life had come to defeat and Nazi occupation. It also considers the dissident intellectuals of the day, and the way some of them fled to America while others remained and experienced wartime life and its fortunes. The story is told (in retrospect) by Joe Lunn, a young science master at the local grammar school. He has literary ambitions, a group of bohemian friends – nonconforming provincial intellectuals, some of them homosexual – and a vivid and troubling girlfriend, Myrtle, who is trying to lure him into marriage, an institution he doesn't believe in. The group is advised by an Oxford friend, Robert (plainly C. P. Snow), who warns them Hitler will invade soon, and they (one of them is Jewish) will be the first victims. All mean, sooner or later, to go into exile in the USA. Yet they are provincials, living in a pleasant and familiar England, with its own weather, social climate, habits and customs. The day-to-day world of love affairs, meetings with friends, local pleasures, finally becomes far more important than grand history. Despite the dangers, they stay just as they are, amid commonplace life and the general ordinariness. Finally Joe, Myrtle, his friends and his pupils enter the world of war, where everything changes. Happily history has supported their choice; they survive the war, and go on and on.

Scenes from Provincial Life (the title is borrowed from the subtitle of George Eliot's *Middlemarch*, 'A Study of Provincial Life') is, like the novels of Philip Larkin, a work of appreciative realism, a highly comic and lyrical celebration of the ordinary over the extraordinary, the everyday over the grand march of politics and history. It celebrates the tones, the amusements, the morality of ordinariness, of innocent bohemia and suburban life, the daily work of a grammar school, the problems of a job. It prefers scepticism to romanticism, sense to sensibility, comedy to historical tragedy. And because of the way the world had gone, the book could be the beginning of a sequence: Cooper produced three more volumes following the course of Joe Lunn's life (a fourth has now been added). In wartime Joe becomes, with Robert, scientific adviser to the government in Whitehall, and plays his part in the development of the atomic bomb; he also becomes a married man. *Scenes from Metropolitan Life* – a book that was completed by 1951 but not published, because of a threat of libel, until 1962 – tells the story, and takes us on from the provinces into the metropolitan world, the corridors and clubs of Whitehall, the life of the 'Establishment'. *Scenes from Married Life* (1961) is (very unusually in modern fiction) the celebration of a happy marriage (not to Myrtle), in which Joe Lunn considers the private life and emotions of a public man. *Scenes from Later Life* (1983) brings him near to retirement. All these stories are told by Joe, a lastingly witty narrator and wise observer; a comic hopefulness and sense of good humour everywhere prevails. This is realism used not for the purposes of reportage or political protest, but for comic purposes, and to celebrate the ordinariness of common life. Cooper (himself a scientist) confessed himself a warm admirer of H. G. Wells: 'I loved it, enshrining Wells' message of optimism,' writes Joe Lunn of Wells's *The History of Mr Polly*. The link was significant: Cooper also shared Wells's scientific optimism, his sexual vitalism, his feeling that the world was progressively opening up to fresh ideas and new talents. Like Wells (and like his friend C. P. Snow), Cooper told the story of the 'new men', often with scientific educations, who were inheriting the age.

Scenes from Provincial Life was, according to John Braine, a much younger writer, a 'seminal book'. Certainly its distinctive tone opened the way for a whole sequence of novels that dealt with tradition and change, class and classlessness, provinciality and metropolitanism, optimism and alienation, exclusion and opportunity, considering changing British life with a new curiosity. Writers like Alan Sillitoe, David Storey, Stan Barstow and Stanley Middleton, also writing of provincial scenes, acknowledged its influence. It was part of a line of works of social fiction that explored the story of a post-war Britain gradually emerging from the class world of the past, coming out of wartime and national service into post-war austerity, then into rising affluence, changing in class allegiance and class attitudes. New social heroes – spendthrift factory workers, aspiring clerks and librarians, hopeful scholarship boys, would-be bohemians – appeared, reflecting the changing composition and improved opportunities of a society where, perhaps, there was room at the top. It suggested the social consensus of the after-war period, until the Suez Crisis of 1956, the emergence of 'Anger', the growth of Youth Culture and the rise of the New Left began to point the way to the Sixties.

3

In 1959, when a fresh generation of novelists had made their presence felt in Britain, William Cooper published, in John Wain's *International Literary Annual*, a polemical article in which he set out to explain his literary credo and the mood of the decade. 'During the last years of the war a literary comrade-in-arms [C. P. Snow] and I, not prepared to wait for Time's ever-rolling stream to bear Experimental Writing away, made our own private plans to run it out of town as soon as we picked up our pens again – if you look at the work of the next generation of English novelists to come after us, you'll see we didn't entirely lack success for our efforts,' he wrote. He then added: 'We had our reasons for being impatient. We meant to write a different kind of novel from that of the Thirties and we saw that the Thirties Novel, the Experimental Novel, had got to be brushed out of the way before we could get a proper hearing.' In some ways the argument is odd: Cooper and Snow were themselves Thirties novelists, and the Experimental Novel is mostly associated with the Twenties. Yet the point being made is clear: the new post-war writing lay in a different tradition from that of the Bloomsbury generation. 'Putting it simply, to start with: the Experimental Novel was about Man-Alone; we meant to write novels about Man-in-Society as well. (Please note the "as well"; it's important. We had no qualms about incorporating any useful discoveries that had been made in the course of Experimental Writing; we simply refused to restrict ourselves to them),' Cooper observed.[2] The uncompromising tone of the polemic probably has something to do with the place where the article appeared, a journal highly sympathetic to contemporary experimentalism and the work of writers like Beckett and Alexander Trocchi. But similar arguments were put by other writers at the time, including Philip Larkin, Angus Wilson, Kingsley Amis and Pamela Hansford Johnson, C. P. Snow's novelist wife, author of *An Impossible Marriage* (1952). If there were strong experimental tendencies alive in the Fifties, there were anti-experimental tendencies as well.[3]

Some of the challenge was blind to the range and international complexity of the Modern movement, especially in times when modern European literature was still hard to acquire; the Modern experiment was often seen as identical with Bloomsbury itself. Angus Wilson would remark later that many of these responses brought critical misjudgement (about the worth of Virginia Woolf's fiction, for instance) and came from 'reasons which are really extraneous to the novel but have something to do with the social battle inside England, and should never have played a part in deciding the form'. But there were other important issues. One was the recognition that the Modernist rejection of the Victorians and Edwardians represented an old generational battle, a finished war of children against their

2 William Cooper, 'Reflections on Some Aspects of the Experimental Novel', in John Wain (ed.), *International Literary Annual*, 2 (London, 1959).
3 There is an excellent account of this in Rubin Rabinowitz, *The Reaction Against Experiment in the English Novel* (New York, 1967).

fathers, sexual liberators against moralists, freethinkers against believers. Thus it was again possible to create a continuity between contemporary fiction and the tradition, to draw with profit on the work of Dickens or Thackeray, Kipling or Forster. The 'experimental novel', with its emphasis on inwardness and psychology, had lost touch with the social span of narrative. In 1950 Wilson himself published a witty pastiche of Woolf's famous essay on the modern novel, 'Mr Bennett and Mrs Brown', in which she attacked the realists for seeing the material nature of a character but not her inner life. Wilson considered the problem of a latter-day Woolfian heroine, 'Mrs Green', with 'her good tweeds, her untidy grey hair, her interesting beauty', who lived in a cottage in the country and devoted her life, and fiction, to the pattern of the clouds, the odd behaviour of the servants, the distant prospect of the poor. Her task was to refine life into poetry; all life that lay outside her enchanted sensitivity was relegated to a human jungle beyond. What was being revived was one of the debates of earlier on in the century, Spender's war between the 'moderns' and the 'contemporaries'. Now, though, it was being waged in reverse; it was the 'moderns' who represented the tradition and the convention, and the 'contemporaries' who were trying to do something new. Perhaps the most important fact was indeed that, after the great upheaval, the upturning, the banging and shaking of the Modern, post-war novelists in Britain were still able to see some contact with the literary tradition, with long-standing themes and conventions. One issue in particular was that of character: the survival of the humanist self of liberal culture in the fiction of the present. However, as Angus Wilson was able to observe in another essay in 1961: 'The traditional English novel as practised by the great Victorians – the novel with strong social connections, the novel of man in the community rather than man in isolation or in coterie, the novel, above all, of firmly constructed narrative and strong plot rather than verbal or formal experiment – has made a triumphant return in England in the last ten years.'[4]

---

4 See Kerry McSweeney (ed.), Angus Wilson, *Diversity and Depth in Fiction: Selected Critical Writings* (London, 1983), and the group of essays entitled 'The View From the Fifties'. Wilson argues that the return to a more social, realistic and narrative fiction was 'a logical result of the interlocking of subject and form rather than any dogmatic

Later, when he had changed his views on the matter, Wilson spoke of a 'tyranny of neo-traditionalism in English novel-writing', and looked toward a new era of experiment. But where had the new 'traditionalism' come from? Here the literary critics had helped, in a post-war debate about fiction in which interest in the social, moral and liberal function of the novel was growing ever stronger. In 1948 F. R. Leavis, then the most influential critic in Britain, published *The Great Tradition*, a study of the British novel. Today, when criticism is infinitely cosmopolitan and pluralist, the book looks narrow and prescriptive; but it discerns a clear 'great tradition' of social and moral realism, of fictional 'maturity', running from the eighteenth to the twentieth century: its key figures are Jane Austen, Dickens (in one book, *Hard Times*), George Eliot, Joseph Conrad and D. H. Lawrence, who becomes the exemplary twentieth-century novelist. Leavis was concerned with the novel as a central critique and analysis of humanity, society and culture; he was highly critical of Bloomsbury and its influence, and the culture of a society corrupted by mass culture, diminishing the novel as a serious form. Leavis's passionate opinions were part of a general reassessment of the novel, which was being elevated to higher status in critical judgement; the New Criticism, originally mostly concerned with poetry, was now giving fiction an increased attention. A more urbane view of the novel came from the American critic Lionel Trilling, in another influential book, *The Liberal Imagination* (1950), a post-war reaction to the ideological Marxist criticism and opinion of the Thirties. Trilling – he had earlier published an excellent book on E. M. Forster, a strong influence on Fifties fiction – perceived the novel as a social and moral form, higher than politics, deeper than a social report. It saw the world in its variousness and multiplicity, and was capable of grasping at the mystery and muddle that lay beyond ideology or intellectual certainty. It was not a realist form, but a form with a deep social sense of the

---

devotion to the traditional English novel. If stream-of-consciousness, interior mono-logue of the more orthodox kind, cinematic treatments of time and other experimental forms are less used – and for my part I believe that this is only a temporary rejection of over-exploited devices still rich in promise – it is because their defects of cumbrousness and monotony have become apparent.'

realities. 'The novel, then,' he said, 'is a perpetual quest for reality, the field of its research being always the social world, the material of its analysis being always manners as the direction of man's soul.' Such was the novel in Europe, the novel of Cervantes, Fielding, Balzac, Dickens, Tolstoy; in this form it had, he admitted, never really established itself in America, where the novel, born in the era of Romanticism and Gothic, and dealing less with society than nature or Utopia, took the form of the 'romance'. But if the social novel had been neglected in American fiction, it was vigorously alive in British. The European novel – not just the work of Dickens and George Eliot but of Cervantes, Stendhal, Balzac and Tolstoy – took social and historical existence seriously, and observed manners as a fundamental aspect of morals and metaphysics. In its concern for the individual self and the power of society it was the expression of the liberal imagination, the spirit of humanism. Other strong works of the Fifties, by György Lukács, Harry Levin and other critics, emphasized the power of realism and the dialogic nature of fiction. The most notable work of all, *Mimesis: The Representation of Reality in Western Literature*, by the German critic Erich Auerbach, appeared in translation in 1953. The book ends with an excellent essay on Virginia Woolf, in which he reflects on the atmosphere of historical pessimism which surrounded the dispersal of reality into multiple and multivalent reflections of consciousness, though also on the way her novels open out to 'the reality and depth of every moment to which we surrender ourselves without prejudice'. Auerbach argues that Modernism was itself a form of modern realism, and that the new literary epoch would find its own way to mimesis. In the Fifties, if – like me – you were interested in criticism, manners, morals and the novel, the issue of realism and the tradition was real indeed.[5]

5 Erich Auerbach, *Mimesis: The Representation of Reality in Western Literature* (Princeton, 1953; originally published in German, Berne, 1946). It seems important to stress that the new debate on realism was different from the political debate of the Thirties on the subject; the powerhouse of history now generated a different kind of light. In *The Creative Element* (1953), Stephen Spender notes that in the Thirties one had to accept 'modern consciousness of politics as a universal fate'. Now it was possible to see literature having an independent existence without supposing literature, history and politics were not intertwined. This was the significance of the new "liberalism":

4

Over the Fifties the social theme flourished, one of the most significant figures being Angus Wilson himself: the *enfant terrible* turned into one of the central writers of the decade. In 1952 he published his first novel, *Hemlock and After*, reputedly written in four weeks (Wilson was now a full-time civil servant, Deputy Superintendent of the Reading Room of the British Museum). The novel is about the anxieties of post-war liberalism, and, as its Socratic title suggests, about the role of the intellectual and the writer as modern man of letters, something Wilson himself was in the process of becoming. Bernard Sands is a well-known fifty-seven-year-old writer and 'moral scourge' at the high point of success. Now he has acquired unconditional government support for his plan to set up a centre for young writers at Vardon Hall, a Georgian mansion in the commuter countryside, and a suitable symbol of post-war Britain itself (a rival bidder wanted to turn the house into a hotel-cum-brothel). Sands seeks to co-opt bureaucracy for freedom, authority for enlightenment, but his progressive ideas conceal moral and sexual confusions. At the same time he begins to glimpse contradiction and hypocrisy in his own life and character. He has engaged in homosexual affairs, but married; now his wife has retreated into neurotic introversion. Over the summer of the events he becomes haunted by a sense of evil which his enlightened liberalism cannot encompass, a 'growing apprehension of evil that had begun . . . to disrupt his comprehension of the world'. Evil and wickedness do not always yield to reason. Then, waiting for a homosexual friend in Leicester Square, he sees a young homosexual arrested for hustling, and feels 'a hunter's thrill'. Sands sees his own life may well be built on sand: 'Truly, he thought, he was not at one with those who exercised proper authority. A humanist, it would seem, was more at home with the wielders of the knout and the rubber

---

'The point really is that a moral view of society can be stated without any concern for political action of any kind, whereas directly politics enters in, social action and taking sides are involved.'

truncheon.' His crisis resembles that of the vision of 'nothing behind nothing' that afflicts and destroys Forster's Mrs Moore in *A Passage to India*, and the book belongs in the same tradition of moral fiction, though its satirical edge and its radical invention of character (like the outrageous Mrs Currie) is distinctive. The book is seated firmly in the moral and psychological preoccupations of his time, when existential self-knowledge, the need for commitment and the unreliable realms of the psyche became areas for fiction. The book was widely acclaimed as a distinctive portrait of contemporary society and the crises of modern liberalism. Wilson had turned from satiric gadfly into a leading successor to Waugh or Forster, a writer of depth and edge.

In 1955 Wilson found himself sufficiently established to give up his museum post and become a full-time writer, quickly producing a play, *The Mulberry Bush*. performed at the Royal Court in 1956. In the same year he published a much more ambitious novel, *Anglo-Saxon Attitudes*, which took its epigraph from Carroll's *Through the Looking Glass*: 'He's an Anglo-Saxon Messenger – and those are Anglo-Saxon attitudes. He only does them when he's happy.' The book satisfied all the hopes and expectations of the critics; it was a splendidly panoramic, a truly Dickensian, English novel. It turns on an Anglo-Saxon deception: an archaeological dig for the remains of a seventh-century Bishop Eorpwold, who is found clutching a priapic object. All this unlocks contemporary anxieties, especially in Gerald Middleton, a retired professor of history in a state of moral inertia, who suspects that the bishop's problem is not a seventh-century dilemma but a twentieth century fraud done by a friend (having worked at the British Museum, Wilson was well aware of the Piltdown skull forgery of 1953). Middleton is aware of his own moral and existential deficiencies, not least in his family life (he has 'neither the courage to walk out of the marriage he hated, nor the resolution to sustain the role of father decently'). Moral crises are in any case, declares one of the shrewder characters, 'just an English parlour game . . . and what's so *ghastly* is that it's got into our literature'. All human action is compromised, and the novel is the story of 'large numbers of people playing louder and louder games to disguise from themselves the earthquake surface on which they live' – although some do come to 'some kind of grace'. Middleton attempts it, but the force of the book lies in the 'large numbers of people' in the story, which is a portrait of many layers of British society: the hypocritical middle classes, the academic community, corrupt underworlds of petty crooks and hustling homosexuals, more and more parts of a world that seems to reach out far beyond the limits of conscience. Here, as in the previous novel, the sense of evil is strong, though Middleton ends the book seeking a self-recovery, searching for 'the good faith of humane study, in a world rapidly losing its humanity.'

As critics at the time observed, few novelists since Dickens (of whom Wilson wrote an excellent study) had attempted a novel on so panoramic and inclusive a scale. In 1957 Wilson published a new story collection *A Bit Off the Map*, which had some amusement with the Angry Young Men, and followed it with another substantial novel, *The Middle Age of Mrs Eliot* (1958), where, as the title itself suggests, the debt appears to be less to Dickens than the author of *Middlemarch*. This is the story of Meg Eliot, a woman curiously like the Mrs Green of Wilson's Virginia Woolf parody, or Mrs Dalloway herself, the 'metaphysical hostess': a wealthy socialite, middle-aged, married, active in good works, a keen reader of novels, whose pleasant life is suddenly destroyed when her husband is killed at a foreign airport as he tries to intervene in a random episode of international terrorism. The theme is that sanctioned by so much Victorian fiction, the need to confront life itself, in all its variety and scale. Yet books don't help; in fact they are the escape route, and Wilson uses the apparatus of the traditional novel not just to write one but to question. Meg is forced to pass through psychic as well as social breakdown in order to face a different world and a half-mysterious and different England, as well as the intricacies of human relationships, until she is able to say that 'the modern world won't be able to take me by surprise so easily again'. Narrow British lives have to open up to new and chaotic realities. The story has a strong satirical edge, but Meg is a central heroine ('myself', Wilson said) and the book is the story of her courage. It is also a story about how the literary myths of the past that have solaced Meg can enclose us and make us fail to see the new realities. Wilson's two large novels of the Fifties had so far established him as a leading figure, a sharp-edged, wide-ranging recorder of contemporary life, his fiction owing as much to George Eliot or E. M. Forster as it did to Dickens in its moral urgency. But as the Sixties began, Wilson signalled a sharp change in his work. In 1961 he published *The Old Men at the Zoo*, a nightmare invasion fantasy set in the future as a new European war breaks out, and dealing with the release of evil inside a bureaucratic institution which is a version of the nation itself. Wilson, always an intelligent and never a simplistic writer, wrote the book, he said, in reaction against the 'tyranny of neo-traditionalism' that had developed in the Fifties novel; and it would pave the way toward a much more experimental phase in his work, discussed in the following chapter.

5

But for the moment Britain did seem to be, as Lionel Trilling had said, the scene of a revival of social fiction, and many writers appeared to be in agreement with Wilson when he said that 'No sharpening of the visual image, no increased sensibility, no deeper penetration of individual consciousness ... could fully atone for the frivolity of ignoring man as a social being.' Cooper was right; his own spirited social comedy, along with Snow's heavier public record and Wilson's 'liberal' fiction, seemed to mark the tone and direction of the Fifties novel. In *The Struggle of Albert Woods* (1956) and *Memoirs of a New Man* (1966), about 'goings on in the world of science and technology', Cooper developed the story of social ascent in the changing and more scientific (and bureaucratic) world of post-war Britain. So did Snow, in his 'Strangers and Brothers' sequence (1940–70), an extended, eleven-volume *roman-fleuve* that carried its tale from the Great War to the post-war present. Snow's theme began in his earlier novel *The Search* (1934), the story of a young lower-middle-class scientist who makes his way from Leicester to London and from provincial drabness to society and influence. 'Strangers and Brothers' is told by Lewis Eliot, former provincial outsider, eventually university lecturer, lawyer, scientist, bureaucrat, government adviser and minister in Harold Wilson's Labour government during the Sixties, when the white heat of the scientific revolution became political policy. This is twentieth-century social history seen with a Wellsian passion by someone who has moved from the outside to the inside, and can wisely tell us of the peculiar customs and habits that affect men and women in love and society, legal and academic communities, above all those well-meaning academics, scientists, bureaucrats and politicians who attempt to make reason, justice, equality and progress prevail in human affairs, and who finally prevail in post-war Britain, though they rarely succeed in their aims.

Key volumes target some of the essential moments in this process. The early books are about Leicester and the political debates of the Thirties. *Time of Hope* (1947) goes back to the Utopian Wellsianism of the years before the Great War, and leads to Lewis Eliot's quest for success in London. The tale moves on to post-war tasks and modern crises. *The Masters* (1951) is a fine academic novel about the contention inside a Cambridge college when it comes time to appoint a new master; no doubt Tom Sharpe's excellent farce *Porterhouse Blue* (1974), a wild comedy of Englishness, owes much to it, but it has been rightly called 'a paradigm of the political life'. *The New Men* (1954) notably deals with the problems of moral conscience, scientific doubt and political realism that attend the birth of the British atomic bomb, and deals with a crucial phase in post-war history. *Corridors of Power* (1964) directly addresses the experiences Snow had when he did become, as his character Eliot had long dreamed, a consultant to ministers and a politician himself, and the story touches on the shattering effects of the Suez Crisis as well as the political claims of a scientific view of the world. Collectively, the novels are part of an extended exploration of the relations between public and private, historical and personal, the dutiful and the sexual. A key theme is the question of reason and unreason; as a scientist Snow believed in reason and intelligence; as a social witness he saw the power of the irrational. It was particularly evident in the famous Moors Murders case, which becomes the subject of *The Sleep of Reason* (1968); and throughout the sequence folly, madness, sexual extremism and mortality itself are never far away. Yet the novels are above all a story of human progress, through science and social justice; by comparison with Cooper's fiction, Snow's can sometimes seem forbidding. 'I had kept an interest in success and power which was, to my friends, forbiddingly intense,' Eliot says in *Homecomings* (1956); so he has, and that is perhaps the one great limitation of the sequence.

The *roman-fleuve* or the saga novel was a form congenial to the Fifties, though not all versions were as realistic and public as Snow's. Yet part of its fascination was as a form of social history for a generation whose lives had started in Edwardian days or the Twenties, and had seen the world go through several great revolutions, above all the Second World War and the post-war social transformation. Nobody told it all better than Anthony Powell, the first volume of whose 'Dance to the Music of Time' sequence, *A Question of Upbringing*, came out in 1951, to close twelve volumes later with *Hearing Secret Harmonies* in 1975; Powell's tale eventually covered an even longer span than Snow's, and came from a different corner of society. Powell himself had been to Eton and Oxford, worked in publishing and film, kept company with the 'Brideshead Generation', published some splendid comic novels (*Afternoon Men*, 1931, *Venusberg*, 1932), lived in Fitzrovia and served in the army in wartime. He was ideal witness to the strange transpositions of fate that sacrificed some of those he knew to death and disaster, others (not necessarily the best) to post-war opportunity and promotion. Sometimes compared with Proust's *Remembrance of Things Past* for its obsession with time and the strange textures of society, the sequence is in fact highly classical: hard, contemporary, satirical, observant, with tight and filmic techniques. Classical too is the concern with time itself: the title of the sequence comes from a Wallace Gallery painting by Nicholas Poussin (so admired by Anthony Blunt), showing a group of dancers strutting their stuff to time's tune. We can now read the twelve books as a coherent and structured sequence, but that is not how they were written. The project was made to deal with happenstance; it grew and changed as the shifts of post-war history added new matter, and hence it danced with the music of time.

The story begins classically enough, in 1921 at Eton, in the school-days of Nicholas Jenkins, the narrator. But all is dominated by a lesson given somewhat earlier, in the nursery schoolroom of a later volume, *The Kindly Ones* (1962): 'I recall Miss Orchard's account of the Furies. They inflict the vengeance of the gods by bringing in their train war, pestilence, dissension on earth; torturing, too, by the stings of conscience. This last characteristic, I could plainly see, made them sufficiently unwelcome guests.' Unfolding over fifty years, 400 characters and an amazing variety of social, political, sexual, commercial and military situations, it can be seen as an account of the decline of the British upper classes through the 'great changes', half a century of crises: the economic disasters of the Thirties, the slaughter of the Second World War, the rise of the new men in the post-war cosmos and the fate of those new political and sexual players who thus emerge. Yet all is seen in glimpses, flashes, scenes of humour and oddity, wit and surprise; and all is observed, through the medium of Jenkins, with the greatest detachment and irony. It was 'the most important effort in fiction since the war', said Kingsley Amis; for Evelyn Waugh it was the only reason for going on living, in bad times. The long story takes us, stylistically, from an older naturalism to a harder Modernism (Powell is a master of styles); socially, through the passage from a structured social order to a post-war and a postmodern world. Jenkins is endlessly tolerant and highly satirical, engaged and indifferent, constantly shifting in viewpoint and timescale. His friends, enemies and other associates suffer many fates: suicide, madness, terror, penury, sexual and social humiliation. Wealth turns to poverty, rank breeds its grudges. The quiet survivor Jenkins is set against the rogue Kenneth Widmerpool, himself one of the avenging furies and one of the great characters of modern British fiction. Despised at school, he stalks the high places of rank and power. His opportunities come in wartime, and then, chameleon-like, he appears in various positions of power in post-war Britain; at one stage as the Vice-Chancellor of a new university, at another as a likely Russian spy. Jenkins, too, is a great chameleon, shifting from scene to scene, angle to angle, technique to technique, borrowing all the styles that come his way even as he seeks life's secret harmonies. A great human comedy, 'A Dance to the Music of Time' would become one of post-war fiction's finest works.

Other important sequences began about the same time. In 1949 Doris Lessing, born in Persia (Iran) of British parents, growing up in Southern Rhodesia (Zimbabwe), where she married twice, arrived in Britain, carrying the manuscript of a novel, *The Grass is Singing*, published in 1950. The bomb-battered England she arrived in seemed to her a strange country; her colonial experience, her left-wing politics, her feminist sentiments and her journey all formed part of her five-volume sequence 'The Children of Violence', which appeared between 1952 and 1969, and covered a time-span from the Thirties to the millennium. The central character is Martha Quest, who gives her name to the first novel. She grows up in 'Zambesia', she marries, joins a Marxist cell in South Africa, and comes to Britain, where she joins new political groups. Martha has radical dreams of a new social order, a 'four-gated city', and the stories are strongly political. Dealing with the role of the individual in the formation of a good community, the 'individual conscience in relation to the collective', they are also about women and their sense of absence from real history. Martha's self-discovery is a central theme; the novels are written over the period when Lessing herself embraced and then discarded Marxism and Stalinism, and when political awareness dissolved into psychological and Utopian awareness, until the author finally acquired the 'cosmic' viewpoint that would in time lead her to a later space-sequence, 'Canopus in Argos'.

By the mid Fifties, then, the direction of British fiction did not seem too hard to characterize. It was, broadly speaking, anti-experimental, or at least no longer Modernist; it was anti-romantic, and went for classical hardness, clarity, observation, satire. It was social but anti-ideological, or in other words liberal, and generally realistic in its treatments and choice of subjects. It was engaged with the world as it was, the here and now, the life of the ordinary. It was interested in manners, customs, classes, communities, social types, histories, social practice. It valued 'character' and followed the randomness of real life. Some of the manners of past fiction had returned: the social breadth and crowded splendour of the novels of Dickens and

Thackeray, the comic realism and materialism of Wells and Bennett. It was less a metaphysic or a philosophical inquiry than a form of social exploration and expression. Its interest in the ordinary and the provincial often made it seem, well, ordinary and provincial. The homage to a longer tradition of British fiction now led writers like Cooper and Snow to express the conviction that the work of Joyce, Woolf and Dorothy Richardson had diverted the river of fiction, that 'stream-of-consciousness' had blocked the flow of the novel. As writers came to see later, this rejection had a price in narrowing representation. In time it would come to seem that along with Modernism were being discarded many of the depths beneath the surfaces: the challenge of life beyond the text, the challenge of the word within it, the complexities of society, the confusions of value, the perils of form and discourse, the multiplicity of narrative, the slippages of the word – all matters that would have to be returned to again.

6

Was there, then, a trend emerging: something that might be called the Fifties British novel? Not everybody thought so. In August 1954 the *Observer* newspaper undertook a not unfamiliar exercise and ran a series of articles on the topic 'Is the Novel Dead?' Sir Harold Nicolson inaugurated the debate, arguing that, because the novel was no more than two hundred years old, it was simply 'a transitory response to certain conditions'. As he magisterially explained: 'The ancients did not write novels since they were so busy with art, politics, administration and war that they never achieved the special type of tranquillity in which the art of fiction becomes creative and relevant.' And in present conditions of untranquillity, the novel had once more grown quite irrelevant. In one of the several replies, Alan Pryce-Jones did suggest this kind of Ovidian gloom could easily be overdone, since 'it needs only one or two oustanding novels to appear for us to be told that English fiction is in the beginning of a remarkable revival'. And some cursory investigation could well have suggested to the commentators, most of whom did incline to the view that the novel was quite dead, that the Fifties were already becoming an era of interesting first novels and dawning reputations. Thus in 1950, which had seen Cooper's *Scenes from Provincial Life* and Lessing's first novel, *The Grass is Singing*, Barbara Pym brought out her comedy *Some Tame Gazelle*, and Barbara Comyns *Our Spoons Came from Woolworths*. In 1951, Festival of Britain year, Nicholas Mosley published his first novel, *Spaces of the Dark*. In 1952, the year of *Hemlock and After*, Paul Scott, recorder of the dying of the Indian Raj, published *Johnnie Sahib*, and Thomas Hinde *Mr Nicholas*. In 1953 Ian Fleming set 007, James Bond, off on a lively career in *Casino Royale*, and John Wain published *Hurry On Down*, a novel soon to be associated with the rising school of 'Anger', which in fictional terms came to full notice in the following year, 1954, the year of Nicolson's funerary sermon – and also, as it happened, of some quite remarkable fictional debuts. Indeed, one future Nobel prizewinner, a literary knight and literary dame were already waiting in the wings. For in that year William Golding published *Lord of the Flies*, Kingsley Amis *Lucky Jim* and Iris Murdoch *Under the Net*.

Over the rest of the decade these signs of fresh talent and fictional revival would continue. In 1955 came Nigel Dennis's witty *Cards of Identity*, Ruth Prawer Jhabvala's *To Whom She Will* and Dan Jacobson's *The Trap*. In 1956 Anthony Burgess began publishing fiction with his Malayan novel *Time For a Tiger*, Roger Longrigg published a satire on modern advertising, *A High-Pitched Buzz*, and Frederic Raphael *Obbligato*. The next year, 1957, was notable for the publication of Muriel Spark's first novel *The Comforters*, John Braine's bestselling *Room at the Top*, Colin MacInnes's multi-cultural London novel *City of Spades*, Christine Brooke-Rose's *The Languages of Love*, Hugh Thomas's *The World's Game* and Keith Waterhouse's splendid Northern comedy *Billy Liar*. In 1958 Alan Sillitoe established himself with *Saturday Night and Sunday Morning* and John Berger published *A Painter of Our Time*. V. S. Naipaul came to print in 1959 with *Miguel Street*, as did Andrew Sinclair with *The Breaking of Bumbo* and Simon Raven with *The Fathers of Death*; there was even a first novel by the present author. Some notable debuts were seen in 1960: David Storey with *This Sporting Life*, Raymond Williams with

Border Country, Edna O'Brien with *The Country Girls* and Stan Barstow with *A Kind of Loving*. In the years immediately thereafter, other notable figures emerged, including John Fowles, Margaret Drabble, A. S. Byatt, Angela Carter, David Lodge and John Le Carré. And, not too surprisingly, Harold Nicolson's gloomy and Waugh-like reflections on the end of things were replaced by a quite different kind of argument. Now all the talk was of a Fifties revival, and the dawn of the post-war movement; the issue was no longer whether the novel was dead but what sort of life it was living. In 1954 the *Spectator* magazine had already identified a 'New Movement' in British poetry, which included a number of the novelists – Larkin, Amis, Wain – mentioned above, its poets being noted for their restraint, classicism and rejection of romanticism, and its links already made with the new novel. By 1956, after the success of Osborne's *Look Back in Anger*, which marked a similar revolution in 'New British Drama', the latest trend was 'Anger'. Related attempts were made to characterize the Fifties novel, via the social origins of the authors and the status of their heroes. Since many of these books were about the changing culture and the new meritocracy, this was the literature of the 'Angry Young Men'. It was, famously, a simplification and finally a falsification; it clearly did not matter that many of the writers were not angry, many were not young and a good many were women.

In truth the important thing about the Fifties was that there was a revival of fiction publishing, that many of the authors were new and that they wrote of their own generation and culture. The books themselves, and the writers who produced them, were highly various, a fact that would become very clear as their careers continued. There was a trend toward social fiction, and a disposition to exploit the link between contemporary fiction and the traditions of the novel, so that as Cooper and Snow paid their homage to H. G. Wells, and Angus Wilson to Dickens and George Eliot, so did John Wain and Margaret Drabble to Arnold Bennett, Kingsley Amis to Henry Fielding, William Golding to R. M. Ballantyne and Alan Sillitoe and David Storey to D. H. Lawrence. Equally, though, John Wain celebrated Flann O'Brien, Iris Murdoch Raymond Queneau and Samuel Beckett, and many writers spoke of their links with contemporary American fiction

7

There are still several good reasons why Kingsley Amis's *Lucky Jim* – a remarkably funny and original book that had been round sixteen publishers before it appeared in 1954 – should come to seem perhaps the exemplary Fifties novel. 'I was only trying to write a funny novel, while having a few knocks at groups of people I disliked, people who are entrenched in power through no merit of their own,' Amis explained himself. The story of Jim Dixon, the young history lecturer in a red-brick provincial university (Amis himself, son of a City of London clerk, was now lecturer in English at Swansea, though the university here is Leicester) who is inwardly and comically at odds with the fusty, Bloomsbury-fied academic, artistic and social culture of his elders but not betters, captured a powerful contemporary mood. In most ways the book is a traditional romantic comedy: Jim is the comic innocent, the young man who finds himself in someone else's court and discovers the emperor has no clothes; so he wins comedy's ancient blessings, good luck, good fortune, the good girl, just like his historic predecessor, Henry Fielding's Tom Jones. Amis was plainly a very English writer, and was always glad to say so.[6] The book's innovations lay not in its form or its experimental shape, but in its voice. Jim Dixon is a bored and philistine meritocrat lifted by social opportunity into a world he cannot accept or entirely understand, but who needs to survive in enemy country because he doesn't know his luck. As with Holden Caulfield in J. D. Salinger's *The Catcher in the Rye* (1951), he does have an innocent's natural instinct for the honest over the phoney, and can undercut with his innocent eye and vernacular voice the culture and pretensions of those who represent the established, the adult, the dominant and corrupted world. As history lecturer in a backwater university, he finds his philistine values more

---

6 Amis also challenged the claims of experimental fiction: 'The idea about experiment being the life-blood of the English novel is one that dies hard. "Experiment" in this context boils down pretty regularly to "obtruded oddity", whether in construction . . . or in style; it is not felt that adventurousness in subject matter or attitude or tone really counts.'

honest than those of the madrigal-singing and recorder-playing faculty who surround him. He fails to accept either the academic or the social values of his seniors, not least those of his Head of Department, Professor Welch, who announces himself on the telephone as 'History speaking'. He performs most of his revolt in silence or in secret, pulling faces or writing insults on the bathroom mirror. Finally, when he has wonderfully disgraced himself with a drunken lecture on 'Merrie England', which he claims has never existed, he opens his mouth and makes his revolt plain – and duly gets comedy's reward, in the form of a good job in London and the book's prettiest and most desirable girl.[7]

The force and comic impact of the book lie in a number of basic substitutions it performs. A plain and common-sense contemporary prose replaces literary prose; a dissenting account of almost every situation is substituted in Dixon's mind for the language in which it publicly presents itself. The romantic Oxbridge novel turns into something else, the campus novel, set in a place where custom has no credit, rank is not guaranteed and culture has not been secured, and where rapid social transition is taking place. Jim Dixon's personal horizons are narrow, his attitudes provincial and ordinary, his engagement to his academic subject quite incidental ('the medieval papers were a soft option in the Leicester course,' he explains). Words like 'culture', 'art' and 'academic' sound offensively in his ears; his basic theory of life, culture and society is that 'nice things are nicer than nasty ones'. Through his viewpoint cultural issues that are normally framed in one language can be more simply re-framed in another ('He remembered a character in a modern novel . . . who was always feeling pity moving in him like a sickness, or some such jargon. The parallel

7 Amis gives an account of the origins of the book – it came from a visit to the common room at Leicester with his friend Philip Larkin, who said someone ought to do something about this – in his essay on Larkin in *Memoirs* (London, 1991): 'Jim Dixon's surname has something to do with ordinariness, but at the outset it had more to do with Dixon Drive, the street where Philip's digs were. Yes, for a short time I was to tell his story. The fact that, as it turned out, Dixon resembles Philip not in the smallest particular . . . witnesses to the transmuting power of art. Philip came into *Lucky Jim* in quite another way. In 1950 or so I sent him my sprawling first draft and got back what amounted to a synopsis of the first third of the structure and other things besides . . .'

was apt; he felt very ill'). If, as some of the reviewers said, Dixon is an intellectual rebel, it is hardly against the contemporary culture, which he loves. It is against approved high culture, aestheticism and bohemianism, indeed the hangovers of Bloomsbury ('No, not Bloomsbury,' he decides when thinking of a place in London – in the American edition at least, for British ones have 'No, not Chelsea'). And art is an adversary of ordinary and commonplace life, which is what he understands and speaks out of. His enemies end up looking like Lytton Strachey or André Gide; his friends have ordinary troubles and plain unpretentious attitudes. If his cultural prejudices ('filthy Mozart') sometimes sound barbarian, they might best be compared with Mark Twain's European adventures with his innocents abroad ('when I had seen one of these martyrs I had seen them all'). Dixon is narrow, but he stands for the plain contemporary truth-teller; his innocent language and his prejudices form an empirical morality in which common sense is better than pretension, ignorance better than self-deceit. It was perhaps his blunt normality (coupled with the fact that many of the jokes in the book are wonderfully good) that made him a hero to many readers of the day. Yet when he wrote the book Amis was himself a serious university teacher of literature, as well as a literary critic and a fine poet; and built somewhere into all his novels is a sense of serious (or at any rate literary-critical) purpose. As one tradition is put into disrespect, it is possible to create another. He described his own intentions as 'writing novels within the main English-language tradition . . . about understandable characters in a straightforward style'; his many books would express many homages to that tradition, to its moral realism, its common sense, its spirit of comedy.

Amis's second book, *That Uncertain Feeling* (1955), is set (just possibly in honour of Philip Larkin) around a Welsh public library. It manages some useful satire at the expense of Dylan Thomas and his Welsh romanticism, as well as telling the story of an adulterous affair that brings home some of the importance of domestic ordinariness. He then won the Somerset Maugham Travelling Prize, intended to send British writers abroad to widen their horizons. Ironically enough, Maugham had himself described the young Fifties 'Angries' as 'scum'; more ironically yet, abroad was never going to widen the horizons of Kingsley Amis. *I Like it Here* (1958) is the result: a story about a writer named Garnett Bowen (his name the name of two earlier writers, though he is no exiled Modernist) who goes to write in Portugal, suffers at the hands of various phoneys and meets the world of 'bloody abroad'. Portugal, he feels, would be improved if moved to somewhere like Eastbourne, and more than Jim Dixon he is a hero of prejudice: anti-foreign, anti-Bloomsbury, anti-Modernist, anti-London. The 'here' Bowen likes is not Portugal but contemporary Britain, and this is undoubtedly an insular book (Amis announced that his books were all about 'what it means to be English'). There are good comic set-pieces, but the tone is over-ironic, the hero has his extreme limitations and passes on into a sequence of shit-heroes of a decidedly Waugh-like kind. More importantly, the book opens out into a parodic literary text, filled with intertextual jokes about Henry James, Conrad, Proust and Joyce. Bowen is plagued by an expatriate writer by the Jamesian name of Strether, who discourses on the banality of life in huge experimental sentences. Lisbon, though, offers one great literary reward, for in a city cemetery lies the grave of Henry Fielding. Bowen and Amis are moved to homage of the great eighteen-century author who proved the novel could express 'a moral seriousness that could be made apparent without evangelical huffing and puffing', and Amis is able to demonstrate his own moral serious-ness, presented through the same engines of satire and comedy.

At the end of the Fifties, Amis changed tack and produced a book, *Take a Girl Like You* (1960), which still ranks among his finest. The reference point here is not Henry Fielding but Samuel Richardson, author of *Pamela* and *Clarissa*; the book is based on the Richardson-ian plot of romance, seduction and rape, seen from the female point of view, and leading finally to male repentance and virtue. The story is seen through the eyes of a strong and interesting heroine, Jenny Bunn, and addresses issues of moral change, shifting gender relations and sexual habits in a world changed by the contraceptive pill. Amis's later works were commonly accused of misogyny, but this novel takes its heroine deeply seriously, confronting her with another Amis shit-hero, Patrick Standish, a local Casanova who is himself associated with a psychology of mortal fear: his grasping at love is part of his fear of death. Here Amis is unlocking some of the themes that would run through later work. Several novels from the Sixties – *I Want It Now* (1968), *Girl, 20* (1971) – deal observantly with changing manners and styles in the era of sexual liberation. Meanwhile Amis's sharp sense of human mortality and the urgency of personal salvation were distilled in other works: in the powerful ghost story *The Green Man* (1969) and the highly moving story of old people *Ending Up* (1974). In 1964 Amis had left academic life, and he was now one of the most productive of full-time writers, trying a splendid repertory of genres, from detective story to spy fiction, and charting social and sexual change and his own increasing misanthropy – for the former radical reformer had grown older into an amusing but stylishly grumpy figure. But, though he would be eternally the author of *Lucky Jim*, his books never lost their quirky authority. Later titles confronted rather than celebrated the changing ordinary world, but a spirited comedy remained. In books like *Jake's Thing* (1978) and *Stanley and the Women* (1984) he examined the changing world of gender relations and their impact on the troubled male psyche. In 1986 *The Old Devils* – the book with which he won the Booker Prize – showed his cantankerously mortal sensibility, still capable of sustaining what had now become the dark comedy of life into older years, when the once comically angry young man had turned into an even angrier and a very mortal one. The comic touch changed but it never disappeared: as is wisely said in *Stanley and the Women*, 'The rewards for being sane may not be very many but knowing what's funny is one of them.' Amis died in 1995, with a literary succession of sorts assured: his son Martin was now one of the leading novelists of a newer generation.

Probably the most significant thing about *Lucky Jim*, always Amis's most famous book, was that (like *The Catcher in the Rye*) it put a new generation into literature. The change it represented was cultural; it shifted the registers of fiction, put a new paradigm into play. In that sense Fifties fiction *was* a genre, expressed in other related books. John Wain's *Hurry On Down* had appeared a year before *Lucky Jim*, but grew lost in its shadow; it remains an important novel, more realistic and more urgent than Amis's. Its anti-hero Charles Lumley is in revolt against his grammar-school upbringing and his university education, which promises a life of convention, and like the hero of Orwell's *Keep the Aspidistra Flying* he decides not to go 'up' to a conventional life in society, but 'down'. He tries to purge his class background by taking a variety of odd jobs – window cleaner, hospital orderly, chauffeur, drug courier, nightclub bouncer – to end up finally in the highly fashionable but classless occupation of a BBC radio comedy scriptwriter. Lumley is another common-sense outsider hero, with a lot of social and literary hostilities to gratify; he has a grainy truthfulness too, which makes the story closer to realistic picaresque. Wain observes the battle of society, between the classes and the generations, but has to confess that the war of society and self must at last end neutrally, in a draw. Wain, a significant poet, critic and teacher, wrote several more novels, generally returning to similar themes: the limitations of bourgeois society, the problems of the artist in a philistine age. A persistent concern – as in *A Travelling Woman* (1959) – was with the moment of rebellion against the limitations of ordinary life. One of the best of them, *The Contenders* (1958), deals with provincial bohemian life in the Potteries: 'It's because the provinces accept dreariness that London can boast of its brilliance,' someone observes. The book shows a respectful indebtedness to Arnold Bennett as a writer of the region, and Wain drew on an eclectic span of influences, including at times Joyce and Beckett. Yet like other writers of the time he stressed the importance of realism: 'A serious novel is an invented story about the truth, not a fantasy,' he said.

In similar spirit it was left to other new writers of the Fifties to explore the detail: the shifting local landscapes, townscapes, cityscapes; the revival of local and working-class cultures; the eyeline taken from the underwritten standpoint of young people and working-class or lower-middle-class life. If many books displayed a spirit of rebellion or social protest, others seemed more frankly accepting of a society in which a new affluence was available but an older sense of alienation and deprivation remained. A notable success of the time was John Braine's *Room at the Top* (1957), the story of Joe Lampton, who exploits his looks and sexual magnetism to make his way upward out of the drab Yorkshire world of 'Leddersford' to London and success. Braine's is a purely materialist version of the story: the prose devotes itself to descriptions of clothes and cars, and the book just saves itself from being a male version of female popular romance (pure celebration of bodies and commodities) by its evident social topicality. Joe is a simplified and updated version of Julien Sorel, in Stendhal's *The Scarlet and the Black*, whose ascent exposes the amoral vacancy both of the hero and the society. Later novels by Braine celebrated the James Bond-like gratifications of life at the 'top', always an elusive site in British society. A better and much more amusing version of the fable is found in Keith Waterhouse's *Billy Liar* (1959), another Yorkshire tale where the young hero fantasizes about a successful life 'anywhere but here'. Both writers were part of a new regionalization of fiction that was, John Wain suggested, renewing literary culture; and a good number of new writers from the provinces – Alan Sillitoe, Stan Barstow, David Storey, Sid Chaplin, Barry Hines – emerged around this date. Yorkshire did as thriving a trade in authors as it once did in muck and brass. Sillitoe and Stanley Middleton wrote of Nottingham and the Midlands, Beryl Bainbridge of Liverpool, Melvyn Bragg of the Lake District, David Lodge of Birmingham ('Rummidge'), Raymond Williams of the Welsh borders. Being provincial was another way of being an outsider, excluded from the mainstream of British cultural life.

Some of these books represented what seemed to be a return to the working-class fiction of the Thirties – though by now the subject-matter had changed. Of these books Sillitoe's *Saturday Night and Sunday Morning* (1958), by a Nottingham working-class author who had already written eight novels before this was accepted, is among the most notable, a powerful tale about the situation of the post-war working class. The central character is Arthur Seaton, who works a capstan lathe in a Nottingham bicycle factory. Wage-rises make him increasingly affluent, but he hangs on to old working-class resentments and hatred for all authority ('don't let the bastards grind you down'). He wants to take his pleasures, financial and sexual, have his fun, and cheat the world before it cheats him. His weapon is cunning, but his pay packet and his sexual needs limit his rebellion, and he has to admit that by comparison with his father he lives in a better world

('No more short-time like before the war or getting the sack if you stood for ten minutes in the lavatory reading . . .'). He lives, in fact, in a world of Saturday night pleasures and Sunday morning repentance, and his anarchist passion for freedom is finally stifled in the usual way, by having to get married. He ends the story beside the canal bank, himself a caught fish, with a few vague ambitions: 'Me, I'll have a good life, plenty of work, plenty of booze and a piece of skirt every month till I'm ninety.' *The Loneliness of the Long Distance Runner* (1958) is Sillitoe's novella about a young Borstal boy also struggling against prison and authority to find a personal freedom; his skill as a runner displays both his isolation and his physical strength. David Storey caught working-class life quite as powerfully in *This Sporting Life* (1960), where, once again, sport – this time rugby-league football – becomes the way out of a confined northern world: Arthur Machin has both sporting and artistic interests, but in the end, like Arthur Seaton, he sees life in purely material terms. Storey himself came from a Wakefield mining family, was a professional footballer and studied at the Slade School of Art. His fiction has a strong mythic sense, and he produced several very ambitious and remarkable novels: *Radcliffe* (1963), a hugely panoramic and original work set in a highly physical northern landscape, dealing with the conflict of the aesthetic and the material, the body and the spirit, the masculine and feminine, in the tradition of the Brontës and D. H. Lawrence; *Pasmore* (1972), the story of a miner's son who becomes a university teacher; and *Saville* (1976), about the moral disintegration of contemporary England (it won the Booker Prize).

The Fifties closed on a significant crop of novels, from Stan Barstow's *A Kind of Loving* (1960), set in the fast-changing Yorkshire working community of 'Cressley', to Raymond Williams's thoughtful and analytical *Border Country* (1960), about an intelligent boy growing up with the same roots as Williams, on the borders of England and Wales. Other borders, between class and class, city and country, province and metropolis, were part of the story. Williams – a leading cultural critic and lecturer in English at Cambridge – clearly saw that what lay behind these tales was a long revolution, a democratic cultural revolution that had gone on in Britain since the eighteenth century, and been fought out in the world of arts and ideas. Williams also explored this over the generations in two highly influential books, *Culture and Society* (1958) and *The Long Revolution* (1961), which in turn would have a significant effect on literary studies. So too did another key book, Richard Hoggart's *The Uses of Literacy* (1957), a critical and cultural exploration of the rise in educational and cultural opportunities, and its potential impact on a new age of culture. These three critical works sometimes read like novels, and they certainly helped in the reading of them. For surely one reason why realism flourished again in the Fifties was that it opened up the contemporary cultural record, and led to new access across the borders – of class, region and cultural experience. Along with these strengths came the weaknesses: without a sense of form, a power of imagination, a creative and critical energy, fiction easily becomes social documentation, reportage, autobiography. The best writers of the Fifties, and those who had the greatest creative survival, were those who did ask more of their genre, and pushed beyond social report to aesthetic inquiry, as a good number did in the Sixties. In the meantime there were other writers of the day who made very doubtful realists, not least of them William Golding, whose allegorical first novel came out at the same time as *Lucky Jim*.

8

Lord of the Flies (1954) was one of the great novels of the Fifties, yet in no obvious sense was it a Fifties novel; one reviewer would find in Golding 'a sullen distaste for the contemporary'. It was a book that belonged in that half-timeless tradition Robert Louis Stevenson called 'romance', and (like Stevenson's fiction) it drew heavily on the Victorian boys' book tradition for its story and situation. The book most immediately in the background was R. M. Ballantyne's *The Coral Island* (1858), the story of a highly resourceful group of British boys, led by Ralph Rover, who are shipwrecked and marooned on an isolated Pacific island, whose lives are threatened by savages but are rescued by a missionary. Golding had worked in theatre and published a volume of poetry before serving in the navy in the Second World War. He then became a Salisbury schoolmaster, a quick lesson in the matter of assuming the heroic innocence of children. No less disillusioning had been the moral crisis brought on by the war, when, as Golding said, one acquired 'a terrible desperate knowledge of what human beings are capable of'. Golding's fable is a powerful latter-day rewriting of Ballantyne's story (there are many direct parallels and references to it), fitting to his own moral and metaphysical disillusion and the climate of the post-Holocaust, post-nuclear age. In Golding's version, the boys are marooned not by shipwreck but by a plane crash; the time is the future, in the aftermath of a nuclear war. Marooned on the island, the boys attempt to create a self-sufficient order, but this founders in the face of terror, cowardice, rivalry, wickedness and pure evil. Convictions collapse, decencies fail, and the boys revert toward a condition of savagery, culminating in the murder of Piggy. Another boy, Ralph, reflects on 'the end of innocence, the darkness of man's heart'. This is no story of adventure or youthful resourcefulness, but a highly pessimistic, and indeed religious, vision of human evil. It lies well outside all ideas of Victorian optimism, all liberal expectations of human progress. The Lord of the Flies, the figure the boys fear, is Beelzebub, and Golding always made clear the point of the book, and his view of mankind: 'Man's nature is sinful and his state perilous.' It was a view that would shape all his novels, most of them in some sense fables. They are not primarily concerned with the social but the moral and metaphysical world; they have little concern with manners and *mores*; they take place in distinctive, enclosed, allegorical spaces, often in enclosed communities, on the borders of history, even before the coming of the human world.

In *The Inheritors* (1955) Golding deals with the encounter between Neanderthal Man and *Homo sapiens*. The book was also provoked by an earlier text, in this case H. G. Wells's *Outline of History*, which had suggested that Neanderthals were gross ogres with cannibal tendencies, an exemplary case of the ignoble savage. Golding not only humanizes the Neanderthals, but questions the progressive or Utopian version of evolution. At the same time the book questions the nature of human language, seeking to explore a world at the dawn of speech (and sin). *Pincher Martin* (1956) is about a torpedoed sailor (alive or dead?) marooned alone on a rock in the mid Atlantic, his Calvary. The rock itself becomes a substitute for the universe and for former society, his past arrayed before him in illusory flashback, so that he is 'islanded in pictures' like 'a row of trailers of old films'. The tale is a purgatory, and so is the related novel *Free Fall* (1959), Golding's next book, the story of the guilty artist Sammy Mountjoy, also told largely by flashback: the story involves a Gestapo interrogation in a wartime prison camp, where questions of the nature of being and consciousness, sin and guilt, body and soul, are explored. Then, with *The Spire* (1964), Golding changed subject matter, and the vision of his work seemed to change too. The book is about the building of a cathedral spire, obviously based on that of Salisbury, where the spire is added against all the odds, since its foundations lie in a pit of slime. The metaphysical implications are clear, but Golding is particularly interested in the aspirations of Jocelyn, the dean who causes the spire to be built. He is himself like the cathedral, a man or a Christ lying on his back with his body in the slime and his dreams and devotions in the sky. The pull downward to purgatory and upward to paradise governs the plot and the remarkable descriptions of medieval building that play an important part in the novel. Perhaps aware that his critics wondered whether he was able to write a social novel, Golding undertook one in *The Pyramid* (1967); the pyramid in question is British society, seen as static and oppressive. During the Seventies, after a period of silence, Golding undertook another large-scale 'Condition of England' novel, and *Darkness Visible* appeared in 1979. The book, which starts in the apocalypse of the Blitz and a firestorm, is a work rich in Miltonic and apocalyptic allusions, complex time-shifts and wild action. Much of it is obscure; this is Golding's most difficult and so perhaps most unsatisfying novel.

Golding, a remarkable novelist, is never likely to be remembered for his social portraiture, which is not the essence of his work. Like Graham Greene, if for quite different theological reasons, he was a latter-day writer trained in a grand metaphysical Christianity who could address questions of good and evil, being and wholeness, creativity and sin in a corrupted and Godless age. His work stands well outside the liberal and humanistic traditions of British fiction, and apart from much of contemporary social writing. He said once that his books should be regarded not as fables but myths – for fable is 'an invented thing out on the surface whereas myth is something that comes out of the roots of things in the ancient sense of being a key to existence, the whole meaning of life, and experience as a whole'. This very large claim was entirely fair. Golding's works have a grand timelessness, a sense of being concerned with capturing the nature of 'experience as a whole'. But they are also plainly struggles of creation, passionately written works in which character, subject, story and meaning are guided not by rules of direct and clear representation but by allegorical structures and powerful energies of being and becoming. Some of his fiction – above all *Lord of the Flies* – has great mythic clarity; other works remain obscure mysteries. Happily, toward the end of his life Golding had a late extraordinary burst of creation. He produced the 'Maritime Novels' – *Rites of Passage* (1980), *Close Quarters* (1987), *Fire Down Below* (1989) – which are discussed in more detail later. Set on an old sailing ship voyaging to the convict colony of Australia at the time of the Napoleonic Wars, they deal with essential Golding themes: the ambiguity of human nature, the powerful tug of primitivism and savagery, the uncertainty of hope or progress, the formless nature of all experience. But more powerfully than the earlier novels, they also suggest the value of quest, search, creativity and aspiration, even if, as always, these things are strangely secured in human nature. The trilogy was perhaps his finest, and certainly his most hopeful, work; appropriately it surely had much to do with the fact that in 1983 he won the Nobel Prize for Literature.

9

And then there was another writer whose first novel also appeared in 1954, and who did not fit in with the predominantly social cast of British fiction in the mid Fifties – even though she was described, for a very brief while, as an Angry Young Man. Iris Murdoch was hardly angry, not exactly young and by no means a man. She was born in 1919 in Dublin, went to Badminton School and Oxford, joined the civil service and worked for the relief organization UNRRA in Britain, Belgium and Austria as the war ended in Europe. She studied philosophy at Cambridge, taught at Oxford, wrote a book on Sartre, and then (having had five earlier novels rejected) published *Under the Net* in 1954. The book does not conceal its origins. The story is, it is true, told by a male narrator who is an outsider, something of a rebel, 'a professional unauthorized person', an intellectual anti-hero in a cycle of despair and downward descent; there were several surface similarities to the work of Amis and Wain. It is dedicated to the French surrealist and member of Oulipo, Raymond Queneau, whose surrealist influence is everywhere apparent; the hero is an admirer of Queneau and Beckett, and, like the author, well aware of the linguistic speculations of Wittgenstein as well as the contemporary French existential novels of Sartre and Camus, with which it conducts a lively debate. (Murdoch had written very thoughtfully about Sartre's endeavours to devise the modern philosophic novel, above all in *La Nausée*, and praised Camus's fiction as 'a serious attempt on the truth'). Jake Donaghue is an Irish bohemian hack who translates novels from the French, above all the work of one Breteuil, whose work he doesn't like, leaving him in a condition of bad faith. As a writer, he is concerned with his own silence, and his own relation to the world, and is engaged in some kind of strange double quest – which on the one hand takes him off on a curious love chase for two sisters, Anna and Sadie Quentin, and on the other takes him into a philosophical search into the nature of language, directing him toward a lost old friend Hugo Belfounder. He has a sidekick called Finn, who comes from and returns to Ireland. In the manner of surrealism the novel is set in two oddly overlapping Londons, one 'necessary' and the other 'contingent', in a cold cure research centre, a mime theatre, a film studio and in illusory Paris itself. One of the characters is a film-star dog called Mister Mars, another edits a magazine called *The Silencer*. Where *Lucky Jim* is self-consciously provincial, *Under the Net* is just as self-consciously cosmopolitan. Where in Amis's novel the world feels real and literal, and art is always the poor relation to life, in

Murdoch's the world is strange, magical and illusory, and art in its tricks and illusions is the essential paradox of life.

Under the Net is a brilliant first novel and one of the most important and considered books to come out of Britain in the Fifties. It still looks like that after thirty or so more books from its author, amounting to a spirited, often comic but in the end fundamentally serious quest into the modern nature of art, illusion, fiction and the novel. The 'realistic' element in the book that linked it to 'Angry' novels – the drifting, the down-and-out existence, the bohemian scene, the concern with money and new socialist politics – are superficial only. It is a philosophical novel, though not in the Sartrean sense.[8] The ghost of Sartre is everywhere in it, and it has an existential tone. Yet it steadfastly refuses to be Sartrean, above all refusing all sense of boredom and futility. If Sartre, according to Murdoch, seems horrified by 'the rich over-abundance of reality', Murdoch revels in it. Where Sartre's hero in *La Nausée* is 'metaphysical by temperament' and lives coldly, Murdoch's does the opposite, addressing the confusing relationships of the world. Sartre's tragic inability to write a great novel afflicts us all, Murdoch had said, and that has something to do with the problem of theory or abstraction: 'We know the real lesson to be taught is that the human person is precious and unique; but we seem unable to set it forth except in terms of ideology and abstraction.' Such, in effect, is Jake's problem in *Under the Net*, and his elaborate and fanciful quest is as much philosophical as it is humanistic or social or moral. If this is not quite a philosophical novel, and in part is challenging whether there can really be one (just as Hugo Belfounder is 'devoid of general theories'), it is certainly a kind of fiction in which contem-

---

8 As Murdoch explained to Frank Kermode: the book 'plays with a philosophical idea. The problem which is mentioned in the title is the problem of how far conceptualizing and theorizing, which from one point of view are absolutely essential, in fact divide you from the thing that is the object of the theoretical attention.' She added that the wealth of social detail was not essential: 'That was just self-indulgence. It hadn't any particular significance.' Frank Kermode, 'The House of Fiction: Interviews With Seven Novelists' (1963), in Malcolm Bradbury (ed.), *The Novel Today: Contemporary Writers on Modern Fiction* (London, rev. ed., 1990). (The novelists are Murdoch, Greene, Angus Wilson, Compton-Burnett, Snow, Wain and Spark. Iris Murdoch's essay 'Against Dryness', 1961, is also reprinted in this volume.)

porary philosophical questions are central. There are many debates in the novel: about the nature and limits of language, word and silence, act and image, art and illusion, figure and referent.[9] And the book opened up a career that would move through many genres and styles, many forms of invention, many different scenes and stages for testing the nature of art, illusion, the true and the good. Elsewhere Murdoch was debating the contemporary fate and nature of the liberal novel, especially in a 1961 essay 'Against Dryness'. 'We no longer see man against a background of values, of realities which transcend him,' she wrote, comparing the spirit of Victorian and contemporary fiction. 'We picture man as a brave naked will surrounded by an easily comprehended empirical world. For the hard idea of truth we have substituted a facile idea of sincerity.' The modern novel had become split between a 'journalistic' fiction, realistic and contingent, where straightforward stories were enlivened with empirical facts (this would apply to Fifties realism), and the 'crystalline', metaphoric rather than metonymic, where novels were consoling quasi-allegorical objects portraying the human condition (Woolfian modernism?). Neither seems to be a fully fit house for portraying the human person, nor for creating a contemporary moral philosophy, or a true sense of the purpose of art and the sovereignty of good.

Murdoch's fit house for free characters would, over the years, prove to be an ever more exotic and unusual place. She used the phrase, in fact, in an earlier essay, 'The Sublime and the Beautiful Revisited' (1959), where she remarked that novels are portraits of human personalities constructed in words, so 'A novel must be a fit house for free characters to live in; and to combine form with a respect for reality with all its contingent ways is the highest art of prose.' These concerns are laid down in a great variety of ways in her first group of novels, published in striking profusion as the Fifties ended: *The Flight from the Enchanter* (1956), *The Sandcastle* (1957), *The Bell* (1958). It was

9 In one of the book's many 'Silencer' dialogues we have a clue to the title, which also seems to allude to Wittgenstein: 'All theorizing is flight. We must be ruled by the situation itself and that is unutterably particular. Indeed it is something to which we cannot get close enough, however hard we may try as it were to crawl under the net.'

not simply the speed but the variety and richness of these novels that was remarkable. *The Flight from the Enchanter* was begun before *Under the Net*, and originally the characters were largely refugees, reflecting Murdoch's wartime and post-war experience. The book keeps its European and post-war flavour, quite unlike *The Sandcastle*, which is a pleasant and often exotic love romance, or *The Bell*, set in an enclosed religious community in Gloucestershire, in which the lesson is plain: 'Those who hope, by retiring from the world, to earn a holiday from human frailty, in themselves and others, are usually disappointed.' They display a move from a Sartrean existentialism to a concern with the endurance of personality and a due sense of the 'unutterably particular'; they also grow increasingly exotic, making much use of the powers of enchantment, charisma, faith, fantasy and dream. By the early Sixties there was a further change of tone. *A Severed Head* (1961), one of her most interesting books, is a sharp romantic comedy where the object of irony seems to be, very visibly, the Woolfian world of Bloomsbury. Antonia, one of the central characters, is a minor figure from the Bloomsbury scene; she possesses 'a metaphysic of the drawing room', and has 'a sharp appetite for personal relations'. The novel finally shifts these characters out of their 'gentler world' into one 'remote from love and remote from ordinary life'. The variety and fluency of writing continued: over the Sixties Murdoch published almost a novel a year, nearly always producing something very different in setting if not in overall preoccupation from the book before. The characters multiplied, the metaphysics sharpened. As Robert Scholes was to observe, with a wisdom rather greater than that of most of her critics, Murdoch was writing not some variant of realism but a modern fiction of 'fabulation', which freely employed or dispensed with realistic elements, drew on fantasy, symbolism and elaborate literary and artistic reference, had an operatic sense of decor and a love of dramatic pastiche, and all this in the interests of constructing a new and original myth, seriously pursued. And – as we shall see – Murdoch's later fiction did everything to show that, having found the fit house for her characters to live in, she was capable of making it into a grand and ever-changing imaginary theatre in which the human drama could tease and explore love, personality, morality and the power of beauty, art and goodness.

10

Iris Murdoch was not the only novelist whose work, in the critical climate of the Fifties, was hard to grasp. 'No Angry Young Woman?' cried one reviewer in great disappointment when Muriel Spark published her first novel, *The Comforters*, in 1957. The answer was no: the novel was a deliberate undermining of fiction's realist illusion. In her origins Spark was already an unusual and confusing case of the British writer. Born in Edinburgh, she was a Jewish Scot who had some dry Calvinist influences, and who in 1956 had become a convert to Catholicism ('One afternoon I did it'); there is some confusion about her family background to this day. In the post-war years she had soon become a significant figure in London bohemia, writing literary biographies, doing hack-work and establishing herself as a serious poet. Her move into the novel followed on her conversion, and her first novel plainly draws on the work of Evelyn Waugh and Graham Greene, above all the self-conscious, metafictional Greene of *The End of the Affair*, his most teasing work. Having picked up on the metatextual and metaphysical complexities of recent Catholic fiction, she now went on to add some notes that were entirely her own. So if one part of her novel deals with her own movement from the highly raffish world of London bohemia (an environment of which she would become the great chronicler) to the no less unusual world of the London Catholic community, another part of the book is greatly concerned with the odd metaphysics of novels, where God-like people called authors create and control the universes of other people they call characters: in Catholicism the fit house for free characters has a great many surprises in store. Though the book is decorated with a wonderful apparatus of occultism, and the plot reaches into smuggled diamonds and blackmail, its subject is quite explicit; as she told Frank Kermode in the 'House of Fiction' interview, it was 'a novel about writing a novel'. 'I don't claim my fictions are truth,' she added, 'they are fictions out of which a kind of truth emerges.'[10] Which perhaps explains why Caroline Rose, a central character who is writing a solemn and no doubt useful book called *Form in the Modern Novel*, discovers she is 'having difficulty with the chapter on Realism', or why, in various sudden intrusions into the book, we are told 'the characters in this book are all fictions'.

Caroline also feels that someone is typing her story up above (someone is) and she constantly challenges her own position in the plot of the novel; as in Greene's *The End of the Affair*, the matter of higher or Godly and lower or literary plotters is regularly raised. Paradoxes of faith and questions of individual free will are evidently also part of the paradoxes of modern metafiction: 'I intend to stand aside and see if this novel has any form apart from this artificial plot,' insists Caroline. 'I happen to be a Christian.' Evelyn Waugh greatly admired the book; it is not hard to see why, since it extended his own brand of black humour and his fascination with memento mori into splendid new quandaries. Here was a new writer who knew fiction, and a black-hearted Catholic writer who was wonderfully hard, grotesque, unrelenting. Spark's second book, *Robinson* (1958), was a heavy reworking of the Crusoe story, set on an island in the mid Atlantic; it now looks like something of a distraction from a career magnificently resumed and extended in *Memento Mori* (1959), a glorious black farce about a group of elderly people, most of them interlinked in the past, and most of them trying to forestall death by leading absurdly youthful lives, who are telephoned by a supernatural voice, different for each one of them, observing 'Remember you must die.' Spark tackles her subject with humour, if not cosmic indifference, and from this time onward a distinctive and teasing black humour becomes her essential voice. It is there in *The Ballad of Peckham Rye* (1960), where the social scene changes, but not the sense that lives are lived under threat. Over time Spark would prove a vivid novelist of London and its subcultures; Peckham Rye and its commercial culture

10 See Frank Kermode, 'The House of Fiction': Interviews With Seven Novelists' (1963), reprinted in Malcolm Bradbury (ed.), *The Novel Today: Contemporary Writers on Modern Fiction* (London, rev. ed., 1990).

provide society and scene, and Dougal Douglas or Douglas Dougal (his name changes depending on whether he is north or south of the Thames), a diabolic figure with warning horns on his head, transforms local lives and causes local deaths. In her next novel *The Bachelors* (also 1960), we are in Hampstead and its world of hard-working intellectual bachelors, who are likewise confronted by a visitor, Patrick Seaton, medium of the Interior Spiral of the Wider Infinity, whose presence has equally dangerous results.

By 1961, when she published her most successful novel, *The Prime of Miss Jean Brodie*, Spark had clearly perfected her style and found her ideal kind of subject. Now she returned to her Edinburgh origins, and the strange pre-war world of academic seriousness, sharp-edged Calvinism and ideological and metaphysical confusion. Miss Jean Brodie, brilliant teacher at the excellent Marcia Blaine Academy for Girls, is in her prime – intellectual, educational and sexual. The girls in her set, the Brodie set, are brilliant creatures, each one famous for something, whether it be sex, religion or fatness. With her prissy elegance, her determination to be a female role model, her right-wing and half-fascist opinions, Miss Brodie wins them over with her style and experience. Then the girls rebel and Miss Brodie is betrayed; who has been the Judas? The tight and finely structured tale, told in several time-zones (flashback, flash forward), is a lesson in fickle fate, an account of the paradoxes of good and evil, honour and treachery, with a dark denouement. Spark was to remain an important and innovative writer, her later books being some of the most interesting and playful fictions of the Sixties. And no British novelist has better explored the idea of the novel as its own metaphor: a metaphor for the human condition, as displayed in the relation of writer to text, predestined plot to present existence, destiny to freedom, and the function of an ending, fiction's own intrinsic memento mori. Fiction was a central part of the inescapable black comedy that is human life itself. And in her work, even before the Sixties started, some of its fundamental themes – fictional play, metafictional inquiry – were already quite clearly promised.

11

Which all meant that in a time that was said to have dispensed with experiment and been in thrall to realism, something else was happening to fiction. And, from the handy Sparkian perspective of wise hindsight, it is now possible to see that with many of the most interesting starts and burgeoning careers of the Fifties – a decade finally notable for exactly that – more than is usually acknowledged was happening. It was a decade of realism, when the post-war world and the post-war generation saw itself newly depicted in fresh fiction. It was a time of return to the 'liberal' novel, the novel of character and personality, and a time of the reconstruction of the tradition, when writers of an earlier period of realism, the Victorian and Edwardian ages, were recuperated and made visible. Yet as time passed the most important new writers of the period, including Angus Wilson, William Golding, Doris Lessing, Kingsley Amis, Iris Murdoch, David Storey and Muriel Spark, whose careers grew over the following decade, turned into very doubtful examples of the fictional culture with which they were too readily identified. Amis proved a highly various and plural writer, experimenting with many genres, from detective fiction to spy story; at the same time his comic realism mutated into a Waugh-like irony. Wilson grew ever more experimental, departing from depiction of Anglo-Saxon attitudes to literary pastiche and elaborate playful fantasy. Murdoch went on to a remarkable and expansive career, one of the most interesting in modern British fiction. Spark became a wonderful mocking metaphysician of the novel.

Other new careers started as the decade progressed. One of the most important was that of Anthony Burgess (John Anthony Burgess Wilson), another Catholic writer of different temper. From Lancashire recusant background, he went to a Catholic school in Manchester and then to Manchester University, and hoped to become a musician. He did war service and afterwards went to the then-British colony of Malaya (Malaysia), where he became a distinctly dissident education officer working for the colonial service. He had earlier written a novel,

A Vision of Battlements, though it did not appear until 1965. Now he began his 'Malayan Trilogy' – *Time for a Tiger* (1956), *The Enemy in the Blanket* (1958), *Beds in the East* (1959) – which established his reputation. The sequence was a rich academic comedy, filled with a true linguist's fascination with the grand spectacle of the world's many languages (here Malay and Urdu, Tamil and Chinese). The stories deal with a rather annoying British expatriate teacher called Victor Crabbe, but are comic tales of the dying of the Pacific Raj; Malaya gained independence as the books came out, in 1957. They are literate texts, already showing Burgess's fascination with the great linguisticians of the novel, above all James Joyce. In 1959, diagnosed with a brain tumour, Burgess was sent back to Britain for treatment, having been told he had a year to live. To use the year profitably and leave his wife an income, Burgess produced five novels: *The Doctor is Sick* (1960), *The Worm and the Ring* (1961) and *The Wanting Seed* (1962) as Anthony Burgess, and *One Hand Clapping* (1961) and *Inside Mr Enderby* (1963) as Joseph Kell. There was no tumour: Burgess had five novels, several styles, two literary identities and a habit of prolific invention. Enderby, a poet with bowel problems that required him to write in the lavatory, became a recurrent character. Writing became an untiring habit conducted under any circumstances; it has been estimated that Burgess's writing output ran to something like 150,000 words a year, though this is probably an under-estimate. This included major books like *A Clockwork Orange* (1962), a splendid novel of a crime-ridden dystopia, based on an invented youth language called Nadsat. Burgess would go on to write over fifty books, a good many on the big scale: another Fifties writer who helped shape the future of modern fiction.

The Fifties were, or so it seemed, the decade when the novel – in Britain and elsewhere – was no longer novel. It would have been truer to judge that, in the wake of the end of the Modern movement, novelists were finding that the genre was as various as it always has been. In a time of changing social order, British fiction returned to questions of representation, regionality and culture, questions of character and social portraiture, issues of the moral purpose and political vision of the novel. The debate about the liberalism of the

7

Crossroads – Fiction in the Sixties: 1960–1969

– fuck all this lying look what im really trying to write about
is writing not all this stuff about architecture trying to say
something about writing about my writing im my hero though
what a useless appellation, my first character then im trying to
say something about me through him albert an architect when
whats the point in covering up covering up pretending . . .

B. S. Johnson, *Albert Angelo* (1964)

This story I am telling is all imagination. These characters I
create never existed outside my own mind. If I have pretended
until now to know my characters' minds and innermost
thoughts, it is because I am writing in (just as I have assumed
some of the vocabulary and 'voice' of) a convention universally
accepted at the time of my story; that the novelist stands next
to God. He may not know all, yet he tries to pretend he does.
But I live in the age of Alain Robbe-Grillet and Roland Barthes;
if this is a novel, it cannot be a novel in the modern sense of
the word.

John Fowles, *The French Lieutenant's Woman* (1969)

Realistic novels continue to be written – it is easy to forget
that most novels published in England fall within this category
– but pressure of scepticism on the aesthetic and epistemological premises of literary realism is now so intense that many
novelists, instead of marching confidently straight ahead, are
at least considering the two routes that branch out from the

crossroads. One of these routes leads to the non-fiction novel, and the other to what [Robert] Scholes [in his book *The Fabulators*] calls 'fabulation'.

David Lodge, *'The Novelist at the Crossroads'* (1971)

1

'The Sixties' are no longer a historical decade; perhaps they never quite were. The image of a radical and transforming era, when the protests and resentments of the rebels without a cause moved to direct action and near-revolution, and changed the culture, politics and consciousness of the Western world, has become so firmly engrained that it is hard to set it aside for the actual history of the decade. In 1960, fifteen years after the war ended, the American people elected to office by a very tight margin a youthful president, John F. Kennedy: the first truly post-war leader they had yet had. In his inaugural address, Kennedy spoke of the 'New Frontier' that lay ahead of the new generation, 'a frontier of unknown opportunities and perils . . . I am asking each of you to be pioneers on that new frontier.' America's future prospects were high. It was a great international power, post-war affluence continued, the nation was in fact entering one of its longest periods of continuous economic growth. The suburbs prospered, the cities spread. Nine out of ten families had a television set, most had a car, and the post-war baby boomers were now in college. At the White House Kennedy's 'Camelot' court was young, intelligent and attractive to writers and intellectuals. The eminent poet Robert Frost in a White House poem spoke of 'a golden age / Of which this noonday's the beginning hour'. In 1960 a leading political scientist, Daniel Bell, had published an influential book, *The End of Ideology*, arguing that the ideological politics that had dominated the first half of the century had no further relevance to the affluence and social progress of the second half; a new post-ideological consensus had grown in the West from consumer affluence and social contentment. Certainly there were social problems (J. K. Galbraith's *The Affluent Society*, 1958, observed a new type of society based on private wealth and public squalor) but they no longer provoked ideological interpretation or radical action.

The new American writing of the time seemed to share the Kennedy spirit in its fascination with a grandly imperial, intellectually vigorous, globally energetic America, even if the dissents of the Fifties continued (the Beat Generation) and many ironic voices were sounding.[1] On the international scene Kennedy inherited formidable problems. The Cold War now intensified, and the perils were growing greater than the opportunities. The first man in space – Russian – circled the globe as the Sixties began; the space race accelerated, not just toward the goal of putting a man on the moon, but in the form of a rising nuclear threat as the capability of intercontinental missiles extended. In 1959 Khrushchev rescinded the Four-Power Agreement on Berlin and proposed to make it a free city. In fact he handed over power to the East German government, who, faced with a constant drain of workers from the workers' paradise, decided to close the checkpoints and build the Berlin Wall; it would remain in place for the next thirty years. Khrushchev's international policies grew ever more aggressive; as the Communist economies grew and influence expanded, he said, 'the international situation will change radically'. Soon tension moved closer to home, as Fidel Castro, who in 1959 had taken power in Cuba and established a Communist regime, threw in his lot with Russia. In 1961 Kennedy allowed the CIA to mount what proved to be a futile invasion attempt at the Bay of Pigs. There soon followed the Cuban missile crisis, as Khrushchev shipped Russian missiles to the island. This raised the climate of nuclear terror right across the world, and was the greatest and most dangerous stand-off of the Cold War. And if Kennedy faced major problems abroad, he also found many at home. His liberal policies and 'New Frontier' vision had summoned high expectations of social change. In 1960 the radical Students for a

---

1 Morris Dickstein, in his *Gates of Eden: American Culture in the Sixties* (New York, 1977), notes of the writing of this time, when major books by John Updike (*Rabbit, Run*, 1960), Joseph Heller (*Catch-22*, 1961), Norman Mailer (*The Presidential Papers*, 1963) and Thomas Pynchon, (*V*, 1963) appeared: 'Grandiose and experimental in form, these books partook of some of the imperial buoyancy of the Kennedy years. But their vision sometimes had a bleak, dead-end character that belied any official optimism.'

Democratic Society (SDS), activist, anti-capitalist and anti-war, was founded, and became influential in radicalizing the campuses. Kennedy had promised Civil Rights legislation, and in the South lunch-counter sit-ins began a sequence of increasingly violent protests about black segregation, which culminated in the 1963 'March on Washington', peacefully led by Martin Luther King, when 250,000 African-Americans publicly asserted their rights.

By now everyone was expecting more – especially the young, the poor, the displaced, the free-spirited, the black. As Bob Dylan sang, the times they were a-changing, for post-war cautions were transforming into grand Utopian claims. The Beat and Hippie movements of the Fifties became the 'counter-culture' of a whole new generation, a youth generation radicalized by their own gurus, student leaders and radical celebrities, their own protest music. They demanded new freedoms: peace, no arms race, sex, music, drugs, free speech, obscenity, nakedness, revolution, pleasure, trips, instant Utopia, instant revelation. Old anarchist gurus like Herbert Marcuse and William Reich offered visions of a psychic libertarian and erotic revolt against the age of mechanism and the repressed world of 'one-dimensional man'.[2] When the birth control pill was made available in 1960, it seemed to offer the promise of sexual Utopia. But it was also clear the role of women had changed, and new claims for female liberation grew; Betty Friedan published her influential book *The Feminine Mystique* in 1963. Social and cultural history was being rewritten, and the sense of rising danger and absurdity, of international tension and domestic turbulence, the growing division between old and young and rich and poor, the feeling that America was split between different versions of itself, between the conservative and the radical, created a sense of unreality. The Sixties were the heyday of post-war American fiction, when the great reputations rose: Bellow, Roth, Updike, Heller,

---

2 Influential liberationist texts include Norman O. Brown, *Life Against Death* (Middletown, Conn., and London, 1959), Herbert Marcuse, *One-Dimensional Man: Studies in the Ideology of Advanced Industrial Society* (Boston and London, 1964) and Charles A. Reich, *The Greening of America* (New York, 1970). In Britain R. D. Laing's *The Divided Self* (London, 1960) and *The Politics of Experience* (London, 1967) had similar influence.

Vonnegut, Burroughs, Pynchon, Kesey, Doctorow, Brautigan, Barth. In a famous essay of 1961, Philip Roth declared that American realities had grown so absurd they were pre-empting the work of the novelist: 'The actuality is continually outdoing our talents, and the culture tosses up figures almost daily that are the envy of any novelist.' In another important essay a year later Saul Bellow observed that the forces of power, mass and public energy in America had grown so powerful they had driven the private self into hiding: this is the essential theme of his finest novel, *Herzog* (1964), about an intellectual hero driven by the reality instructors into a splendidly productive madness.[3] One of the chief sites of the counter-cultural revolution was the arts, which grew more extreme in subject matter, more bitter in humour and, in many cases, more collaborative and performance-oriented. New theatre, poetry and art groups multiplied: Off-Off Broadway, Living Theatre, the New York School of Poets, Black Mountain, Op Art, Pop Arts, the New Realists (Andy Warhol established himself with a major exhibition in 1962). The Sixties turned into the age of acid rock and folk music, mass concerts, improvised and sudden events, public happenings, street theatre, love-ins, drugs, sex, psychedelic fantasy – part of the new 'youth revolt' and 'revolution of consciousness' that ran on through the decade.

Then on 22 November 1963, John Kennedy was shot in Dallas – the first of a series of tragic political assassinations that took place in an increasingly unsettled, dangerous decade. As Lyndon B. Johnson inherited office and promised a reforming 'Great Society', his political problems grew. Protest at home was turning more extreme; radical groups became committed to violence, and there were black riots in the ghettoes of American cities. Meanwhile Johnson not only inherited but escalated American involvement in the war in Vietnam. By the mid Sixties a rising movement of disaffection and protest was already spreading across the world. Student riots in Tokyo, the rise of the British 'New Left', British and European protest marches against nuclear weapons, which turned into anti-American protests against

3 The essays by Roth and Bellow are both reprinted in Malcolm Bradbury (ed.), *The Novel Today: Contemporary Writers on Modern Fiction* (London, rev. ed., 1990).

the Vietnam War, and the protests against the use of American global power by young Americans themselves, all marked the appearance of an international 'youth intelligentsia' who saw themselves as harbingers of general social change. The Black Power movement and the SDS grew more organized, activist and violent; soon student revolt was affecting nearly every university campus in the USA and Western Europe. As the war in Vietnam grew more brutal and genocidal, the 'military-industrial complex' and the nuclear missile seemed to stand for the new America, and public figures virtually acknowledged that the country was caught in a war from which it could not extricate itself. Everything came under challenge, not least prevailing ideas about reality or history itself. Indeed, a kind of grand historical undermining runs through much of the American fiction of the times. In Joseph Heller's black-humour novel *Catch-22* (1961), the world of war is absurd, humanly and philosophically; the only logic is personal escape. In Ken Kesey's *One Flew Over the Cuckoo's Nest* (1962), madness is preferable to social common sense, and society is the real madhouse, repressing the instincts of the self. In Richard Brautigan's Californian hippie novel *A Confederate General at Big Sur* (1964), the modern 'confederate general' is in revolt against the American military-industrial complex, and his weapon is creative play and indeterminacy, so that the book ends up with 'more endings, faster and faster until this book is having 186,000 endings per second'. In *The Crying of Lot 49* (1966), Thomas Pynchon portrays the American technical wasteland and its over-plenitude, then suggests some possible hidden code in the redundancy and senseless history. In Norman Mailer's *Armies of the Night* (1968), about the anti-Vietnam march on the Pentagon, history is fiction and fiction is history. In Kurt Vonnegut's *Slaughterhouse Five* (1969), about the firebombing of Dresden, there is 'nothing to say about a massacre', and the story is perceived from the imaginary planet of Tralfamadore, where stories work the other way round.

In 1968 – the year of a new American election that brought Richard Nixon, Kennedy's challenger in 1960, to presidential office amid student protests across the country – the Sixties peaked. Riots broke up the Democrat presidential convention in Chicago. Perhaps America had stirred the forces of change, but they were everywhere. In Paris in May came the *événements*, and students and workers tore up the streets in revolt against the dominant state. Campuses right across Europe came to a halt over any and every issue: student rights and representation, free speech, the bombing of Cambodia, the ending of capitalism, the dissolving of the centralist state. It felt like a fatal year. Kennedy's brother Robert and Martin Luther King both fell to assassins. Baader-Meinhof terrorist outrages spread across Germany. This was also the year of the Prague Spring, when Russian tanks entered Prague to crush the democratic Czech Revolution and trap and execute its leaders. This was the peak and the trough of 'the Sixties'. It was a radical idea, based in part on a culture of Western affluence, the opportunities it offered and the disillusions it bred. It became a free-standing notion, standing for a general image of 'youth' and 'liberation', of lifestyle revolution, supported by style and fashion, music and icon, sit-ins and love-ins, concerts and protests, a youth underground to challenge the overground. It drew on drugs and psychedelic experience, gatherings and impromptu events, Utopian expectations and inter-galactic space-age dreams. It was permissively libertarian, erotic and sexual; one went to bed for a good deal in the Sixties. It united new politics and new arts, high and pop cultures, the historic avant-garde and the new arts of the day. It saw a revolt against most things from parenthood to science, the commercial corporation to the military-industrial complex. The mythic Sixties are this generational cultural rebellion, which was a product of rising expectations, a period of extended affluence, its ideologies and Utopian passions primarily fed not by disadvantaged workers but by other groups who felt culturally disadvantaged (ethnic minorities, blacks, women, gays) or by students and young people in general, and not necessarily in search of material reward but for the rewards of a 'new consciousness'. A ferment of ideas (old and new, sophisticated and naive, anarchistic and high conservative, idealistic and brutal) developed, and ran through popular culture and the arts. The arts, particularly those that were radical, free-style, improvised, self-discovering, communal, often felt like the front edge of Sixties revolution.[4]

Yet the Sixties saw another, even more powerful revolution. It came from the new affluence, the new technologies, the application of modern sciences and systems, the rise of a new international web of commercial and communications networks, from goods and shopping malls, theme parks and movie houses, mass entertainments. Sometimes the counter-culture was part of this, in pop music, new radio and music stations, TV shows; sometimes commercial mass culture seemed the adversary, a symbol of all that was bland and repressive. As Marshall McLuhan observed in two internationally influential books, *The Gutenberg Galaxy* (1962) and *Understanding Media* (1964), what was happening was more than a change in cultural attitudes; it was a fundamental change in the nature of culture itself.[5] A print-based linear era was ending, yielding to an age of the technological stimulation of consciousness and cultural experience. The medium itself was the message; the sign and signature of things was changing, the image and the icon altering, the human figure shifting in relation to the technological landscape. It was the end of an old book-based humanism, the beginning of the tribalized global village. And in fact this was the inescapable revolution, the Western late modern or postmodern social experience, the cultural logic of late capitalism. Over the Sixties both revolutions became – if somewhat more slowly than in America – part of British life. The new politics had strong links with the British 'New Left': the *New Left Review* was founded in 1960, and it represented, as Stuart Hall put it, 'the imaginative resistance of people who live under capitalism'. It was also intricately engaged with popular and mass culture and the rapid changes of social behaviour that were taking place in an increasingly affluent world. In Britain too, where in 1959 another Conservative government was elected, affluence was growing, as it was across all

---

4 A good contemporary study is Theodore Roszak, *The Making of the Counter-Culture* (New York, 1969); also see A. Matusow, *The Unraveling of America* (New York, 1984).
5 Marshall McLuhan, *The Gutenberg Galaxy: The Making of Typographic Man* (Toronto, 1962) and *Understanding Media: The Extensions of Man* (New York, 1964).

of western Europe. New educational opportunities were growing available as universities expanded and increased in number, and taught new subjects, including 'cultural studies'. Commercial development of communications and the media multiplied; commercial television had started in Britain in 1955, and grew powerfully during the Sixties, while the BBC took a more aggressive and independent role. The age of mass culture became dominant: a collectivity, it was said, quite unique to late modern technological society.

When in 1962 Anthony Sampson, in *An Anatomy of Britain*, offered a progress report on the contemporary 'Condition of England', he similarly saw a modernizing society where the old Establishment values still retained power but were dissolving fast. The nation had entered an era of mass economic growth and 'galloping consumption'. 'Within two years,' he explained, 'the credit squeeze ended, skyscrapers rushed up, supermarkets spread over cities, newspapers became fatter or died, commercial TV began making millions, shops, airlines, even coal and banks had to fight for their lives. After the big sleep many people welcomed any novelty; any piece of Americanization seemed an enterprising change . . .' His book and many another study surveyed the current 'Condition' as the struggle of a nation trapped between a declining, evocative, imperial past and an accelerating American-style commercial democratic future: probably in the European Community, to which Britain applied (unsuccessfully) in 1961. With new values and new commodities came the new technologies; now there was a car in many British garages and a television set in almost every home – so opening a window on the state of the rest of the nation, its amusements, its celebrities, its tastes and its styles. Regionality and local difference began to dissolve, and a consumer collectivity to grow. Shopping centres rose; the countryside went under concrete. The age of mechanical reproduction had arrived, in which the old stratifications of high and mass culture, good and bad taste, better and worse, were reincorporated within one continuous and seamless frame. Mass culture had its own rewards and accompaniments: it depended on rapid stylistic consumption, ephemerality, generational tastes and quick obsolescence, the tastes and involvements of the young. It hence quickly assimilated the counter-cultural, and the new arts and new media, the anarchist underground and the youth revolution, protest and style, began to merge, till it came to appear that the old avant-garde, the new counter-culture and the great media revolution were all simply one and the same.

By the end of the Sixties it was clear that a deep transformation had altered life and culture in the capitalist and consumerist West. The new technological revolution and the cultural revolution developed together, shaped by new affluence, commodities, changing demographic patterns and rising expectations. Style had become a badge, an empowerment, a declaration of identity. The arts themselves, as makers and custodians of style and freewheeling invention, had played a serious part. The result was a new kind of experimentalism, less avant-garde than counter-cultural, but mostly to do with the release of new forms and cultural inhibitions, in the interests of creating new icons, images, interpretations, dreamwork, fantasy, concepts of self and myths of reality. The arts were becoming multi-cultural, multi-dimensional, plural, provisional. Forms, genres and hierarchies were breaking down or crossing over. Old ideas of the value of high cultural icons and objects were being replaced by the values of an age of multiple reproduction, where old or iconic forms could be freely multiplied, manipulated, quoted, pastiched, parodied, ironized or subverted in a culture of plenitude. Now there was a consciousness revolution and a consciousness industry; style was itself a commodity offered for widespread purchase and possession. Such was the global village, which was less a village than a complex and very hi-tech international profit-taking conglomerate. But in it no style was stable, no form permanent, no tradition indivisible, and everything borrowed freely from everything and everyone else in a glut of iconography.

And what about the novel? It was dead, of course. And so, as Marshall McLuhan said, was the book itself, the printed institution on which the novel depended. Writers, if they did write books, were left with what John Barth called 'the literature of exhaustion', where all the forms were used up. Language was slipping: 'What does language have against me – me that has been good to it, respecting its little peculiarities and nicilosities, for sixty years,' asks the narrator of one of Donald Barthelme's stories. The experimental British writer

B. S. Johnson explained that the nineteenth-century narrative novel was 'exhausted, clapped out', and a new random literature was needed to reflect the disorderly nature of truth and the modern chaos. Yet it seemed that if old stories were complete and done for, new ones were already needed: mixed stories, Möbius strips, generic crossovers or even returns to the grand story-banks of narrative, like *The Arabian Nights* or *Don Quixote*, as well as to films, genre fiction, the media arts. Playing with forms and folk tales, writers now started hunting back through the labyrinths of narrative to find new journeys or forking paths. As David Lodge observed in his essay 'The Novelist at the Crossroads', novelists, summoned in the Fifties back to the tradition of the realistic novel, now found that passion abating ('For one thing, the novelty of the social experience the fiction of that decade had fed on – the break-up of a bourgeois-dominated class society – has faded. More important, the literary theorizing behind the "Movement" was fatally thin').[6] Now there were new temptations: the non-fiction novel, fabulation, metafictionality, in a time when history and the real became ambiguities and fictionality a value in its own account. Now theatre flourished on new and experimental relationships with its own theatricality, poetry turned to performance and the novel forewent much of its status as grand narrative and saw itself as a more open, provisional form. One result was that, in America, France and Britain too, there was a period of interesting fictional innovation, when it came to seem that something like a new post-war, or postmodern, experimental style was being formed.

6 David Lodge, 'The Novelist at the Crossroads', in *The Novelist at the Crossroads and Other Essays on Fiction and Criticism* (London, 1971). Also reprinted in Malcolm Bradbury (ed.), *The Novel Today: Contemporary Writers on Modern Fiction* (London, rev. ed., 1990). Lodge notes various kinds of alternative to realism: the fabulation, or the fantastic and allegorical novel and the genre novel; the non-fiction novel; the self-conscious, self-begetting or problematic novel.

2

According to Philip Larkin in his poem 'Annus Mirabilis', there was no doubt at all when the Sixties started in Britain. It was in 1963, the year when sexual intercourse began: 'rather late for me – /Between the end of the Chatterley ban/ And the Beatles' first LP.' The trial that ended the long-lived ban on publication of D. H. Lawrence's last novel, *Lady Chatterley's Lover*, took place in 1960: one of several important obscenity trials that, both in Britain and America, punctuated the decade, suggesting a kind of belated victory for frankness and the Modern movement, though also for contemporary writers like William Burroughs (*The Naked Lunch*, Paris 1959), Alexander Trocchi (*Cain's Book*, 1962) and for that matter Vladimir Nabokov's American novel *Lolita*. The Beatles (MBE, 1965) indeed had a chart hit with *Please Please Me* in 1963: the year, as it happened, of the John Profumo sex-and-spy scandal, which dissolved into an amazing British farrago of classical decadent Cliveden aristocracy, high-class prostitution, establishment high jinks, sex therapy, Russian espionage and House of Commons principles, all of which deeply embarrassed the Macmillan government. 'It *is* a moral issue,' said, rather helplessly, *The Times* – though in the same year the liberal Bishop of Woolwich published an Anglican humanist's permissive version of Christianity, *Honest To God*, which more or less said it wasn't. In 1961 the contraceptive pill became available in Britain – as did the Pilkington Report on the future of television broadcasting, the founding of the post-war 'new universities' and the loss of the farthing from the currency.

Even literary criticism was changing fast, turning into literary theory. The strong moral note – and the accompanying disapproval of modern mass culture – that had sounded from F. R. Leavis and *Scrutiny* – gave way to the permissively sociological criticism of the Sixties. As Raymond Williams put it in *The Long Revolution* (1961), the British way of life, 'from the shape of our communities to the organization and content of education, and from the structure of the family to the status of art and entertainment, is being profoundly affected by the interaction of democracy and industry, and the extension of communications'. And now there was Paris, not just the scene of the great *événements* but of literary theory. For 1968 was also the year when the philosophy of Structuralism – an assemblage of literary and semiotic theory, anthropology, post-Existentialist philosophy, psychoanalysis – began to give way to the latter-day philosophy of Deconstruction, which would dominate many of the ideas of the Seventies. Deconstruction was a new philosophical universe which emptied plenitude; it was a universe of gaps, slippage, absences, its signs and signals shifting, its centres vacated, its texts eternally delayed or deferred. Sartre's empire of signs had been in crisis since 1953, when Barthes published *Writing Degree Zero* (it happened to appear in English in 1967). Barthes was no Sartrean or Existentialist: 'the Sartrean novel gives the novel the ambiguity of a testimony that may well be false.' He was also a semiotician, a reader for whom the world of signs was found everywhere; indeed Barthes read everything – a plate of steak, a wrestling bout, a sauce bottle – as if it were *Finnegans Wake*. It proved the world was a text, the text was a world, and writing was not *lisible* but *scriptible*, not what reads itself to us, but what we read – meaning that literature could be 'openly reduced to the problematics of language, and that is all it can now be'. Fiction was not a humanist insight, a true report, or a philosophic utterance; it could not reconcile word with object or text with history. It was simply left with its character as writing itself: 'man's direct experience of what surrounds him without his being able to surround himself with a psychology, a metaphysic'. Character withdrew into consciousness, consciousness into fragmentation, world into text. Barthes's key essay, 'The Death of the Author', itself came in 1968; it argued that there was no way a writer could locate him or herself in the larger textual machine that was writing's real activity as a real 'author'. In the world of signs, literature was a text and the writer was written, by language itself. In later Deconstructive versions, the need is to move beyond texts to grammatology, or a science of writing in general.[7]

7 Useful discussions of these matters are in John Sturrock, *Structuralism and Since: From Lévi-Strauss to Derrida* (Oxford, 1979), and Christopher Norris, *Deconstruction: Theory and Practice* (London and New York, 1982). Terence Hawkes, *Structuralism and Semiotics* (London and New York, 1977) observes: 'We live in a world of signs,

Novelists have no particular reason to read the philosophers or academic critics, and (quite sensibly) only a few of them do. But it seemed at least that the new theorists and the new novelists shared something of a climate in common, as American writers like Ronald Sukenick published books with titles like *The Death of the Novel and Other Stories* (1969), or the novelists of the French *nouveau roman* – Alain Robbe-Grillet, Michel Butor, Nathalie Sarraute, Marguerite Duras and Claude Simon – wrote novels from what Sarraute called an 'era of suspicion' when simple representation appeared to be possible no longer. What the *nouveau roman* was meant to show, Robbe-Grillet explained, was that we live alone with 'the smooth, meaningless, amoral surface of the world'. Those who accused the novelist of committing a crime against humanism should know the only crime committed was 'stating that there is in existence in the world something that is not man, that takes no notice of him, and has nothing in common with him'. Thus the *nouveau roman* came close to Beckett's idea of a writing devoted to 'nameless things' and 'thingless names', a post-literary literature without characters or conventional psychology, merely a text or a mode of perception. In 'The Novel as Research', another essay published in 1968, Michel Butor explained it differently: the novel had now become a 'laboratory of narrative', devoted not to realism but the quest for reality, and 'far from being opposed to realism, as short-sighted critics often assumed, [it] is the *sine qua non* of a greater realism'.[8]

Similar notions were emerging, rather more playfully, in other places: the USA in particular.[9] 'The obtaining of such local ingredients as would allow me to inject a modicum of average "reality" (one of

---

and of signs about signs. A growing awareness of this situation has involved modern man in a momentous change of perspective which has gradually forced him to accept that in such a world "reality" inheres not in things themselves, but in the relationships we discern between things . . .'

8 Roland Barthes, 'The Death of the Author', (from *Image, Music, Text*) reprinted in David Lodge (ed.), *Modern Criticism and Theory: A Reader* (London, 1988). Michel Butor, 'The Novel as Research', reprinted in Malcolm Bradbury (ed.), *The Novel Today: Contemporary Writers on Modern Fiction* (London, rev. ed., 1990).

9 I have discussed American 'metafiction' at length in my *The Modern American Novel* (London and New York, rev. ed., 1992).

the few words that mean nothing without quotes) into the brew of individual fancy,' was how Vladimir Nabokov explained he had 'invented America' in *Lolita*, a book and a writer of enormous influence in the Sixties, along with Beckett and Borges. The Sixties debate about 'metafiction' has been extensively described by now.[10] As Patricia Waugh rightly said, such debates about the nature of fiction's text have been a familiar feature of the novel's history at times when culture and sensibility change and writers and audiences are pleased to see the genre's conventions tested or undermined; this is one reason why the novel *is* novel. What is clear is that during the Sixties a good many writers returned to a self-examining approach to fiction: in some cases to suggest the crisis of narrative in the face of the 'unreality' of contemporary history; in others to explore the limits of the book and writing; in still others to make a new assertion of the inventive power of fictions or narrative, which were capable of challenging the more official fictions known as history, politics, biography, documentary or news. Whenever reality is in doubt, fiction is renewed, suggested Ronald Sukenick in *The Death of the Novel*: 'The contemporary writer – the writer who is acutely in touch with the life of which he is a part – is forced to start from scratch: Reality doesn't exist. God was the omniscient author, but he died; now no one knows the plot . . .' Over the Sixties, in France, in Italy, in Latin America, in Britain too, 'metafiction', 'fictive fiction', 'fabulation' or 'postmodern fiction' had plainly arrived.

In the British fiction of the time, as well as the American, such issues became powerful – though, because one tradition always varies from another, the questions and answers were often rather different. As many of the British writers of the Fifties had suggested, had even passionately argued, realism did have a singularly powerful place in the history of the English novel, which had a fictional tradition that had long been more socially curious, culturally expansive, narratively

---

10 Above all in Patricia Waugh, *Metafiction: The Theory and Practice of Self-Conscious Fiction* (London, 1984). Also see Margaret A. Rose, *Parody/Meta-Fiction* (London, 1979), Linda Hutcheon, *Narcissistic Narrative: The Metafictional Paradox* (Waterloo, Ont., 1980), and Brian McHale, *Postmodernist Fiction* (London, 1987).

richer than most. It had often seemed the novel was what the British had instead of a philosophy, that it represented the native empiricism in its narrative action. By the nineteenth century the 'Victorian novel' had become the great national repository of a huge cultural narrative, stabilized by its liberal or Whiggish balance of the personal stories of many individual lives and those larger social processes we call history. It had acquired critical mass, narrative authority, the divine power of authorship. It was a currency that readily turned reality into fiction, and made fiction feel like reality. It made reality tolerable and history personal. And the novelists of the Fifties who had to some degree reacted against Modernism or found it to be a tired tradition had found it perfectly natural to return there, reinstating what had never properly gone away: plot and character, onward and direct chrono-logical storytelling, strong social setting, a sense of community, tra-dition and history, the author's own narrative authority. They had preserved round, sympathetic, identifiable characters and probable situations, the world as familiarity – recuperating the long-term and probably the most lasting conventions of fictional storytelling. Now, in the Sixties, these narrative types and practices were being looked at again, under the influence of a changing history, a shifting culture, a new and powerful and philosophical literary theory. Beckett and the speculative arguments of the writers of the *anti-roman* – the novel against the novel, the place where, as Sartre put it, the novel contested with itself – acquired a new importance, even if on peculiarly British terms.

David Lodge was reasonably typical when he observed that, though drawn to metafiction, he retained a modest faith in realism, finding the elaborate code of decorum that covered the writing of realistic fiction a source of strength. Nor did he accept the assumption that history and reality were so appalling, the human state so disastrous, that realism could no longer be a response. The code underlying realism, he observed, is liberalism: that which assumes we are rounded and competent individuals, conscious of our own reality and that of others, able to balance identity and world; and that most of our lives are not spent *in extremis*. British fiction was not willing to let humanism, fictional character and a sense of common reality go easily.

Nor did it generally share the apocalyptic sense of living in an age of distorted history so common in American writing, nor French convictions that word and sign were in terminal crisis. The gravitational tug of liberal realism generally remains in the most important novels of the Sixties, even experimental ones. But no less clear is an extension of the fascination with the fractures and experimental resources of the novel which had already begun in the work of writers like Angus Wilson, Iris Murdoch, Anthony Burgess and Muriel Spark. The preoccupation was no doubt partly a matter of a new generation of writers increasingly setting out to explore and extend the possibilities of their genre. But it was plainly stimulated by the new debate about the novel, narrative and the nature of fictions that arose internationally over the decade. 'If you want to be true to life, start lying about the reality of it,' wrote John Fowles, one of the most important and interesting of Sixties British writers, in a note to himself as he wrote his pastiche Victorian romance, *The French Lieutenant's Woman* (1969).[11] 'I live in the age of Alain Robbe-Grillet and Roland Barthes,' the novelist's 'I' observes in that book; 'If this is a novel, it cannot be a novel in the modern sense of the word.' Fowles was hardly alone in his concerns. Over the Sixties the younger British novelists, some new, some established in the previous decade, began increasingly to explore the fictional genres, turning to pastiche and parody, fantasy and Gothic. They also began to explore the limits of fiction by writing self-conscious books, where the status of the author, the structure of

---

[11] 'Notes on an Unfinished Novel', in John Fowles, *Wormholes: Essays and Occasional Writings* (London, 1998), also reprinted in Malcolm Bradbury (ed.), *The Novel Today: Contemporary Writers on Modern Fiction* (London, rev. ed., 1990). In this essay Fowles goes on to comment: 'Alain Robbe-Grillet's polemical essay *'Pour un nouveau roman'* (1963) is indispensible reading for the profession, even where it provokes no more than total disagreement. His key question: *Why bother to write in a form whose key masters cannot be surpassed?* The fallacy of one of his conclusions – that we must discover a new form to write in if the novel is to survive – is obvious. It reduces the purpose of the novel to the discovery of new forms, whereas its other purposes – to entertain, to satirize, to describe new sensibilities, to record life, to improve life, and so on – are clearly just as viable and important. But his obsessive pleading places a new stress on every passage one writes today. To what extent am I a coward by writing within the old tradition? To what extent am I being panicked into avant-gardism?'

the text, the line of plot, the certainties of ending, were challenged, all with a freedom very different from the mood of the Fifties.

3

What were surely the two most important 'metafictional' novels to come from the British Sixties encased the decade, one coming near to the beginning, the other close to the end of it. In 1962 Doris Lessing suddenly interrupted the realistic and political narrative of her 'Martha Quest' sequence of novels, 'The Children of Violence' (1952–69), after the third volume to write what would prove her most ambitious work of fiction. Up to this point she had seemed primarily a political novelist, depicting from a left-wing viewpoint social and racial events in southern Africa, and their implications for post-war and post-colonial Britain. But *The Golden Notebook* was something very different: a multi-layered narrative about 'free women' which asked questions about the nature of stories themselves. Lessing's central character, Anna Freeman Wulf, is close to being autobiographical; she has published a successful novel about Africa, and is dissatisfied with the work she has done, just as she is dissatisfied with her own state of being and her life as a woman. She is 'at a pitch when words mean nothing'. She observes in the notebooks she keeps that the function of the novel has somehow changed. The novel in the tradition of Thomas Mann, 'who used the novel for large philosophical statements about life', has given way to a less thoughtful and considered novel of serial information: 'Most novels, if they are successful at all, are original in the sense that they report the existence of an area of society, a type of person, not yet admitted to general literate consciousness,' she reflects, and hopes for a new kind of book – 'powered with an intellectual or moral passion strong enough to create order, to create a new way of looking at life'. It seems to her the first task is dissolution, a consideration of how when we write we organize and comprehend life and ourselves. So what is needed is a 'formless account' that will set things down before they become literature: 'Why not simply the truth?' But then there are many truths, and those about present existence are often sterile, chaotic, fragmentary. They dissolve into elements – social, historical, political, sexual, sociological, psychological, autobiographical – that can provide explanatory stories, but never seem to cohere as a whole. This is especially so from Anna's point of view as a woman, since her desire for personal completeness and wholeness seems to be dissolving under the pressures of modern life and her own conflicting expectations. She cannot unify her life, as woman, wife, lover, mother or political radical; she is suffering both from a psychological and a literary breakdown. If, perhaps, she needs therapy, she also needs a new kind of story – an account or a narrative that does not simplify, sanitize or entrap. The answer seems to lie in her notebooks, where she records different experiences, devises different kinds of stories.

Thus *The Golden Notebook* acquires a complicated structure, one Lessing later attempted to clarify in a highly interesting preface she added to the book. The novel contains five 'notebooks', each one written in a different style, each divided into four sections. A frame story called *Free Women* is by and about Anna Wulf, also the author of the notebooks, which are intercut into the main story. The Black Notebook deals with her life in southern Africa and her earlier novel. The Red Notebook deals with her political life and her growing disillusionment with and final departure from the Communist Party. The Yellow Notebook is an attempt to fictionalize her life under the name of 'Ella'. The Blue Notebook deals with the crucial theme of her breakdown and her psychoanalysis. These stories intersect with, mirror, transform or parody one another, or mime different modes of storytelling. As one critic put it, Lessing in the novel 'took narrative apart and laid it out to find a new beginning'; and, as Lessing says herself in the preface, Anna needs to separate things out like this for fear of 'chaos, formlessness – breakdown'. But the way onward is *through* breakdown, and the ultimate goal is to achieve the ideal or Golden Notebook. This begins to appear, in part in the form of the story of Anna's relationship and affair with Saul Green, an American writer-expatriate in London. He too is in crisis and, though they are not able to settle down together, his storytelling does begin merging with hers. He acquires a story from her, she gains one from him. So, out of it all, in a kind of circular motion, the tale *Free Women* begins to emerge, which leads back to the story of the notebooks.

A story about the making of a story, the problems of creating and constructing it, *The Golden Notebook* is no doubt a work of 'metafiction'. Yet the term does less than justice to the complexity of the task the novel undertakes: attempting to explore the many facets and fragments of one plural or divided personality, to capture the social, cultural and gender disorder of the London world Anna lives in, to struggle beyond the segments to a way of fiction that is emotionally coherent and whole. The fragmentary nature of the book thus itself simply represents a stage, a phase of multiplicity and pluralization in the life of a central character evidently close to the author, who is then seeking to move onward. This is no attempt at fictive play, and it is not a self-conscious anti-novel. Anna firmly rejects what she calls 'anti-humanist bullying', and the problem is not with contemporary fiction but with her own loss of completeness as a consciousness, as a woman, as a political person, as a writer. To accept that we live in a state of linguistic collapse would be the same as accepting permanent breakdown, whereas Anna/Lessing's aim is to create literary, psychological, communitarian wholeness: 'an end to the split, divided, unsatisfactory way we all live'. Many of the ideas are Laingian, and influential in the Sixties, when the notion of journeying through breakdown to new and visionary wholeness was strong.[12] Thus the book *The Golden Notebook* may be left to its own fragmentation; meanwhile its writer can go forward to new forms and possibilities. Conventional realism is insufficient for the task, and *Free Women* is itself not the final answer. So the novel remains suspended in a state of its own making, while suggesting that further steps can and must be taken.

---

12 R. D. Laing's *The Divided Self* (1960), which drew on Kierkegaard and Sartre, was an attempt by a noted clinical psychotherapist to 'demystify' madness by exploring the schizophrenic personality as a source of self-creation. Later books like *The Politics of Experience* (1967) linked madness to family life, personal sickness to social sickness, and explored the belief that madness reflected the repressions of an oppressive form of society. By the later Sixties Laing became an influential and radical guru, a figure in the 'anti-psychiatry' movement and a promoter of Indian philosophy.

The Golden Notebook – the work where, one critic said, Lessing 'took narrative apart and laid it out to find a new beginning' – is one of the most powerful of post-war British novels: a complex and many-layered literary text which is also a vivid portrait of a remarkable woman, for whom elements of personal incompleteness, political responsibility and psychoanalytical curiosity create a crisis in self and discourse, here encountered. It has rightly been seen as a work of feminist sensibility, and as the most remarkable work by a woman to appear in Britain since Virginia Woolf's (though the solemnity, the social concern and the moral urgency bring it closer to the work of George Eliot). It is centrally concerned with the opening out of female identity; yet Lessing has been understandably worried by the limitations of a feminist reading. The book is not simply about a crisis of discourse, subjectivity, female identity; it is also an attempt to explore, as she thought the novel should, the moral, intellectual and emotional crisis of a fragmenting and apocalyptic age. This produced the book's ambitious reach, its multiplicity of codes (the historical, the political, the personal, the literary, the aesthetic) and, in the 'Golden Notebook' itself, an androgynous merging of male and female narrative. Lessing called the writing of the book a traumatic passage, and for her it was a transformation in her own sense of herself as a writer; like Anna, she is on the way to other, future things. It can certainly be seen as the turning point of the 'Children of Violence' sequence, which from this point changes radically in form, attitude and subject. The last two volumes are no longer realistic political stories of the past, but stories about the self and our apprehension of the future. Laingian notions of redemption through breakdown, madness or illness take over, in a society moving toward some kind of disaster or apocalypse. Meanwhile the story concentrates on those who, like Martha, are capable of accepting some new awareness, those who 'have included history in themselves and have transcended it'. From this time on Lessing's work largely departs from earlier social and political realism. It acquires a kind of visionary humanism and Utopianism, looks to fresh sources of vision, more fantastic and hallucinatory modes of writing, and deals with a world that seemed to suffer a double breakdown: a collapse of societies and systems, probably into another age of war, and a more personal process of the disintegration and reintegration of consciousness.

Lessing followed the sequence with a row of novels dealing in visionary fashion with social crisis, mental breakdown and personal quest. In *Briefing for a Descent Into Hell* (1971) – a book Lessing described as a work of 'inner space fiction' – a middle-aged classics professor from Cambridge, Charles Watkins, is hospitalized for psychiatric treatment after he has a breakdown on Waterloo Bridge. His vision and consciousness shift beyond the earth into space-time; finally he is briefed by various contending and often satirical voices for his return to the world. *The Summer Before the Dark* (1973) is a related story about the middle-aged wife of a well-known neurologist, mother of four children, who believes life and identity have passed her by. By way of dream and hallucination, and a fresh acceptance of her middle-aged female identity, she too breaks through into new existence. The most striking and successful of this group of books is *Memoirs of a Survivor* (1974), a dystopian fantasy set in a collapsed future world, where the cities of England are left polluted, dangerous and crime-ridden after nuclear war. An unnamed woman enters a second world beyond the walls of her room, which leads into more and more rooms, here and elsewhere, now and then. She finds a child, finds a way to new consciousness and awareness, and finds it is possible to walk 'Out of this collapsed little world into another order of world altogether.' By now Lessing was something of a public guru herself, and was willingly taking her own fiction out of this collapsed little world and into another order of world altogether. Her concerns were less purely political than cosmic, less social than apocalyptic, less descriptive than transcendental. She had something far more important to do than simply please us with easy stories. The result was another highly ambitious project for the early Eighties, her 'space fiction' 'Canopus in Argos'.

Of this five-volume sequence – consisting of *Shikasta* (1979), *The Marriages Between Zones Three, Four and Five* (1980), *The Sirian Experiments* (1980), *The Making of the Representative for Planet 8* (1982) and *The Sentimental Agents* (1983) – she said: 'I feel I have been set free both to be as experimental as I like, and as traditional.' Possibly what today seems most traditional about it is what at the time seemed the most experimental: the employment – in the manner of, say, Ursula Le Guin's 'Earthsea' stories – of the types, devices and nearly cartoon-like characters of popular science fiction and other-world space adventure. Lessing's intentions were, as always, high-minded and visionary: 'I found a new world for myself, a realm where the petty fates of planets, let alone individuals, are only aspects of cosmic evolution . . .' she explained. 'Cosmic evolution' is the subject, and the inter-galactic cosmos of science fiction and New Age fantasy gave her epic materials to play with. Three galactic empires attempt to control or reorganize the earth (a Third World War has taken place); the earth itself is simply one small instance of life and society in the greater evolution of cosmic time and consciousness, where planets heat or freeze, grand inter-planetary dynasties emerge, higher states of being evolve. Lessing uses the form freely, not to tell sensational or adventurous tales, but to engage both in meditation on our human existence and Swiftian satire on earthly affairs. The point is to create a 'new' fiction, beyond realism, conventional political opinion, familiar identity: transcendental fiction. Happily Lessing had not entirely left this earth behind. Cloaked as 'Jane Somers' she wrote two novels largely concerned with the dilemmas of ageing: *The Diary of a Good Neighbour* (1983) and *If the Old Could* (1984). She revisited political Utopianism in *The Good Terrorist* (1985), set among a family of squatters, where radicalism spills over into vengeful revolutionary violence. In *The Fifth Child* (1988) she dealt with a happy family with four children that produces a fifth demon child, possibly as a result of the fantasies of the mother. In *Love Again* (1998) she returned to Africa, and Utopianism. No material seemed inappropriate, no theme unavailable; her work reaches across forms, from the early radical politics to the sagacities of Sufism, and has a deeply-earned sense of lasting wisdom. However, *The Golden Notebook* – the book that opened the way and made the transition, in the opening phase of the Sixties – remains the book we are likely to respect and remember most. The fragmentary work that was meant as a way to healing is, in its variety, confusion and indirection, surely her deepest and most personal book, as well as a flamboyantly self-analytical late twentieth-century novel: a metafiction.

4

If Doris Lessing, at the beginning of the consciousness-expanding Sixties, used metafiction as a way to discover a new fictional wholeness, then John Fowles, in *The French Lieutenant's Woman*, published in 1969 at the more cynical end of the decade, used it for a different purpose – to explore the wonder and fascination of the fictional itself. Born in 1926, Fowles served after the war in the Royal Marines and then studied French literature (and Existentialism) at Oxford; his novels and stories would always display strong French influences (see the stories of *The Ebony Tower*, 1974). Then, fallen out of love with his own claustrophobic Englishness, he became a language teacher abroad, first at the University of Poitiers, then at an English-style school on the Greek island of Spetsai, though he finally returned to teach in Britain. In 1963 he published his first novel, *The Collector*: a decidedly Nabokovian work of aesthetic and decadent atmosphere, dealing with what was to be a fundamental theme of Fowles's writing, the pursuit of the elusive and enigmatic female who is the obscure object of desire. It is about a young clerk, Frederick Clegg, a collector of butterflies, who decides to capture and imprison a girl, Miranda, with whom he has fallen in love; the tale is about enchantment, possession and the male desire to entrap. Fowles tells it this way and that from both viewpoints, that of the prisoner and the collector, the enchanter and the enchanted, the symbol and the one who tries to hold and contain it. The story has a rich aesthetic flavour, but ends gothically and grimly; it is Fowles's most sensational book. But its subject led directly to that of his splendid second novel *The Magus* (1966): an enormous and ambitious attempt to deal with romance and modern history, desire and psychoanalysis, gender and sexuality, and the powers of fantasy, myth and fiction-making.

The Magus opens realistically enough in London, the story of Nicholas Urfe, an inexperienced young Englishman described as representing something 'passive, abdicating, English in life', who tries to purge a failed guilty love affair from his life by taking a teaching post on the Greek island of 'Phraxos'. The episode begins ordinarily, but then the atmosphere starts to change. Urfe slowly finds he has entered a world of the enchanted or fantastic, where 'second meanings hung in the air, ambiguities, unexpectedness'. Narratives multiply, odd recreations of events from the past occur; the island is full of strange sounds and mysteries. Then Urfe is taken up by the magus, or magician, of the title, Conchis, the Prospero of the island. He creates a series of 'god-games', masques or strange theatricals that surround and engulf Urfe. Some of them reveal the ambiguous history of Conchis himself, or the history of the island, scene of wartime Nazi atrocities and more atrocities in the Greek Civil War, and of the bitter century. But if Urfe is being given an education in magic, or theatricality, enchantment and illusion, he is also being taken far deeper, into a deep psychotherapy or mytho-therapy. He becomes increasingly exposed to the problems of his own English nature, his limitations and repressions, his failure in love and desire, the limits and delusions of his male sexuality and his damaging relationship with Alison, the girl in London he has abandoned, the existential problems of choice and human freedom. The ambiguous role of the magus Conchis, the maker of god-games, is central to the drama. At one level he is the priest, the wise man, the therapist; but he is also the trickster, the counterfeiter, the manipulator of illusions and the corrupter of souls. In a sense he is the novelist himself; at one point he is described as 'a sort of novelist *sans* novel'. His illusions are less a theatrical unreality than a complex illusion from a world where probability is suspended. He represents his own creator, as magician, inventor, weaver of games, but also as man of deceptions, liar, stealer of freedoms. Nicholas accepts the fictionality that surrounds him, as an ambiguous and yet also a purgative fiction, that 'all here is illusion' and 'the masque is only a metaphor'. Yet his life, his world and his self-knowledge have been transformed. The obscure object of desire returns, in the mysterious figure of a second Alison; when Urfe returns to the 'real' world of London the mysterious god-games do not totally cease. Significantly, Fowles was not entirely satisfied by the ending, and in 1977 he revised the novel and changed it – with the metafictional result that it now has two endings, according to choice. *The Magus* – a book about the complex, elusive and yet deeply important power of fictions and fiction-making – is a remarkable novel, one of the most significant works of the British Sixties, as much for its psychoanalytic intensity as for its fictional playfulness. It was in every sense a deliberate step beyond 'Englishness', and the work that established Fowles as a major novelist – though, alas, it took the English critics some time to see the point. Today we would no doubt call it a work of 'magical realism', and indeed it does have a kind of postmodern echo in a more recent novel dealing with a somewhat similar subject, Louis de Bernières's *Captain Corelli's Mandolin* (1995).

The Magus is an important novel. But *The French Lieutenant's Woman* is Fowles's masterpiece, a return to the Victorian novel and therefore to the site of that realism from which much modern fiction has been struggling to diverge. 'It started four or five months ago, as a visual image,' Fowles wrote of the book when it was still unfinished. 'A woman stands at the end of a deserted quay and stares out to sea . . . It was obviously mysterious. It was vaguely romantic. It also seemed, perhaps because of the latter quality, not to belong to today.' It was not, Fowles said, intended as a historical novel. As he noted to himself: 'You are not trying to write something one of the Victorians forgot to write; but perhaps something one of them failed to write. And: Remember the etymology of the word. A novel is something new.' Thus the Victorian novel Fowles sets out both to reconstruct and deconstruct is not the novel of any single Victorian novelist – Dickens, the Brontës, Thackeray, Trollope, Wilkie Collins, George Eliot or Hardy. All are alluded to, all contribute something, but essentially this is the Victorian novel as archetype, subjected to analysis and reinterpretation. Fowles seizes on all that Victorian fiction has to offer to the later novelist: its narrative capaciousness, vividness of character, its scale and detail, a sense of life as an orderly process of opening and closure, even while acknowledging that no contemporary writer could or should write as the Victorians did. He constructs the novel – set just a hundred years earlier, in 1867 – in terms of many Victorian conventions and interpretations; he also probes its doubts, hypocrisies, gaps and silences from the standpoint of someone who can know what the Victorians could not, placing his characters' world back in a distinctive stage of the longer historical evolution of which so much more was known and in which modern people find themselves. He can observe, as historical facts, its instinctive assumptions, ideas of religion and science, divine intervention in lives, human nature and evolution, as well as its codes of authorship, storytelling, character, moral self-understanding, sexual reticence. And he can do this from the standpoint of an author who has read Sigmund Freud, knows modern Existentialism and accepts that the age he belongs to is that of Barthes and Robbe-Grillet. The story is set in the 1860s because that, too, is an age when realities were collapsing in the face of the evolutionary theories of Lyall and Darwin. 'Just as we "live with the bomb", the Victorians lived with the theory of evolution. They were hurled into space. They felt themselves infinitely isolated.' So, says Fowles, a man, a scientist, existentialist before his time, walks down a quay and 'sees that mysterious back, feminine, silent, also existentialist . . .'

The French Lieutenant's Woman is a remarkably doubled work: an endeavour by an ambitious author to recover, examine, question and challenge the value of the Victorian novel for his own time, while seeing his time itself in the light of Victorian origins. One result is superb pastiche, telling one of the Victorian era's central fables – a male hero faced with the choice between fair lady and dark lady, between social duty and danger, sentiment and sensuality, order and confusion – with, at times, the voice of the Victorian god-narrator. At the same time a more chameleon author is present, who no longer 'stands next to God', though he does sometimes resemble Conchis, as magus, forger, impresario. The story is undermined, as it were, from within as well as from without. The figure at the end of the Cobb at Lyme Regis is Sarah Woodruff, the 'French lieutenant's woman', who is existential, self-created, and who has willed herself to be a fallen woman, an outsider, an outcast, a *femme fatale*, with a far greater and a more modern independence than the confining age would normally allow (though such figures do appear in Victorian fiction). 'No insult, no blame, can touch me,' she says, and inside the story she creates her own life story, which in turn is a lesson for Charles. She is allowed an independent discourse, an existential will, and remains continuously a mystery; this breaks opens the narrative, prevents its natural closure and constructs a creative challenge to the activities of a modern author. Yet there is a real historical intimacy. By setting the story in a time of doubt and contradiction, after Lyall, Darwin and Marx, Fowles is creating a world in which the twentieth century was born. The fable goes on to trace historical change: the break-up of the Victorian world-picture, the departure from mid-Victorian respectabilities to the aesthetic decadence of the Pre-Raphaelites and early Moderns. Sarah eludes Charles only to reappear in the painting studio of the Rossettis, and in the era of the New Woman. By the time the story is done, the Victorian world is already ending. The book is both homage and critique; we can read it as a Whiggish Victorian tale of unfolding laws of progress and emancipation, and as a story of repression and layers of social and sexual hypocrisy. Yet though the modern and the liberated and emancipated always seem to have the edge over the past, we can also see social loss as well as gain; the book suggests to us that in destroying the Victorian 'other', the labyrinthine realm of the forbidden, the modern spirit has also destroyed much in the way of complexity and pleasure.

In the same way, his playfully and cleverly modernized text sometimes sustains and sometimes destroys the illusion of the real and familiar so important to Victorian fiction; though that fiction itself then questions the depthless surfaces, emptied realities, narrative thinness and high self-consciousness of postmodern fiction (this is one reason why many readers often prefer to read it as, essentially, a reprinted Victorian novel and ignore the 'postmodern' interventions). Fowles waits until Chapter 13 to break the illusion he is so carefully cultivating: 'Who is Sarah? . . . I do not know. These characters I create never existed outside my own mind. If I have until now claimed to know my characters' minds and thought, it is because I am writing in (just as I have assumed some of the vocabulary and "voice" of) a convention universally accepted at the time of my story; that the novelist stands next to God.' But if this convention can no longer be sustained in intellectual logic, it is within the power of fiction to perform it, and the novelist shows us it can actually be done. He continues to give us a narrative quite as substantial as those of any of the great Victorians, even while he interrupts in order to present himself with various contemporary masks and impostures: as structuralist critic, spokesman for Existentialism, sceptical and revisionist historian, Freudian interpreter, fop and dandy, pasticheur, impresario, faker, cheat. He enters a running text, stops and starts the action, intrudes later sociological knowledge or subsequent historical fact. He presents, in the middle of the novel, an appropriate Victorian ending to the tale: the sober and responsible hero, faced with the choice of two women, one far more appropriate than the other, sacrifices the rebel and *femme fatale*, marries the pallid, rich, virtuous lady, and lives not happily but perfectly successfully ever after: 'They begat, what shall it be – let us say seven children.' But it will no longer do, because the existential drive of the story, the nature of modern sexual and gender values, the belief that the Victorians sacrificed their libidos and their souls to repression and sublimation, makes the ending untenable. So it is dispensed with: a fresh stage of the action begins, when Charles's labyrinthine quest for Sarah, the female enigma, resumes, across Britain, the USA and a significant slice of late Victorian history. That gives the impresario novelist the chance for two more endings, placed side by side for our pleasure at the close. One ends in marriage, one in Sarah's independence; according to mood, we may prefer one over the other. But the real point is not that they offer a choice to the reader but an existential 'freedom' to the two main characters; they are left indeterminate, free to 'emerge' as they wish from the end of the story.

This, of course, creates a new postmodern paradox. The characters are themselves fictions, made of words, so there is nowhere for them to go next (except, of course, into the film version). Fowles affirms the existential message of his ambiguous ending: 'Fiction is woven into all . . . I find this new reality (or unreality) more valid.' Yet the breaking of the frame does not destroy the 'Victorian' dimension of the novel, and the way in a collusion of reader and writer we acknowledge the fictive reality of the characters, the power of scene, setting, custom, convention and story. And the postmodern self, the present-day trickster, is itself a fiction, making a claim on our sense of (unreal) reality. The implications of the book seem clear; like a good few late twentieth-century British writers, Fowles is glad to retain much from the Victorian novel – its narrative scope, its social breadth, its fascination with character, its respect for society – at the same time as he admits, in a parallel story, 'The Enigma' (*The Ebony Tower*, 1974), that 'Everything is fiction.' Fowles's ending to *The French Lieutenant's Woman* is a liberal ending, drawn from the middle ground, where most British writers seem happiest to settle; it asserts the 'presence' of the characters of the novel, the importance of their selfhoods and their stories, as well as the postmodern character of modern authorship and the magical trickery of the fictive. So were Fowles and Lessing 'postmodern' novelists, writing 'metafiction'? Perhaps not quite, though Fowles's endeavour to make the Victorian novel into the 'pretext' of a postmodern fiction comes closest. Perhaps the clearest account of Fowles's view is seen in his portrait of the artist Breasley in the story 'The Ebony Tower'. His way to an art of the present is by way of appropriating all he can manage from the art of the past: 'Behind the modernity of many of his surface elements stood both a homage and a kind of thumbed nose to a very old tradition' – a definition of the ironic quotability that has been a major element of Postmodernism.

When, therefore, in *Daniel Martin* (1977), Fowles turned to a contemporary subject and another portrait of the artist – Daniel Martin is a screenwriter – it was the more traditional and realistic features that struck the critics. Here again was density of social representation, close concern with character, anxiety about selfhood and personal and cultural identity: Fowles said himself that the book was his 'exploration of what it means to be English', and that he felt it to be a humanist work, whereby the novel is regarded with a certain Victorian depth and seriousness. Indeed, he suggests, Martin belongs to the last generation in Britain that carries the Victorian century 'since the twentieth did not begin until 1945'. In *Mantissa* (1982) – the title means 'something playful' – he again explored the many modes of modern writing, and developed his sense of the great enigma; here the female muse who leads the way knows everything about fictions. With *A Maggot* (1985) once more he turned the other way, back to another historical subject – the beginnings of the Shaker sect – and to the role of another powerful woman, Ann Lee. Now the narrative method was different, using documentary research and historical fact; the result is actually a highly effective piece of historical recuperation. Fowles rightly asserted that in the end it was not his task or wish to be a literary theorist; his aim was the imaginative writing of fiction as a serious activity from the viewpoint of the now. But his books wonderfully raised the paradoxes of fiction and the problematic recovery of the historical subject, and they have had great influence on British fiction since. The attempt to create a serious artistic and philosophical bridge between deconstructive present and constituted past has remained important to many writers, as works ranging from Lindsay Clarke's virtuoso historical recreation *The Chymical Wedding* (1989) to A. S. Byatt's *Possession* (1990), from Peter Ackroyd's cunning *Hawksmoor* (1985) to Adam Thorpe's *Ulverton* (1992) show. A. S. Byatt has nicely called such novels works of 'greedy rewriting', recuperating the difficult past – 'The past is a foreign country; they do things differently there,' L. P. Hartley put it in *The Go-Between* (1953) – into narrative usable in the present. 'Furtive nostalgia', this has been called, often by critics who feel the novel's sole subject is the contemporary. But it has been a means not only of recreating past narrative or returning to past ways of life, but of creatively relating fiction to earlier codes and traditions. It was largely thanks to Fowles that a powerful debate about fictiveness raged through British culture at the dawn of the Seventies; also due to him that the intricate and self-examining historical novel became one of the strong forms of the Eighties and the Nineties.[13]

Yet, whatever the distinctive concerns of both writers, Lessing and Fowles were producing fiction co-equal with other self-conscious fiction of similar date. Both foreground modern anxieties: they reflect on the process of composition, the nature of fictionality, the role and perspective of author, the task of narrative, the status of 'character' as a real and discernible subject in fiction. They examine the canon,

---

13 'I don't like total obsession with form, with the "look of the thing",' Fowles says in an interview in *Wormholes* (see note 11 above), when asked about 'the postmodern text'. 'By "content", I suppose I mean seriousness. All writers are rather like prostitutes; they know they have to sell by physical appearance, though underneath they may have far more serious intentions and meanings.' Also: 'I dislike in any novel a too-overt use of theory. I'd say more realism, not more fantasy, sci-fi and all the rest, is what is needed in the next century.'

they explore realism as exploded illusion. Both have some discernible quarrel with the notion of Englishness, and yet both have some sense of being distinctively in the tradition. Lessing interestingly acknowledged a historical connection with George Eliot, even if 'the penalty she paid for being a Victorian woman was that she had to be shown to be a good woman even when she wasn't'. Fowles pays his own homage to the corporeal substantiality of Victorian fiction; so did others like Angus Wilson, Margaret Drabble, A. S. Byatt. Neither *The Golden Notebook* nor *The French Lieutenant's Woman* aspired to be a pure fictionalist text, written after the end of narrative, the failure of referentiality or the death of the subject. Anna acquires not less but more character and complexity as the text 'she' produces multiplies and fragments. Sarah Woodruff, muse to Charles and the novelist, acquires ever more 'existential' independence as the fictive nature of the text is being emphasized. The aim of Lessing's fractured narrative is to create a new vision and a new reality; Fowles sees narratives as 'god-games' that can create a sense of larger realities once the performance is over. Both writers emphasize from their different standpoints the generative role of the female imagination or muse, partly stressing the androgyny of fiction, but also stressing the deconstructive nature of excluded or half suppressed stories, and the way the imagination needs to deepen to comprehend a larger and less predictable sense of reality. So both writers push realism toward a much more problematic status: into the realm of the self-examining, the fleeting, the sceptical, the androgynous, the disruptive. Both refuse to dispense with the realist code entirely. The result is that their books are both novels and anti-novels, part of a new compendium of fiction that was now emerging as issues left over from the Victorian and the Modern novel began to intersect in a new compound.

5

Certainly, fed by new academic theory and the emergence of a new generation of splendidly experimental works from the USA, France, Italy and Germany, the debate about the frontiers of fiction enlarged wonderfully during the Sixties. To the British novelist Christine Brooke-Rose, now living and teaching in Paris, it seemed that back in Britain the 'anti-novelists' and experimentalists made 'a sparse alignment compared with the vast body of 'straight' novelists', and no doubt this was true. Brooke-Rose was a translator of Robbe-Grillet, a good and witty Structuralist and Deconstructionist literary theorist, with a special interest in the uncanny, the fantastic and the intertextual. She was also an anti-novelist with a cross-Channel flavour, some of her fiction being written in a kind of inter-language between English and French. Her first novel, *The Languages of Love* (1957), is very much a book of the Fifties, a satirical academic comedy set around London University, but it clearly displays her concern with the language of fiction and the paradoxes of interpretation. Then in the Sixties came a group of novels – *Out* (1964), *Such* (1966), *Between* (1968), *Thru* (1975), later collected in 1986 as *The Christine Brooke-Rose Omnibus* – which were essentially books of signs. In the Parisian spirit of semiotic theory as well as that of the *nouveau roman*, these are experiments in language and the complexities of textual interpretation. In *Thru*, a very texty text indeed, there are visual icons and charts, as well as solemn discussions of noise and redundancy. There are plenty of intertextual references, theoretical textbook arguments drawn from linguistic scholars like Ramon Jakobson, charts, flow-plans and other typographical experiments, and, since a text does not have to have an author, a final catalogue of 'authors', starting with Adam. Brooke-Rose insists that all texts are made of language, that language has its own analysable devices, and therefore all fictions are of the same order; this is quite literally a metafiction, using the fundamental devices.[14] Other books in the sequence show further aspects, and pick up on some of the familiar and fantastic games of story. Many more books followed, including *Amalgamemnon* (1984), which suggests that all stories can in one sense be amalgamated into one. *Textermination*

---

14 As Linda Hutcheon points out in *Narcissistic Narrative: The Metafictional Paradox* (Waterloo, Ont., 1980), a significant group of metafictional novels (by writers like Borges, Nabokov, Butor, Barth, Barthelme) have this analysis of narratological, linguistic and fiction-making structures in common: 'The "rules" of fiction-making come into play as the overt subject of much modern metafiction.'

(1991), with its typically punning title, is a later tour de force of inter-woven texts and textualities, based around a literary congress devoted, naturally, to the future of the novel. Brooke-Rose, like many, has grown increasingly interested in the disruptive or the fantastic, and has defended 'magical realism' as what she calls the innovative genre of 'palimpsest history', which, mingling realism with history, fantasy with spiritual revelation, has renewed the life of the novel. It helps in reading her to know a good deal about the development of French and inter-national literary theory and its preoccupations, on which her novels over the years provide a witty meta-commentary. That said, she is an important figure who has brought 'critical fiction' closer to the heart of British writing.[15]

More home-grown and far less directly theoretical British versions were also on offer during the Sixties, often echoing contemporary French, American or Latin-American experiments. 'Literary forms do become exhausted, clapped out,' said B. S. Johnson, an important and interesting writer whose tragic suicide in 1975 cut off an exciting career. 'That is what seems to have happened to the nineteenth-century narrative novel too . . . No matter how good the writers are who now attempt it, it cannot be made to work for our time, and the writing of it is anachronistic, invalid, irrelevant and perverse.'[16] Johnson explained that the tradition that fascinated him was Irish (he was 'besotted by Irish writers like Sam Beckett, James Joyce and Flann O'Brien'), though the great creator was Laurence Sterne, the eighteenth-century author of *Tristram Shandy*, parent of them all, maker of the first great anti-novel. Johnson's first novel was *Travelling People* (1963), where each chapter is told in a different style, including the use of letters and screenplay formats. His methods grew ever more

---

15 Some of her most important criticism is collected in *A Rhetoric of the Unreal: Studies in Narrative and Structure, Especially of the Fantastic* (Cambridge, 1981).
16 He adds: 'Present-day reality is markedly different from, say, nineteenth-century reality. Then it was possible to believe in pattern and eternity, but today what most characterizes our reality is the probability that chaos is the most likely explanation; while at the same time recognizing that even to seek an explanation represents a denial of chaos.' B. S. Johnson, Introduction to *Aren't You Rather Young to be Writing Your Memoirs?* (1973); reprinted in Malcolm Bradbury (ed.), *The Novel Today: Contemporary Writers on Modern Fiction* (London, rev. ed., 1990).

experimental, using typographical play, blank pages, holes in pages; and the books contain many self-conscious references to novel-writing, telling truths and telling lies. The aim was to break up the familiar narrative illusion of the conventionally structured linear novel, and echo randomness, chaos and therefore truth. *Alberto Angelo* (1964) employs the device of holes cut in pages to let the story-time and scene be interrupted. But it is apparent there is something quixotic about the endeavour, since the aim is not to prove fiction's lie but to get closer to truth, document, real life. His aim, he said, was 'truth in the form of a novel': 'fuck all this lying look what im really trying to write about is writing . . .' he declares, 'im trying to say something not tell a story telling stories is telling lies and i want to tell the truth . . .' *The Unfortunates* (1969, and recently reissued) is perhaps the most interesting (and moving) experiment of all; the novel appeared in a box consisting of twenty-seven unbound 'sheets' which could be shuffled by the reader. The story within is a very intimate one, based on true details of the death from cancer of a close friend in Nottingham (which means there does seem to be a 'right' way to read the apparently random story). *Christie Malry's Own Double-Entry* (1973) is a surreal black comedy about a man revolting against the slights and insults of his life, and is printed in two columns: external events in one, violent reactions to them in another. *See the Old Lady Decently* (1975) is about his mother and England, both in the process of dying. Here Johnson manages a link between his two primary concerns: 'experiment' on the one hand, the rejection of fiction for an autobiographical truth on the other. The problem is that it is hardly easier to tell the 'truth' within the framework of metafiction than it is in conventional realism. Alas, this book, which was intended to be part of a projected 'Matrix Trilogy', was Johnson's last; a promising, adventurous and, in retrospect, very important career was halted suddenly by his suicide.

During the Sixties the book began breaking its borders and boundaries in a great many ways, rejecting sexual reticence or sliding off the edge of the page. There was the interesting experimental fiction of Ann Quin in *Berg* (1964) and *Passages* (1969). In Eva Figes's feminist experiments in *Equinox* (1966), *Winter Journey* (1967) and *B* (1972), the text represented a rejection of 'patriarchal attitudes'. 'Having begun with an interest in the fragmentary nature of remembered experience I have found myself increasingly involved in the making of new connections,' Figes later explained in Giles Gordon's anthology of experimental writing, *Beyond the Words: Eleven Writers in Search of a New Fiction* (1975). Related experiments appeared in Brigid Brophy's *Flesh* (1962) and *In Transit* (1969), and Angela Carter's flamboyant early novels *Shadow Dance* (1965) and *The Magic Toyshop* (1967). Though still relatively realistic by comparison with what was to come, Carter's early books drew on the heritage of Gothic, the culture of camp, the work of the French surrealists, the realm of legend and folk tale, as well as the modern fantasy of such writers as Mervyn Peake (the 'Gormenghast' trilogy, 1946–59) and the science fiction 'New Wave'. Contributing to the same collection, *Beyond the Words*, another writer, Alan Burns, explained his experimental and radical fiction – *Europe After the Rain* (1965), *Celebrations* (1967), the multi-voiced parodic *Babel* (1969) – as being about 'the network of manipulations that envelops the citizens and makes them unaware accomplices in the theft of their liberty'. Burns drew on the science-fiction fantasy and the 'cut-up, fold-in' method of William S. Burroughs, though his works eventually became fact-based satires on political events. In the 'surrealist fantasy' *Dreamamerika!* (1972) he creates a collage text about the Kennedy family; *The Angry Brigade* (1973) is a 'documentary', dealing with the British terrorist group by way of real interviews. In a number of writers – David Caute, John Berger – 'experiment' was a way of leaking political facts from a disordered and often terrible era of history into a fiction fascinated by collage, documentary, random methods and complicated textual interweavings. There were Nicholas Mosley's thoughtful, randomized novels *Accident* (1965) and *Impossible Object* (1968), Robert Nye's lively *Doubtfire* (1967), Julian Mitchell's experimental *The Undiscovered Country* (1968), and Alan Sheridan's *nouveau roman*-like *Vacation* (1972). Gabriel Josipovici's text-experiment *The Inventory* (1968) was built from a series of lists, and his *Möbius the Stripper* (1974) employs a text shaped as a Möbius strip (a device already used by John Barth in his *Lost in the Funhouse*).

In the meantime it was growing clearer that one important and interesting place where the new experiment was surfacing was in the ever-inventive world of science fiction and science fantasy, where – with the emergence of a 'new wave' developed in the pages of *New World* magazine after the energetic Michael Moorcock became editor in 1964 – the genre was breaking free of many of its pulp conventions, just as it had in America in the work of writers like Kurt Vonnegut and Ray Bradbury. Here was a fresh space where the displacement activity of the fantastic could be freely employed, where frontiers could be probed, where the detritus of new technologies and space race militarism could be introduced into hyper-real, fantastical, apocalyptic and dystopian worlds, as such serious writers as Doris Lessing now showed. One of the most notable as well as prolific practitioners was J. G. Ballard, whose 'atrocity novels' – *The Drowned World* (1962), *The Drought* (1965), *The Crystal World* (1966) – owed much of their stylized and alienating character to surrealist and pop art. By the end of the decade, also drawing on the 'cut-up, fold-in' method of Burroughs, he began a series of 'condensed novels' collected in *The Atrocity Exhibition* (1970). They drew, again, on Kennedy's assassination, the Vietnam War, Marilyn Monroe, Ronald Reagan and other icons for a harsh and satirical vision of a dystopian society; they also opened out into a new mythology of urban dreck, violent solitude and eroticized technology that fed Ballard's fiction of the Seventies. In the hands of Ballard, Brian Aldiss and Moorcock himself, science fiction was becoming an ever more self-conscious and experimental instrument for exploring unease, blankness, sadness, mechanical massing – the aggressively mechanical and hostile environment of an imaginative world where, as Julio Cortazar put it, 'nothing is missing, not even, and especially, nothingness, the true solidifier of the scene'. An alternative landscape, a mirrored universe, a realm of dislocation and fantasy, science fiction was becoming a region of the anti-novel itself, not least in the early fiction of powerful feminist surrealists and writers of female Gothic like Angela Carter. Fiction was resorting increasingly to the grotesque, the fabulous, the Gothic, the fantastic, the hostile and the uncanny, to the invention of imaginary worlds that were neither in reality nor history, space nor time. As in Lessing's work, avant-garde fiction and genre fiction were crossing over, growing closer together. Whether driven by political anger or a sense of fictive experiment, writers felt increasingly released from conventional and restricting codes of signification and familiarity. They were turning to the strange and grotesque, along with pastiche and parody, and the playful indeterminacy of the postmodern text. Habitual genres no longer stood secure; the boundaries of both the serious and the popular or genre novel were changing – so passing a quite different legacy to the new novelists of the Seventies.

6

'But the English novel is not an aesthetic novel, it is a social novel,' protests Herr Birnbaum, a rather obnoxious minor character who appears in Angus Wilson's most ambitious novel of the Sixties, *No Laughing Matter* (1967). '*The Forsyte Saga* has great importance as a mirror of the British bourgeoisie,' he adds, in the course of a novel that is filled with distorting mirrors of the British bourgeoisie and the dissidents, disorderlies and drop-outs who also feel they deserve reflection. Herr Birnbaum is, of course, perfectly right; and realism had certainly not gone away, in British fiction or anywhere else. But the comment is, like everything in this book, highly self-conscious; Wilson himself had been changing course over the decade, moving from social fiction to something a good deal more fragmentary and experimental. His early fiction had indeed been 'social' rather than 'aesthetic', work of speculative liberalism rather than a literature of extremity. It was as if his tactics of irony and social mimicry, his awareness of hypocrisy, self-delusion and evil, had disturbed the moral order of his fiction. With *The Old Men at the Zoo* (1961) the tone had entirely changed, as Wilson tried, as he said, to react against the 'tyranny of neo-traditionalism'. This apocalyptic story is about nuclear war, the collapse of an order, the breakdown of authority and certainty, the end of a stage of Englishness. The old men who run the London Zoo, Wilson's symbol of England, are forlorn figures, obstinately failing to see change or danger; meanwhile the dangerous animals run out of control. To some reviewers the book was a brilliant portrait of a dying British establishment, to others a grotesque fantasy. Wilson took the chance to explain that his fiction had double origins: he may have been a moralist in the George Eliot mould, but mixed with that was 'a great lump of Dickensianism . . . I have got this . . . grand guignol side.' With *Late Call* (1964) Wilson returned to George Eliot's spirit and social themes, in a story about an England that has transformed over half a century from an Edwardian stability to a socialist Utopia, which is in fact an emptily liberal New Town impermanence, ripe for satire. But above all this is a sympathetic tale, about an elderly and uneducated woman, Sylvia Calvert, who has moved uncomplainingly through the changes and is an image of England herself. Sylvia makes no claims for herself: 'I'm nobody. I always have been.' But her life is a challenge to the sparky new liberalism of Carshall New Town, and she is one of Wilson's strong heroines, demanding a life deeper and more profound than the glossy new world on offer.

No Laughing Matter represents a much more daring and impertinent assault on the story of the century, a return to the grand guignol side. Once again the founding period lies just before the Great War, indeed in 1912, when the Wild West exhibition is held at London's Earls Court. In a brilliant opening, Wilson introduces his central family, the Matthews, who, standing before the carnival mirrors at the exhibition, find themselves rendered distorted and absurd. This is amusing, but is, perhaps, no laughing matter. For this was Wilson's largest venture yet in writing the late twentieth-century 'Condition of England' novel, a long history of things seen through the eyes of a single family (as it were, modern Forsytes) whose fragmentation is here already predicted, and who offer us a strange history of British culture from the age of Edwardian and Forsyte-ian security to the age of nuclear unease and strange economic miracle, of 'hire-purchase Hoovers and sleeping-pill salvation', in which the present novel is written. The book follows the fortunes of the six Matthews children as they pass through modern times: two World Wars, the Fascist marches through London's East End in the Thirties, the Marxism of the same decade, and the culture of Appeasement, the Suez Crisis, the dawn of the age of mechanical reproduction and the postmodern global village. In its way the bourgeois novel survives, but in a distorted or stunted form that dismayed quite a few of Wilson's familiar readers. The dominant image is of the Hall of Mirrors, where identities are multiplied, distorted, parodied. The bourgeois saga was now a different kind of chronicle, mirroring the lifetime and the dysfunctional family life of the author writing it, in paradoxical form – and, in the process, allowing many others to write it too. For the text refuses to lay down a firm realistic surface. As the tale is packed throughout with distorting mirrors, so it is also packed with pastiches and parodies. Entire segments are flamboyantly told in the manner of other writers, past and present: Jane Austen and Samuel Beckett, Bernard Shaw and Noel Coward, Terence Rattigan and Harold Pinter. If life is a theatre, and the world is a stage filled with strange costumes and distorting mirrors, then the Matthews children over the years become brilliant, camp, self-aware actors in their own domestic psycho-drama and in the theatre of modern society. Some become writers, some businessmen. Some marry, some stay single, some are gay. All are a club of skilled game-players, experts at devising worlds of their own for the purposes of survival. By the end of the book their old identities have slipped away and, dispersed to different parts of the globalizing new world, they have become full inhabitants of a postmodern world of refractions, distortions, fragments, multiple selves and plural cultures.

With its brilliant range of registers, its multiple stories, its games and trickeries, its mixture of grotesque and history, *No Laughing Matter* has claim to be Wilson's finest novel, and certainly his best late work. It also marked a decisive change in his writing and his relationship with the audience. The Sixties, if in different guise, also provided the backdrop to his next novel, *As If By Magic* (1973), a remarkable yet even more unsettling book, Wilson's most obvious attempt at Postmodernism. A number of the characters are students at a new university (Wilson taught literature in one, the University of East Anglia in Norwich) at the hippie time, when new lifestyles are tried out, sexual relationships are highly permissive and provisional, and the young are seeking wisdom and spiritual nourishment from the gurus of India and the East. The story of the drop-out student Alexandra, travelling to India with two lovers and a baby, is paralleled with the story of Hanno, a genetic biologist and a repressed Anglo-Scot, who hopes that a new miracle rice he has bred, called Magic, will solve the problems of Third World famine and poverty. This is, quite deliberately, a global novel; Wilson was himself a famous writer travelling the world as author and lecturer, and he was also in revolt against the parochial and limited character of contemporary, London-based, bourgeois fiction. This new interconnected multiverse, this new pluralism, was the material with which the novelist had to cope. And if the book is wonderfully bold in reach, it is also daring in subject; Hanno is gay, and this is Wilson's most Rabelaisian novel, a transgressive story from a writer pushing at the edges of the acceptable in fiction, and unwilling to believe in or offer literature as simplification or consolation. Alexandra has studied English literature, but knows that books are no perfect guide to life. Nor is Hanno's Magic the panacea it appears, since it aids corporations and rich farmers and drives the poor off the land. Hanno's interest in the Far East has a strong sexual element – he travels abroad to meet 'The Fairest Youth in the World' – and it ends in absurdity and then disaster. The book does not simply reveal the multiplicity of cultures, stories, meanings; it touches on the conflict, danger and violence that can underlie this. Today, perhaps, *As If By Magic* is most interesting and illicit as an explicitly gay novel; one reason, no doubt, why it cost Wilson some of his audience and his popularity.

Wilson published his last novel, *Setting the World on Fire*, in 1980. By now he was Britain's most famous man of letters. Many younger writers were influenced by him, including Margaret Drabble, the present writer, Martin Amis and Ian McEwan, who had been his writing student. In the book – 'a melodramatic finale', Anthony Burgess prophetically called it – he returns to the subject of England, seen as critically as ever, and in the light of yet another complex metaphor. It is the story of the great mansion of Tothill House, built by Vanburgh and hidden in the centre of Westminster, close to the heart of government. The present owners have theatrical interests, and a key event is the restaging of Lully's opera *Phaethon* (who nearly did set the whole world on fire). The main theme of this dense novel is the chaos and violence out of which both civilization and art arise. They are incendiary, apocalyptic, like the characters in the book, all of whom aim, figuratively and literally, at 'setting the world on fire'. The book predicted the angrily apocalyptic writing of a good deal of British fiction over the Eighties, when many writers reacted against the age of Thatcherism, a distrust Wilson shared. In 1985, unhappy with present-day Britain, Wilson and his companion Tony Garrett left Britain for Provence, with various novels already planned. The move tragically coincided with the onset of a serious disease, labyrinthitis; he was now unable to write. At the end of the decade he returned to Britain and died in a Suffolk nursing home in 1991. His remarkable career showed a distinctive shape, his work a complete logic. The mischievous satirist of the Forties turned into the splendidly liberal and social novelist of the Fifties, recorder of the Anglo-Saxon attitudes; and then, in the Sixties, the complex mythmaker of a pluralizing, troubled, international world, when notions of literature, virtue and Englishness all had to be rewritten. Wilson remained a liberal writer, concerned with the need for human maturity and complete self-awareness. Three, certainly, of his books are classics: *Anglo-Saxon Attitudes* for its Dickensian portrait of British society in its liberal virtues and its rich hypocrisies; *The Middle Age of Mrs Eliot*, the work of a powerful and compassionate imagination; and *No Laughing Matter*, a multi-voiced, mimicking, self-questioning yet wonderfully full version of that complex, still unfinished and ever developing thing: the 'Condition of England' novel.

7

For most of the major writers who had emerged from the Fifties, the Sixties were to be a time of change. Iris Murdoch – like Wilson, one of the key British novelists of the last half of the century – had never regarded the novel as a simple form of imitation, though, also like Wilson, she had looked back to the great novelists of the nineteenth century – Dickens, Dostoevsky, Tolstoy – for a sense of the rich and human powers of fiction. But if, for her, the novel was indeed to be a fit house for free characters to live in, that house could be remarkably ornate, rich and strange. Robert Scholes described her books as 'fabulations', and her various novels of the Sixties certainly fit the description. There were many of them; it seemed a year could not go by without a book from her, and there were eight by the time the decade was done. They were, as Scholes said, 'artistic' rather than 'realistic', 'more concerned with ideas and ideals, less concerned with things'. Murdoch used the kitty of forms with the greatest freedom: the Bloomsbury novel of intuitions and sensibilities, the Jamesian novel of manners, the exotic love romance, the strange Gothic fantasy, the fiction of modern history. If *A Severed Head* (1961) was a very witty Bloomsbury parody, focused around a London wine merchant nicely called Martin Lynch-Gibbon, then *An Unofficial Rose*, published in the same year, was a serious love romance, seeing love (the 'unofficial rose') as a tempestuous or illicit passion which can create havoc but also confer freedom; the book is also concerned, as Murdoch expressed it, with 'the invigorating presence of shapely human wills'. *The Italian Girl* (1964) is a rather more conventional love story, but then *The Red and the Green* (1965) is not: in fact it is an extremely intricate tale of intrigue, politics, love and danger during the 1916 Easter Rising in Ireland, where all the action is set, in an unusual and allegorical mingling of genres. The tone then changed. *The Time of the Angels* (1966) and *The Nice and the Good* (1968) represent a return, but with a new quality of philosophical seriousness and density, to what could now be recognizably thought of as the Murdochian novel. By now her books were famous for their complex mixtures of love, marriage, adultery, high seriousness, art, extravagance, meditation, sexual and religious charisma. They held wise and powerful characters, complex and deceptive ones, false prophets and true saints, large problems of human virtue and goodness. Who but Murdoch would think of calling a modern novel *The Nice and the Good*? And, though the forms could be very various, there was something to be thought of as Murdochland, quite as distinctive as Greeneland. It was sophisticated, intelligent, deeply bourgeois; readers sometimes wondered how her characters earned a living. In it recurred certain kinds of household, certain kinds of person: the Near-Saint, the Failed Priest, the Charismatic Philosopher, the Fatal Enchanter, the Love Prisoner, the Bookish Bureaucrat, the Radiant Woman, the Ascetic, the Sensualist, the Haunted Child, the Wise Dog, the Deathbed Contemplative. It was filled with objects, clothes, possessions, styles, haircuts, works of art, fine terraces, splendid gardens, lawns and grounds. It led on to complicated places: art galleries, museums, the Post Office tower, the many pubs of London.

Murdochland was a baroque and highly sexualized world. Yet its complicated, labyrinthine and ever-changing love relationships led to remarkable encounters and provoked the most elaborate quasi-symbolic themes: the nature of power and possession, the way we act virtuously or badly, the way we perceive the existence of others, the way we create or destroy realities, the need for the good, the beautiful and the true. Murdoch clearly believed in Plato's vision, that art was by nature dangerous precisely because it could present ideal forms and complex moral truths. Her imagination was both one of ornate and fantastic gifts and of very metaphysical passions and curiosities, in which tales of love and relationship and community are ritualized, turned into something splendidly ceremonial. Meanwhile metaphor, symbol and often quite obscure and pictorial allegory are there to shape her stories into a complete and distinctive vision. Questions of love, ethics, virtue, goodness; of self-deception and the deception of others, evil and moral wickedness; of how to define the real and name the true; all found their place. Philosophical and political questions emerged early, in *Under the Net*; religious questions clearly appeared in *The Bell*. Murdoch's best book of the Sixties was *Bruno's Dream* (1968), less playful, much darker and at times Beckettian; it is a dying old man's meditation on memory, love and death in a world without religious certainties, though 'love still existed and it was the only thing that existed'. Bruno (an expert on spiders) attempts to reconcile himself with his family, and unsettles the world. 'The great deaths of literature are few, but they show us with an exemplary clarity the way art invigorates us by a juxtaposition, almost an identification, of pointlessness and value,' Murdoch was to reflect in her philosophical study *The Sovereignty of Good* (1970); the book is a serious attempt at the project, and led the way into the later novels. For around this point Murdoch's work changed again, and – as her best critics agree – a new and larger scale of interests and tactics began to emerge in her writing. The writer was departing from an earlier existentialism to a more Platonic, indeed perhaps ultimately a more religious, view of the world. At the same time the books, instead of being mostly exotic love romances, concern themselves more with art and death, since, as Bradley Pearson would put it in one of her best novels of the Seventies, *The Black Prince* (1973), 'all art is a struggle to be, in a particular sort of way, virtuous'. Murdoch's best and most virtuous books still lay ahead.

If Lessing and Fowles, Wilson and Murdoch were re-examining the conventions of the realist, humanist and philosophical novel in ways appropriate to changing times, Muriel Spark was certainly doing no less for the Catholic novel. From her first book *The Comforters* on, she had shown herself preoccupied by the nature of fiction and fictionality (Caroline in that book hears the novelist next door, typing, talking to herself and inventing her), though for reasons very different from John Fowles. Fowles might like to see the novelist as a new kind of god, no longer omniscient and decreeing, and with freedom as his first principle, not authority; Spark preferred to see the writer as something closer to an obscure and providential figure who is devoted to working out the divine plot of the world, and not in the least bit interested in freedom at all. Over the years she had been developing her own hard, anti-psychological manner of writing, which showed great interest in but small sympathy with her characters, and always emphasized the power of plot. Her most famous book, *The Prime of Miss Jean Brodie* (1961), deals with the charismatic Edinburgh teacher who, during her 'prime' in the Thirties, turns her class into a splendid elite, until she is finally betrayed, Judas-like, by one of them. The book is a classic of style. Though psychology is absent, time is ever-present: time as it was then, is now, and will be. The novel uses the device of the flash-forward to indicate that the outcome is settled, all is determined, what begins must end, and all the characters are plotters in a yet larger plot. In the following book, *The Girls of*

Slender Means (1963), Spark recreates, quite as vividly, London at the end of the war, in the strange hiatus between VE and VJ days. The war is over, but not over, 'all the nice people in England are poor', and good girls have slender means. This turns into another black allegory about plots and destinies. When an unexploded bomb finally goes off in the grounds of the May of Teck Club, where nice girls with slender means can stay, it is only those with the very slenderest – the thin ones who can squeeze through a small window – who escape. Clearly, as her fiction grew more assured, Spark felt free to delight in the strange and absurd arbitrariness of stories, and the novelist's ability to administer it as she chose, using her role in relation to characters and plots with grim wit and much black humour.

Like a number of more recent writers, Spark – much of whose work was published in *The New Yorker* – crossed the Atlantic in the early Sixties to live in Manhattan (*The New Yorker* provided her with an office), and remained for three years. In retrospect, or so her ironic novella *The Hothouse on the East River* (1973) would suggest, she found the city extreme and the experience purgatorial. Her next novel was *The Mandelbaum Gate* (1965), set in Jerusalem at the time (1961) of the trial of Adolph Eichmann for complicity in the Holocaust. The book – which is plainly autobiographical and explored her own history, emotions, faith and divided allegiances – seemed to repudiate the earlier hard manner; it is long and self-analytical, with a strong religious concern, a sense of being divided in loyalties between Catholic and Jewish, pro-Israeli and pro-Palestine; it displayed a complexity to the author we had not yet seen. It even contained an attack on the *nouveau roman* as a false course: 'repetition, boredom, despair, going nowhere for nothing'. And while it was true these books were plotless, and hers highly plotted, theirs without psychology but a distinct centre of perception, a vacant space for seeing, and hers with a controlling author, nonetheless the kind of fiction she had written so far seemed to be kin to new French fiction, with its hard and indifferent surfaces, its insistence on the dominance of the text. But this, her longest and most open novel, was followed by some of her shortest and most exact. By this time, in 1966, Spark had moved to an apartment in Rome, and she has remained in Italy ever since. It gave a new distance and a far greater cosmopolitanism to her fiction, which changed constantly in era and location, and increasingly contained figures from the *dolce vita* world. The three pared-down novels that came from this period – *The Public Image* (1968), *The Driver's Seat* (1970) and *Not to Disturb* (1971) – represent some of her most interesting and original work. Essential parables of modern fiction, they sit at the centre of her art, for by now Spark was quite sure of her powers and the paradoxical views of fiction and person she meant to explore. All are works of pure plot and precise economy. The text lays its causalities bare and becomes the chief presence. And no writer has ever seemed surer about where things are going, how they will work out and why these words are like this. They are also – perhaps this is what makes them of the Sixties – chill tales of moral absence, where lives are robbed of all humanity and conducted in a world of empty things. Here the self is a public image, an icon, a void, an outward spectacle designed for consumption. And there is surely now an analogy between this fiction and the *nouveau roman*, since here characters become simply objects in a world filled with other objects. The essential difference is that Spark clearly holds to a religious-absurdist view of the world: that evils are punished, events are predetermined and life ends in death.

Perhaps the greatest joke is that the characters know they are in just this kind of world and behave accordingly. They understand they are not self-authored, but live in an alien fiction. Sometimes they speculate about their role in the story, sometimes they challenge their author over control of their fates. Annabel Christopher, in *The Public Image*, is an actress who accepts her role as public icon as a fiction. But by getting pregnant she is able to consider the question of whether there is, as it were, a life inside her – and seeks, to ambiguous effect, to query her fate. In the macabre *The Driver's Seat* Lise travels from the north of economic miracle Europe to the south on an obscure journey. Her fate has been determined; her author has decided she will be found mysteriously dead. Lise, a dissenting character, sets out to control and manage the situation; if she cannot change the ending she can at least make sure it is arrived at on her own terms; in the end she effectively commits suicide without sin. In *Not to Disturb*, the servants in the Gothic big house are both informed and literary enough (they even have agents) to manage the story and turn away chance strangers or anyone who might interrupt the predetermined outcome of a classic Gothic plot. Endings, usually meaning death, cannot be changed. But the way to them, their meaning, the tricks and intricacies, the devices and occasions, sometimes can. The characters are readers in the text and, as Frank Kermode put it, generally have to do most of the interpretation, long before the critic gets there. Spark's real spiritual home or base-camp was now Italy, where a fair number of her novels were set. Later novels – *The Takeover* (1976), *Territorial Rights* (1979) – increasingly became stories of a blanked-out, over-moneyed Euro-world where only materialist concerns matter, emptiness is the only essence, life is a secular parody of divine intentions and everyone wishes to appropriate the property of everyone else. One of her most brilliant books, *The Abbess of Crewe* (1974), is a comic satire on Richard Nixon and the Watergate scandal, all set in a very secular nunnery. Other novels – *Loitering With Intent* (1984), *A Far Cry from Kensington* (1988) – were splendid returns to the bomb-blasted post-war London of Grub Street or the time when she worked in black propaganda, splendid training for the novelist. *Reality and Dreams* (1996) showed that, twenty novels on, she had lost none of her cunning. Set in the Nineties, at a time when 'the century is getting old, very old', and the world is downsizing, it is the story of an ageing director who falls off his crane during filming and has to confront the discrepancies between realities and dreams. As his vengeful half hippie daughter Marigold ('worthy as any man or woman in the works of George Eliot') says, 'Few people realize what redundancy can lead to.' The characters of the novel, shifting between roles in films and roles in life, are constantly inventing and destroying themselves, creating themselves and making themselves redundant, in a dance of human deceivers. Perhaps mindful of Graham Greene's observation that 'with the death of James, the religious sense was lost to the English novel, and with it the importance of the human act', Spark has written accordingly. Her novels are worlds where there is no apparent moral law and decadence is universal, though to her cool eye no more than to be expected. Life is a black comedy unfolding in a strangely divine universe; yet somewhere is a hunger for truth, purpose, reality. Spark is a virtuoso of the arts of fiction and fictionality, but also more. Her grids, her plots, her self-conscious fictions, her empty realities are not just clever texts but moral satires on the meaning – or meaninglessness – of life, and the world of contingent reality, of redundancy, makes moral and religious truths. If Iris Murdoch is the late modern metaphysician of character in the novel, then Muriel Spark is the eschatalogist of modern plot.

8

There can be no doubt that British fiction in the Sixties was passing through a phase of intense self-consciousness. It is equally apparent in the work of Spark's interesting and very different co-religionist Anthony Burgess. Where Spark was spare, Burgess was prolix; where Spark hoarded invention, Burgess spilled it in quantity. In the Fifties the 'Malayan Trilogy' had shown him to be a clever comic realist who was fascinated by languages and etymologies: 'comic novels about man's tragic lot', he called them. The threat of death from a brain tumour then started a period of frenzied literary production which was not to cease till his death in 1993 (indeed, not all was done then, for he left behind a remarkable and fiery verse novel in ottava rima, *Byrne*, published posthumously in 1995). The early Sixties thus opened on a period of remarkable fertility, with the year 1962 alone seeing two of his finest and most long-lived novels, *A Clockwork Orange* and *The Wanting Seed*. Both depart realism; both are dystopian fantasies, tales of social disaster. *A Clockwork Orange*, today a classic, is Orwellian in spirit, yet without the grimness: in a dulled socialist society where all streets are dangerous and gang crime rules, language has declined to a 'droog' argot; Burgess renders it brilliantly as a code for the book. Meanwhile his murderous teenage rebels require 'rehabilitation', a concept Burgess questions out of the complexities of his own Catholic faith. *The Wanting Seed* brings similar moral and religious questions to another great social problem, over-population; the novel is set in a Malthusian England where contraception is obligatory and homosexuality encouraged as a dis-couragement to childbearing; then counter-revolution brings about the opposite problem, of gross and obligatory sexual libertarianism. Burgess seemed to be joining the ranks of those serious writers who (like Lessing and Amis) were turning to science fiction. But he was moving in other directions too. In 1963 came the first of the Enderby novels, *Inside Mr Enderby*, tales of the rogue hero F. X. Enderby, post-Joycean artist, lecher poet, obsessed with art, language, sex, death and his own bowels. Enderby would return in several more novels, until he ended up in *The Clockwork Testament, or Enderby's End* (1974), only to be resurrected in *Enderby's Dark Lady* (1984); good ideas never die.

By now Burgess had most of his chief themes in place: a polymathic and polyglot fascination with language; a Catholic sense of sin linked with a realist's sense of society and a modernist's sense of disaster; an obsession with the rogue artist, who appears again and again, from Enderby to Byrne; a sense of the gross, ridiculous, unbidden and embarrassing sources and origins of art. And Burgess had not studied music, taught languages and learned them, read and re-read James Joyce and other related experimental heroes for nothing. He was a latter-day Joycean, except that where Joyce preserved his avant-garde purity and sought to rise out of history into myth, with language as experimental discourse, pure form, Burgess was the expert in pro-lixity. In the end he produced over sixty works of every conceivable kind: fiction, poetry, memoir, fantasy, literary criticism, screenplay, stage play, opera, concerto. There were novels about Shakespeare (*Nothing Like the Sun*, 1964), Marlowe, Keats, screenplays on Cyrano, Shelley, Byron. There was a 'musical' novel, *Napoleon Symphony* (1974), in which the tale of the Little General is played off against the musical score of Beethoven's 'Eroica' Symphony. Over the Sixties and Seventies the adventures of Structuralism entered his writing, and there are books of codes and lexical systems, cryptically called *MF* and *Abba Abba*. *MF* (1971) draws on Claude Lévi-Strauss's anthro-pology and his fascination with incest taboos, to give us a book of riddles and gender problems so complex it took Frank Kermode to decode it. Later on came the most ambitious and capacious books of all: *Earthly Powers* (1980), about papal sins and modern history; *The End of the World News* (1983), an intellectual spanning of the century which takes on Freud and Trotsky; and *The Kingdom of the Wicked* (1985), another massive recreation of history as fiction. These are discussed later; but by the Sixties Burgess had already become a postmodern storehouse of contemporary writing, opening out the world of past authorships, narratives, languages and discourses, codes and tactics for every kind and level of literary use.

This rising self-consciousness was one remarkable quality of mainstream British fiction over the Sixties; we can justly say a significant rediscovery of the novel and its possibilities was now occurring. Realism was under test in Wilson and Fowles; gender and utopianism in Lessing; character and aesthetic philosophy in Murdoch and Spark; fictional language and trope in Burgess. Where was it leading? The novelist, David Lodge famously said in 1969, now stood at the crossroads: 'the pressure on the aesthetic and epistemological premises of literary realism is now so intense that many novelists, instead of marching confidently straight ahead, are at least considering two routes that branch off in opposite directions . . .': one toward neo-documentary, fiction as history, history as fiction; the other toward fabulation. Often the paths then met again further on, generating a changed but renewed faith in realism. Or so he explained his own novels, which were split neatly between contemporary realism and playful and comic metafiction. Lodge (who taught literature at the University of Birmingham) had established himself as a realistic novelist in 1960 with *The Picturegoers*, about young Catholics struggling with the moral problems of their faith in South London. *Ginger, You're Barmy* (1962) dealt with conscription into the army under National Service, a key experience for a generation. Then with *The British Museum is Falling Down* (1965) – though about a perfectly realistic subject, Catholic parents struggling with the perils of contraception – he turned to a playful, parodic, metafictional form to tell the story of Adam Appleby, Catholic and research student, who is working in the great domed library of the British Museum, at the heart of Bloomsbury. Adam soon finds himself inside the fictions he so diligently studies: the book develops through a splendid series of parodies – of Virginia Woolf, D. H. Lawrence, Franz Kafka, Ernest Hemingway, Graham Greene and more – where the hard realities of pinched marriage and child-rearing are set against the greater grandeurs of fiction. As Adam realizes: 'Literature is mostly about sex and not much about having children; life is the other way round.' The book ends on a parody of *Ulysses*, Molly Bloom's famous modernist soliloquy no longer closing with the great orgasmic and life-affirming 'yes', but a rather more ironic and postmodern 'perhaps'. In later work – most notably the fine 'campus novels' *Changing Places* (1975), *Small World* (1984) and *Nice Work* (1988) – he moves freely between the two modes, the difference between them embodied in the difference between the world of his chosen city 'Rummidge' (plainly Birmingham) and the world of conferences, congresses and Californian academic dreams and pleasures in which hyper-reality is set free as fact and theory. Other books, like *Therapy* (1995), reveal much more about the late twentieth-century Catholic trying to deal with the problems of love, writing and growing older, trying to understand the nature of life's pilgrimage. Again they move freely between both modes. As he himself suggested, Lodge can be best described as an experimental realist; and this was a place where many of his literary contemporaries also seemed willing to settle.

By the close of the Sixties, British fiction was a very eclectic church. Realism had by no means died, and many of the most interesting writers developing during the decade depended on it and its traditions in one way or another. One of the most interesting novelists to emerge in the early Sixties was Margaret Drabble, whose first group of novels – *A Summer Bird-Cage* (1963), *The Garrick Year* (1964), and *The Millstone* (1965), about unmarried motherhood – tightly portray the experiences of intelligent young women, latter-day heirs to Emma Woodhouse and Dorothea Brooke, most of them newly out of university, as they enter the contemporary world of marriage, family, career, new feminist ideas and expectations. At a time when women's needs and desires were becoming more articulate in fiction, they were largely read as feminist works. Drabble came from Sheffield in Yorkshire, her sister being the novelist A. S. Byatt; the 'commonsense' North (embodied in her novels in the city of 'Northam') was always to be a point of reference. She had also been taught by F. R. Leavis at Cambridge; she acknowledged a debt to Arnold Bennett, another novelist from the provinces, of whom in 1974 she wrote a biography (another later dealt with Angus Wilson, to whom she also felt much indebted). As she said: 'I'd rather be at the end of a dying tradition which I admire than at the beginning of a tradition which I deplore'; she felt the task of the novelist was the 'transfiguration of the every-day', and that we are all part of a human community in which we must play a role. The concern with social history and the great community grew in her novels, through *Jerusalem the Golden* (1967) and *The Waterfall* (1969). By the Seventies (*Realms of Gold*, 1975, *The Ice Age*, 1977) she was becoming a large and inclusive chronicler of contemporary life and social history, writing with clear political and moral passion about the scenes of the day: financial scandals, changing sexual *mores*, the decline of moral confidence and social hope, the cruelties and silences of British society, the divisions of England, between class and class, north and south. While A. S. Byatt, publishing her first novel *Shadow of the Sun* in 1964, grew into one of the strongest experimentalists in female fiction, Drabble became one of the strongest recording angels, writing a dense socio-moral portrait of an entire age.

There was, similarly, Melvyn Bragg, whose first novel *For Want of a Nail* (1965) was a powerful portrait of a Cumberland scholarship boy very like his author. Like Drabble, Bragg carried the weight of the serious British cultural historian that had come to writers from critics like Leavis, Richard Hoggart and Raymond Williams. Bragg, too, retained a firm and productive faith in the values of the realistic and regional novel, despite his role as a major figure in contemporary television and national politics, and his engagement with the spirit of modern and postmodern experiment. Despite other activities he managed to produce fiction of great and interesting variety. 'The Cumbrian Trilogy' (*The Hired Man*, 1969, *A Place in England*, 1970, *Kingdom Come*, 1980) is a long history of British regional and metro-politan life over the twentieth century. *Love and Glory* (1983) deals with the media world of London; *The Maid of Buttermere* (1987) returns to Cumberland (now Cumbria) and its literary past. Like other writers, including Beryl Bainbridge, he also reported on contemporary society, exploring in *Speak for England* (1976) the paradox that runs deep in British society: that despite the processes of change, modernization, globalization, media influence that have dissolved the sense of history, landscape and personal and domestic history, many English people still retain an intense sense of connection with their history, customs, landscape and family, and that this is relevant to the novel. For other writers, a change and the coming of a new unreality could not come soon enough. For Angela Carter, the old realities and public myths were there to be deconstructed and demonu-mentalized, and the doors of literature to be thrown open to trans-formation, fantasy. Her novels *Shadow Dance* (1965) and *The Magic Toyshop* (1967) began the journey; the spirit of folklore and fantasy, magic and grotesque writing, started to take a central place in her work. A spell in Japan, and the intellectual influences of feminism, Post-Structuralism and Deconstruction, also helped. By *Fireworks: Nine Profane Pieces* (1974), her work is essentially about transforma-tion, shattered mirrors, new being. Gothic was the thing: 'cruel tales, tales of wonder, tales of terror, fabulous narratives that deal directly with the imagery of the unconscious – mirrors, the externalized self, forsaken castles, haunted forests: forbidden sexual objects,' – so she began to describe her work.

The tradition of the novel had widened, new reference points emerged. British fiction had become part of a broader experiment everywhere. Its codes of realism had been questioned or were being dissolved. Narrative means and methods multiplied, novels refracted a random and harder world. While fiction asserted its own fictionality, it also incorporated the materials of the supposedly factual codes: journalism and reportage, history-writing and biography. It also turned again to folk tale, dream-story, fairy tale, science fiction. Self-consciousness had come, the sign had wavered, but humanism had not necessarily departed. Many of the most interesting books of the Sixties were experiments in fabulation and metafiction; they were also about humanism's authenticity and the realms of moral, social and metaphysical truths. If challenged, realism was not entirely dis-avowed. Fiction ranged from the minimalism of Beckett to the fictional playfulness of Fowles; from Lessing's multiple notebooks to Murdoch's ornate baroque; from Wilson's mimicry and parody to Spark's cool black irony; from Johnson's realistic fragmentations to Angela Carter's transgressive 'tales of wonder, tales of terror'. Yet for most writers the novel's task was the same: finding a structure for the exploration of experience, wisdom, truth. The human figure had not disappeared; concern for character remained one mark of British fiction. These were not the abstractified texts of the French *nouveau roman*, subjectless writing purged down to perception; they were mostly works of liberal experimentalism opening to fresh psychological curiosity, a new view of the creative imagination, a widened sense of subject; Lodge was probably right about the British 'aesthetics of compromise'. In 1992 he revisited the subject of his essay again, to find that things had changed only a little. What he called 'crossover fiction', merging realistic and experimental, had become 'a salient feature of writing today'. And not just in British fiction, for the compound terms of more recent literary discussion – 'magical realism', 'dirty realism', 'hyper-realism' – suggest this had turned into a general line for international fiction as it approached the close of the twentieth century.[17]

---

17 'The Novelist Today: Still at the Crossroads', in Malcolm Bradbury and Judy Cooke (eds.), *New Writing*, no. 1 (London, 1992). Lodge adds: 'The astonishing variety of styles on offer today, as if in an aesthetic supermarket, includes traditional as well as innovative styles, minimalism as well as excess, nostalgia as well as prophecy.'

8

The Ice Age – Fiction in the Seventies: 1969–1979

> Those who had been complaining for the last twenty years
> about the negligible rise in the cost of living did not of course
> have the grace to wish that they had saved their breath to cool
> their porridge, because once a complainer, always a com-
> plainer, so those who had complained most when there was
> nothing to complain about were having a wonderful time
> now . . . Margaret Drabble,
> *The Ice Age* (1977)

> I wonder what sort of person I can be?
> Martin Amis, *The Rachel Papers* (1973)

1

After the Swinging Sixties, the Sagging Seventies. Rarely has a decade
acquired less obvious character in popular memory and mythology
than the Seventies, a time that now seems more like a dull passage
between the dying of the Sixties and the sudden coming of the entrepreneurial Eighties. Though much of the euphoria waned quickly after
the events of 1968, the fantastic change that did not and never could
quite happen, the Sixties died gradually. Though the politics of that
decade grew more extreme and violent, it had been a time of creative
euphoria and invention, and this swept internationally across the arts.
By the dawn of the Seventies fresh realities imposed themselves. In
1969 American astronauts made the first moon landing – a 'giant step
for mankind' – and images of the new space frontier were transmitted

all over the globe. But though major space projects by the USA and Russia would continue over the next decade, they were a severe drain on both economies. In 1968, as Richard Nixon was elected to the presidency, the television newscaster Walter Cronkite announced: 'It seems now more certain than ever that the bloody experience of Vietnam is to end in a stalemate. This summer's almost certain stand-off will either end in real give-and-take negotiations or terrible escalation; and for every means we have to escalate, the enemy can match us.' Despite Nixon's attempt to extricate the nation, America's Vietnam War had several years to run, and the last departure in 1975, with American helicopters frantically airlifting their allies from a defeated Saigon, marked the final humiliation. For the first time the USA had been defeated in foreign war. Other scenes of conflict were escalating. In Northern Ireland the 'Troubles' that would dominate British and Irish politics for the next thirty years began. In 1973 came the Yom Kippur War when Egypt and Syria attacked Israel. One significant consequence was a control of oil production which affected all Western economies, bringing inflation, recession, collapsing production and unemployment. The long-running economic miracle that had funded political and cultural excitement over the last decade had come to an end. In 1974, as a result of press investigations into the 'dirty tricks' surrounding Nixon's election victory, the Watergate scandal turned critical. Faced with impeachment, Nixon became the first American president to resign from office; presidential authority and government in effect collapsed for the rest of the decade. In 1975 civil war broke out in Lebanon; by the end of the decade Russian troops had invaded a now Communist Afghanistan and, like the Americans in Vietnam, had become embedded in long-lasting guerrilla war. Iran saw the Islamic revolution of the Ayatollah Khomeini, and Americans saw their diplomats being held hostage by the new regime in Tehran.

In Britain the mood of 'swinging London' did not survive. 'It swings; it is the scene,' *Time* magazine had said of 1966 London, surveying the pop scene, the youth cult, underground theatre, the hippie stores of Carnaby Street and the style boutiques like Biba in Kensington, the fading of the Establishment, the rise of satire, self-parody and pluralism. The Britain of the Seventies had a different feel: the 'Ice Age', Margaret Drabble called it in her 1977 'Condition of England' novel of the same title. Confident assumptions about growth in living standards no longer seemed so certain; as the international recession grew, the mood was one of decline. In 1974 Edward Heath took Britain into the European Economic Community after two rebuffs, but it was now a Britain already economically enfeebled by sterling crisis, balance-of-payments deficits and low productivity, unsure of its relationship with the expanding economic and political world. As Drabble said in her novel, the Ice Age came 'when the flow had ceased to flow; the ball had stopped rolling'. The conflict between rising hopes and deteriorating economy destabilized successive British governments: the Wilson Labour government, the Heath Conservative government and the Callaghan Labour administration at the end of the decade. All culminated in the 'Winter of Discontent' of 1978–9, when the public unions withdrew their services; sewage disposal ceased, rubbish piled in the streets, the dead lay unburied. It brought the collapse of the Labour government and the emergence of Margaret Thatcher, riding in a new spirit on a new set of priorities.

If the Sixties were the age of Aquarius, the time of the collective counter-culture, the Seventies became perceived as the 'Me Decade'. 'After the political turmoil of the Sixties, Americans have retreated to purely personal preoccupations,' wrote the American cultural commentator Christopher Lasch, defining 'the culture of narcissism'.[1] The new mood, Lasch said, marked a diminishing of serious politics, the fading of a serious sense of history and reality. It was a time of postmodern culture in the form of a preoccupation with the presentational, the empty, the ironic. The emphasis now fell not on the system but on the environment, not on power politics and international forces but on 'relational' issues, such as the disintegrating family, the individual state of consciousness, therapies and encounters, and above all issues of gender, sexual identity and cultural politics

---

1 Christopher Lasch, *The Culture of Narcissism: American Life in an Age of Diminishing Expectations* (New York, 1979).

that developed as the feminist movement grew. For such issues had become central in America after publication of Kate Millett's *Sexual Politics* in 1969. Similar issues and controversies emerged in Britain after the publication in 1970 of Germaine Greer's *The Female Eunuch* and Eva Figes's *Patriarchal Attitudes*. These issues of gender, new consciousness and personal relationship had much influence on the fiction of the decade. Meanwhile in the fiction market-place there was some considerable feeling that the serious novel itself was losing out to the self-help climate of the times. This feeling, and a concern to invigorate the debate about the novel, unquestionably had a good deal to do with the founding of the Booker Prize for Fiction, which covered not simply British novels but those by writers of other countries writing centrally in English – 'the Commonwealth, Eire, Pakistan, Bangladesh, or South Africa', according to the rules. It also had to do with the fact that the Booker company had an 'Authors' Division', holding the copyrights of such writers as Ian Fleming, Agatha Christie, Georgette Heyer and Harold Pinter, which were making large returns. It began in 1969, and from the first its choices were disputed. The most significant novel that year was surely John Fowles's *The French Lieutenant's Woman*, which did not reach the shortlist, though Iris Murdoch's *The Nice and the Good* and Muriel Spark's *The Public Image* did. So the first Booker went to P. H. Newby's *Something to Answer For*; it started contentiously, and so it remains. To some critics it has seemed to give the serious novel a powerful new foothold in contemporary culture; to others it has shifted the novel from the realm of art to that of commerce, brought absurd rivalries into literary debate and stimulated the sale of certain lucky and selected fictions at the expense of others that are as good or in many cases better. At times absurd choices, bitter rivalries, obvious misjudgements, nepotism and prejudiced opinion on the part of the judges, or a feeling that the literary debate and the eternal argument that always surrounds fiction has been vulgarized and distorted, have led to serious calls for the abandonment of the prize (though often from critics who somehow take a different view in the following year).

Yet all that said, the prize, now joined by many others (the

Whitbread, the Saga, the Orange), became a central part of modern fictional culture, has encouraged support for serious fiction when publishers feared its audiences were departing and made contemporary fiction a matter of public debate. It drew attention to the wide range of fiction published in English, with London as cultural capital, and widened public understanding of the nature and spread of the novel. Famously, many of the books chosen were drawn from the post-colonial or post-imperial experience (it used to be said you needed to write about India, South Africa or Guyana to win), and the subject-matter runs like a continuous theme through the early awards. V. S. Naipaul won in 1971 for his book *In a Free State*, part novel, part document, mostly a group of three multi-cultural stories, set in the USA, Britain and Africa; a later book, the admirable *A Bend in the River*, a story from the heart of darkness, set in Africa and with allusions to Conrad's novella, was shortlisted in 1979. In 1973 J. G. Farrell won the prize for his fine novel about the Indian Mutiny, *The Seige of Krishnapur*; in 1974 the liberal South African novelist Nadine Gordimer, for a symbolic fable about the possession and use of African lands, *The Conservationist*; in 1975 Ruth Prawer Jhabvala, for her Indian tale *Heat and Dust*; in 1977, Paul Scott, author of the 'Raj Quartet', for his novel about the British in India after Independence, *Staying On*. It took most of the decade for the Booker to establish itself, as prize money rose, press coverage grew and the books chosen began to sell significantly. At the same time the choice of winners and shortlisted authors showed something of the real variety of current British fiction. In 1972 John Berger (so politically Left he gave half the prize money to an activist protest movement, the Black Panthers) won for the experimental *G.*, an eroticization of history, a history of eroticism, a complex reworking of the Don Juan tale set around the Great War and relating sex to political crisis. Other experimental works – Nicholas Mosley's *Impossible Object* (1969), David Storey's dramatic *Saville* (1976) – won or were shortlisted. Controversy has always surrounded the prize, but it eventually became a key cultural institution, rivalling the Prix Goncourt in France, though with far less predictability. Which is why anyone who keeps some accountancy of the modern British novel needs to attend to it; the list of titles is a useful and illuminating chart of the good fiction published in Britain and the Commonwealth from the dawn of the Seventies on.[2]

2

The Seventies may indeed have been the 'Me Decade', but to look at the strong titles of the decade is to see the importance of what Bernard Bergonzi called the genre of 'fictions of history'. The centrality of the theme of Empire and post-imperialism was noted by J. G. Farrell, who remarked that the close of the Empire had been signalled 'when the Labour Prime Minister, Harold Wilson, announced the final homecoming of the British legions' in January 1968, with the departure from Aden (the last significant furling of the flag would not occur until near the end of the millennium, in Hong Kong). Born in Liverpool in 1935, Farrell published several novels in the Sixties, including *The Lung* (1965), about his own experiences as a polio victim, before he began a sequence of novels about people 'undergoing history'. The books of his 'Empire Trilogy' were all set at moments of imperial crisis. *Troubles* (1970) deals with the fading power of the Anglo-Irish ascendency living in a Dublin hotel, the Majestic, in 1919–21. *The Siege of Krishnapur* deals with the Indian Mutiny of 1857, while *The Singapore Grip* (1978) treats the greatest imperial crisis of all, the hapless surrender of Singapore to Japanese forces in early 1942 – for Winston Churchill, the worst moment of the war. As Farrell sought to emphasize, all are contemporary works as well as historical novels (*Troubles* deals by implication with the Ulster Troubles, just begun), works of formal experiment and symbolic exploration as well as of historical recreation. *Troubles* also owes something to a live tradition, the Anglo-Irish fiction of Elizabeth Bowen, Henry Green, the

2 A list of Booker Prize winners to date is given at the back of this book. Also see Richard Todd's interesting study *Consuming Fictions: The Booker Prize in Britain Today* (London, 1996), and *Booker 30: A Celebration of 30 Years of the Booker Prize for Fiction, 1969–1998* (London, 1998).

admirable William Trevor or Iris Murdoch (*The Red and the Green*). But it has its own Gothic intensity, the whole tale being dominated by the metaphor of the malign, disintegrating Hotel Majestic itself. Set back in Victorian times, *The Siege of Krishnapur* involves larger problems of re-creation; parody and various motifs are used to explore Victorian confidence and its disintegration. One is the Great Exhibition of 1851, held in Hyde Park at the grand Crystal Palace, another the pervasive and endemic diseases that spread through the Indian world of the story. *The Singapore Grip* is about Pacific colonialism but also the tale of a fantastic society, where ambiguities multiply from the title onward (the grip variously refers to the influenza, Britain's colonial grasp on the region and the sexual skills of the whores of Singapore). Farrell – who died in an accident on a fishing trip to Ireland in 1979 – left behind the manuscript of a last novel, *The Hill Station* (unfinished, published posthumously, 1981). Here sickness has become the dominant metaphor (it had been the running theme of all the novels). These are fictions of a significant historical disintegration which has not simply been chronicled but reimagined as experience, for those there at the time, and then given fictional shape by a writer with a great historical imagination and a strong sense of perspective from the present.

Quite as powerful was the 'Raj Quartet' Paul Scott had been writing over the Sixties and Seventies: *The Jewel in the Crown* (1964), *The Day of the Scorpion* (1968), *The Towers of Silence* (1971) and *A Division of the Spoils* (1975). Born in London in 1920, Scott served in the Indian army during the Second World War; of the thirteen novels he wrote up to his death in 1978, just after receiving the Booker, most are about or refer to India, which is central to the lives of nearly all his characters. Earlier books like *The Corrida at San Felieu* (1964), a significant postmodern tale about a novelist writing a novel, showed his interest in experimental and Faulknerian techniques; and the structure of the central work 'The Raj Quartet' is itself highly complex, with personal subjectivities, individual stories, separate time-schemes being placed against large and shifting historical events. The main period of the story is from wartime to Independence, the final stage of British rule. The books start from a metaphor drawn from

E. M. Forster's *A Passage to India*: 'This is the story of a rape, of the events that led up to it and followed it and the place in which it happened,' *The Jewel in the Crown* begins. We also learn: 'There are the action, the people and the place; all of which are inter-related but in their totality incommunicable in isolation from the moral continuum of human affairs.' The rape seems to accelerate the rapid decline of the Raj, leaving behind a mystery about whether British and Indians are drawn together in love, aggression or hate. As in Forster, India is seen as a dense and obscure reality; the mystery is one most of his characters wish to understand and penetrate. It is also a vast illusion or mirror, through which Britons reflect a strange image of themselves. The central characters – Britons, Eurasians, Indians – are lost between cultures, never sure where is home. Like Farrell, Scott is interested in history not just as process or inevitability but in the light of the different states and consciousnesses through which it is lived as reality; it is motion, maze, labyrinth, pointing toward hope or disaster. From such fragments we make up the greater sum: 'Only from the air can one trace a pattern, a design, an abortive human intention.' In what proved his last book, *Staying On* (Booker Prize, 1977), a splendid coda, Scott examined the last stage before all that had been central to his world seemed over: the tragi-comic story of two minor British characters out of the epic span of the 'Quartet' who stay on in India, trying to retain their lives, their hopes, their values and their curiosity as the world dissolves around them and the next India (soon to appear in fiction) takes shape.

It was clear enough that British modern history contained many viewpoints. And it was not simply about fading glorious pasts but a very real present, a continuous shaping process that still had to be understood in its variousness, pointing a way beyond colonialism or imperialism. V. S. Naipaul, a major writer from Trinidad who came to Britain to study at Oxford as the Fifties began, had written an early sequence of Caribbean novels beginning with *The Mystic Masseur* (1957), a book touched with the kind of narrative complexity we today call magic realism. The three stories of *In a Free State* (1971) deal with the wider world of his more recent experience, and not just with political change but a new culture of rootlessness – Indians in the USA, West Indians in Britain, Englishmen in Africa. His fine novel *A Bend in the River* (1979), looking at the strange juxtapositions of tradition and change in post-colonial Africa, displays the unease of a sharp political writer as well as the talents of an observant novelist. Naipaul went on to use fiction and non-fiction, journalism and imaginative history to explore the worlds of Africa, India, the Caribbean and South America at various moments of disastrous or fruitful intersection. Naipaul's arrival in Britain from the Caribbean just preceded a significant process of settlement, for during the Fifties a number of writers from Trinidad and elsewhere in the Caribbean came to Britain: George Lamming (author of *In the Castle of the Skin*, 1953, and *The Emigrants*, 1954) from Barbados, Samuel Selvon (*An Island is a World*, 1955, *The Lonely Londoners*, 1956) and James Berry from Trinidad, Wilson Harris ('The Guyana Quartet' written 1960–63, collected in one volume 1985) from Guyana. Writers like Rumer Godden, Ruth Prawer Jhabvala (*Heat and Dust*, 1975) and Anita Desai (*Bye Bye Blackbird*, 1971, *Clear Light of Day*, 1980) successfully wrote across Anglo and Indian culture; their work created a climate that helped establish the new 'post-colonial' generation of Indian writers of the Eighties and the Nineties.

There were other important histories. The great narrative of divided Europe in the era of the Cold War had generally been left to those most in the know: the makers of spy stories. The post-war spy tale had acquired its sensational character in the Fifties, with Ian Fleming's flamboyant James Bond. It came to flower over the Sixties, when in 1962 Len Deighton published *The Ipcress File*, followed a year later by John Le Carré's bestselling, informed, revealing novel *The Spy Who Came in from the Cold*. These writers did not only offer an insider's glimpse of the conspiratorial looking-glass world of the Cold War; they also depicted the troubled and distorted ideas of patriotism, split loyalties, confused codes of honour, moral self-deceit and seediness that ran through societies on both sides of the Iron Curtain ('We're all the same you know, that's the joke,' Le Carré's novel observes). In 1965 Le Carré explored with distaste and moral suspicion the entire post-war intelligence community in *The Looking-Glass War*; and now in the Seventies some of his finest work appeared.

Tinker, Tailor, Soldier, Spy (1974) presents his two great spymaster adversaries, George Smiley ('Looks like a frog, dresses like a bookie') and Karla, as 'two halves of the same apple', and they begin to play out their intricate and conspiratorial relationship, a quest that would take a trilogy of novels to resolve. Le Carré's unease, his sense of ravaged patriotism and corrupted honour, came out again in *The Honourable Schoolboy* (1977), second volume of the trilogy; his sense of the moral seediness of the age is explored in *A Perfect Spy* (1986), the most autobiographical of his novels. Le Carré refined a popular genre: but he was a significant heir not just of Erskine Childers or John Buchan but of Graham Greene and Arthur Koestler. His sombre tales of Cold War intrigue are both an allegory of two hostile systems conspiratorially interlocked and an inquiry into the moral state of post-war Britain and the post-war world. They explore a British Establishment that in various fashions had been corrupted from within: by divided allegiances in the Thirties, by the fading of patriotic confidence in wartime, by the post-war obsession with nuclear competition, secrecy and dirty tricks, creating a paranoid world that would increasingly have a part in mainstream fiction – in, for example, the novels of Ian McEwan.

If spy fiction moved ever closer to the mainstream, so did science fiction, especially in the work of the 'New Wave' writers like J. G. Ballard and Michael Moorcock. Over the Seventies, following on from his political fantasy *The Atrocity Exhibition* (1970), Ballard produced some of his most notable work, emerging as the surrealist pop-artist of new urban landscapes, techno-horrors, postmodern dreck. His landscape was the world of concrete motorways, high-rise apartment blocks, abandoned film studios, advertising hoardings, inner-city derelictions. Popular celebrities, dead icons and communal urban myths fed his fiction. Ballard described *Crash* (1973) as a technological porn novel; it deals with sexual fantasies triggered by a fatal crash on a motorway, and *Concrete Island* (1974) is a version of the same theme. *High Rise* (1975) is a dystopian fable set in a 'vertical city', a high-rise apartment block. *The Unlimited Dream Company* (1979) is about a fantastic sexual Utopia set in and around Shepperton film studios, that modern park where unlimited dreams are in theory constructed. Ballard insisted that he belonged to the illegitimate tradition of the novel, in the form of popular or pulp fiction; his style and themes were conceived for his own distinctive audience. Yet his gift for surreal fantasy influenced many other writers, above all Angela Carter, another key novelist of the Seventies. It was a surprise to its author when his strongest and most personal book, *The Empire of the Sun* (1984), won the *Guardian* Fiction Prize; it is the story of a child learning the arts of survival in a Japanese prison camp in Shanghai during wartime, where he becomes a distant witness to the explosion of the atomic bomb over Nagasaki, and is one of the strongest novels of the Eighties. To most of the 'New Wave' writers, recent history and the formation of the postmodern science and technology-based consumer society, the society of the high-rise, the motorway and the concrete island, was as grotesque as any fantasy, provoking the novelist into new acts and forms of the imagination. 'I believe that science fiction is the authentic literature of the twentieth century, the only fiction to respond imaginatively to the transforming nature of science and technology,' Ballard explained.

3

For the Seventies there were other highly important stories to tell. Over the Sixties women writers had increasingly begun to explore the rising expectations and the distinctive perceptions that came from female writing in a time of social change and increasing artistic and intellectual confidence. *The Golden Notebook* had told a story of free women, and then, with ever more expansive invention, Lessing had taken the subject into the galaxy itself. In a different fashion Margaret Drabble had explored the minutiae of thoughtful middle-class female lives, with their liberal, conflicting aspirations and frequent disappointments. Her early books were sharp miniatures, vivid portrayals of the lives of well-educated and serious young women, making their careers, exploring their sexual identities and needs. Over the Seventies, Drabble's firm moral realism and sharp social curiosity widened into a thoughtful culture-reading of an age which was sinking into an affluent materialism, and beginning to lose much of its historic family life and its domestic networks. Men and women alike led lives quite different from those of their parents; in *The Needle's Eye* (1972) one character feels 'his whole life – the clothes he wore, the car he drove, the way he spoke, the house he lived in – was an act of misrepresentation'. The novel shows her widening concerns, taking in a range of stories and social classes, the divide between northern and southern England, the growth of modern commerce and inter-nationalism. *Realms of Gold* (1975) uses archaeology as a metaphor to explore the underlying structures of British life, above all the role and traditions of women's lives within it. But Drabble's chief novel of the Seventies was *The Ice Age* (1977), a large, chilly vision of a Britain in a state of social collapse and moral sterility, dominated by financial scandals and property development; the social world and the social theme dwarf the lives of individuals and destroy humanism. Then with *The Middle Ground* (1980) Drabble began a fiction of 'shapeless diversity' that would look at women's lives and issues in the light of the state of broader society: the moral emptiness, the lack of humanity, the failure of trust, the weakening of identity. By the late Eighties she was ready to undertake a major trilogy – *The Radiant Way* (1987), *A Natural Curiosity* (1989), *The Gates of Ivory* (1991) – which put her increasingly in the light of the tradition of George Eliot, another morally serious writer of the 'middle ground' between individual and society, hope and despair, class and class, men and women, in a world where the issue of justice for women was part of the issue of justice for all. At a time of rising political dissatisfactions, her work felt ever more powerful. 'We live in an uncharted world, as far as manners and morals are concerned, we are having to make up our morality as we go,' she commented. 'Our subject-matter is enormous, there are whole new patterns to create.'

While highly aware of new arguments about the nature of fiction, Drabble was deliberately constructing her own in the light of the nineteenth-century tradition. So, to start with, was her sister A. S. Byatt, whose first novel, *Shadow of a Sun*, about a daughter growing up in the heavy shadow of a novelist father, appeared in 1964. From fathers to sisters: *The Game* (1967), besides being a dense literary work that draws on the world of the Brontës, is unmistakably a work about personal and sisterly literary rivalries. Byatt – a lecturer in English and American literature at London University, and a significant literary critic – has always been a novelist of intense and wonderful literariness: a highly modern writer still guided by what she called her 'greedy' relationship with the fictions of the past. She had chosen, she said, to explore the symbolic connection that exists between past writings and forms and contemporary writing, in order to test 'the ambiguous power and restrictiveness of the tradition'. In 1978 she began her most ambitious project – a set of multi-layered novels about a revised and contemporary Elizabethan age which took twenty years to complete – with *The Virgin in the Garden*. Rich, allusory, ripe for decoding, the sequence covers the period between the coronation of the new Queen Elizabeth in 1952 and a Post-Impressionist exhibition held in London at the end of the Eighties, meanwhile drawing on a repertory of techniques and complex references both to Elizabethan and Victorian literature, and much concerned both with female experience and the imagery and iconography of womanhood. Her work would move in a variety of directions – into long novels, brief and distilled novellas, the short story – until in 1990 she published her most successful novel *Possession*, about present and past. Victorian and American literature affected her writing, and one particular homage she expressed in two critical books, devoted to Iris Murdoch.

As for Murdoch herself, her own fiction took on a new character over the Seventies. Key critics date the change at different times, but more or less agree on what it is.[3] The familiar themes remained, the distinctive flavour, the concern with character, the exploration of the novel as a fit house for free characters to live in. But her books now displayed, as one critic, Elizabeth Dipple, points out, a fresh 'spatial luxuriousness that made plot and action seem far less significant, while the concern with romantic love shaded into something more complex'. Her themes grew increasingly ritualized, drawing on a number of fundamental and recurrent sources of imagery: houses and

---

3 See in particular Elizabeth Dipple, *Iris Murdoch: Work for the Spirit* (London, 1982), and Peter Conradi, *Iris Murdoch: The Saint and the Artist* (London, 1986).

entire unusual communities, great paintings, landscapes, animals, sea, water, caves. Certain key pairings become of great importance: the nice and the good, the nun and the soldier, the sacred and the profane. The great ritual forms of art, opera, music, comic and tragic drama, are scarcely hidden allusions behind the text. A key book here was *Bruno's Dream* (1968), a meditation on love and death in a world without its old sacred meanings, so that 'love still existed and it was the only thing that existed'. Several of the books of the Seventies have clear links with the plays of Shakespeare. *A Fairly Honourable Defeat* (1970), a tale of jealousy and deceit, draws its parallels from *Othello*. *The Black Prince* (1973), which is one of Murdoch's finest novels, owes a good deal to *Hamlet*, and reflects on Shakespeare's significance. Bradley Pearson, the narrator of this complex story, acknowledges that 'by his own meditation on the problem of his identity' Shakespeare actually created 'a new language, a special rhetoric of consciousness', which advanced the complexity of art. 'I wanted to produce a sort of statement that might be called my philosophy,' Bradley also observes, saying that this means that his story will be one of considerable (and tricky) complexity: 'And then one asks, how can this also be "true"? Is the real like this, is *it* this?' This is a tale of high self-consciousness, human and textual, for the world of the real upsets all Bradley's grand designs, so that his narrative becomes 'a literary failure'. Yet another voice comes in at the end to see matters differently: 'Art is not cosy and is not mocked. Art tells the only truth that ultimately matters. It is the light by which human things can be mended. And after art there is, let me assure you all, nothing.'

In 1978 came *The Sea, The Sea*, which won the Booker Prize. Here the allusions are to *The Tempest*, the play in which art is both celebrated and abjured. Again love is the central kingdom, but it is past love seen under the contemplation of the solitary present: the story of a theatre director, Charles Arrowby, who gives up the magic of the stage for the tranquillity of a retreat by the sea, an 'image of inaccessible freedom'. The story is set round a great Edwardian house with a view over yellow rocks, a testing watery cauldron, a swimming place, and a small village where the odd unexpected visitor can be housed. Spareness is all; even Charles's diet comes from a textbook for minimalist gourmets. But the isle is full of noises, the past is not done with, there is even a sea monster to worry about, and various lost loves from the past. The book is about the dark chills of loving, the conflicts of egotism and sacrifice, desire and death. Late in the book Charles too reflects on Shakespeare's powers, to create a work where 'magic does not shrink reality and turn it into tiny things to be the toys of fairies'. Murdoch's own work too was now a great theatre, in which the largest matters could be handled: the fictional world is a magic place or a Platonic illusion, narrative is filled with mystery and paradox, serious rituals of knowledge and the exploration of the nature of reality can be performed. The sureness passed on into the following novels: *Nuns and Soldiers* (1980), *The Philosopher's Pupil* (1983), *The Good Apprentice* (1985), *The Book and the Brotherhood* (1987). In *The Philosopher's Pupil*, a key figure, the Philosopher, returns. Here the stage is again splendidly elaborate: the spa town of Ennistone (given its name, we are told, because the novel's narrator is called, naturally, N.). Murdoch writes, with all the grandeur of a nineteenth-century novelist, a story that could only be told about the twentieth. Chapters are called 'Our Town', 'The Events in Our Town', 'What Happened Afterwards', but the town is unusual. Its entire culture is based on water, and it stands over hidden springs. The philosopher, John Robert Rozanov, is the presiding genius; he too has been away and forsworn his philosophy. When he returns, he proves to have feet of clay, and his philosophical powers are an illusion. He dies at the hands of a pupil, his last book floating away in the waters of the baths. Philosophy yields to love and confusion; meanwhile Murdoch lays bare the labyrinthine underground network of springs, ladders, caves and pipings that create the erotic spirit of Ennistone baths. Likewise books are invented things, but they also have truth to love, wholeness, plenitude and the greater reality. At the end of the book, the narrator, N., concludes:

The end of any tale is arbitrarily determined. As I now end this one, someone may say: but how on earth do you know all these things about all these people? Well, where does one person end and another begin? It is my role in life to listen to stories. I also had the assistance of a certain lady.

When Iris Murdoch, that 'certain lady', died in 1999, at the age of seventy-nine, she had created twenty-seven novels: a remarkable production for a great serious novelist comparable, as she became, with the great fictionalists of the past. The prolixity, the constant starting over again, was an important part of the achievement. So was the basic seriousness; she had started life as a philosopher, and through fiction she ended as one, making the novel the best place where thought, ideas, imaginings and human apprehensions could be explored. Her books are all placed in the realm of the imaginary, with its own distinctive laws; they are all concerned with the problem of the real, the nature of selfhood, the question of character and identity, the principle of love, the encounter with darkness in the form of guilt, corruption, cruelty, anguish and death. All this means her fiction poses the question of the usefulness and value of art itself. The human creature, Murdoch said, is a 'word child'. The only means for reaching reality and the ideal is through language, and 'the quality of a civilization depends on its ability to discern and reveal truth, and this depends on the scope and purity of its language'. Her books are pursuits of form, but not to represent linguistic crisis, or reach the obscure or the unspoken; they are meant as wise encounters with the density of experience, renewing our contact with the real. She published her last novel, *Jackson's Dilemma*, in 1995, as she was already succumbing to Alzheimer's disease: a tragic misfortune for one of the most intellectual of our novelists and one of the most brilliant and engaging of modern minds.

4

'New patterns', new types of discourse, new adventures were an important theme of the writing of the Seventies, especially among women writers whose work had been invigorated by feminism, the growth of new publishing imprints and the recovery of many of the classics of women's fiction. For some the great change could not come soon enough, the old myths dismantled and deconstructed. Some, like Elizabeth Jane Howard, Penelope Mortimer, Nell Dunn and Maureen

Duffy, saw the task as one that could be fulfilled largely within the terms of realism. Others, like Emma Tennant, looked to fantastic forms and borderline experiment to bring about the regendering of fiction. Of these, surely the most notable was Angela Carter, who had begun writing during the sixties under the influence, amongst other things, of 'New Wave' science fiction. Her early work (*Shadow Dance*, 1965, *The Magic Toyshop*, 1967) displayed her departure from realism, her interest in fairy tale and erotic themes. By the Seventies, influenced by her experiences in Japan, her interest in Post-Structuralism and Deconstruction, surrealism and Gothic fantasy, her work greatly changed and enlarged. Later it was charged with the spirit of 'magical realism', fiction where elements of history and magic merge, dream and magic freely penetrate realistic narrative. Gabriel García Márquez's *One Hundred Years of Solitude* was published in Spanish in 1967, in English in 1978, and quickly became influential. In 1972 Carter published *The Infernal Desire Machines of Doctor Hoffman*, which was based on a double joke: there was the clear reference to the great German romantic fantasist, E. T. A. Hoffman, and his famous and disturbing tales, but also to a second Dr Hoffman who was familiarly known in certain circles as a drugs guru. Written while she was still in Japan, the book was, she said, meant as a 'flux of mirages', its theme being that 'everything it is possible to imagine can exist'. *The Passion of New Eve* (1977) shifted the setting to a futurist America, taking another classic myth explored by Villiers de l'Ile Adam in his *L'Eve future* of a hundred years earlier. A work of the postmodern world, it is a story about a man–woman 'living legend' set in an America disintegrating into its own dream-fantasies and movie-myths, mirrored selves and doubled images, 'a series of enormous solipsisms'. Even so, out of this theatrical carnival new myths, a new Eve, can be born. In 1979 Carter produced *The Sadeian Woman*, a strong-minded feminist reading of Sade, exploring the need to release fiction into the dangerous spaces of assertive female sexuality. In the same year she brought out *The Bloody Chamber and Other Stories*, rewriting the fairy-tale tradition of Perrault, the Grimm Brothers and others in feminist terms. Flamboyantly retold, the famous stories – 'Beauty and the Beast', 'Red

Riding Hood' – become radical feminist myths, power and energy totally reversed. Captor turns victim, beast becomes heroine. Her fiction began to establish a fantastic new Gothic iconography – a panoply of dolls and toys, puppets and clowns, animals and birds, popular icons and symbols, circuses and music halls, mythic figures from Dracula to the Hollywood movie queens – that allowed her anti-patriarchical and sexually transfiguring fictions to become a form of radical surrealism. Fantasy was a form of freedom, worth taking very seriously, and she made it into serious literature. And her new way of writing would be seen at its best in the two large novels that came at the end of her career, *Nights at the Circus* (1984) and *Wise Children* (1991).

No less wicked, rather more frankly comic, was Beryl Bainbridge, who had published her first novel *A Weekend With Claude* in 1967. Over the Seventies she wrote some of her finest and funniest books: *Harriet Said* (1972), *The Dressmaker* (1973), *The Bottle Factory Outing* (1974), *Sweet William* (1975), *Injury Time* (1977). 'I write about the sort of childhood I had, my parents, the landscape I grew up in: my writing is an attempt to record the past,' she has said. But the past is curious country: who before she wrote *Young Adolf* (1978) would have known that Adolf Hitler grew up partly in Liverpool, where his North Country sister-in-law began recommending brown shirts? In Bainbridge's fiction stories that start in common domestic realism generally evolve into comic fantasy, striking surprise and, very often, death or violence. Born in lower-middle-class Liverpool, growing up in the war years, Bainbridge's world is shaped by pre-war, wartime and post-war politics, and history is never far off. In her world nuclear families collapse, sieges and hostage-takings interrupt domestic life, and the strange constantly attacks the world of the familiar. Bainbridge's special gift is to write a comic fiction that, rather like Muriel Spark's, incorporates the extreme within the perfectly familiar, so domesticating Gothic fiction and undomesticating all the reliable comforts of the traditional family novel. As her fiction developed, history – stories taken from the past – became ever more important. *Watson's Apology* (1984) deals with a Victorian murder case; later books – *Every Man for Himself* (1996), *Master Georgie*

(1998) – deal with the sinking of the Titanic (in a way vastly superior to the film version) and the Crimean War.

Many notable female and feminist careers flourished over the Seventies, deeply changing the flavour of the novel. Books by Elaine Feinstein, Alice Thomas Ellis, A. L. Barker, Bernice Rubens, Susan Hill, Emma Tennant and Rose Tremain changed the scale and terms of female representation, enriching the stock of feminist myth and discourse. One of the most striking and effective of these writers is Fay Weldon, whose first book, *The Fat Woman's Joke*, appeared in 1967; her next two novels were titled *Down Among the Women* (1971) and *Female Friends* (1975). Here she laid claim to a world of her own, the world of professional women with their own jealousies and anxieties, desires and fantasies; it was a world she explored to fascinating and often very savage effect in what now seem her best books – *Praxis* (1978), *Puffball* (1980) and *The Life and Loves of a She-Devil* (1983). A number of these are stories of female revenge either on the opposite sex or their own, her characters showing a frantic and inventive resentment of a world that has sidelined or misdefined them; they show the intimate world of female concerns as well as changing gender values and *mores*. They are also interesting demonstrations of the limits and possibilities of literary technique. Weldon's style is distinctive. The tone is hard and cool, the dialogue stylized, tales are angled and told from this way and that: 'watching me, watching you'. Stories sometimes fold into other stories, and in *Praxis*, her most ambitious and to my mind most interesting novel, we move from first person to third person narration to get new angles on the tale. Weldon's later books, like *The Cloning of Joanna May* (1989), about genetic engineering (a girl finds she has four identical sisters) and set 'in a year of strange events', are satires on modern culture and 'the temporary nature of our lives'. If Weldon's work shows signs of over-productivity or repetition, the central vision is a strong one, the stylish alienations brilliantly done. It is perhaps best summed up in almost the closing lines of *Praxis*: 'She wrote, she raged, grieved and laughed, she thought she nearly died; then, presently, she began to feel better.' For Praxis herself enjoys the modern female revolt into writing that passed through writing in the Seventies, as a new generation of writers less bound by the social history of the past were beginning to make their mark.

5

Even so, two of the most interesting writers of the new generation did still manage to be male. One was Martin Amis, son of Kingsley Amis, who in a fascinating process of dynastic turnover published his first novel *The Rachel Papers* in 1973, when he was twenty-four. Amis had lived in Britain and the USA, gone a separate way from his father, read English at Oxford (a first, naturally), worked in an art gallery, advertising and literary journalism. His first novel is the personal narrative of Charles Highway, still only on the edge of twenty, who has a similar life-journey in mind, and hopes to become a literary wunderkind. Like his father's *Lucky Jim*, the book won Amis the Somerset Maugham Prize. The book shares with the story of Jim Dixon a laddish hero and a firm grip on contemporary culture; in other ways the two writers could hardly have seemed more dissimilar. Charles is truly literary, to the point of seeing himself as something of a fiction. He is obsessed by plotting – particularly to get into Oxford and a girl called Rachel Noyes. He has his own writerly understanding of modern life, 'that it's so mediated that authentic experience is harder to find'. But fiction is not, which is why Charles is perhaps clearly visible to us now as the Angry Young Man of Postmodern Times, born to an age of sex, drugs, extreme situations, self-conscious narcissism. He is quite as ambitious as his author, and his prose is skilled and self-challenging. 'I had begun to explore the literary grotesque,' Charles explains, 'in particular the writings of Charles Dickens and Franz Kafka, to find a world full of bizarre surfaces and sneaky tensions with which I was always trying to invest my own life.' Charles has also been reading a lot of American fiction, like his creator. In the end he gets his warning, obviously to be ignored: 'Literature has a kind of life of its own,' his tutor tells him. 'You can't just use it . . . ruthlessly, for your own ends.' Neither character nor author is fully persuaded; Amis's second novel *Dead Babies* (1975) was, as its title aims to declare, distinguished by its willingness to exploit and shock. The term applies to the six central characters, who live in a world of sexual lassitude and exhaustion, where even two-night stands have become a rarity. Drunk, stoned, drugged, sick, their lives are a self-destructive orgy of sex and drugs. Appleseed Rectory, the main setting, is 'a meeting place of shifting outlines and imploded vacuums; it is a place of lagging time and false memory, a place of street sadness, night fatigue and cancelled sex.' If the tone is satirical, all ends in grim and bloody tragedy. The book is again full of literary allusions; it carries self-conscious addresses from the author, plays games with fictionality, exploits murder story conventions and draws on several remarkable sources, including Denis Diderot's *Rameau's Nephew*, a classic story of the undercutting double. This 'postmodern trickiness', as Amis calls it, became a central feature not just of his own writing but of many contemporaries and imitators over the following years.

There was deep disorder rooted somewhere in Amis's world, and his next work, *Success* (1978), went on to explore it. The novel, with its two male narrators, who are in various fashions doubles of each other, is full of sexual activity and sexual distaste, a grotesque, decadent text, playing wonderfully complicated games with voice and narrative identity, and splendid rills of language. It was clear enough Amis had every kind of self-consciousness – literary, social, sexual, stylistic; it was even possible that these were the writings of a bitter and angrily serious moralist. The charged prose also disclosed multiple literary origins and borrowings; Amis's writing was shaped by powerful readings of many writers, above all Saul Bellow and Vladimir Nabokov, on both of whom Amis wrote essays, and with whom as individuals and texts he built up intricate relations. With the next book, *Other People: A Mystery Story* (1981), Amis complicated his materials. The book begins with a mystery, a blanking-out of identity; we are following the breakdown of a girl, Mary Lamb, and her condition of nominal aphasia, which turns the universe into a kind of *nouveau roman*, afflicts the novel too. Mary has no recollection of who she is or where she comes from: she is thus identityless. In the process of her disintegration and destruction, the gap between herself and others is obscured. Amis later said that the novel is about the girl's death, which is the double of her life (which she lived as Amy Hide). At the same time there is a dominant narrator guiltily responsible for the story. With this book Amis's work became more cunningly perplexing. Questions of the breakdown of self, the naming of reality, the borders of identity, are part of the 'mystery' that his stories deal with, and so is the sense of living in a corrupted, baffling, decaying, materially damaged world.

In 1975 another very distinctive writer established himself no less outrageously. This was Ian McEwan, who at the age of twenty-seven published a first volume of stories, *First Love, Last Rites*; a second very similar collection, *In Between the Sheets*, appeared in 1978. Not since Angus Wilson had a major career started with two volumes of stories rather than a novel. It is significant that Angus Wilson taught McEwan – as did the present author – when he became the first student of creative writing at the University of East Anglia in 1969–70. McEwan was quite as willing as Amis to undertake disturbing and disruptive themes: strange adolescent sex fantasies, concern with death, dismemberment, violence, perversion, madness. Many of the stories are set somewhere near the frontiers of childhood, seen not as an innocent but as an underground world. Many are fantasies, highly solipsistic; they move in unexpected directions, through strange distortions and surprises, into complex grotesquerie. Like Amis, with whom he was quickly compared, McEwan was a technically complex and intricate writer, confidently opening stories out beyond their realistic surfaces into worlds of psychic oddity and intensity. He too used shocking material, though it was evidently under the control of something like reticence; he too appeared an unwilling recorder of a disintegrative world, a world that provoked only alienation, detachment, nausea, 'desolate couplings'. The finest story, 'Psychopolis', is appropriately set in the city of narcissistic nothingness, Los Angeles, postmodernism's unreal city, and shows off its glossy surfaces, inner tensions, empty pluralism. In 1978 McEwan produced his first novel, *The Cement Garden* – a Gothic tale told from the child's-eye viewpoint of a household where both parents die and are buried under the garden, so leaving the young people free to explore their emerging sexuality, incestuous, regressive and transgressive impulses, their own universe. 'I did not kill my father, but I sometimes felt I had helped him on his way,' confesses the book's fourteen-year-old narrator Jack; the book has a sense of psychological and Oedipal truth that was to become a mark of McEwan's more mature fiction. In *The Comfort of Strangers* (1981), McEwan signalled a change, at least of the underlying perspective. The story is set in an imaginary, water-borne European city which is clearly Venice, a literary home to the elusive and sinister. It is an impressionist, nightmare fable of labyrinthine and dangerous relationships, shading from first normality toward an ever more ominously promised fulfilment of 'a violence that is in the air', and is born from a fundamental dislocation of sexual and gender roles and feelings which have 'distorted all relations, all truth'.

By the turn of the Eighties, Amis and McEwan had both established themselves as important writers, troubling and self-conscious visionaries of a world in which dangerous psychological energies moved. Methods of the grotesque, visions from fantasy and dream, feelings of extremity seemed all that could serve to deal with the social and psychological landscapes of times when actuality leaked into the world of the thriller, the self was unable to define itself as a part of society, moral coherence was gone. 'Why do death, murder and victimization appear so frequently in Amis's fiction?' asked one critic, reflecting on what he called 'narrative homicide', a sense of the vengeful nature of the storytelling act. Though hardly a complete answer, it indicated the high self-awareness that went into the themes and methods. Both writers were opening out to a new spirit in British fiction, where writers again crossed the frontiers and broke the limits, attempting to open the novel to a psychological realm in which the sense of crisis was felt. Fantasy is a mode of artistic dissolution, breaking down borders of familiarity, control and identity, opening the door to otherness, acknowledging and defining unconscious forces, at times admitting to a silencing of language and a loss of order and signification. It was a means of freeing British writing from constraints that had long been familiar; it would enlarge during the Eighties, over a time when British fiction – growing ever less 'British'–

would see reality, history and society less as firm givens than part of a fantasy or dream-like disorder, to which its novelists had to attend.

6

As the Seventies closed, a familiar ritual was performed; various soundings were taken to consider whether the English novel was living or dying. In the closing issue of Ian Hamilton's lively Seventies magazine *The New Review*, which shut down in 1978, fifty-six novelists and critics were summoned to reflect on the current state of fiction. Given the historic lessons of this particular type of accountancy, it was no doubt predictable that the results would be very depressing. No one read novels now, it was generally agreed, but perhaps that was because no good new writers appeared any more; the critics remained as blind-eyed as ever, and British fiction was failing to adjust to modern times or to respond to the widening and internationalizing world and its climate of experiment, typified by Thomas Pynchon and Gabriel García Márquez. And when in 1980 the new (or rather renewed) Cambridge magazine *Granta*, edited by Bill Buford, ran a similar symposium, at greater length, on the 'End of the English Novel', similar views flourished. Since the magazine was becoming the outlet for recent American fiction, especially that called 'Dirty Realism', they were not entirely surprising. Apparently British fiction was never more parochial, a tiny parish with its own rules, boundaries and unremitting class preoccupations – while, at the same time, in the USA and Latin America, a great postmodern experiment was flourishing. A few critics did notice the widening of subject matter, the growing plurality of voices, the variety of Englishnesses, the new feminist energies and arguments, and the appearance over the Seventies of a large number of new young writers. Meanwhile, in the same issue, *Granta* published: a segment of a forthcoming novel by Salman Rushdie, which appeared the next year as *Midnight's Children*; a feminist fairy tale from Angela Carter; another fragment from a novel of self-creating language, *Riddley Walker*, by Russell

Hoban, which began, in distinctive speech, 'On my naming day . . .'; and a postmodern speculation by Christine Brooke-Rose. By way of useful warning, the American critic James Gindin did observe that the assumption that American fiction was always superior to British should not be taken for granted. Very likely something was indeed ending: a certain familiar notion of Britishness that had served sensibilities ever since the war, along with the themes, conventions and images that had come to express it. What was surely not ending was the British novel. As the Eighties began, it was in a very clear state of revitalization, from writers old and new, and new angles, new viewpoints, new experiments would go on flourishing over the next decade.

across the Atlantic, film-star Republican President Ronald Reagan, one of the oldest American presidents ever, won office from an enfeebled Jimmy Carter to enter the Oval Office for two terms. A new happy marriage of political minds was celebrated, a re-formed Special Relationship. The Eighties started in step on both sides of the ocean. Both administrations took up office with a fresh, determined conservative mandate, a revised social and economic theory. Both marked a deliberate endeavour to reject or overcome the economic disasters (oil crisis, falling currencies, national humiliations), false directions and faded political dreams of the decade just gone. The British Seventies had ended in a 'Winter of Discontent' that brought society to a halt and displayed the dangers of union power. Similar feelings of discontent and impotence stoked the American 1980 election, as inflation rose, unemployment soared and the 'Great Society' stagnated. The nation was suffering many humiliations: the withdrawal from Vietnam, the scandals of the presidency, then the Iran hostage crisis, which decent but weak President Carter had failed to resolve. The Seventies went down under lost hopes, growing social division, economic problems, fading radical dreams. Impatient voters on each side of the Atlantic looked for something new. There was indeed work to be done; the problem, if you sought employment in a downturning economy, was to find it. A new agenda of social, economic and cultural policies was, though, soon at hand to help the Eighties on their way. Much of it was born of a reaction against the Sixties, the decade that, with its Utopian myths, its freed sexualities, its instinctive anarchism, its dreams of a style-and-consciousness revolution and its own new variants of repressive tolerance had assumed a modern cultural transformation that unending affluence could easily support.

Over decades dominant cultural languages had changed radically. The Fifties largely read culture with a moral vocabulary, the Sixties with a radical sociological one, the Seventies with the language of personal consciousness. The Eighties spoke the language of economics, read culture with a discourse based on myths of money. Not radical sociologists nor personal consciousness gurus but post-Keynesian economists of the Chicago school provided the times with their working rate of exchange. Their theory, 'Monetarism', dominated not simply the economic but the social and cultural atmosphere of the day. Welfare State values that had run their course through the post-war years proved to be seriously over-spent. New economic fictions (money fictions are as fictional as any other fictions) now took over, and were applied to all manner of things, not least the world of culture and the arts, which rapidly became commodified in remarkable ways. The age of the 'free market' constructed as commodities much that had been perceived as of independent social value or moral necessity. The world marketed itself to itself in a universe of service and consumption. Like it or not (and most writers and intellectuals definitely did not, since apart from the intrinsic humanism of their calling they were now mostly reared either in the Welfare State sensibility of the Fifties, or the radical-revolutionary agendas of the Sixties), 'Thatcherism' proved a powerful and dominant philosophy, and the 'Thatcher Revolution' a real political revolution which brought much in the post-war Lib-Lab consensus to an end.

Margaret Thatcher could never naturally consent to consensus. As she correctly observed in 1979, Old Testament prophets never said: 'Brothers, I want a consensus.' The times required, she said, 'conviction politics'; these she had to offer. 'Liberal values' lost severely in credit, and if most intellectuals assumed the direction of progress was toward an ever greater egalitarianism or the proletarian society, the run of the decade suggested it was not. The revolution that was reviving the Western economies and asserting the strength of international capitalism was not a proletarian but a bourgeois revolution, based on the individual rather than the state, the market rather than the command economy, personal enterprise rather than collective aid. At the same time the old manufacturing base of Britain was eroding as the times moved toward a hi-tech service economy. Manufacturing moved its centres into the paced-up advancing economies of the Second World and the Pacific Rim, or even the Third World. The class, labour and gender stratifications that had marked Britain for decades were in change, like the ideologies they generated. The traditional Lib-Lab view had emphasized common collectivity, the 'great society' that redistributed wealth among all members. The new order emphasized individualism, enterprise and entrepreneurship, and sought to roll back the frontiers of the state. In a phrase much quoted against her, Mrs Thatcher said society 'did not exist'. She may fairly be presumed to mean that the individual was prior to or equal to the collectivity of the state, that she was rolling back the 'nanny state' that organized the interests of all. And in truth, in the Eighties, a triumphant moment in the evolution of latter-day capitalism, society did not quite exist. The age built its temples and monuments in the form of investment banks, new stock exchange buildings, shopping malls, science parks, headquarters for multinational corporations and new communications conglomerates. Beside these stood many of the less well-endowed lots of culture: declining universities, closing theatres, under-endowed schools and struggling hospitals. Public spaces deteriorated, parks closed, crime increased, drugs problems intensified, and the sociologists observed, along with a growth in personal wealth and the endless multiplication of designer commodities, the rise of a new 'underclass'.

By releasing enterprise, business endeavour, growth in the service and banking sectors, and by freeing their economies to the energies of global capitalism and modern media and communications, Thatcher and Reagan began to regenerate their societies. At the same time pressure grew on socialist economics, the command economies of the Communist bloc. At the start of the Eighties Cold War intensified, as Ronald Reagan condemned the 'evil empire' and raised the missile stakes with 'Star Wars'. In fact the rising demands of defence spending were bankrupting the Russian economy, further drained by the fact that the true Russian currency was not the rouble but the dollar, many of them banked abroad by the *nomenklatura*. Russia was also disastrously over-committed in Afghanistan, and the leakage of frontiers in the age of satellite and digital communication meant that the glossy self-imaging of designer corporate capitalism could not be excluded from the far side of the Curtain. In 1985 the USSR acquired an intellectual, economically numerate Party Secretary, Mikhail Gorbachev, who resumed détente. A policy of *glasnost* (greater openness) began, along with a major reconstruction (*perestroika*) of the Soviet system. The ideological stasis in Central and Eastern

Europe, the chilly freeze of history brought by the Cold War, began to thaw. In 1988 a 'democratic' system was established in the USSR itself, along with a prospect of autonomy for the regions. Gorbachev was urging the adoption of a market economy and the Iron Curtain that ran across Europe north to south was falling fast; in November 1989 the Berlin Wall came down. In 1991, after an aborted Communist counter-coup, Gorbachev resigned as president, on the day before the Soviet Union was dissolved.

The post-war world was over, the Cold War was done. Modern corporate capitalism had triumphed, though it was less than clear to many – not least the Russian planners whose attempt to introduce the 'free market' was proving expensive – what it was. Meanwhile in Western Europe a new boom gave fresh impetus to the idea of a European economic, political and cultural community, and the dream of an affluent united Europe with common corporate interests became real. In fact the nation state was fast dissolving, though Mrs Thatcher's Britain was a patriotic place, ostensibly secure in interests and historical identity. A war in the Falklands and an aggressive policy on cooperation with Europe asserted as much: Britain was Britain, a long-term democracy with a sovereign identity, and not Europe. The rhetoric concealed much fundamental transformation: Eighties Britain was a fast-changing scene. Old manufacture was dying, historic male employment falling away. In parts of the nation gentrification and growth advanced: hi-tech industries, service industries, traffic, motion, travel, leisure, fast food and gourmet eating all boomed. Other regions away from southern England declined and entire communities collapsed. If the Sixties had the hippie, the Eighties had the yuppie. Psychedelic shapes converted to straight lines, flared jeans to sharp suits, sex (now tainted with the plague of AIDS) to money. Money was no longer hard and metallic; it was the plastic card, the cash dispenser, the share portfolio, the fast-changing figures on the VDU as London locked into Wall Street and the Hang Seng talked to the Dow and the Nikkei. The erotics of trading grew; the Big Bang came at last. In 1986 the London Stock Exchange was deregulated, opening the markets to international intervention and rapid boom, not too long after followed by slump. Meanwhile in the

North and the Midlands, old manufacturing sites were becoming industrial sheds, distribution centres, shopping malls for a new goods-based, high-spending economy. Communications, publishing and new technologies grew, and the book itself turned into a profitable High Street designer commodity. Other fundamental changes were also observed, not least the extent to which Britain, as a result of post-colonial immigration and increasing movement of peoples, had become a pluri-cultural society. For a time the buzz of the dealing room, the bleep of the mobile phone, the thrill of the personal computer, the chatter of the wine bar, the pleasure of designer labels and gourmet restaurants, the thrill of the high-rise apartment in Docklands, seemed the essential spirit of the Eighties.

So did Mrs Thatcher herself – often unpopular, yet unquestionably the most influential political figure in Britain since the Second World War. She was unprecedentedly elected for two further terms; her prime-ministerial career ran right across the decade. When she was ousted from office in 1990, the fall came neither from a disillusioned electorate nor a strong Opposition, but dismay from within her own party with her Old Testament prophecies and often abrasive style; as well as from growing party division over the future of British national identity, within or outside Europe, and awareness that the changes of her own decade had undermined many of her own policies. In Britain her fall felt like the end of an era. But it was very clear that an era had ended worldwide. In Eastern Europe the Marxist interpretation of history and economics no longer served as sufficient explanation; an ideological age was over. While Communist leaders were dislodged, often imprisoned, in some cases killed, across Eastern Europe, an uncertain new order started taking shape. Forty-five years of post-war history ceased as its monuments fell, its statues tumbled, its streets and squares were renamed, its frontiers redrawn, its statehoods removed. Likewise the mental maps that had served several generations since the end of the Second World War no longer worked. This was, historians said, a 'New World Order' (it soon became a New World Disorder). It was, proposed Francis Fukuyama, perhaps 'The End of History': 'What we may be witnessing is not just the end of the Cold War, or the passing of a particular period of post-war history, but the end of history as such: that is, the end point of mankind's ideological evolution and the universalization of Western liberal democracy as the final form of government,' he suggested. For a moment it seemed that the values of the free society, the independent nation and the humanistic self had triumphed, and the Nineties started on a high plateau of hope. Like everything in history, or even after it, it was not to last.

2

In literary culture, the Eighties can now be seen as a seriously interesting as well as rapidly changing time. In British terms the Eighties define a clear episode: the well-marked epoch between Margaret Thatcher's 1979 election to office and her fall from grace eleven years later. It was a time of reappraisals and ideological restructurings; also the period when much else in the world order was transforming, not least the novel and cultural life itself. It was a time of many doubts and dark prophecies – above all from writers and intellectuals who in general cluster toward the leftward end of the thinking spectrum, and who had little love for the Thatcherite mood.[1] 'It's suddenly chic to be rich, and unchic to be a socialist,' observed Margaret Drabble, noting the breakdown of the Lib-Lab consensus that had run through post-war British political life. It seemed almost improper, she added, to complain that all was not well, yet the writer always has an awkward 'natural curiosity about what's going on underground'. This 'natural curiosity' became a common theme of Eighties writing, not least in Drabble's own work. In the Thatcher years she produced

[1] A characteristic reaction to her came from Anthony Burgess, writing with 'a terrible objectivity' from Monaco in the Scandinavian magazine *Scanorama* in October 1989. Observing a market economy England divided between North and South, old and young, rich and poor, culture and cash, he noted: 'There is a piquancy in seeing the most successful politician of the age as a member of a sex traditionally downtrodden. The trouble with her is that, despite the allure and the purposefulness, she is not likeable. Churchill, with all his faults, was even loveable. So was the cuckolded Edwardian dandy Harold Macmillan. But we have had ten years of a lady who chills the heart and stultifies the national imagination.'

some of her biggest, bleakest, most realistic novels about the state of the nation, where decent liberalism is broken down by corporatism or a culture of moral chaos. Her first novel for the Eighties suggests by its title, *The Middle Ground* (1980), the position her fiction was still seeking to inhabit. Her socio-political sequence, *The Radiant Way* (1987), *A Natural Curiosity* (1989) and *The Gates of Ivory* (1991), portrayed critically and gloomily a world where public and private split apart, cities lose order and become apocalyptic, while death, global crisis and a sense of impending catastrophe impinge on the decent and intelligent bourgeois lives that have been central to her fiction, so that they begin to splinter in despair and confusion.

She was hardly alone in her vision. Most writers of the era of Thatcherism saw it as a time of disaster, decay, human neglect, lost wholeness: even those who had already judged the world to be in this condition before she governed it. Salman Rushdie's novel *The Satanic Verses* (1988) was, of course, to win its author a tragic fate as his sceptical and fictionalist view of all texts, including those sacred to Islam; yet the primary theme of this novel was in fact the fragmentation of an incoherent but increasingly migrant and multi-cultural Britain, dominated at this time by one 'Mrs Torture'. Meanwhile images of urban crisis and historical apocalypse intensified in British fiction, as if in a return to the mood that had shaped the fiction of Decadents and Naturalists a hundred years earlier. Bonfires of the vanities appeared in British fiction, as they did now in American. Angus Wilson's *Setting the World on Fire* (1980) seemed to set an apocalyptic and incendiary trend. Peter Ackroyd's *Hawksmoor* (1985) is a tale of London Gothic, with strange crimes and odd codes of architecture stalking the churchyards of the city of London, as a famous eighteenth-century church architect and a modern detective cover the same ground. Paul Bailey's *Gabriel's Lament* (1986) is another novel which creates apocalyptic London with Dickensian depth and intensity. Michael Moorcock's *Mother London* (1988) draws together the Dickensian city with the age of the Blitz and then the new age of the Eighties. Martin Amis's *London Fields* (1989), consciously contemporary, sees the city as lost Arcadia, a killer-haunted metropolis hung on the edge of some great ecological holocaust (Amis commented: 'If you are interested in ugliness and sleaze [as he was], London is the place to be,' though some said New York). Geoff Dyer's *The Colour of Money* (1989) offered a streetwise angle on London's chaos and decline. Justin Cartwright's *Look at it This Way* (1990) considered it as a carnivorous jungle. Iain Sinclair in his documentary black humour fiction *Downriver* (1991) knowingly explored its hidden corners, weird extremities and strange intersections. In Angela Carter's dissenting, ambitious and deliberately raucous *Wise Children* (1991), which shows London as a city split completely in two by its river, just like Budapest, two worlds are displayed in overlap: one established, one provisional, one on the right and the other on the wrong (which of course is the right) side of the tracks.

Thatcher's Britain was finding its place in fiction; and the Eighties were after all to prove a highly vigorous and productive era in the novel. New writers, new versions and new styles emerged in great numbers; at the same time their manners were often carapaces over social dismay. Even before she came to office, Martin Amis appeared to specialize in wonderfully Thatcherite titles (*Success*, 1978). Once she came to power, surely no writer better caught the note of her era, with its apocalyptic anxieties, sense of moral loss, its cynicism, greed and underlying alarm. In *Money: A Suicide Note* (1984), Amis tapped a perfect title for the times. 'As Saul Bellow said [here was the great guru of the age of excess accumulation, where more "it" always means less "we"] it seemed for a while in the Eighties that money was the one thing that didn't stink,' Amis explained. 'Everything was questionable, but money was a vital substance you knew where you were with.' Money entered many of the titles; though theatre largely shifted to high-presentation musicals, Caryl Churchill's play *Serious Money* did catch a similar note ('Sexy greed *is* the late Eighties'). Money is everywhere in Amis's novel; 'While making love, we often talk about money,' explains its grubby anti-hero narrator, John Self. 'I like it. I like dirty talk.' An artist of tacky TV commercials and pornographic film-scripts, Self lives firmly in the present, as opposed to the past and the future: 'The future's futures have never looked so rocky. Don't put money on it. Take my advice and stick to the present.

It's the real stuff, the only stuff.' John Self, 'this prole, this Goth, this foul-mouthed Clockwork Orange,' as one reviewer called him, devotee of junk-food, junk-money, junk-work, junk-nature and junk-self, was plainly a figure for the times.[2] Treated in part as the target of Amis's satirical and disappointed moralism, he is also a version of the author as fragmentary and disintegrating self; even his voice and setting is transatlantic, and this is a tale of two apocalyptic cities, London and Manhattan. Amis himself was now a figure for the late century urban-decadent romantic, cultivating all the special flavours of disillusionment, cosmic weariness, end-of-the-world news. Taking his own – or Self's – advice, he did stick largely to the present and his hard style, mordant wit, vividly rolling constructions and weary ways became the most imitated style of the day. He was hardly alone in his disaffections: the political fury behind Angela Carter's novels, the dark notes of Ian McEwan's chilling Eighties tales, where an innocence perhaps never there is in the process of being corrupted by false politics, bad history, the sado-masochistic struggles of sex and gender, desire and perversity, were also part of the mood. In the Eighties, fiction set in the present generally emerged as a tale of large-scale dismay.

There was admittedly a paradox here. In this age of commerce over culture, profit over public service, drama was declining, serious theatre yielding to box-office musical, TV drama leaving contemporary issue screenplays in favour of classic nostalgia or formatted genre (though the Granada version of Waugh's *Brideshead Revisited* was, for all its gloss, serious in its social history, and was shortly followed by an extended and brilliant adaptation of *The Jewel in the Crown*). Yet fiction was in fact enjoying a time of revitalization. The novelist was

---

2 'One of the chief glories of Martin Amis's elaborate, enticing, subtle, irritating, overpowering new fiction is the astonishing narrative voice he has devised, the jagged, spent, streetwise, gutterwise, gutteral mid-Atlantic twang, the buttonholing, earbending, lughole-jarring monologue with "all the energy, the electricity . . . all the hustle and razz" of midtown, fastfood, fastback, fastfuck Manhattan, of the dangerous districts uptown where everything is frazzled, charred, blistered (like the narrator), the sleaze and grate of louche London-on-the-make . . .' wrote Eric Korn in *The Times Literary Supplement* (5 October 1984).

fashionable, the book was back. New user-friendly bookstores opened in the Thatcherite high-street, and publishing and communications takeovers enlarged the worth of literary properties, including writers like Amis or Rushdie. The fattening newspapers and magazines were busy with literary chatter; the hype of literary prizes and public signings lifted the profile of literary writers, especially when they were young and comely, or addressed themselves straight to the youth generation. Hence certain writers, above all the most bitter ones, strangely acquired the appearance and celebrity of Thatcherite entre-preneurs, assuming the rewards of literary fame, financial success, and growing as famous for the sale of film rights (or the film-scripts Hollywood now purchased them to write) as for their novels them-selves. For the novel was sexy again; its works refracted a streetwise portrait of changing and style-consuming times. Novelists were them-selves an economic miracle, anti-Thatcher Thatcherite icons in an age of 'lifestyles', 'role-models' and a culture of consumption, emulation, stylistic competition, presentation, glossy and mannered 'success'. Literary fiction competed with blatantly commercial genre fiction in the charts. 'Postmodernism' became a name not for obscure and baffling experiments done in Paris but an elegant commodity that put smart novels along with designer restaurants, art museums, crumpled Italian suiting and upmarket foreign foods. All this contributed to the distinctive mood – best characterized as post-liberal irony – that ran through much of the writing. The Eighties resembled the Fifties in the flourish of new writers, fictional energy and general air of stylish stylistic discovery that abounded.

Even so, while some writers were making the very most of John Self's advice that the present was 'the real stuff, the only stuff', a good many British novelists were once again turning back to history. Retrospective fiction now became highly popular; the quarrel with the Victorian age seemed entirely over and done. Even as Mrs Thatcher sought to restore 'Victorian values' (commercial enterprise coupled with stable family life), and while the Victorian classic authors (Dickens, the Brontës, Thackeray, Trollope) enjoyed a significant revival, novels perhaps influenced by John Fowles's powerful re-creation of the past in the present began to revisit an age when individualism felt stronger and social values clearer. The End of Empire was still a key theme: unsentimentally treated, for instance, in the novels of Barry Unsworth, who in the splendid *Pascali's Island* (1985) looked at the waning of imperial Venice, in *Sugar and Rum* (1988) at the Liverpool slave trade, in *Sacred Hunger* (Booker Prize, 1992) at the terrible voyages of the Middle Passage. Dying empires, fading lives, glimpses of greater things, filled the novels of the Anglo-Irish author William Trevor (*The Silence in the Garden*, 1988); the wickedly witty fiction of Molly Keane (*Good Behaviour*, 1981, *Loving and Giving*, 1988) also caught the decline of the Irish Protestant ascendancy. The wars of the century became an essential subject, captured in J. L. Carr's archaeological novel *A Month in the Country* (1980) and Isabel Colegate's *The Shooting Party* (1980), set, like many novels now, in 1913, with the aristocratic age finally dying as the Great War approached. These are fine writers, and these are fine books. But they soon brought the familiar complaint that writers were evading the present by returning to tired forms and old verities: '. . . it seems to me that the main thrust of the best new writing of the first years of the Eighties has been backward, into the past,' one critic, Hugh Hebert, complained in the *Guardian*, reflecting that novelists were also reverting to 'the traditional novel, with its burgher-like literary virtues'.

Yet the past was not only a foreign country where they did things differently, but difficult and perplexing literary territory; and many of these books were hardly conventional returns to the burgher novel Angus Wilson's Herr Birnbaum celebrated. In a splendid and picto-graphic book, *A Humument* (1980), the painter Tom Philips took a late Victorian social novel – W. H. Mallock's *A Human Document* (1892) – and by over-painting some words and highlighting others constructed a visual, random, provoking narrative that was a post-modern media collage. Peter Ackroyd, writing a biography of Dickens, used *Little Dorrit* as the foundation for creating a new version of the story on a modern film-set in *The Great Fire of London* (1982). David Lodge's *Nice Work* (1988) returned to the Victorian 'Condition of England' novel and the industrial novel of Mrs Gaskell, Disraeli and others to explore the 'Two Nations Britain' of his own day. A

Marxist-feminist lecturer at Rummidge University in the industrial Midlands knows just how to deconstruct this kind of fiction, but is then asked to shadow the plain-speaking managing director of a local engineering company; so two New Nations meet, along with two styles of fiction, self-conscious and realistic. These meetings seemed frequent in Eighties fiction, where postmodern experiments frequently assimilated or merged with traditional narrative. In her ambitious *Possession* (Booker Prize, 1990) A. S. Byatt built similar bridges between Victorian romance and artistry and the contemporary world of feminist and deconstructive thought. Possibly it was less that novelists were reverting to old forms and narrative certainties, than making the past relevant to the present and making history past and present the material of literary examination. For the nature of history and history-writing was an issue among novelists, British, American and Latin American, as it was too among historians themselves. 'There are times when you have to disentangle history from fairy tale,' Graham Swift observes in *Waterland* (1983), one of the best books of the era, and a tale about the unreliable and watery layers of history amid which all present lives are lived. Serious questions of literary 'archaeology', a term that grew fashionable in the decade, were important elements in the experiment of Eighties fiction.

Often the subject was less history than the morbid ghosts left to us by history: the two world wars, the Holocaust, the Nuremberg Trials – 'It is this ordinariness I must capture,' observes the narrator of Graham Swift's *Out of This World* (1988). The atomic explosions of Hiroshima and Nagasaki recur and recur: 'the light was a premonition of his death,' reflects J. G. Ballard in his memoir *The Empire of the Sun*. The chilly mirror world of Cold War hostilities has been explored in the novels of John Le Carré, and in *The Little Drummer Girl* (1983) he took on a new age of terrorism and looked at another modern scene where undercover operations and espionage played a big part, the Arab–Israeli conflict. The traumas of apartheid South Africa, the apparently irresolvable and cruel troubles of Northern Ireland and the dangers of nuclear disaster were recurring themes. Forty-five years of Cold War peace had still not driven away the nuclear horrors and the image of the Holocaust or loosened their hold on fiction (thus

of history. So are the works of Julian Barnes, a student of French literature: *Flaubert's Parrot* (1984), *Staring at the Sun* (1986), *A History of the World in 10½ Chapters* (1989). 'Postmodern trickiness' was, if anything, a general convention among serious young writers by this date. 'The self is not a steady voice that has need for itself any more,' Martin Amis explained, justifying the elaborate structure of *Money*, where 'John Self' (a version, presumably, of Martin Amis) meets not just Martin Amis but his female twin Martina Twain, 'It's a babble, various gibbering needs and envies.' With this fragmentation went, he explained, a breakdown of the old literary borders of genre, meaning that fiction was now a grotesque and multiple form of comedy and parody: 'all sorts of things are getting into the comic novel that shouldn't be there, like rapists and murderers. There's a kind of promiscuity of style which is perhaps characteristic of the collapse of various structures in society and fiction.'

Amis is talking here about something – the mixing and merging of styles, genres, cultural layers and levels, in other and more topical words 'intertextualization' or 'crossover' – that had been the strong preoccupation of American postmodernists since the Sixties. According to John Barth, we lived in the age both of the literature of exhaustion and the literature of replenishment. According to André Malraux, writing some time earlier, it was the time of the 'imaginary museum', where all styles were available simultaneously, without order or hierarchy. Postmodern manners were now an achieved part of British fiction. Texts constantly asserted their self-conscious fictionality; authors intruded into their stories or crossed over with their characters; fictions merged with facts or documentaries; old tales changed place with new ones; literary high culture traded with streetwise pop styles. There was no end to the works that proclaimed the death of the author, the collapse of the self, the end of humanism; worked the borders of the grotesque and fantastic; employed schlock, horror, pornography; borrowed in style and spirit from the multimedia, multi-styled, multi-cultural plenitude. The term 'Postmodernism' was itself a movable feast, for the argument around it was changing again. As books on the matter jostled the Jane Fonda hip-and-thigh diets in the bookstores, it came to mean less the ironic self-consciousness of artists than an overall state of culture: the 'post-modern condition' itself. This was the title of a book by the French cultural philosopher Jean-François Lyotard (1979), which appeared in English in 1984.[3] Lyotard explained that there were no longer any Grand Narratives which philosophers could construct or human beings depend on; totalizing explanations no longer set the scene, and the great ideologies had gone, leaving narrative in charge in its eclectic variety. As Lyotard put it: 'Simplifying to the extreme, I define *postmodern* as incredulity toward meta-narratives.' Another influential French philosopher Jean Baudrillard argued that the texture of the age was one of 'hyper-reality', where surfaces were without depths, images held no inner content, selves had no centre, and in the great and surreal theme-park which is the Disneyland world of the cybernetic future 'power will only belong to those with no origins and no authenticity, who know how to exploit the situation to the full'. Another Marxist critic from the world of American critical affluence, Fredric Jameson, offered analytically 'to take postmodernism for what it says it is', and gave a compelling if densely worked account of its Americanized, variegated, surface-layered mass-cultural and multi-cultural phenomena, exemplified by glitz architecture (Los Angeles' Westin Bonaventura Hotel), shopping fever, MTV, video culture, computer art and design, body art, theme-park history, root-less nostalgia, cyberpunk and 'blank parody', or the knowing and yet ignorant cannibalization of the styles of the past. Jameson offered a substanceless (in most senses) world in which life was lifestyle, presentation replaced people, statement was always quote, history was instant nostalgia and every building was scaffolded in pastiche. It was a world of icons, screens and surfaces. It displayed, he said, a

3 Jean-Francois Lyotard, *The Postmodern Condition: A Report on Knowledge*, trans. G. Bennington and B. Massumi (Manchester, 1984). (Lyotard was also the biographer of André Malraux, to whose own theories of earlier date his bear a resemblance.) Other books mentioned are Jean Baudrillard, *America* trans. C. Turner (London, 1988), and Fredric Jameson, *Postmodernism: Or, the Cultural Logic of Late Capitalism* (Durham, NC, 1991). I have discussed the topic in relation to modern American fiction (where 'reality is a decadent and absurd fantasy in the midst of plentitude') in *The Modern American Novel* (London and New York, rev. ed., 1992).

process of 'global gentrification' where everything was digested as fashion, design or style.

It was some such culture that quickly became processed as the fictional world of the Eighties. John Self is a self without a self, and a consumer of culture in its every aspect without possessing a culture. Contemporary culture is generally seen as decentred. George Orwell had seen England as a family with the wrong members in control; now there was no family, no familiarity, no control. The apocalyptic note is characteristic of much Eighties writing: it wrote of a culture which was random and 'junk', where time was often dislocated and oppressive hints of danger, disaster, crisis were universal. There was a sense of recent history as essentially a history of catastrophes leading to more catastrophe, and dark themes present in fiction since the Fifties seemed to intensify. Science fiction had been exercising considerable influence on post-war fiction, and now it came even closer to the literary novel. With the publication of *The Empire of the Sun* (1984), set in Shanghai before and during the war, based on his own childhood experience, J. G. Ballard became a mainstream novelist. His work and that of writers like Amis, Iain Banks or Ian McEwan no longer seemed in different traditions or separated by cultural layers. Degraded cities, ravaged fields, dying clouds, polluted landscapes, drug-trashed visions once seemed the special preserve of science fiction; now they filled many novels. 'Flies get dizzy spells and beeze have booze problems,' writes Amis in one of the fine perorations of *Money*. 'Robin redbreasts hit the deck with psychosomatic ulcers and cholesterol overload. In the alleys, dogs are coughing their hearts out on snout and dope.' In Ian McEwan's *The Child in Time* (1988), set in a future where Thatcherism has gone to the extremity, the rot is found even in the weather, which creates 'a sense of crisis and excitement'. The London of Rushdie's *The Satanic Verses* is going surreally crazy in an extravagant heatwave. So common now was end-of-the-world news, disaster vision, that it became a relief to find writers who possessed the sceptical arts of comedy – as did Amis himself, Rushdie at best, Angela Carter, William Boyd, David Lodge and Howard Jacobson, who knew when extremity was extravagance.

British 'postmodernism' was, it seemed, following the course of

American, which had gone through a cycle from Sixties black humour and fictionalist playfulness to a grotesque, extreme, heightened realism that was concerned with the late modern urban scene, seen as violent, criminal, estranging and deeply depersonalizing, to the point of emptying out the self. Eighties British fiction often showed a similar temper; much of it had a *fin-de-siècle* feel, and often it echoed the styles and tropes of the previous *fin de siècle*, where the clock seemed stopped on the very edge of danger. Thus Angela Carter set her wonderfully elaborate novel *Nights at the Circus* (1984) on the trans-figuring moment of the turn into the twentieth century; her heroine Fevvers is a garrulous reflection of the different and radical images that can surround a figure described as a 'child of the century'. Millennial thoughts run everywhere through Martin Amis's apocalyptic urban novel from the late Eighties, *London Fields* (1989), which is set in 1999, when cyclonic winds blow and there are rumours of a Second Coming, though this story of death for everybody becomes the story of a murder. Amis explains he had thought of calling the book *Millennium*, but 'everything is called *Millennium* just now'. And so it was. Corrupted Utopias, collapsing cities and urban terrors were widespread. Gothic violence, the grotesque, the fantastic and the uncanny were back from the tomb. Innocence here is generally corrupted, psychic extremities and pathologies are frequently explored. Violence erupts suddenly, atrocities are never far distant, accidents are everywhere, death stalks a dead world. The old figures of Gothic culture – Dracula, Frankenstein's monster, Vlad the Impaler, Jekyll and Hyde, Jack the Ripper (now in the fashionable guise of 'the serial killer', marauding urban man who brings random danger out of city darkness) – were dusted down from roles in earlier fictions and popular movies and recycled as the stuff of postmodern narrative, with a mixture of the sinister and the grand literary effect. Thus Clive Sinclair, a very Nabokovian and playful writer, incorporated Vlad the Impaler and other Gothic figures into his meta-textual *Bibliosexuality* (1973); later books like *Blood Libels* (1985) and *Cosmetic Effects* (1989) both explore the lush gallery of grotesque subject-matter and a brooding and sinister sexuality in a spirit of elaborate and comic fictionality. Iain Banks used a wide variety of bizarre psycho-sexual horrors in *The Wasp Factory* (1984) and *Walking on Glass* (1985). Patrick McGrath neatly assimilated his subject-matter into his title in his highly mannered Gothic novel *The Grotesque* (1989). Iain Sinclair's *Downriver* (1991) 'shows the city in the grip of a psychotic crisis', says Angela Carter. And the radical violence of gender relations is tilted in the female direction in the revisionist Gothic of her own novels, where fantasy, narrative richness and strange and protean transformations and magickings break down conventional values, conventional gender referents, fixed and stable fictional types – all in the best interests of the illicit and the illegitimate as the best source of fiction.

As happened in the 1890s, these destabilizing notes – Gothic gloom, historical despair, psychic disturbance, cosmic dismay – were accompanied by a buoyant sense of literary replenishment, a reaching out to all kinds of genres and all sorts of styles. Besides Gothic mannerism there was strong influence from Latin American 'magic realism' and the related styles developed in Central and Eastern Europe during the Communist era. 'Magic realism' is important, said the Czech novelist Milan Kundera, because it transforms but does not deny historical and political realities; it is a fiction marked by 'our special humour: a humour capable of seeing history as grotesque'. The distorted worlds of modern history were now familiar in British fiction: in Lisa Saint Aubin de Terán's novel of domestic imprisonment on a hacienda in Venezuela, *Keepers of the House* (1982), Nicholas Shakespeare's *The Vision of Elena Silves* (1990), as imaginary fictional playground in Louis de Bernières's *The War of Don Emmanuel's Nether Parts* (1990). The troubled, now fast-shifting political world of Central and Eastern Europe also became an important setting, in books from my own *Rates of Exchange* (1983) to Brian Moore's *The Colour of Blood* (1987), Bruce Chatwin's haunting *Utz* (1988) and Tibor Fischer's later, very knowing *Under the Frog* (1992). Britain was now in 'Europe', which became an important subject in the fiction of Chatwin, McEwan, Julian Barnes, Anita Brookner and Penelope Fitzgerald. Africa also took on high visibility, especially in its troublespots: William Boyd wrote *A Good Man in Africa* (1981) and *An Ice-Cream War* (1982); Christopher Hope powerfully explored his native South

Africa in *Kruger's Alp* (1984) and *The Hottentot Room* (1986). Nadine Gordimer, the radical South African novelist who had won the Booker for *The Conservationist* in 1974, published *Burger's Daughter* in 1979 (it was banned after the Soweto Riots) and *A Sport of Nature* in 1987; in 1991 she was awarded the Nobel Prize for Literature. South Africa was a land of major English-language writers, including André Brink and J. M. Coetzee, who published *Waiting for the Barbarians* in 1980, and whose powerful *Life and Times of Michael K.* won the Booker in 1983. Other scenes became familiar: Hilary Mantel wrote of Dubai in *Eight Months on Ghazzah Street* (1988) and Penelope Lively of Egypt in *Moon Tiger* (Booker Prize, 1987).

Increasingly the English novel, as Martin Amis said, was 'starting to go into places where the English novel didn't go, and was being too fastidious about'. This went along with a new era of travel-writing, rivalling the Thirties: Bruce Chatwin, Paul Theroux, Colin Thubron and Jonathan Raban, all also novelists, were among the best performers. British-based writers now came from a widening variety of origins and sources. With one-third of its population made up of ethnic minorities, London was a pluri-cultural world city. Paul Theroux, Russell Hoban and Rachel Ingalls were American-born writers based in Britain. Many writers were of African, Caribbean, Indian or Pakistani origin, or else were bicultural. Some, like George Lamming and Samuel Selvon, belonged to the Windrush generation, of those who came over in a tide of post-war migration into Britain. Salman Rushdie was born in Bombay to a liberal merchant family that later moved to Karachi, Pakistan, and was educated at Rugby and Cambridge; Vikram Seth was born in India, Adam Zameenzad in Pakistan, Timothy Mo in Hong Kong, Kazuo Ishiguro in Japan. African writers often spent time in Britain, including the Nigerian Chinua Achebe, whose remarkable novel *Things Fall Apart* had appeared in 1958. The literary-cultural mixture was fed by many things: the social mixture of post-colonial British society, the globalization of cultural relationships, the spread of international Anglophobe fiction and the feeling that, as Rushdie put it, contemporary writing was sailing on the 'sea of stories'. The reference points of English-language fiction were widening greatly. Ireland had always been a great centre of fiction, to the point where its tradition often seemed distinctive and independent. Yet the relationship stayed close, and now to the work of well-established writers like William Trevor, Edna O'Brien and Molly Keane were added the works of a generation of Irish writers whose fiction played a big part in the culture of the Eighties: John Banville (*Kepler*, 1980, *Mefisto*, 1986, *The Book of Evidence*, 1989), John McGahern (*The Pornographer*, 1979, *Amongst Women*, 1990), Claire Boylan (*Black Baby*, 1988), Neil Jordan, (*The Past*, 1980, *The Dream of a Beast*, 1983), Roddy Doyle (*The Commitments*, 1988), Deirdre Madden (*The Birds of the Innocent Wood*, 1988), Patrick McCabe (*The Butcher Boy*, 1992). And the conflicts and horrors of Ulster provoked other important fiction, from Bernard Mac Laverty (*Lamb*, 1980, *Cal*, 1983), Maurice Leitch (*Silver's City*, 1981) and Glenn Patterson (*Burning Your Own*, 1988, *Fat Lad*, 1992).

The nationalities and the regions of the British mainland were also developing a new writing. Scots fiction prospered as rarely before, some of the writing self-consciously regional, some powerfully experimental or international in spirit. Alan Massie, who had written splendid historical fiction, treated Scots subjects in such books as *One Night in Winter* (1984). Glasgow acquired a remarkable and innovative writer in Alasdair Gray, a novelist and artist whose postmodern fictions include *Lanark* (1981), *1982, Janine* (1984) and his 'up-to-date nineteenth-century novel' *Poor Things* (1991). James Kelman brought a new, grainy, disaffected vernacular into his treatments of working-class Glaswegian life, in *The Busconductor Hines* (1983) and especially *A Disaffection* (1989). Jeff Torrington wrote about the Glasgow Gorbals in *Swing Hammer Swing* (1992), and Liz Lochhead, Janice Galloway and A. L. Kennedy all chronicled the spirit of contemporary Scots life. Wales had its own novelists: Kate Roberts, writing in Welsh, Bruce Chatwin (*On the Black Hill*, 1982), Russell Celyn Jones (*Soldiers and Innocents*, 1990). And, perhaps encouraged by a new sense of nature and history, the rural-regional novel began to return. In different ways Graham Swift's splendid Fenland tale *Waterland* (1983), Lindsay Clarke's East Anglian fantasy *A Chymical Wedding* (1989), D. J. Taylor's powerful mixture of rural and urban *Great Eastern Land* (1986) and Adam Thorpe's *Ulverton* (1992) showed that, in the greening age, the regional novel still belonged within British fiction mythology. For all Mrs Thatcher's leadership, Eighties Britain was a land in the process of fragmenting. As internationalism grew, so did the sense of diversity, the qualities of principality, county, place and region. British fiction in the Eighties thus felt less like the fiction of a communal and agreed culture than the fiction of multiplying cultures, each adding to the sea of stories and shaping new myths of what Britain and British fiction could be.[4]

4

Perhaps, once again, nothing better revealed the state and the changing nature of British fiction as the Eighties started than the Booker Prize for Fiction. It had now become a televised public event, with growing influence over taste, opinion, book sales, literary directions and controversy. The Eighties opened with a visible contest between two writers who were now giants from the Fifties generation – the senior generation of novelists that included Lessing, Murdoch, Spark, Wilson, Kingsley Amis and John Fowles. In 1980 Anthony Burgess published *Earthly Powers* and William Golding *Rites of Passage*. Both were major novels, showing these writers at the height of their powers. The passion for telling and retelling, recreating and adapting, reconstructing and deconstructing that ran through Burgess's work was now producing novels of epic dimension. *Earthly Powers* begins boldly: 'It was the afternoon of my eighty-first birthday, and I was in bed with my catamite when Ali announced that the archbishop had come to see me.' Told over eighty-one chapters and 600 pages by the narrator Kenneth Toomey, Catholic, pederast, writer and bearer of modern experience, the book distilled a great deal of the literary, the political, the sexual and the cultural history of the world in the twentieth century. With familiar Burgess prolixity, much of everything

---

4 Interesting general surveys of the fiction of the period can be found in Peter Kemp's essay 'British Fiction of the Eighties' and Valentine Cunningham's 'Facing the New', both in Malcolm Bradbury and Judy Cooke (eds.), *New Writing*, no. 1 (London, 1992).

is in it: the Pope is here, the rise of Fascism, the Holocaust, religion and voodoo, the spread of strange sects and beliefs. It deals with crime, sin, darkness, the power of evil and its possible moral purpose in making us feel sentient. Two more novels from the Eighties, *The End of the World News* (1983) – which takes its title from the closing phrases of the BBC World Service evening news and its material from many of the great figures of the century – and *The Kingdom of the Wicked* (1985), showed Burgess writing at the highest level of his ambitions. Golding's novel had an equally significant place in its author's career. In 1979 Golding broke a long literary silence with *Darkness Visible*, a book of strong power and vision, though inescapably obscure. *Rites of Passage* posed no such difficulties; it was a novel of moral strength and great clarity, the story of a voyage to the Australian colonies on an old hulk in the time of the Napoleonic wars and the early stages of convict settlement. It would in fact form the first volume of the 'maritime trilogy' that belongs with the very best of Golding's work and was his major late-life achievement, leading to the award of the Nobel Prize. Both men had several more years of significant writing; both men, it so happened, died in the same year, 1993. It is never easy when two distinguished writers are in the same competition, and the result only confirmed Burgess's exiled sense of himself, for in the event it was Golding who won the prize.

A year later the prize took the form of another contest, this time between younger writers virtually unknown beforehand. Both were contemporary, highly experimental works from the new generation and the new manner. One was D. M. Thomas's *The White Hotel*, a surreal psychological work by a writer who had chiefly been known as a poet and a Russianist, though he had published two previous novels, including the lively and surrealistic *The Flute-Player* (1979). The other was Salman Rushdie's *Midnight's Children*, a huge and remarkable novel by an Indian-born and British-educated author who had so far only published one rather dry and little-noticed novel, *Grimus* (1975) (it turned out there had been one previous novel not accepted for publication). The books shared a good deal in common. Both could be described as variant versions of 'magic realism', and both were written with great freedom and invention. Both deal with fundamental and important historical events. Thomas's novel explores the psycho-history of Europe, the rise of psychoanalysis and anti-Semitism, Communism and Fascism, and ends with the genocide at Babi Yar. Rushdie's novel derives from the key moment of Indian Independence, on the midnight of 15 August 1947, and the release of a new national India and a new potential. The books also appeared in a year when the novel seemed particularly exciting, when there were strong signs of a new generation and a new spirit in writing, and the books we read (for I was chair of the Booker judges that year) inspired an enormous confidence and also an unusually long shortlist of seven. The books seriously considered were Doris Lessing's *The Sirian Experiments* (volume three of 'Canopus in Argos'), Muriel Spark's *Loitering With Intent*, Alasdair Gray's brilliant and experimental Scots novel *Lanark*, two highly self-conscious texts by Maggie Gee (*Dying in Other Words*) and Gabriel Josipovici (*The Air We Breathe*), Graham Swift's *Shuttlecock*, Christopher Priest's *The Affirmation*, George Steiner's long and controversial novella *The Portage to San Cristobal of A. H.*, J. G. Ballard's *Hello America*, Michael Moorcock's *Byzantium Endures*, William Boyd's *A Good Man in Africa*, John Banville's *Kepler*, A. N. Wilson's *Who Killed Oswald Fish?*, Martin Amis's *Other People* and Ian McEwan's *The Comfort of Strangers* – plainly a lively year for fiction.

The novels by Thomas and Rushdie stood out as the two most remarkable books of the year. Seriously experimental, *The White Hotel* interweaves documentary 'fact' with fictional fantasy, pastiche reporting with powerful and original poetry, to tell the story of Lisa Erdman, a patient of Sigmund Freud in Vienna, eventually to perish in the massacre of Ukrainian Jews at Babi Yar in 1941. The story reaches across the psycho-sexual and political history of the dark twentieth century; it includes a brilliantly pastiched Freudian case history, a fine erotic poem 'Don Giovanni' and a baroque sequence of erotic imaginings intricately linked to the horrors slowly gathering in the Europe and Russia of the *belle-époque* years of the century. Sexual Utopia and regression to the womb – one meaning of the White Hotel of the title – conflict with the death-bringing energies of the age; conflict between sexual Utopia and modern death becomes the main theme. A scholar of Russian fiction and poetry, Thomas was able to appropriate techniques familiar to Russian writing – improvisation, fantastic characterization, deep psychological intensity – to the normally calmer surfaces of British fiction. His concern with erotic psychology (a lasting preoccupation of his subsequent fiction) is linked with an interest in multiple storytelling, open narrative, dream-writing; these themes and techniques would develop into a sequence of 'improvisational' novels done in the manner of Pushkin (whose poetry Thomas translated), but now applied to great crises of modern history. The sequence – *Ararat* (1983), *Swallow* (1984), *Sphinx* (1986), *Summit* (1987) and *Lying Together* (1990) – juggles with a striking group of international storytellers in competition with each other, using a wonderful variety of styles of storytelling. It plays splendidly with the idea of literature as an art of complex improvisation, while also dealing with the twentieth century as the age that has eroticized death and massacre, in such terrible events as the massacres of the Armenians from Ararat and the conspiracies, espionages and mutually assured destructions of the Cold War. Thomas's later work (*Pictures at an Exhibition*, 1993, etc.) continues to deal with big modern themes: the Kennedy assassination, the Nazi death camps, the Soviet Gulags (he was also the biographer of Alexander Solzhenitsyn). But the creative fluency of the earlier work – *The White Hotel*, and then *Russian Nights* – represents his major endeavour to internationalize, poeticize, above all psychologize the British novel.

In several senses *Midnight's Children* represented a new narrative start. 'Forty years ago the independent nation of India and I were born within eight weeks of one another,' Rushdie later explained. 'This gave rise to a family joke – that the departure of the British was occasioned by my arrival on the scene – and the joke, in turn, became the germ of a novel, *Midnight's Children*, in which not just one child, but one thousand and one children born on the midnight hour of freedom, the first hour of 15 August 1947, were comically and tragically connected to the birth of a nation.' Thus, if the dying of British imperial India had previously been a familiar theme in British fiction, his book now turned on the moment of India's post-imperial rebirth;

he was heir to a new subject, the India after the Raj. It had also plainly not slipped Rushdie's attention that *The Arabian Nights* – ur-book of storytelling, sourcebook of so much narrative, where the cunning narrator Scheherazade daily delays her own death by telling more and more stories, many spawned out of earlier stories – is made up of one thousand and one tales told over one thousand and one nights. One thousand and one, the novel reminds us, is 'the number of night, of magic, of alternative realities'. The children of India's famous midnight are themselves stories, the multiplication of all these new tales representing India's best hope: after all, India is 'a mass fantasy', a 'collective fiction'.[5] One of the children, Saleem Sinai, is the book's narrator: dreamer, victim, trickster, comedian, changed in the cradle, he is devious, cunning, inventive. He also has 'problems with reality': 'I had entered into the illusion of the artist, and thought of the multitudinous realities of the land as the raw unshaped material of my gift.' He eventually splits into fragments, perhaps reflecting E. M. Forster's view that no single story can ever capture the 'many-headed monster' of India. At one level an angry and bitter satire – Saleem tells how the children's magic powers are virtually extinguished by racial and religious conflict and above all by the 'Black Widow', Mrs Gandhi, who turns into the wicked witch of fable, cursing her people – the book was also a celebration of stories and their power. It was difficult to unpack, never an easy read. Yet, as is quite clear today, it is also a major modern classic. This was the book that duly won the prize.

Rushdie was an internationalist writer. He drew heavily on the Indian art and tradition of oral storytelling (as have a good many Indian writers since), the great story kitty of Arab and Mediterranean tale-telling, but he was no less at home with the experimentalism of the great novels of the European and Latin-American traditions or, as he said, 'the novel's polyglot family tree'. Here are the multiple

---

5 As the novel tells us: '. . . a nation which had never previously existed was about to win its freedom, catapulting us into a world which, although it had five thousand years of history, although it had invented the game of chess and traded with Middle Kingdom Egypt, was nevertheless quite imaginary; into a mythical land, a country which would never exist except by the efforts of a phenomenal collective will – except in a dream we all agreed to dream.'

narratives of *The Arabian Nights*, the threaded tales of the Decameron, the fantastic adventures of Cervantes's Don Quixote and the intellectual voyagings of Sterne's Tristram Shandy, the influence of Joyce and Beckett, Borges, Carlos Fuentes, Márquez, all linking the book with European fictional experimentalism – 'postmodernism', 'magic realism' – as well as the ancient seas of story. Rushdie would make this richness of background very visible later, not least in his playful tale for children, *Haroun and the Sea of Stories* (1990). And it was this vast interweaving – of narratives, voices, traditions, cultures, languages, of story sources, stories of faith and stories of amusement, historical fictions, timeless fictions, sacred fictions, profane fictions, which wandered across the ranges of discourse and language, used the digressiveness of oral story and the textual self-teasing of the tradition of written fictional narrative – it was all this that made the book feel like a fresh start for the twentieth-century novel, especially in Britain. With it Rushdie confidently established himself as a major writer, one of the most important to emerge anywhere in the early Eighties; and it was very much to the point that the book was as much a European or Western work as it was an Indian or an Arab one, so the globalization of modern culture is as much a presence as the narrative plenitude that Saleem is celebrating as he reaches his tale's end.[6]

Rushdie followed this book with the no less ambitious *Shame*, told by a strange 'sidelined hero', Omar Khayyam Shakil, who is born not

---

6 In an essay ' "Errata": Or, Unreliable Narration in *Midnight's Children*', Rushdie, reflecting on the mistakes intentional and unintentional that occur in the book, says: 'When I began the novel . . . my purpose was somewhat Proustian. Time and migration had placed a double filter between me and my subject, and I hoped that if I could only imagine vividly enough it might be possible to see beyond those filters, to write as if the years had not passed, as if I had never left India for the West. But as I worked I found that what interested me was the process of filtration itself. So my subject changed, it was no longer a search for lost time, had become the way we remake our past to serve our present purposes, using memory as our tool. Saleem's greatest desire is for what he calls meaning, and near the end of his broken life he sets out to *write himself*, in the hope that by so doing he may achieve the significance the events of his adulthood have drained from him.' See *Imaginary Homelands: Essays and Criticism 1981–1991* (London, 1991).

of one but three mothers, and set in a Pakistan which is both fantastic and very real and contemporary (Rushdie knew this Muslim country; his relatives had moved there, and he visited in the early Seventies). It is an oppressed, dictator-led country that puts the narrator to 'shame', since he is unable to change it, except through an act of the imagination: 'Realism can break a writer's heart,' he explains. But that is why we need fantasy; there are other modes of writing, other ways of telling significant stories: 'Like all migrants, I am a fantasist,' he says, 'I build imaginary countries and try to impose them on the ones that exist'; he also adds that he is 'only telling a sort of modern fairy tale, so that's all right; nobody need get upset . . .' People of power, religious leaders and those who read books in a different fashion did, however, get upset; indeed each of the early novels was banned in one country or another, whether because of the strongly satirical approach Rushdie took to real political figures (Mrs Gandhi, Bhutto, Zia) or his sceptical view of sacred materials, which to some seemed like using First World liberalism to attack the Third World. They became even more upset when Rushdie published his next, even more ambitious novel, *The Satanic Verses* (1988), which is described as a 'burlesque for our degraded, imitative times'. This was another 'migrant's tale', and Rushdie has described the migrant mentality, where no single world seems real or home-like, as the typical late twentieth-century sensibility. It is also another story about story-telling, opening with the magic descent to earth of two key characters from a jumbo jet flying over Britain, brought down by a terrorist bomb. There is a Miltonic as well as a postmodern metaphor about how angels, devils and other messengers descend on us from the heavens, with legends, myths, stories, prophecies good and bad, how divine and diabolic narratives contend and constantly confuse us, and how we fall out of one world into another. Out of this arises the task of the storyteller, which is to 'name the unnameable, to point out frauds, to take sides, to start arguments, shape the world and stop it going to sleep'. A fable for and from multi-cultural times, the book is set in India, Arabia and in a very racially tense Britain where London becomes Babylondon and Mrs Thatcher is Mrs Torture, and considers British racism and its state of degraded modernity.

Above all, the book is a fantasy, playing games with flight, time travel, life and death, dream and reality. We are not sure when we are in a 'real story' or a 'dream-narrative'. Fictions are wrapped inside fictions. Characters realize they are 'moving through several stories at once'. They die and resurrect, breaking the boundaries of self. Once more a variety of narrative traditions – myths and sacred texts, theologies of life and death or heaven and hell – interfuse, presuming that the novelist sailing on the sea of stories can create a new imagination and a new cultural belonging. In the event, book and author were moving to a tragic fate. The book's use of the so-called 'satanic verses' of the Koran, and the treatment of the prophet Mohammed as a historical rather than a divine figure, offended Moslems in Britain and elsewhere. As a result of their opposition to the book, copies of which were publicly burned, the Iranian Ayatollah Khomeini, four months away from his own death, and a few months before the ending of the Cold War, pronounced on 14 February 1989 the famous *fatwa*, a religious edict of death on a secular British author. Violence and threats of it followed in many countries, and Rushdie was driven into hiding in Britain. This is not a place to explore the political or religious dimensions of the issue, which had serious consequences not just for Rushdie but for all cultural and political relations between the traditions of Western liberalism and fundamentalist Islam. Ironically enough, it secured Rushdie's reputation as a leading world writer, a major figure of the late modern imagination, comparable with Solzhenitsyn, Kundera and Klima in his political sufferings, and to Márquez, Fuentes, Eco or Calvino in his scale of writing. It also shocked British and Western minds into considering what fictions are for, and where their essential values lie. Since the European Renaissance, novels had been intimately linked with the spirit of humanism, scepticism and individualism. They tell tales of personal lives through the playful god-games of narrative, producing not sacred truths or real tales but fictions that declare themselves as fictional, imaginary things that help us to better understand the nature of the real. In modern commodity culture novels can be trivial, toy-like, cheap goods hawked for profit or celebrity. In other cultures they can be controlled messages advancing state ideology. They can also be among the most profound and independent explorations of human experience, the means through which we come to moral and metaphysical understanding of our own experience, see society, history or consciousness afresh, give order and shape to our personal and public lives. If in recent times some of our best writers – Rushdie notable among them – have explored the fictionality of fiction, the deconstruction of fables, the cultural plenitude of story, that does not mean their fictions are irrelevant to history, or are not a response to its pressures and conflicts. Indeed, until the end of the Cold War in 1989 a large part of experimental modern fiction had arisen from the repression, or attempted repression, of writing and writers. Now Rushdie joined their number.

Remarkably he was not silenced by his grim circumstances; indeed, he went on to produce major work. In 1990 came the delightful fable *Haroun and the Sea of Stories*, a child-like tale about fiction's enterprise. It involves a search for the sea of stories on the moon Kahani, where the stories come from; the sea always risks being polluted or misused, but there are generally stories in abundance, because 'new stories come from old – it is the new combination that makes them new'. In 1995 he produced another major novel which was partly a reflection on his present situation, *The Moor's Last Sigh*, comparable in richness, idea and compassion with *Midnight's Children*. The new storyteller is Moraes Zogoiby, another Scheherazade who is trying to save his own skin; he too has his oddity, since he lives his life at double speed. His family are illegitimate descendants of Vasco da Gama, and though much of the story is set in the present the tale reaches back to the key moment indicated by the title. For in 1492, as Columbus sailed to America and the New World opened up to the West, the Moors in Spain were driven at last from the Alhambra and an era of medieval multi-culturalism came to an end. The Moor's last sigh is Boabdil's, as he gazes in tears on the lost wonderland of Granada, a city of Indo-European stories that reached through the Mediterranean, the Arab world and India. The book also explores India's rich, plural history, especially that of Bombay, 'city of mixed-up, mongrel joy'. Moraes Zogoiby the Moor is a modern mongrel too, 'a jewholic anonymous, a cathjew nut, a stewpot, a joy', a case of Joycean interfusion. His family are traders, merchants, painters and writers, one version of Indian identity, though not one that pleases the new Nationalists (a bitter portrait of one such political adventurer ensues). The story is filled not just with stories in plenitude, from here and everywhere, a mongrel spawning, as in much of Modernism; it is packed too with strange new art objects that acquire mythic status. Moraes finally does a Columbus in reverse. But stories have enemies, and, back in Spain, Moraes is held hostage by a mad painter, Vasco Miranda, who forces him at gunpoint to produce more and more stories, including this one, to survive. Moraes ends up as the sum of all the storytelling heroes and heroines: from Scheherazade to Cervantes, Rip Van Winkle to Finn McCool, waiting to tell even better stories in a better time, 'sleepers waiting their moment of return'.

At the end of 1999 Rushdie produced his 'millennial novel', *The Ground Beneath Her Feet*, discussed later. But what was already clear by the dawn of the Nineties was that Rushdie was a major late twentieth-century storyteller, a 'migrant writer' working in the hybrid and Babelian world of stories in an age of transit, an age after the death of God where there are no longer eternal and sacred texts or secure Grand Narratives, simply a multiplicity of human fictions. He also belongs with those writers who have found themselves in voluntary or involuntary exile or banishment, for whom exile and difficulty had created the literary pluralism, the sense of history, the crisis of literary responsibility that had run like a dark theme through the modern century. As he said himself: 'those of us who have been forced by cultural displacement [and now banning and *fatwa*] to accept the provisional nature of all truths, all certainties, have perhaps had modernism forced on us.' His is an English-language fiction, but written in times when those who use the language no longer directly inherit or care to use its previous myths and histories, its narrative conventions and story types, and therefore look to new ones – exactly like many of the earlier Modernists. Rushdie stressed in 1982, shortly after the success of *Midnight's Children*, that he was an 'international' writer who considered the novel an international form, at a time when writers could find parents anywhere: 'It is perhaps one of the more pleasant freedoms of the literary migrant to be able to choose his own parents,' he wrote. 'My own – selected half consciously, half not – include Gogol, Cervantes, Kafka, Melville, Machado de Assis; a polyglot family tree, against which I measure myself, and to which I would be honoured to belong.'[7] The world is a sea of stories, sacred and profane, on which we voyage beyond familiar ports and landfalls to make new moral and metaphysical discoveries. Yet, as Rushdie discovered, not all accept the tradition of individual scepticism embodied in much of the history of the Western novel. What Rushdie had inherited was not only the spirit of Joycean and Modernist plurality but a humanist faith in the power of fictions to explore our place and fate in this divided and not always progressive world, and the belief that we may acquire some larger human wholeness – the liberal aim that E. M. Forster expressed in *A Passage to India* sixty years earlier, though he also saw the danger of emptiness, muddle, the senseless 'ou-boum' of the caves. Rushdie's own pluralism came from a new age, the age when, as he said, the Empire strikes back, recolonizing the imperial centres. The writer, Rushdie observes, depends on an 'inner multiplicity, this crowd within', which is 'often very difficult for artists to bear, let alone explain', for 'the creative process is not unlike the process of free societies, which are by their very nature divided, plural, even quarrelsome'. If Rushdie's misfortunes had any merit, it was to remind Western writers of the heritage and seriousness of fiction's tradition of moral discovery, humanistic exploration and intellectual freedom.

5

Rushdie is an international writer in the large sense of the word, an author whose work transcends any single source or location. But he is also part of the widening ethnic and stylistic multi-culturalism that has been changing Britain, and for that matter the idea of the British

---

7 See the title essay of Rushdie, *Imaginary Homelands: Essays and Criticism, 1981-1991* (London, 1991). Other quotations from Rushdie have been taken from this collection.

novel. From the Fifties the cultural range had been slowly widening, and colonial, then post-colonial, commonwealth and dominion litera- ture had been a fundamental if sometimes ambiguous part of British writing. But by the Eighties the cultural mood had changed, and the Empire was indeed striking back. A significant number of bicultural or pluri-cultural novelists emerged in Britain, their work drawing on a mixture of traditions and a variety of cultural experience. Timothy Mo – who was born in Hong Kong in 1950, after British rule returned, and who came to London at the age of ten – was plainly a novelist of two empires, Chinese and British, and his early work captured some of the main crossing-points with a sharp comic vision, then, more recently, with huge epic sweep. His first novel, *The Monkey King* (1980), is set in contemporary, booming, decaying Hong Kong, a growth city where the oldest traditions, customs and loyalties live side by side with massive speedy modernization. His second, *Sour Sweet* (1982), looks at another divided culture, but this time in London's Chinatown, where the Chen family are again subject to opposing forces, the ancestral claims of the Triad gangs and the whims of the unpredictable English. The third book returned to the subject, but now with a broader historical sweep. *An Insular Possession* (1986) is a key story of Hong Kong, the malarial island scarce fit for settlement that became a British treaty possession as a result of the Opium Wars between Britain and China. Mo interweaves fact and fiction, true and invented letters and records, telling the story of the emerald colony with great action and vividness. An even more important story of colonial inheritances and Pacific crisis is found in *The Redundancy of Courage* (1991), Mo's most powerful and pro- phetic novel. It is set in 'Danu' (plainly East Timor) as the Portuguese empire in the Indonesian archipelago recedes, and violence and mas- sacre erupt. Hopes of independence are destroyed by a bloody invasion from neighbouring Indonesia. The central character, Adolph Ng, observes both an appalling violence and the moral transformation of his friends and comrades; the tone is of modern historical tragedy, occasionally touched with comedy but rooted in deep political dismay. Mo remains a major writer. In 1995 he published another political novel of the Pacific, *Brownout on Breadfruit Boulevard*, set in the

473

Philippines, but it is his two earlier novels that most sum up the Pacific experience in the fading of the age of colonialism.

At first sight, nothing could seem further away from Mo's epic and increasingly political intentions than the restrained, economical, half-hidden fiction of another writer working at the crossing point of a European and Pacific tradition, Kazuo Ishiguro. Born in the city of Nagasaki, Japan, a decade after the nuclear attack, he moved with his family to Britain at the age of six, and grew up in the pleasant city of Guildford. Nearly all of his life has been spent in Britain, and English is his first language; yet his Anglo-Japanese inheritance has been quite as powerful as Mo's Anglo-Chinese one. The peculiar reticence and intricate mannerism of his novels owe something to the tradition of the Japanese novel, though they owe quite as much to Ishiguro's own careful aesthetic invention. Every one of his books touches some of the large historical events of the century, in the Pacific or Europe, but always indirectly, at an angle, and from the standpoint of a few chosen moments or glimpses taken from the perspective of the displaced figure or the quiet observer, or those who lead routine, quiet or dutiful lives. The main story of Ishiguro's first novel *A Pale View of Hills* (1982) is gently told by a Japanese widow, Etsuko, who lives in a confusing and alien England, but it takes us back to a distant summer in Nagasaki just after the war, when the city is being reconstructed, individual lives being remade. The atomic horror is never clearly mentioned, but everywhere implied. There is an odd secret somewhere in the memories – as a strange consequence of what is half remembered, a daughter has committed suicide. At the same time Etsuko's memories of the lives of other people have a confusing similarity to the unrevealed events of her own. A similar reticence and indirection of method is there in *An Artist of the Floating World* (1986). This time the novel is entirely set in a Japan Ishiguro had not himself revisited since childhood, much of it at a time before the war which well preceded his birth. This is another first-person narrative, a collage of memories and experiences recorded by Masuji Ono, an artist who won fame in the Thirties, at a time when Japan had invaded China and had imperial ambitions across the Pacific. Ono was then 'an artist of the floating world', catching impressions from life's underside, 'things intangible and transient', 'pleasurable things that disappear with the morning light'. But, evidently, in 'troubled times', as Japanese ambitions grew and militarism intensified, Ono has done his duty. Now in the post-war world, Ono is old, eminent, a repository of memories, greatly respected and also, we sense, greatly suspected. Again it is what the story does not say, the facts that are not mentioned, the details unrevealed, that matter. Aesthetic and moral betrayal are everywhere implied, but the heart of the story has to be deduced. For, after all, Ishiguro too is an artist of the floating world, dealing in impressions, 'things intangible and transient', rather than in clear-cut plots.

With *The Remains of the Day* (1989), his third and so far most successful novel (it won the Booker Prize and sold a million copies), Ishiguro remarkably shifted in subject and scene; the book moves not only from Japan to class-bound as well as fog-bound England, but deals chiefly with a period in British life, the Thirties, which Ishiguro could not have known. The narrator is Stevens, a butler in an aristocratic household, who follows an historic (and near-Japanese) code of deference, obedience and reticence; he always does his duty. In 1956 (the year of the Suez Crisis) he travels across Britain on a late-life journey, following his memories. Gradually we understand the way in which he has respectfully colluded in the appeasement politics and the pro-Fascist sentiments of his eminent employer, Lord Dartington, as a result of his dutiful obedience. As with Ono, long-engrained codes of respect have made him passive before historic moments of choice; this also applies more directly to his personal life, in which he has always civilly repressed feelings, sexual sentiments and personal affections, even feeling it his duty to leave his dying father to serve at a dinner party arranged by his employer. The slow journey he takes brings home to him (and even more so to the reader) the rule of civil self-suppression he has lived by, always leaving things unsaid. A possible love affair and marriage are now, alas, not to be retrieved. But the same reticence is observed by the narrative code of this precisely told tale in which Jamesian precision and Japanese aesthetic economy merge. So successful was the book (and the Merchant-Ivory film made from it) that readers were surprised when Ishiguro's next novel *The Unconsoled* (1995) proved a different kind of enterprise. It was a strange, experimental, mid-European book, about a musician trying to find his way about an unnamed, alien city, where nothing is reliable, identities and meanings multiply, and deceptions and confusions abound. In 2000 Ishiguro seemed, very successfully, to unite the two manners in *When We Were Orphans*, where the story is again largely set in the Thirties and the scene is a double one: the Shanghai of the Bund or International City, in the time of opium trading and of growing civil war and impending Japanese invasion; and the London of smart parties, polite Englishness and the problem-solving detective, like Sherlock Holmes or Lord Peter Wimsey, who could put the wronged world to rights.

Ishiguro too said his work was a contribution to the modern 'international novel', and in that aim he is very far from alone. He evidently belongs with a good number of other writers – V. S. Naipaul, Rumer Godden, Ruth Prawer Jhabvala, Anita Desai, Vikram Seth, Michael Ondaatje – who have married British and other forms and traditions of fiction and storytelling, to the point of creating an internationalized and late modern fictional voice and style. Though some writers have found the cultural melting pot a dangerous place – like the Kenyan writer Ngugi wa Thiong'o who lived in Britain and published several important English-language novels (including *Petal of Blood*, 1977) before returning to Kenya to write stories in Kikuyu – others, like the Nigerian author Chinua Achebe (whose splendid first novel *Things Fall Apart* (1958) became a classic of English-language African writing, and whose *Anthills of the Savannah* (1987) was shortlisted for the Booker), have been able to explore their own culture and folklore while assimilating international themes and interests. Achebe's most significant heirs have been the Nigerian playwright and novelist Wole Soyinka (winner of the Nobel Prize in 1985) and the novelist and poet Ben Okri. Okri was born in Minna, Nigeria, but educated in Britain, where he remains resident. His first novel *Flowers and Shadows* (1980) is the story of a boy's painful growing-up in a small Nigerian town like his own. With *The Landscapes Within* (1981), which tells the story of a Nigerian painter, Okri began to release some of the rich, free, imaginative, pluri-cultural poetry that would guide his later work. He became best-known for the novel *The Famished Road*, which won the Booker Prize in 1991: the book, narrated by a 'spirit child', Azaro, who has returned from the dead, is a work of African 'magic realism', a vast and inventive amalgam of folklore, mystery, spirit and dream, packed with wonderful and fantastical characters, a story of the power of the imagination to struggle against the problems of life and death. In 1993 he published *Songs of Enchantment*, and through the Nineties in a sequence of richly imaginative novels, including the appropriately titled *Infinite Riches* (1998), he added significantly to the stock of English-language African-based fiction. Also Nigerian and living in London, Buchi Emecheta realistically recorded, in books like *Second-Class Citizen* (1974) and *Destination Biafra* (1982), the battles of tradition and modernity both in Africa and within migrant culture, treating both the conflicts and wars of contemporary Nigeria, and harsh experiences of racism and sexism in London.

Such writing displayed the increasingly significant and central part the developing novel was playing throughout the post-colonial world; it also demonstrated that this writing from what Rushdie called the age of 'migration' was playing inside British culture itself. It was a world that for two or three generations had been breeding its own distinctive multi-cultural writers, its own distinctive stories – often not of buoyant migration but of disillusionment. Caryl Phillips, born in St Kitts but brought up in Britain, wrote of the homelessness and disordered migrant identities of those who came from Africa to the Caribbean, the Caribbean to Britain or Europe, in a sequence of novels – *The Final Passage* (1985), *Higher Ground* (1986), *A State of Independence* (1986), *Cambridge* (1991) – that traces the passage from slavery to the lost or difficult selfhoods of the present. Hanif Kureishi, a British-Asian film-maker born in Bromley, explored the confusions of modern cultural identity as they emerge during adolescence in *The Buddha of Suburbia* (1990): a wonderfully comic tale of a Pakistani boy ('an Englishman born and bred – almost') growing up in London's suburbia. *The Black Album* (1995) is set amid the confusions and recriminations of the Rushdie affair, and tensely and interestingly explores the issue from both sides. Adam Zameenzad, born in Pakistan

477

and settled in Britain, made his fictional debut with the ironic and teasing *The Thirteenth House* (1987), and then in *Cyrus Cyrus* (1990), a spectacular book showing much of the experimental flamboyance and grandeur of Rushdie, he devised a wondrous tale of human and cosmic good and evil, shifting scenes and changed identities, set in India, California and London. Zameenzad described it as a tale of 'images of sex and survival, death and after-death, madness and genius, as relived within the dark, unfathomable recesses of the black hole in his mind by Cyrus Cyrus, one of the most notorious men the century has produced'. Vikram Seth, a remarkable writer who lives variously in Bombay, Britain and the United States, displays some of the contrasts of global village multi-cultural fiction: its elaborate use of scene, technique, cultural forms, and its essential cultural mobility. His poetic novel *The Golden Gate* (1986) is told, entirely and unusually, in the sonnet form; the story deals with life in San Francisco and Silicon Valley in the cyber-age. *A Suitable Boy* (1993) is a vast chronicle of post-Independence Indian life set in Bombay, and one of the most startling works of the early Nineties. Bombay now seemed an outpost of Hollywood, of London, of Canada. 'Bombay was central; all rivers flowed into its human sea,' Rushdie wrote in *The Moor's Last Sigh*. 'It was an ocean of stories; we were all its narrators, and everyone talked at once.' All the writers, all the voices, also became part of post-colonial British fiction, and it became ever harder to determine its edges, or know whether the British novel had turned into something else, an internationalized literature written in English, which was now taking its place.

6

For at the same time British fiction was shifting culturally, growing more international from within. 'If I stare into his face I can make out the areas of waste and fatigue, the moonspots and boneshadows you're bound to get if you live in the twentieth century,' reflects John Self, the unlikeable anti-hero of Martin Amis's *Money: A Suicide Note*, commenting on his literary creator, 'Martin Amis'. And here was an author who, unlike his father, did not feel lucky, did not like it here, who did not find the ordinary familiar or rewarding, and who wrote of some aimless, placeless, essentially midatlantic world in a state of what he called the late twentieth-century 'suspense', when everything old was tired and used and everything new was spent and weary. His own strongest literary influences were international, all his most admired writers Russian or American. He wrote about characters or narrators who were as fractured as Rushdie's: multiple Amises, figures called John Self, Nichola Six or Keith Talent who can be trusted not to be trusted, and who are no longer the rounded characters of realist fiction, but Pynchon-like names with a high textual presence – traumatized, fragmentary, rootless figures, belonging neither here nor there, always in the presence of technology or engaged in acts of passage, suffering from contemporary excess, waste and fatigue, citizens of the failing urban jungles on either side of the Atlantic Ocean in the age of endless travel and transactional globalism. They are afflicted by identity problems, difficulties of naming or finding, nameless crises in general. In their world nothing is real or whole, the present is perpetual, without real past or real future, since 'something has gone wrong with modern time'. 'I am a thing made up of time lag, culture shock, zone shift,' Self explains. *Money* is a topically titled story of the big ambiguous symbol of the Eighties (Self wants to direct a movie called variously *Good Money* and *Bad Money*, and belongs in a world where everyone is fleecing each other). It's an Anglo-American tale of doubles and orphans, refracting cities (London and New York), shuttling planes. When Self jumbos across the Atlantic, he appropriately finds there is a Martin Amis waiting on each side, equipped with imagery, cultural education and literary antecedents to match. This and all of Amis's later books are narrated in a high-lit, raunchy, vernacular and yet intensely literary Anglo-American discourse. It is extravagantly inventive, word-spinning, culturally acquisitive; it has rolling tropes, a generous supply of apocalyptic images, rich funds of street and club talk crossed with high literariness, Jamesian self-composure, knowing intertextual references.

Amis already had some claim to be considered the prose stylist for a generation, and he has freely acknowledged he draws some of his method and manner from the hyper-real prose of Saul Bellow, while the great ironist and playmaster of modern fiction Vladimir Nabokov is here too. In 1987 Amis produced the story collection *Einstein's Monsters*, nearly all about post-nuclear crisis, which seemed to offer some explanation for his distinctive and weary world of fragmentation and 'time disease', and his 'paranoid style'. He acknowledged the influence of his scientific reading and of science fiction, especially J. G. Ballard, and noted the way it always functions completely realistically within its dystopian context. For Amis the world of *Einstein's Monsters* – 'we're hurtling toward an entropy watershed' – is the late twentieth-century condition; it may seem a belated recognition, but it is set within the notion of an age that cannot advance in time. Beside these, there seem to be other important debts, and surely not least to the fiction of Muriel Spark, whose ironic distance from her stories, clear abstract games to do with author, authority, character, plot, life, death, eternity, and above all time, past, present and future, seem closely related. For Amis's later work is not just about the world but how the fiction of it is made, proportioned, dealt out, and the combinatorial games that can be played with the great toys of fiction – author, plot, character, etc. – so that they are managed, manipulated, given metaphoric value. Amis's last novel of the Eighties was *London Fields* (1989), set just ten years further on, at the cusp of the millennium, which is surrounded by all the iconography of apocalyptic disaster (Alasdair Gray's *Lanark* uses a similar theme). In the spirit of *Einstein's Monsters*, Amis suggests that the millennium will this time bring about the end of the world because last time 'Nobody had the hardware'; now they do. It also seems that the age has been catastrophic for fifty or more years, that nothing has changed in history since the events of 1945 ('it seemed possible to argue that Hitler was still running the century – Hitler the great bereaver'). But in the end *London Fields* is a murder story. The book's would-be narrator is Samson Young, an American writer arrived in London to write a story: 'This is the story of a murder,' he says. 'It hasn't happened yet, but it will.' But (as in Spark's *The Driver's Seat*), the book is a chronicle of a death foretold where the female victim knows much of the plot already and manipulates it, in her own destructive self-interest. All depends on the fictionalist assumption that the walls of fiction are never solid, so a character can collude with an author, or a plot be transformed. The characters in the story know they are icons or simulacra, in this type of tale or that. Some have Pynchonesque literary names like Analiese Furnish, Trish Shirt and Guy Clinch. Stories can come free of their frames, and 'time's arrow' can be fired in various directions, so that apocalypse never comes. In fact *Time's Arrow*, said Amis, was a possible title for the book. Instead it became the title of his next one, published in 1991.

During the Eighties the themes of Amis's books and Ian McEwan's increasingly seemed to converge. McEwan's work depended less on literary sensationalism and outrageous flamboyance; there was a growing depth of feeling and awareness of evil and inner emptiness, a sense of the moral weight of violence. *The Comfort of Strangers* (1981) is a confidently mature novel, a disturbing work of Venetian Gothic, where sexual tension and hidden gender-war turn into a self-gratifying and yet senseless violence. It was followed by several powerful screenplays; then came the appearance of *The Child in Time* (1988), a book of much greater sensitivities. As in Amis's fiction, it is set in a future English world, a degraded Thatcherite Britain, where there is licensed begging, private ambulance services, an armed police force (not a bad set of prophecies); and this plot too depends on a striking 'time-slip'. But this is McEwan's most social novel to date; here what had essentially been private concerns, personal fantasies and psychic disorders become public and political ones. Childhood, always central in McEwan's fiction, is the main theme, but now no longer seen as an angle on a hard adult world from a child's perplexed and ambiguous point of view, but as an element in the ambiguous world of contemporary family life. The story involves the abduction of a child from a supermarket, a grim road accident and the regression of an adult to his own failed and tattered boyhood. Stephen Lewis, a writer of children's books who has lost both wife and daughter, is the protagonist. The theme of the novel – the nature of childhood, the welfare of children – is seriously considered and carefully worked; the reintegration of the child within the adult, and the regeneration of male, female and child through love. This was a book that laid down many of the themes of McEwan's fiction of the Nineties, where questions of the malign powers and the restoration of hope and virtue would be posed.

7

'Writing novels is more like writing history than we often choose to think,' Frank Kermode once wrote. 'The relationship between events, the selection of incident, even, in sophisticated fictions, the built-in scepticism as to the validity of procedures and assumptions, all these raise questions familiar to philosophers of history as problems relating to historical explanation.' It has also often been said that writing history is more like writing novels than we choose to think since, as the historian Hayden White observed, real events never present themselves to us as a story, they do not narrate or advance themselves – writers of history do that. And, as the century drew closer to its end, the question of history – the history essentially of the troubled and terrible century, of how to see it and how to write it – became of ever greater concern to those who wrote 'sophisticated fictions'. The shape of the century, the story of a modern age when progress became either ambiguous or entirely disastrous, when humanity corrupted itself and radical and progressive dreams disappeared and died, was a recurrent theme in Eighties fiction, so that it came to seem that no novel would do that did not go back to wartime (the Great War, the Second World War, the conflicts in Spain, Korea, Vietnam, the Death Camps, the Holocaust), or the End of Empire, or the last glimpse of the Edwardian wonderland before so many things went wrong. The principle was not new; the novel has always been a form of history, as its titles often said (*The History of Tom Jones*, etc.). But questions of what we mean by history, how we shape it, interpret it, tell it, distort it, how we amend it by our own place in the present, are constantly in change. And such concerns will sharpen when writers feel they are near the close of an epoch, either at the end of history or at a time when it changes or transforms.

'We have to keep scooping, scooping up from the depths this remorseless stuff that time leaves behind,' says Tom Crick in Graham Swift's *Waterland* (1983), one of the best of a good many novels of the Eighties that attended to how we recuperate the past. Swift had established himself with *The Sweetshop Owner* (1980), set in a northern town, about a man who feels himself to be a powerless witness to larger dramas: wartime, love, history. In *Shuttlecock* (1981) he wrote a psychological thriller about a police archivist working in a department of 'dead crimes' who comes to realize that one crime lies in his family history, with his father, a war hero for his work with the French Resistance, the suspect. Untrustworthy fathers and dead crimes were the stuff of the twentieth-century world, and they play a large part in Swift's later fiction, where modern people live in the 'aftermath', the shadow of corrupted history. With *Waterland*, his most perfect and most thoughtful book, Swift found the ideal subject: the flat, flooded, man-made, secretive landscape of the Cambridgeshire and Norfolk fenlands – 'a landscape, which of all landscapes, most approximated to nothing', according to the history teacher Tom Crick. History is the story's chief concern – a word that means many things: a great system of human progress, an inquiry, a narrative about the past, an interesting personal story. The book itself is all those things, playing different ideas of history. As for the past, it is itself a 'waterland', yielding not a stable body of facts but a wealth of pasts hidden, drowned, suppressed; water-soaked corpses; 'dead crimes'. Tom explores different layers, with his own pupils, and increasingly in his own life. Chapter titles pose the problems: 'About the Question Why', 'About the Explanation of Explanation', 'Who Says?' The book shares postmodern writing's long-standing fascination with history as fiction; but it is also about something more personal – history as recuperation, about how we can rediscover and use what past or memory have left for us.

Waterland appears to deal with a timeless natural landscape in remote rural England; in fact Swift's fenland waterland is a layered and complex place with a strange history. In *Out of This World* (1988) he moved to some of the bigger political events of the twentieth century, again concerned with the difficulty and ambiguity of making a true record. Harry Beech is an aerial photojournalist who has learned to fly above history – 'out of this world'. He takes aerial photographs of the bombed cities of the Second World War, then of the 'ordinariness' of the Nuremberg Trials that followed it. As he confesses, all records depend on the perspectives from which they are seen; but they also depend on the technologies of record. Photographs themselves are not objective images; they change over time, the sepia monochrome of wartime giving way to the flared colour images of the post-war world. Through such shifting records and changing icons, layer on layer of the dark phases of twentieth-century history can be set into a great postmodern collage: the wartime bomber raids and the Apollo mission, the Nuremberg Trials and the Vietnam War. And Beech himself is not, after all, 'out of this world.' His father was an arms manufacturer, another unreliable dead father; his daughter is going through a psychic crisis occasioned by Beech's own indifference to real facts and sufferings. Dead crimes, past and present, guilt and responsibility, the deadened feeling of somehow living in history's aftermath, the feeling that we have all suffered some 'bomb damage' we cannot escape, however hard we try to fly up 'out of this world': these are the themes of the novel, as Swift, here and in novels to come, attempts to create what he calls an archaeology of the past, usable in the 'here and now'.

Strange and radical contrasts between the past and present were just as central to Peter Ackroyd's fiction. A leading literary scholar and critic, a splendid biographer (Dickens, T. S. Eliot), Ackroyd emerged as one of the strong writers of the Eighties. His theme was less the relation between modern individuals and their history than the connection between narratives and codes, a present writer or situation and a previous author or text, a 'pre-text'. Ackroyd was not just a good scholar and a tracer of intricate literary connections, but a superb creator of literary pastiche. In his first novel *The Great Fire of London* (1982) this text was Charles Dickens's *Little Dorrit*, being filmed in the story, which then points the way to many of the locations (Marshalsea Prison, etc.), influences various characters and steers Ackroyd's vision of London, packing what would be his own favourite location with dense Dickensian associations. *The Last Testament of*

Oscar Wilde (1983) offers in Wildean fashion a tale Oscar simply failed to write, the virtuoso version of the story of his tragic last days in Paris, as Sebastian Melmoth. But Ackroyd's most complex book is another brilliant London novel, *Hawksmoor* (1985). It works on several stunning displacements. Nicholas Hawksmoor (1661–1736) was a real figure, former clerk to Sir Christopher Wren, who became a leading eighteenth-century architect, creator of parts of All Souls College, Oxford, and many fine London churches, a number destroyed in the great fires of the Second World War. But this Hawksmoor is fictionalized and transformed as Nicholas Dyer, an eighteenth-century architect and Satanist who uses human sacrifices in constructing these same churches, and who tells his own story. Meanwhile Hawksmoor has become a twentieth-century London detective superintendent, a kind of latter-day Sherlock Holmes, who is investigating a series of mysterious killings at the same churches. The story is cut between the two eras, and told in two languages, layered into each other to create a sinister and Gothic novel. In *Chatterton* (1987) the layers are not two but three. We follow the again famous story of the death of the seventeen-year-old Thomas Chatterton, poet and faker, creator of the spurious 'Rowley' poems (it is possible that the death was faked). Another layer tells the story of the well-known sentimental painting by Henry Wallis depicting Chatterton's death. A third layer is a contemporary story exploring art, forgery and mystification. Like William Gaddis's brilliant American novel *The Recognitions* (1955), this is an intricate and experimental tale about art as lying and counterfeiting, since art is 'the lie that tells the truth'.

In *First Light* (1989) Ackroyd shifted the scene from his most familiar and often sinister location, London, to nature and Dorset, the literary ghost in the story to Thomas Hardy. This is a tale of the investigation of two quite different 'archaeologies'. One is the excavation of a neolithic barrow; the other is the investigation of a giant star at a nearby astrophysics observatory. Earth and sky, the human universe and the stellar one, the ancient past and the topical ideas of new science in the age of quarks, black holes and revisionist theories of time (two chapters are entitled 'The Uncertainty Principle') make the book another form of complex layering. Like many fiction writers of this generation, Ackroyd is fascinated by new scientific ideas, set against a sense of history. His critical articles make the case for an experimental, self-conscious and post-realist fiction; his own complex books are not just counterpoints of past and future but of historical codes and styles with modern ones. And he always makes splendid use of the battery of devices available in the skilful novelist's repertory in the age of metafiction: pastiche, parody, punning, inter-textuality. Yet, interestingly in a writer who complained of English fiction being too in love with its own Englishness, he has also been a distinctively English novelist. He explored this himself in *English Music* (1992), an elaborate dialogue of a novel, set in Clerkenwell, treating a variety of writers, painters and architects, touching on a mixture of myths, motifs and traditions, exploring various aspects of their Englishness; then in *The House of Doctor Dee* (1993) he took up one of Clerkenwell's most famous and in some ways most sinister residents, the Elizabethan necromancer John Dee. More recently Ackroyd wrote *The Plato Papers* (1999), described as a novel, though the French would call it a *conte philosophique*. Set in the distant future, AD 3700, it tells of a philosopher called Plato who sets about reconstructing the Age of Mouldwarp (1500–2300). This includes our own time, which survives only in odd traces: a fragment of a novel by Charles Darwin called *Origin of Species*, the comic routines of Sigmund Freud and Oedipus, who do a stand-up show called *Jokes and Their Relation to the Unconscious*, and so on. What the philosopher of the future can study is the age's distinctive language, though it now needs total decoding (*rock music*: the sound of old stones; *recreation ground*: an area of the city selected for the restoration of past life, etc.). Plato the philosopher is finally able to time-travel back to our own London, and bring his report back into the half-world of the cave. Sometimes whimsical, sometimes profound, Ackroyd had devised yet another tale of layer upon layer, past and present and future.

Ackroyd's fiction, especially the early work, owes much to French literature and French literary theory. So does the fiction of Julian Barnes, another very important novelist to emerge at the start of the Eighties. His first book, *Metroland* (1980), set in Paris amid the revolutionary *événements* of May 1968, is a postmodern echo of the story of Wordsworth and Annette Vallon, and is about a modern sentimental education. In 1982 he published *Before She Met Me*, essentially a learned and academic murder story (Barnes interspersed his 'serious' novels with streetwise mysteries about a bisexual ex-cop, written under the pen-name of Dan Kavanagh). But his first major book was *Flaubert's Parrot* (1984), half a critical text, half a human narrative. Based around studies, speculations and games concerning the great mid nineteenth-century French realist Gustave Flaubert, creator of *Madame Bovary* ('c'est moi'), it also opens the door to the spirit of fictional postmodernism. Flaubert famously worked with a stuffed parrot on his desk, 'a fluttering, elusive emblem of the writer's voice'. He also ended one of his greatest tales, *Un Coeur Simple* (*A Simple Heart*), with an extraordinary metaphor, of the Holy Ghost as parrot ('as she breathed her last breath she thought she saw, as the heavens opened for her, a gigantic parrot hovering over her head'). The parrot becomes the crux of Barnes's tale, as the academic narrator, Geoffrey Braithwaite – a modern Charles Bovary, cuckolded by a wife who commits suicide – pursues his researches and theories. Braithwaite discovers that the parrot exists in numerous variants and copies. At the same time the text he creates also takes numerous forms. It is a research and a meditation, an examination paper on Flaubert, a latter-day absurdist commentary. It follows Flaubert's strange adventures, his journey to Egypt, his meticulous literary obsessions. The text as a whole plays with real and fictional, devises new rules, breaks up its own discourse. 'This is how it was,' begins Barnes's next novel, *Staring at the Sun* (1986), as if the questioning of realism has now been dispensed with, and the book can take its stance on safe ground. Like Graham Swift's *Out of This World*, published two years later, it looks from the viewpoint of the airman at the world of the Second World War. But this too is a novel of several time-layers, from the Great War to the twenty-first century, depending on the future for its apocalyptic outcome.

Barnes's next book, *A History of the World in 10½ Chapters*, part novel, part essay, is one of his most interesting. As its title suggests, it raises the question of history in its largest sense. History, we are told, is 'just voices echoing in the dark; images that burn for a few centuries then fade; stories, old stories that sometimes seem to overlap; strange links, impertinent connections'. Barnes plays with the limits and forms of fiction, the techniques of reportage; but the main concern is with those 'strange links, impertinent connections'. The story of Noah's Ark begins the narrative, but told from the woodworm's point of view, and from this various sea-going tales are spun. Some are literary fabulations, some are brilliant artistic essays, one in particular on the famous Géricault painting *The Raft of the Medusa*. Autobiographical recollections, parodies and footballing memoirs are linked together not by conventional associations but by mythic or metaphoric ones. The narrator is concerned with the randomness of history, the utter confusion of the deposits it leaves behind, the need for 'love'. And 'love', or rather the story of a triangular sexual relationship in the age of modern banking and AIDS, told from the different viewpoints and voices of the three lovers, is the material of *Talking it Over* (1991), a book in which, as one of the characters says, it is all 'my word against anyone else's'. In 1993 Barnes published a novel of a very different kind, *The Porcupine*, one of the first works of serious fiction to explore the situation of Eastern Europe after the coming down of the Berlin Wall and the fall of the Communist dictators. The deposed leader of a former Balkan Communist state (the tale is plainly about Todor Zhivkov of Bulgaria, and indeed the book was first published in that country) is brought to trial, creating a dispute about history seen under the guise of old ideologies and new realities. The trial is a struggle of postmodern fictions, a novel of the New World Order. At the end of the Nineties Barnes, by now one of the most intelligent, cosmopolitan and precise of British writers, produced a satire, *England, England* (1998), about a theme park England replicated on the Isle of Wight, a dark and mocking commentary on the nation, and the times.

Other writers speculated with considerable pleasure on the relationship between the real and the fictional, history and the fantastic. One was David Lodge, who – over the years when, like other writer-academics, he had been living at the crossroads and working with Structuralism – developed his campus fictions into a trilogy. *Changing Places: A Tale of Two Campuses* (1975), shows Morris Zapp, high-powered academic from Euphoria State, changing places with drab Philip Swallow from Rummidge. The two different worlds also breed different discourses: Rummidge in the industrial Midlands is realism in action, Euphoria is postmodernism by the Pacific. Technically ambitious as well as funny, the book shows American fictiveness crossing with British social realism. It ends appropriately in mid air over the Atlantic, turned into the format of a film-script. By *Small World* (1980) the academic world and its philosophies have changed. Literary scholars have developed Francophilia and are engaged on a love affair with Structuralism, Post-Structuralism and Deconstruction, and the age of the big congress and the super-academic is here. The book is self-consciously based on the classic structure of the medieval quest romance – except that postmodern heroes and heroines no longer go on love-quests or pilgrimages but on conferences, touring the Global Campus, the 'travelling caravan of professors with international contacts, lightweight luggage and generous conference grants'. The book thus contains not just a pleasant sexual pursuit conducted by way of literary allusions, but much satire of the fashionable literary-theoretical ideas, partly displayed in the opinions of two hotshot critics. One is Morris Zapp, now returned as celebrity professor; the other is the decidedly sinister Michel Tardieu, French Deconstructor, both of whom play their part in deconstructing the novel's own plot. By *Nice Work* (1985) all ideas have changed, not least because of the arrival of theoretical feminism. The book moves between the academic world of postmodern and post-feminist ideals and the male world of industry and practical work: in other words, between contemporary criticism and one of its favoured objects of study, the Victorian novel. A feminist lecturer, Robyn Penrose, who specializes in the Victorian industrial novels of the 1840s, takes part in a shadow scheme and enters the world of the factory floor, grainy reality and a down-to-earth industrial manager, Vic Wilcox. In the world of Thatcherism, the two nations meet and learn something from each other. Two later novels, *Paradise News* (1991) and *Therapy* (1996), have explored ageing, the Catholic faith and the idea of pilgrimage and paradise (*Paradise News* is set in a classic paradisial Utopia, Hawaii). Lodge's novels, like his criticism, have been both

chosen to depict her ascent from behind – bums aloft, you might say; up she goes, in a steatopygous perspective, shaking out about her those tremendous red and purple pinions large enough, powerful enough, to bear up such a big girl as she . . .' Fevvers is the streetwise pop version of *art nouveau* erotic ambiguities, and the novel is about slippages, fantasies and aerial dreams, some stage-managed by Fevvers, some by the novelist herself. It takes us from London to St Petersburg and Siberia, from the world of the music hall to the world of the legendary forests, from the city of the smoke to the land of the bears. Like Fevvers herself ('How does she do it?' 'Do you think she's real?'), the story is a refusal of fixity and stable setting, a universe of trickery, alive and slippery with an invention that has no need to stop. Clocks can halt on command, toys become trains, Fevvers grow wings. In fact *Nights at the Circus* is a version of the modern novel in a form that Carter well understood – the carnivalesque.

The same is true of her final novel, *Wise Children* (1991), her largest book, and another enterprise in spectacle, travesty, saturnalia, masquerade. It's a wise child, they say, that knows its own father; the identical Chance twins in the story certainly have an ambiguous relationship with theirs. Born on the wrong side of the blanket to 'the imperial Hazard dynasty that bestrode the British theatre like a colossus for half a century', they are the love-children of Sir Melchior Hazard, famous Shakespearean (and therefore 'legitimate') actor. Legitimacy and illegitimacy in modern British culture are the book's main theme; the Chance twins are 'illegitimate in every way – not only born out of wedlock, but we went on the halls, didn't we?' They belong in the alternative world of music hall, the seaside postcard, pantomime and vaudeville, which is also the world of the ugly dame, the dirty joke, the sexual innuendo, travesty, clowning and cross-dressing. They live on the wrong side of the tracks, south of the river, or in other words in the working-class, alternative part of London. There are legitimate Hazard descendants, mostly male; there are Chance descendants, mostly female ('Chance by name, Chance by nature'). Self-invention and female regeneration is another central theme. Pantomime, Carter once said, is 'the carnival of the unacknowledged and the fiesta of the repressed', and the story is in part a pantomime reworking of Shakespeare's tales (it is set partly on the Chance twins' seventy-fifth birthday, which is also Shakespeare's birthday), not in a solemn homage but in the form of outrageous carnival. ('There was singing and dancing all along Bard Row that day and we'll go on singing and dancing till we drop in our tracks.') The allegorical meanings are not obscure: the legitimate Hazards are a theatrical royalty and their global touring is a version of imperialism; the illegitimate Chances are a second Britain of far greater ambiguity, anti-imperial, anti-patriarchal, a radical dissolution of culture. 'Millennia get strange before the end,' Carter said, and so it seemed; this was British 'magic realism', where reality and history could be transformed and rewritten, taken over the edge. Carter died in February 1992 at the early age of fifty-one, not very long after her finest book appeared. A last book of stories, *American Ghosts and Old World Wonders* (published posthumously, 1993), explored two of the essential landscapes of her distinctive and Gothic universe, extending our sense of her transgressive literary vitality.

In a similar way other landscapes were expanding. Doris Lessing's 'Canopus in Argos' novels belong to the early Eighties, and they too observe a world in fundamental change, where the fatal misuse of energies has ruined the planet Shikasta (Earth) and made it necessary for wiser visions and policies to be pursued elsewhere in the cosmos, not least with the use of a new consciousness led by women. While some writers like Zoë Fairbairns (*Stand We at Last*, 1983) and Sarah Maitland (*Virgin Territory*, 1984) wrote a polemical feminist fiction, other writers like Fay Weldon explored the issues with a good deal of technical trickery and, often, great satirical bite. Weldon, a prolific writer, had all the techniques and genres at her disposal, as well as an observant eye for society and domestic manners, angles and viewpoints. Her chief books of the Eighties were *The Life and Loves of a She-Devil* (1983), a tale of bitter rivalries where a less attractive woman pursues and kills a more approved and conventional heroine; and *The Cloning of Joanna May* (1989), a latter-day version of the Frankenstein myth. Another significant figure was Michèle Roberts, of Anglo-French Catholic background, who published her first feminist novel *A Piece of the Night* in 1978. A number of her books amend the biblical myths: *The Visitation* (1978) rewrote the Virgin Birth tale, *The Wild Girl* (1984) is a revised 'fifth gospel' story of Mary Magdalene and in *The Book of Mrs Noah* (1987) the Ark is filled with female writers, seizing the moment after God has writer's block. Another powerful reviser is Marina Warner, author of an important critical study *Monuments and Maidens: The Allegory of Female Form* (1985). Her fiction (it starts with *In a Dark Wood* in 1977) has been both scholarly and striking. *The Skating Party* (1982) derives its contemporary story from the ambiguities of lost frescoes dicovered in the Vatican; *Indigo* (1992) revises the story of Caliban's mother, Sycorax, from *The Tempest*, and looks at the subsequent history of the Caribbean over the age of slave-trading and colonialism. Feminist revisionism over the next few years took a variety of forms. Emma Tennant considered Thomas Hardy's most famous female in *Tess* (1993), part of a vogue for critical prequels and sequels that included Susan Hill's *Mrs De Winter* (1993), a revisiting of Daphne du Maurier's *Rebecca*. Entire genres were increasingly feminized. P. D. James, Ruth Rendell and Joan Smith all applied female or feminist angles to crime fiction and, in her second guise as 'Barbara Vine', Rendell wrote some of the strongest psychological fiction of the day (*A Dark-Adapted Eye*, 1986).

Works of strong and original experiment also appeared. In 1981 Maggie Gee published *Dying in Other Words*, a powerful novel about the violent death, by deeds and words, of the central female character, and about the problematics of language, the blanknesses of female representation. But the most significant and promising experimental writer of the day appeared to be Jeannette Winterson, who published *Oranges Are Not the Only Fruit* in 1985. A remarkable tale about a girl growing up in a highly strict Pentecostal family in Lancashire, using many experimental interventions and interludes, it depicts the fascination with signs and symbols such an education leads to, as well as the kind of gender revolt it produces, as its heroine breaks loose through a series of lesbian relationships and an entry into writing. Winterson, like Carter, insisted on being 'boundariless', and attempted to break the borders of fact and fiction, reality and fantasy, in a number of highly self-conscious fictions that explored the unwritten meanings of the body, complex sexualities and sensualities, the nature of love and desire. Her books are often highly playful; *Boating for Beginners* (also 1985) is a splendid travesty of the story of Noah and his Thatcherite enterprise in creating a boat-building business even as he tries to attend to the instructions of Yahweh the Unpronounceable. *The Passion* (1987) – Gore Vidal hailed her on the strength of it as 'the best young writer I've read in twenty years' – is a more complex, highly mirrored postmodern experiment, brilliant and unusual. One part of the story is set in the early nineteenth century as Napoleon invades Russia, the other part in the deceptive city of Venice. A key character is Napoleon's chicken-chef, another a bisexual Venetian courtesan who is born with webbed feet and walks on water. History becomes a place of burlesque, confusion of sexual identity and the complex indulgence of passion.

Her later novels deal with words and signs, history and fantasy, the reading and revising of the 'text' of the body, the giving to writing of a more complex physicality. *Sexing the Cherry* (1989) is freely and frame-breakingly set both in the English Civil War in the seventeenth century and the present, and moves between the realms of fact and fiction, opening out to Rabelaisian fairy tale, literary meditation and political commentary. *Written On the Body* (1992) is a postmodern, ambiguous love story written by a predatory, ungendered but probably female narrator, and is about the multiple meanings of love and the different ways in which we read the body. A married Australian lover is now dying of leukaemia, and the plotless text becomes a hymn not just to the sexual wonder but the decomposition of the human body. *Arts & Lies* (1994) is a Calvino-like fiction made of collage and scraps, told by multiple voices; and Winterson expressed her lesbian aesthetics clearly in the essays of *Art Objects: Essays on Ecstasy and Affrontery* (1995), the title being as good a definition of her attitude as we have. Winterson is a powerful, baroque and thoughtful writer of a time when, working under the influence of feminist, Foucault-ian and Lacan-ian theory, feminists have been rewriting many myths and texts, or revising the representation of gender and the body. The problem with her more recent work is that the experimentalism of the serious and exploratory novelist seems to have given way to the self-conscious narcissism of the high-profile celebrity, along with an old-fashioned Pentecostal conviction that only her own personal speaking-in-tongues is of any artistic interest. The great rewriting, in its various forms – transgression, travesty, parody and what Winterson calls 'affrontery' – was one of the themes of the Eighties, and had great significance for the depiction and interpretation of sex and gender in fiction, and for the growing sense of literary freedom that ran right through the decade.[8]

9

An important consequence of all this was its broad effect on sexual and gender representation in fiction, in the work of male as well as female authors, and in the work of the many women writers, including Doris Lessing and A. S. Byatt, who did not want to be simply identified as feminist. 'I strenuously resist categorization as a "woman's writer" and the notion that women should address themselves only to women's problems, as this strikes me as limiting and inhibiting, a kind of literary sexism in itself,' remarked Rose Tremain, a highly important novelist who (having written a thesis on women's suffrage) established herself in the mid Seventies with *Sadler's Birthday* (1976), the bleak and compassionate story of a butler who, having sacrificed most of his life for others, is now dying in the stately home he has inherited from his employers, a labyrinth of unfurnished rooms (the book bears an interesting resemblance to Kazuo Ishiguro's later *The Remains of the Day*). Tremain's fiction, which includes *Letter to Sister Benedicta* (1978), *The Cupboard* (1981), about the life of a radical woman novelist, and *The Swimming Pool Season* (1985), set in France, was to remain notable for its moral understanding, its sense of the pains and discords of human life and its androgynous sympathies (Tremain is one of those striking novelists who can recount a fiction as convincingly from the male as the female viewpoint). The anatomy

---

8 Several of the writers mentioned above, and the general issues surrounding their work, are excellently discussed by Lorna Sage in her *Women in the House of Fiction: Post-War Women Novelists* (London, 1992).

of the human heart became, symbolically and actually, the cental subject of her finest novel from the Eighties, *Restoration* (1989). It was her first historical novel, set in the age of and round the court of King Charles the Second, and including in its drama the Great Plague and the Great Fire of London. It is the story of Robert Merivel, an anatomist, much exploited court favourite, 'fool' and victim of the highly unreliable king. Merivel himself is obsessed with the human heart, which he sees visibly through the wall of a chest, a living, beating organ of feeling which is, paradoxically, itself without feeling. Merivel bears this in mind as he nervously tells his own story as it unfolds: 'I am also in the middle of a story which might have a variety of endings, some of them not entirely to my liking.' Merivel is a good enough man, with his own disturbing lusts and a troubled sense of humanity. He is also a natural cuckold; the king uses him to take an unwanted mistress off his hands and thus he earns himself the reward of a fine Norfolk estate. He is under royal command not to consummate the marriage, but his human heart betrays him; he makes the mistake of falling in love with his own wife. In the end, working with lunatics and plague victims, Merivel goes on trying to understand the complex truths of the human heart. So does the book, jewelled, intricate, vividly symbolic; one of the finest British books of the Eighties.

Tremain's work developed powerfully in the Nineties. Her next novel, *Sacred Country* (1992), bears a small but significant inward resemblance to *Late Call* and other novels by Angus Wilson (she was his student at the University of East Anglia). It starts in traditional, rural, scarce-changing Norfolk in 1952 at the beginning of the New Elizabethan Age; King George VI has died, and the young queen is crowned, suggesting a new promise and a time of change. The change sought by Mary Ward, a farmer's daughter, is to her sexuality; she wishes to be a man. Like Virginia Woolf's *Orlando*, the novel becomes a story of transsexuality, and runs from a settled rural England to the Country-and-Western universe of Nashville, Tennessee, and the Grand Ol' Opry. Her transsexuality relates to and resembles that state of androgyny the novelist herself defines as part of the writer's powers. *The Way I Found Her* (1997), another strong story of growing up, is this time told by a thirteen-year-old boy who goes to Paris with his mother, a literary translator working on a book by a famous and intriguing female Russian novelist, and who is subtly initiated into the mysteries of Paris, gender, sex, life and literature. Then in *Music and Silence* (1999) Tremain returned to the historical novel; the story is set round the Danish court of King Christian IV in the year 1629, where another observing young man, the English musician Peter Claire, who plays with the royal orchestra in the cellar below the state rooms, becomes increasingly involved in the difficult world of royal affairs, as a perfectionist king and a selfish queen contend with each other. Again the book is measured, meditative, surprising, much concerned with the needs of art, the oddities of sex and the complex and intricate world of music and its opposite, silence. Tremain is a splendid, symbolically vivid, always unusual novelist not of the politics of relationships, but of their often bitter subtleties, and her novels are indeed anatomies, tales of strong and interesting characters and the strange ways of human nature.

In the end, what distinguishes much of the women's writing that flourished so strongly over the Eighties was not only its feminist concerns and its intensive re-exploration of female discourse, iconography and social subject, but its narrative range and discovering variety. One of the most interesting writers of the decade was Penelope Fitzgerald (1916–2000), another novelist of the intricacies of human nature. She came to fiction late, at the age of fifty-eight, having already written works of scholarship and biography. Her first novel, *The Golden Child*, was based around the Tutankhamun Exhibition held at the British Museum. Her second book, *The Bookshop* (1978), was shortlisted for the Booker, and she won the prize the next year for her third book, *Offshore*, a tale of a group of London bohemians who live on houseboats moored on the River Thames, filled with wit and a sense of human ironies. *Human Voices* (1980) is a remarkable, Muriel Spark-like tale knowingly set in the strange bureaucracy of BBC broadcasting during wartime, and the London of the Blitz. She took up several wry historical subjects: *Innocence* (1986) is a novel set in Florence in the Fifties and the past, and *The Beginning of Spring* (1988), the story of a Moscow-born Englishman with a small business, deals with personal relations in the context of the last days of Tsarist Russia, trembling with revolution. The finest book came right at the end, when she published *The Blue Flower* (1995), a remarkable portrait of the strange, perverse German writer Novalis (whose emblem was a blue flower), an essential source of the romantic and Gothic imagination. Like all her books, the novel was technically skilful, an art of indirection and compression; it won numerous prizes, not least the American National Book Critics Circle Award, recognition of a major career in writing. Fitzgerald died at the age of eighty-three in 2000.

Fitzgerald's is part of a modern fiction of form and restraint, as far distant as possible from Angela Carter's world of the carnivalesque, the illegitimate and general creative overspill as it would be possible to go – unless one turned to the work of Anita Brookner, a distinguished art historian, biographer of Watteau and David, as well as one of the great postmodern experts of a fiction of order, structure, angle of vision, self-restraint. Her first book was *A Start in Life*, published at the beginning of the Eighties, notable for its recession, its Jamesian precision and sense of style. This was followed by subtle works like *Hotel du Lac*, which won the Booker Prize in 1984, the story of a middle-aged woman observing the world from a continental hotel terrace as she closes down an affair with a married man. In Brookner's work, restraint is a kind of irony, recessiveness a subtlety, modesty a delicate withdrawal from the scene; at the same time her female characters are aware of the domesticities and small tyrannies that have shaped them, and that things might well have been different: 'It seems to me my own youth was passed in a dream, and that I only came to see the world as it was when it was already too late,' reflects one of her characters in *Brief Lives* (1990). Most of her books – *A Misalliance* (1986), *Latecomers* (1988), *Incidents at the Rue Langier* (1995) – vividly portray moments in the lives of highly intelligent, generally lonely and frequently self-sacrificing women, often *émigrée* or Jewish, living in families of complicated obligations. The viewpoint of her novels is frequently that of the woman as observer, the woman who leads life by a kind of literary or bookish decency, only to find that the one who does not claim opportunities is at a disadvantage to those less reticent women who demand more from life: 'immodesty . . . always gains concessions', it is wisely and wrily observed in *A Misalliance*.

Then there is the fiction of Penelope Lively, who also turned to adult fiction late (there were earlier stories for children), and whose novels make memory, loss, the archaeology of personal lives, and human history central themes. In 1979 she published *Treasures of Time*, about an archaeologist, while *According to Mark* (1984) explores the paradoxes of biography. In 1987 her novel *Moon Tiger* – an ageing woman historian's personal and professional recollections of Egypt here turn into a medley of conflicting voices – won the Booker Prize. Egypt and travel are favourite settings, and *Cleopatra's Sister* (1993) invents a whole new society. Lively's fiction is decidedly international; so too is that of Hilary Mantel. Her novels range from a sharp and often amusing exploration of various contemporary societies – *Eight Months on Ghazzah Street* (1988) is set in Dubai – to powerful historical novels: *Fludd* (1989) and *The Giant O'Brien* (1998). Lisa Saint Aubin de Terán moved from the shifting 'magic realism' of her Venezuelan novel *Keepers of the House* (1983) and its Italian successor *Slow Train to Milan* (1984) by way of a number of high-Gothic tales to the large span of her generational novel *Joanna* (1990). The reinvigoration of women's fiction had an obvious consequence; the latter part of the Eighties and the turn into the Nineties saw the emergence of a large number of new women writers. They included Elspeth Barker (author of the vivid and Gothic *O Caledonia!*, 1991), Georgina Hammick, Candia McWilliam, Jenny Diski (*Happily Ever After*, 1991), Lucy Ellmann, Jane Rogers (*Mr Wroe's Virgins*, 1991), Deirdre Madden, Helen Simpson, Kathy Page, Janice Galloway, A. L. Kennedy (*Looking for the Possible Dance*, 1993) and Esther Freud (*Hideous Kinky*, 1992). They were able to draw on the new literary freedoms that had developed over the Eighties, both in freer and more assertive depiction of gender and sexuality and in their use of formal play, delight in fantasy, generic crossover. The same applied to the new wave of gay and lesbian fiction – the writing of Jeannette Winterson, Adam Mars-Jones, Alan Hollinghurst (*The Swimming Pool Library*, 1988) – which came toward the end of the decade.

The Eighties was a time of particularly powerful change in British fiction, as the writers of an older generation that had been writing since the Fifties were joined by a medley of new voices. The climate of change came not least because of underlying social, sexual and cultural shifts that were taking place beneath the apparently highly conservative surface of Thatcherism. They marked, in fact, a kind of triumph of commercial and cultural international capitalism, when forms and *mores* were more and more shaped by an age of catholic, pluri-cultural and global values. Images and icons now came less from linear national traditions than from the imagery of an age dominated by flicker and screen, rock music and movies, celebrity icons and fashion myths; meanwhile individual lives were changing in the presence of increasing wealth, multiplying commodities, a general individualization and feminization of culture. The book itself adapted to changing culture; older publishing houses clustered together in great communications conglomerates, large bookstores opened on the high streets, new audiences were cultivated. Said one influential and feminist publisher, Carmen Callil: '. . . the second fifty years of the century . . . have been a period as sublime and exciting as any other for the novel. The mass market paperback came to its own during these fifty years. Books have benefited from a revolution in publishing and printing and selling methods; the computer has waved a magic wand over most publishing processes; authors have more rights, and many, if still too few, earn more money.'[9] It was a transforming time for fiction and authorship, for the emergence of young new talents and promising and well-paid literary careers. For all its streetwise gloom and millennial anxiety, the vigour of British fiction was apparent, and this had been an expansive period for the novel. The interesting question, as the world changed entirely at the end of the decade (the Berlin Wall came down, Thatcher fell, the ideological age ended) was how this would shape the fiction of the Nineties.

9 Carmen Callil and Colm Tóibín, *The Modern Library: The 200 Best Novels in English Since 1950* (London, 1999).

10

Millennial Days:
1989–2001

A word about the title. Several alternatives presented themselves. For a while I toyed with *Time's Arrow*. Then I thought
Millennium would be wonderfully bold (a common belief:
everything is called *Millennium* just now). I even flirted, late
at night, with *The Death of Love*...

> Martin Amis, 'Note' to *London Fields* (1989)

Reading is always this: there is an object that is there, a thing
made of writing, a solid, material object, which cannot be
changed, and through this thing we measure ourselves against
something else that is not present, something that belongs to
the immaterial, invisible world, because it can only be thought
or imagined, or because it was once and is no longer ... Or
that is not present because it does not yet exist, something
desired, feared ... Reading is going toward something that is
about to be, and no one yet knows what it will be.

> Italo Calvino, *If On a Winter's Night a Traveller...* (1981)

Thus they went on living in a reality that was slipping away,
momentarily captured by words, but would escape irremediably
when they forgot the values of written letters.

> Gabriel García Márquez,
> *One Hundred Years of Solitude* (1967)

1

The year 1999 was a year for the making of lists. The twentieth century, inventive, modernizing, terrible, was coming to an end. So was twentieth-century literature, which in one apocalyptic moment (celebrated by a rubberized dome at Greenwich and a hi-tech River of Fire on the Thames that somehow failed to burn) passed from present to past, contemporary to classic. A hundred years of modernity, and modern fiction, were closing; there was no clear certainty of what would come next. A 'Millennium' is an artificial invention, a calendar fiction, an aspect of Western Christian chronology born of a faith now less and less believed in, a narrative imposition on the seamless flow of space and time. Even the date is up for revisionist dispute; the brand-new epoch surely starts in 2001, not 2000. Yet millennial sentiments are, and always have been, real enough. Apocalyptics are part of our power to give shape and meaning, structure and purpose, beginnings and middles and endings to the random plot of time; and the sense of passage is profound.[1] So it had seemed at the dawning of the twentieth century when, in a striking rush of change, it appeared history was altering entirely, a fresh modern age was to hand. Even more so at the end not of one but of two epochs: of a hundred years of speeded-up modernity, a thousand of evolving modern history, through the Dark and Middle Ages to our present age of Science and Democracy, Worldwide Web and Internet – a long passage of religion and superstition, reason and enlightenment, progress and reaction, reform and revolution, European hegemony, deep social change, scientific hypotheses and discoveries that have

---

1 Waiting for the end is an old human custom; on this see Norman Cohn, *The Pursuit of the Millennium* (London, 1990). Felipe Fernández-Armesto's more recent and fascinating account, *Millennium* (London, 1995), looks back over the last thousand years and considers the likely future. Paul Kennedy, *Preparing for the Twenty-First Century* (New York, 1993), looks as a historian at the implications for the new century of political, economic and demographic change; while Harold Bloom, *Omens of Millennium: The Gnosis of Angels, Dreams and Resurrection* (London, 1997), looks at the extraordinary history of millennial imaginings.

altered human nature, horrific conflicts that have destroyed our hopes and Utopian dreams. In the year 1000, modernity, Britain and the genre of the novel did not even exist. Our literary traditions and the idea of literary modernity are evolutionary products of the ages between. Some halfway through the millennium the novel as a central form of imaginative expression came into being in Europe, related to a growing individualism, an empirical, scientific view of experience, a personalized sense of the world. In the past three centuries it became an important carrier of experience, amending its nature to suit the facts of historical existence, types of society, moral and political values, degrees of freedom, perceptions of love and gender, order and value, comedy and tragedy, reality and fantasy, that seemed to form a sufficient fiction for the times.

In the early twentieth century, Western fictions grew modern too. As we have seen, the novel shrugged off many elements of its Victorian role as burgher epic, solid text of God-like realism, the great instrument of social representation. It found a new character among the relativities and uncertainties of an age when revolutions dawned, when space and time, progress and expectation, desire and imagination were shifting. The radical changes of the 1890s – new printing technologies, means of distribution, readers and audiences, the growth of fresh narrative mechanisms and fresh popular genres – reshaped every printed object. Poetry grew aesthetic and symbolist, the novel split between serious and popular. In late James, Conrad, Lawrence and Joyce, serious fiction entered experiment and obscurity, as popular writers from H. G. Wells and Arnold Bennett to Elinor Glyn and John Buchan grew rich and famous on evolving genres: boys' imperial adventure, women's popular romance, children's fantasy, detective fiction, science fiction, ghost stories, Gothic horror. In the years between 1900 and the Great War, when a futurist or millennarian view of the century grew, much literature responded to the conditions of modernity itself: the self-conscious age of accelerating science and medicine, urbanism and secularism, reform and revolution, which then turned into the age of horrific war and genocide, collapse of monarchs and empires, mass slaughter, fundamental ideological conflict. By the Twenties, when the disturbing character of the century had grown evident and its destructive energies plain, a series of self-questioning works appeared – Joyce's *Ulysses*, Proust's *Remembrance of Things Past*, Mann's *The Magic Mountain*, Virginia Woolf's *Mrs Dalloway*, Faulkner's *The Sound and the Fury*, Kafka's *The Trial*, Hemingway's *A Farewell to Arms* – which changed our notions of the novel, and radically restructured its forms.

Less obscure transformations grew obvious in fiction: the perception of history, the sense of human promise, the rules of romance and emotion, sexual, class, ethnic and international inter-relations, the sense of manners and custom. And the new techniques and styles arose not just from the intricate mechanics of such devices as stream-of-consciousness, collage-writing or the reproduction of involuntary memory, but from film, history-writing, journalism and reportage. Literary modernity was dissolving into an age of technological mass culture. New forms of publication – especially the cheap paperback, pioneered by Allen Lane's Penguin Books in the Thirties – and distribution also changed the world of the book. The balance between genres changed: poetry lost much of its epic status, though major poets (Ted Hughes, Philip Larkin, Seamus Heaney, Derek Walcott) emerge to this day. It was the novel that increasingly became the vehicle both of serious and popular narrative expression, and in an age of internationalization what had started primarily as a European or Mediterranean genre became a global form. From the *émigré* disorientations of the turn of the century, then the revolutionary and totalitarian years, when Conrad fled Poland and Nabokov Russia, many of the great writers came from between or across cultures: Canetti, Mann and Nabokov, Borges and Márquez, Kundera and Solzhenitsyn, Rushdie writing migrant tales of East and West, Toni Morrison drawing on African, Caribbean and Afro-American legend. Novels, magical and tricky histories, have spread by global transit and translation, the smuggling of manuscripts, *samizdat*. By the end of the twentieth century the novel had necessarily and visibly adapted to a great realignment of world culture and an age of new technologies – which had threatened to dispense with it altogether for hotter media. It had adapted to new values, changed systems and patterns of communication, different audiences, the modern marketplace. The final years of the century, the age of IMAX film and digital television, the Internet, the website, the interactive screen, saw an explosion of systems of communication and an unprecedented acceleration of the print and post-print media. More stories were told in more languages, sign systems and technologies to a wider and more international spread of audiences for more pleasure and profit than ever before. Medium fed on medium, narrative on narrative, in a vast crossover of narrative myths and types, icons and genres. Some called this the great dumbing down, the end of the Gutenberg tradition, the collapse of the canon.[2] Others saw it as an explosion of creativity, the demo-cratization of imaginative expression, the triumph of the book and the novel.

The century's end was an age of prizes, a time for assessing modern achievements. When in 1997 Waterstone's bookshop and Channel Four television polled 25,000 British readers on the hundred most important books of the century, the results surprised in several ways. The list had no poetry and little non-fiction; forms of the novel took centre stage. J. R. R. Tolkein's *The Lord of the Rings*, an elaborate learned children's fantasy, written in 1954–5, headed the list, and Tolkein's other lasting work *The Hobbit* was at number nineteen. Other books read first in childhood – Orwell's *Animal Farm*, Kenneth Grahame's *The Wind in the Willows*, A. A. Milne's *Winnie the Pooh* – held high place, but so did darker fictions: Orwell's *Nineteen Eighty-Four* at number two, Aldous Huxley's *Brave New World* at fifteen. Modernity had turned into classic: *Ulysses*, forbidden to the British reader in the Twenties, read only by experts in the Fifties, was at number four, Márquez's magic realist classic *One Hundred Years*

2 As Sven Birkerts puts it in *The Gutenberg Elegies: The Fate of Reading in an Electronic Age* (London, 1994): 'The influx of electronic communications and information-processing technologies, abetted by the steady improvement of the micro-processor, has suddenly brought on a condition of critical mass. Suddenly it seems as if everything is poised for change; the slower world many of us grew up in dwindles in the rearview mirror. The stable hierarchies of the printed page – one of the defining norms of that world – are being superseded by the rush of impulses through freshly minted circuits . . . living as we do in the midst of innumerable affiliated webs, we can say that changes in the immediate sphere of print refer outward to the totality; they map on a smaller scale the riot of societal forces.'

of Solitude at number eight. Modern American novels took very high place (Heller's *Catch-22*, Salinger's *The Catcher in the Rye*, Alice Walker's *The Color Purple*); so did Irvine Welsh's Scots drugs-and-lowlife *Trainspotting*, though the film version was just released. What seemed apparent was the novel's survival – and the multiplicity of its use. Yet still the question returned: was the novel alive or dead? For the *émigré* Czech novelist Milan Kundera, author of *Days of Laughter and Forgetting*, the answer was clear. The end of the political age, the rise of a commodity literary culture, had killed it as a serious form: 'The children of the novel have abandoned the art which shaped them. Europe, the society of the novel, has abandoned its own self.' As a Czech living under Communism, Kundera had already known one 'death of the novel': 'a violent death (inflicted by bans, censorship, and political pressure) in the world where I spent much of my life and is usually called totalitarian'. Under commodity capitalism he sees another, a superfluity of unnecessary fiction, the trivialization of its purpose:

But now, in another order, comes a different kind of death; there are novels written by graphomaniacs that, by discovering nothing, fail to place themselves within the sequence of discoveries that is the true history of the novel: the novel does not die, it falls away from history, because it has no real function. The death of the novel is in part a fantasy that comes when Modernism turns into kitsch, and the future and the media are everything – and we withdraw modern fiction from the four-centuries history of the novel.[3]

And yet, as Salman Rushdie observed, the novel's health had never looked greater, especially if we accepted that its function had changed, its centre shifted, away from the European heartland where the humanist novel was forged. What, Rushdie argued, is now emerging is 'a decentred, trans-national, interlingual, cross-cultural novel'. Today the problem, Rushdie declared, is not the end of the book, not the death of the reader; it is 'the bewilderment of the reader. In Britain

---

3 Milan Kundera, *The Art of the Novel* (London, 1988), and also *Testaments Betrayed* (London, 1995).

[in 1995] over 8,000 new novels were published. Eight thousand! It would be extraordinary if eighty of them were good. It would be a cause for universal celebration if eight of them – if one of them! – were great. Publishers are over-publishing because good editors have been fired or not replaced, and obsession with turnover has replaced the ability to distinguish good books from bad . . .' What we need is simple, he says, to separate the good from the bad, the temporary from the lasting: 'We need a return to judgment.'[4]

2

Apocalyptics, retrospectives, grand reckonings have always happened as times have turned. All modern centuries have ended in radical change, a shift in styles and technologies, intimations both of strange hopes and dystopian glooms. The eighteenth century ended in an age of revolutions (the American, the French, the Industrial), the collapse of nations, *anciens régimes*, monarchies, empires; a profound change in human expectation and sensibility challenged religion and authority, changed scientific understanding and altered the sense of human consciousness; all this was plainly expressed in arts themselves revolutionary, the arts of the Romantic Revolution. The nineteenth century, as I suggested at the start, closed on an equally radical change: the revolution of Modernity, which shattered so much of the nineteenth-century world-view, dismantled icons and monuments, dislocated tradition, began – in arts, sciences, politics, philosophy, architecture, technology, the visible appearance of cities – the Triumph of the New. The modern project sent planes into the skies, lit streets with electricity, put motor vehicles on city roads, electric trains underneath

---

4 Salman Rushdie, 'The novel is not dead. It's just buried', in the *Observer*, 18 August 1996, p. 15. Rushdie is responding to some recent observations by George Steiner: 'We are getting very tired in our novels . . . Genres rise, genres fall, the epic, the verse epic, the formal verse tragedy. Great moments, then they ebb. Novels will continue to be written for quite a while but, increasingly, the search is on for hybrid forms, what we will call rather crassly fact fiction . . . What novel can today quite compete with the best of reportage, with the very best of immediate narrative?'

them. It changed perspectives on space and time, transformed science. The Modern revolution in the arts was in some ways a revolt against history: the nightmare from which Stephen Dedalus was trying to awake. It was not just the narrow repressions of history and politics, religion and nationality that restrained the arts; the task of the artist was to leave history and read the transcendental signatures beyond. The modern novel was more than a report or a history; it was a radical adventure in form, in sign, in language, and it broke with familiarity to set the creative imagination in process.

This was one of the serious projects of modernity, the making of a modern literature. That project itself is now more than a century long, and is itself historical. As George Steiner said, 'we come after', in modernity's shadow, 'postmodern' times. In the event, the century of modernity was also the terrible century, and the history of its wars, cruelties and disasters by far overshadows its other achievements. Modern times and 'the shape of things to come' were quite as extreme and visionary as the utopians of a century past predicted, and quite as disastrous as the dystopians feared. If Utopia and Dystopia have played a large part in modern history and politics, they have played just as great a part in our fictions.[5] The visionary images of an age of the new that ran through science and religion, politics and the arts, and did so much to shape them, have now mostly grown familiar, clichés at the end of their lives. The first great marker was a monument, the raising of the Eiffel Tower in 1889, a celebration of the French Revolution one hundred years earlier, and in its abstraction a metaphysical cathedral of modernity, according to Umberto Eco in his novel *Foucault's Pendulum*. In the next twenty-five years, to 1914,

---

5 For an excellent representation of the theme, see John Carey (ed.), *The Faber Book of Utopias* (London, 1999). As Carey notes, though the pursuit of Utopia, the ideal society, has lasted long in history, it has been particularly potent in the twentieth century. Utopia means no place, but is often taken to mean 'good place'; hence it has spawned its opposite, Dystopia, 'bad place'. The twentieth century has given us much of both: the future fictions of H. G. Wells, the *Brave New World* of Aldous Huxley, George Orwell's *Nineteen Eighty-Four*, but also joyous space fantasies, feminist Utopias (the universal worship of the goddess, or worlds without men), Las Vegas and Disneyland itself. Most millennarian fantasies are forms of Utopianism, and the book has a lively topicality.

the speed of hope and expectation accelerated enormously, the *belle époque* and *art nouveau* flourished, and modernity dawned in a mixture of clean futurist hope and exotic decadence. Then in August 1914 it collapsed into the long drawn-out battlefronts of the Great War.

'What a disappointment the twentieth century has been,' reflected Winston Churchill as early as 1922. 'How terrible and how melancholy is the long series of disastrous events which have darkened its first twenty years.' The years to 1939 saw a Modernist interregnum, a new era of modernity: fragmentary, chaotic, despairing, ideological. Then, twenty-five years on, it too collapsed into war, the greatest crisis of the century, in which the modern had now become the militaristic and the totalitarian. Thus the shadows that fell over the century's second half were not just those of the new arts that had dissolved representation or opened expression to new notions of perception and consciousness, but those of the ideologies and competitions of a century which, in 1945, left a continent and large parts of the world in ruins. All political geography changed; the great map of the world imagined by Hitler at the start of the war, where the new German Empire possessed Europe and the British Empire much of the rest of the world, shifted into the age of the two hostile superpowers, Russia and America, each attempting to create new spheres of influence. Europe was no longer the core of history; a Second and a Third World emerged in the wake of old colonialisms. By the mid Sixties, twenty-five years further on still, the new post-war arts were coming alive again in an era of radical populism and youth culture, born from nuclear anxiety and Cold War gloom, and hoping for a new Age of Aquarius. In 1989, a hundred years after the Eiffel Tower went up, the Berlin Wall came down, ending an entire phase of modern history. The surprise was massive; almost no political commentator had predicted the sudden collapse of Communism or the speed of the change. This, said American President George Bush, was the New World Order, the achievement of the century. And it was, said the political analyst Francis Fukayama, the end of history, when the nightmare we had been trying to wake from had at last reached its conclusion, beyond ideology, brinkmanship and confrontation. The post-war world had come to an end.

3

The euphoria did not last long; it took only a very short span of years for the excitement to dissolve. The New World Order very soon proved itself to be the New World Disorder, as boundaries shifted and nations examined their own identities, as past alliances and allegiances fractured and the map of the world looked as chaotic as ever. The Nineties began with signs of reconciliation, promises of progress, and old conflicts appeared to be reaching resolution in South Africa, the Middle East, Ireland. Yet as often the End of History created a return to the old wounds of history, and the calendar often did not advance but rolled remorselessly back. Unsettled scores and conflicts reopened, old crisis sites were revisited: Sarajevo, Kosovo, the Czech and Yugoslav borders, the Baltic states, the Arab borders, the flashpoints of 1945 and 1939, 1918 and 1914, 1871 and 1848. Unions and nations dissolved (the Czechs, the Yugoslavs). In 1991 Mikhail Gorbachev, the last Soviet president, resigned, and days later the USSR no longer existed. The statues of modern icons (Lenin, Stalin) fell, the names of cities changed (Leningrad to St Petersburg, Stalingrad to Volvograd). The political leaders of the Eighties – Gorbachev, Thatcher, Reagan, Bush, Kohl, Mitterrand – began disappearing from the political stage. As real nuclear terrors faded, their fictional counterparts took their place: Einstein's monsters. The world's problems – industrial pollution, environmental crisis, global warming – had not gone away. Apocalyptic signs abounded: plagues (AIDS and drugs) and earthquakes seemed to spread, weather patterns shifted, cities decayed. Human pleasures were human pains: food and drinks, sex and smoking, all came with health warnings. New visions arose of the technological wilderness, the age of dreck, crime-ridden, drug-crazed cities, wasted landscapes, ethnic cleansing, modern genocide, tribal slaughters, rising seas, shrinking ice-caps, urban surveillance, genetic interference, human cloning, cyberspace. Sensations of transition, anxiety and uncontrollable energies and disorders had always haunted the ends of centuries; this one was no exception.

Certainly if the Cold War had been a stand-off between two of the dominant ideologies of the later age of Modernity, Marxist-Leninism and liberal capitalism, one seemed to have triumphed over the other. The Soviet system, invented by Stalin on the principles of the geopolitics of terror, had given way under the greater wealth and investment, the richer inventiveness, the social openness, the sheer and glossy consumer attractiveness of the Americanized and capitalist West. Yet capitalism had its pains as well as pleasures, and destabilization started at once. War returned to the Arab world in the Gulf, then by 1991 in a splintering Yugoslavia. Czechoslovakia divided in 1993. Russia, the CIS, attacked the breakaway state of Chechnya for the first time in 1994. In the West the triumph of capitalism generated an economy of fortunate affluence, as the Clinton administration succeeded in generating a period of remarkable economic boom, largely based on high-speed technological innovation in silicon-based companies and the global spread of the communications marketplace. Yet in many parts of the world the free market proved far from free; it failed to regenerate the Russian economy, and constant economic instability afflicted the growth of the Pacific Rim. Europe expanded into a new identity, the twelve-nation club becoming twenty-five and then more. It created problems of identity for the member nation states, above all for those like Britain which, having survived war and invasion over centuries, had an extended history of nationhood and sovereignty. Fragmentation, regionalism and insistent forms of cultural diversity both enriched and divided many of the member states, even as they tried to adapt to the new free economy, the world of deregulation and global competition, and a new relationship with the dominant USA.

For Britain the Nineties were a time of great political uncertainty. The strengthening of Europe and the decline of the classic idea of the nation state was weakening faith in the Union which, ever since the Act of Union of 1707, had given Britons their identity. The Conservative administration of the Nineties, under John Major, found the issue of double identity (British and European) only divided their party. When the mismanaged entry of the pound sterling into the European Exchange Rate Mechanism weakened all the gains of the British economy, the party was left enfeebled and divided; ironically the greatest achievement of the Thatcher era, the financial deregulation which made Britain a major player in the new global economy, was now weakening her own party, as well as the sense of national identity. Cultural diversity continued to increase, as the well-established migrant communities in Britain (Caribbean, African, Indian, Pakistani, Asian, Arab) became a growing political and cultural force. The weakening nation state intensified claims for devolution or outright independence in Scotland, Wales and Northern Ireland. The icons of unity – the monarchy, the established Church, the hereditary aristocracy who as peers made the second chamber of Parliament – faced increasing challenge. So did religion, marriage, the stable and traditional family. Definitions of culture changed too: it no longer represented a classic canon or a definable national tradition, or a set of elite judgements and values. As the innumerable magazine culture supplements found it expedient to make clear, culture was youth-style, fashion, rap, body-piercing, nudity, designer labels, supermodels, gourmet eating, alternative therapies, organic vegetables, sports and fitness. In the universities, courses in English Literature somehow became courses in Cultural or Media Studies or Feminism or Gay Iconography. The new society presented itself in playful and feminized guise. It was youth-centred, present-centred, narcissistic, relational, glutted with goods, information, styles and redundancy. Somehow, as the fiction of decades had been suggesting, something had gone from the core of British life, a sense of its historical, traditional and substantial reality. The familiar, the domestic, the usual, the sovereign, gave way to the fleeting, the permissive, the illusory, the transitional, the plural. It was a culture with no firm centres and many powerful and assertive peripheries, a compound of multiple myths, needs and interests.

It was on some such politics – the reconciling politics of the middle ground in a plural and populist time – that the New Labour government of Tony Blair came to office on 1 May 1997, after eighteen years of Conservative rule. Blair was 'rebranding' Britain. As he took office an imperial age ended. On another post-imperial midnight, 30 June 1997, the Union flag was furled in Hong Kong, the glittering entrepreneurial outpost in the China Seas that Britain had held ever since the treaty of Nanjing in 1842. The 'Last Post' sounded and the Union Jack came down; the band played 'The East is Red' and the Chinese flag went up – though the former colony remained a special development zone devoted to capitalism in a changing communist world. A few weeks after empire ended, Diana, Princess of Wales, died in a car accident in Paris, creating a mood of national mourning and a sense of increased transition. Blair's national 'rebranding' of 'Cool Britannia', trying to create the spirit of a modernizing, populist, multi-cultural, egalitarian, non-racist Britain ever impatient with the entrenched 'forces of conservatism' that for many actually were the real England, was complicated by the processes of devolution within the old Union. The founding of a Scottish parliament, a Welsh assembly, a new assembly based on a peace process in Northern Ireland, along with the pressure from ethnic and religious communities, and increasing divisions between urban communities and countryside, North and South, made the question of common culture and historical identity a complex issue, especially for the English themselves, that part of the Union that had in effect sacrificed its sense of nationhood to the larger Britishness, or else to regional loyalties.

Thus Britain at the end of the twentieth century was a profoundly different nation from that which had ruled much of the world at the beginning of it. It had lost its empire and many of the things that gave it a common identity: easy patriotism, pride in power and world leadership, confidence in science, industry, manufacture and commerce, a sense of leadership in style and in the arts. It still made a high claim to leadership, in political values, culture, invention and creativity, and it possessed the fortune to be linguistically and on the whole artistically and culturally in tune with the now dominant superpower, the USA. In its language most of the linguistic transactions of the world were now performed: English was spoken on all the six continents, and five-sixths of all English-language speech acts were performed by those using English not as mother tongue but as second language. The Empire had indeed struck back in other ways: London was now a truly multi-cultural city, one-third of its population being from ethnic minorities. Thus Blair's 'Cool Britannia' was a representation of a different cultural agenda shaped over the previous decades: it was largely populist, post-colonialist, multi-culturalist, feminist. Gay rights, women's rights, green issues, global perspectives, new age and alternative sensibilities and dot.com. awareness now largely presided, at least in the world as seen from Islington, and this was a Britain that could celebrate itself over the turn of the millennium. The ideal site was found at Greenwich, on the line of the zero meridian of longitude, the home of mean time, at the core of the old empire and the site which, in their attempt to destroy Western civilization, the anarchists of Conrad's *The Secret Agent* attempt to blow up. Here a stately pleasure dome was decreed, designed by Richard Rogers, creator of the postmodern Beaubourg in Paris. A dome, classic symbol of aspiration and inclusiveness, was decided on. Brunelleschi's dome for the Duomo in Florence had represented a triumph of faith and workmanship over gravity. Michelangelo's for St Peter's, Rome, displayed exact mathematical mastery over the perils of curvature's stress and strain. Wren's St Paul's in London was a triumphant expression of rational faith in a resurrected London. Soufflot's Panthéon in Paris became a celebration of human talent and genius, a fitting resting place for the likes of Voltaire. Paxton's Crystal Palace of 1851 was a triumphant glass-and-ironwork conservatory glittering over the industrial invention of an age.

Rogers's rubber-topped dome on the Thames opposite the new commercial London was a triumph of a rather different order: a large-scale circus tent, where clowns, furry dolls, interactive games, danger rides and prosthetic acrobats filled a windy interior. Faith was represented by doubt, and science by chaos. The book was notable by its absence. It was the *Nights at the Circus* view of history and the present: was it fact or was it fiction? Found lightweight by many, it would eventually require the rescuing help of a Frenchman from Euro-Disneyland; nothing could have been more postmodern. In 1998 Julian Barnes had written a satirical novel, *England, England*, in which the whole nation had become an imaginary museum, a set of symbols, sites and icons, from the Tower of London to Stonehenge, that could be placed on the Isle of Wight and turned into a theme park; now it was here. The turning moment came, the cyber-clock ran backwards to zero; the centuries span, the millennium arrived.

Planes did not drop from the skies, as promised; nor did hospitals close, office blocks shut down or the millennium computer bug arrive and bring global meltdown. Horsemen did not appear, locusts did not arrive, the Internet did not cease, nor the world economy collapse. The Nikkei and the Dow continued, the clock went on ticking. The terrible century had come to an end and something else had taken its place. It had invented, often out of wartime, remarkable technologies that had moved human beings into the galaxies and allowed amazing means of global communication, multiplying and accumulating daily. Past ways of life, past nationhoods and empires, past realities and familiarities, had been steadily eliminated. The cake of custom had been broken, the rules of family and domesticity fractured, the sense of person and gender destabilized; all this had entered the novel. The 'tradition of the new' had indeed become our form of history and, as Karl Mannheim promised, we had indeed learned 'to tell by the cosmic clock of history what the time is'. By now the sense of mythic excitement that had so long surrounded the idea of the year 2000 (or 2001), the dawn of the future space-century, had dissolved into something more complex. Now the time moved on, and the literature of modern history moved backward, into the past, into the age of the modern, and the postmodern, as we started the unnamed and yet to be written age of what comes after the after.

4

The novel in the last decade of the old millennium was seeing some striking changes too. A significant number of the leading writers who had shaped the course of post-war British fiction died in the decade: Graham Greene in 1991, both Angus Wilson and Angela Carter in 1992, William Golding and Anthony Burgess in 1993, Kingsley Amis in 1995, V. S. Pritchett in 1997, Iris Murdoch in 1999, Anthony Powell and Penelope Fitzgerald in 2000. Many of the radical new writers who stood for the critical edge of fiction a decade or so earlier now represented the mainstream state of fiction. It was a time of expanding bookstores, increasing publication of books and magazines, new ventures in new writing, and it offered singular opportunities to young writers. Yet where the Eighties had started out in a mood of political gloom but cultural excitement, the Nineties seemed gloomy altogether, perhaps a reflection of recessionary times. Publishers were more nakedly commercial, rivalries more intense, critics more savage. Papers like the *Guardian* often seemed to merge their book and their obituary pages, surer than ever that we had reached the end of the British novel. 'Contemporary British fiction, as everyone knows . . . is in a sad state,' announced the then fiction editor, Richard Gott, considering a 1993 listing of the 'Best of Young British Writers' devised by *Granta* magazine, remarking that it lacked the distinction of a similar list issued ten years earlier, which had been criticized in just the same way. Writing in the same newspaper, James Wood regularly and sometimes justifiably deplored the 'harmless hoax that the endless new fiction, from Michael Ignatieff to Paul Watkins, belongs in the same world as the great classics'. Familiar complaints were regularly rehearsed: British fiction had lost all sense of a subject; it lacked the vernacular energy of American fiction, the radical imagination of Indian fiction, the surreal splendour of Latin-American, the political and historical vigour of Irish. It displayed a lack of interest in contemporary history, a lack of attention to the moral life of modern Britain. William Leith argued that Britain had faded off the fictional landscape: 'these days, it doesn't make a good backdrop for stories . . . Not writing about contemporary Britain seems to be a growth industry . . . you wonder – if England seems a more diluted, washed-out kind of country these days, maybe that's because it is.'[6]

Some of the pessimism was merited (there was certainly a significant trivialization of fiction); some was not. The pessimism came in part from the sense that some essential notions of the novel and its Britishness were dissolving, leaving writers who came from other cultural frontiers (Scotland, Ireland, the Indian subcontinent) with the advantage of historical confidence; it also reflected the view that the innovations of fiction in the Eighties had become matters of cliché and convention. In a highly generational and media-based culture,

6 William Leith, 'Where Nothing Really Happens', *Independent on Sunday* 2 May 1993.

preoccupied with journalism and fashion, the novel was becoming an outpost for a now much more highly educated, computer-literate and culturally aggressive generation. There was no shortage of new writers, no decline of fictional publication; expanding bookshops were filling with new titles by new and youthful authors. Novels were read more widely than ever before; one of the cultural surprises was their sheer plurality. The Nineties were the age of the busy high-street bookstore, the literary festival, the promotion of author and book as commodity. Writing fiction became a sexy activity, an instrument of youth, attention, celebrity; thus many of them were written (or so it was claimed) by alternative comedians, catwalk models, politicians and media figures. The climate of over-promotion, hype and celebrity interview easily obscured all that was serious about the novel. Marketing and advertising shaped the market, the nature of literary reputation; literary prizes became the high-profile face of fictional competition.[7] As D. J. Taylor complained in his *After the War: The Novel and England Since 1945*, the novel became far less literary: too engaged with the marketplace, the style-scene, generational culture, nepotism, author profiling and hype. This is true; yet the sheer display, the prizes, the exhibitions, the launches, the signings, suggested not that the novel was in trouble, but in its own postmodern way doing rather well.[8] One result was certainly the growth of popular and generic fiction: familiar genres were recycled for the contemporary scene; stories aped other stories; sequels and prequels extended them; feminist or gay revisionists reworked them. In an age of celebrity and growing book-talk, fattening magazine supplements and book pages, fiction

---

7 Richard Todd explores this in *Consuming Fictions: The Booker Prize in Britain Today* (London, 1996).
8 D. J. Taylor. *After the War: The Novel and England Since 1945* (London, 1993). Taylor asks: 'why devote so much attention to an art-form which everyone admits is in a wretched state, and in which large numbers of intelligent people have lost interest?' His argument is that the downhill slide of the novel matches that of Britain itself, and shows the same failings: lack of social understanding; absence of fascination with region, place, community; want of vision, vigour of language and reporting what it cannot even bother to believe in, the condition of Englishness. The strength of the book lies in its social reading of post-war fiction, and its clear account of the kind of Britain that springs from the pages.

grew ever more commercial. Yet the literary classics were never in more extensive supply, and the striking fact was that in an age dominated by film, television, video and Internet, the book continued to prosper.

In truth, what the climate most resembled was that of just a hundred years before, as this narrative of modern British fiction started. In 1884 Henry James, reflecting on the future in 'The Art of Fiction', had said that no one thing any longer defined what novels were: 'They are as various as the temperaments of men, as they reveal a particular mind, different from the others.' He also said: 'It must be admitted that the field at large suffers discredit from overcrowding. I think, however, that this injury is only superficial, and that the superabundance of written fiction proves nothing against the principle itself.' By the 1890s the sense of plurality was becoming widespread, with the growth of literacy, the emergence of cheaper books and rapid printing methods. The future of fiction pointed in many directions; what struck the critics, then as now, was not the one direction the novel was taking, but the atmosphere of contentious variety. Aesthetic argument pointed in different directions: followers of Zola headed toward scientific reportage and the political criticism of Naturalism; the disciples of Aestheticism moved toward a psychologized and formalized self-consciousness. Traditional forms and genres continued; new types and amazing outrages abounded. Historic genres, like children's romance, were renewed; new genres, like science fiction and serious crime-writing, were evolved. Gothic fiction was popular again, as popular sensationalism, but also as a way of dealing with the strange frontiers of a culture in great change. New media, publishing houses and magazines, printing and marketing methods, new libraries and new bookstores changed the marketplace; some said serious fiction was gone for ever. It was possible to think the opposite – the growing resources of fiction made it possible to see it as a fresh form for serious art. As *mores*, values and opportunities changed, it was also, as Elaine Showalter said, a period of 'sexual anarchy'. Issues of decadence, homosexuality, transvestism and psychological abnormality, as well as feminism, dominated the decade. Many of the most challenging books were written by women; a sense of psychological and sexual complexity and ambiguity grew. When sexual and religious certainties break down, Showalter remarks, fictional certainties change as well. And what is clear in retrospect is that these confusing, plural, decadent and finally self-critical times were also aesthetically highly productive; out of them much that belongs to 'modern' fiction was born.'

A hundred years on, much had changed completely. The old imperial world power, Henry James's 'place in the world where there is most to observe', had seen its role and influence decline, its empire dissolve. A society of class, rank and deference, it had seen its hierarchies give way to new classlessness, its social relationships and interconnections transform. A confidently male society, it had seen life and culture feminized. Once the major source of invention and manufacture, it had watched most of these hard industries pass elsewhere, first to the USA and then to the Second World; the modern economy was based not on manufacture but service and science. The post-war years in particular brought attrition of power, decline in confidence and weakening of older certainties. In some ways it had grown more inward as a society, conscious of its own historical problems and difficulties. In other respects it was never more international; its economy, commerce and society were part of the globalized world. These changes are clearly reflected in the stories it has told about itself, persistently rewritten and renegotiated over the years. Inevitably, in the globalizing world, these stories have interfused with alternative stories from elsewhere, out of a different sense of tradition, a different perspective on reality, myth and history: Ameri-

---

9 Elaine Showalter, *Sexual Anarchy: Gender and Culture at the Fin de Siècle* (London, 1991). Showalter observes: 'The end of centuries seem not only to suggest but to intensify crises ... But why should the ends of centuries have special meanings and feelings or manifest common patterns? ... In a famous book, Frank Kermode argued that 'the sense of an ending' is a myth of the temporal that affects our thought about ourselves, our histories, our disciplines and our fictions: "We project our existential anxieties onto history; there is a real correlation between the ends of centuries and the peculiarity of our imagination, that it chooses always to be at the end of an era." The crises of the *fin de siècle*, then, are more intensely experienced, more emotionally fraught, more weighted with symbolic and historical meaning, because we invest them with the metaphors of death and rebirth that we project onto the final decades and years of a century.'

519

can fiction, South American fiction, Caribbean fiction, Indian fiction, African fiction, Irish fiction and the other literatures we broadly call 'post-colonial'. One result has been that the same kind of pluralism that shaped the novel in the 1890s is on display again. Fiction has taken on a vast variety of voices, forms and manners; 'postmodern' ways have increasingly entered the British novel. Along with this came the postmodern problem, random openness to all styles, all attitudes, all kinds of performance, along with equal randomness of judgement about what is serious, worthwhile, valuable, authoritative. Writers looked in many different directions: backward to history and the tradition, forward to experimental styles.

The striking feature of fiction in Britain as the millennium turned was, then, sheer diversity: the mixed and plural origins from which it came. The Nineties saw a fresh generation of novels from the Indian subcontinent: the work of the Bombay writer Amit Chaudhuri, author of *A Strange and Sublime Address* (1991), *Afternoon Raag* (1993) and *Freedom Song* (1998), and the powerful work of Bapsi Sidhwa (*The Ice-Candy Man*, 1992), the realistic Calcutta fiction of Raj Kamal Jha (*The Blue Bedspread*, 1999), the cosmopolitan fiction of Rohinton Mistry (*A Fine Balance*, 1995), who went to live in Canada, and of Vikram Chandra, whose panoramic *Red Earth and Pouring Rain* was one of the best books of 1995, and the magic fantasy of Arundhati Roy's *The God of Small Things* (1997), unthinkable without the influence of Salman Rushdie, and the winner of the Booker for 1997. Many new writers emerged from Africa, including the Tanzanian novelist Abdulrazak Gurnah (*Paradise*, 1996). Writers in South Africa – André Brink, J. M. Coetzee, Nadine Gordimer and others – adjusted to deal with the new historical situation following the election of Nelson Mandela as president of a new South Africa in 1994. Remarkable new writers came from the Caribbean, like the Guyanan Fred d'Aguiar (*Feeding the Ghosts*, 1998) and Indo-Caribbean David Dabydeen, also from Guyana, author of the novels *The Intended* (1991) and *The Counting House* (1996).[10] Yet some of

10 David Dabydeen also edited *The Black Presence in English Literature* (Manchester, 1985) and, with N. Wilson-Tagoe, *A Reader's Guide to West Indian and Black British Literature* (London, 1988).

the most striking pluri-cultural writing came from closer to home, or rather the edge of home. For understandable reasons, writing from Ireland and above all from Ulster acquired an increasing relevance, a commanding sense of history. Important books came from several young writers over the decade, telling stories of the past and present of the 'Troubles': Bernard Mac Laverty's *Cal* (1983) and *Grace Notes* (1997), Danny Morrison's *West Belfast* (1989), Glenn Patterson's *Fat Lad* (1992), *Black Night at Big Thunder Mountain* (1995) and *The International* (1999), Robert MacLiam Wilson's *Ripley Bogle* (1989) and the terror-filled *Eureka Street* (1996), Seamus Deane's deeply disturbing *Reading in the Dark* (1996), Philip McCann's quirky, morbid tales of Ireland North and South in *The Miracle Shed* (1995), and the more delicate and shaded novels of Deirdre Madden (*Remembering Light and Stone*, 1992). A nation itself in rapid change, Ireland acquired a fiction of striking plurality, from Anne Enright's urban comedy *The Wig My Father Wore* (1995) to the varied work of Joseph O'Connor (*True Believers*, 1991), Carlo Gebler (the grim historical tale of the Ireland of the potato famine, *How to Murder a Man*, 1998), Colm Tóibín (*The South*, 1990, *The Blackwater Lightship*, 1999) and the postmodern Ireland of Robert Cremins's *A Sort of Homecoming* (1998). Ireland and Dublin found their own contemporary and popular laureate in Roddy Doyle, author of the vernacular Dublin trilogy *The Commitments* (1987), *The Snapper* (1990) and *The Van* (1991), whose *Paddy Clarke Ha Ha Ha*, the tale of a ten-year-old boy watching his parents' marriage break up, won the 1993 Booker Prize.

Scotland had long pursued a literary language and culture of its own; to a degree it had found one in the fiction of Lewis Grassic Gibbon and George Mackay Brown. But now it had a lively and inventive new surrealist in Alasdair Gray, whose *Lanark* (1981) was one of the important books of the Eighties, and who now exploited his Glasgow background as well as his skills as a visual illustrator in books like *Poor Things* (1992), *A History Maker* (1994) and *Mavis Belfrage* (1996), stories about lost identities. James Kelman, author of *The Busconductor Hines* (1984), developed a new hard-man vernacular, a kind of contemporary Lallans; in 1994 he won the Booker

Prize with *How Late it Was, How Late*, the long, violent monologue of a drunk in a Glasgow prison. Jeff Torrington's *Swing Hammer Swing!* (1992), set in the Gorbals, reinforced the view that there was a new, contemporary Glasgow novel. It found its Edinburgh equivalent, radical vernacular and all, in Irvine Welsh's *Trainspotting* (1993), a portrait of drug-ridden, disaffected young people; Welsh became a cult novelist for this and later youth-oriented books like *The Acid House* (1994), *Ecstasy* (1996) and *Filth* (1998), about a corrupt Edinburgh policeman. So did Iain Banks, writing of the world of pop music, punk and the cyberfuture in grim fantasies like *The Wasp Factory* (1984), *Against a Dark Background* (1993) and *Feersum Endjinn* (1994), which invents a crossover language somewhere between Scots and cyberspeak. Janice Galloway wrote an experimental work of Scots feminism in *Foreign Parts* (1994); A. L. Kennedy's witty style, easygoing vision of sexuality and sudden gestures of violence were displayed in *Looking for the Possible Dance* (1993), set on a train between Glasgow and London, *So I am Glad* (1995) and *Original Bliss* (1997). In Andrew O'Hagan's *Our Fathers* (1999), the paradoxes and confusions of Scots literary, cultural and linguistic identity are finely explored through past and present.

And the Nineties were indeed an age of sexual anarchy. New books by new women writers – Janet Galloway's *Foreign Parts* (1994), Lesley Glaister's *The Private Parts of Women* (1996), Lucy Ellmann's *Man or Mango?* (1998) – depicted forms of successful and independent existence or an angry assertive sexuality quite different from their predecessors. Gay writing flourished, in the work of writers like Alan Hollinghurst (*The Swimming Pool Library*, 1988, *The Folding Star*, 1994) and Paul Magrs (*Does it Show?*, 1998); in Jeannette Winterson's *Written on the Body* (1992) and the black, Scots and lesbian Jackie Kay's *The Trumpet* (1998). Laddish women stimulated tales of the world of laddish men, notably Nick Hornby's *Fever Pitch* (1992) and *High Fidelity* (1995). There were other interesting crossovers, for instance in crime fiction, where female investigations became an important theme (e.g. the novels of Minette Walters, Frances Fyfield). Some of the most interesting books of the Nineties looked like one thing, then turned out to be quite another – crossover narratives, like

Dava Sobel's topical book *Longitude* (1999), about the development of an accurate naval chronometer by John Harrison, which reads equally well as fact or fiction. John Lanchester's *The Debt to Pleasure* (1996), one of the best books of the Nineties, is explained thus: 'This is not a conventional cookbook.' So the narrator Tarquin Winot explains, though the story he tells does seem to consist of the subtle recipes of an epicurean food writer as he travels from the Hotel Splendide in Portsmouth to Provence – until this slowly turns out to be the story of a random poisoner. In Andrew Motion's *Wainewright the Poisoner* (2000), the process is reversed; the autobiography of a true (and very literary) murderer of the Romantic period is made into fiction. Fact grew closer to literary narrative, history-writing to the narrative of the present, as the book not only sustained but extended its appeal into the twenty-first century.

5

For all the preoccupation with the contemporary if not the forth-coming that ran through the pre-millennial Nineties, history and the novelist's relationship with the past remained an important inquiry. In 1990 the Booker Prize was won by A. S. Byatt for her novel *Possession: A Romance*, her cleverest, most sure-footed work of fiction. It was both a highly intelligent and an engagingly popular novel, linking critical and feminist awareness with the romantic appeal of historical fiction. The basic enterprise, the relationship between Victorian writing and literary postmodernism, owed something to one of the most important books of twenty years earlier, John Fowles's *The French Lieutenant's Woman*, but Byatt now brought to the subject a new critical intelligence and a fascination with feminist and deconstructive ideas that had concerned so many modern minds. *Possession* is indeed a 'romance', but (as in David Lodge's *Small World*, another related novel) the term is quite precisely used. 'When a writer calls his work a romance,' Nathaniel Hawthorne explained in his preface to *The House of the Seven Gables* (1851), it need hardly be observed he wishes to claim a certain latitude, both as to its fashion and material, which he would not have felt entitled to assume, had he professed to be writing a Novel. The latter form of composition is presumed to aim at a very minute fidelity, not merely to the possible, but to the probable and ordinary course of man's experience. The former – while, as a work of art, it must rigidly submit itself to laws, and while it sins unpardonably so far as it may swerve aside from the truth of the human heart – has fairly a right to present that truth, to a great extent, under circumstances of the writer's own choosing or creation.

It is Hawthorne's point (and the passage is quoted in Byatt's novel) that romance is not simply an exotic plot, but a specific kind of relationship between the real and the fictive, and that it is often the attempt 'to connect a bygone age with the present that is flitting away from us. It is a legend prolonging itself . . .' The romance proposes a new or different relationship between emotion and social reality. It is also, as the Victorian writer Christine LaMotte reflects in the story, 'the land where women are free to express their true natures'.

The question of female expression is crucial to Byatt's story. It starts off as a modern academic adventure, as a male and female researcher, Roland Michell and Maud Bailey (their names are old romance names), stumble across evidence of the hidden lives of two mid-Victorian poets, Randolph Ash and Christine LaMotte, who prove to have had an affair. It starts an intricate plot of literary detection that takes the reader through Yorkshire (the Brontës, etc.), Lincolnshire (Tennyson, etc.), to literary London and Brittany, as well as through various Victorian writings and a number of beautifully pastiched letters, poems and texts. There are strange overlappings of past and present. Each age has its own kind of story, but the two begin to cross over, passing between a Victorian romantic conception of the self and the postmodern view of it as 'a discontinuous machinery and electrical message-network of various desires, ideological beliefs and responses, language-forms and hormones and pheromones'. Like Byatt's collected stories about moments of crucial encounter in the Victorian period, *Angels and Insects* (1992), the book makes an ironic criticism of much contemporary literary and psychological theory and the drab deconstructive discourse in which it is expressed. It attaches real value to a recovery of the 'romantic' creative principle, the fire of art and imagination that brings sensibility and imaginative possession to a dead, abstracted, over-textualized, over-politicized world. A learned book from a truly scholarly writer, very alert to modern international experiment, *Possession* draws much on the relationship between Robert Browning and Elizabeth Barrett, the self-imprisoned princess of Wimpole Street, which at first was conducted entirely through letters ('I love your verses with all my heart ... and I love you too,' Browning wrote by way of self-introduction to Elizabeth Barrett, who took several months to meet him in the flesh[11]). Two poets read each other as 'texts'. And if the word 'romance' is central to the story, so is the word 'possession' – which can refer to ownership, inspiration, sexual possession, the desire to have, the knowledge that one has been taken over, possessed. We can possess the past, through archives and letters; we can also be possessed by it; old writings and new can interweave, and stories affect stories to come. Connections are stranger than we generally presume. Here, by way of an illegitimate Victorian child, there is a direct link between an illicit Victorian relationship (and what is written about it) and the 'postmodern' present (and 'postmodern' is another key word in the text).[12]

Possession, we can take it, is a novel of 'historical fabulation' – a

11 Suitably *Possession* came out just after there had been a revival of interest in the Browning/Barrett courtship, following the publication of Daniel Karlin (ed.), *Robert Browning and Elizabeth Barrett: The Courtship Correspondence* (Oxford, 1989).

12 Some of the intricacies of the novel are delightfully observed by John Sutherland in 'What Really Happened in 1868?' an essay in his *Where Was Rebecca Shot?: Puzzles, Curiosities & Conundrums in Modern Fiction* (Oxford, 1998): '*Possession* is an extra-ordinarily knowing novel, in the manner popularized by Umberto Eco's *The Name of the Rose* (1980). Byatt's narrative picks up innumerable echoes of actual literary history. Randolph Ash, man and poetry, seems to owe much to Robert Browning. The affair with LaMotte recalls Browning's relationship (only revealed in the late twentieth century) with Julia Wedgwood. As a poet, Christabel strongly recalls Christina Rossetti. And the business of the buried manuscripts recalls G. H. Lewes's love letters which George Eliot had buried with her. More morbidly, it recalls Dante Gabriel Rossetti's first burying the manuscripts of his *House of Life* sonnets with Elizabeth Siddal, then having them dug up again when he decided, after all, that the world, rather than the corpse of his lover, should have the fruits of his genius.'

term Byatt used when she reflected on how many British novelists had turned to the form at the end of the century, turning away from contemporary themes, obsession with cultural events and sexual relationships. Writers today, she argued, are 'interested in history and its relation to fable; they are interested in tricks of consciousness, dreams, illusions . . .'[13] They are 'fabulists in the European tradition'. Writers she includes are Angela Carter, especially for her revisionist fairy tales, Barry Unsworth (*Pascali's Island*, 1980, *Sacred Hunger*, 1992), Penelope Fitzgerald (*Innocence*, 1986, *The Blue Flower*, 1995), Julian Barnes (*History of the World in 10½ Chapters*, 1989, *The Porcupine*, 1993), Rose Tremain (*Restoration*, 1989, *Sacred Country*, 1992), Hilary Mantel (*Fludd*, 1989, *A Place of Greater Safety*, 1992), Kazuo Ishiguro (*The Unconsoled*, 1995), Louis de Bernières (*The War of Don Emmanuel's Nether Parts*, 1990, *Captain Corelli's Mandolin*, 1995), Lawrence Norfolk (*Lemprière's Dictionary*, 1991, *The Pope's Rhinoceros*, 1997) and Tibor Fischer (*Under the Frog*, 1992, *The Collector Collector*, 1997). And this represents a significant sweep from the novels of the Nineties: a time when, even more than in the Eighties, there was a sophisticated return to historical subjects of all kinds. What Byatt perceives in her 'historical fabulators' is not just a return to history but a playful tricky lightness, a sense of profitable opposition between factual and fictive, past and present, the world of solid facts and the world of impermanence. Thus, she says of Penelope Fitzgerald's fiction, objects are rescued from vanishing, glitter with surreal reality. These fabulators are, Byatt says, 'grown-up and elegant; they are metaphysical makers of imaginary time and space and objects, who reflect on what they are doing.'[14]

13 A. S. Byatt, 'Parmenides and the Contemporary English Novel', in *Literature Matters*, 21 (December, 1996), published by the Literature Dept. of the British Council, London, pp. 6–8. Also see her literary essays in *Passions of the Mind* (London, 1991).
14 In Fredric Jameson's difficult and extended but rewarding study *Postmodernism: Or, the Cultural Logic of Late Capitalism* (Durham, NC, 1991), a book I find the more remarkable as I re-read it, Jameson reflects on the difference between modern historical fabulations and the conventions of much earlier historical fiction going back to Walter Scott: 'Such fabulations – not unexpectedly cheered on by a whole generation of ideologues complacently but with relish announcing the death of the referent, if not the end of history itself – also clearly enough show signs of that release and euphoria of the

6

It is true that – despite the fashionable view that, as J. G. Ballard put it, 'any novel not set within the last ten minutes is practically costume drama' – a return to history became a dominant theme of British fiction as the century moved to its close. Following his own theme that past lives leave traces everywhere, Graham Swift in *Ever After* (1992) also returned to Victorian times. An Oxford don feels betrayed by the death of his father, who commits suicide over his wife's infidelity. He researches the life of an ancestor who lived in the age of Darwin and Lyell, to find he too had ruined his life in a search for truth. In *Last Orders* (1996), the book with which Swift won the Booker Prize, a group of pub friends decide to commemorate a dead friend, a butcher, by conveying his ashes from London to Canterbury. This turns into a comic Chaucerian pilgrimage, ending when they finally deposit the remains from Margate Pier. There are other literary influences too – not least that of William Faulkner's *As I Lay Dying*, a modernist story of a funeral journey which treats the elusive and fragmentary influence of the past and its place in the unfixed universe of the present. History and the traces it leaves also increasingly became the theme of Beryl Bainbridge's work: in *Master Georgie* (1998) she carries her British characters off to the carnage of the Crimean War, the first European war to be photographed – it ends with photographic images of the living posing amid the dead.

For if history, for British novelists, still meant coming to terms

---

postmodern to which we have already referred ... These historical fantasies, unlike those of certain other epochs (as in the pseudo-Shakespearean historical romance of the early nineteenth century), do not aim essentially at the derealization of the past, the lightening of the burden of historical fact and necessity, its transformation into a costumed charade ... Nor does postmodern fantastic historiography seek, as in naturalism, to diminish the grisly and deterministic historical event into the minute workings of natural law ... its very invention and inventiveness endorses a creative freedom with respect to events it cannot control, by the sheer act of multiplying them; agency here steps out of the historical record itself into the process of devising it; and new multiple or alternate strings of events rattle the bars of the national tradition and the history manuals whose very constraints and necessities their parodic force indicts.'

with the Victorian inheritance, it also meant coming to terms with modernity and modern wars. Allan Massie wrote powerfully of the Second World War in *A Question of Loyalty* (1989) and *The Sins of the Father* (1991), and Pat Barker returned to the First in her 'Regeneration' trilogy (*Regeneration*, 1991, *The Eye in the Door*, 1993, *The Ghost Road*, Booker Prize, 1995), one of the strongest sequences of the Nineties. The trilogy looks back to the battle front and home front, and mixes fact and fiction, drawing on both real figures (Wilfred Owen, Siegfried Sassoon, Robert Graves, the psychologist William Rivers, diagnostician of 'shell-shock') and imagined ones. A key setting is Craiglockhart Hospital in Edinburgh, where shell-shocked men came for treatment so they could be regenerated and sent back to the front. Barker deals with the reverse side of war, the secrets that lie behind patriotism, courage, comradeship: that is, with pacifism, cowardice, psychosis, homosexual relations. War is seen from a modern psycho-sexual, indeed a feminist perspective. Just as powerful is Sebastian Faulks's Great War novel *Birdsong* (1993), which deals with the destruction and horror of the Western Front in 1916, when all attempts to break the deadlock of war were ending in collective slaughter, and the only relief was that when the guns fell silent the birds strangely began to sing. In *Charlotte Gray* (1999) Faulks returned to war as his subject, this time dealing with the experience of a British woman agent working in occupied Vichy France, in a world of hope, love, confusion and betrayal.

Yet, as Byatt says, stranger versions of history were fascinating contemporary novelists. One of the finest novels of the Nineties (still not fully appreciated) was Lawrence Norfolk's *Lemprière's Dictionary* (1991), a novel quite comparable in scale, intelligence and literary playfulness to the work of Thomas Pynchon or Umberto Eco. Exploiting the plots of detective fiction and of literary investigation, it tells the story of John Lemprière, a real eighteenth-century dictionary-maker, the record of whose life is obscure. In the novel the dictionary becomes a secret code, somehow involved in the fortunes of the emerging East India Company and so of the British Empire in the Pacific. The result is a book of postmodern play, clever decipherments, historical knowledge; so is Norfolk's next novel, *The Pope's*

Rhinoceros (1995), about how a rhinoceros was involved in resolving various papal problems in Spain. Penelope Fitzgerald's *The Blue Flower* (1995), deviously telling the strange story of Novalis, is no less clever and playful, and another major novel of the decade. If these books ironized the past, Jim Crace brilliantly found a modern poetry for recreating it, most notably in *Quarantine* (1997), his account of Jesus' forty days of quarantine in the desert. The ingenious restoration of history became an important concern among younger writers, two of the most brilliant books being Andrew Miller's *Ingenious Pain* (1997), the story of a giant who becomes a doctor and visits the court of Catherine the Great, and Mick Jackson's *The Underground Man* (1997), the surreal tale of the fifth Duke of Portland, whose agoraphobia was so great he built a vast network of tunnels beneath his Welbeck estate to avoid coming into the light of common day. The reconstitution of significant histories, the decrypting of their secrets, the unlocking of their passages: these became central themes of fiction – and not just in Britain but in, for example, the works of Thomas Pynchon, Don DeLillo and E. L. Doctorow in the USA – as the century closed and the millennium turned.

Historical fiction was itself merging with something else – the growing interest in Latin American 'magical realism'. Some writers, like Nicholas Shakespeare (*The Vision of Elena Selves*, 1989, *The Dancer Upstairs*, 1995), wrote directly about modern Latin American history, while others took the spirit of its fiction as a guide. Pauline Melville's brilliant *The Ventriloquist's Tale* (1997) deals with a hundred years of strange and magical Brazilian life and history through a remarkable narrator, the Ventriloquist. He tells us first he is a realist – 'Facts are king. Fancy is in the doghouse' – only, gradually, to acknowledge the greater wisdom of the old Portuguese proverb: 'Beyond the equator everything is permitted.' Others drew the same lesson. Louis de Bernières, wonderfully well-read in South American fiction, produced three novels (*The War of Don Emmanuel's Nether Parts*, 1990, etc.) set in an imaginary South American country where the traces of old conquistadores cross with the era of drug traffickers and radical revolutionaries. It was, however, when he changed not his style but his scene, moving his narrative to the Greek Ionian island of Cephalonia (Homer's Ithaca) and dealing with episodes of real history – the occupation of the islands first by the Italians and then by the Germans during the Second World War – that he produced a major novel, *Captain Corelli's Mandolin* (1995). The era is treated by John Fowles in *The Magus*, where the subject of German atrocities is explored as symbol of modern guilt. De Bernières too deals with the matter, though, with a magicality comparable to that of Michael Ondaatje in *The English Patient*, the horror and cruelty are gradually transformed into something else. The book was to become one of the big bestsellers of the Nineties, another 'historical fabulation'.

Then in 2000 Kazuo Ishiguro returned to the novel with a yet stranger kind of fiction about the problems of the past and the nature of Englishness. *When We Were Orphans* tells the story of a young English boy, Christopher Banks, who grows up in the international Bund district of Shanghai in the early years of the century. He has Chinese and Japanese friends, and his father is an international businessman, his mother an opponent of the opium trade. From childhood he wonders about his identity: should he 'become more English'? 'I think it would be no bad thing if boys like you did grow up with a bit of everything . . .' his uncle advises him. 'So why not become a mongrel? It's healthy.' His parents disappear; he becomes, like most of the characters in this book, an 'orphan'. Returned to England, he acquires a public school education, and turns during the Thirties into a socialite and a 'celebrated detective', solving crimes, dispensing justice, in Peter Wimsey-like fashion. He tells his own story with a mannerist prose that is a pastiche of the British adventure and detective novel, the very English tone of Conan Doyle, Dorothy Sayers or John Buchan; Ishiguro's prose has always had a borrowed voice inside it, a quality of anglophone pastiche. It is when he returns to Shanghai in 1937 to use his skills to trace what has happened to his parents that his English rectitude and modern history collide. The Pacific is dissolving into war; Chinese nationalists and revolutionaries fight each other, and the Japanese have invaded; the world he has known is over. Amid the shattered battle fronts of a city in wartime he tries to pursue his investigation, and he does find certain answers, though at the price of a love affair he is conducting. His actions and the style in which he tells them seem so inappropriate to what is happening it could appear like a postmodern joke. Yet Christopher's quest is serious; so is his sense that 'for those like us, our fate is to face the world as orphans, chasing through long years the shadows of vanished parents. There is nothing for it but to try and see through our missions to the end, as best we can, for until we do, we will be permitted no calm.' *When We Were Orphans* is a novel of history as disconnection, and of the peculiar remoteness of an old Englishness, which at the same time holds within itself the power of telling a story.

7

Despite this, British fiction had not done with the quest for contemporaneity; after all, there was always Martin Amis. By the Nineties he had become perhaps the most admired, most copied, most suspected of all the British novelists. As Will Self, a novelist plainly under the influence, put it, every British male writer under forty-five wanted to be Amis – for the louche assurance, the easy swing of the voice, the transatlantic style, but above all the sheer contemporaneity. 'You don't select material,' Amis explained. 'It selects you . . . my version of the truth is these things that come before my eyes.' Amis is indeed a very male writer, irksome to many female readers in the same way Nineties sisterly 'aren't-men-terrible' fiction alienated male readers. But the material of the modern world – metropolitan, cosmopolitan, transatlantic – readily came his way, and it was always clear he had the style to match it – sharp, witty, edgily ironic in a British way; vernacular, relaxed, flowing in an American way. It is a prose of a distinctive kind, a language of the here and now: 'Maybe it's the attitude of the prose that people copy – the prose responding helplessly, but intensely, to the society around it,' he suggested. Amis was first with the millennium, putting his imprimatur on it as early as *London Fields* (1989); like the murder in that book, the great apocalypse hasn't happened yet, but it will. Amis writes with a Hardy-like fatalism in the modern late scientific world, tainted in every way. Nor has the end of the Cold War dispensed with the age of Einstein's monsters. As Amis put it in a collection of essays, *Visiting Mrs Nabokov* (1993), 'The nuclear age has survived its Deterrence period and is entering a new phase, one we can confidently – but not safely – call Proliferation.'

Amis's first book from the Age of Proliferation was *Time's Arrow: Or, The Nature of the Offence* (1991), history in reverse; starting from the present as the rewind button is hit, the story starts moving 'backwards'. The book is plainly indebted to *Slaughterhouse Five* (1969), Kurt Vonnegut's most intimate novel, about the firebombing of Dresden, to which he was personally a witness. Since there is 'nothing to say about a massacre', Vonnegut tells part of the story from the viewpoint of the imaginary planet Tralfamadore, where novels work differently – laws of cause and effect reverse, bombs do not fall to earth but rise from it to fly into bomb-bays, bullets return to guns. Following Tralfamadorian principles, *Time's Arrow* too deals with the unspeakable, the Holocaust. The tale of a Nazi war criminal fled to America whose life history is pursued in reverse, the book is a formidable exercise in literary skill, reversing the dominant code of narrative that drives fiction forward, creating the pressure of the sentence, paragraph, chapter, the pulse of fictional expectation. Here the world turns upside down and moves from crime to innocence, victims from extermination to survival, and gross medical experiments are rescue operations with benign results. Food is regurgitated, garbage men do not collect but strew garbage, the scenes of Auschwitz turn into Resurrection tales. A dystopian narrative becomes a utopian one. Amis has the urgency of a moral satirist, desiring to redeem guilt and restore innocence; but the book is above all a tour de force, a brilliant exercise in inversion and postmodern skills, making the Holocaust a trope. A critic defined Amis's style, with its fascination with the 'unpresentable', as one of 'adoring revulsion'. Though it is a strong, pained, satirical address to what is plainly perceived as a monstrous age, it also has the air of being an attitude and technique waiting to be engaged by it, making this clever novel morally ambiguous.

Amis followed with a far more personal book, a tale of literary middle age, *The Information* (1995). 'The information' is street-smart knowledge of our current situation, our nothingness, the awareness that the new science makes our existence a mere speck in the schemeless scheme of things. The central theme is the literary rivalry induced by an unjust fate that comes to all writers: ageing. The book's chief character, Richard Tull, turns forty and is rotting with middle age and envy; he is a 'necromode' smelling of his own death. His reputation is in decline; when he submits a new book called *Untitled*, 'with its octuple time scheme and its rotating crew of sixteen unreliable narrators', agent and publisher are struck down by sudden disease on reaching page nine. He is also a literary critic – when he reviews a book, it stays reviewed – and planning a study called *The History of Increasing Humiliation*, about the historic decline of literary heroes: 'First gods, then demi-gods, then kings, then great warriors, great lovers, then burghers and merchants and vicars and doctors and lawyers. Then social realism: you. Then irony: me. Then maniacs and murderers, tramps, mobs, rabble, flotsam, vermin.' Tull has a tennis-playing partner and literary rival, Gwyn Barry, who is more amenable, popular and accessible, and is going from success to success – bitterly distressing to Tull, since he is 'not a contemporary guy' like himself. The book is brilliant as literary satire, superb on the humiliations of the literary life in the world of bookshop readings, American celebrity tours, radio and TV interviews, postmodernist tattle and the oppressive power of political correctness in this multi-cultural world where writers now have names like Shanana Ormulu Davis and Johnny Two Moons, and it doesn't help to be white, male, middle-aged and British. Amis is also brilliant on apocalyptic decay and degradation on both sides of the Atlantic; the streets of London (the darker reaches of Notting Hill) and New York City are as dangerous and absurd as they ever have been in his writing, abysses of drugs, sick pigeons, jogging, street crime. All of these injustices, the emptiness of the universe, the facts of mortality, need avenging. *The Information* is a revenger's comedy; in this world of literary and urban degradation, cultural slippage, cosmic depression, millennial anticipation, it is possible on the street to get a writer killed, for the price of eight book reviews.

The critic James Wood, commenting on Amis's style of postmodern satire, observed that one problem with his work is that he has expressed the wish to become an American novelist, writing like Saul Bellow or Vladimir Nabokov, yet his subject is Britain, a culture without a national myth or a high dream, so the one note left to him is irony. Certainly Tull is an expert in irony, including self-irony. His own flaw, he explains, is 'he wasn't innocent enough. Writers are innocent . . . Even Proust was innocent. Even *Joyce* was innocent.' But Tull, like Amis, has an excess of 'information'; he 'is always an adjective ahead of his subjects; always an adjective ahead of wonderment'. Yet, Wood adds, 'At his best, his satiric knowingness is not just cleverness, but a deep literary gift.'[15] The desire to 'become an American novelist' presumably had much to do with Amis's next book, *Night Train* (1997), a hard-boiled crime tale set entirely in an unnamed 'second-echelon American city'. The heroine, a child-abused Irish-American female cop called Mike Hoolihan, announces herself: 'I am a police.' Her voice is an elaborate, attempted feminization of Dashiell Hammett, and the styles of hard-boiled detective fiction are extensively pastiched. At the same time, having been accused of misogynistic writing, Amis presumably delighted in creating a strong female narrator with a gender-bending name. The victim of the mysterious crime she investigates is also female, Jennifer Rockwell, a highly successful astronomer married to a professor of philosophy. The investigation leads Hoolihan down a sequence of false trails, but also into contemplation of the disturbing cosmos, more of the disturbing scientific 'information' that had disoriented Richard Tull: 'What we're seeing out there, the stars, the galaxies, the galaxy clusters and superclusters, that's just the tip of the iceberg . . . At least 90 per cent of the universe consists of dark matter, and we don't know what dark matter is . . .' she is told. 'I'm trying to give you an idea of the kinds of thing Jennifer thought about.' This is a cosmic crime, which is why the book is not quite a detective story – since 'the information' can only lead to ambiguity, or a dead end. Amis has always had a

---

15 High praise from Wood, an interesting if over-demanding critic with a conviction that American fiction has outsmarted British, in 'Martin Amis: The English Imprisonment', in *The Broken Estate: Essays on Literature and Belief* (London, 1999).

good deal of the enraged satirist, perhaps the nearest thing to a latter-day Swift modern British fiction has produced. But he is also a postmodern ironist, heavy with the information – meaning there is little point in indignation since the universe itself is clearly at a dead end.

Amis's fiction had a familiar counterpoint in the work of Ian McEwan; but over the Nineties their work seemed to diverge. While Amis's work moved toward irony, McEwan's increasingly took on a compassionate humanism – though this did not deter him from dealing in strong themes. His first book of the Nineties, *The Innocent* (1990), was an immediate response to the climate created by the fall of the Berlin Wall. The bulk of the story is set back in the mid Fifties; Berlin a typical late twentieth-century location, fated to be endlessly revisited. McEwan had dealt with the theme of spying and wartime codes in a TV play, *The Imitation Game*, set at Bletchley Park, the place where in effect the war was won, the modern computer born. *The Innocent* is based around another true episode in the history of Sigint, the CIA's attempt to construct an elaborate listening post tunnelled under the Berlin Wall. McEwan uses this to tell the story of a painful personal initiation: a young British soldier Leonard Marham, twenty-five and still a virgin, a 'kind and gentle Englishman who knew so little about women and learned so beautifully', loses his innocence in the arms of a German girl, Maria. Growing sexual awareness makes him realize he has an instinct for sexual domination; then Maria's husband reappears, and is killed in the ensuing fight. It becomes necessary to dismember his body and dispose of it in the tunnel. The two stories, the political and the personal, entwine, as they generally do in McEwan's later work. The book ends on an allegorical coda, when Leonard comes back to Berlin after the Wall is down. The finale seems to suggest the possibility of renewing a love relationship that violence, suspicion and political division have destroyed. A similar theme, the trace of old wartime crimes and divisions, lay behind McEwan's next novel, *Black Dogs* (1992), which also alludes to the coming down of the Wall. But the story is chiefly set in the Languedoc region of France, and concerns a woman on honeymoon who sights two dogs said to have been used by the

Gestapo to intimidate French prisoners. For the rest of her life the sight remains, as proof of 'A malign principle, a force in human affairs that periodically advances to dominate and destroy the lives of individuals and nations'. Fifty years on, in the world of the Nineties, she senses the black dogs are still there, 'fading as they move into the foothills of the mountains from where they will return to haunt us, somewhere in Europe, in another time'.

McEwan's two novels of the late Nineties also deal with the world of love and danger. *Enduring Love* begins dramatically: a helium balloon breaks free of its moorings and carries off a ten-year-old boy. The attempt to save him brings death to one of the rescuers ('the little stick figure flowed or poured outward across the ground, like a drop of viscous fluid'), and opens a tale of human vulnerability; one rescuer, Joe Rose, finds himself stalked by another, Jed Parry. As in Amis, there is much consideration of the scientific nature of the cosmos; Joe is a science journalist. He finds no less mystery in the cosmos of love, above all the problems and dangerous paradoxes of de Clérambault's Syndrome, the stalkers' powerful delusional conviction that despite all proof one is loved by someone distant. The scientific papers attached to the story note that 'the pathological extensions of love not only touch upon but overlap with normal experience, and it is not easy to accept that one of our most valued experiences [loving and being loved] may merge into pathology.' *Amsterdam* (1998) – the book that won McEwan the Booker Prize – is set in 'the Augustan age of rock and roll', and deals with the lovers of a forty-year-old woman who meet at her funeral after she dies of mental disease. Little of the story is set in Amsterdam; the main scene is the world of press, publishing and politics, and turns on a potential scandal affecting a xenophobic British Foreign Secretary. Again the book has a vivid social vision, a concern with the obscure nature of desire, and has a strong moral seriousness. If Amis retained the spirit of fiction's satirical bad boy, McEwan now became the latter-day humanist, concerned with the need for the human spirit to confront its own dangerous impulses. The writer's task becomes a form of fragile modern science and the novel is the book of modern life: 'as a work unfolds, it teaches you its own rules, it tells how it should be written;

at the same time it is an act of discovery, in a harsh world, of the extent of human worth.'

Amis and McEwan are both intensely, sometimes even oppressively, 'contemporary' writers, and the influence they have exerted over others has much to do with the sense they have of living in an age of the disastrous, the unpresentable, the nihilistic: the drained-out darkened world of 'maniacs and murderers, tramps, mobs, rabble' that Richard Tull understands as part of 'the information'. They helped other writers write the Nineties as an age of extremity – the era of Quentin Tarantino, David Lynch, David Cronenberg, a time for the dark, *noir*, grotesque, extreme, where the postmodern met the posthuman. Many writers took up the new Gothic; one of the more influential, Patrick McGrath, entitled an early book *The Grotesque* (1989) and another *Asylum* (1996). Drugs played a serious part in the contemporary vision of brutal and grotesque sensibility, as in the fiction of Irvine Welsh. Another extremist of grotesque satirical energy, Will Self, established himself with a book called *The Quantum Theory of Insanity* (1991), and turned from psycho-therapeutic lunacies to a fiction of bodily extravagancies and transformations in *Cock & Bull* (1992). Self's universe of nastiness is inventive, at best truly satirical; like Wyndham Lewis his writing works best when the satirical rather than scatological energy is running high, and his later books – *My Idea of Fun: A Cautionary Tale* (1993), *The Sweet Smell of Psychosis* (1996) and *Great Apes* (1998) – are of varied quality. Extremity usually works best when the touch is light, as it is, for instance, in the fiction of Toby Litt, one of the strong reputations of the late Nineties. The stories of *Adventures in Capitalism* (1997) are postmodern teases: the strange tale of Sherlock Holmes and a legless Moriarty; the mysterious tale of how Mr Kipling came to bake his cakes, or how Michel Foucault got his Death of the Subject's come-uppance at an S and M club – all this set amid the world of late capitalism's glut of designer commodities, videos and CDs, Gap and Prada. In *Beatniks: An English Road Movie* (1998), Litt brings the plot of Jack Kerouac's *On the Road* to Britain (the adventurous journey from Bedford to Brighton). *Corpsing* (2000), his most assured work, is a brilliant thriller, set in a contemporary, millennial London of designer restaurants, easy drugs, modems and mobile phones, fashion models and TV shoots. The book is a genre story of investigation; but it is also about the postmodern body and its vulnerability. Flesh is the stuff both of the fashion magazine and the path lab, and the body is an iconic object of erotic manipulation and of mutilation. The story starts in a fashionable designer restaurant; as Conrad Redman dines with his ex-lover Lily, a gunman comes and fires six shots, killing Lily and badly wounding Redman. In a cunning suspense plot from the whodunnits, he investigates the truth. The result is a novel of cruel and painful cleverness, told at a cool post-humanist distance – a stylish, troubling work of millennial postmodernism.

8

What, then, is the state of the novel – the British novel – as the world enters the new millennium? It is, in several different senses, 'postmodern': smart, experimental, self-mocking and historically analytical and retrospective all at once. It is the fiction not of a future yet to come, but a future that has already happened, and been incorporated into the present. The age of Modernity, the tactics of Modern writing, has been and is now over. Modern history itself has been transformed into a storehouse of images and icons, become, in many cases, the stuff for literary archaeology and the arts of literary pastiche. Fictional experiment has long since ceased to be an avant-garde outrage and become an available convention. The great kitty of stories is now in a state of overstock. As Salman Rushdie puts it in *Haroun and the Sea of Stories* (1990), what Haroun sees in the water is

a thousand thousand thousand and one different currents, each one a different colour, weaving in and out of one another like a liquid tapestry of breathtaking complexity; and Iff explained that these were the Streams of Story, that each coloured strand represented and contained a single tale. Different parts of the Ocean contained different sorts of stories, and as all the stories that had ever been told and many that were still in the process of being invented could be found here, the Ocean of the Streams of Story was in fact the biggest library in the universe.

Fiction is in fact in a state of plenitude, its stories coming from many directions. Certain themes have become routine diet: apocalyptic cities, gender wars, gay and lesbian relations, marital collapse, feminist self-discovery, football fever, serial killers, child abuse, New Age consciousness, laddish girls and girlish lads. Hard satire has largely replaced social comedy, dark horrors have replaced familiar lives. Serious literary fiction is under profound pressure from the commercial; Grand Narratives are giving way to more plural and playful themes.

Like modern Britain itself, the modern novel has come a long way from the age of fiction Henry James encountered, when the twentieth-century adventure of the novel was about to begin. Yet many of the developments would surely not have surprised him. As the twentieth century turned, he was invited to consider the prospects, and wrote a (long-buried) essay on the subject of 'The Future of the Novel'. The novel had become, he noted, 'a surprising example . . . of swift and extravagant growth, a development beyond the measure of every early appearance. It is a form that has had a fortune so little to have been foretold at its cradle.' In short the fairies at fiction's christening evidently had little idea of what they were doing when they blessed such an open and complex new genre. James too was writing in an age of new publishing, and of all the books the novel, good and bad, penetrated fastest and furthest – 'Penetration appears to be directly aided by mere mass and bulk.' Every kind of fiction prospered: stories for children, stories for men and stories for women by women ('the innumerable women who, under modern arrangements, fail to marry – fail, apparently, even, largely, to desire to'), fiction for the popular reader ('the sort of taste that used to be called "good" has nothing to do with the matter'), fiction for the serious mind. So many ways of writing and producing books that almost anyone can do it, since 'almost any variety is thrown off and taken up, handled, admired'. Yet while problems of quality worried, the sheer excess was encouraging, for 'The more we consider it the more we feel that the prose picture can never be at the end of its tether until it loses the sense of what it can do. It can do simply everything, and that is its strength and its life . . . Till the world is unpeopled there will be an image in the mirror. What need more immediately concern us, therefore, is the care of seeing the image shall continue various and vivid.'[16]

A hundred years on, in quite different historical, moral and scientific circumstances, when the world is a different place and Britain a strikingly different nation, many of these observations stay true. The novel survives, proliferates, penetrates. It remains a form located somewhere between the literary and the popular, moral, social and philosophical meditation or artistic experiment and the endless generic repetition that allows so many books to flow from the presses and be sold and resold. It is both a higher form of knowledge (as D. H. Lawrence said, the bright book of life that tells a greater truth than does the priest or the philosopher) and a soft form of entertainment, where 'good' certainly has nothing to do with the matter. Children still buy and read; women who won't marry and dislike present arrangements still write. We expect some of our novelists to be gurus, moralists, wise observers, great explorers, visionary prophets; we also like them to be comedians, supermodels or some form of celebrity. We want our novels to be works of wisdom; we also like them to make great Christmas presents. The novel has survived beyond the death of heavy metal type, consorted with film, television, the computer age. It survives into the times of fast new information highways, self-publishing screens, the traffic of Internet, though clearly it has been changed by all such innovations. It has outlasted the death of many things – the Death of the Novel, the Author, the Subject, the Word. The new technologies, styles and cultural values, the contemporary 'information', have not silenced it; instead they have entered it, keeping an image in the mirror even in the de-peopling void. Its boundaries and frontiers are not shrinking but expanding, as national boundaries and heritages open and cultures

16 Henry James, 'The Future of the Novel', in Leon Edel (ed.), *Henry James, The Future of the Novel: Essays on the Art of Fiction* (New York, 1956).

globally interfuse. For James, the novel, with its peculiar mixture of social observation and commerce, its dependence on destiny, history and custom, was especially an Anglo-Saxon or a European form. Today for many reasons it has lost much of its defining 'Britishness', and a good deal of its Europeanness. Yet for good or ill English remains the dominant fictional language, used not just to tell tales of British society or the 'Condition of England', but to tell what Rushdie calls 'migrant tales' and Pauline Melville 'ventriloquist's tales'. London is a major publishing capital, and a classic home of the modern novel – which itself comes from multiple sources, many ethnicities, the different and variegated streams that feed the Ocean of Stories. More books are published than ever before (over 6,000 titles a year) for more readers than ever before.

If critics have any use at all (and we should always wonder), then they can usefully remind us that we have been here, or somewhere similar, before. That has been one reason for telling this story, from one age of change and disintegration, a century back, when science and technology were transforming lives, old faiths and the Victorian grand narratives were dissolving, changing sexual and gender roles were undermining all sense of the real, the stable and the familiar. The arts of the time showed the trembling of the veil, the shimmers of novelty, the dawning of the modern; and the novel seemed peculiarly well-adapted to telling its story. It became a story of very great achievements: the experimental late fictions of Henry James, the novels and stories of Conrad, Joyce's aesthetic revelations, Lawrence's prophetic despairs, Forster's desires for cultural unity, Woolf's fragments, her 'matches struck in the dark'. The modern novel before 1945 created a new sense of fiction's power and significance; in the period since then major writers – Beckett, Lowry, Golding, Wilson, Murdoch, Fowles, Rushdie – have seriously advanced the form and our sense of the novel as a bright book of life. Now, as always, present prospects for the novel lie in the traffic between change and custom, new voices and the tradition. The development of fiction in the post-war era has left several major generations in place. Many significant writers from the generation of the Fifties and Sixties – Doris Lessing, Muriel Spark, Margaret Drabble, V. S. Naipaul, John Fowles,

Alan Sillitoe, J. G. Ballard, A. S. Byatt, David Lodge, Fay Weldon, Penelope Lively, Beryl Bainbridge – are still at work. So are the new writers of the next two decades, who have become a mainstream: Ian McEwan, Martin Amis, Salman Rushdie, Timothy Mo, Julian Barnes, Peter Ackroyd, Marina Warner, Graham Swift, Rose Tremain, Kazuo Ishiguro, Alasdair Gray. Then there are their strong successors: Jeannette Winterson, Hilary Mantel, Lisa Saint Aubin de Terán, Alan Hollinghurst, Jim Crace, James Kelman, Adam Thorpe, Pat Barker, Lawrence Norfolk, Bernard Mac Laverty, A. L. Kennedy, Pauline Melville, Nicholas Shakespeare, Tibor Fischer, Sebastian Faulks, Louis de Bernières, John Lanchester, David Dabydeen, Fred d'Aguiar, Vikram Chandra, Toby Litt.

Whatever the pressures, the novel does remain various and vivid. It depends on one of the world's most brilliant communications technologies: the book. It is capable of expressing a subtlety, truth and intimacy, a creative consistency and energy, that cannot be had from television screenplay or film. It is capable of profound human influence, moral and political wisdom; we still want our novelists to be priests, prophets or gurus, to take us into the depths. The novel is above all a fiction, and a fiction is a distinctive form of text: not pure narrative, not history, not biography, not reportage, but a scene of dialogue, drama, creative discovery. Since we are all storytellers, we understand the meaning and power of its activities. Which is why, as we go onward toward the unpeopled void, we still seek the image in the mirror.

The British Novel 1878–2001:
A List of Major Works

The following list of authors and titles is intended to indicate the wide variety as well as the quality of British fiction published since the 1870s. It reaches well beyond the authors it has been possible to cover in the text, but, though full, it remains, of course, personal and selective. Not all works by each author are included.

Ackroyd, Peter (1949   )
The Great Fire of London (1982), *Hawksmoor* (1985), *Chatterton* (1987), *First Light* (1989), *The House of Doctor Dee* (1993), *Dan Leno and the Limehouse Golem* (1994), *Milton in America* (1996), *The Plato Papers* (1999).

Aldington, Richard (1892–1962)
Death of a Hero (1929), *The Colonel's Daughter* (1931).

Aldiss, Brian (1925   )
A Report on Probability A (1968), *The Hand-Reared Boy* (1970), *A Rude Awakening* (1978), *Helliconia Spring* (1981), *Remembrance Day* (1993).

Ambler, Eric (1909–1998)
The Dark Frontier (1936), *Epitaph for a Spy* (1938), *Journey into Fear* (1940), *The Night-Comers* (1956), *The Intercom Conspiracy* (1970), *Doctor Frigo* (1974), *The Care of Time* (1981).

Amis, Kingsley (1922–1995)
Lucky Jim (1954), *That Uncertain Feeling* (1955), *Take a Girl Like You* (1960), *One Fat Englishman* (1963), *The Anti-Death League* (1966), *The Green Man* (1969), *Ending Up* (1974), *Jake's Thing* (1978), *The Old Devils* (1986), *Difficulties With Girls* (1988), *The Russian Girl* (1992), *You Can't Do Both* (1994).

Amis, Martin (1949   )
The Rachel Papers (1973), *Dead Babies* (1975), *Success* (1978), *Money* (1984), *London Fields* (1989), *Time's Arrow* (1992), *The Information* (1995), *Night Train* (1997).

Arlen, Michael (Dikran Kouyoumdjian) (1895–1956)
The London Venture (1920), *Piracy* (1922), *The Green Hat* (1924).

Bailey, Paul (1937   )

At the Jerusalem (1967), *Trespasses* (1970), *A Distant Likeness* (1973), *Old Soldiers* (1980), *Gabriel's Lament* (1986), *Sugar Cane* (1993), *Kitty and Vergil* (1998).

Bainbridge, Beryl (1934   )

A Weekend with Claud (1967), *Harriet Said* (1972), *The Bottle Factory Outing* (1974), *Sweet William* (1975), *Injury Time* (1977), *Young Adolf* (1978), *An Awfully Big Adventure* (1989), *The Birthday Boys* (1991), *A Quiet Life* (1993), *Every Man for Himself* (1996), *Master Georgie* (1998).

Ballard, J. G. (1930   )

The Atrocity Exhibition (1970), *Concrete Island* (1974), *High Rise* (1975), *The Unlimited Dream Company* (1979), *Empire of the Sun* (1984), *The Day of Creation* (1987), *Running Wild* (1988), *The Kindness of Women* (1991), *Rushing to Paradise* (1994), *Cocaine Nights* (1997).

Banks, Iain (1954   )

The Wasp Factory (1984), *Walking on Glass* (1985), *The Bridge* (1986), *The Player of Games* (1988), *The Use of Weapons* (1990), *Feersum Endjinn* (1995), *Whit* (1995), *Inversions* (1999).

Banville, John (1945   )

Kepler (1981), *Mefisto* (1986), *The Book of Evidence* (1989), *Ghosts* (1993), *The Untouchable* (1997).

Barker, A. L. (1918   )

John Brown's Body (1969), *Relative Successes* (1984), *Zeph* (1993).

Barker, Pat (1943   )

Union Street (1982), *Century's Daughter* (1986), *The Man Who Wasn't There* (1989), *Regeneration* (1991), *The Eye in the Door* (1993), *The Ghost Road* (1995), *Another World* (1999).

Barnes, Julian (1946   )

Metroland (1980), *Flaubert's Parrot* (1984), *Staring at the Sun* (1986), *A History of the World in 10½ Chapters* (1989), *The Porcupine* (1992), *England, England* (1999).

Barstow, Stan (1928   )

A Kind of Loving (1960), *Joby* (1964), *The Watchers on the Shore* (1966), *A Raging Calm* (1968), *Just You Wait and See* (1986).

Bates, H. E. (1905–1974)

The Fallow Land (1932), *Thirty Tales* (1934), *My Uncle Silas* (1939), *Love for Lydia* (1952), *The Purple Plain* (1947), *The Darling Buds of May* (1958).

Bates, Ralph (1899–2000)

Lean Men (1934), *The Olive Tree* (1936).

Beckett, Samuel (1906–1989)

More Pricks Than Kicks (1934), *Murphy* (1938), *Molloy* (Paris, 1951), *Malone Dies* (Fr., Paris, 1951, trans. 1956), *The Unnamable* (Fr., Paris 1953, trans. 1959), *Watt* (Paris, 1953), *How It Is* (Fr., Paris, 1961, trans. 1964).

Bedford, Sybille (1911   )

A Legacy (1957), *A Compass Error* (1968), *Jigsaw* (1989).

Beerbohm, Max (1872–1956)

Zuleika Dobson, Or An Oxford Love Story (1911).

Bell, Adrian (1901–1980)

The Cherry Tree (1932), *The Balcony* (1934).

Belloc, Hilaire (1870–1953)

Four Men (1911), *The Green Overcoat* (1912).

Bennett, Arnold (1867–1931)

A Man From the North (1898), *Anna of the Five Towns* (1902), *The Grand Babylon Hotel* (1905), *The Old Wives' Tale* (1908), *Clayhanger* (1910), *Hilda Lessways* (1911), *Riceyman Steps* (1923).

Benzie, Alex (1961   )

The Year's Midnight (1996), *The Angle of Incidence* (1999).

Berger, John (1926   )

A Painter of Our Time (1958), *The Foot of Clive* (1962), *Corker's Freedom* (1964), *G.* (1972), *Pig Earth* (1979), *Lilac and Flag* (1990), *To the Wedding* (1996).

Blacker, Terence (1948   )

Fixx (1989), *Revenance* (1997).

Blackwood, Caroline (1931–1996)

Great Granny Webster (1977), *Corrigan* (1984).

Bowen, Elizabeth (1899–1973)

Encounters: Stories (1923), *The Hotel* (1927), *The Last September* (1929), *Friends and Relations* (1931), *The Cat Jumps and Other Stories* (1934), *The House in Paris* (1935), *The Death of the Heart* (1938), *The Heat of the Day* (1949), *A World of Love* (1955), *Collected Stories* (1980).

Boyd, William (1952   )

A Good Man in Africa (1981), *An Ice-Cream War* (1982), *Stars and Bars* (1984), *The New Confessions* (1987), *Brazzaville Beach* (1990), *The Blue Afternoon* (1991), *The Destiny of Nathalie 'X'* (1995), *Nat Tate: An American Artist* (1998), *Armadillo* (1999).

Bradbury, Malcolm (1932–2000)

Stepping Westward (1965), *The History Man* (1975), *Rates of Exchange* (1983), *Doctor Criminale* (1992), *To the Hermitage* (2000).

Bragg, Melvyn (1939   )

For Want of a Nail (1965), *The Hired Man* (1969), *A Place in England*
(1970), *The Nerve* (1971), *The Silken Net* (1975), *Love and Glory* (1983),
The Maid of Buttermere (1987), *Crystal Rooms* (1992), *Credo* (1996), *The
Soldier's Return* (1999).

Braine, John (1922–1986)

Room at the Top (1957), *The Vodi* (1959), *The Jealous God* (1964), *The Queen
of a Distant Country* (1972), *The Pious Agent* (1975), *The Two of Us* (1984).

Brierley, Walter (1900–1972)

Means-Test Man (1935), *Danny* (1940).

Brophy, Brigid (1929   )

Hackensacker's Ape (1953), *Flesh* (1962), *In Transit* (1969).

Brooke-Rose, Christine (1926   )

The Languages of Love (1957), *The Dear Deceit* (1960), *Out* (1964),
Between (1968), *Thru* (1975), *Amalgamemnon* (1984), *Xorandor* (1986),
Remake (1997).

Brookner, Anita (1928   )

A Start in Life (1981), *Look at Me* (1983), *Hotel Du Lac* (1984), *Fraud*
(1992), *A Family Romance* (1993), *A Private View* (1994), *Incidents at the
Rue Langier* (1995), *Visitors* (1997).

Brown, George Mackay (1917–1996)

A Time to Keep (1969), *Greenvoe* (1972), *Magnus* (1973), *Time in a Red
Coat* (1985), *The Golden Bird* (1987), *Vinland* (1992), *Beside the Ocean of
Time* (1994).

Buchan, John (1875–1940)

Prester John (1910), *The Power House* (1913), *The Thirty-Nine Steps*
(1915), *Greenmantle* (1916), *Mr Standfast* (1919).

Burgess, Anthony (1917–1993)

Time for a Tiger (1956), *The Enemy in the Blanket* (1958), *The Wanting Seed*
(1962), *The Clockwork Orange* (1962), *Nothing Like the Sun* (1964), *MF*
(1971), *Abba Abba* (1977), *Earthly Powers* (1980), *The End of the World
News* (1982), *The Kingdom of the Wicked* (1985), *Byrne* (1995, post.).

Burn, Gordon (1948   )

Alma Cogan (1991), *Fullalove* (1995).

Burns, Alan (1929   )

Celebrations (1967), *Babel* (1969), *Dreamamerika!: A Surrealist Fantasy*
(1972), *Revolutions of the Night* (1986).

Butler, Samuel (1835–1902)

Erewhon, Or Over the Range (1872, enlarged 1901), *Erewhon Revisited*
(1901), *The Way of All Flesh* (1903, post.).

Byatt, A. S. (1936   )

Shadow of a Sun (1964), *The Game* (1967), *The Virgin in the Garden* (1978), *Still Life* (1985), *Sugar and Other Stories* (1987), *Possession: A Romance* (1990), *Angels and Insects* (stories, 1992), *The Matisse Stories* (1993), *The Djinn in the Nightingale's Eye* (fairytales, 1995), *Babel Tower* (1996).

Carr, J. L. (1912–1994)

A Day in Summer (1964), *A Month in the Country* (1980), *The Battle of Pollock's Crossing* (1985), *What Hettie Did* (1987).

Carter, Angela (1940–1992)

Shadow Dance (1965), *The Magic Toyshop* (1967), *The Infernal Desire Machines of Dr Hoffmann* (1972), *The Passion of New Eve* (1977), *Nights at the Circus* (1984), *Wise Children* (1991).

Cartwright, Justin (1945   )

Interior (1988), *Look at it This Way* (1990), *Masai Dreaming* (1993), *In Every Face I Meet* (1995), *Leading the Cheers* (1998).

Cary, Joyce (1888–1957)

Aissa Saved (1932), *The African Witch* (1936), *Mister Johnson* (1939), *Herself Surprised* (1941), *To Be A Pilgrim* (1942), *The Horse's Mouth* (1944), *A Fearful Joy* (1949), *Prisoner of Grace* (1952).

Caute, David (1936   )

At Fever Pitch (1959), *The Decline of the West* (1966), *The Occupation* (1971).

Chatwin, Bruce (1940–1989)

On the Black Hill (1982), *The Songlines* (1987), *Utz* (1988).

Chaudhuri, Amit (1962   )

A Strange and Sublime Address (1991), *Afternoon Raag* (1993), *Freedom Song* (1997).

Chesterton, G. K. (1874–1936)

The Napoleon of Notting Hill (1904), *The Club of Queer Trades* (1905), *The Man Who Was Thursday: A Nightmare* (1908), *The Innocence of Father Brown* (1911).

Childers, Erskine (1870–1922)

The Riddle of the Sands (1903).

Christie, Agatha (1890–1976)

The Mysterious Affair at Styles: A Detective Story (1920), *The Murder of Roger Ackroyd* (1926), *The Mystery of the Blue Train* (1928), *Lord Edgware Dies* (1933), *Death on the Nile* (1937), *Ten Little Niggers* (1939).

Clark, Lindsay (1939   )

Sunday Whiteman (1987), *The Chymical Wedding* (1989).

Coe, Jonathan (1961   )

What a Carve Up! (1994), *The House of Sleep* (1997).

Compton-Burnett, Ivy (1892–1969)

Dolores (1911), *Pastors and Masters* (1925), *Brothers and Sisters* (1929), *A House and Its Head* (1935), *Manservant and Maidservant* (1947), *A Father and His Fate* (1957), *The Mighty and Their Fall* (1961), *A God and His Gifts* (1963).

Colegate, Isabel (1931   )

Orlando at the Brazen Threshold (1971), *News from the City of the Sun* (1979), *The Shooting Party* (1980), *Deceits of Time* (1988).

Comyns, Barbara (1909–1992)

Our Spoons Came from Woolworths (1950), *The Juniper Tree* (1985), *Mr Fox* (1987).

Conrad, Joseph (Josef Korzeniowski) (1857–1924)

Almayer's Folly (1895), *The Nigger of the 'Narcissus'* (1897), *Lord Jim* (1900), *Nostromo* (1904), *The Secret Agent* (1907), *Under Western Eyes* (1911), *Chance* (1913), *Victory* (1915), *The Shadow Line* (1917), *The Arrow of Gold* (1919), *The Rescue* (1920).

Cooper, Lettice (1897–1994)

The Lighted Room (1925), *National Provincial* (1938), *Late in the Afternoon* (1973), *Unusual Behaviour* (1986).

Cooper, William (Harry Hoff) (1910   )

Trina (as H. S. Hoff) (1934), *Scenes from Provincial Life* (1950), *The Struggles of Albert Woods* (1952), *Disquiet and Peace* (1956), *Young People* (1958), *Scenes from Married Life* (1961), *Memoirs of a New Man* (1966), *Scenes from Metropolitan Life* (1982), *Scenes from Later Life* (1983), *Immortality at Any Price* (1991).

Crace, Jim (1946   )

Continent (1986), *The Gift of Stones* (1988), *Arcadia* (1992), *Signals of Distress* (1994), *Quarantine* (1997), *Being Dead* (1999).

Dabydeen, David (1956   )

The Intended (1991), *Disappearance* (1993), *The Counting House* (1996), *A Harlot's Progress* (1999).

D'Aguiar, Fred (1960   )

Dear Future (1996), *Feeding the Ghosts* (1998).

Day Lewis, Cecil (1904–1972)

The Friendly Tree (1936), *Starting Point* (1937), *Childs of Misfortune* (1939).

Deane, Seamus (1940   )

Reading in the Dark (1996).

De Bernières, Louis (1954)

The War of Don Emmanuel's Nether Parts (1990), *Senor Vivo and the Coca Lord* (1991), *The Troublesome Offspring of Cardinal Guzman* (1992), *Captain Corelli's Mandolin* (1995).

Deighton, Len (1924)

The Ipcress File (1962), *Spy Story* (1974), *The Berlin Game* (1983), *The Mexico Set* (1984), *London Match* (1985).

Dennis, Nigel (1912)

Cards of Identity (1955), *A House in Order* (1966).

Desai, Anita (1937)

Fire On the Mountain (1977), *Clear Light of Day* (1980), *In Custody* (1984), *Feasting, Fasting* (1999).

Diski, Jenny (1947)

Nothing Natural (1986), *Then Again* (1990), *Monkey's Uncle* (1994).

Douglas, Norman (1868–1952)

Siren Land (1911), *South Wind* (1917).

Doyle, Arthur Conan (1859–1930)

A Study in Scarlet (1887), *The Sign of Four* (1890), *The White Company* (1891), *The Adventures of Sherlock Holmes* (1892), *The Memoirs of Sherlock Holmes* (1894), *The Return of Sherlock Holmes* (1905).

Doyle, Roddy (1958)

The Commitments (1988), *The Snapper* (1990), *Paddy Clarke Ha Ha Ha* (1993), *The Woman Who Walked Into Doors* (1996), *A Star Called Henry* (1999).

Drabble, Margaret (1939)

A Summer Bird-Cage (1963), *The Garrick Year* (1964), *The Needle's Eye* (1972), *The Realms of Gold* (1975), *The Ice Age* (1977), *The Middle Ground* (1980), *The Radiant Way* (1987), *A Natural Curiosity* (1989), *The Gates of Ivory* (1991), *The Witch of Exmoor* (1996), *The Peppered Moth* (2001).

Duffy, Maureen (1933)

That's How it Was (1962), *The Paradox Players* (1967), *Capital* (1975), *Londoners* (1983), *Change* (1987), *Illuminations* (1991), *Occam's Razor* (1993), *Restitution* (1998).

Du Maurier, Daphne (1907–1989)

Jamaica Inn (1936), *Rebecca* (1938), *Frenchman's Creek* (1941), *The Flight of the Falcon* (1965).

Du Maurier, George (1834–1896)

Peter Ibbotson (1892), *Trilby* (1894).

Dunmore, Helen (1952)

Zennor in Darkness (1993), *A Spell of Winter* (1995), *Talking to the Dead* (1996), *Your Blue-Eyed Boy* (1998), *With Your Crooked Heart* (1999).

Dunn, Nell (1935   )

Poor Cow (1967), *Tear Their Heads Off Their Shoulders* (1974), *The Only Child* (1978), *My Silver Shoes* (1996).

Durrell, Lawrence (1912–1990)

The Black Book (Paris, 1938), *Justine* (1957), *Balthazar* (1958), *Mountolive* (1958), *Clea* (1960), *Monsieur, Or the Prince of Darkness* (1974).

Egerton, George (Mary Chavelita Bright) (1859–1945)

Keynotes (stories, 1893), *Discords* (stories, 1894), *Symphonies* (stories, 1897).

Ellis, Alice Thomas (1932   )

The Sin Eater (1977), *The Twenty Seventh Kingdom* (1982), *Unexplained Laughter* (1985), *The Clothes in the Wardrobe* (1987), *The Inn at the Edge of the World* (1990), *Pillars of Gold* (1992).

Emecheta, Buchi (1944   )

In the Ditch (1972), *Second Class Citizen* (1974), *The Joys of Motherhood* (1979), *A Kind of Marriage* (1986).

Enright, D. J. (1920   )

Academic Year (1955), *Figures of Speech* (1965).

Farrell, J. G. (1935–1979)

A Man From Elsewhere (1963), *A Girl in the Head* (1967), *Troubles* (1970), *The Siege of Krishnapur* (1973), *The Singapore Grip* (1978), *The Hill Station* (1981, post.).

Faulks, Sebastian (1953   )

A Trick of the Light (1984), *The Girl at the Lion d'Or* (1988), *A Fool's Alphabet* (1992), *Birdsong* (1993), *Charlotte Gray* (1999).

Feinstein, Elaine (1930   )

The Circle (1970), *Children of the Rose* (1975).

Figes, Eva (1932   )

Equinox (1966), *Winter Journey* (1967), *B.* (1972), *Ghosts* (1988), *The Knot* (1997).

Fischer, Tibor (1959   )

Under the Frog (1992), *The Thought Gang* (1994), *The Collector Collector* (1997).

Fitzgerald, Penelope (1916–2000)

Offshore (1979), *Human Voices* (1980), *At Freddie's* (1982), *Innocence* (1986), *The Beginning of Spring* (1988), *The Gate of Angels* (1990), *The Blue Flower* (1995).

Fitzgibbon, Constantine (1919   )

The Arabian Bird (1949), *When the Kissing Had to Stop* (1960).

Firbank, Ronald (1886–1926)

Caprice (1917), *Valmouth* (1919), *Prancing Nigger* (1924), *Concerning the*

Eccentricities of Cardinal Pirelli (1926), *The Complete Firbank* (1961).
Fleming, Ian (1908–1964)
Casino Royale (1953), *Thunderball* (1961).
Foden, Giles (1967   )
The Last King of Scotland (1998).
Ford, Ford Madox (Ford Madox Hueffer) (1873–1939)
The Brown Owl: A Fairy Story (1892), *The Inheritors* (with Joseph
Conrad, 1901), *The Fifth Queen* (1906), *A Call* (1910), *The Good Soldier*
(1915), *Some Do Not . . .* (1924), *No More Parades* (1925), *A Man
Could Stand Up –* (1926), *The Last Post* (1928), collected as 'Parade's
End'.
Forster, E. M. (1879–1970)
Where Angels Fear to Tread (1905), *A Room with a View* (1907), *Howards
End* (1910), *The Celestial Omnibus and Other Stories* (1911), *A Passage to
India* (1924), *Maurice* (1971, post.).
Forster, Margaret (1938   )
Georgy Girl (1965), *The Bogeyman* (1965), *Mother Can You Hear Me?*
(1979), *Marital Rites* (1981), *Lady's Maid* (1900), *Mother's Boys* (1990),
Shadow Baby (1996).
Forsyth, Frederick (1938   )
The Day of the Jackal (1971), *The Odessa File* (1972), *The Dogs of War*
(1974), *The Fourth Protocol* (1984), *The Negotiator* (1989), *The Fist of God*
(1994).
Fowles, John (1926   )
The Collector (1963), *The Magus* (1965: rev. ed., 1977), *The French
Lieutenant's Woman* (1969), *Daniel Martin* (1977), *A Maggot* (1985).
Frayn, Michael (1933   )
The Tin Men (1965), *The Russian Interpreter* (1966), *Sweet Dreams* (1973),
The Trick of It (1989), *Now You Know* (1992), *Headlong* (1999).
Freud, Esther (1963   )
Hideous Kinky (1992), *Peerless Flats* (1993).
Fry, Stephen (1957   )
The Liar (1991), *Making History* (1997).
Galloway, Janice (1956   )
The Trick is to Keep Breathing (1989), *Foreign Parts* (1994).
Galsworthy, John (1867–1933)
The Man of Property (1906), *The Country House* (1907), *In Chancery*
(1920), *To Let* (1921), *The Forsyte Saga* (1922).
Garnett, David (1892–1981)
Lady Into Fox (1922), *A Man in the Zoo* (1924).

Gebler, Carlo (1954   )

The Eleventh Summer (1984), *Work and Play* (1987), *The Glass Curtain* (1991), *How to Murder a Man* (1998).

Gee, Maggie (1948   )

Dying in Other Words (1981), *Light Years* (1985), *Grace* (1988), *Ice People* (1998).

Gerhardie, William (1895–1977)

Futility (1922), *The Polyglots* (1925), *Of Mortal Love* (1936).

Gibbon, Lewis Grassic (James Leslie Mitchell) (1901–1935)

Sunset Song (1932), *Cloud Howe* (1933), *Grey Granite* (1934), all reprinted as *A Scots Quair* (1945).

Gibbons, Stella (1902–1992)

Cold Comfort Farm (1932).

Gissing, George (1857–1903)

Workers in the Dawn (1880), *The Unclassed* (1884), *Demos* (1886), *Thyrza* (1887), *The Nether World* (1889), *New Grub Street* (1891), *The Odd Woman* (1893), *In the Year of the Jubilee* (1894).

Glaister, Lesley (1956   )

Honour Thy Father (1990), *Trick or Treat* (1991), *Partial Eclipse* (1994), *The Private Parts of Women* (1997).

Glanville, Brian (1931   )

The Reluctant Dictator (1952), *The Bankrupts* (1958), *A Second Home* (1965), *The Financiers* (1972).

Glyn, Elinor (1864–1943)

Three Weeks (1907), *Elizabeth Visits America* (1909), *It* (1926).

Godden, Rumer (1907–1998)

Black Narcissus (1939), *The River* (1946), *An Episode of Sparrows* (1955), *Thursday's Children* (1984).

Golding, William (1911–1993)

Lord of the Flies (1954), *The Inheritors* (1955), *Pincher Martin* (1956), *The Spire* (1964), *Darkness Visible* (1979), *Rites of Passage* (1980), *The Paper Men* (1984), *Close Quarters* (1987), *Fire Down Below* (1989).

Gordon, Giles (1940   )

The Umbrella Man (1971), *Girl with Red Hair* (1974).

Gosse, Edmund (1849–1928)

The Secret of Narcisse (1892), *Father and Son* (autobiography, 1907).

Grand, Sarah (Frances McFall) (1854–1943)

The Heavenly Twins (1893), *The Beth Book* (1897).

Graves, Robert (1895–1985)

I, Claudius (1934), *Claudius the God* (1934), *Antigua, Penny, Puce* (1935).

Gray, Alasdair (1934   )
Lanark (1981), *1982, Janine* (1984), *The Fall of Kelvin Walker* (1985), *Poor Things* (1992), *A History Maker* (1994), *Mavis Belfrage: A Romantic Novel* (1997).

Green, Henry (1905–1985)
Blindness (1926), *Living* (1929), *Party-Going* (1939), *Caught* (1943), *Loving* (1946), *Concluding* (1948).

Greene, Graham (1904–1991)
The Man Within (1929), *It's a Battlefield* (1934), *Brighton Rock* (1938), *The Power and the Glory* (1940), *Nineteen Stories* (1947), *The Heart of the Matter* (1948), *The End of the Affair* (1951), *The Quiet American* (1955), *A Burnt-Out Case* (1961), *The Comedians* (1966), *The Human Factor* (1978), *Monsignor Quixote* (1982).

Greenwood, Walter (1903–1974)
Love on the Dole: A Tale of Two Cities (1933).

Gunesekera, Romesh (1954   )
Monkfish Moon (stories, 1992), *Reef* (1994), *The Hourglass* (1998).

Gurnah, Abdulrazak (1948   )
Paradise (1994).

Haggard, H. Rider (1856–1925)
King Solomon's Mines (1885), *She* (1887), *Allan Quatermain* (1887), *Montezuma's Daughter* (1893), *Heart of the World* (1896).

Hamilton, Patrick (1904–1962)
Rope (1929), *Gaslight* (1939), *The West Pier* (1951).

Hanley, James (1901–1985)
Boy (1931), *Sailor's Song* (1943), *Winter Song* (1950), *Collected Stories* (1953), *The Welsh Sonata* (1954), *Say Nothing* (1962), *A Woman in the Sky* (1973).

Hardy, Thomas (1840–1928)
Under the Greenwood Tree (1872), *Far From the Madding Crowd* (1874), *The Return of the Native* (1878), *The Mayor of Casterbridge* (1886), *The Woodlanders* (1887), *Wessex Tales* (1888), *Tess of the D'Urbervilles* (1891), *Jude the Obscure* (1896).

Harkness, Margaret ('John Law') (1861–1921)
A City Girl (1887), *Out of Work* (1888), *A Manchester Shirtmaker* (1890).

Harris, Wilson (1921   )
The Guyana Quartet (1960–63), *Black Marsden* (1972), *Carnival* (1985), *Resurrection at Snow Hill* (1993), *Jonestown* (1997).

Hartley, L. P. (1895–1972)
Simonette Perkins (1925), *The Shrimp and the Anemone* (1944), *The*

Go-Between (1953), *The Hireling* (1957), *Facial Justice* (1960), *The Betrayal* (1966).

Heath, Roy A. K. (1926   )

A Man Came Home (1974), *The Murderer* (1978), *From the Heat of the Day* (1979), *One Generation* (1981).

Hill, Susan (1942   )

Strange Meeting (1971), *Bird of Night* (1972), *In the Springtime of the Year* (1974), *The Woman in Black* (1983), *Air and Angels* (1991).

Hines, Barry (1939   )

Kestrel for a Knave (1968), *The Gamekeeper* (1975), *Looks and Smiles* (1981).

Hollinghurst, Alan (1954   )

The Swimming Pool Library (1988), *The Folding Star* (1994), *The Spell* (1998).

Holtby, Winifred (1898–1935)

The Land of Green Ginger (1927), *South Riding* (1936).

Hope, Christopher (1944   )

Kruger's Alp (1984), *The Hottentot Room* (1986), *Black Swan* (1987), *My Chocolate Redeemer* (1989), *Serenity House* (1992).

Hopkins, Bill (1928)

The Divine and the Decay (1957).

Hornby, Nick (1957   )

Fever Pitch (1992), *High Fidelity* (1995).

Howard, Elizabeth Jane (1923   )

The Beautiful Visit (1950), *The Long View* (1956), *After Julius* (1965), *Something in Disguise* (1969), *Odd Girl Out* (1972), *Getting it Right* (1982), *The Light Years* (1990), *Confusion* (1993), *Falling* (1999).

Hudson, W. H. (1841–1922)

The Purple Land That England Lost (1885), *A Crystal Age* (1887), *Green Mansions* (1904).

Hughes, Glyn (1935   )

Where I Used to Play on the Green (1981), *The Hawthorn Goddess* (1984), *The Antique Collector* (1990).

Hughes, Richard (1900–1976)

A High Wind in Jamaica (1929), *In Hazard* (1938), *The Fox in the Attic* (1961).

Humphreys, Emyr (1919   )

The Little Kingdom (1946), *The Gift* (1963), *Salt of the Earth* (1985), *Bonds of Attachment* (1991), *The Gift of a Daughter* (1998).

Hunt, Violet (1866–1942)

The Workaday Woman (1906), *White Rose of Weary Leaf* (1908), *The Tiger Skin* (1924).

Huxley, Aldous (1894–1963)
Crome Yellow (1921), *Antic Hay* (1923), *Those Barren Leaves* (1925), *Point Counter Point* (1928), *Brave New World* (1932), *Eyeless in Gaza* (1936), *Time Must Have a Stop* (1945).

Isherwood, Christopher (1904–1986)
All the Conspirators (1928), *The Memorial* (1932), *Mr Norris Changes Trains* (1935), *Goodbye to Berlin* (1939), *The Berlin Stories* (collection, 1946), *The World in the Evening* (1954), *Down There on a Visit* (1962), *A Single Man* (1964).

Ishiguro, Kazuo (1954   )
A Pale View of Hills (1982), *An Artist of the Floating World* (1986), *The Remains of the Day* (1989), *The Unconsoled* (1995), *When We Were Orphans* (2000).

Jackson, Mick (1960   )
The Underground Man (1997).

Jacobson, Dan (1929   )
The Trap (1955), *The Price of Diamonds* (1957), *The Beginners* (1966), *The Rape of Tamar* (1970), *The Confessions of Joseph Baisz* (1977).

Jacobson, Howard (1942   )
Coming from Behind (1983), *Peeping Tom* (1984), *Redback* (1986), *The Very Model of a Man* (1992).

James, Henry (1843–1916)
Roderick Hudson (Boston, 1876; 1879), *The American* (1877), *The Europeans* (1878), *Washington Square* (1881), *The Portrait of a Lady* (1881), *The Bostonians* (1886), *The Princess Casamassima* (1886), *The Tragic Muse* (1890), *What Maisie Knew* (1897), *The Awkward Age* (1899), *The Wings of a Dove* (1902), *The Ambassadors* (1903), *The Golden Bowl* (1904), *The Art of the Novel* (prefaces, ed. R. P. Blackmur, 1934), *The Future of the Novel* (essays, 1956).

James, P. D. (1920   )
Cover Her Face (1962), *Unnatural Causes* (1967), *The Black Tower* (1975), *Death of an Expert Witness* (1977), *Innocent Blood* (1980), *The Skull Beneath the Skin* (1982), *A Taste for Death* (1986), *Devices and Desires* (1989), *The Children of Men* (1992), *Original Sin* (1994), *A Certain Justice* (1998).

Jameson, Storm (1891–1986)
The Single Heart (1932), *Women Against Men* (stories, 1933), *Love in Winter* (1935).

Jenkins, Elizabeth (1905   )
The Tortoise and the Hare (1954), *Honey* (1968).

Jhabvala, Ruth Prawer (1928   )

To Whom She Will (1955), *The Householder* (1960), *A New Dominion* (1972), *Heat and Dust* (1975), *Three Continents* (1987).

Johnson, B. S. (1933–1973)

Travelling People (1963), *Albert Angelo* (1964), *Trawl* (1966), *The Unfortunates* (1968), *House Mother Normal* (1971), *Christie Malry's Own Double-Entry* (1972), *See the Old Lady Decently* (1975).

Johnson, Pamela Hansford (1912–1981)

World's End (1937), *Too Dear for My Possessing* (1940), *An Impossible Marriage* (1954), *The Unspeakable Skipton* (1959), *Night and Silence, Who Is Here?* (1962), *Cork Street, Next the Hatters* (1965), *The Bonfire* (1981).

Johnston, Jennifer (1930   )

The Captains and the Kings (1972), *How Many Miles to Babylon?* (1974), *The Invisible Worm* (1991), *The Illusionist* (1995).

Jones, Russell Celyn (1955   )

Soldiers and Innocents (1990), *Small Times* (1992), *An Interference of Light* (1995), *The Eros Hunter* (1998).

Jordan, Neil (1950   )

The Past (1982), *The Dream of a Beast* (1983).

Josipovici, Gabriel (1940   )

Möbius the Stripper (1974), *The Echo Chambers* (1978), *In the Fertile Land* (1987).

Joyce, James (1882–1941)

Dubliners (1914), *A Portrait of the Artist as a Young Man* (New York, 1916; London, 1917), *Ulysses* (Paris, 1922; New York, 1934; London, 1936), *Finnegans Wake* (New York, 1939; London, 1946).

Kelman, James (1946   )

The Busconductor Hines (1984), *A Chancer* (1985), *A Disaffection* (1989), *How Late it Was, How Late* (1994), *The Good Times* (1998).

Kennedy, A. L. (1965   )

Looking for the Possible Dance (1993), *So I Am Glad* (1995), *Original Bliss* (1997), *Everything You Need* (1999).

King, Francis (1923   )

The Dividing Stream (1951), *The Widow* (1957), *The Last of the Pleasure Gardens* (1965), *A Domestic Animal* (1970), *The Action* (1978), *Frozen Music* (1987), *Woman Who Was Good* (1988).

Kipling, Rudyard (1865–1936)

Plain Tales from the Hills (Calcutta, 1888; 1890), *The Light That Failed* (1890), *The Jungle Book* (1894), *The Second Jungle Book* (1895), *Stalky*

& Co. (1899), *Kim* (1901), *Just So Stories* (1902), *Puck of Pook's Hill* (1906).

Koestler, Arthur (1905–1983)

The Gladiators (from German, 1939), *Darkness at Noon* (1940), *The Age of Longing* (1951).

Kureishi, Hanif (1954   )

The Buddha of Suburbia (1990), *The Black Album* (1996).

Lanchester, John (1962   )

The Debt to Pleasure (1996), *Mr Phillips* (2000).

Larkin, Philip (1922–1985)

Jill (1946), *A Girl in Winter* (1947).

Lawrence, D. H. (1885–1930)

The White Peacock (1911), *The Trespasser* (1912), *Sons and Lovers* (1913), *The Prussian Officer and Other Stories* (1914), *The Rainbow* (1915), *Women in Love* (New York, 1920; London, 1921), *The Lost Girl* (1920), *Kangaroo* (1923), *The Plumed Serpent* (1926), *Lady Chatterley's Lover* (Florence, 1928; London, 1932), *The Virgin and the Gypsy* (1930), *Phoenix* (essays) (1936, post.), *Mr Noon* (1985, post.).

Le Carré, John (David Cornwell) (1931   )

The Spy Who Came in from the Cold (1963), *The Looking-Glass War* (1965), *Tinker, Tailor, Soldier, Spy* (1974), *The Honourable Schoolboy* (1977), *The Little Drummer Girl* (1983); *A Perfect Spy* (1986), *The Russia House* (1989), *The Night Manager* (1993), *Our Game* (1995), *The Tailor of Panama* (1996), *Single & Single* (1999).

Lehmann, John (1907–1987)

Evil Was Abroad (1938).

Lehmann, Rosamund (1903–1990)

A Dusty Answer (1927), *A Note in Music* (1930), *An Invitation to the Waltz* (1932), *The Weather in the Streets* (1936), *The Ballad and the Source* (1944), *The Echoing Grove* (1953).

Le Queux, William (1864–1927)

Guilty Bonds (1890), *A Madonna of the Music Halls* (1897), *The Invasion of 1910* (1906).

Lessing, Doris (1919   )

The Grass is Singing (1950), *Martha Quest* (1952), *The Golden Notebook* (1962), *Briefing for a Descent Into Hell* (1971), *Memoirs of a Survivor* (1974), *Shikasta* (1979), *The Good Terrorist* (1985), *The Fifth Child* (1987), *Love Again* (1997).

Leverson, Ada (1862–1933)

Love's Shadow (1908), *Tenterhooks* (1912), *Love at Second Sight* (1916), collected as *The Little Ottleys* (1962).

Lewis, C. S. (1898–1963)
Out of the Silent Planet (1938), *Voyage to Venus* (1943), *That Hideous Strength* (1945).

Lewis, Norman (1908   )
The Day of the Fox (1955), *The March of the Long Shadows* (1987).

Lewis, Wyndham (1882–1957)
Tarr (1918), *The Childermass* (1928), *The Apes of God* (1930), *Snooty Baronet* (1932), *The Revenge for Love* (1937), *Rotting Hill* (1951), *The Human Age* (1955).

Litt, Toby (1968   )
Adventures in Capitalism (1997), *Beatniks: An English Road Movie* (1998), *Corpsing* (2000).

Lively, Adam (1961   )
Blue Fruit (1988), *The Burnt House* (1989), *The Snail* (1991), *Sing the Body Electric* (1993).

Lively, Penelope (1933   )
The Road to Lichfield (1977), *Judgement Day* (1980), *Next to Nature, Art* (1982), *According to Mark* (1984), *Moon Tiger* (1987), *Passing On* (1989), *Cleopatra's Sister* (1993).

Lodge, David (1935   )
Ginger, You're Barmy (1962), *The British Museum Is Falling Down* (1965), *Out of the Shelter* (1970, rev. ed. 1985), *Changing Places* (1975), *How Far Can You Go?* (1980), *Small World* (1984), *Nice Work* (1988), *Paradise News* (1991), *Therapy* (1995).

Lowry, Malcolm (1909–1957)
Ultramarine (1933), *Under the Volcano* (1947), *Dark as the Grave Wherein my Friend is Laid* (1968 post.), *Lunar Caustic* (1968, post.), *October Ferry to Gabriola* (1971, post.).

Macaulay, Rose (1881–1958)
The Furnace (1907), *Told By an Idiot* (1923), *Crewe Train* (1926), *Keeping Up Appearances* (1928), *Staying With Relations* (1930), *The Towers of Trebizond* (1956).

McEwan, Ian (1948   )
First Love, Last Rites (stories, 1975), *In Between the Sheets* (stories, 1978), *The Cement Garden* (1978), *The Comfort of Strangers* (1981), *The Child in Time* (1987), *The Innocents* (1990), *Black Dogs* (1992), *Enduring Love* (1997), *Amsterdam* (1998).

McGahern, John (1934   )
The Barracks (1963), *Nightlines* (1971), *The Leavetaking* (1974), *The Pornographer* (1979), *Amongst Women* (1990), *The Power of Darkness* (1991).

McGrath, Patrick (1950   )
The Grotesque (1989), *Spider* (1990), *Dr Haggard's Disease* (1993), *Asylum* (1996).
Machen, Arthur (1863–1947)
The Great God Pan (1894), *The House of Souls* (stories, 1906).
McIlvanney, William (1936   )
Doherty (1975), *The Big Man* (1985), *Strange Loyalties* (1991).
Macinnes, Colin (1914–1976)
To the Victors the Spoils (1950), *City of Spades* (1957), *Absolute Beginners* (1959), *Mr Love and Justice* (1960).
Mackay, Shena (1944   )
An Advent Calendar (1971), *Redhill Rococo* (1986), *The Laughing Academy* (stories, 1993), *The Orchard on Fire* (1995).
Mackenzie, Compton (1883–1972)
Carnival (1912), *Sinister Street* (1914), *Extraordinary Women* (1928).
Mac Laverty, Bernard (1942   )
Lamb (1980), *Cal* (1983), *Grace Notes* (1997).
McWilliam, Candia (1955   )
A Case of Knives (1988), *A Little Stranger* (1989), *Debatable Land* (1994).
Madden, Deirdre (1960   )
The Birds of the Innocent Wood (1988), *Hidden Symptoms* (1988), *Remembering Light and Stone* (1992), *Nothing is Black* (1994).
Magrs, Paul (1969   )
Does it Show? (1998).
Manning, Frederic (1882–1935)
Her Privates We: By Private 19022 (1930).
Manning, Olivia (1911–1980)
The Wind Changes (1937), *School for Love* (1951), *A Different Face* (1953), *The Doves of Venus* (1955), 'The Balkan Trilogy' (1960–65), 'The Levant Trilogy' (1977–8).
Mansfield, Katherine (1888–1923)
In a German Pension (stories, 1911), *Bliss and Other Stories* (1920), *The Garden-Party and Other Stories* (1922).
Mantel, Hilary (1952   )
Eight Months on Ghazzah Street (1988), *Fludd* (1989), *A Place of Greater Safety* (1992), *A Change of Climate* (1994), *An Experiment in Love* (1995), *The Giant, O'Brien* (1998).
Mars-Jones, Adam (1954   )
The Waters of Thirst (1993).

Massie, Alan (1938   )

Change and Decay in All Around I See (1978), *The Death of Men* (1981), *A Question of Loyalties* (1989), *The Hanging Tree* (1990), *Tiberius* (1991), *These Enchanted Woods* (1993), *The Ragged Lion* (1994), *King David* (1995).

Maugham W. Somerset (1874–1965)

Liza of Lambeth (1897), *Mrs Craddock* (1902), *Of Human Bondage* (1915), *The Moon and Sixpence* (1919), *Cakes and Ale* (1930), *The Razor's Edge* (1944).

Mayor, F. M. (1872–1932)

The Third Miss Symons (1913), *The Rector's Daughter* (1924).

Melville, Pauline

The Ventriloquist's Tale (1997), *The Migration of Ghosts* (1999).

Meredith, George (1828–1909)

Modern Love (1862), *The Egoist* (1879), *The Tragic Comedians* (1880), *Diana of the Crossways* (1885).

Middleton, Stanley (1919   )

A Short Answer (1958), *Harris's Requiem* (1960), *Two's Company* (1963), *Apple of Eve* (1970), *Holiday* (1974), *In a Strange Land* (1979), *Recovery* (1988).

Miller, Andrew (1960   )

Ingenious Pain (1997), *Casanova* (1999).

Mistry, Rohinton (1952   )

Such a Long Journey (1991), *A Fine Balance* (1997).

Mitchell, Julian (1935   )

Imaginary Toys (1961), *A Disturbing Influence* (1962), *The White Father* (1964), *The Undiscovered Country* (1968).

Mo, Timothy (1950   )

The Monkey King (1978), *Sour Sweet* (1982), *An Insular Possession* (1986), *The Redundancy of Courage* (1991), *Brownout on Breadfruit Boulevard* (1995).

Morgan, Charles (1894–1958)

The Fountain (1932), *The Voyage* (1940), *The River Line* (1949).

Moorcock, Michael (1939   )

The Chinese Agent (1970), *Byzantium Endures* (1981), *Mother London* (1988), *The Laughter of Carthage* (1984), *Jerusalem Commands* (1992).

Moore, Brian (1921–1999)

The Lonely Passion of Judith Hearne (1955), *The Luck of Ginger Coffey* (1960), *An Answer from Limbo* (1963), *The Emperor of Ice Cream* (1966), *Catholics* (1972), *The Doctor's Wife* (1976), *Cold Heaven* (1983), *The Colour of Blood* (1987), *Lies of Silence* (1990), *No Other Life* (1993).

Moore, George (1852–1933)
A Modern Lover (1883), *A Mummer's Wife* (1885), *A Mere Accident* (1887), *Esther Waters* (1894), the 'Hail and Farewell' trilogy (1911–14).
Morris, William (1834–1896)
The Dream of John Ball (1888), *News from Nowhere* (1890), *The Wood Beyond the World* (1895).
Morrison, Arthur (1863–1945)
Tales of Mean Streets (1894), *A Child of the Jago* (1896), *To London Town* (1899), *The Hole in the Wall* (1902).
Mosley, Nicholas (1923   )
Spaces of the Dark (1951), *The Rainbearers* (1955), *Accident* (1965), *Impossible Object* (1968), *Natalie, Natalia* (1971), *Imago Bird* (1980), *Hopeful Monsters* (1990).
Mottram, R. H. (1883–1971)
The Spanish Farm (1924), *The Spanish Farm Trilogy, 1914–18* (1927).
Munro, H. H. ('Saki') (1870–1916)
The Chronicles of Clovis (1911), *The Unbearable Bassington* (1912).
Murdoch, Iris (1919–1999)
Under the Net (1954), *The Bell* (1958), *A Severed Head* (1961), *An Unofficial Rose* (1962), *The Red and the Green* (1965), *The Nice and the Good* (1968), *The Black Prince* (1971), *A Word Child* (1975), *The Sea, The Sea* (1978), *The Philosopher's Pupil* (1983), *The Book and the Brotherhood* (1987), *The Green Knight* (1993).
Myers, L. H. (1881–1944)
The 'Clio' (1925), *The Near and the Far* (1929), *The Root and the Flower* (1935).
Naipaul, V. S. (1932   )
The Mystic Masseur (1957), *A House for Mr Biswas* (1961), *The Mimic Men* (1967), *In a Free State* (1971), *Guerrillas* (1975), *A Bend in the River* (1979), *The Enigma of Arrival* (1987), *A Way in the World* (1994).
Newby, P. H. (1918   )
A Journey to the Interior (1945), *Picnic at Sakkara* (1955), *The Barbary Light* (1962), *Something to Answer For* (1968), *Leaning in the Wind* (1986).
Norfolk, Lawrence (1963   )
Lemprière's Dictionary (1991), *The Pope's Rhinoceros* (1997).
Nye, Robert (1939   )
Doubtfire (1967), *Falstaff* (1976), *Faust* (1980), *Voyage of the Destiny* (1982), *The Late Mr Shakespeare* (1998).
O'Brian, Patrick (1914–2000)
Master and Commander (1970), *Treason's Harbour* (1983), *The Reverse of the Medal* (1986), *The Wine-Dark Sea* (1993), *The Commodore* (1994).

O'Brien, Edna (1932   )

The Country Girls (1960), *Girls in Their Married Bliss* (1964), *August is a Wicked Month* (1965), *The Love Object* (1968), *Johnny I Hardly Knew You* (1977).

O'Brien, Flann (Brian O'Nolan) (1911–1966)

At Swim-Two-Birds (1939), *The Dalkey Archive* (1964), *The Third Policeman* (1967).

O'Faolain, Sean (1900–1991)

A Nest of Simple Folk (1933), *Midsummer Night Madness* (1982), *The Heat of the Sun* (1983).

O'Hagan, Andrew (1968   )

Our Fathers (1999).

Okri, Ben (1959   )

Flowers and Shadows (1980), *Incidents at the Shrine* (1986), *Stars of the New Curfew* (1988), *The Famished Road* (1991), *Songs of Enchantment* (1993), *Astonishing the Gods* (1995), *Dangerous Love* (1997), *Infinite Riches* (1998).

Orwell, George (Eric Blair) (1903–1950)

Burmese Days (1934), *A Clergyman's Daughter* (1935), *Keep the Aspidistra Flying* (1936), *Coming Up for Air* (1939), *Animal Farm* (1945), *Nineteen-Eighty-Four* (1949).

'Ouida' (Marie Louise de la Ramée) (1839–1908)

Moths (1880), *Wanda* (1883).

Parks, Tim (1954   )

Tongues of Flame (1986), *Loving Roger* (1987), *Home Thoughts* (1987), *Cara Massimina* (1994), *Mimi's Ghost* (1995), *Europa* (1997), *Destiny* (1999).

Patterson, Glenn (1961   )

Burning Your Own (1988), *Fat Lad* (1992), *Black Night at Big Thunder Mountain* (1995), *The International* (1999).

Peake, Mervyn (1911–1968)

Titus Groan (1946), *Gormenghast* (1950).

Philips, Tom (1937   )

A Humument: A Treated Victorian Novel (1980: rev. ed., 1987).

Phillips, Caryl (1958   )

The Final Passage (1985), *A State of Independence* (1986), *Cambridge* (1992), *Crossing the River* (1993).

Powell, Anthony (1905–2000)

Afternoon Men (1931), *Venusberg* (1932), *From a View to a Death* (1933), *What's Becoming of Waring?* (1939), 'A Dance to the Music of Time' (12 vols., 1951–75), *The Fisher King* (1986).

Powys, J. C. (1872–1963)

Wood and Stone (1915), *Wolf Solent* (1929), *A Glastonbury Romance* (1933), *Weymouth Sands* (1934, 1963).

Powys, T. F. (1875–1953)

Mr Weston's Good Wine (1927), *Unclay* (1931).

Pratchett, Terry (1940   )

The Colour of Magic (1983), *Sourcery* (1988), *Men at Arms* (1993), *Soul Music* (1994), *The Witches Trilogy* (1995).

Priest, Christopher (1943   )

Indoctrinaire (1970), *Inverted World* (1974), *The Affirmation* (1981), *The Extremes* (1998).

Priestley, J. B. (1894–1984)

The Good Companions (1929), *Angel Pavement* (1930), *Festival at Farbridge* (1951), *Lost Empires* (1965), *The Image Men* (1968).

Pritchett, V. S. (1900–1997)

Dead Man Leading (1937), *Mr Beluncle* (1951), *Key to My Heart* (1963), *Collected Stories* (1982), *More Collected Stories* (1983).

Pym, Barbara (1913–1980)

Some Tame Gazelle (1950), *Excellent Women* (1952), *Less Than Angels* (1955), *A Glass of Blessings* (1958), *Quartet in Autumn* (1977), *The Sweet Dove Died* (1978), *An Academic Question* (1986, post.).

Quin, Ann (1936–1973)

Berg (1964), *Three* (1966), *Passages* (1969), *Tripticks* (1972).

Raban, Jonathan (1942   )

Foreign Land (1985).

Raphael, Frederic (1931   )

Obbligato (1956), *The Trouble with England* (1962), *Glittering Prizes* (1976), *After the War* (1988).

Raven, Simon (1927   )

The Feathers of Death (1959), the 'Alms for Oblivion' sequence (1964–75), *The Troubador* (1992), *The Islands of Sorrow* (1994).

Read, Piers Paul (1931   )

Game in Heaven With Tussy Marx (1966), *The Junkers* (1968), *The Professor's Daughter* (1971), *A Married Man* (1979), *The Villa Golitsyn* (1981), *A Season in the West* (1988), *On the Third Day* (1990), *A Patriot in Berlin* (1995).

Reid, Forrest (1875–1947)

The Kingdom of Twilight (1904), *Uncle Stephen* (1931), *The Retreat* (1934), *Young Tom* (1944).

Rendell, Ruth (1930   )

Shake Hands for Ever (1975), *Make Death Love Me* (1979), *An Unkindness of Ravens* (1985), *A Dark-Adapted Eye* (as Barbara Vine, 1986), *Heartstones* (1987), *Talking to Strange Men* (1987), *Asta's Book* (as Barbara Vine, 1994), *Simisola* (1994).

Rhys, Jean (1894–1979)

Postures (1928, reissued as *Quartet*), *After Leaving Mr Mackenzie* (1930), *Voyage in the Dark* (1934), *Good Morning, Midnight* (1939), *Wide Sargasso Sea* (1966).

Richardson, Dorothy (1873–1957)

Pointed Roofs (1915), *Backwater* (1916) and further volumes collected as 'Pilgrimage' (4 vols., 1938, 1967).

Roberts, Kate (1891–1985)

Traed Mewn Cyffon (Welsh, 1936), *Haul a Drycin* (Welsh, 1981).

Roberts, Michèle (1949   )

A Piece of the Night (1978), *The Wild Girl* (1984), *The Book of Mrs Noah* (1987), *Daughters of the House* (1992), *Flesh and Blood* (1994), *Impossible Saints* (1997), *Fair Exchange* (1999).

Rogers, Jane (1952   )

Separate Tracks (1983), *Mr Wroe's Virgins* (1991), *Promised Lands* (1995).

Rolfe, Frederick ('Baron Corvo') (1860–1913)

Hadrian the Seventh (1904), *The Desire and Pursuit of the Whole* (1934, post.).

Roy, Arundhati (1959   )

The God of Small Things (1997).

Rubens, Bernice (1927   )

Set on Edge (1960), *The Elected Member* (1969), *Spring Sonata* (1979), *Birds of Passage* (1987), *A Solitary Grief* (1991), *Yesterday in the Back Lane* (1995).

Rumens, Carol (1944   )

Plato Park (1987).

Rushdie, Salman (1947   )

Grimus (1975), *Midnight's Children* (1981), *Shame* (1983), *The Satanic Verses* (1988), *The Moor's Last Sigh* (1996), *The Ground Beneath Her Feet* (1999).

Saint Aubin de Terán, Lisa (1953   )

Keepers of the House (1982), *The Slow Train to Milan* (1983), *The Tiger* (1984), *Black Idol* (1987), *Nocturne* (1992).

Sansom, William (1912–1976)

Fireman Flower (1944), *Something Terrible, Something Lovely* (1948), *The Body* (1949), *The Face of Innocence* (1951), *A Bed of Roses* (1954), *The Cautious Heart* (1958), *The Stories of William Sansom* (1963).

Sassoon, Siegfried (1886–1967)

Memoirs of a Fox-Hunting Man (1928), *Memoirs of an Infantry Officer*

(1930), *Sherston's Progress* (1936), collected as *The Complete Memoirs of George Sherston* (1937).

Sayer, Paul (1955   )

The Comforts of Madness (1988), *The Absolution Game* (1992).

Sayers, Dorothy (1893–1957)

Clouds of Witness (1927), *Lord Peter Views the Body* (1928), *The Nine Tailors* (1934), *Gaudy Night* (1935), *Busman's Honeymoon* (1937).

Schlee, Ann (1934   )

The Vandal (1979), *Rhine Journey* (1980), *Laing* (1987).

Schreiner, Olive (1855–1920)

The Story of an African Farm (1883), *From Man to Man* (1927, post.).

Scott, Paul (1920–1978)

Johnnie Sahib (1952), *The Alien Sky* (1953), *A Male Child* (1956), *The Birds of Paradise* (1962), *The Jewel in the Crown* (1966), *The Day of the Scorpion* (1968), *The Towers of Silence* (1971), *A Division of the Spoils* (collected as *The Raj Quartet*, 1976), *Staying On* (1977).

Sebald, W. G. (1944   )

The Emigrants (1993; trans. 1996), *The Rings of Saturn* (1995; trans. 1998), *Vertigo* (1999; trans. 1999).

Self, Will (1961   )

The Quantity Theory of Insanity (1991), *Cock & Bull* (1992), *My Idea of Fun: A Cautionary Tale* (1993), *Grey Area* (stories, 1994), *Junk Mail* (1995), *The Sweet Smell of Psychosis* (1996), *Great Apes* (1998).

Seth, Vikram (1952   )

The Golden Gate: A Novel in Verse (1986), *A Suitable Boy* (1993), *An Equal Music* (1999).

Shakespeare, Nicholas (1957   )

The Vision of Elena Silves (1990), *The High Flyer* (1993).

Sharpe, Tom (1928   )

Riotous Assembly (1971), *Indecent Exposure* (1973), *Porterhouse Blue* (1974), *Wilt* (1976), *The Great Pursuit* (1977), *Vintage Stuff* (1982).

Sillitoe, Alan (1928   )

Saturday Night and Sunday Morning (1958), *The Loneliness of the Long-Distance Runner* (1959), *The Ragman's Daughter* (stories, 1963), *The Death of William Posters* (1965), *The Flame of Life* (1974), *The Storyteller* (1979), *Out of the Whirlpool* (1987), *Snowstop* (1993).

Sinclair, Andrew (1935   )

The Breaking of Bumbo (1959), *My Friend Judas* (1959), *Gog* (1967), *Magog* (1972), *King Ludd* (1988).

Sinclair, Clive (1948   )

Bibliosexuality (1973), *Hearts of Gold* (stories, 1979), *Blood Libels* (1985), *Augustus Rex* (1992).

Sinclair, Iain (1943   )

White Chappell, Scarlet Tracings (1987), *Downriver* (1991).

Sinclair, May (1863–1942)

The Helpmate (1907), *The Three Sisters* (1914), *The Tree of Heaven* (1917), *Mary Oliver: A Life* (1919), *The Life and Death of Harriett Frean* (1922), *A Cure of Souls* (1924).

Smith, Stevie (1902–1971)

Novel on Yellow Paper (1936), *Over the Frontier* (1938), *The Holiday* (1949).

Snow, C. P. (1905–1980)

Death Under Sail (1932), *The Search* (1934), *Strangers and Brothers* (1940), *The Masters* (1951), *The New Men* (1954), *Homecomings* (1956), *Corridors of Power* (1964), *The Sleep of Reason* (1968), *Last Things* (1970), *The Malcontents* (1972).

Spark, Muriel (1918   )

The Comforters (1957), *Memento Mori* (1959), *The Ballad of Peckham Rye* (1960), *The Prime of Miss Jean Brodie* (1961), *The Girls of Slender Means* (1963), *The Public Image* (1968), *The Driver's Seat* (1970), *Not to Disturb* (1971), *The Hothouse by the East River* (1973), *Territorial Rights* (1979), *Loitering With Intent* (1984), *The Stories of Muriel Spark* (1986), *A Far Cry from Kensington* (1988), *Symposium* (1990), *Reality and Dreams* (1997).

Stevenson, Robert Louis (1850–1894)

The New Arabian Nights (1882), *Treasure Island* (1883), *The Strange Case of Dr Jekyll and Mr Hyde* (1886), *Kidnapped* (1886), *The Black Arrow* (1988), *The Master of Ballantrae* (1889), *Catriona* (1893), *Weir of Hermiston: An Unfinished Romance* (1896, post.).

Storey, David (1933   )

This Sporting Life (1960), *Flight into Camden* (1960), *Radcliffe* (1963), *Pasmore* (1972), *Life Class* (1974), *Saville* (1976), *A Serious Man* (1998).

Swift, Graham (1949   )

The Sweetshop Owner (1980), *Shuttlecock* (1981), *Waterland* (1983), *Out of This World* (1988), *Ever After* (1992), *Last Orders* (1996).

Taylor, D. J. (1960   )

Great Eastern Land (1986), *Real Life* (1992), *English Settlement* (1996), *Trespass* (1998).

Tennant, Emma (1937   )

Hotel de Dream (1976), *Women Beware Women* (1983), *Tess* (1993).

Thomas, D. M. (1935   )

The Flute-Player (1979), *The White Hotel* (1981), *Ararat* (1983), *Swallow* (1984), *Sphinx* (1986), *Summit* (1987), *Pictures at an Exhibition* (1993).

Thomson, Rupert (1955   )

Dreams of Leaving (1987), *The Insult* (1996).

Thorpe, Adam (1956   )

Ulverton (1992), *Still* (1995), *Pieces of Light* (1998).

Thubron, Colin (1939   )

The God in the Mountain (1977), *Emperor* (1978), *A Cruel Madness* (1984), *Falling* (1990), *Turning Back the Sun* (1991).

Tóibín, Colm (1955   )

The South (1995), *Story of the Night* (1997), *The Blackwater Lightship* (1999).

Tolkien, J. R. R. (1892–1973)

The Hobbit (1937), *The Lord of the Rings* (3 vols., 1954–5), *The Silmarillion* (1977).

Tomlinson, H. M. (1873–1958)

Gallion's Reach (1927), *All Our Yesterdays* (1930).

Trapido, Barbara (1941   )

Brother of the More Famous Jack (1982), *Noah's Ark* (1984), *Temples of Delight* (1991), *Juggling* (1994).

Tremain, Rose (1943   )

Sadler's Birthday (1976), *Letter to Sister Benedicta* (1978), *The Cupboard* (1981), *The Swimming Pool Season* (1985), *Restoration* (1989), *Sacred Country* (1992), *The Way I Found Her* (1997), *Music and Silence* (1999).

Tressell, Robert (Robert Noonan) (1870–1911)

The Ragged-Trousered Philanthropists (1914, post.).

Trevor, William (1928   )

The Old Boys (1964), *The Boarding House* (1965), *Mrs Eckdorf in O'Neil's Hotel* (1969), *The Children of Dynmouth* (1976), *Fools of Fortune* (1983), *The Stories of William Trevor* (1983), *The Silence in the Garden* (1988), *Two Lives* (1991), *Felicia's Journey* (1994), *Death in Summer* (1998).

Trocchi, Alexander (1923–1984)

Cain's Book (1962).

Unsworth, Barry (1930   )

The Hide (1970), *Mooncranker's Gift* (1973), *The Rage of the Vulture* (1982), *Pascali's Island* (1980), *Stone Virgin* (1985), *Sugar and Rum* (1988), *Sacred Hunger* (1992), *Morality Play* (1995), *After Hannibal* (1997).

Upward, Edward (1903   )

Journey to the Border (1938), *In the Thirties* (1962), *The Railway Accident and Other Stories* (1969), *The Rotten Elements* (1969), *No Home But the Struggle* (1977).

Wain, John (1925–1994)

Hurry On Down (1953), *Living in the Present* (1955), *A Travelling Woman* (1959), *Strike the Father Dead* (1962), *A Winter in the Hills* (1970), *The Pardoner's Tale* (1978).

Walpole, Hugh (1884–1941)

Mr Perrin and Mr Traill (1911), *Rogue Herries* (1930).

Warner, Marina (1946)

In a Dark Wood (1977), *The Skating Party* (1982), *The Lost Father* (1988), *Indigo* (1992).

Warner, Rex (1905–1986)

The Wild Goose Chase (1937), *The Professor* (1938), *The Aerodrome* (1941).

Warner, Sylvia Townsend (1893–1978)

The Espalier (1925), *Mr Fortune's Maggot* (1927).

Waugh, Evelyn (1903–1966)

Decline and Fall (1928), *Vile Bodies* (1930), *A Handful of Dust* (1934), *Scoop* (1938), *Brideshead Revisited* (1945), *The Loved One* (1948), *Men at Arms* (1952), *Officers and Gentlemen* (1955), *Unconditional Surrender* (1961), (these three collected and revised as *Sword of Honour*, 1965), *The Ordeal of Gilbert Pinfold* (1957).

Webb, Mary (1881–1927)

Gone to Earth (1917), *Precious Bane* (1924).

Weldon, Fay (1931)

The Fat Woman's Joke (1967), *Down Among the Women* (1971), *Female Friends* (1975), *Praxis* (1978), *The Life and Loves of a She-Devil* (1984), *The Shrapnel Academy* (1986), *The Rules of Life* (1987), *Affliction* (1994), *Splitting* (1995).

Wells, H. G. (1866–1946)

The Time Machine: An Invention (1895), *The Invisible Man: A Grotesque Romance* (1897), *The War of the Worlds* (1900), *Kipps* (1905), *In the Days of the Comet* (1906), *Tono-Bungay* (1909), *Ann Veronica: A Modern Love Story* (1909), *The History of Mr Polly* (1910), *The Country of the Blind and Other Stories* (1911), *The New Machiavelli* (1911).

Welsh, Irvine (1958)

Trainspotting (1993), *The Acid House* (1994), *Ecstasy* (1997), *Filth* (1998).

Wesley, Mary (1912)

The Sixth Seal (1969), *The Camomile Lawn* (1984), *Harnessing Peacocks* (1985), *A Dubious Legacy* (1993), *An Imaginative Experience* (1994).

West, Rebecca (Cecily Fairfield) (1892–1983)

The Return of the Soldier (1918), *The Judge* (1922), *Harriet Hume* (1929), *The Thinking Reed* (1936), *The Fountain Overflows* (1956), *The Birds Fall Down* (1966).

White, T. H. (1906–1964)

The Sword in the Stone (1938), *The Once and Future King* (1958).

Wilde, Oscar (1854–1900)

The Happy Prince and Other Tales (1888), *The Picture of Dorian Gray* (1891).

Williams, Charles (1886–1945)

Descent into Hell (1937), *All Hallows' Eve* (1945).

Williams, Nigel (1948   )

My Life Closed Twice (1977), *Class Enemy* (1982), *Black Magic* (1988), *The Wimbledon Poisoner* (1991).

Williams, Raymond (1921–1988)

Border Country (1960), *The Volunteers* (1978), *The Fight for Manod* (1979), *Loyalties* (1985).

Williamson, Henry (1895–1977)

The Beautiful Years (1921), *Dandelion Days* (1922), *The Dream of Fair Women* (1931), the 'A Chronicle of Ancient Sunlight' sequence (1951–69).

Wilson, A. N. (1950   )

The Sweets of Pimlico (1977), *The Healing Art* (1980), *Who Was Oswald Fish?* (1981), *Wise Virgin* (1982), *Scandal* (1983), *Love Unknown* (1986), *Incline Our Hearts* (1988), *A Watch in the Night* (1997), *Dream Children* (1998).

Wilson, Angus (1913–1992)

The Wrong Set and Other Stories (1949), *Such Darling Dodos* (1950), *Hemlock and After* (1952), *Anglo-Saxon Attitudes* (1956), *The Middle Age of Mrs Eliot* (1958), *The Old Men at the Zoo* (1961), *Late Call* (1964), *No Laughing Matter* (1967), *Collected Short Stories* (1987).

Wilson, Robert McLiam (1964   )

The Dispossesed (1992), *Eureka Street* (1997).

Winterson, Jeanette (1959   )

Oranges Are Not the Only Fruit (1985), *Boating for Beginners* (1985), *The Passion* (1987), *Sexing the Cherry* (1989), *Written On the Body* (1992), *Art & Lies* (1994), *Gut Symmetries* (1997).

Wodehouse, P. G. (1881–1975)

The Man With Two Left Feet (1917), *My Man Jeeves* (1919), *The Clicking of Cuthbert* (1922), *The Inimitable Jeeves* (1923), *Young Men in Spats* (1936), *Summer Moonshine* (1937), *The Code of the Woosters* (1938).

Woolf, Virginia (1882–1941)

The Voyage Out (1915), *Night and Day* (1919), *Jacob's Room* (1922), *Mrs Dalloway* (1925), *To the Lighthouse* (1927), *The Waves* (1931), *The Years* (1937), *Between the Acts* (1941), *The Common Reader* (essays, 1925; 2nd series, 1932).

Zameenzad, Adam (1947   )

The Thirteenth House (1987), *Love, Bones and Water* (1989), *Cyrus, Cyrus* (1990).

Select Bibliography

General

This list concentrates on general studies of modern fiction, twentieth-century British literary culture, period studies and works on aesthetic trends and groupings. Works on individual writers are not listed; readers wanting specialist works on literary theory, etc., will need other bibliographies. Twentieth-century British fiction, especially up to 1939, is well-studied ground. A key source is I. R. Willison (ed.), *The New Cambridge Bibliography of English Literature, Vol. 4: 1900–1950* (Cambridge, 1972); also E. C. Bulkin, *The Twentieth Century Novel in English: A Checklist* (Atlanta, Ga., 2nd edn, 1984), and Randall Stevenson, *The British Novel in the Twentieth Century: An Introductory Bibliography* (London, 1988). Other good reference sources are John Richetti (ed.), *The Columbia History of the British Novel* (New York, 1994) and four volumes in the extensive *Dictionary of Literary Biography*: Jay Halio (ed.), *Vol. 14: British Novelists Since 1960* (2 vols., Detroit, 1983), and Bernard Oldsey (ed.), *Vol. 15: British Novelists 1930–1959* (2 vols., Detroit, 1983); also D. L. Kirkpatrick (ed.), *Reference Guide to English Literature* (Chicago and London, 2nd edn, 1991). Susan Windych Brown (ed.), *Contemporary Novelists* (Chicago and London, 6th edn, 1996), is an indispensible, regularly updated record of living writers. Also see James Vinson (ed.), *Twentieth Century Fiction* (Chicago and London, 1983), and Hans Bertens et al. (eds.), *Post-war Literature in English* (Groningen, 1988 onward), a fine, loose-leaf updated record and interpretation.

Other key reference works include Paul Schellinger (ed.), *Encyclopedia of the Novel* (2 vols., Chicago and London, 1998), Mark Hawkins-Dady (ed.), *The Readers' Guide to Literatures in English* (Chicago and London, 1996), Andrew Michael Roberts, *The Novel From its Origins to the Present Day* ('Bloomsbury Guides to English Literature', London, 1993), Lionel Stevenson, *The History of the English Novel: Yesterday and After* (New York, 1967), and Boris Ford (ed.), *The New Pelican Guide to English Literature, Vols. 7*

& 8 (Harmondsworth, 1988). Also see Eugene Benson and L. W. Connolly (eds.), *Encyclopedia of Post-Colonial Literatures in English* (2 vols., London and New York, 1994), Kathleen Wheeler (ed.), *A Guide to Twentieth Century Women Novelists* (Oxford, 1997), and Virginia Blain, Patricia Clemens and Isobel Grundy (eds.), *The Feminist Companion to Literature in English* (London, 1990). There is more detailed background on individual authors or texts in the many series devoted to the subject: 'Macmillan Casebooks', 'Prentice-Hall Twentieth Century Views', 'Routledge Critical Heritage', etc. The Methuen 'Contemporary Writers' series (eds. Malcolm Bradbury and Chris Bigsby) was a pioneering series in the study of contemporary authors; also see the Macmillan 'Women Writers' series, the Harvester 'Key Women Writers' series and the British Council/Northcote House series 'Writers and Their Work'. In the age of CD ROM and the website there is more information available than ever: see *Contemporary Authors on CD* (Galenet).

On Modernism, see Peter Nicholls, *Modernisms: A Literary Guide* (London and Berkeley, 1995), Randall Stevenson, *Modernist Fiction: An Introduction* (London and New York, 1992), V. Kolocontroni, J. Goldman and O. Taxidou (eds.), *Modernism: An Anthology of Sources and Documents* (Edinburgh, 1998), and Christopher Butler, *Early Modernism* (Oxford, 1994). A key and inclusive account with an extensive bibliography is Malcolm Bradbury and James McFarlane (eds.), *Modernism: 1890–1930* (Harmondsworth, rev. edn, 1989). A valuable sourcebook is Richard Ellmann and Charles Feidelson Jr. (eds.), *The Modern Tradition: Backgrounds of Modern Literature* (New York and London, 1965); also see Stephen Spender, *The Struggle of the Modern* (London, 1963), Irving Howe (ed.), *The Idea of the Modern in Literature and the Arts* (New York, 1967), Cyril Connolly's personal *The Modern Movement: 100 Key Books from England, France and America, 1880–1950* (London, 1965) and Edmund Wilson's classic study *Axel's Castle* (New York, 1931). Also Rita Felski, *The Gender of Modernity* (Cambridge, 1995), and Bonnie Kime Scott (ed.), *The Gender of Modernism: A Critical Anthology* (Bloomington, Ind., 1990). And note A. Bullock, O. Stallybrass and S. Trombley (eds.), *The Fontana Dictionary of Modern Thought* (London, 3rd edn, 1998).

Useful general studies of modern British fiction include Walter Allen, *The English Novel: A Short Critical History* (Harmondsworth, 1954) and *Tradition and Dream: A Critical Survey of British and American Fiction from the 1920s* (Harmondsworth, 1965), Malcolm Bradbury, *Possibilities: Essays on the State of the Novel* (Oxford and New York, 1973) and *No, Not Bloomsbury* (London, 1987), Anthony Burgess, *The Novel Now: A Students' Guide to Contemporary Fiction* (London, 1967), David Daiches, *The Novel and the Modern World* (Chicago, rev. edn, 1960), Leon Edel, *The Psychological Novel 1900–1950* (New York, 1955), G. S. Fraser, *The Modern Writer and His World* (Harmondsworth, rev. edn, 1970), W. J. Harvey, *Character and the Novel* (London, 1965), David Lodge, *Language of Fiction: Essays in Criticism and Verbal Analysis of the English Novel* (London, rev. edn, 1984) and *The Modes of Modern Writing: Metaphor, Metonymy and the Typology of Modern Literature* (London, 1977), Frederick R. Karl and M. Magalener, *A Reader's Guide to Great Twentieth Century English Novels* (New York and London, 1959), John Orr, *The Making of the Twentieth Century Novel* (London, 1988), Mark Schorer (ed.), *Modern British Fiction* (Oxford, 1942), J. I. M. Stewart, *Eight Modern Writers* (Oxford, 1963), and George Woodcock (ed.), *Twentieth Century Fiction* (London, 1983).

On various key themes, trends, genres and developments in modern fiction, see Kingsley Amis, *New Maps of Hell: A Survey of Science Fiction* (London, 1961), Nicola Beauman, *A Very Great Profession: The Women's Novel 1914– 1939* (London, 1983), David Cairns and Shaun Richards, *Writing Ireland: Colonialism, Nationalism and Culture* (Manchester, 1988), Glen Cavaliero, *The Rural Tradition in the English Novel 1900–1939* (London, 1977), Claud Cockburn, *Bestseller: The Books that Everyone Read 1900–1939* (London, 1972), Margaret Crossland, *Beyond the Lighthouse: English Women Writers in the 20th Century* (London, 1981), Mary Eagleton and D. Pierce, *Attitudes to Class in the English Novel from Walter Scott to David Storey* (London, 1979), Jeremy Hawthorn (ed.), *The British Working Class Novel in the Twentieth Century* (London, 1984), Edward James, *Science Fiction in the Twentieth Century* (Oxford, 1994), A. A. Mendilow, *Time and the Novel* (London, 1952), Elaine Showalter, *A Literature of Their Own: British Women Novelists from Brontë to Lessing* (London, 1978), Sharon Spencer, *Space, Time and Structure in the Modern Novel* (New York, 1971), Julian Symons, *Bloody Murder: From the Detective Story to the Crime Novel* (London, 1972), and (on the thriller) Colin Watson, *Snobbery With Violence* (London, 1971).

On the general background, see Malcolm Bradbury, *The Social Context of Modern English Literature* (Oxford, 1971), José Ortega y Gasset, *The Dehumanization of Art and Other Essays* (London, 1972), John Oliver Perry (ed.), *Backgrounds to Modern Literature* (San Francisco, 1968), Wylie Sypher, *Loss of the Self in Modern Literature and Art* (New York, 1947) and Raymond Williams, *The Long Revolution* (London, 1961) and *Culture and Society: 1780–1950* (London, 1959). An invaluable study of the whole period is James Joll, *Europe Since 1870: An International History* (London, rev. edn, 1990). Also see E. J. Hobsbawm, *The Age of Empire 1875–1914* (London, 1987), Norman Stone, *Europe Transformed: 1878–1918* (London, 1983), and David

Thompson, *England in the Twentieth Century* (Harmondsworth, 1970). Now the twentieth century is over Martin Gilbert offers an entire and powerful history of the entire period, year by year, in his three-volume *A History of the Twentieth Century: Volume 1: Empires in Conflict 1900–1933* (London, 1997), *Volume 2: Descent Into Barbarism 1933–1951* (London, 1998), *Volume 3: Challenge to Civilization 1951–1999* (London, 1999).

1. The Turn of the Novel: 1878–1900

On the fiction of the period a fine background study is Peter Keating's *The Haunted Study: A Social History of the English Novel, 1875–1914* (London, 1989), which also contains a valuable listing of the chief fiction published between 1875 and 1915; also see John Sutherland, *The Longman Companion to Victorian Fiction* (London, 1988), and Douglas Hewitt, *English Fiction of the Early Modern Period 1890–1940* (London, 1989). For 'the turn of the novel', see Alan J. Friedman, *The Turn of the Novel: The Transition in Modern Fiction* (New York and London, 1966), William C. Frierson, *The English Novel in Transition 1885–1940* (Norman, Okla., 1942), Stephen Kern, *The Culture of Time and Space, 1880–1918* (London, 1983), John A. Lester, *Journey Through Despair 1890–1914: Transformations in British Literary Culture* (Princeton, 1968), D. R. Schwartz, *The Transformation of the English Novel 1895–1920* (London, 1989), David Trotter, *The English Novel in History 1895–1914* (London, 1993), and Raymond Williams, *The English Novel from Dickens to Lawrence* (London, 1970).

For the atmosphere of the 1890s see M. Bradbury, D. Palmer and I. Fletcher (eds.), *Decadence and the 1890s* (London, 1979), Barbara Charlesworth, *Dark Passages: The Decadent Consciousness in Victorian Fiction* (Madison, Wis., 1965), Holbrook Jackson, *The Eighteen Nineties* (London, 1913; reissued 1988), Elaine Showalter, *Sexual Anarchy: Gender and Culture at the Fin de Siècle* (New York, 1990, London, 1991), and John Stokes, *In the Nineties* (London, 1989). On fantasy and Gothic note David Punter, *The Literature of Terror* (London, 1980), and Victor Sage, *Horror Fiction in the Protestant Tradition* (London, 1988). On fiction and the Empire, see Martin Green, *Dreams of Adventure, Deeds of Empire* (London, 1980), Alan Sandison, *The Wheel of Empire: A Study of the Imperial Idea in Some Late 19th Century and Early 20th Century Fiction* (London and New York, 1967), and Patrick Brantlinger, *Rule of Darkness: British Literature and Imperialism, 1830–1914* (Ithaca, NY, 1988). On fiction and feminism, see Gail Cunningham, *The New Woman and the Victorian Novel* (London and New York, 1978), Patricia

Stubbs, *Women and Fiction: Feminism and the Novel, 1880–1920* (London, 1981), and Ann L. Ardis, *New Women, New Novels: Feminism and Early Modernism* (New Brunswick, NJ, 1990). On 'future fiction' see I. F. Clarke, *The Pattern of Expectation: 1644–2001* (London, 1979), and his *Voices Prophesying War: Future Wars 1763–3749* (London, rev. ed., 1992).

For the changing ideas of the era, see Leo Henkin, *Darwinism in the English Novel, 1860–1910* (New York, 1963), and H. Stuart Hughes, *Consciousness and Society: The Reorientation of European Social Thought, 1890–1930* (London, 1959). E. J. Hobsbawm's *The Age of Empire, 1975–1914* (London, 1987) gives an overview of the period.

2. The Opening World: 1900–1915

A good many of the works cited above also deal with the fiction of the 'transitional' period of 1900–1915; also note David Trotter, *The English Novel in History, 1895–1920* (London and New York, 1993). More detailed studies of the Edwardian period are Richard Ellmann (ed.), *Edwardians and Late Victorians* (New York and London, 1960) and *Eminent Domain: Yeats Among Wilde, Joyce, Pound, Eliot and Auden* (London, 1968), Samuel Hynes, *The Edwardian Turn of Mind* (Oxford, 1969), and Simon Newell Smith (ed.), *Edwardian England 1901–1914* (Oxford, 1964). On Edwardian fiction see John Alcorn, *The Nature Novel from Hardy to Lawrence* (London, 1977), John Batchelor, *The Edwardian Novelists* (London, 1982), William Bellamy, *The Novels of Wells, Bennett and Galsworthy 1890–1910* (London, 1971), Jefferson Hunter, *Edwardian Fiction* (Cambridge, Mass., 1982), Frank Swinnerton, *The Georgian Literary Scene* (London 1938, rev. edn, 1969).

Early Modernism has been extensively studied; see above and the bibliography of M. Bradbury and J. McFarlane (eds.), *Modernism, 1890–1930* (Harmondsworth, rev. ed., 1989). Further useful studies are Hugh Kenner's *A Sinking Island: The Modern English Writers* (London, 1988), Stan Smith, *The Origins of Modernism* (Brighton, 1988), and Allon White, *The Uses of Obscurity: The Fiction of Early Modernism* (London, 1981). More specialist works are M. Chelford et al. (eds.), *Modernism* (Urbana, Ill., 1986), Joseph Chiari, *The Aesthetics of Modernism* (London, 1970), Donald Gordon, *Expressionism: Art and Idea* (New Haven, 1987), Hilton Kramer, *The Age of the Avant Garde* (London, 1974), Michael Levenson, *The Genealogy of Modernism* (Cambridge, 1984), and Stella K. Tillyard, *The Impact of Modernism* (London, 1988).

3. The Exciting Age: 1915–1930

On the literature of wartime, see Bernard Bergonzi, *Hero's Twilight: A Study of the Literature of the Great War* (London, 1965), Paul Fussell, *The Great War and Modern Memory* (New York and London, 1975), M. S. Greicus, *Prose Writers of World War I* (London, 1973), and Holger Klein (ed.), *The First World War in Fiction* (London, 1976). General studies of the Twenties include Humphrey Carpenter, *The Brideshead Generation: Evelyn Waugh and His Friends* (London, 1989), and Martin Green, *Children of the Sun: A Narrative of 'Decadence' in England After 1918* (London, 1977). There are innumerable studies of Bloomsbury, one of the best being Leon Edel, *Bloomsbury: A House of Lions* (New York, 1979). Virginia Woolf's own diaries are an ideal record: Anne Oliver Bell (ed.), *The Diaries of Virginia Woolf* (5 vols., London, 1977–84). Also note Margaret Crossland, *Beyond the Lighthouse: English Women Writers in the 20th Century* (London, 1981). On the European Modern movement, see Noel Riley Fitch, *Sylvia Beach and the Lost Generation: A History of Literary Paris in the 20s and 30s* (London, 1984).

Twenties Modernism has also been extensively explored; see titles on the subject cited above. Studies that concentrate specifically on the fiction of the Twenties include Frank Kermode, *Puzzles and Epiphanies: Essays and Reviews 1958–61* (London, 1962), Sean O'Faolain, *The Vanishing Hero: Studies in Novelists of the Twenties* (London, 1956), and S. J. Greenblatt, *Three Modern Satirists: Waugh, Orwell and Huxley* (New Haven, 1965).

4. Closing Time in the Gardens: 1930–1945

Of this once critically neglected period accounts have multiplied. Quite the best is Valentine Cunningham's wide-ranging and splendidly documented *British Writers of the Thirties* (Oxford and New York, 1989), with excellent bibliography. Cunningham also edited *The Spanish Front: Writers on the Civil War* (London, 1986). Also see Andy Croft, *Red Letter Days: British Fiction in the 1930s* (London, 1990), John Baxendale and Christopher Pawling, *Narrating the Thirties* (London and New York, 1996), Janet Montefiore, *Men and Women Writers of the 1930s: The Dangerous Flood of History* (London, 1996), and Samuel Hynes's classic *The Auden Generation: Literature and Politics in England in the 1930s* (New York, 1972; London, 1976). Other important studies are John Lehmann, *New Writing in Europe* (Harmondsworth, 1940) and Stephen Spender, *The Thirties and After* (London, 1978), and various memoirs – Lehmann, *The Whispering Gallery* (London, 1955), Isherwood, *Lions and Shadows* (London, 1938), Spender, *World Within World* (London, 1951).

On the importance of politics in the period, see Bernard Bergonzi, *Reading the Thirties: Texts and Contexts* (London, 1978), David Caute, *Illusion: An Essay on Politics, Theatre and the Novel* (London, 1971), J. Clark et al. (eds.), *Culture and Crisis in Britain in the Thirties* (London, 1979), Richard Johnstone, *The Will to Believe: Novelists of the 1930s* (Oxford, 1982), John Lucas (ed.), *The 1930s: A Challenge to Orthodoxy* (Brighton and New York, 1978), J. A. Morris, *Writers and Politics in Modern Britain* (London, 1977), Malcolm Muggeridge, *The Thirties* (London, rev. edn, 1967), Julian Symons, *The Thirties: A Dream Revisited* (London, rev. edn, 1975), and Alan Swingewood, *The Novel and Revolution* (London, 1975). Other important dimensions are explored in Paul Fussell, *Abroad: British Literary Travelling Between the Wars* (New York and London, 1980), Robert Graves and Alan Hodge, *The Long Weekend: A Social History of Great Britain 1918–1939* (London, 1940), C. L. Mowat, *Britain Between the Wars 1918–1940* (London, 1955), and A. J. P. Taylor, *The Origins of the Second World War* (London, 1964). Also see Robert Hewison's important *Under Siege: Literary Life in London 1939–1945* (London, 1977).

5. The Novel No Longer Novel?: 1945–1954

The story and interpretation of post-war British fiction was slow to be written. Among the chief early works are James Gindin, *Post-war British Fiction: New Accents and Attitudes* (London, 1962), Alfred Kazin, *Contemporaries: Essays* (London, 1963), Richard Kostelanetz (ed.), *Contemporary Literature* (New York, 1964), and Frederick R. Karl, *A Reader's Guide to the Contemporary English Novel* (London, rev. edn, 1965). Bernard Bergonzi's *The Situation of the Novel* (London, 1970) and his *Wartime and Aftermath: English Literature and its Background* (London, 1993) are both valuable. Malcolm Bradbury in *Possibilities: Essays on the State of the Novel* (Oxford and New York, 1973) and *No, Not Bloomsbury* (London, 1987) explores contemporary fiction; Malcolm Bradbury (ed.), *The Novel Today: Contemporary Writers on Modern Fiction* (London, 1977, rev. ed., 1982) contains important essays by contemporary novelists (including Iris Murdoch, John Fowles, Angus Wilson, etc.); and also see the essays of Malcolm Bradbury and David Palmer (eds.), *The Contemporary English Novel* (London, 1979). Many of these books are relevant to the next several chapters.

Other important works on or including discussion of various aspects of post-war British fiction are André Brink, *The Novel: Language and Narrative from Cervantes to Calvino* (London, 1998), Stephen Connor, *The English Novel in History, 1950–1995* (London, 1996), Andrzej Gasiorek, *Post-War British Fiction: Realism and After* (London, 1995), David Leon Higdon, *Shadows of the Past in Contemporary British Fiction* (London, 1984), Gabriel Josipovici, *The World and the Book* (London, 1971), Alan Kennedy, *The Protean Self: Dramatic Action in Contemporary Fiction* (London, 1974), Frank Kermode, *Puzzles and Epiphanies: Essays and Reviews 1958–61* (London, 1962), *Continuities* (London, 1968), *Modern Essays* (London, 1971) and *History As Value* (Oxford, 1988), David Lodge, *The Novelist at the Crossroads and Other Essays* (London, 1971), *The Modes of Modern Writing: Metaphor, Metonyomy, and the Typology of Modern Literature* (London, 1977), *Write On: Occasional Essays, 1965–85* (London, 1986), *The Art of Fiction* (1992) and *The Practice of Writing* (1996). Also Neil McEwan, *The Survival of the Novel: British Fiction in the Later Twentieth Century* (London, 1981), Alan Munton, *English Fiction of the Second World War* (London, 1989), Lorna Sage, *Women in the House of Fiction: Post-War Women Novelists* (London, 1992), Margaret Scanlan, *Traces of Another Time: History and Politics in Postwar British Fiction* (Princeton, 1990), Alan Sinfield (ed.), *Society and Literature 1945–70* (London, 1983), Randall Stevenson, *The British Novel Since the Thirties: An Introduction* (London, 1986), and Patrick Swinden, *The English Novel of History and Society 1940–1980* (London, 1984). The British Council produced regular guides to British post-war fiction, regularly updated, including Henry Reed, *The Novel Since 1939* (London, 1946), P. H. Newby, *The Novel 1945–50* (London, 1951), Walter Allen, *The Novel Today* (London, 1955), Anthony Burgess, *The Novel Today* (London, 1963) and Michael Ratcliffe, *The Novel Today* (1968). An important recent study is D. J. Taylor, *After the War: The Novel and English Society Since 1945* (London, 1993).

On the Forties as a period, see Andrew Sinclair, *War Like a Wasp: The Lost Decade of the Forties* (London, 1989), and Woodrow Wyatt (ed.), *The Way We Lived Then: The English Story in the 40s* (London, 1989). Also see Bryan Appleyard's overview of the post-war period, *The Pleasures of Peace: Art and Imagination in Post-war Britain* (London, 1989), Robert Hewison, *In Anger: Culture in the Cold War, 1945–1960* (London, 1981), and Peter Hennessy, *Never Again: Britain, 1945–1951* (London, 1993). Raymond Williams's *Culture and Society, 1780–1950* (London, 1958) and its sequel *The Long Revolution* (London, 1961), capture the post-war climate and political and cultural attitudes, as does Richard Hoggart's *The Uses of Literacy*

(London, 1957), and Richard Titmuss's *Essays on the Welfare State* (London, 1958).

6. No, Not Bloomsbury: 1954–1960

A number of the books on post-war fiction cited above also deal with the Fifties. An important study of the lively fictional arguments of the time is Rubin Rabinowitz, *The Reaction Against Experiment in the English Novel, 1950–1960* (New York, 1967), and a fine study is Blake Morrison, *The Movement: English Poetry and Fiction of the 1950s* (London, 1980). Also see Malcolm Bradbury, *The Social Context of Modern English Literature* (Oxford and New York, 1971). On the decade as a whole, see Kenneth Allsop, *The Angry Decade: A Survey of the Cultural Revolt of the 1950s* (London, 1958), Peter Lewis, *The Fifties* (London, 1958), John Russell Taylor, *Anger and After: A Guide to New British Drama* (London, 1962), and Colin McInnes, *England, Half English* (London, 1961). Also see Boris Ford (ed.), *The Cambridge Cultural History of Britain, Vol. 9: Modern Britain* (Cambridge, 1998).

Other important books are Al Alvarez, *Under Pressure* (London, 1965) and Tom Maschler (ed.), *Declaration* (London, 1958). Also see Harry Ritchie's interesting *Success Stories: Literature and the Media in England, 1950–1959* (London, 1988).

7. Crossroads – Fiction in the Sixties: 1960–1969

Studies of British fiction from the Sixties onward are still limited, though the record improves yearly. As said in the opening section, various publications record the work and careers of contemporary writers. The British Council continued to publish good surveys of contemporary writing: Ronald Hayman's *The Novel Today, 1967–1975* (London, 1976), and its successor, Alan Massie's *The Novel Today: A Critical Guide to the British Novel, 1970–1989* (London, 1990). The British Council and the Book Trust also began to publish a set of 'Contemporary Writers' pamphlets featuring individual authors, now available on website. Bibliography can be found in reference texts cited at the beginning (*Contemporary Novelists, Twentieth Century Fiction, British Novelists Since 1960*, etc.) and critical opinion can be traced in Irving Adelman and Rita Dworkin, *The Contemporary Novel: A Checklist of Critical Literature on the British and American Novel Since 1945* (Metuchen, NJ, 1972).

Several works cited above deal generally with post-war fiction. But also see David Leon Higden, *Shadows of the Past in Contemporary British Fiction* (Athens, Ga., 1985), James Macmillan (ed.), *The British and Irish Novel Since 1960* (London, 1991), Bruce King (ed.), *The Commonwealth Novel Since 1960* (London, 1991), Andrzej Gasiorek, *Post-War British Fiction: Realism and After*, (London, 1995), Margaret Alexander, *Flight from Realism: Themes and Strategies in Postmodernist British and American Fiction* (London, 1990), and David Rubin, *After the Raj: British Novels of India Since 1947* (Hanover, 1986). Also see entries for the next two chapters. There are various important collections of essays by leading authors, including Anthony Burgess's *Homage to QWERTYUIOP* (London, 1986), A. S. Byatt's *Passions of the Mind: Selected Writings* (London, 1991), Angela Carter's *Nothing Sacred* (London, 1982) and *Expletives Deleted* (London, 1992), John Fowles's *Wormholes: Essays and Occasional Writings* (London, 1998), David Lodge's *The Modes of Modern Writing: Metaphor, Metonymy, and the Typology of Modern Literature* (London, 1977), and Angus Wilson's *Diversity and Depth: Selected Critical Writings*, ed. Kerry McSweeney (London, 1983).

For the rise of experimental metafiction, see Patricia Waugh, *Metafiction: The Theory and Practice of Self-Conscious Fiction* (London and New York, 1984), and also Robert Alter, *Partial Magic: The Novel as a Self-Conscious Genre* (Berkeley, 1975), Robert Scholes, *The Fabulators* (New York, 1967), later heavily revised as *Fabulation and Metafiction* (Chicago and London, 1979), Linda Hutcheon, *Narcissistic Narrative: The Metafictional Paradox* (Waterloo, Ont., 1980), and David Lodge's *The Novelist at the Crossroads and Other Essays, 1965–85* (London, 1986).

On Sixties culture see A. Alvarez, *Beyond All This Fiddle* (London, 1968), Bryan Appleyard, *The Culture Club: Crisis in the Arts* (London, 1984), Christopher Booker, *The Necrophiliacs* (London, 1969), Giles Gordon (ed.), *Beyond the Words* (London, 1975), Dick Hebdige, *Subculture: The Meaning of Style* (London, 1979), Robert Hewison, *Too Much: Art and Society in the Sixties: 1960–75* (London, 1986), George Melly, *Revolt Into Style* (London, 1970), Jeff Nuttall, *Bomb Culture* (London, 1968), C. H. Rolph (ed.), *The Trial of Lady Chatterley* (Harmondsworth, 1961), and Theodore Roszak, *The Making of the Counter-Culture* (New York, 1969). On cultural theory see Marshall McLuhan, *The Gutenberg Galaxy: The Making of Typographical Man* (Toronto, 1962), and *Understanding Media: The Extensions of Man* (New York and London, 1964). On British society see Anthony Sampson, *Anatomy of Britain* (London, 1962), Eric Butterworth and David Weir (eds.), *The Sociology of Modern Britain* (London, 1970), Vernon Bogdanor and Robert Skidelsky, *The Age of Affluence 1951–1964* (London, 1978), Alan

Sked and Chris Cook, *Postwar Britain: A Political History* (Harmondsworth, 1979), and Elizabeth Wilson, *Only Halfway to Paradise: Women in Postwar Britain, 1945–68* (London, 1980).

8. The Ice Age – Fiction in the Seventies: 1969–1979

Many of the books cited above also deal with the Seventies. But see also Philip Whitehead, *The Writing on the Wall: Britain in the Seventies* (London, 1985), and Christopher Lasch, *The Culture of Narcissism* (New York, 1978). On the rise of feminism see Kate Millett, *Sexual Politics* (London, 1969), Germaine Greer, *The Female Eunuch* (London, 1970), and Mary Ellmann, *Thinking About Women* (London, 1979), as well as works listed in the following sections. On literary theory see Jonathan Culler, *Structuralist Poetics* (London, 1975), John Sturrock, *Structuralism and Since: From Lévi-Strauss to Derrida* (Oxford and New York, 1979), and Christopher Norris, *Deconstruction: Theory and Practice* (London, 1982), and also Peter Ackroyd, *Notes for a New Culture: An Essay in Modernism* (London, 1976).

9. Artists of the Floating World: 1979–1989

The fiction of the Eighties is treated in several of the more recent titles cited above, such as Steven Connor's *The English Novel in History, 1950–1995*, Margaret Alexander's *Flight From Realism* and Lorna Sage's *Women in the House of Fiction*. An interesting if very polemical and critical account is D. J. Taylor's *A Vain Conceit: British Fiction in the Eighties* (London, 1989), deploring the departure from realism and a fiction of Victorian scope. For the issue of social change and 'Thatcherism', see Dennis Kavanagh, *Thatcherism and British Politics: The End of Consensus* (London, rev. edn, 1988), Hugo Young and Anne Sloman, *The Thatcher Phenomenon* (London, 1986), and Anthony Sampson, *The Changing Anatomy of Britain* (London, 1972).

As this and previous and following chapters suggest, a key issue in the writing of the Seventies and Eighties was the argument – conducted first by academic critics but then by cultural commentators generally – over 'Postmodernism'. A large literature exists and some titles are cited above. But see in particular Fredric Jameson, *Postmodernism: Or, the Cultural Logic of Late Capitalism* (Durham, NC, 1991), Margaret A. Rose, *The Post-Modern and the Post-Industrial* (Cambridge, 1991), Charles Jencks (ed.), *The Post-Modern Reader* (London, 1992), Thomas Doherty (ed.), *Postmodernism:*

A Reader (London, 1996), Hans Bertens, *The Idea of the Postmodern: A History* (London, 1990), and the useful book by Steven Connor, *Postmodernist Culture: An Introduction to Theories of the Contemporary* (London, 1989). Other important books on the much discussed topic include Douwe Fokkema's *Modernist Conjectures: Modernism and Postmodernism* (Amsterdam, 1984), Ian Adam and Helen Tiffin (eds.), *Past the Last Post: Theorizing Post-Colonialism and Postmodernism* (New York, 1991), and Douglas Hofstadter's fascinating *Godel, Escher, Bach: An Eternal Golden Braid* (Harmondsworth, 1980).

One important and useful consequence of the debate about postmodernism was that it focused attention on the nature of contemporary fiction and fictionality and also brought it within the orbit of current theoretic and academic speculation. Here are some of the most interesting books about postmodern fiction: Margaret Alexander, *Flight from Realism: Theories and Strategies in Postmodernist British and American Fiction* (London, 1990), Robert Alter, *Partial Magic: The Novel as a Self-Conscious Genre* (Berkeley, 1975), Christopher Butler, *After the Wake: An Essay on the Contemporary Avant Garde* (Oxford, 1980), Neil Cornwell, *The Literary Fantastic: From Gothic to Postmodernism* (New York, 1990), Diane Elam, *Romancing the Postmodern* (London, 1992), Linda Hutcheon, *Narcissistic Narrative: The Metafictional Paradox* (Waterloo, Ont., 1980) and *A Theory of Parody* (London and New York, 1985), Rosemary Jackson, *Fantasy: The Literature of Subversion* (London, 1981), Alison Lee, *Realism and Power: Postmodern British Fiction* (London, 1990), Brian McHale, *Postmodernist Fiction* (London, 1987), E. J. Smythe, *Postmodernism and Contemporary Fiction* (London, 1991), Patricia Waugh, *Metafiction: The Theory and Practice of Self-Conscious Fiction* (London and New York, 1984) and *Practising Postmodernism/Reading Modernism* (London and New York, 1992), and Alan Wilde, *Horizons of Assent: Modernism, Postmodernism and the Ironic Imagination* (Baltimore and London, 1981). On magical realism see Louis P. Zamora and Wendy B. Faris (eds.), *Magical Realism: Theory, History, Community* (Durham, NC, 1995).

On two of the most important issues of the Eighties, post-colonialism and feminism, there is a fast-growing literature. On post-colonialism see Bill Ashcroft et al., *The Empire Writes Back* (London, 1989), Michael Valdez Moses, *The Novel and the Globalization of Culture* (New York, 1995), Homi Bhabha, *The Location of Culture* (London, 1994), Elleke Boehmer, *Colonial and Postcolonial Literature: Migrant Metaphors* (Oxford, 1995), Iain Chambers and Lidia Curti (eds.), *The Post-Colonial Question* (London, 1996), Michael Gorra, *After Empire: Scott, Naipaul, Rushdie* (Chicago, 1997), Bruce

King (ed.), *The Commonwealth Novel Since 1960* (London, 1991), and Patrick Williams and Laura Chrisman, *Colonial Discourse and Post-colonial Theory* (London, 1993). On feminism, see Marleen S. Barr, *Feminist Fabulation: Space/Postmodern Fiction* (Iowa City, 1992), Toril Moi, *Sexual/Textual Politics: Feminist Literary Theory* (London, 1985), Sally Munt (ed.), *New Lesbian Criticism: Literary and Cultural Readings* (New York and London, 1992), Lorna Sage, *Women in the House of Fiction: Post-war Women Novelists* (London, 1992), Elaine Showalter, *A Literature of Their Own: British Women Novelists from Brontë to Lessing* (London, 1978), Elaine Showalter (ed.), *The New Feminist Criticism: Essays on Women, Literature and Theory* (London, 1986), Dale Spender (ed.), *Feminist Theories: Three Centuries of Women's Intellectual Traditions* (London, 1983), Janet Todd, *Gender and Literary Voice* (London, 1981), Michelene Wandor, *On Gender and Writing* (London, 1983). Also see Mark Lilly (ed.), *Lesbian and Gay Writing: An Anthology of Critical Essays* (London, 1990).

10. Millennial Days: 1989–2001

Not surprisingly, despite vast interest in the state of contemporary culture, there is not yet a well-developed serious literature on the fiction of the Nineties and the turn of the millennium. Among various end-of-century books that attempted to take stock of recent literature was Carmen Callil and Colm Tóibín, *The Modern Library: The 200 Best Novels in English Since 1950* (London, 1999) – a subjective yet interesting list with an internationalist perspective including much writing from Ireland, Australasia, India, Canada, and the post-colonial world, from all of which important contemporary fiction has emerged. (Since some of this writing is not within the frame of the present volume, it serves as a significant reminder of how international the scene of fiction in English now is.) Among good critical books to appear over the Nineties, James Wood's *The Broken Estate: Essays on Literature and Belief* (London, 1999) is interesting for its seriousness and a persistent (if wildly excessive) disquiet with the idea of English fiction as such, which he considers has lost the battle with the 'word-coining powers'. See also Theo d'Haen and Hans Bertens (eds.), *British Postmodern Fiction* (Amsterdam, 1993), and Richard Todd's interesting *Consuming Fictions: The Booker Prize in Britain Today* (London, 1996). As often, much of the most interesting critical and creative commentary comes from the meditations of writers themselves, including Italo Calvino, *Six Memos for the Next Millennium* (London, 1992), Milan Kundera, *Testaments Betrayed* (1995), Salman

Rushdie, *Imaginary Homelands: Essays and Criticism 1981–1991* (London, 1991), A. S. Byatt, *Passions of the Mind: Selected Writings* (London, 1991), Martin Amis, *Visiting Mrs Nabokov and Other Excursions* (London, 1993), and André Brink, *The Novel: Language and Narrative From Cervantes to Calvino* (London, 1998).

In the Nineties many ideas from the fiction and criticism of earlier decades became central and institutional: Post-Colonial Studies, Women's Studies, Gay and Lesbian Studies, Media and Cultural Studies, new forms of British Studies and Creative Writing remodelled the literary curriculum. Many studies arising from this work have been mentioned already. One result was a supply of reference and research material: thus on Post-Colonial Studies Eugene Benson and J. W. Connolly (eds.), *Encyclopedia of Post-Colonial Literatures in English* (London, 1994); likewise on Women's Studies see Jennifer Breen, *In Her Own Write: Twentieth Century Women's Fiction* (London, 1990), Joanne Shattuck, *The Oxford Guide to British Women Writers* (Oxford, 1993), and Lorna Sage (ed.), *The Cambridge Guide to Women's Writing in English* (Cambridge, 1999).

Happily, in these times of high visibility and extensive cultural news, far more attention is paid today to new and younger writers, experimental texts, work from small presses and regional outlets, and the fast-changing directions of contemporary fiction and general cultural activity. For writing emerging at present, useful sources are issues of the magazine *Granta*; the anthologies of new writing, *First Fictions*, published irregularly by Faber; and the annual collections *New Writing* (London, for the British Council) which have appeared since 1992. Leading booksellers like Waterstones publish pamphlets and writer aids and assist reading parties, and there are informative websites. The invaluable *Writers and Their Work* series, published by Northcote House and the British Council, has lately been updated to include many volumes on contemporary writers, including Jean Rhys, William Golding, Doris Lessing, Chinua Achebe, John Fowles, Salman Rushdie, David Lodge and Ian McEwan.

The Booker Prize, 1969–2000

1969 P. H. Newby, *Something To Answer For*
1970 Bernice Rubens, *The Elected Member*
1971 V. S. Naipaul, *In a Free State*
1972 John Berger, *G.*
1973 J. G. Farrell, *The Siege of Krishnapur*
1974 Nadine Gordimer, *The Conservationist*
     Stanley Middleton, *Holiday*
1975 Ruth Prawer Jhabvala, *Heat and Dust*
1976 David Storey, *Saville*
1977 Paul Scott, *Staying On*
1978 Iris Murdoch, *The Sea, The Sea*
1979 Penelope Fitzgerald, *Offshore*
1980 William Golding, *Rites of Passage*
1981 Salman Rushdie, *Midnight's Children* (also Booker of Bookers)
1982 Thomas Kenneally, *Schindler's Ark*
1983 J. M. Coetzee, *Life and Times of Michael K.*
1984 Anita Brookner, *Hotel du Lac*
1985 Keri Hulme, *The Bone People*
1986 Kingsley Amis, *The Old Devils*
1987 Penelope Lively, *Moon Tiger*
1988 Peter Carey, *Oscar and Lucinda*
1989 Kazuo Ishiguro, *The Remains of the Day*
1990 A. S. Byatt, *Possession*
1991 Ben Okri, *The Famished Road*
1992 Michael Ondaatje, *The English Patient*
     Barry Unsworth, *Sacred Hunger*
1993 Roddy Doyle, *Paddy Clarke Ha Ha Ha*

1994 James Kelman, *How Late it Was, How Late*
1995 Pat Barker, *The Ghost Road*
1996 Graham Swift, *Last Orders*
1997 Arundhati Roy, *The God of Small Things*
1998 Ian McEwan, *Amsterdam*
1999 J. M. Coetzee, *Disgrace*
2000 Margaret Atwood, *The Blind Assassin*

Index

The letters *e.* and *n.* after page references indicate epigraphs and footnotes.

READ MORE IN PENGUIN

In every corner of the world, on every subject under the sun, Penguin represents quality and variety – the very best in publishing today.

For complete information about books available from Penguin – including Puffins, Penguin Classics and Arkana – and how to order them, write to us at the appropriate address below. Please note that for copyright reasons the selection of books varies from country to country.

In the United Kingdom: Please write to *Dept. EP, Penguin Books Ltd, Bath Road, Harmondsworth, West Drayton, Middlesex UB7 0DA*

In the United States: Please write to *Consumer Services, Penguin Putnam Inc., 405 Murray Hill Parkway, East Rutherford, New Jersey 07073-2136.* VISA and MasterCard holders call 1-800-631-8571 to order Penguin titles

In Canada: Please write to *Penguin Books Canada Ltd, 10 Alcorn Avenue, Suite 300, Toronto, Ontario M4V 3B2*

In Australia: Please write to *Penguin Books Australia Ltd, 487 Maroondah Highway, Ringwood, Victoria 3134*

In New Zealand: Please write to *Penguin Books (NZ) Ltd, Private Bag 102902, North Shore Mail Centre, Auckland 10*

In India: Please write to *Penguin Books India Pvt Ltd, 11 Community Centre, Panchsheel Park, New Delhi 110017*

In the Netherlands: Please write to *Penguin Books Netherlands bv, Postbus 3507, NL-1001 AH Amsterdam*

In Germany: Please write to *Penguin Books Deutschland GmbH, Metzlerstrasse 26, 60594 Frankfurt am Main*

In Spain: Please write to *Penguin Books S. A., Bravo Murillo 19, 1°B, 28015 Madrid*

In Italy: Please write to *Penguin Italia s.r.l., Via Vittorio Emanuele 45/a, 20094 Corsico, Milano*

In France: Please write to *Penguin France, 12, Rue Prosper Ferradou, 31700 Blagnac*

In Japan: Please write to *Penguin Books Japan Ltd, Iidabashi KM-Bldg, 2-23-9 Koraku, Bunkyo-Ku, Tokyo 112-0004*

In South Africa: Please write to *Penguin Books South Africa (Pty) Ltd, P.O. Box 751093, Gardenview, 2047 Johannesburg*

ART AND ARCHITECTURE

Ways of Seeing   John Berger

Seeing comes before words. The child looks before it can speak. Yet there is another sense in which seeing comes before words ... These seven provocative essays – some written, some visual – offer a key to exploring the multiplicity of ways of seeing.

The Penguin Dictionary of Architecture
John Fleming, Hugh Honour and Nikolaus Pevsner

This wide-ranging dictionary includes entries on architectural terms, ornamentation, building materials, styles and movements, with over a hundred clear and detailed drawings. 'Immensely useful, succinct and judicious ... this is a book rich in accurate fact and accumulated wisdom' *The Times Literary Supplement*

Style and Civilization

These eight beautifully illustrated volumes interpret the major styles in European art – from the Byzantine era and the Renaissance to Romanticism and Realism – in the broadest context of the civilization and thought of their times. 'One of the most admirable ventures in British scholarly publishing' *The Times*

Michelangelo: A Biography   George Bull

'The final picture of Michelangelo the man is suitably three-dimensional and constructed entirely of evidence as strong as Tuscan marble' *Sunday Telegraph*. 'An impressive number of the observations we are treated to, both in matters of fact and in interpretation, are taking their first bows beyond the confines of the world of the learned journal' *The Times*

Values of Art   Malcolm Budd

'Budd is a first-rate thinker ... He brings to aesthetics formidable gifts of precision, far-sightedness and argument, together with a wide philosophical knowledge and a sincere belief in the importance of art' *The Times*

READ MORE IN PENGUIN

ARCHAEOLOGY

The Penguin Dictionary of Archaeology
Warwick Bray and David Trump

The range of this dictionary is from the earliest prehistory to the civilizations before the rise of classical Greece and Rome. From the Abbevillian handaxe and the god Baal of the Canaanites to the Wisconsin and Würm glaciations of America and Europe, this dictionary concisely describes, in more than 1,600 entries, the sites, cultures, periods, techniques and terms of archaeology.

The Complete Dead Sea Scrolls in English Geza Vermes

The discovery of the Dead Sea Scrolls in the Judaean desert between 1947 and 1956 transformed our understanding of the Hebrew Bible, early Judaism and the origins of Christianity. 'No translation of the Scrolls is either more readable or more authoritative than that of Vermes' *The Times Higher Education Supplement*

Ancient Iraq Georges Roux

Newly revised and now in its third edition, *Ancient Iraq* covers the political, cultural and socio-economic history of Mesopotamia from the days of prehistory to the Christian era and somewhat beyond.

Breaking the Maya Code Michael D. Coe

Over twenty years ago, no one could read the hieroglyphic texts carved on the magnificent Maya temples and palaces; today we can understand almost all of them. The inscriptions reveal a culture obsessed with warfare, dynastic rivalries and ritual blood-letting. 'An entertaining, enlightening and even humorous history of the great searchers after the meaning that lies in the Maya inscriptions' *Observer*

READ MORE IN PENGUIN

RELIGION

The Origin of Satan Elaine Pagels

'Pagels sets out to expose fault lines in the Christian tradition, beginning with the first identification, in the Old Testament, of dissident Jews as personifications of Satan ... Absorbingly, and with balanced insight, she explores this theme of supernatural conflict in its earliest days' *Sunday Times*

A New Handbook of Living Religions
Edited by John R. Hinnells

Comprehensive and informative, this survey of active twentieth-century religions has now been completely revised to include modern developments and recent scholarship. 'Excellent ... This whole book is a joy to read' *The Times Higher Education Supplement*

Sikhism Hew McLeod

A stimulating introduction to Sikh history, doctrine, customs and society. There are about 16 million Sikhs in the world today, 14 million of them living in or near the Punjab. This book explores how their distinctive beliefs emerged from the Hindu background of the times, and examines their ethics, rituals, festivities and ceremonies.

The Historical Figure of Jesus E. P. Sanders

'This book provides a generally convincing picture of the real Jesus, set within the world of Palestinian Judaism, and a practical demonstration of how to distinguish between historical information and theological elaboration in the Gospels' *The Times Literary Supplement*

Islam in the World Malise Ruthven

This informed and informative book places the contemporary Islamic revival in context, providing a fascinating introduction – the first of its kind – to Islamic origins, beliefs, history, geography, politics and society.

READ MORE IN PENGUIN

PHILOSOPHY

Brainchildren   Daniel C. Dennett

Philosophy of mind has been profoundly affected by this century's scientific advances, and thinking about thinking – how and why the mind works, its very existence – can seem baffling. Here eminent philosopher and cognitive scientist Daniel C. Dennett has provided an eloquent guide through some of the mental and moral mazes.

Language, Truth and Logic   A. J. Ayer

The classic text which founded logical positivism and modern British philosophy, *Language, Truth and Logic* swept away the cobwebs and revitalized British philosophy.

The Penguin Dictionary of Philosophy   Edited by Thomas Mautner

This dictionary encompasses all aspects of Western philosophy from 600 BC to the present day. With contributions from over a hundred leading philosophers, this dictionary will prove the ideal reference for any student or teacher of philosophy as well as for all those with a general interest in the subject.

Labyrinths of Reason   William Poundstone

'The world and what is in it, even what people say to you, will not seem the same after plunging into *Labyrinths of Reason* ... holds up the deepest philosophical questions for scrutiny in a way that irresistibly sweeps readers on' *New Scientist*

Metaphysics as a Guide to Morals   Iris Murdoch

'This is philosophy dragged from the cloister, dusted down and made freshly relevant to suffering and egoism, death and religious ecstasy ... and how we feel compassion for others' *Guardian*

Philosophy Football   Mark Perryman

The amazing tale of a make-believe team, *Philosophy Football* is the story of what might have happened to the world's greatest thinkers if their brains had been in their boots instead of their heads ...

READ MORE IN PENGUIN

LANGUAGE/LINGUISTICS

Language Play David Crystal

We all use language to communicate information, but it is language play which is truly central to our lives. Full of puns, groan-worthy gags and witty repartee, this book restores the fun to the study of language. It also demonstrates why all these things are essential elements of what makes us human.

Swearing Geoffrey Hughes

'A deliciously filthy trawl among taboo words across the ages and the globe' *Observer*. 'Erudite and entertaining' Penelope Lively, *Daily Telegraph*

The Language Instinct Stephen Pinker

'Dazzling ... Pinker's big idea is that language is an instinct, as innate to us as flying is to geese ... Words can hardly do justice to the superlative range and liveliness of Pinker's investigations' *Independent*. 'He does for language what David Attenborough does for animals, explaining difficult scientific concepts so easily that they are indeed absorbed as a transparent stream of words' John Gribbin

Mother Tongue Bill Bryson

'A delightful, amusing and provoking survey, a joyful celebration of our wonderful language, which is packed with curiosities and enlightenment on every page' *Sunday Express*. 'A gold mine of language-anecdote. A surprise on every page ... enthralling' *Observer*

Longman Guide to English Usage
Sidney Greenbaum and Janet Whitcut

Containing 5000 entries compiled by leading authorities on modern English, this invaluable reference work clarifies every kind of usage problem, giving expert advice on points of grammar, meaning, style, spelling, pronunciation and punctuation.

READ MORE IN PENGUIN

LITERARY CRITICISM

The Penguin History of Literature

Published in ten volumes, *The Penguin History of Literature* is a superb critical survey of the English and American literature covering fourteen centuries, from the Anglo-Saxons to the present, and written by some of the most distinguished academics in their fields.

New Bearings in English Poetry   F. R. Leavis

'*New Bearings in English Poetry* was the first intelligent account of the work of Eliot, Pound and Gerard Manley Hopkins to appear in English and it significantly altered critical awareness . . . Leavis gave to literary criticism a thoroughness and respectability that has never since been equalled' Peter Ackroyd, *Spectator*. 'The most influential literary critic of modern times' *Financial Times*

The Uses of Literacy   Richard Hoggart

Mass literacy has opened new worlds to new readers. How far has it also been exploited to debase standards and behaviour? 'A vivid inside view of working-class culture and one of the most influential books of the post-war era' *Observer*

Epistemology of the Closet   Eve Kosofsky Sedgwick

Through her brilliant interpretation of the readings of Henry James, Melville, Nietzsche, Proust and Oscar Wilde, Eve Kosofsky Sedgwick shows how questions of sexual definition are at the heart of every form of representation in this century. 'A signal event in the history of late-twentieth-century gay studies' Wayne Koestenbaum

Dangerous Pilgrimages   Malcolm Bradbury

'This capacious book tracks Henry James from New England to Rye; Evelyn Waugh to a Hollywood as grotesque as he expected; Gertrude Stein to Spain to be mistaken for a bishop; Oscar Wilde to a rickety stage in Leadsville, Colorado . . . The textbook on the the transatlantic theme' *Guardian*

READ MORE IN PENGUIN

LITERARY CRITICISM

The Practice of Writing   David Lodge

This lively collection examines the work of authors ranging from the two Amises to Nabokov and Pinter; the links between private lives and published works; and the different techniques required in novels, stage plays and screenplays. 'These essays, so easy in manner, so well-built and informative, offer a fine blend of creative writing and criticism' *Sunday Times*

A Lover's Discourse   Roland Barthes

'May be the most detailed, painstaking anatomy of desire we are ever likely to see or need again ... The book is an ecstatic celebration of love and language ... readers interested in either or both ... will enjoy savouring its rich and dark delights' *Washington Post*

The New Pelican Guide to English Literature   Edited by Boris Ford

The indispensable critical guide to English and American literature in nine volumes, erudite yet accessible. From the ages of Chaucer and Shakespeare, via Georgian satirists and Victorian social critics, to the leading writers of the twentieth century, all literary life is here.

The Structure of Complex Words   William Empson

'Twentieth-century England's greatest critic after T. S. Eliot, but whereas Eliot was the high priest, Empson was the *enfant terrible* ... *The Structure of Complex Words* is one of the linguistic masterpieces of the epoch, finding in the feel and tone of our speech whole sedimented social histories' *Guardian*

Vamps and Tramps   Camille Paglia

'Paglia is a genuinely unconventional thinker ... Taken as a whole, the book gives an exceptionally interesting perspective on the last thirty years of intellectual life in America, and is, in its wacky way, a celebration of passion and the pursuit of truth' *Sunday Telegraph*